Proceedings

33rd Annual IEEE /ACM
International Symposium on Microarchitecture

MICRO-33 2000

10-13 December 2000
Monterey, California, USA

Cover photo courtesy of the Monterey Bay Aquarium and the Monterey Bay Visitors and Convention Bureau. Copyright belongs to the Monterey Bay Aquarium.

Proceedings

33rd Annual IEEE/ACM
International Symposium on Microarchitecture
MICRO-33 2000

10-13 December 2000

Monterey, California, USA

Sponsored by
IEEE TC–MARCH
ACM SIGMICRO

With the generous support of
COMPAQ, IBM, INTEL, S3 INCORPORATED, SGI, and HEWLETT-PACKARD

Los Alamitos, California

Washington • Brussels • Tokyo

Copyright © 2000 by The Institute of Electrical and Electronics Engineers, Inc.
All rights reserved

Copyright and Reprint Permissions: Abstracting is permitted with credit to the source. Libraries may photocopy beyond the limits of US copyright law, for private use of patrons, those articles in this volume that carry a code at the bottom of the first page, provided that the per-copy fee indicated in the code is paid through the Copyright Clearance Center, 222 Rosewood Drive, Danvers, MA 01923.

Other copying, reprint, or republication requests should be addressed to: IEEE Copyrights Manager, IEEE Service Center, 445 Hoes Lane, P.O. Box 133, Piscataway, NJ 08855-1331.

The papers in this book comprise the proceedings of the meeting mentioned on the cover and title page. They reflect the authors' opinions and, in the interests of timely dissemination, are published as presented and without change. Their inclusion in this publication does not necessarily constitute endorsement by the editors, the IEEE Computer Society, or the Institute of Electrical and Electronics Engineers, Inc.

IEEE Computer Society Order Number PR00924
ISBN 0-7695-0924-X
ISBN 0-7695-0926-6 (microfiche)
ISSN 1072-4451

Additional copies may be ordered from:

IEEE Computer Society	IEEE Service Center	IEEE Computer Society
Customer Service Center	445 Hoes Lane	Asia/Pacific Office
10662 Los Vaqueros Circle	P.O. Box 1331	Watanabe Bldg., 1-4-2
P.O. Box 3014	Piscataway, NJ 08855-1331	Minami-Aoyama
Los Alamitos, CA 90720-1314	Tel: + 1 732 981 0060	Minato-ku, Tokyo 107-0062
Tel: + 1 714 821 8380	Fax: + 1 732 981 9667	JAPAN
Fax: + 1 714 821 4641	http://shop.ieee.org/store/	Tel: + 81 3 3408 3118
http://computer.org/	customer-service@ieee.org	Fax: + 81 3 3408 3553
csbooks@computer.org		tokyo.ofc@computer.org

Editorial production by Anne Rawlinson Jacobs

Cover art production by Alex Torres

Printed in the United States of America by The Printing House

Table of Contents
33rd Annual International Symposium on Microarchitecture
MICRO-33

Foreword ix

Committees xi

Reviewers xiii

Keynote Speakers

A Whole New Ballgame–Supercomputing on Two AA Batteries 3
    David Baker
    BOPS Inc.

Breathing Life into a Paper Tiger 5
    Darrell Boggs
    Intel

Defect Tolerant Molecular Electronics: Algorithms, Architectures, and Atoms 7
    Phil Keukes
    Hewlett-Packard

Memory Hierarchy I
Session Chair: Ronny Ronen, Intel

Eager Writeback — A Technique for Improving Bandwidth Utilization 11
    H.-H. S. Lee, G. S. Tyson, and M. K. Farrens

Silent Stores for Free 22
    K. M. Lepak and M. H. Lipasti

A Permutation-Based Page Interleaving Scheme to Reduce Row-Buffer
Conflicts and Exploit Data Locality 32
    Z. Zhang, Z. Zhu, and X. Zhang

Predictor-Directed Stream Buffers 42
    T. Sherwood, S. Sair, and B. Calder

Superscalar Architecture I
Session Chair: Gary Tyson, University of Michigan

On Pipelining Dynamic Instruction Scheduling Logic 57
    J. Stark, M. D. Brown, and Y. N. Patt

The Impact of Delay on the Design of Branch Predictors 67
    D. A. Jiménez, S. W. Keckler, and C. Lin

Improving BTB Performance in the Presence of DLLs 77
   S. Vlaovic, E. S. Davidson, and G. S. Tyson

Efficient Checker Processor Design 87
   S. Chatterjee, C. Weaver, and T. Austin

Compilation

Session Chair: Carol Thompson, Hewlett-Packard

An Integrated Approach to Accelerate Data and Predicate
Computations in Hyperblocks 101
   A. Eichenberger, W. Meleis, and S. Maradani

Accurate and Efficient Predicate Analysis with Binary Decision Diagrams 112
   J. W. Sias, W. W. Hwu, and D. I. August

Modulo Scheduling for a Fully-Distributed Clustered VLIW Architecture 124
   J. Sánchez and A. González

Accelerator Architecture

Session Chair: Tom Conte, North Carolina State University

Two-Level Hierarchical Register File Organization for VLIW Processors 137
   J. Zalamea, J. Llosa, E. Ayguadé, and M. Valero

PipeRench Implementation of the Instruction Path Coprocessor 147
   Y. Chou, P. Pillai, H. Schmit, and J. P. Shen

Efficient Conditional Operations for Data-Parallel Architectures 159
   U. J. Kapasi, W. J. Dally, S. Rixner, P. R. Mattson, J. D. Owens, and B. Khailany

Flexible Hardware Acceleration for Multimedia Oriented Microprocessors 171
   F. Vermeulen, L. Nachtergaele, F. Catthoor, D. Verkest, and H. De Man

Low-Power Design

Session Chair: Rajiv Gupta, University of Arizona

Very Low Power Pipelines Using Significance Compression 181
   R. Canal, A. González, and J. E. Smith

A Static Power Model for Architects 191
   J. A. Butts and G. S. Sohi

A Framework for Dynamic Energy Efficiency and Temperature Management 202
   M. Huang, J. Renau, S.-M. Yoo, and J. Torrellas

Dynamic Zero Compression for Cache Energy Reduction 214
   L. Villa, M. Zhang, and K. Asanović

Memory Hierarchy II

Session Chair: Mike Smith, Harvard University

Register Integration: A Simple and Efficient Implementation
of Squash Reuse 223
   A. Roth and G. S. Sohi

The Store-Load Address Table and Speculative Register Promotion 235
   M. Postiff, D. Greene, and T. Mudge

Memory Hierarchy Reconfiguration for Energy and Performance in
General-Purpose Processor Architectures 245
    R. Balasubramonian, D. Albonesi, A. Buyuktosunoglu, and S. Dwarkadas

Frequent Value Compression in Data Caches 258
    J. Yang, Y. Zhang, and R. Gupta

Dynamic Translation and Multithreading

Session Chair: Kemal Ebcioğlu, IBM

A Study of Slipstream Processors 269
    Z. Purser, K. Sundaramoorthy, and E. Rotenberg

Relational Profiling: Enabling Thread-Level Parallelism
in Virtual Machines 281
    T. Heil and J. E. Smith

Calpa: A Tool for Automating Selective Dynamic Compilation 291
    M. Mock, C. Chambers, and S. J. Eggers

Increasing the Size of Atomic Instruction Blocks Using Control
Flow Assertions 303
    S. J. Patel, T. Tung, S. Bose, and M. M. Crum

Superscalar Architecture II

Session Chair: Bob Colwell, Intel

Reducing Wire Delay Penalty through Value Prediction 317
    J.-M. Parcerisa and A. González

Compiler Controlled Value Prediction Using Branch Predictor
Based Confidence 327
    E. Larson and T. Austin

Instruction Distribution Heuristics for Quad-Cluster,
Dynamically-Scheduled, Superscalar Processors 337
    A. Baniasadi and A. Moshovos

Performance Improvement with Circuit-Level Speculation 348
    T. Liu and S.-L. Lu

Author Index 357

Foreword

As the chairpersons for this year's symposium, we would like to welcome you to Monterey and to MICRO-33. Through more than a dozen generations of processors and more than a million-fold increase in performance/dollar, this meeting, first a workshop and now a symposium, has led the way in introducing and exploring new ideas in microarchitecture. Once again, we have an exciting program that highlights emerging research in high-performance processor microarchitecture, embedded microarchitecture, and compiler optimization. In addition, we have keynote presentations that range from the most visible mainstream processor architecture today to perhaps one of the longest-reaching views of the future of computing.

Micro has attracted some of the best research from both academia and industry in the form of 110 high-quality papers on research topics that are central to modern microarchitecture. This presented a difficult challenge to the program committee, whose job was to select the best papers among those received. The program committee used a large team of reviewers as consultants to generate the material used in the review process. This material was gathered and organized using a review database hosted at North Carolina State University by Tom Conte, and personally administered by Gary Allen Smith whose efforts were central to the program committee's success.

The program committee and their carefully selected reviewers provided a vast experience base of individuals able to fairly judge the research quality of submitted papers. Because they are experienced authors, the program committee was fully aware of the important and controversial nature of their assignment. It is the authors' hard work and creativity, and their sponsors' funding, which fuels a successful and high-quality conference. A diligent and fair review process is central to success. A total of 590 reviews were generated for the 110 papers received, or an average of over 5.3 reviews per paper. All but a few papers received at least 5 reviews. The committee finally selected 31 papers for publication. We sincerely hope that these papers contain important ideas and results that will contribute to future successful research and product development efforts.

The Monterey that we meet in today is a far different place from the sardine-packing fishing port described by Steinbeck. As the fertile Pacific fishing grounds that once made the city successful ran dry, the locals redirected their energy and ingenuity into developing new opportunities. This is a city that has reinvented itself several times, most recently as a center of marine research and as a premier tourist destination. This conference and its participants are constantly engaged in a similar process. In the extreme pace of processor development, companies rapidly absorb the ideas and innovations generated by the microarchitecture research community and integrate them into mainstream technology. Every few years we must begin to address new problems and develop new areas for research. This type of change is always a challenge for both individual researchers and the research community. The organizers of Micro have tried to create an environment that encourages this type of exploration while still demanding the scientific rigor that defines good research. This has allowed Micro to reinvent itself many times over the past 33 years and we hope that it will continue to do so.

It takes many enthusiastic people to put together a successful conference. Kevin Skadron has been an exceptional resource, putting together the proceedings and handling much of the registration procedure. Kyle Vannucci of S3 handled many of the local arrangements, a daunting task given the volume of corporate activity in Northern California. Kemal Ebcioğlu has been vigilant in advising us on every stage of the organizational process and gently harassing us when we fall behind schedule. Ronny Ronin, Ilan Spillinger, and Gabby Silberman provided details of Micro-32 along with comprehensive feedback about the successes and failures of every aspect of their endeavor. Tom Conte has helped with many of the details. Chris Newburn assembled the teams to organize the workshops. We thank them all for their hard work in making this conference successful.

Silicon Valley executives often use Monterey as a location for strategic retreats, a quiet place to go to think about the future and thoughtfully discuss their direction in it with their peers. We would like to encourage the "executives" of the microarchitecture research community to use this week in the same way, as time to think about and discuss the future directions of our research, of our research community, and of this meeting.

Finally, we gratefully acknowledge the support of Compaq, IBM, Intel, S3 Incorporated, SGI, and Hewlett-Packard who have provided funds either to support the conference activities or to support student travel grants to the conference.

Andrew Wolfe
General Chair

Michael Schlansker
Program Chair

Committees

General Chair
Andrew Wolfe, *S3 Incorporated*

Program Chair
Michael Schlansker, *Hewlett-Packard*

Program Committee

Pradip Bose, *IBM*

Bob Colwell, *Intel*

Tom Conte, *North Carolina State University*

Henk Corporaal, *Delft*

Jim Dehnert, *SGI*

Kemal Ebcioğlu, *IBM*

Joel Emer, *Compaq*

Keith Farkas, *Compaq*

Rajiv Gupta, *University of Arizona*

Wen-mei Hwu, *University of Illinois*

Lizy John, *University of Texas at Austin*

Richard Johnson, *Transmeta*

Roy Dz-ching Ju, *Intel*

Vinod Kathail, *Hewlett-Packard*

Bill Mangione-Smith, *University of California at Los Angeles*

Hans Mulder, *Intel*

Yale Patt, *University of Texas at Austin*

Ronny Ronen, *Intel Israel*

André Seznec, *IRISA/INRIA*

Jim Smith, *University of Wisconsin*

Mike Smith, *Harvard University*

Guri Sohi, *University of Wisconsin*

Lothar Thiele, *ETH Zurich*

Carol Thompson, *Hewlett-Packard*

Gary Tyson, *University of Michigan*

Mateo Valero, *Universitat Politecnica de Catalunya, Spain*

Pen-Chung Yew, *University of Minnesota*

Steering Committee
Chair: Richard Belgard, *Consultant*

Kemal Ebcioğlu, *IBM*

Tom Conte, *North Carolina State University*

Matthew Farrens, *University of California at Davis*

Wen-mei Hwu, *Univeristy of Illinois*

Yale Patt, *University of Texas at Austin*

Ronny Ronen, *Intel Israel*

Jim Smith, *University of Wisconsin*

Finance Chair
Tom Conte, *North Carolina State University*

Publications Chair
Kevin Skadron, *University of Virginia*

Workshops/Tutorials Chair
Chris Newburn, *Intel*

Reviewers

Mohammad Abdallah
Santosh G. Abraham
Shail Aditya
Dave Albonesi
Gary Allen
Don Alpert
Erik Altman
David August
Todd Austin
Eugene B. John
Maury Bach
Iris Bahar
Ronald Barnes
Todd M. Bezenek
Ravi Bhargava
Jim Bondi
David Brooks
Mary Brown
J. Adam Butts
Alper Buyuktosunoglu
Gregory T. Byrd
Brad Calder
Doug Carmean
Rob Chappel
Robert Chappell
Mark Charney
Dong-Yuan Chen
Li-Ling Chen
Ben-Chung Cheng
Joe Coha
Joseph Coha
Aviad Cohen
Robert Cohn
Jean-Francois Collard
Jamison Collins
Bob Colwell
Daniel Connors
Marie T. Conte
Tom Conte
Seth Copen
Jesus Corbal
Henk Corporaal
John Crawford
Darren C. Cronquist
Kevin Crozier
Alex Dean
Jim Dehnert
Carole Dulong

Jim Dundas
Kathleen Durant
Kemal Ebcioglu
Susan Eggers
Michael Eisenring
K. Ekanadham
Joel Emer
Philip Emma
Todd Erdner
Mattan Erez
Brian L. Evans
Babak Falsafi
Jesse Fang
Paolo Faraboschi
Keith Farkas
Manoj Franklin
Dan Friendly
Chao-ying Fu
Jordi Garcia
Somnath Ghosh
John Glossner
Antonio Gonzalez
Jose Gonzalez
David Greene
Jonas Greutert
Matthias Gries
Dirk Grunwald
Michael Gschwind
Rajiv Gupta
Siamack Haghighi
Kim Hazelwood
Timothy Heil
Gerolf Hoflehner
John Holm
Urs Holzle
Wei-Chung Hsu
Guillaume Huard
Rick Hudson
Hillery Hunter
Wen-Mei Hwu
Hans Jacobson
Lizy John
Teresa Johnson
Richard Johnson
Norman P. Jouppi
Stephan Jourdan
Roy Dz-ching Ju
Toni Juan

James A. Kahle
Mahmut Kandemir
Vinod Kathail
Hong-Seok Kim
Sangwook Kim
Thomas Kistler
Artur Klauser
Ralph Kling
Allan Knies
Jens Knoop
Prabhakar Kudva
Dattatraya Kulkarni
Konrad Lai
Viktor Lapinskii
Sergei Larin
Josep L. Larriba-Pey
Daniel Lavery
Corinna Lee
Hsien-Hsin S. Lee
Jenq-Kuen Lee
Yong-Fong Lee
Tao Li
Rappoport Lihu
Mikko Lipasti
Daniel Litaize
Jack Lo
Geoff Lowney
Chi-Keung Luk
Scott Mahlke
Bill Mangione-Smith
Srilatha Manne
Peter Markstein
Joe Matarazzo
Matthew Mattina
Sally McKee
Avi Mendelson
Bilha Mendelson
Matthew C. Merten
Harit Modi
Teresa Monreal
Jaime Moreno
Shubu Mukherjee
Hans Mulder
Kalyan Muthukumar
Ravi Nair
Tin-Fook Ngai
Avinoam Nomik
Erik Nystrom

Soner Onder
Emre Ozer
Enric Pastor
Sanjay J. Patel
Yale Patt
Jih-Kwon Peir
Marco Platzner
Matt Postiff
Paul Racunas
Damu Radhakrishnan
Tripura Ramesh
Alex Ramirez
Norman Ramsey
Parthasarathy Ranganathan
B. Ramakrishna Rau
Steve Reinhardt
Gabriel Rivera
Ronny Ronen
Steven Roos
Roni Rosner
Amir Roth
Jesus Sanchez
Yiannakis Sazeides
Michael Schlansker
Rob Schreiber
Andre Seznec
John P. Shen

Tim Sherwood
Bishara Shomar
Tatiana Shpeisman
John W. Sias
Mukund Sivaraman
Anand Sivasubramaniam
Mikhail Smelyanskiy
Jim Smith
Mike Smith
Guri Sohi
Viji Srinivasan
Jared Stark
Don Steiss
Pratap Subrahmanyam
Roman Surgutchik
Deepu Talla
Lothar Thiele
Carol Thompson
Mark C. Toburen
Josep Torrellas
Omri Traub
Marc Tremblay
Jenn-Yuan Tsai
Francis Tseng
Jordi Tubella
Gary Tyson
Bob Valentine

Mateo Valero
Madhavi Valluri
N. Vijaykrishnan
T. N. Vijaykumar
Victor Vinyals
Stevan Vlaovic
David Wall
Hong Wang
Perry Wang
Zheng Wang
Richard Weiss
John-David Wellman
Youfeng Wu
Byung-Sun Yang
Pen-Chung Yew
Adi Yoaz
Huiyang Zhou
Craig Zilles

Keynote Speakers

A Whole New Ballgame–Supercomputing on Two AA Batteries

David Baker
BOPS Inc.

Breathing Life into a Paper Tiger

Darrell Boggs
Intel

Defect Tolerant Molecular Electronics: Algorithms, Architectures, and Atoms

Phil Keukes
Hewlett-Packard

Memory Hierarchy

Eager Writeback - a Technique for Improving Bandwidth Utilization

Hsien-Hsin S. Lee[†]   Gary S. Tyson[†]   Matthew K. Farrens[‡]

[†]ACAL, EECS Department
University of Michigan
Ann Arbor, MI 48109
{*linear, tyson*}@eecs.umich.edu

[‡]Department of Computer Science
University of California
Davis, CA 95616
farrens@cs.ucdavis.edu

Abstract

Modern high-performance processors utilize multi-level cache structures to help tolerate the increasing latency of main memory. Most of these caches employ either a *writeback* or a *write-through* strategy to deal with store operations. Write-through caches propagate data to more distant memory levels at the time each store occurs, which requires a very large bandwidth between the memory hierarchy levels. Writeback caches can significantly reduce the bandwidth requirements between caches and memory by marking cache lines as *dirty* when stores are processed and writing those lines to the memory system only when that dirty line is evicted. Unfortunately, for applications that experience significant numbers of cache misses due to streaming data, writeback cache designs can degrade overall system performance by clustering bus activity when dirty lines contend with data being fetched into the cache.

In this paper we present a new technique called *Eager Writeback*, which re-distributes and balances memory traffic by writing and "cleaning" dirty cache lines prior to their eviction. Eager Writeback can be viewed as a compromise between write-through and writeback policies, in which dirty lines are written later than write-through, but prior to writeback. We will show that this approach can reduce the large number of writes seen in a write-through design, while avoiding the performance degradation caused by clustering bus traffic in a writeback approach.

I. INTRODUCTION

Caches are very effective at reducing memory bus traffic by intercepting and handling most of the read requests generated by the processor. However, caches must deal with both reads *and* writes to memory. Support for writes (stores) tends to be simple – on a store the data item is either written into both the cache and through the cache hierarchy to the memory (referred to as a *write-through* policy), or it is written into the cache exclusively and the data item is written out to memory only when the cache line is evicted (known as a *writeback* policy.)

Caches employing a write-through policy generate memory traffic every time a store occurs in the program. Since it would largely defeat the purpose of having a cache if the processor had to block on each store until the write completed, write-through caches use a structure known as a *store buffer* or *write buffer* [10] to buffer writes to memory. Whenever a write occurs, the data item is written into both the cache and this structure, allowing the processor to continue executing without blocking (until the store buffer becomes full). The store buffer will send its contents to memory as soon as the bus is idle.

Writeback caches, on the other hand, generate memory traffic much less frequently. When a store occurs in a writeback cache the data value is written into the corresponding line in the cache, which is then marked *dirty*. Writes to memory occur only when a line marked *dirty* is evicted from the cache (usually due to a cache miss) in order to make room for the incoming data item.

Whenever there are many consecutive misses (caused by context switches, or working set changes, or by certain graphics algorithms and applications, for example) the writeback cache can find itself blocked waiting for a dirty line to be written to memory. This is the same problem faced by the write-through cache, and can be dealt with in much the same manner by adding a writeback buffer. However, there are certain classes of programs which suffer from memory delay penalties that even a large writeback buffer cannot eliminate. For example, many newer applications (e.g. 3D graphics or multimedia) have enormous incoming data streams. In these programs, the stream of incoming data items can cause many conflict cache misses and trigger the eviction of many dirty lines. This dirty writeback traffic must compete for available memory bandwidth with the arriving data, and often impedes the delivery of the data to the processor. For programs where overall performance is bound by memory bandwidth, this competition for bandwidth can have a substantial negative impact.

In this paper we propose a modification to the writeback policy which spreads out memory activity by selectively writing some dirty lines to memory whenever the bus is free, instead of waiting until that line in the cache is replaced. This early writing of dirty lines to the memory system reduces the potential impact of bursty reference streams, and can effectively re-distribute and balance the memory bandwidth and thereby improve system performance.

II. BACKGROUND

As discussed in the introduction, caches that employ a writeback policy reduce memory traffic by delaying the transfer of data to memory as long as possible. Many modern microprocessors using a writeback cache policy incorporate a writeback (or cast-out) buffer, which is used as temporary storage space for holding dirty cache lines while the data request that caused the eviction is serviced. Upon eviction, a dirty cache line is deposited into the writeback buffer, which usually has the highest bus scheduling priority among all types of non-read bus transactions. Once the writeback buffer fills up, subsequent dirty line replacements cannot take place. As a result, their corresponding data demand fetch operations cannot be committed into the cache, and the processor pipeline stalls waiting for the dependent data.

It is possible to alleviate this problem somewhat by using existing cache hardware. *Non-blocking caches* have been proposed by Kroft [7] which use a set of *miss status holding registers* (MSHRs) to manage several outstanding cache misses. When a cache miss occurs in a non-blocking cache, it is allocated an empty MSHR entry. Once the MSHR entry is allocated, processor execution can continue. If none of the MSHRs are available (i.e. a structural hazard [6] exists due to resource conflicts), the processor will have to block until an MSHR entry becomes free.

By adding data fields to the MSHRs, it would be possible to use them to temporarily store returning cache lines. This would allow fetched data to be immediately forwarded to the appropriate destination registers, and help overcome the situation where the cache cannot be written to because the writeback buffer is full. However, this scenario delays MSHR deallocation and can lead to processor stalls on a cache miss if there are no free MSHRs.

In addition, in a modern computer system memory bandwidth is not exclusively dedicated to the host processor. There are often multiple agents on the bus (such as graphics accelerators or multiple processors) issuing requests to memory over a short period of time. In a contemporary multimedia PC platform with an Accelerated Graphics Port (AGP) interface running a graphics-centric application, for example, the graphics accelerator shares system memory bandwidth with the host processor in order to retrieve graphics commands and texture maps from the system memory. A typical system architecture of a contemporary multimedia PC system is illustrated in Figure 1.

In a common 3D graphics application, the processor reads instructions and triangle vertices, performs the specified computations, and then stores them with rendering state commands back into AGP memory space. The graphics accelerator then reads these commands out of AGP memory for rasterization. In addition to the command traffic, the graphics accelerator also reads a large amount of texture data (which constitutes the major portion of AGP traffic on the bus). These textures are mapped onto polygon surfaces to increase the visual realism of computer-generated images.

Current cache designs have difficulty in efficiently managing the flow of data in and out of the cache hierarchy in these data intensive applications. Buffering techniques, including write buffers and MSHRs can help, but do not alleviate the problems of clustering bus traffic caused by writeback data. In the next section we introduce a new technique designed to distribute the writes of dirty blocks to times when the bus is idle.

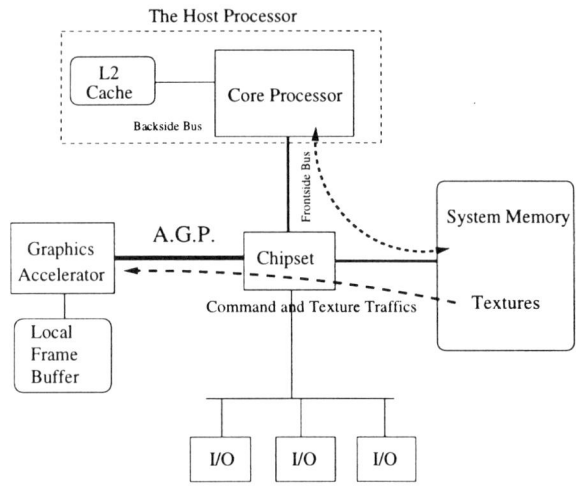

Figure 1: A Multimedia PC Architecture.

III. EAGER WRITEBACK

1 Overview

To address the performance drawbacks of a conventional writeback policy, we are proposing a new technique called *Eager Writeback*. The fundamental idea behind Eager Writeback is to write dirty cache lines to the next level of the memory hierarchy and clear their dirty bits earlier than in a conventional writeback cache design, in order to better distribute bandwidth utilization and alleviate memory bus congestion. If dirty cache lines are written to memory when the bus is less congested, there will be fewer dirty lines that require eviction during peak memory activity.

In essence, we are speculating that certain dirty lines will not be re-written before eviction and thus there is no need to wait until eviction time to perform the cache line write. An Eager Writeback will never impact the correctness of the architectural state even if the operation that triggers it was wrongly speculated - if our speculation is incorrect and we write too often, we approach the limiting case of write-through cache behavior. If we do not speculate often enough, we approach writeback cache behavior. However, in either case we do not violate any correctness constraints.

This work is similar in spirit to that of Lai and Falsafi [8], in which they identify cache lines in a shared memory system that can be speculatively self-invalidated in order to hide the invalidation time and reduce the coherence overhead. However, we are applying the idea to uniprocessor caches instead of DSM machines, which enables us to use a far simpler mechanism to identify which lines should be speculatively written out.

In order to select the best "trigger" to cause an eager writeback, we examined the probability of rewriting a dirty line in a set-associative cache when it was in a given state (MRU through LRU) for the well-known SPEC95 benchmarks [5] and four applications from the lesser-known X benchmark suite [9]. The X benchmark suite consists of four applications representing different graphics algorithms based on X Windows. X-DOOM, a popular video game, uses a polygon-based rendering algorithm. POV-ray is a

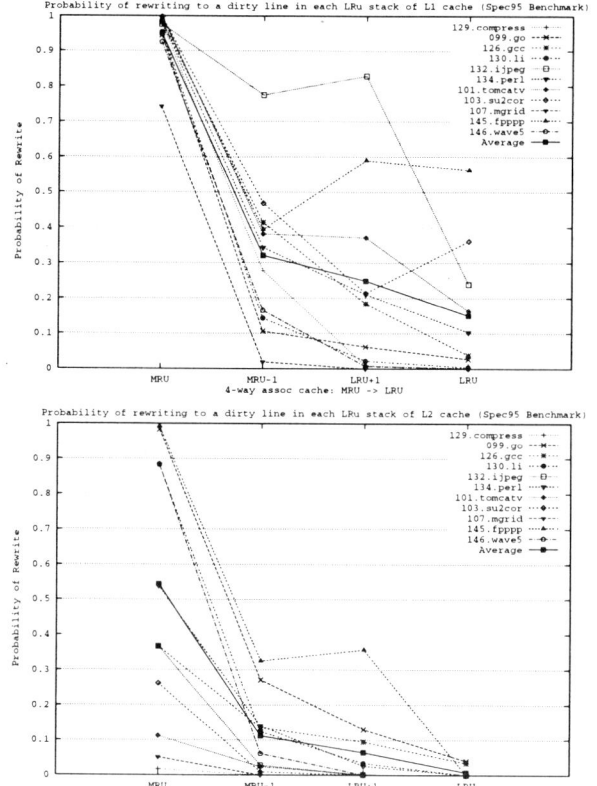

Figure 2: Probability of writing to a dirty line in each LRU stack of L1 and L2 caches (SPEC95)

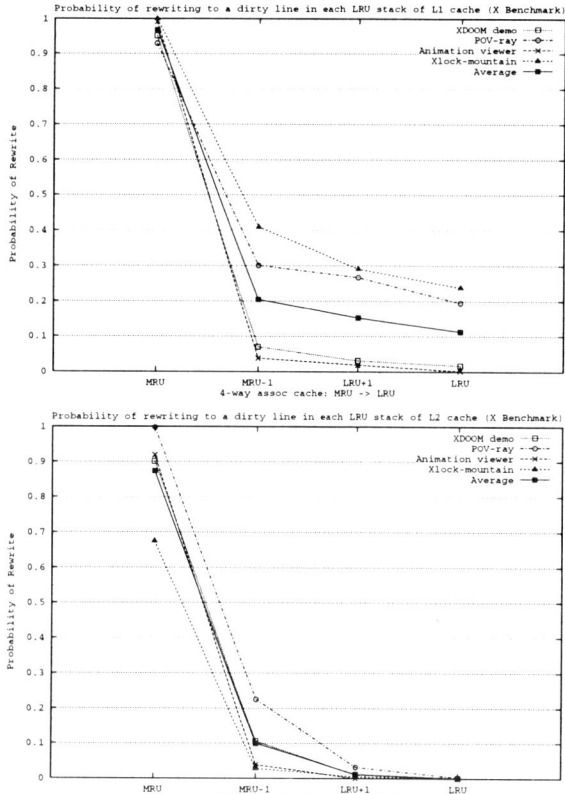

Figure 3: Probability of writing to a dirty line in each LRU stack of L1 and L2 caches (X benchmark)

public domain ray tracing package developed for generating photo-realistic images on a computer. xlock, a popular screen saver, renders a 3D polygonal object on the screen. The final application is an animation viewer which processes an MPEG-1 data stream to display an animated sequence.

Our results indicate that cache lines that have been marked dirty and reach the LRU (Least Recently Used) state in a 4-way set-associative data cache are rarely written to again before they are evicted. In Figure 2 and Figure 3, we show the probability of a line that was marked dirty being written to again as it moves from the MRU (Most Recently Used) state to the LRU state for both L1 and L2 caches. The cache configurations are described in Table 1. The graph on the top in Figure 2, for example, shows that in the L1 cache the average probability (the solid line) of a dirty line in the LRU state being re-written is 0.15, while the similar probability for a dirty line in the MRU state is 0.95. The probabilities of re-dirtying lines in the LRU state are even lower in the L2 cache - in fact, close to 0 as shown in the graphs on bottom of Figure 2 and Figure 3.

These figures indicate there are some programs (such as *fpppp* and *su2cor*) that have a fairly high probability of writing to dirty lines after they have entered the LRU state, however. In order to further evaluate these cases, we looked at the ratio of the number of times a dirty line in the LRU state is written to, normalized to the number of times a dirty line in the MRU state is written to. The results are presented in Figure 4, which shows that while the probabilities may be high, the actual number of these occurrences is negligible compared to the rewriting that occurs when a line is in other states (MRU, MRU-1, etc.). These trends held across a wide range of cache configurations, and imply that once a line enters the LRU state it becomes a prime candidate for Eager Writeback, since it has a very low occurrence of being written to again.

2 Design Issues in Eager Writeback Caches

There can be many different approaches to deciding when to trigger an Eager Writeback. As was shown in the previous section, one obvious candidate is to use the transition of a dirty line into the LRU state as a trigger point for an Eager Writeback. For example, when a cache set is being accessed and its corresponding LRU bit is being updated,

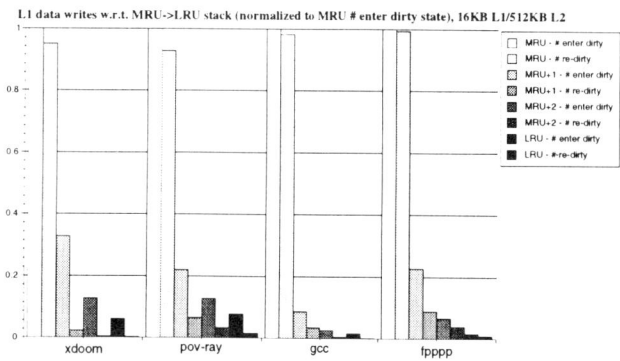

Figure 4: Normalized number of writes and rewrites to a dirty line in each MRU-LRU state

the line can be checked to see if it is marked dirty. If it is, then a dirty writeback can be scheduled, and the dirty bit can be reset.

If the writeback buffer is full at this point, two approaches can be considered; (a) simply abort the Eager Writeback - the actual dirty writeback will take place later when the line is evicted, or (b) perform the eager writeback when an entry in the writeback buffer becomes free. This provides the ability to perform eager writeback anytime between when a line is marked LRU and when it is evicted.

To provide this capability using a minimum of hardware, we chose to implement an *Eager Queue* which holds attempted eager writebacks which were unable to acquire writeback buffer entries. Whenever an entry in the writeback buffer becomes available, the Eager Queue checks the cache set on the top of the queue to see if the dirty bit of the LRU line in the indexed set is set. If it is, the line is moved into the writeback buffer.

An alternate implementation considered during this research was *Autonomous Eager Writeback*. This implementation used a small independent state machine which autonomously polled each cache set in round-robin fashion and checked the dirty bit of its LRU line, initiating eager writeback on those lines when the writeback buffer was not full. Whether eager queues or the autonomous state machine is more feasible is highly dependent on the processor and cache organization. For this study we present results for the more conservative approach which used eager queues.

IV. SIMULATION FRAMEWORK

Our simulation environment was based on the SimpleScalar tool set [1], a re-targetable execution-driven simulator which models speculative and out-of-order execution. The machine employs a Register Update Unit (RUU), which combines the functions of the reservation stations and the reorder buffer necessary for supporting out-of-order execution [11]. Separate address and data buses were implemented and their contentions were all modeled appropriately. Writeback buffers were implemented between cache hierarchies. All the binaries used were compiled using the SimpleScalar GCC compiler that generates code in the portable ISA (PISA) format.

The microarchitectural parameters used in our baseline processor model are shown in Table 1. Table 2 lists the latencies of each functional unit modeled in the simulation. A non-blocking cache structure, writeback buffer and eager queue associated with each cache level were added to the simulator for this study. The number of entries in each buffer was re-configurable from 1 to 256, and varied from simulation to simulation.

A pseudo-Rambus DRAM model was used in the external memory system. This single-channel RDRAM with 64 dependent banks can address up to 2GB of system memory. In the model, 32 independent banks can be accessed simultaneously (contiguous banks share the same sense amplifier for driving data out of the RAM cells). Row control packets, column control packets and data packets can be pipelined and use separate busses. RDRAM address remapping [4] was modeled to reduce the rate of bank interference. The peak bandwidth that can be reached in our RDRAM model is 1.6GB/sec.

A simplified uncacheable write-combining (or write-coalescing) memory [2][3] was implemented as well for the purpose of correctly simulating our benchmark behavior. Whenever a data write to an uncacheable region results in an L1 cache miss, the write operation will immediately request access to the bus and drive data out to the system memory directly (skipping a next-level cache look-up). Only cache line writes are modeled - any partial cache line update will be treated as a full cache line write in the simulator.

For modeling multiple agents on the memory bus, a memory traffic injector was also implemented. This injector allowed us to imitate the extra bandwidth consumed by other bus agents by configurable periodic injections of data streams onto the memory bus.

1 Benchmarks

In order to evaluate the effectiveness of the Eager Writeback technique, we ran extensive simulations on the SPEC benchmark suite and two programs representative of future graphics and streaming applications. Concentrating the analysis on these small, representative kernels enables us to illustrate the potential benefits of our scheme in far greater detail than can be achieved running an entire application.

The first of these kernels is a 3D geometry processing pipeline (*mini-geometry*), which is present in most triangle-based rendering algorithms [13]. Two different geometric rendering configurations were simulated, one which was very simple (i.e. ambient light with no external light sources), and one which included multiple diffuse light sources. The ambient light configuration reduces the computational requirements of the algorithm in order to maximize frame rate at the expense of image realism[1]. The multiple light source configuration increases the computational demands, reducing the relative impact of bus utilization as the processor spends more time processing between each data element request.

The second kernel represents the class of streaming data algorithms which work with large data sets. This kernel

---

[1]This would be preferred in real-time 3D applications (e.g. Doom or Quake) when processor performance is lacking.

Processor Parameters	Cycles in Processor Clocks
1st Level I- and D-Cache	3 clks, thruput = 1 clk
2nd Level Cache	18 clks, thruput = 10 clks
I- and D-TLBs	2 clks, thruput = 1 clk
Backside bus arbitration	4 clks
Frontside bus arbitration	10 clks
RDRAM Trcd, RAS-to-CAS	20 clks
RDRAM Tcac, CAS-to-data return	20 clks
RDRAM Trp, Row Precharge	20 clks
INT ALU latency/thruput	1 / 1
INT multiplier latency/thruput	3 / 1
INT divider latency/thruput	20 / 19
FP ALU latency/thruput	2 / 1
FP multiplier latency/thruput	4 / 1
FP divider latency/thruput	12 / 12

Table 2: Latency Table (in core clocks) of Functional Units in the Baseline Processor.

Processor Architectural Parameters	Specifications
Core frequency	1 GHz
1st Level I-Cache	2-way 16KB, virtual-index physical-tag
1st Level D-Cache	4-way 16KB, virtual-index physical-tag
2nd Level Cache	Unified, 4-way 512KB, physical-index physical-tag
Cache line size	32 bytes
I- and D-TLBs	2-way 8KB
Backside bus	500 MHz (half-speed), 8B wide
Frontside bus	200 MHz, 8B wide
Memory model	Rambus DRAM (peak: 1.6 GB/s)
Branch predictor	2-level adaptive, 10-bit gshare
Instr. fetch/decode/issue/commit width	8 / 8 / 8 / 8
Load/Store Queue size	32
Register update unit size	64
Memory port size	2
INT/FP ALU size	4 / 4
INT/FP MULT/DIV size	1 / 1

Table 1: Summary of the Baseline Processor Model.

```
MINI-GEOMETRY()
while ( frames )
  for ( objects in each frame )
    for ( every 4 vertices )
      /* Transformation */
      tx = m11 * InV[]x + m21 * InV[]y + m31 * InV[]z + m41;
      ty = m12 * InV[]x + m22 * InV[]y + m32 * InV[]z + m42;
      tz = m13 * InV[]x + m23 * InV[]y + m33 * InV[]z + m43;
      w  = m14 * InV[]x + m24 * InV[]y + m34 * InV[]z + m44;
      OutV[]rw = 1/w;
      OutV[]tx = X_offset + tx * OutV[]rw;
      OutV[]ty = Y_offset + ty * OutV[]rw;
      OutV[]tz = tz * OutV[]rw;
      /* Texture coordinates copying */
      OutV[]tu = InV[]u;
      OutV[]tv = InV[]v;
      /* Lighting Loop */
      IDr = IDg = IDb = 0.0;
      for ( every light source )
        dot = LDir[]x * InV[]nx + LDir[]y * InV[]ny + LDir[]z * InV[]nz;
        IDr = IDr + Ambient_r + Diffuse_r * dot;
        IDg = IDg + Ambient_g + Diffuse_g * dot;
        IDb = IDb + Ambient_b + Diffuse_b * dot;
      OutV[]cd = ((int)IDr << 24)|((int)IDg << 16)|((int)IDb << 8|α)
/* Device driver loop */
for ( each transformed and lit vertex )
  /* Assume Tri-Strip triangles */
  /* Copy entire OutV records to graphics AGP memory */
  GfxCommand[vertex - 2] = OutV[vertex - 2];
  if (even - numberedvertex)
    GfxCommand[vertex] = OutV[vertex];
    GfxCommand[vertex - 1] = OutV[vertex - 1];
  else
    GfxCommand[vertex - 1] = OutV[vertex - 1];
    GfxCommand[vertex] = OutV[vertex];
```

Figure 5: Algorithm of the mini-geometry pipeline

This kernel consists of three nested loops wrapped by two outer loops which iterate through frames and 3D objects in the world space. The first innermost loop processes vertices for each 3D object assuming the entire object is modeled by a single triangle strip. The basic functions performed inside this loop are *transformation, lighting,* and *rendering command output*.

The *transformation* function projects the new location of each vertex on screen through a 4x4 matrix multiplication and a viewport transformation. The *lighting* function calculates the interaction of each vertex with light sources and generates the color intensity for each vertex. This calculation involves a dot product between the light direction vector and the vertex normal vector using a Phong illumination model [12]. A single parallel light source with diffuse only components is assumed in the lighting model. For a parallel light source, per-vertex normal transformations can be replaced by an inverse transformation of the light source location on a per-scene basis, thus eliminating a large number of computations. A color packing conversion then packs four single-precision floating-point RGBA color intensities into a packed 4-byte integer. (We assume the machine ISA supports four wide SIMD computation).

After finishing with all the vertices in one object, a loop imitating the functionality of a device driver is invoked (the *command output* function). This driver loop breaks one triangle strip into individual triangles and copies these transformed and lit vertices to the uncacheable graphics memory.

processes a large array of data, performing both reads and writes, generating frequent cache misses as well as many dirty writebacks (behavior common to many current streaming applications). In a real program the data would have some computation performed upon it – however, in order to highlight the behavior of the memory system in this kernel no actual computations are performed.

1.1 Mini-Geometry Pipeline

The 3D geometry processing pipeline, shown in Figure 5, is representative of a very frequently used algorithm in most triangle-based rendering engines. Geometry processing, consisting of intensive floating-point operations on a large quantity of data (mostly vertices that describe the geometry of each 3D object), is mainly performed by the processor. It is one of the two key portions of a three-dimensional graphics rendering pipeline (the other portion being rasterization, which is typically performed by a dedicated graphics accelerator nowadays).

1.2 Streaming Kernel

The *Streaming* kernel is presented in Figure 6, and consists of three inner loops that exercise the L2 cache. The first loop writes data into $array_A$. The second loop reads data from $array_A$, performs some floating-point computation and passes the results to inner loop invariant array elements. Finally the third loop accesses a new array ($array_B$), displacing elements of $array_A$ from the cache.

This program is designed to represent the typical behavior of many streaming applications. However, as pointed out previously, in order to highlight the interaction of Eager Writeback and the memory system in this uniprocessor, no actual computational work is performed per data read.

```
STREAMING()
    float arrayA[MAX], arrayB[MAX];
    for (m = 0; m < loop; m + +)
        for ( arrayA[i] ∈ each set of L2 cache )
            write arrayA[i] to way 0;
            write arrayA[i + 1 * 8 * set_size] to way 1;
            write arrayA[i + 2 * 8 * set_size] to way 2;
            write arrayA[i + 3 * 8 * set_size] to way 3;
        for ( arrayA[j] ∈ each cache line in L2 cache )
            read arrayA[j];
            compute arrayA[j];
            write arrayA[m];
        for ( arrayB[k] ∈ each set of L2 cache )
            read arrayB[k] into way 0;
            read arrayB[k + 1 * 8 * set_size] into way 1;
            read arrayB[k + 2 * 8 * set_size] into way 2;
            read arrayB[k + 3 * 8 * set_size] into way 3;
            write arrayAa[m];
```

Figure 6: Algorithm of the Streaming Kernel

V. SIMULATION RESULTS AND ANALYSIS

For each kernel studied, we present two different data sets, one with no memory contention from other potential bus agents, and one with artificially injected memory traffic.

1 Spec95 Benchmarks

Table 3 shows the simulation results for the SPEC95 benchmark suite using 3 configurations - Baseline, Eager and Free Writeback. The Baseline case uses a single entry writeback buffer, while Free Writeback models a system in which dirty writebacks do not generate any memory traffic on the bus (thus serving as an upper bound on performance.)

Looking at the table it is apparent that there is little performance gain possible for the programs in this suite, since the difference in the cycle count between the baseline case and the upper bound is negligible. This is not surprising, since it is well-known that the SPEC95 benchmark suite is not a good candidate for memory system performance studies primarily due to its small working set size. For the rest of this study we will focus on the benchmarks that more aggressively exercise the memory system, and are arguably more representative of future workloads.

2 Analysis of Mini-Geometry Pipeline

2.1 Without Injected Memory Traffic

Table 4 contains the number of mini-geometry pipeline execution cycles for a variety of memory configurations. In this table, each row represents a different combination of writeback buffer size and lighting conditions, while the columns contain different writeback strategy cycle counts. The first column, *Baseline*, shows the cycle count using a conventional writeback policy. The next 6 columns contain the results for 3 different variations of the *Eager Writeback* scheme and the speed-up of each scheme over the baseline case, with each scheme identified by the size of its *Eager Queue* (EQ). The simplest design choice is EQ=0, in which Eager Writebacks are dismissed if the writeback buffer is full. The other two cases can queue up attempted eager writebacks within Eager Queues of specified sizes. The rightmost column contains the Free Writeback case, which as stated earlier is the upper bound to available performance.

There are several things of interest to note in this table. Perhaps most significantly, it can be seen that increasing the depth of the writeback buffer has virtually no impact

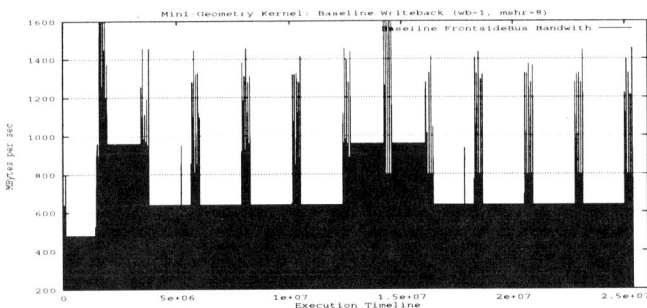

Figure 7: Memory Bandwidth Profile by *Baseline Writeback* for Mini-Geometry Pipeline (No light)

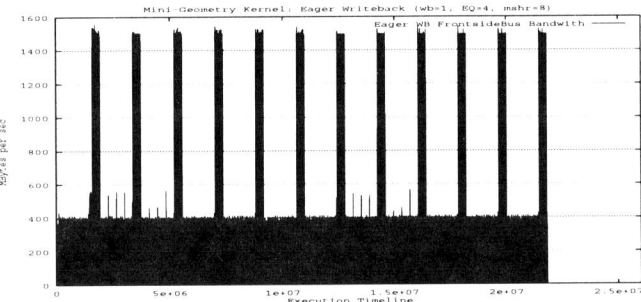

Figure 8: Memory Bandwidth Profile by *Eager Writeback* for Mini-Geometry Pipeline (No light)

on the performance of the Baseline case. In fact, going from 1 to 256 entries in the writeback buffer only improves performance by 0.17%. This is because a large number of dirty writebacks are competing for bandwidth with the demand fetches, and the bus congestion can not be alleviated by a deeper writeback buffer.

On the other hand, adding Eager Writeback scheme increases the performance of the system by 4.9% to 16.2% (depending on the light sources and the depth of the Eager Queue). For the simplest case of no Eager Queue and a single entry writeback buffer, the speedup ranges from 6.2% (for no light source) to 4.9% (with 3 light sources). This speedup is smaller than for the other cases, because many eager writebacks are dropped due to the lack of space in the writeback buffer. When the Eager Queue size is increased (or the number of writeback buffer entries is increased), the speedup achieved approaches the upper bound.

The "bandwidth shifting" effect is quite apparent in Figure 7 and Figure 8. These two figures present the utilization profile of memory bandwidth requested by the processor using the Baseline (Figure 7) and Eager Writeback (Figure 8) configurations, running the mini-geometry pipeline. The y-axis plots the instantaneous bandwidth versus the execution timeline on the x-axis, which was calculated by sampling the data phase on the memory bus every 2000 core clocks (e.g. if 1600 bytes are seen on the bus in 2000 core cycle period, its instantaneous bandwidth is 800MB/sec for a 1GHz processor).

The 12 broad spikes that saturate the peak RDRAM bandwidth in Figure 8 occur within the driver loop, where ren-

sim cycle	Baseline	Eager		Free Writeback	
benchmark	cycles	cycles	speedup	cycles	speedup
go	4106741898	4106316586	1.000	4105050891	1.000
gcc	1425690611	1423578223	1.001	1419981686	1.004
li	401639628	401635232	1.000	401481752	1.000
ijpeg	2125521487	2123322070	1.001	2117908634	1.004
perl	3705579465	3701065936	1.001	3683430936	1.006
tomcatv	5436594306	5436670500	1.000	5436456381	1.000
su2cor	4625207540	4625248569	1.000	4625117247	1.000
mgrid	2138832527	2132120132	1.003	2061823555	1.037
fpppp	8404705112	8410760399	0.999	8404047239	1.000
wave5	2221747518	2208702430	1.006	2179225372	1.020

Table 3: Performance of SPEC95 Benchmarks. (WB buffer = 1, EQ = 4)

write buffer size	Baseline cycles	Eager (EQ=0) cycles	speedup	Eager (EQ=4) cycles	speedup	Eager (EQ=256) cycles	speedup	Free Writeback cycles	speedup
No light, WB Buf=1	25364637	23876911	1.062	21838002	1.162	21837952	1.162	21798206	1.164
No light, WB Buf=4	25320139	21820627	1.160	21820566	1.160	21820566	1.160	21798206	1.162
No light, WB Buf=256	25320139	21820566	1.160	21820566	1.160	21820566	1.160	21798206	1.162
3 diff. lights, WB Buf=1	30643341	29200004	1.049	27176616	1.128	27176333	1.128	27134147	1.129
3 diff. lights, WB Buf=4	30643153	27158044	1.128	27158049	1.128	27158044	1.128	27134147	1.129
3 diff. lights, WB Buf=256	30643153	27158044	1.128	27158044	1.128	27158044	1.128	27134147	1.129

Table 4: Simulated cycles of Mini-Geometry Pipeline.

dering command output is being written into the write-combining graphics memory while eager writebacks of dirty lines are concurrently taking place. Since within the driver loop there is still some computation occurring, the bandwidth is not fully utilized, and eager writeback writes can use the available idle slots and maximize bandwidth. Conversely, in the baseline case, the same writebacks occur within the geometry computation loop. This means these requests compete for the bus with the return of the data requested by vertex loads, and thus slow down the processing. This maximization of the utilization of the bandwidth during the driver loop leads to a lower and sparser average memory bandwidth in Eager Writeback than in the Baseline case outside the driver loop[2].

The overall performance improvement is obviously gained from the shifting of dirty writeback traffic to where this traffic does not impede the return of any data on the critical path of performance. This can be seen in Figure 9, which presents an execution profile of the benchmark. In this figure the sequence of vertex data load requests appears on the y-axis, and the cycle upon which the corresponding data item returns is plotted on the x-axis. As execution begins, the profiles of Baseline and Eager Writeback are completely overlapped, because data is returning at the same time for both schemes. Beginning at around 2.6 million cycles, these two curves start to deviate from one other, and continue to diverge as execution time increases. The first deviation indicates the location where data returns of the Baseline model were getting delayed because of dirty writeback contentions. The speedup due to Eager Writeback as measured is around 16%.

By looking carefully at this figure it is possible to distinguish the geometry computation loop from the device driver loop on each curve. The segments with shorter but

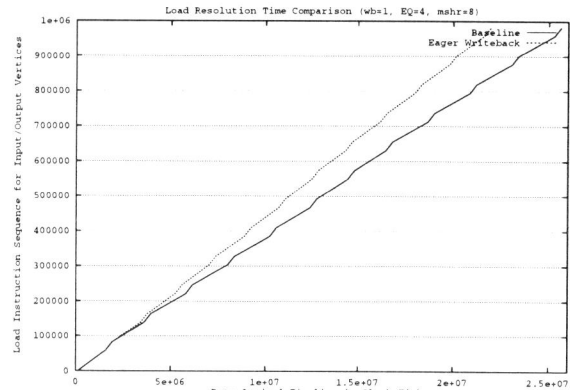

Figure 9: Load Response Time for Input Vertex in Mini-Geometry Pipeline

steeper slopes are where the driver loop is executing. The steepness of the slope occurs because the requested data was returned faster (since the loop read the output vertices generated in the transformation and lighting stages from the L2 cache directly, rather than from memory).

Table 5 shows how Eager Writeback affects the performance bottleneck in the Register Update Unit (RUU) of the processor. The layout of this table is similar to Table 4, and contains the number of cycles the processor is stalled due to the RUU being full. As the table shows, Eager Writeback is able to remove a substantial number of stall cycles due to a full RUU and keep the execution pipeline running smoother. These stalls are reduced because in conventional writeback schemes dirty writebacks are competing with demand fetches for available bandwidth, causing delays in data arrival and the filling of the reservation stations in the RUU. The eager writebacks shift the dirty writes to an earlier time, freeing up the bandwidth to handle just data reads and reducing the pressure on the RUU.

---

[2]It should be emphasized that the total bandwidth required by a system using Eager Writeback is not reduced; rather, it is re-distributed by the early eviction of dirty cache lines.

RUU Full cycles	baseline	Eager (EQ=0)		Eager (EQ=4)		Eager (EQ=256)		Free Writeback	
	cycles	cycles	improved	cycles	improved	cycles	improved	cycles	improved
No light, WB Buf = 1	8404023	6678659	20.5%	4452469	47.0%	4452265	47.0%	4409553	47.5%
No light, WB Buf = 4	8375679	4439397	47.00%	4439226	47.00%	4439226	47.00%	4409553	47.35%
3 diffuse lights, WB Buf=1	8045791	6541028	18.7%	4361651	45.8%	4361259	45.8%	4313710	46.4%
3 diffuse lights, WB Buf=4	8033850	4344799	45.92%	4344670	45.92%	4344653	45.92%	4313710	46.31%

Table 5: Resource Hazard Improvement of Mini-Geometry Pipeline.

2.2 With Injected Memory Traffic

In order to evaluate the effectiveness of Eager Writeback in a real system, we implemented a memory traffic injector which we used to model other bus agents requesting the memory bus and consuming memory bandwidth. For this study, we injected three different external bandwidths using two different injection frequencies onto the bus during the simulations. The external bandwidths chosen were 400MB/sec, 800MB/sec and 1.2GB/sec. For each bandwidth configuration, data was injected at a high frequency (every 400 processor clock cycles) and a low frequency (every 3200 processor clock cycles). Data was injected onto the bus in blocks - for example, in the 800MB high frequency case, every 400 cycles the injector took over the bus and held it until it had completed transferring 320 bytes of data. The injections are uniformally distributed throughout the simulation.

The results for simulations of the mini-geometry pipeline using no light sources are shown in Table 6. The top line of the table is the base case with no injected memory traffic, while the other entries are for the different injected bandwidths at the different frequencies. In this table we can see that (as expected) memory traffic injection causes extra stall cycles in the RUU. In addition, as the amount of injected bus traffic increases, the opportunity to do Eager Writeback decreases and the RUU stalls climb dramatically.

The table also shows that Eager Writeback provides virtually no speedup when a bandwidth of 0.8GB/sec is injected at the higher frequency, while the same bandwidth injected at a lower frequency allows a speedup of 11%. By examining the dirty writeback bandwidth utilization profile of this scenario (Figure 10 and Figure 11), one can see that many eager writebacks (i.e. the spikes) are prevented from occurring by the higher frequency injection. The advantages of Eager Writeback are lost and it performs almost on par with the baseline scenario, due to more frequent bus contention.

3 Streaming Kernel

The mini-geometry pipeline highlighted the problem of implicit dirty writebacks causing loss of performance due to delays in receiving data. Finite memory peak bandwidth is another serious performance issue, which is exposed by the Streaming kernel.

3.1 Without Injected Memory Traffic

Table 7 contains the results of simulation runs of the Streaming kernel, presented in the same format used in Table 4. For this benchmark, an eager queue of length 0 (EQ=0) is enough to approximate the optimal case of no dirty writeback traffic at all. Further size increases of the EQ provide

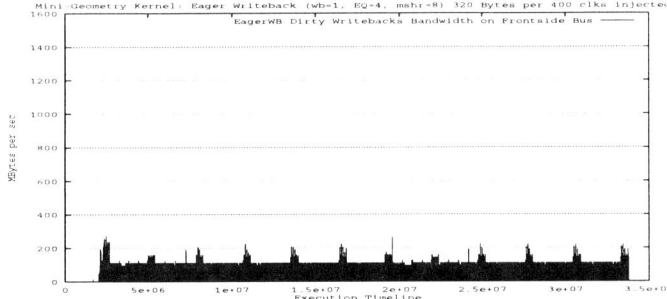

Figure 10: Dirty WB L2-to-Mem Bandwidth with 320B/400clks Injection (*Eager*) for Geometry

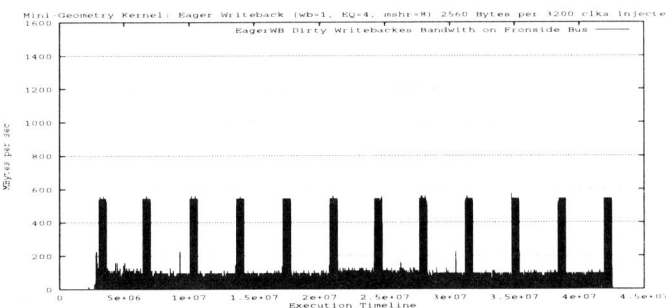

Figure 11: Dirty WB L2-to-Mem Bandwidth with 2560B/3200clks Injection (*Eager*) for Geometry

only marginal performance gains.

Looking at the memory bandwidth utilization profiles for this kernel (Figure 12 and Figure 13), we see three spikes that appear repeatedly in both writeback schemes (because the outer loop contains three iterations). The spikes are much wider in the Baseline case, however, indicating the program is spending more execution cycles in these phases. Examining the algorithm, it is clear these spikes are related to the time during the third inner loop where incoming $array_B$ data items collide and share memory bandwidth with the induced dirty writebacks of $array_A$. Because the finite memory bandwidth (1.6 GB/sec in this study) must be shared between both memory accesses[3], the rate of demand fetches for $array_B$ in the third inner loop is (theoretically) cut in half and thus the overall performance degrades.

Figure 12 also shows three bandwidth grooves where memory bus bandwidth has dropped to zero. These correspond to the second inner loops, where all data references hit in

---
[3]Read and write turnarounds between demand fetch and dirty writeback streams also prevent peak memory bandwidth from being achieved.

bandwidth	sim cycles			RUU Full cycles		
injection (no light)	Baseline	Eager	speed-up	Baseline	Eager	improved
0 GB/sec	25364637	21838002	1.16	8404023	4452469	47.0%
0.4GB/sec (160B/400clks)	27323771	25434535	1.07	10529817	8448695	19.76%
0.8GB/sec (320B/400clks)	33567580	33775835	0.99	16760998	17024045	-1.6%
1.2GB/sec (480B/400clks)	60699573	59162773	1.03	44206642	42864369	3.0%
0.4GB/sec (1280B/3200clks)	32539684	28636072	1.14	15604083	11364679	27.2%
0.8GB/sec (2560B/3200clks)	47365936	42559653	1.11	30356564	25269290	16.8%
1.2GB/sec (3840B/3200clks)	87400980	83426435	1.05	70248220	66015191	6.0%

Table 6: Memory Traffic Injection to Mini-Geometry Pipeline. (EQ = 4)

sim cycle write buffer size	Baseline cycles	Eager (EQ=0)		Eager (EQ=4)		Eager (EQ=256)		Free Writeback	
		cycles	speedup	cycles	speedup	cycles	speedup	cycles	speedup
WB buf = 1	10230328	9054559	1.130	9053851	1.130	9053851	1.130	9045154	1.131
WB buf = 4	10067331	9052957	1.112	9052957	1.112	9052957	1.112	9045154	1.113
WB buf = 256	10223055	9052821	1.129	9052821	1.129	9052821	1.129	9045154	1.113

Table 7: Simulated cycles of Streaming Kernel.

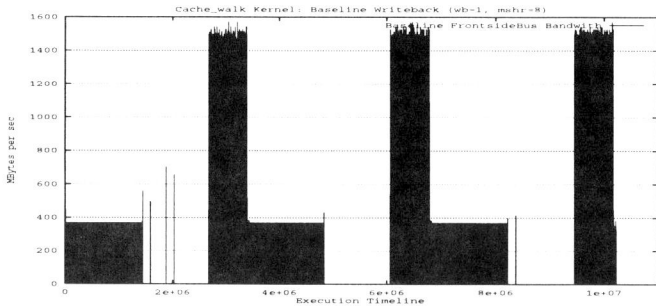

Figure 12: Memory Bandwidth Distribution by *Baseline Writeback* for Streaming Kernel

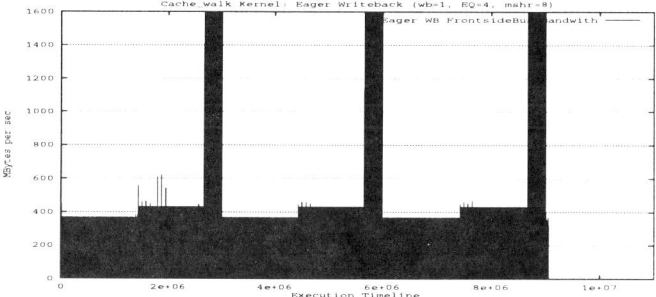

Figure 13: Memory Bandwidth Distribution by *Eager Writeback* for Streaming Kernel

the cache. To take advantage of this available resource, Eager Writeback fills these bus idle states with early evictions of dirty data cache lines (as shown in Figure 13). By shifting these bandwidth requests to idle cycles, the memory bandwidth during the course of the third inner loop can be fully dedicated to the demand fetches of $array_B$, speeding up the cache fill requests.

As was done for the mini-geometry pipeline, we examined how Eager Writeback interacted with internal processor resources when running this benchmark. Table 8 shows that the Load/Store Queue is used heavily by this benchmark, and that Eager Writeback can remove more than half of the stalls due to a full Load/Store Queue. As the LSQ is kept less full, instructions are able to leave the Instruction Fetching Queue (IFQ) faster and as a result cycles lost due to a full IFQ are reduced substantially.

3.2 With Injected Memory Traffic

We also repeated the experiments involving injecting memory traffic onto the bus for this benchmark program. The results are shown in Table 9, and indicate that higher frequency injection seems to have a greater impact on the Baseline case than on the Eager Writeback case. The number of simulated cycles for the Baseline case using high frequency injection increases faster than for the Eager Writeback case, while the increase stays roughly the same for both schemes while injecting lower frequency traffic.

The reason the cycle count climbs faster for the Baseline case than for the Eager Writeback case can be understood by analyzing Figure 14. This figure contains an execution profile of the Streaming benchmark, plotting the arrival time for each load instruction. Each curve can be divided into 3 repeated patterns, which bear the following three piecewise line segments: flat (zero increment), steep rise, and slowdown knee. These 3 line segments correspond to the three inner loops in the benchmark.

The first loop contains only data stores, so the load instruction count stays flat as execution time continues. The steep vertical climb corresponds to the second inner loop, which has a high number of cache hits (a large number of loads completing in a short period of time). Finally, the third segment represents the behavior of the third loop, which loads another array that misses in both the caches.

This third segment, shown as a knee in the curve, reveals the reason for the performance deviation between Baseline and Eager Writeback. Figure 15 shows a close-up view of part of Figure 14, focusing on the knees of the curve. The slopes ($\tan\theta$) of these knees are the key - the flatter the slope, the longer it will take to complete. Comparing the slope changes between Baseline and Eager Writeback, it is obvious that the slope of the Baseline segment is much shallower than that of the Eager Writeback segment. This means that for the same number of loads in the third loop, the execution time of the Baseline case was more sensitive to and severely delayed by other transactions, which in this case are composed of the dirty writebacks induced by the

Bottlenecks	baseline cycles	Eager (EQ=0) cycles	improved	Eager (EQ=4) cycles	improved	Eager (EQ=256) cycles	improved	Free Writeback cycles	improved
IFQ Full cycles	5770175	4594401	20.38%	4594631	20.37%	4594631	20.37%	4587638	20.49%
RUU Full cycles	4274868	4260784	0.33%	4260703	0.33%	4260703	0.33%	4258811	0.38%
LSQ Full cycles	1978596	864867	56.29%	866341	56.21%	866341	56.21%	862880	56.39%

Table 8: Resource Constraint Improvement of Streaming Kernel. (Writeback buffer = 1)

bandwidth injection	simulated cycles			IFQ Full cycles			LSQ Full cycles		
	Baseline	Eager	speed-up	Baseline	Eager	improved	Baseline	Eager	improved
0 MB/sec	10230328	9053851	1.13	5770175	4594631	20.4%	1978596	866341	56.2%
0.4GB/sec (160B/400clks)	11807448	10039848	1.18	7340618	5576536	24.0%	2903145	1205358	58.5%
0.8GB/sec (320B/400clks)	15025957	12389159	1.21	10540877	7908077	25.0%	4428473	1882587	57.5%
1.2GB/sec (480B/400clks)	24250335	21412735	1.13	19717746	16880309	14.4%	8309036	5480188	34.05%
0.4GB/sec (1280B/3200clks)	12379290	10991058	1.13	7908538	6521201	17.5%	2030932	1417595	30.2%
0.8GB/sec (2560B/3200clks)	16593748	15115348	1.10	12101456	10622058	12.2%	4264295	2818313	33.9%
1.2GB/sec (3840B/3200clks)	29048835	27135235	1.07	24495295	22585042	7.8%	8903039	7007451	21.3%

Table 9: Memory Traffic Injection to Streaming Kernel. (Eager Queue = 4)

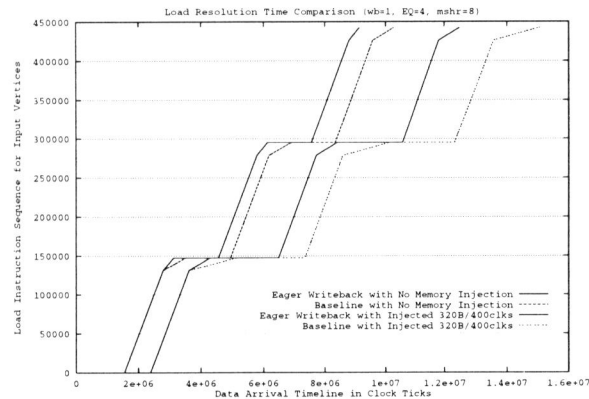

Figure 14: Load Response Time for Data Reads in Streaming Kernel (Higher Frequency Injection)

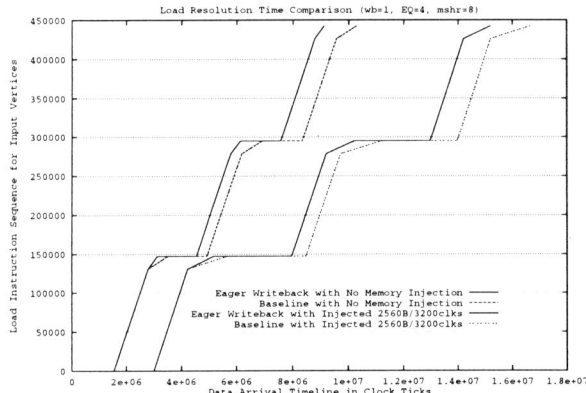

Figure 16: Load Response Time for Data Reads in Streaming Kernel (Lower Frequency Injection)

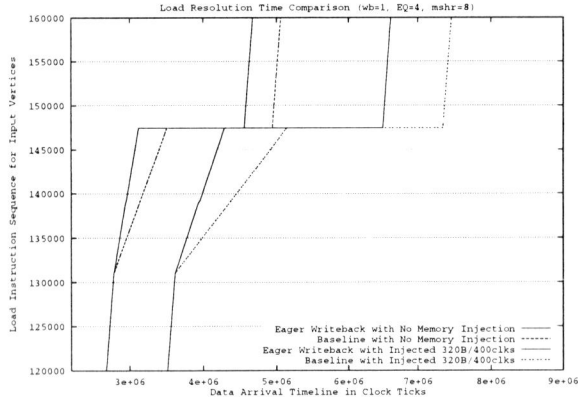

Figure 15: Details of the Load Response Time for Data Reads (Higher Freq. Injection)

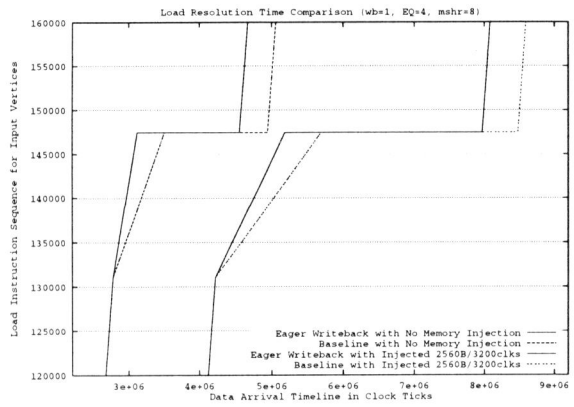

Figure 17: Details of the Load Response Time for Data Reads (Lower Frequency Injection)

loads and the periodic injection of memory traffic. For the Eager Writeback case, the dirty writebacks were mostly completed in the second loop, so the slope of the knee is steeper and the third loop can be completed more swiftly than its Baseline counterpart.

Repeating the same experiment using lower frequency injection (as plotted in Figure 16 and Figure 17) reveals that the slope of the knees of the curve are more similar to one another. As a result, roughly the same number of penalty cycles were added to both Baseline and Eager Writeback, and the speedups due to Eager Writebacks are smaller in Table 9. These results suggest higher frequency interference can deteriorate performance in the baseline case more in a bandwidth-limited code.

VI. CONCLUSIONS

Systems employing write-back caches have to contend with the following two issues: (1) Dirty writebacks contend with demand fetches for bandwidth and can impede the delivery of data, and (2) Finite memory bandwidth shared between demand fetches and implicit dirty writebacks limit the performance of memory bound programs. These performance issues are important to a large and growing class of programs – those that consume large amounts of memory bandwidth and generate many data stores.

In this paper we have presented a new technique for dealing with these issues, called Eager Writeback, which can effectively improve overall system performance by shifting the writing of dirty cache lines from on-demand to times when the memory bus is idle. This time-shifting is accomplished by identifying and speculatively writing ("cleaning") dirty lines whenever the bus is free. We have shown that for a wide variety of programs, once a dirty cache line has entered the LRU state it is rarely written to again. We use this fact to identify the lines that should be speculatively written (although this information could be of interest to many other intelligent cache management techniques as well).

We have shown that applying this technique can alleviate bandwidth congestion and improve performance for two kernels that are representative of these classes of applications. We have shown that when conventional writebacks compete with memory loads and defer the delivery of data, the Eager Writeback technique is able to remove the competition by evicting dirty data earlier. We have also shown that when "finite" memory bandwidth limits overall performance, eager writeback can alleviate this situation by utilizing earlier idle bus cycles. Eager Writeback can be implemented in a number of was - for example, as an additional programmable memory type on top of the exisiting memory types provided by a processor to speed up bandwidth-hungry applications, e.g. 3D games or content-rich applications.

Further investigation of this Eager Writeback mechanism will include the effect this approach has on other system performance issues. For example, Eager writeback can be expected to reduce context switching time overhead by flushing dirty lines in advance of the context switch. In addition, Eager Writeback can push modified data closer to the globally observable memory level earlier to reduce coherence miss latency, and as a result, respond to other processors' requests faster. Similarly, the same analysis performed in this paper can be applied to write-update and write-invalidate protocols in a shared memory system to reduce coherence traffic in a way similar to (but perhaps simpler to implement than) that presented in [8].

VII. ACKNOWLEDGMENTS

This research is sponsored by NSF grant CCR-9812415, NSF Career grant MP-9734023 and generous gifts from IBM and Intel corporations.

VIII. REFERENCES

[1] Doug C. Burger and Todd M. Austin. The SimpleScalar Tool Set, Version 2.0. Technical Report 1342, Computer Science Department, University of Wisconsin-Madison, 1997.

[2] Intel Corporation. Pentium Pro Family Developer's Manual, volume 3: Operating System Writer's Manual. Intel Literature Centers, 1996.

[3] Intel Corporation. IA-64 Architeture Software Developer's Manual, Volume 2: IA-64 System Architecture. Intel Literature Centers, 2000.

[4] Rambus Corporation. Direct Rambus Memory Controller (RMC.dl) Data Sheet. http://www.rambus.com/docs/RMC.d1.0036.00.8.pdf, 1999.

[5] Standard Performance Evaluation Corporation. SPEC CPU95 Benchmarks. http://www.specbench.org/osg/cpu95/, 1995.

[6] John L. Hennessy and David A. Patterson. *Computer Architecture: A Quantitative Approach.* Morgan Kauffmann Publishers, Inc., second edition, 1996.

[7] David Kroft. Lockup-Free Instruction Fetch/Prefetch Cache Organization. In *Proceedings of the 8th Annual International Symposium on Computer Architecture*, 1981.

[8] An-Chow Lai and Babak Falsafi. Selective, Accurate and Timely Self-Invalidation Using Last-Touch Prediction. In *Proceedings of the 27th Annual International Symposium on Computer Architecture*, 2000.

[9] Simplescalar Tool set. X benchmark suite. http://www.cs.wisc.edu/ austin /simple/xbenchmarks.tar.gz, 1998.

[10] Kevin Skadron and Douglas W. Clark. Design Issues and Tradeoffs for Write Buffers. In *Proceedings of the 3th International Symposium on High Performance Computer Architecture*, 1997.

[11] Guri Sohi and Sriram Vajapeyam. Instruction Issue Logic for High-Performance Interruptable Pipelined Processors. *Proceedings of the 14th Annual International Symposium on Computer Architecture*, 1987.

[12] Alan Watt. *3D Computer Graphics.* Addison-Wesley Publishers, 1993.

[13] Paul Zagacki, Deep Buch, Emile Hsieh, Daniel Melaku, Vladimir Pentkovski, and Hsien-Hsin Lee. Architecture of a 3D Software Stack for Peak Pentium III Processor Performance. *Intel Technology Journal*, Q2 1999. http://developer.intel.com/technology/itj/q21999/arcticles/art_4.htm.

Silent Stores for Free

Kevin M. Lepak and Mikko H. Lipasti
Electrical and Computer Engineering
University of Wisconsin
1415 Engineering Drive
Madison, WI 53706
{lepak,mikko}@ece.wisc.edu

Abstract

Silent store instructions write values that exactly match the values that are already stored at the memory address that is being written. A recent study reveals that significant benefits can be gained by detecting and removing such stores from a program's execution. This paper studies the problem of detecting silent stores and shows that an average of 31% and 50% of silent stores can be detected for very low implementation cost, by exploiting temporal and spatial locality in a processor's load and store queues. We also show that over 83% of all silent stores can be detected using idle cache read access ports. Furthermore, we show that processors that use standard error-correction codes to protect data caches from transient errors can be modified only slightly to detect 100% of silent stores that hit in the cache. Finally, we show that silent store detection via these methods can result in a 11% harmonic mean performance improvement in a two-level store-through on-chip cache hierarchy that is based on a real microprocessor design.

1.0 Introduction

A recent study of store value locality notes that many store instructions write values that are either trivially predictable or actually match the values that are already stored at the memory address that is being written. Such stores are called *silent stores*, since they have no effect on system state. While surprising at face value, this discovery is logically consistent with the plethora of recent research on the value locality of load instructions and register-writing instructions (e.g. [6,7,10,15,17]). If indeed the input values that are being loaded from memory exhibit significant value locality, and the register-to-register computation itself exhibits value locality, it follows naturally that the output values being stored back to memory also exhibit significant value locality. Source-level analysis presented in [1] indicates that many silent stores are algorithmic in nature. Results reported in [14] demonstrate that 20%-68% of all store instructions are silent.

Detecting and squashing silent stores can have a number of beneficial effects: reducing the pressure on cache write ports, reducing the pressure on store queues or other microarchitectural structures that are used to track pending writes, reducing the need for store forwarding to dependent loads, and reducing both address and data bus traffic outside the processor chip. Many of these benefits are examined and quantified in [14]. However, there is also a complexity and microarchitectural resource utilization cost associated with detecting silent stores. Namely, to detect the fact that a store is silent, the prior value must first be read out from the memory location, compared to the new value, and then conditionally overwritten in a process called *store squashing*. The simple store squashing approach outlined in [14] simply issues each store instruction twice: first as a read followed by a compare, and later as a store if it is not silent. Though beneficial overall, it is clear that such a simplistic approach places additional pressure on cache ports, particularly when running programs with few silent stores.

Meanwhile, concerns over reliability and the increasing susceptibility of current and future semiconductor technologies to soft errors induced by gamma rays [24,25] and alpha particles [16] have forced additional complexity into the store-handling logic of high-end microprocessors. For example, the latest high-end processors from Compaq and IBM (the Alpha 21264 and PowerPC RS64-III) protect L1 data caches from soft errors with SEC-DED error-correction codes for each aligned 64-bit quantity. Performing sub-64bit stores into SEC-DED-protected caches requires a read-merge-write procedure for recomputing and storing the ECC for the affected 64 bit parcel.

Store handling has also been heavily complicated by the introduction of out-of-order execution in many current processor cores. In order to track pending requests and guarantee that memory ordering rules are not violated, all outstanding uncommitted loads and stores are tracked in complex hardware structures commonly called load queues and store queues. These queues in fact provide a historical and future context for every individual memory reference by surrounding it with memory references that occur near to it in the program order.

The emergence of both SEC-DED protection for transient error recovery and load/store queues to support out-of-order execution create interesting opportunities for a microarchitect searching for low-cost approaches for implementing store squashing. In this paper, we examine some of these opportunities, ranging from embedding silent store detection into the read-merge-write sequence required for subword stores; to read port stealing; to exploiting temporal and spatial locality in the store and load queues; all to perform store squashing for negligible or reasonably low implementation cost. We find that 31% of silent stores can be identified with the simplest approach that exploits temporal locality only, while a more aggres-

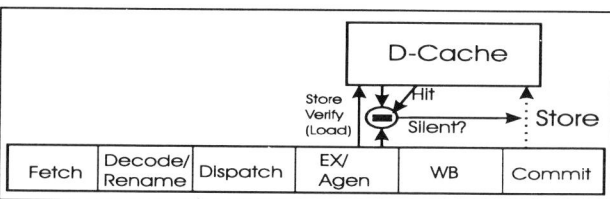

FIGURE 1. A standard store verify consists of load and compare operations in the execute stage..

sive approach that also exploits spatial locality captures an additional 19% on average. Finally, we explore the performance benefits of store squashing in a two-level cache hierarchy with store-through L1 caches that is based on the upcoming IBM Power4 design [13]. In such a configuration, we find that reducing pressure on the memory system can provide up to 56% performance improvement in one benchmark, with a harmonic mean improvement of 11%.

2.0 Free or Low-Cost Squashing Options

Earlier work showed that performance benefit can be obtained by squashing silent stores for both uniprocessor and multiprocessor systems [14]. Throughout this paper, *store squashing* describes the overall process of suppressing a silent store; *store verification* refers to the subtask of detecting that a store is silent. Further, we assume a weakly consistent memory model when describing the various squashing and verification mechanisms. Of course, some optimizations may or may not be possible with stricter consistency models. Further discussion of consistency model issues is generally omitted for the sake of brevity.

2.1 Explicit Store Verifies for All Stores

In order to understand why we would like to exploit free silent store squashing (FSSS), a review of the original proposed mechanism is necessary to understand its implicit assumptions and potential performance problems. As originally explained in [14], referred to in this work as a *standard store verify*, all store operations are converted to explicit loads, comparisons, and conditional stores. A pipeline diagram is shown in Figure 1.

This implementation has some undesirable characteristics. First, explicitly converting all stores to loads increases pressure on the available cache ports in the system and can potentially delay the issue of loads which are likely on the critical path. Second, having a single instruction perform multiple data cache accesses (and potentially cause many data cache misses) will increase scheduler and control logic complexity. Finally, performing more cache accesses (an additional read for each non-silent store) can increase power consumption. Therefore, we would like to find more efficient ways of squashing silent stores.

In the next sections, we present several alternative implementations of store squashing, each more efficient than the standard store squashing mechanism. We use the term *free* rather loosely to indicate that these mechanisms

Table 1: ECC data words and required check bits.

Data-word Size (bits)	ECC Check Size (bits)	ECC-word Size (bits)	ECC Check Bit Overhead
8	4	12	50.0%
16	5	21	31.3%
32	6	38	18.8%
64	7	71	10.9%
128	8	136	6.3%
256	9	265	3.5%

have a qualitatively lower implementation cost than the standard store verify. Detailed assessment of actual implementation complexity is left to future work. We will use the traditional store verify mechanism as the basis for comparison.

2.2 Error Correcting Codes (ECC)

With soft errors in modern microprocessors becoming a larger concern as we move to deeper sub-micron fabrication technologies and higher reliability systems [11,16,21,22,24,25], microprocessor designers are protecting the areas of a chip which are most densely packed with transistors (e.g. caches, memories, etc.) against random alpha-particles and other causes of soft errors. Error checking and correcting (ECC) codes are a very common method for protection against soft errors.

With the incorporation of ECC logic into data caches, even in the L1, as is done in the Alpha 21264 [9] and PowerPC RS64-III [4], silent store squashing becomes much simpler to implement. We return to this point in more detail in Section 3.1 when a possible implementation of squashing in this cache structure is presented, but the basic idea is the following:

ECC using various encoding schemes (we focus on the SEC-DED variety of Hamming based codes [2,20], but the comments made here apply more generally) requires some number of data bits and check bits to enable the correction of errors. The number of check bits is related to the number of data bits by the following function: $n + k \leq 2^k - 1$, where n is the number of data bits and k is the number of check bits. Given the transcendental nature of this function, there is no simple closed form for k, but we illustrate the number of data bits and check bits required for various ECC-word sizes in Table 1.

There is an obvious trade-off between the granularity on which we keep ECC (data-word size) and the overhead of the check bits. In the case of 12 bit ECC-words (8 data bits), there is a 50% increase in storage space as overhead for ECC. For progressively larger ECC-words, the overhead is reduced--down to 3.5% in the case of 265 bit ECC-words (256 data bits). However, this lower overhead does not come without penalty. We can only correct a single bit error and detect a double bit error within the entire ECC-word. Of course, as ECC-word size increases, the probability of multiple errors within a word increases, so ECC is less effective for larger words and a design com-

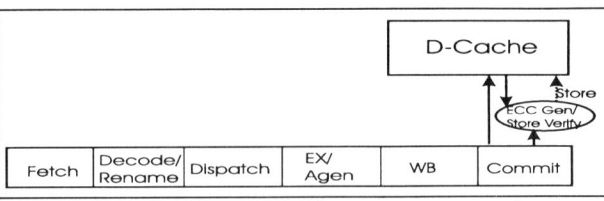

FIGURE 2. ECC store verify occurs at commit.

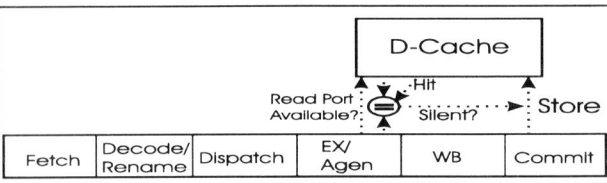

FIGURE 3. Read port stealing performs a load and compare only if a cache port is idle.

promise must be reached. In general, fairly large ECC-word sizes are chosen to minimize overhead and obtain acceptable error coverage. In many modern microprocessors and system busses, 64 bit data-word ECC or larger is used for ease of implementation and because of the configuration of memory systems [9,11]. As a point of reference, the Alpha 21264 and the PowerPC RS64-III implement L1 data cache ECC on quadword (64 bit) data quantities.

The check bits for a data-word are generated when a value is stored into the cache and compared when the value is later read (more detail in Section 3.1). In order to generate correct check bits, all bits in the ECC-word must be available as input to the ECC generation logic. Therefore, if we perform a write operation that is either improperly aligned on ECC-word boundaries, or is a sub-ECC-word write, we must first fetch the rest of the original ECC-word stored at the location, merge in the changes (from the current write), calculate the new check bits, and store the ECC-word.

We can see that in many cases the store operation into an ECC-protected cache really consists of four operations: read original ECC-word, store merge, ECC check bit generation, and new ECC-word store. This realization illuminates the possibility of one type of free silent store squashing (FSSS). Since we are reading the original ECC-word anyway, we can perform a comparison of the new store value to the original value and squash the silent stores. This store verify can be performed in parallel with the store merge and new ECC check bit generation, adding very little delay to the store logic, as will be examined in more detail in Section 3.1.

In comparison to standard store verifies (Section 2.1), we can see that store verifies carried out in ECC logic require no explicit load operation, but rather can simply be performed at commit, as illustrated in Figure 2. The drawbacks of this approach are that a store is squashed relatively late in the pipeline (at commit instead of during the execute stage) so it may not reduce pressure on write buffers; it cannot be removed early from the LSQ; and finally that it cannot capture ECC-word-aligned stores.

2.3 Read Port Stealing

It is well known that programs are non-uniform in the usage of system resources. Therefore, in many cases, some available idle resources can be used for other purposes. We propose an additional use of idle resources; namely, exploiting free cache read ports to implement store verifies. This mechanism is a simple extension of the standard store verify explained in Section 2.1. Since stores must commit in order, it is possible that due to a pipeline stall a store can wait in the LSQ for a long period of time before it completes. If a load port becomes free while the store is waiting to commit, we can use the load port to perform a store verify operation. Because we are using resources that are idle and available, these store verifies are free. If a load port never becomes available before the store is ready to commit, we forego attempting to squash the store and assume it is non-silent.

Relative to standard store verifies, this method has the benefit of not delaying execution of load operations due to resource conflicts. However, it can create additional instruction scheduling difficulties because the policy for issuing a store verify is dependent on resource usage and not just program order or another static scheduling policy. This technique of FSSS is shown in Figure 3.

2.4 Load/Store Queue

In order to obtain high performance, many processors implement aggressive memory systems which require load/store queues (LSQs) to perform store to load forwarding and monitor speculative load operations which may be violations of the architected consistency model. We can exploit locality in the LSQ to obtain FSSS as outlined in the following sections.

2.4.1 Temporal Locality in the LSQ

Store to load forwarding of memory dependences is an optimization commonly implemented in modern microprocessors. In the case of store squashing, a store verify operation necessitates a read. If store forwarding is implemented, we can extend it to squash later stores to the same address as an earlier store in the LSQ (WAW dependence). We can do so without using a cache read port, hence making the squash free.

In a similar fashion, we can also squash stores to memory addresses for which an outstanding load exists in the LSQ. This is possible because the cache access for the load will be performed, obtaining the data value for the store verify. In some sense, we can consider the store verify for the store to be "piggy-backed" on the explicit load operation to the same memory address (WAR dependence). Note that this optimization is also possible for loads which occur later in program order, which generally would have their load value forwarded from the previous store we're trying to squash. This is possible because the usage of the cache port is usually scheduled before it is known whether the value will be forwarded from an earlier store in the LSQ [8,13]. Therefore, since we have scheduled the load for cache access anyway, the load can

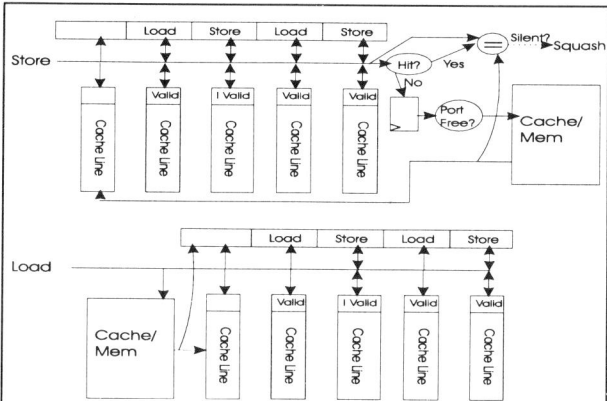

FIGURE 4. Block level LSQ cache design. The temporal and spatial LSQ squashing operations, data allocation, and store forwarding are illustrated for memory operations.

still be performed at no cost. Hence, the store verify is again free in the case of a RAW memory dependence.

2.4.2 Spatial Locality in the LSQ

In a similar fashion, we can expand the scope of stores squashable within the LSQ to addresses that inhabit the same cache line. Given that L1 data caches are on-chip, obtaining wide access to these caches is relatively easy. Therefore, one may imagine each memory operation reading an entire cacheline on any reference because of the high bandwidth available from the L1 cache. Assuming that a memory access reads the entire line from the cache into a *LSQ cache* (shown in Figure 4), we can use the spatially local data to perform additional squashing.

In the case of a WAW dependence, a previous store to the line reads the line into the LSQ cache, and all subsequent stores to that line can be squashed from the LSQ cache. In the case of a WAR and RAW dependences, a similar process occurs--the load operation allocates the line in the LSQ cache, and stores to the same line are squashed from it. We will show in Section 4.4 that a small LSQ cache is especially effective in the case of WAW dependences.

The LSQ cache is similar to the *write cache* proposed in [12], except it contains entire cache lines as opposed to 8 byte quantities and it buffers both load-allocated and store-allocated lines. Also note that since issuing stores is generally not as time critical as issuing loads (because the stores can be buffered at commit) we serialize the lookup in the LSQ cache and the access to the memory system (shown in Figure 4) to avoid unnecessary usage of the data cache port. We can also exploit read port stealing (Section 2.3) and only read data for stores into the LSQ cache if a memory read port is available. Assuming we do so, we also need a separate valid bit both for the LSQ cacheline data and for the entries in the LSQ themselves (shown in the Figure 4) because a store may fail to acquire a free read port, leaving the data invalid. When an access allocates a line into the LSQ cache, we may choose to verify stores already present in the LSQ with the newly allocated data, but this may add complexity to the LSQ

and LSQ cache for additional data paths. We will discuss this further in Section 4.4.

If we assume that the LSQ cache is FIFO allocated and is operated in lock-step with the entries in the LSQ such that when an entry leaves the LSQ its LSQ cache line is also deallocated, we can avoid having explicit tags and dirty bits in the entries (because all necessary address and dirty value forwarding is already available in the LSQ entries for store-forwarding). In the case of a weakly consistent system, it is sufficient for correctness to flush the LSQ cache on memory barriers (and this is most likely very effective because of the small LSQ cache size) and avoid snooping it for invalidates. In more strict consistency models, snooping the LSQ may already be required to detect consistency model violations, so snooping the LSQ cache as well adds no additional complexity [23].

The benefits of squashing in the LSQ relative to standard store verifies are apparent. No additional cache access is required for the load portion of the store verify and squashing stores is free.

3.0 ECC Free Silent Store Squashing

As touched on briefly in Section 2.2, soft errors are a growing concern for microprocessor architects in order to provide highly reliable systems and because of manufacturing concerns [11,16,21,22,24,25]. Having discussed in Section 2 the opportunities for FSSS, in this section we elaborate on the ECC method of FSSS in greater detail. We show three possible mechanisms for protecting L1 data caches from soft errors and illustrate under what circumstances the FSSS techniques can be exploited. We also explore which of the techniques we expect to be most effective for different cache architectures.

3.1 L1 Data Cache with ECC

Soft error protection can be performed in the L1 data cache directly, as is done in the Alpha 21264 [9] and the PowerPC RS64-III [4]. The 21264 and PowerPC RS64-III use 64-bit ECC data words. As shown in Section 2.2, this provides error coverage for relatively low space overhead of approximately 11%. As also outlined in that Section, FSSS is trivially implementable as part of ECC check bit generation for subword writes. In order to illustrate the argument made in Section 2.2, Figure 5 shows a datapath with which ECC may be implemented on a sub-ECC-word store operation in an Alpha-like system. Note that we use 72-bit ECC words (instead of the 71 used in standard Hamming-based codes) because the Alpha uses a slightly modified coding scheme with 72-bit words [9].

Implementation will be slightly different to handle smaller bit width stores, but for ease of illustration, only a 32-bit store is shown. We see the four major operations as discussed in Section 2.2: read the original quadword from the data cache, merge the store data into the input side of the ECC Data Register, generate ECC check bits, and store the quadword and ECC bits. Note that if ECC-word generation takes multiple cycles (as one might expect for

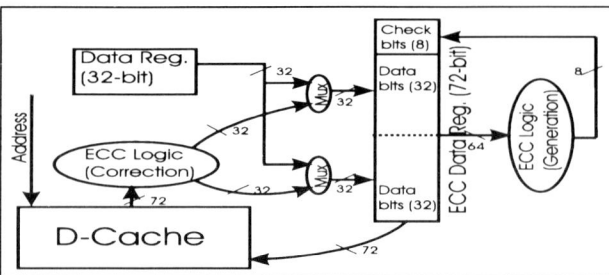

FIGURE 5. L1 data cache ECC-word generation on a sub-ECC-word store.

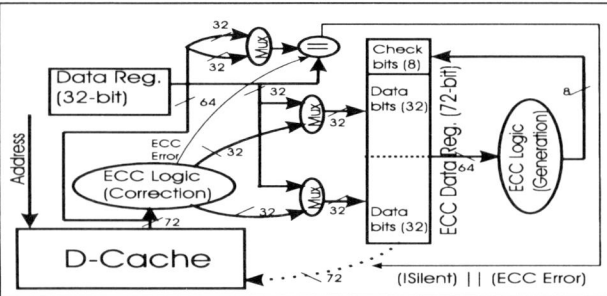

FIGURE 6. L1 data cache ECC-word generation on a sub-ECC-word store with free silent store squashing.

essentially a read-modify-write sequence), we must maintain atomicity of the sequence either through design of the write buffer feeding the ECC logic, or in the logic itself. We have ignored this detail to simplify the diagram.

In Figure 6, we show the implementation of FSSS in the same ECC logic structure as shown in Figure 5. We can see that the changes to the datapath are relatively simple; the addition of an extra multiplexor and a comparator. Figure 6 also illustrates that we cannot perform silent store squashing if an ECC error is encountered on the read of the data value from memory. This is because the corrected value is obtained from the ECC correction logic and therefore must be written back to the memory system. The logic implements the same four steps as described previously. However, the store merge, ECC check bit generation, and new ECC-word store operations may be aborted if it is determined that the store is silent and there is no ECC error. The abort operation can be as simple as not re-acquiring the cache port for the write of the (silent) ECC-word from the ECC Data Register.

The most important aspect of Figure 6 is when the silent store comparison can be performed. From the datapath shown, we can see that the comparison can be performed in parallel with the ECC check bit correction and generation. In general, ECC correction and generation logic consists of trees of exclusive-or gates [20] which have delay on the same order as the 32-bit comparison for squashing. Therefore, FSSS for sub-ECC-word stores can be implemented in an ECC-protected L1 data cache for simply the cost of a few extra gates which should not increase the ECC logic's critical path.

3.2 Store-through L1 Cache with ECC L2

Implementing ECC protection directly is not the only way to combat soft errors in the L1 data cache. In fact, adding ECC protection to the L1 directly can contribute negatively to cycle time because the ECC correction logic is now added to the critical path on load operations to assure usage of corrected values from the cache. Of course, speculation can be used in order to move the ECC check/correction logic off the critical path by speculating that all load values are correct and recovering if the ECC logic reports an error. Of course, this adds control complexity to trigger the recovery [9].

An alternative is to use an L1 cache with simple parity protection and a store-through policy backed up with an ECC L2 cache. The L1 parity protection has a few advantages when compared with ECC in the L1. First, parity can easily be kept on a byte basis with the same overhead as the 72-bit ECC-word as in the 21264 (in both cases the overhead is approximately 13%.) With byte parity in the L1, there are no merging issues with store operations because the smallest atom for memory operations is a byte--therefore stores into the L1 do not require a read-modify-write sequence. The parity for each byte can be calculated very early in the pipeline when the store value is known and can simply be written into the cache. The single bit of parity for each byte provides single error detection on the byte level, as opposed to double error detection over 64 data bits as provided by 64-bit SEC-DED. If an error is detected in the L1 data cache via parity, the correct value is fetched from the ECC L2 cache.

Of course, a major caveat of this approach is the additional bus traffic generated by implementing a store through L1 cache [12]. This traffic can be reduced with techniques like aggressive write combining and other buffering techniques, but special care must be taken to handle the extra L1 to L2 bandwidth requirements. Weaker consistency models allow greater freedom for store combining than stricter models.

In the case of a store-through L1 cache, silent store squashing can have a noticeable performance benefit. To further improve performance, we can use ECC squashing for sub-ECC-word writes in an ECC-protected L2 cache. However, this will not reduce store-through traffic on the L1 to L2 interface. Instead, we rely on the other methods of FSSS--squashing in the LSQ and stealing read ports--in order to reduce store-through traffic. Performance results of the different methods of FSSS for such a memory system configuration are given in Section 4.

3.3 Duplication of L1 Data Cache

We can also obtain single error detection and correction capability in the L1 cache by duplicating it and protecting both copies with parity. If we encounter a parity error on the read of any byte, we can fetch the correct byte from the other copy of the cache to recover from the error. This scheme avoids a read-modify-write sequence for sub-word stores. It also provides effectively double the read-port bandwidth into the L1 data cache because each copy of the data cache can be accessed with loads to arbitrary addresses.

However, this scheme is not without its flaws. First, this scheme has high overhead of 100% compared to a cache with only parity. Second, this scheme does not allow easy scaling of store bandwidth because both copies must be consistent, requiring stores to write both copies.

FSSS can still provide performance benefit in this cache structure because it is biased towards more read ports than write ports. Therefore, we would expect the performance improvement of FSSS in this cache configuration to be similar to results reported in [14] and do not explore this configuration further in this work.

4.0 FSSS Performance Benefit

We have shown in Section 2 and Section 3 that many opportunities exist for FSSS. In this Section, we quantify the performance benefit of the mechanisms compared with a standard architecture. As we have stated previously, the squashing mechanisms we evaluate are *free* (as defined in Section 2.1) so any non-negligible performance benefit is proof that these methods are effective.

We perform only uniprocessor simulations to show proof-of-concept for the proposed mechanisms. Of course, as shown in [14], there are additional savings for communication misses in multiprocessors that are not considered in these results.

4.1 Machine Model

To determine the performance impact of FSSS, we used an execution driven simulator of the SimpleScalar architecture with an enhanced memory system model [5]. The default SimpleScalar does not accurately (or in some cases at all) model finite memory system components such as write buffers, writeback buffers, scheduling of write/writeback traffic over the L1 to L2 interface, etc. Since FSSS focuses on improving memory system performance, modelling these resources accurately is necessary for our results to reflect true performance.

In order to model the increasing demands on a memory subsystem, we used an aggressive out of order design. The configuration of the execution engine is 8 issue; 64 entry RUU; GShare branch predictor with 64K entries, 16 bit global history; 6 integer ALUs, and 2 integer multipliers. The cache configurations are 64KB each split I/D L1 and 512KB unified L2 with latencies 2, 8, and 50 clocks for the L1, L2, and main memory, respectively. The I-cache is 2 way associative with a line size of 64 bytes; The D-caches are 4 and 8 way associative with line sizes of 32 and 64 bytes, respectively. Store to load forwarding is implemented in the simulator with a latency of 2 clocks to match the L1 hit latency. All binaries are SimpleScalar PISA and compiled with SimpleScalar gcc at -O3.

The machine has two fully pipelined general memory access ports each of which can handle either one load or one store per cycle with no address restrictions. If a store has begun verification, we count this store as verified in the percentages reported, but we do not force verification to finish before committing the store. If a store has not finished verifying when it reaches commit, it is assumed to be non-silent and enters the memory system. Read port stealing for squashing occurs regardless of where an address hits in the memory hierarchy. The simulator implements two write buffers outside of the instruction window (i.e. only for committed stores) where committed stores are held until their completion. Aggressive write-combining is implemented in the write buffer so that any store to the same L1 cacheline can be combined with other stores to the same line in the buffer. The LSQ cache only allocates for stores when it can steal a read port.

The L1 cache has a write-through, write-allocate policy backed by a writeback L2. In all cases (except Section 4.5 where we consider this bandwidth specifically) we make the very aggressive assumption that there is a full L1 cache line width interface between L1 and L2 that can begin a new transaction every clock cycle, as might be possible with on-die L2 caches. Both store-through bandwidth and L1 fill bandwidth are modeled over this interface. Fill transactions (i.e. demand misses) take precedence over store-through traffic on this interface.

The memory access configuration of this machine model is similar, though not identical, to the Power4 [13] which implements a store-through L1 and writeback L2 for ECC protection (as outlined in Section 3.2). It is not our goal in this Section to advocate a specific method of error correction, but rather to show how FSSS can be exploited for performance benefit in one possible configuration.

4.2 ECC Squashing

We do not show performance results for this method of FSSS because it does not make sense to complicate the results discussion with two incomparable machine models. As discussed in Section 3, if a store-through L1 cache is implemented for the purposes of error protection, we have no need for ECC in the L1, since the store-through to an ECC-protected L2 provides adequate reliability. In order to meaningfully demonstrate the performance of ECC squashing, we need a writeback L1. Results for a machine model similar to this were published in [14].

However, it should be noted that the key assumption of Section 2.2 and Section 3.1, namely that store operations must be sub-ECC-word for ECC FSSS, is realistic given commercially available processors today. One would expect that no architect would design a system with the maximal store atom size being smaller than the ECC-word-size so that every store incurs a read-modify-write for ECC generation. However, this occurs frequently. The IBM RS64-III (Pulsar) processor, in use in IBM S80 servers and other machines, executes exactly this way when running 32-bit code. In the RS64-III, the L1 cache is ECC protected directly (similar to the manner discussed in Section 3.1) using an ECC-data-word size of 64 bits. In 32 bit mode, the largest integer store atom is 32 bits, hence incurring the read-modify-write on every store [3,4]. Therefore, we expect ECC squashing to provide significant performance benefit in this and similar systems.

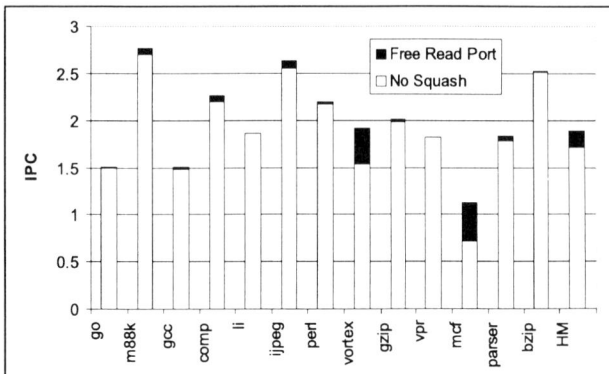

FIGURE 7. Performance improvement of read port stealing vs. no squashing.

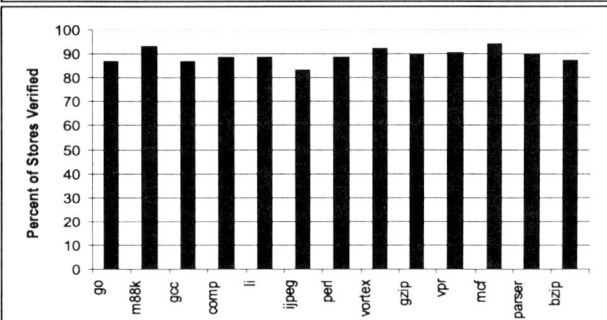

FIGURE 8. Percentage of all dynamic stores verified using only available cache read ports.

4.3 Available Read Port Squashing

Figure 7 shows the performance improvement of read port stealing over the baseline performance with no squashing. We see improvements ranging from a low of 0% in *li* and *vpr* to a high of 56% in *mcf*. The harmonic mean across all benchmarks shows a 10.3% improvement.

It is worthwhile to note that we do not see a performance decrease in any benchmark. This occurs because we are only using cache read ports available after all other ready loads and stores have had a chance to issue/commit. The performance benefit comes primarily from two factors: a) a reduction of bandwidth required between L1 and L2 caches by eliminating store traffic on the interface, and b) reduced pressure on write buffers.

It is also interesting to note how few store squashing opportunities we miss by only using available cache read ports as opposed to trying to squash all stores. In Figure 8 we show the percentage of store operations we are able to store verify for free using read port stealing.

We can see that in all cases, we are able to verify over 83% of store operations using available cache read ports with an average of 89%. This indicates that we are achieving almost all available benefit from squashing that uses the standard store verify, but without impacting performance of critical load and store operations.

4.4 LSQ Squashing

In Figure 9, we show the performance improvement of

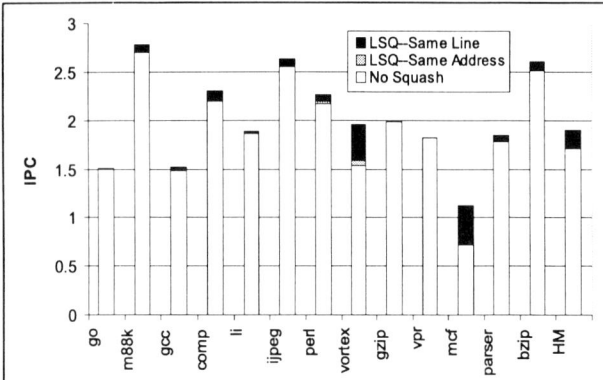

FIGURE 9. Performance of LSQ squashing. The stacked bars indicate the performance of the baseline system (without squashing), same address (temporal) LSQ squashing, and same cacheline (spatial) LSQ squashing, respectively.

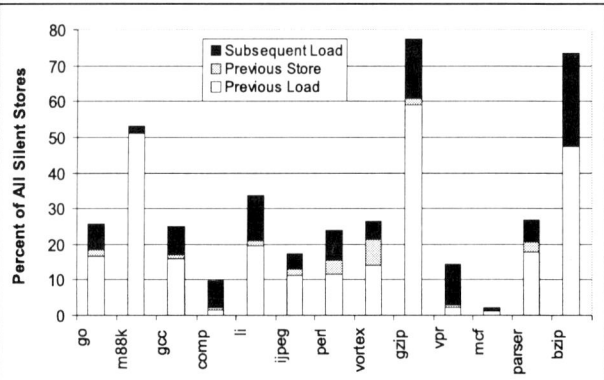

FIGURE 10. Temporal LSQ squashing provided by WAR, WAW, and RAW dependences.

temporal and spatial LSQ squashing over the baseline performance with no squashing (as discussed in Section 2.4.1 and Section 2.4.2, respectively). The stacked bars show the contribution of each mechanism to overall performance. For temporal LSQ squashing, we see improvements in IPC ranging from a low of 0% in *gzip* and *mcf* to a high of 3% in *vortex* with overall performance improved by 0.6% as indicated by the harmonic mean over all benchmarks. When we add spatial LSQ squashing, we see total improvements over the baseline from a low of 0% in *gzip* to a high of 56% in *mcf* with the harmonic mean improving by 11.3%.

When examining temporal squashing, it is interesting to note that most of the stores are squashed by preceding or subsequent load operations (the RAW and WAR dependences discussed in Section 2.4.1), as opposed to previous store operations (WAW dependences), as illustrated in Figure 10. In most benchmarks (except *compress*, *ijpeg*, *vpr*, and *mcf*), temporal LSQ squashing captures over 25% of all silent stores within the dynamic program execution. Some possible explanations for this are provided in [1], and could include program model considerations like stack frame usage. In the results presented in Figure 10, each dynamic silent store is counted at most once (it is present in only one section of the

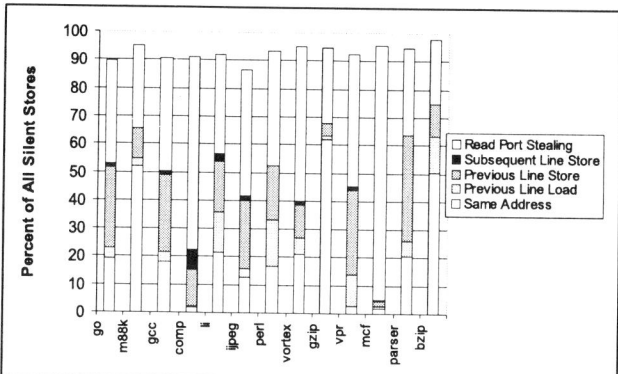

FIGURE 11. LSQ store verifies provided by same address (temporal locality), previous load to line, previous store to line, subsequent store to line, and read port stealing.

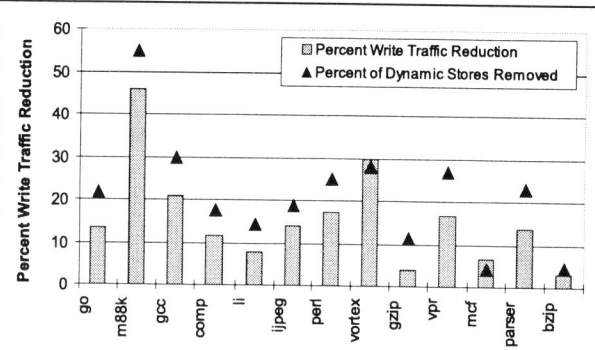

FIGURE 12. Percent reduction of L1 to L2 traffic by performing FSSS. The bars and bullets indicate the percentage of write through traffic reduction and the percentage of total dynamic stores removed, respectively, by FSSS.

stacked bars), with the following priority counting on multiple aliases: previous load (WAR), previous store (WAW), subsequent load (RAW).

In the case of spatial LSQ squashing, the same statement regarding counting of squashable stores holds (a dynamic silent store is only counted once). However, the priority of counting changes slightly due to simulator implementation issues. In this case, the counting precedence is: WAR, WAW, cache line previous load, cache line previous store, RAW, cacheline subsequent load, and read port stealing. We show the results of this method of counting in Figure 11 (results from all same address squashing methods are combined in the Same Address bar for readability and the subsequent line load section is removed because it did not contribute meaningfully). Note that the total percentage of silent stores captured by this mechanism is greater than the results presented in Figure 8 (simple read port stealing) because the LSQ cache is store-allocating using free read ports, as well as exploiting locality in the LSQ. Because LSQ store verifies do not consume a cache port, a port tends to be free more often for additional read port stealing store verifies.

We see that the percentage of same address store verifies decreases over Figure 10, mainly due to counting precedence. Also, substantial previous line store verifies are observed, indicating that the LSQ cache proposed in Section 2.4.2 is useful. These results also indicate, due to the small fraction of subsequent line verifies, that verification from a line allocated by a subsequent access to previous stores in the LSQ is unnecessary for squashing purposes, potentially saving some complexity in the LSQ cache.

Finally, we see that in all benchmarks (except *compress* and *mcf*), over 40% of all silent stores are captured by exploiting locality in the LSQ. Read port stealing for LSQ cache line allocation brings the total percentage of silent stores captured to over 90% (except for *ijpeg*).

In comparing temporal to spatial LSQ squashing, we see only two benchmarks that benefit from temporal squashing (*perl* gains 1.5% and *vortex* 3.3%). It is not until spatial LSQ squashing is applied that we see noticeable improvements in instruction throughput. This occurs because the overall percentage of silent stores detected by the spatial scheme (including free read port squashing) is much higher.

4.5 Increasing Effective Write-Through Bandwidth via FSSS

Given that FSSS can squash many silent stores, it is interesting to examine what kind of trade-offs we can make as an architect with this type of memory system to obtain sufficient throughput between the L1 and L2 caches. We can use the "brute force" method and implement a fully-pipelined, write-combining, cache-line-width interface between L1 and L2 (as used in all results presented so far) which can induce significant circuit design complexity. Or, we can exploit FSSS to obtain "effective" throughput over the L1 to L2 interface with less physical throughput. In order to illustrate this, we present Figure 12 which shows the store-through traffic reduction over the L1 to L2 interface as well as the percentage of dynamic stores removed by FSSS. We see an average traffic reduction of 15% across all benchmarks and up to 45% in *m88ksim*. Since this interface is wide (32B) and fast (single cycle pipelined), it is reasonable to assume that this traffic reduction would lead to a savings in chip power.

Note that, as we would expect, the percentage of write through traffic reduction closely mirrors the percentage of successfully removed, squashed, stores. In the case of *vortex* and *mcf*, the traffic reduction is slightly greater than the percentage of removed stores, which we attribute to second-order increase in write combining efficiency. Because squashed stores do not allocate a write buffer, there are more buffers available for combining non-silent stores. The percentage of removed stores is lower than the overall percentage of silent stores (and also the percentages of squashed stores presented previously) because we do not wait for store verifies to complete before committing stores (explained in Section 4.1). In further experiments not detailed here, we found that although we could decrease traffic by waiting for stores that hit in the L1 to finish verifying, because commit of some stores is stalled

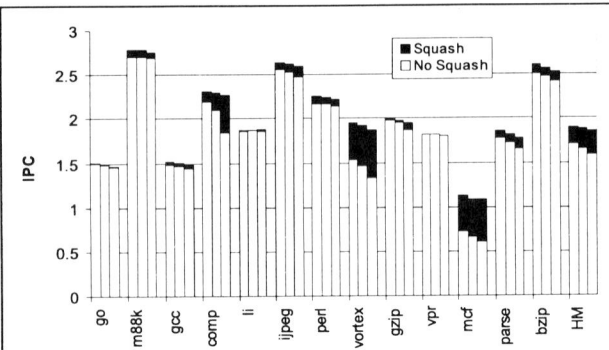

FIGURE 13. Performance comparison between most aggressive FSSS and no squashing for narrower L1 to L2 interfaces. The stacked bars indicate the performance obtained by squashing with 32B, 16B, and 8B wide L1 to L2 interfaces, respectively.

in this case, overall instruction throughput is lower. There is a potential performance vs. power consumption trade-off here that could be exploited in power-aware designs.

In order to determine how effective this bandwidth reduction is on instruction throughput, we present Figure 13, which shows the performance across all benchmarks with varying width interfaces between L1 and L2, with and without FSSS squashing in its most aggressive form (spatial LSQ squashing with read port stealing). We keep the L1 cacheline size at 32B in all simulations, but illustrate the performance of 32B, 16B, and 8B wide interfaces between the L1 and L2. In each case, we are progressively lowering the physical bandwidth of the L1 to L2 interface because in the case of 16B and 8B widths more transactions across the interface are required for a cacheline transfer (two and four transactions for 16B and 8B, respectively). However, we change the write combining width to match the physical interface width so that flushing a write buffer takes only a single cycle.

If we compare FSSS with an interface width of 8B to no squashing with an interface width of 32B, we see that the effective bandwidth (as evidenced by IPC) of FSSS with the 75% lower physical bandwidth interface is more effective than the higher physical bandwidth interface without FSSS (the only exceptions to this are *go* and *gzip*; in these benchmarks, the percentages of silent stores are low, 27% and 16% respectively, leading us to expect less benefit from FSSS). In fact, as evidenced by the harmonic mean, the FSSS low physical bandwidth interface actually provides 9% greater effective bandwidth on average than the fastest physical interface we model. Therefore, we can potentially trade the implementation of FSSS for physical bandwidth. Of course, as also shown, FSSS still provides benefit no matter what physical bandwidth is available. Note that even though the actual reduction in physical bandwidth for the narrower interfaces (50% and 75% for 16B and 8B wide interfaces, respectively) is larger than the percent reductions shown in Figure 12, FSSS also decreases pressure on other hardware structures, such as write buffers, so the performance improvement is not solely due to the reduced L2 bandwidth.

We also observe in Figure 13 that the performance degradation from the widest (32B) to the narrowest (8B) interface is lower in the case of FSSS than for the baseline system with no squashing (40% lower according to the harmonic mean). This occurs because squashing is relatively more effective as the write-combining width narrows. With respect only to physical interface bandwidth, combining and squashing are equivalent. We can either save a transaction over the L1 to L2 interface by combining with a previous store or by squashing the store. However, there is some overlap between the methods (i.e. some stores that are squashed could also have been combined, and vice-versa, as can bee seen in Figure 12 in the difference between removed dynamic stores and reduced write through traffic). Of course, the combining width directly affects the number of stores that can be combined, but does not directly affect the number of squashed silent stores. Therefore, FSSS will capture some stores that can no longer be combined (but can still be squashed at any combining width), so the relative benefit of squashing increases as the combining width decreases along with the width of the L1 to L2 interface.

4.6 Results Discussion

Comparing the performance results for the three FSSS methods simulated for our machine model, we see that read port stealing and aggressive LSQ squashing exploiting both temporal and spatial locality in the LSQ provide nearly equivalent performance, with harmonic mean speedups of 10% and 11%, respectively. This occurs because both methods capture greater than 83% of all silent stores and close to 90% on average, so both methods are suitable for exploiting FSSS for IPC benefit. However, aggressive LSQ squashing reduces the number of store verifies issued to the memory system by 50%, on average (comparing the read port stealing percentages from Figure 8 and Figure 11). Therefore, in a machine model with relatively fewer memory ports, aggressive LSQ squashing may have greater benefit because of reduced port contention. Reducing data cache accesses may also reduce overall power consumption.

Temporal LSQ squashing by itself provides only modest speedup in these benchmarks, less than 1%, because of the low percentage of silent stores captured (31% on average) and the corresponding 9% average reduction in total committed dynamic stores. Therefore, while temporal LSQ squashing has the benefit of never stealing a cache read port, in our machine, solely implementing this mechanism does not seem worthwhile.

5 .0 Conclusion

We make four contributions in this paper. First, we explain why standard store verifies, as initially proposed in [14] have some undesirable characteristics, and introduce the concept of free silent store squashing, which uses existing resources as-is or with slight modification to squash a significant portion of all silent stores. Second, we explain three ways in which we can implement free silent store squashing: i) using pre-existing ECC logic that is present, and will become more prevalent, in current and future microarchitectures; ii) using idle read port stealing to perform store verifies; iii) enhancing an existing load/store queue to exploit temporal and spatial locality for store squashing. We show that in current and next generation microarchitectures that opportunities exist to exploit these mechanisms using real examples from the Alpha 21264 [9], IBM RS64-III [4], and IBM Power4 [13]. We further show that substantial performance benefit can be obtained by exploiting free silent store squashing and that two of the three mechanisms--read port stealing and aggressive LSQ squashing--capture a significant portion of silent stores detected by the standard store verify mechanism (greater than 83% and 89% on average). They do so at a substantially reduced cost for performance benefits averaging 10% and 11% across the SPECINT95 and a subset of the SPECINT-2000 benchmarks for each method respectively. Third, we illustrate that "effective" bandwidth between the L1 and L2 data caches can be increased by free silent store squashing, and indicate that a substantially lower bandwidth physical interface between the two caches provides the same or better performance when performing free silent store squashing. Finally, we provide additional characterizing information about silent stores by showing that, in most benchmarks, greater than 40% of all silent stores can be squashed by simply examining data that are temporally or spatially local to data already existing in the LSQ. We also illustrate that, on average, 31% of silent stores are detected with temporal locality, and an additional 19% are detected with spatial locality, in the LSQ. The work reiterates that silent stores can be exploited for performance improvement and illustrates that taking advantage of the majority of silent stores is relatively easy given current microarchitectures, lowering the barriers to exploiting them in the future.

6.0 Acknowledgements

This work was supported by generous equipment donations from IBM and Intel. Financial support was provided through a graduate student fellowship from Intel and also funds from the University of Wisconsin Graduate School. We would also like to thank the anonymous reviewers for their many helpful comments.

References

[1] G. B. Bell, K. M. Lepak, and M. H. Lipasti. Characterization of Silent Stores. To appear in *International Conference on Parallel Architectures and Compilation Techniques*, October 2000.

[2] R. E. Blahut. *Theory and Practice of Error Control Codes*. Addison-Wesley Publishing Company, Reading, MA, 1983.

[3] J. Borkenhagen. Personal Communication. IBM Server Development. Rochester, MN, June 2000.

[4] J. Borkenhagen and S. Storino. *5th Generation 64-bit PowerPC-Compatible Commercial Processor Design*. IBM Whitepaper, http://www.rs6000.ibm.com, 1999.

[5] D. C. Burger and T. M. Austin. The Simplescalar Tool Set, Version 2.0. Technical Report CS-TR-97-1342, University of Wisconsin, Madison, June 1997.

[6] B. Calder, G. Reinman, and D. Tullsen. Selective Value Prediction. In *Proceedings of the 26th Annual International Symposium on Computer Architecture (ISCA'99)*, volume 27, 2 of *Computer Architecture News*, pages 64–75, New York, N.Y., May 1–5 1999. ACM Press.

[7] B. Calder, P. Feller, and A. Eustace. Value Profiling. In *Proceedings of the 30th Annual ACM/IEEE International Symposium on Microarchitecture*, December 1997.

[8] R. P. Colwell and R. Steck. A 0.6um BiCMOS Processor with Dynamic Execution. In *Proceedings of ISSCC*. 1995.

[9] Compaq Computer Corp. *Alpha 21264 Hardware Reference Manual DS-0027A-TE*. http://www1.support.compaq.com/alpha-tools/documentation/current/chip-docs.html. February, 2000.

[10] J. Gonzalez and A. Gonzalez. Control-flow Speculation Through Value Prediction for Superscalar Processors. In *Proceedings of PACT-99*, October 1999.

[11] IBM Corporation. *Fault Tolerance Decision in DRAM Applications*. Application Note, http://www.chips.ibm.com/products/memory/fault/fault.html. July, 1997.

[12] Norman P. Jouppi. Cache Write Policies and Performance. In *Proceedings of the 20th Annual International Symposium on Computer Architecture*, 1993

[13] J. Kahle. Power4: A Dual-CPU Processor Chip. *Microprocessor Forum*. October 1999.

[14] K. M. Lepak and M. H. Lipasti. On the Value Locality of Store Instructions. In *Proceedings of the 27th Annual International Symposium on Computer Architecture*, June 2000.

[15] M. H. Lipasti and J. P. Shen. Exceeding the Dataflow Limit via Value Prediction. In *Proceedings of the 29th Annual ACM/IEEE International Symposium on Microarchitecture*, December 1996.

[16] T. May and M. Woods. Alpha-particle-induced Soft Errors in Dynamic Memories. *IEEE Transactions on Electronic Devices*, 26(2), 1979.

[17] A. Mendelson and F. Gabbay. Speculative Execution Based on Value Prediction. Technical report, Technion, 1997. (http://www-ee.technion.ac.il/.

[18] C. Molina, A. Gonzalez, and J. Tubella. Reducing Memory Traffic via Redundant Store Instructions. In *Proc. of Int. Conf. on High Perf. Computing and Networking*, pages 1246 1249, April 1999.

[19] A. Moshovos. *Memory Dependence Prediction*. PhD thesis, University of Wisconsin, December 1998.

[20] T.R.N. Rao and E. Fujiwara. *Error-Control Coding for Computer Systems*. Prentice Hall, Englewood Cliffs, NJ, 1989.

[21] E. Rotenberg. AR-SMT: A Microarchitectural Approach to Fault Tolerance in Microprocessors. In *Proceedings of the 29th Fault-Tolerant Computing Symposium*, June 1999.

[22] P. Rubinfeld. Managing Problems at High Speed. *IEEE Computer*, pages 47-48, January 1998.

[23] Kenneth C. Yeager. The MIPS R10000 Superscalar Microprocessor. *IEEE Micro*, April 1996.

[24] J. Ziegler. Terrestrial Cosmic Rays. *IBM Journal of Research and Development*, 40(1):19-39, January 1996.

[25] J. Ziegler et al. IBM Experiments in Soft Fails in Computer Electronics. *IBM Journal of Research and Development*, 40(1):3-18, January 1996.

A Permutation-based Page Interleaving Scheme to Reduce Row-buffer Conflicts and Exploit Data Locality

Zhao Zhang   Zhichun Zhu   Xiaodong Zhang
Department of Computer Science
College of William and Mary
Williamsburg, VA 23187
{zzhang, zzhu, zhang}@cs.wm.edu

Abstract

DRAM row-buffer conflicts occur when a sequence of requests on different rows goes to the same memory bank, causing much higher memory access latency than requests to the same row or to different banks. In this paper, we analyze the sources of row-buffer conflicts in the context of superscalar processors, and propose a *permutation-based page interleaving scheme* to reduce row-buffer conflicts and to exploit data access locality in the row-buffer. Compared with several existing schemes, we show that the permutation-based scheme dramatically increases the hit rates on DRAM row-buffers and reduces memory stall time of the SPEC95 and TPC-C workloads. The memory stall times of the workloads are reduced up to 68% and 50%, compared with the conventional cache line and page interleaving schemes, respectively.

1 Introduction

Concurrent accesses to multiple interleaved memory banks are supported in modern computer systems, where each bank has a row-buffer holding a page of data.[1] With the significant improvement in memory bandwidth, the DRAM access speed is becoming more crucial to determine the memory stall time of a program execution [6]. One effective solution to address this issue is to utilize the available concurrency among multiple DRAM banks, and to exploit data locality available in the row-buffer of each DRAM bank. However, conflicting performance benefits exist between exploiting access concurrency and data locality in the row-buffer. Memory interleaving scheme designs directly determine the effectiveness of the solution. A conventional memory interleaving scheme allocates consecutively addressed data blocks to consecutive memory banks using a modular mapping function. The size of the interleaved data block can be a word, a cache line, multiple cache lines, a page, or multiple pages. In general, using larger interleaved data blocks leads to more data locality in each DRAM row-buffer but lower concurrency among the multiple banks.

Regarding the efforts of exploiting locality, people have proposed techniques to take advantage of the row-buffer, which serves as a natural "cache" with a large block size. Some DRAM manufacturers even add SRAM caches into the DRAM chips. With the improvement of DRAM row-buffers in the accumulative size, exploiting row-buffer locality is becoming more and more effective for memory system performance improvement. One major bottleneck limiting this effort comes from DRAM row-buffer conflicts which occur when a sequence of requests on different pages goes to the same bank, causing conflict misses in the row-buffer. Frequent row-buffer misses can significantly increase access latency and degrade overall performance. Compared with a row-buffer hit, a row-buffer miss may cause additional DRAM precharge time and DRAM row access time, which will be tens of ns on a typical DRAM. Thus, the row-buffer hit time could be 30% to 50% less than a row-buffer miss time.

Regarding the efforts of utilizing concurrency among the DRAM banks, one commonly used technique is to interleave small data blocks among memory banks. However, this approach limits the ability to effectively exploit spatial locality in the row-buffer. To consider the trade-offs between large and small data block interleaving schemes, several schemes are proposed. Block interleaving [10] is such an example used in vector supercomputers with Cached DRAM.

In this paper, we analyze the sources of the row-buffer conflicts in the context of superscalar processors. Then we propose a memory interleaving scheme, called *permutation-based page interleaving*, to accomplish both the objectives of utilizing concurrency for reducing row-buffer conflicts and of exploiting access locality for reusing

---
[1] For Direct Rambus DRAM, the row buffer size is one-half page, and adjacent banks share half-page row buffers with each other.

the data in the row-buffer. The strategy is to generate the memory bank index by XOR-ing two portions of memory address bits. The hardware cost of the interleaving scheme is trivial, and additional runtime overhead involved is negligible. We evaluate the performance of the proposed interleaving scheme for SPEC95 and TPC-C workloads with execution-driven simulations. Compared with existing schemes, we show that the permutation-based scheme dramatically increases the hit rates on DRAM row-buffers and reduces memory stall time of the workloads. The memory stall times of the workloads are reduced up to 68% and 50%, and the execution times are reduced up to 38% and 19%, compared with the conventional cache line and page interleaving schemes, respectively.

We discuss some issues of memory system design in section 2, and analyze the sources of row-buffer conflicts in section 3. We propose a permutation-based page interleaving scheme in section 4. After introducing our experimental environment in section 5, we present performance comparisons between the permutation-based page interleaving and three other existing schemes in section 6. Other related work is discussed in section 7. Finally, we summarize the work in section 8.

2 Memory System Considerations

2.1 Open-page and Close-page Strategies

An access to DRAM consists of *row access* and *column access*. During row access, a row of data (which is also called a page of data) containing the desired data is loaded into the row buffer. During column access, the data is read or written according to its column address. The page can be either open or closed after an access. Both strategies have their advantages and limitations. In the *open-page* strategy, if the next access to the same bank goes to the same page, only column access is necessary.[2] However, if the next access is a row-buffer miss, the DRAM precharge will not start until the request arrives. The *close-page* strategy allows the precharge to begin immediately after the current access. Which strategy will win mainly depends on the access patterns of applications. If the row-buffer hit rate is high, the open-page strategy should be more beneficial.

Most of our discussions in the rest of the paper are in the context of the open-page strategy. We propose a memory interleaving scheme to improve the row-buffer hit rate. Thus, the open-page strategy is a natural choice for our purpose since it reduces the memory access time for page hits.

2.2 Concurrent Memory Accesses

Most DRAM systems nowadays have multiple banks so that DRAM access operations can be performed on different banks in parallel. Contemporary superscalar processors exploit the instruction-level parallelism (ILP) aggressively by performing out-of-order executions, speculative executions, and non-blocking load/store. A superscalar processor may issue multiple memory requests simultaneously. Although the processor can keep running before the outstanding memory requests are finished, its ability to tolerate long memory latency is still limited [22].

All concurrent memory accesses can be classified into the following three categories:

1. *Accesses to the same page in the same bank.* These accesses fully exploit the spatial locality and can be well pipelined. Precharge and row access are needed to initiate the first access. Subsequent accesses only require column access.

2. *Accesses to different pages in different banks.* Since the accesses can be done in parallel, the corresponding operations can also be well pipelined.

3. *Accesses to different pages in the same bank.* These accesses cause *row-buffer conflicts*. Precharge and row access are needed to initiate each access. The operations cannot be pipelined. Thus, the access patterns belonging to this category have much higher latency than those belonging to the first two categories, and only partially utilize the memory bandwidth.

2.3 Framework of Interleaving Schemes

A memory system is characterized by a group of parameters in Table 1. Figure 1 shows the bit representations of a memory address for conventional cache line and page

Parameter	Parameter descriptions
m	the length of the memory address in bits.
Cache-related	Parameter descriptions
C	the cache size in bytes.
S	the number of sets in the cache.
N	the number of blocks in a set.
B	the block size in bytes.
s	the length of the cache set index in bits. $s = \log S = \log C/(BN)$.
b	the length of the cache block offset in bits. $b = \log B$.
t	the length of the cache tag in bits. $t = m - (s + b)$.
Memory-related	Parameter descriptions
K	the number of memory banks.
P	the page size in bytes, which is also the size of the row buffer.
R	the number of pages (rows) in a memory bank.
k	the length of the memory bank index in bits. $k = \log K$.
p	the length of the page offset in bits. $p = \log P$.
r	the length of the page index in bits. $r = \log R = m - (k + p)$.

Table 1: Parameters of a memory system.

---
[2]One cycle is normally required for bus turn-around between read and write accesses.

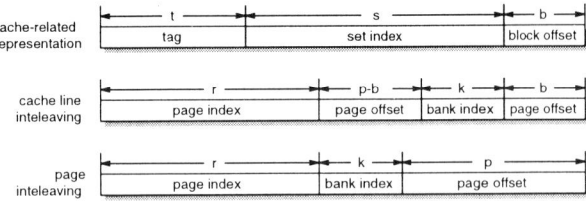

Figure 1: Bit representations of a memory address for both cache addressing and memory addressing with conventional cache line and page interleaving schemes.

interleaving, and gives the relationship between the cache-related representation and the memory-related representation for given memory hierarchical configuration.

The cache line interleaving scheme uses the k bits above the low order b bits (L2 block offset) as the memory bank index. In the uniprocessor system, the processor usually requests data from the memory in a unit of an L2 cache line. The cache line interleaving scheme attempts to access multiple memory banks uniformly (e.g. [5]). However, since continuous cache lines are distributed in different memory banks, this scheme may not effectively exploit the data locality in the row buffer.

The conventional page interleaving scheme uses the k bits above the low order p bits (page offset) as the bank index. This balances between exploiting the data locality in row buffer and referencing memory banks uniformly. However, it may cause severe row buffer conflicts in some typical cases which we will discuss next.

The high order interleaving scheme uses the high order k bits as the bank index. This exploits higher data locality than low order interleaving, but also makes accesses to multiple banks less uniform. In addition, continuous accesses in DRAMs crossing the page boundary will incur precharge and row access. Thus, there is no benefit to exploit spatial locality beyond the page size.

3 Sources of Row-buffer Conflicts

In the conventional page interleaving, there are three major sources for row-buffer conflicts and conflict misses: *L2 cache conflict misses*, *L2 cache writebacks*, and *specific memory access patterns*.

3.1 L2 Conflict Misses

We will use the following example to show that data access patterns causing L2 conflict misses will again cause DRAM row-buffer conflicts and conflict misses under some conditions.

```
double X[T], Y[T], sum;
for (i = 0; i < T; i ++)
    sum += X[i] * Y[i];
```

Without losing generality, we assume the L2 cache is direct mapped, arrays X and Y are contiguously allocated in the memory, and the address distance between $X[0]$ and $Y[0]$ is a multiple of the cache size. Then a pair of data elements $X[i]$ and $Y[i]$ ($i = 0, \cdots, T-1$) will map to the same cache line. Specifically, if a cache line holds E elements, the sequential accesses to $X[0], Y[0], \ldots, X[E-1], Y[E-1]$ will cause L2 conflict misses and generate the following accesses to the main memory:

$$x, y, x, y, \cdots, x, y$$

where x and y are the block addresses of $X[i]$ and $Y[i]$ ($i = 0, \cdots, E-1$), respectively.

What will happen in the DRAM banks for this sequence of memory accesses? To answer this question, we need to look into the bit representations of these addresses. For modern computer systems, the L2 cache size is much larger than the row-buffer (page) size. In addition, the associativity of L2 cache and the number of memory banks are limited. Thus, the bank index is a part of the L2 set index, and the page index comprises the L2 tag (refer to Figure 1).

Since x and y are block addresses mapped to the same cache line, their set indices are the same. Thus, x and y share the same bank index. On the other hand, since x and y are different block addresses, their cache tags must be different. Thus, their page indices are also different. So block addresses x and y are mapped to the same bank but on different pages. In this example, each L2 conflict miss (except the first one) will again cause a DRAM row-buffer conflict miss.

In summary, *any L2 conflicting addresses* (having the same L2 set index but different L2 tags) *are row-buffer conflicting* (having the same bank index but different page indices), providing that the L2 cache size divided by the L2 cache associativity is larger than the accumulated size of all the DRAM row-buffers. For similar reason, in conventional cache line interleaving, any L2 conflicting addresses are also row-buffer conflicting.

3.2 L2 Writebacks

The writeback policy is commonly used in memory systems to preserve data consistency and system efficiency. When an L2 cache miss happens, if the replaced cache block is dirty, it must be written back to the memory or the write buffer before the missed block is read from the memory. Since the read address and the write address belong to different memory locations mapped to the same cache set, they are L2 conflicting addresses. Consequently, they cause a row-buffer conflict under page interleaving. Normally, programs have spatial locality. When a sequence of replacement on dirty cache blocks happens, the reads and writes conflict on the row-buffer and cause frequent row-buffer conflict misses where the pages with the read addresses or the write addresses are replaced and retrieved back and forth.

Write buffers can be used to reduce processor stalls waiting for memory writes [7, 20]. The write buffer can be implemented with read bypass (read misses have higher priority than writes) or with no-bypass. The write buffer with no-bypass will not change the access patterns causing row-buffer conflicts. The write buffer with read bypass can alleviate row buffer conflicts by postponing the writebacks and grouping consecutive reads together. The effectiveness of the write buffer depends not only on its size, but also on when the buffered data are written to the memory. One write policy for reducing the row-buffer conflicts is to write the buffered data to memory only when the number pending writes reaches a threshold. However, since writebacks are not issued immediately when the memory system is free, the delayed writebacks may compete with subsequent reads and increase their latencies. Another write policy is to write the buffered data to main memory whenever there are no outstanding reads. However, the memory access patterns do not change so much in this case. In Section 6, we will show with experiments that using write buffers may reduce row-buffer miss rates but fails to reduce memory stall time effectively.

3.3 Specific Memory Access Patterns

Some specific memory access patterns may cause row-buffer conflicts. For example, when the distance of memory locations between consecutive data elements being accessed is a multiple of the accumulative size of all row buffers of the memory banks, each element is stored in a different page of the same memory bank. Thus, continuous accesses will cause row-buffer conflicts.

4 A Permutation-based Page Interleaving

In order to address the problem of row-buffer conflicts caused by the three sources discussed in the previous section, we introduce a new memory interleaving scheme which generates different bank indices by retaining spatial locality and by reducing row-buffer conflicts. An attractive technique of generating bit patterns used in memory addressing is to XOR the original bit pattern with another bit pattern [14]. Our interleaving scheme is based on this technique.

4.1 The Scheme and its Properties

Our memory interleaving scheme, called *permutation-based page interleaving*, is shown in Figure 2. The low order k bits of the L2 tag and the original bank index are used as the input to a k-bit bitwise XOR logic to generate the new bank index. The page index and the page offset are unchanged. The selection of k bits from the bank index under the conventional page interleaving scheme keeps the same degree of data locality, while the selection of k bits from the L2 tag attempts to make a wide distribution of

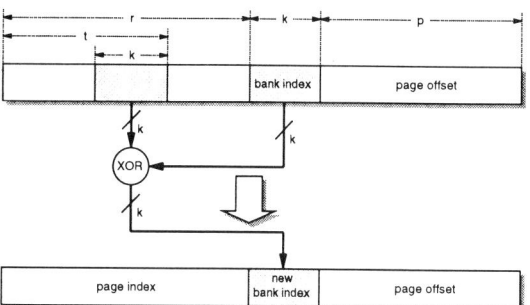

Figure 2: The permutation-based page interleaving scheme

pages among banks for exploiting concurrency. Other design choices could be used with the same mapping principle. We will discuss these later.

Let $\langle a_{m-1}a_{m-2}\cdots a_0\rangle$ be the binary representation of a memory address A. Then the bank index under the conventional page interleaving, I, is $\langle a_{k+p-1}\cdots a_p\rangle$. The new bank index after applying the permutation-based page interleaving scheme, I', is

$$a'_i = a_i \oplus a_{m-t+i-p} \quad \text{for } i = p,\ldots,k+p-1 \quad (1)$$

This interleaving scheme has the following properties, which are useful in achieving the objectives of exploiting both the concurrency and the data locality:

1. *L2-conflict addresses are distributed onto different banks.*

   Given any two L2-conflict addresses, their bank indices in conventional page interleaving are identical, but their t-bit L2 tags are different. As long as the low order k bits of the two tags are different, the k-bit XOR function will produce two different bank indices. Figure 3 shows an example of mapping four L2-conflict addresses onto 16 banks. All the four addresses are mapped onto the same bank in conventional page interleaving. After applying the permutation-based page interleaving scheme, they are distributed onto four different banks.

2. *The spatial locality of memory references is preserved.*

   All addresses in the same page are still in the same page after applying our interleaving scheme.

3. *Pages are uniformly mapped onto multiple memory banks.*

   The permutation-based page interleaving scheme still uniformly maps continuous pages onto multiple memory banks, since the conventional bank index information is used in the mapping. Figure 4 gives an example to show that continuous pages are uniformly mapped onto four memory banks by both the conventional and the permutation-based page interleaving schemes.

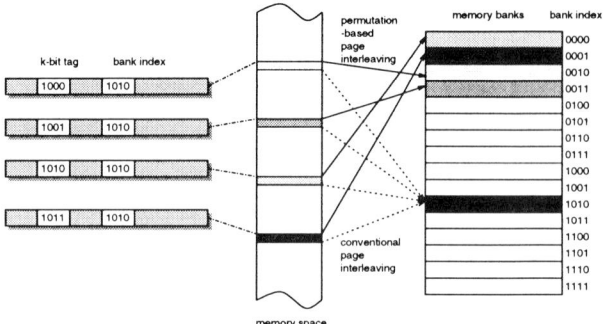

Figure 3: An example of mapping four memory addresses with the conventional page interleaving and the permutation-based page interleaving schemes. Only the k-bit bank index and the low order k-bit of L2 tag are shown for each address.

One would think that spatial locality of memory references could be maintained and page conflicts could be reduced by using only the low order k bits of the L2 tag as the bank index, thus avoiding the XOR operation. The limit of this approach is that it maps a large fraction of the memory space (of the L2 cache size) onto the same bank. This would create hot spots on some memory banks and introduce a new source of page conflicts.

There are several alternatives to the selection of k bits among the t-bit L2 tag. Since programs have data locality, it is more likely that higher order bits of L2-conflict addresses are the same. Our experiments show that choosing the low order k bits achieves or approaches the lowest row-buffer miss rate for all the benchmark programs used.

Other operations such as "add" and "subtract" can also be used to generate the bank index for reducing row-buffer conflicts. However, since this operation is done for each memory access, it should be executed as fast as possible.

We will later show in the paper that the risk for the XOR operation to cause more row-buffer conflicts is very small in practice. A major reason for this is discussed as follows. The memory space can be divided into segments in the unit of the cache size. The XOR operation uses the same k-bit L2 tag for the addresses in each segment. Thus, it does not change the conflicting relationship between any pair of addresses in each segment, which is defined as whether the pair is mapped onto the same row-buffer or not. Our analysis also shows that the XOR operation may increase the chance of conflicts only for addresses in some specific segment boundaries. Since the cache size is sufficiently large in current computer systems, these addresses form a very small subset in the entire memory address space.

4.2 Correctness of the Scheme

The mapping function of a memory interleaving scheme must satisfy the one-to-one property [15]. For a given memory address A, we can obtain its memory location A'

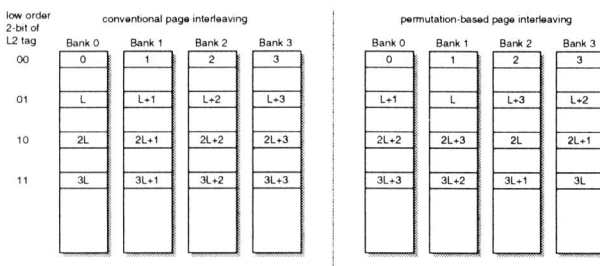

Figure 4: An example of mapping continuous pages onto 4 memory banks under the conventional and the permutation-based page interleaving schemes, where L is the number of pages the L2 cache can hold.

using the permutation-based interleaving scheme by computing its bank index I' using equation (1). Conversely, for a given memory location A', we can obtain its address A by computing $\langle a_{k+p-1}...a_p \rangle$ as $a'_i \oplus a'_{m-t+i-p}$ for $i = p, \ldots, k + p - 1$. In modern computer systems, it is always true that $(s + b) > (k + p)$. Thus, for $i = p, \ldots, k + p - 1$,

$$a'_i \oplus a'_{m-t+i-p} = (a_i \oplus a_{m-t+i-p}) \oplus a_{m-t+i-p} = a_i. \quad (2)$$

Thus, the permutation-based mapping function has the one-to-one property.

4.3 Comparisons with the Swapping Scheme

Zurawski, Murray, and Lemmon [28] present an interleaving scheme that swaps partial bits of the L2 tag and partial bits of the page offset, which is used in the AlphaStation 600 5-series workstations. We call it the swapping scheme in this paper. Wong and Baer [27] study the performance of the swapping scheme for selected SPEC92 benchmark programs by finding the optimal number of bits to be swapped for these programs.

Figure 5 describes the swapping scheme. This scheme maps every 2^n L2 conflict addresses (with the same $\langle a_{p-1} \ldots a_{p-n} \rangle$) to the same page. Thus, if two L2 conflict misses have the same high order n bits in their page offsets, they will cause page hits. However, if two L2 conflict misses have different high order n bits in their page offsets, they will still cause page conflicts. In addition, the swapping scheme may degrade the spatial locality of memory references because the block size of continuous addresses inside a page is decreased from 2^p to 2^{p-n}. The more bits that are swapped using this method, the more conflict misses can be removed, but the less spatial locality is retained. In contrast, the permutation-based scheme reduces page conflicts and preserves data locality at the same time.

The swapping scheme attempts to convert accesses to different pages in the same bank into accesses to the same page. The permutation-based scheme attempts to convert accesses to different pages in the same bank into accesses

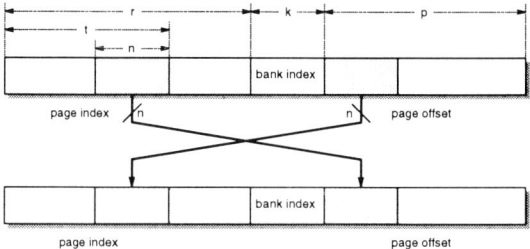

Figure 5: The swapping scheme

to different banks. The permutation-based scheme not only reduces the row-buffer conflicts of current accesses, but also potentially increases the row-buffer hit rates for subsequent accesses.

5 Experimental Environment

Performance evaluation is based on execution-driven simulations. We use the SPEC95 [23] and the TPC-C [24] as workloads, and use SimpleScalar [2] as the base simulator. The database system we have used to support the TPC-C workload is the PostgreSQL (version 6.5) [12].

In order to compare different interleaving schemes, we have modified two programs in the SimpleScalar tool set: *sim-cache* and *sim-outorder*. We use the modified *sim-cache* to measure the row buffer miss rate to compare different interleaving schemes on different memory system configurations at a small simulation cost. This allows us to investigate a wide range of choices. We use *sim-outorder* to measure the execution time and collect detailed statistics of workloads. In addition to the DRAM, the memory controller and a bus with contention are emulated. Bank contention, DRAM precharge, DRAM refresh, and processor/bus synchronization are also considered in the simulation.

We have used *sim-outorder* to configure an 8-way processor, to set the load/store queue size to 32, and to set the register update unit size to 64 in the simulation. The processor allows up to 8 outstanding memory requests, and the memory controller has the ability to accept up to 8 concurrent memory requests. Reads are allowed to bypass writes. The outstanding writes are scheduled to memory modules as soon as there are no outstanding reads. Table 2 gives the major architectural parameters. The 500 MHz processor and the 256-bit (32 bytes), 83 MHz data bus are used in Compaq Workstation XP1000 [4]. All times are converted into processor cycles in the simulation.

6 Performance Evaluation

Using execution-driven simulations with the SPEC95 and TPC-C workloads, we have evaluated the permutation-based page interleaving scheme by comparing it with three

CPU Clock rate	500 MHz
L1 inst. cache	32 Kbytes, 2-way, 32-byte block
L1 data cache	32 Kbytes, 2-way, 32-byte block
L1 cache hit time	6 ns
L2 cache	2 Mbytes, 2-way, 64-byte block
L2 cache hit time	24 ns
memory bus width	32 bytes
memory bus clock rate	83 MHz
number of memory banks	4~256
row buffer size	2~8 Kbytes
DRAM precharge time	36 ns
DRAM row access time	36 ns
DRAM column access time	24 ns

Table 2: Architectural parameters of simulation

other interleaving schemes: cache line interleaving, page interleaving, and swapping.

6.1 Comparisons of Row-buffer Miss Rates

Figure 6 presents the row buffer miss rates of SPEC95 benchmark programs and the TPC-C workload among the four interleaving schemes: the cache line interleaving (*cache line*), the page interleaving (*page*), the swapping interleaving (*swap*), and our permutation-based page interleaving (*permutation*) schemes. The memory system contains 32 memory banks. The row-buffer size of each bank is 2KB. This is a representative high performance memory system configuration [13].

We have following observations based on our experiments:

- Most programs using cache line interleaving have the highest row buffer miss rates compared with three other interleaving schemes. The row-buffer miss rates of ten benchmark programs out of the total nineteen programs are higher than 90% using cache line interleaving. Since cache line interleaving is normally associated with the close-page mode, the high row-buffer miss rates do not necessarily mean poor overall performance.

- All the programs except *su2cor* using page interleaving have lower miss rates than those using cache line interleaving. However, the miss rate reductions are not significant for most programs.

- Our experiments show that the swapping scheme reduces the row-buffer miss rates for most of the benchmark programs compared with page interleaving. However, the row-buffer miss rates of six programs using the swapping scheme are higher than those using page interleaving. This is because the swapping scheme could make programs exploit less locality than page interleaving, as we have discussed in Section 4.

- For almost all programs, our permutation-based interleaving scheme obtains the lowest row-buffer miss

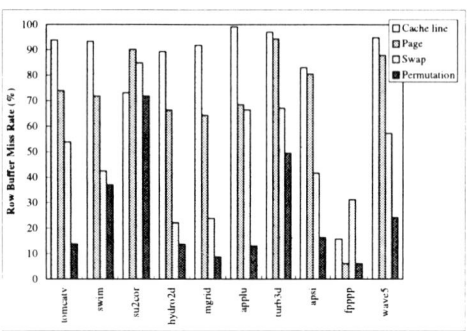
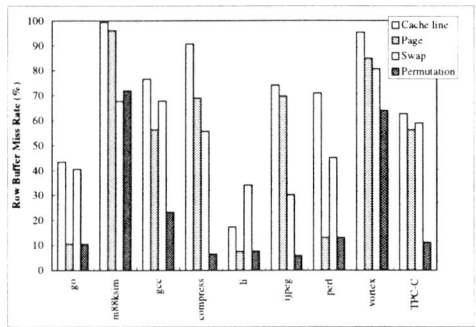

Figure 6: Row buffer miss rates for different interleaving schemes when the number of banks is 32, and the row buffer size is 2KB. The left figure contains SPECfp95 programs, and the right figure contains SPECint95 programs and TPC-C workload.

rates compared with the other three interleaving schemes. The only exception is *m88ksim* whose miss rate is 6% higher than that using the swapping scheme. Our experiments show the permutation-based interleaving scheme significantly reduces the row-buffer miss rates. For example, compared with the best performed interleaving scheme among the other three for each program, the permutation-based interleaving scheme can further reduce the row-buffer miss rate by more than 80% for five programs, and by more than 50% for eight programs.

6.2 Effects of Memory Organization Variations

Changing the number of memory banks and the row-buffer size of each memory bank, we have evaluated the effects of memory system organization variations on the interleaving schemes and on memory performance. Due to the page limit, we only present the performance of selected program *applu*, which is memory intensive and well representative for the group of workloads. Figure 7 shows the row-buffer miss rates of the program using the four interleaving schemes as the number of banks varies from 4 to 256 and the row-buffer size varies from 2 KB to 8 KB.

For each memory system variation, our experiments show that the permutation-based page interleaving scheme reduces the row-buffer miss rate dramatically. For example, when the number of memory banks is 16 and the row-buffer size is 4 KB, the permutation-based interleaving scheme reduces row-buffer miss rates by 82%, 75%, and 72%, compared with the cache-line interleaving, the page interleaving, and the swapping schemes, respectively. We also show that the permutation-based scheme reduces row-buffer miss rate more closely proportional to the increase in the number of memory banks than the other three interleaving schemes. The reason this scheme scales well with the number of memory banks is related to its bank index generation, which is able to widely distribute the conflicted pages among the memory banks. The larger the number of memory banks, the more effective of the permutation-based bank index generation.

6.3 Effects of Write Buffers

Among the nineteen programs we studied, four programs do not have memory write operations. For the rest fifteen programs, the ratios of the number of memory stores to the number of memory loads range from 0.26 to 0.84. Using SPEC95 programs *mgrid* and *applu* as examples, we show the effects of write buffers with different write policies on the row-buffer miss rates. The performance of the other workloads is consistent with that of these two. Figure 8 shows the row-buffer miss rates of *mgrid* and *applu* on a memory system of 32 banks with the row-buffer size of 2KB in each bank. We have compared the following three write policies: *write with no-bypass* (reads are not allowed to bypass writes), *write after reaching the threshold* (writes are scheduled to memory banks only when the number of outstanding writes reaches a threshold — four in our experiments), and *write when memory is idle* (writes are scheduled to memory banks whenever there are no outstanding reads).

As we have discussed in Section 3, postponing writes using write buffers could reduce the row-buffer miss rate. However, our experiments show that the existence of write buffers cannot reduce the row-buffer miss rate as effectively as the permutation-based page interleaving scheme does. For example, when the *write after reaching the threshold* policy is used for program *applu*, the permutation-based scheme can still reduce the row-buffer miss rates by 87%, 65%, and 74%, compared with cache line interleaving, page interleaving, and swapping, respectively.

Although workloads scheduled by the *write after reaching threshold* policy normally get lower row-buffer miss rates than those scheduled by the policy of *write when memory is idle*, the *write after reaching threshold* policy

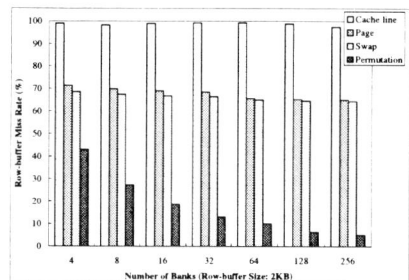 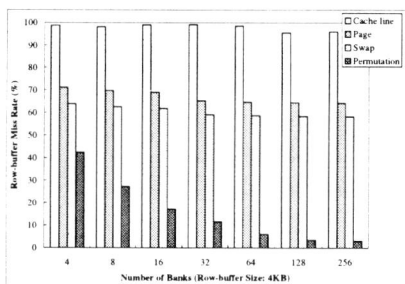 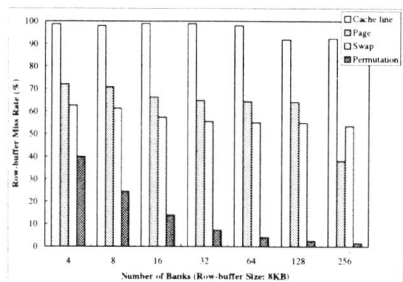

Figure 7: Row buffer miss rates of program *applu* using four interleaving schemes: the cache line, the page, the swapping, and the permutation-based interleaving. The number of memory banks changes from 4 to 256. The performance results in the left figure, the middle one, and the right one correspond to row buffer sizes of 2KB, 4KB, and 8KB, respectively.

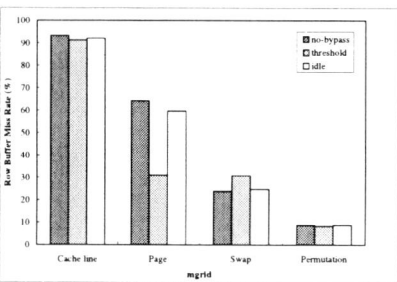

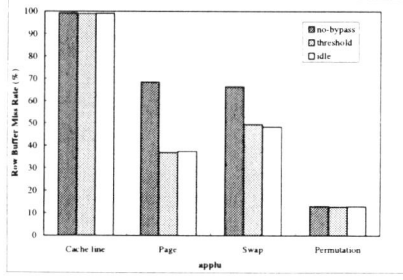

Figure 8: Row buffer miss rates using the three write policies: *write with no-bypass* (no-bypass), *write after reaching the threshold* (threshold), and *write when memory is idle* (idle). The upper figure corresponds to *mgrid*, and the bottom one corresponds to *applu*. The number of memory banks is 32, the row buffer size is 2KB.

may cause higher total execution time due to longer memory stall time. For example, our experiments show that program *mgrid* scheduled by the *write after reaching the threshold* policy reduces the row-buffer miss rate using page interleaving scheme by 48% compared with the policy of *write when memory is idle*, but its total execution time is 12% longer. For this reason, the policy of *write when memory is idle* is used for comparing the overall performance of different interleaving schemes in our study.

6.4 Comparisons of Memory Stall Times

We have measured the memory access portions of CPIs of the SPEC95 programs and the TPC-C workload to compare the four interleaving schemes. In order to show the memory stall portion in each program, we used a method similar to that presented in [1] and [6]. We simulated a system with an infinitely large L2 cache to eliminate all main memory accesses. The difference between the execution time on this "perfect" system and that on a system using the investigated interleaving scheme is defined as the memory stall portion of the program on the system using the interleaving scheme.

We have only studied the SPECfp95 programs and the TPC-C workload because memory accesses only account for a negligible portion in the total execution time for the SPECint95 programs. Figure 9 presents the memory stall portion of the SPECfp95 programs and the TPC-C workload using the four interleaving schemes: the cache line, the page, the swapping, and the permutation-based interleaving schemes. The close-page mode is used for cache line interleaving, while the open-page mode is used for the other three schemes.

Compared with page interleaving, our permutation-based interleaving scheme is able to reduce the memory stall time of these programs by 16% to 50%. The average memory stall time reduction for all the SPECfp95 programs and the TPC-C workload is 37%. Compared with the swapping scheme, our scheme can reduce the memory stall time of these programs by 14% to 53%. The average memory stall time reduction is 33%.

Compared with cache line interleaving, the permutation based interleaving scheme is able to reduce the memory stall time of these programs by 21% to 68%. The only exception is for program *su2cor*, where the memory stall time is increased by 11%. The average memory stall time reduction is 36%. Here is the reason for the exception. Although the permutation-based scheme does reduce the row-buffer miss rate by 8% for *su2cor* compared with the cache line interleaving scheme, the row-buffer miss rate is still as high as 70%. Because cache line interleaving is combined with close-page mode, the precharge can begin

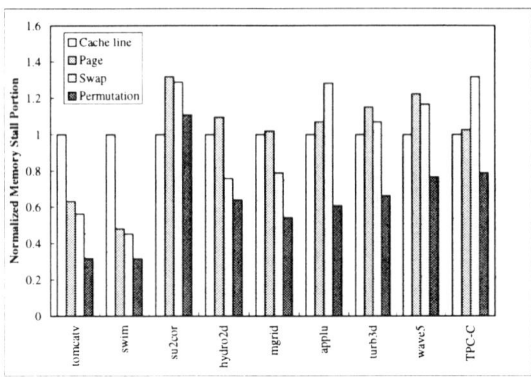

Figure 9: Normalized memory stall portion of the SPECfp95 programs and the TPC-C workload using the four interleaving schemes. All the stall time values are normalized to that using the cache line interleaving scheme. The number of memory banks is 32, and the row buffer size is 2KB.

earlier than in the open-page mode for a row-buffer miss. When the row-buffer miss rate is so high, the benefit of a row-buffer hit cannot offset the penalty caused by late precharge in open-page mode. Thus cache line interleaving outperforms the other schemes which use the open-page mode for this program.

We have also made performance comparisons between cache line interleaving and page interleaving. Among the nine programs we have studied, cache line interleaving outperforms page interleaving for seven programs.

The swapping scheme performs better than cache line interleaving for four programs but worse for five programs. For those four programs, the swapping scheme effectively reduces the row-buffer miss rate so that open-page mode is more beneficial than close-page mode. For most programs, the swapping scheme performs better than page interleaving because the swapping scheme reduces row-buffer conflicts. But for two of these nine programs, the swapping scheme achieves worse performance than page interleaving because data locality cannot be retained after the "swapping".

7 Other Related Work

Hsu and Smith propose and study several memory interleaving schemes which can both increase data locality and avoid hot banks in vector supercomputers with Cached DRAM [10]. There are several other research papers dealing with the bank conflict problem of vector accesses in vector supercomputers. Authors in [8] and [19] attempt to use the prime memory systems to address the conflict issues. Other papers focus on the memory interleaving schemes on vector systems [3, 15, 17, 18, 21, 25]. Authors in [9], [3], and [17] study the skew schemes. Rau, Schlansker, and Yen propose a pseudo-random interleaving technique using the XOR function to randomize the mapping of references to memory modules in [15]. Their scheme can eliminate the occurrence of long clusters due to structured data access. Sohi studies permutation-based interleaving schemes which can improve memory bandwidth for a wide range of access patterns for vector computers [21]. Valero, Lang, and Ayguadé [25] divide the memory address into several portions according to the width of bank index, then XOR all the address portions to generate the bank index. Their method can avoid bank conflict due to power-of-two strides in vector machines. Seznec and Lenfant [18] propose the Interleaved Parallel Scheme, which uses the XOR operation and parameters related to the numbers of processors, logical memory banks, and physical memory banks to induce more equitable distribution over memory banks for a wider set of vectors than the normal mappings.

In contrast to above cited interleaving schemes, our major objective is to reduce the conflicts of DRAM row-buffers. Concurrent accesses to the same bank can be well pipelined in a contemporary DRAM system as long as they hit the row-buffer. In vector machines, concurrent accesses to the same bank always cause bank conflicts and cannot be pipelined.

Besides memory bank interleaving techniques, there are other approaches to address the memory latency problem, such as blocking-free cache, prefetching, thread changing, and data prediction and speculation [26].

8 Conclusion

We have shown that the conflicts and conflict misses of DRAM row-buffers significantly increase memory stall times. We have analyzed their sources in the context of superscalar processors with two levels of caches. Our study indicates that the miss rates of row-buffers are mainly determined by the ways data are interleaved among the memory banks. Conventional schemes, such as cache line and page interleaving, could not effectively exploit both the concurrency of multiple banks and data locality in the row-buffer of each bank. Aiming at achieving the both objectives, we have proposed a memory interleaving scheme, called *permutation-based page interleaving*. By using the fast exclusive-OR operation to generate the bank index, our scheme can dramatically reduce the row buffer miss rates for SPEC95 and TPC-C workloads compared with the two conventional interleaving schemes and an existing optimized commercial scheme. Our execution-driven simulations show that the permutation-based scheme outperforms the cache line interleaving, the page interleaving, and the swapping schemes by reducing the average memory stall times of the workloads by 36%, 37%, and 33%, respectively. In terms of overall performance, the permutation-based scheme reduces the average execution times of the workloads by 12%, 10%, and 8%, compared with the cache line interleaving, the page interleaving, and the swapping schemes, respectively.

The potential performance penalty of the permutation-based scheme is the exclusive-OR operation for generating each memory bank index. For a modern computer system with multiple levels of caches, this operation is not in the critical path, and can be overlapped with operations above this level in the memory hierarchy. Our experiments show that the additional runtime overhead involved is negligible compared with effective reductions of memory stall times. For example, when using the permutation-based page interleaving scheme, the average memory access latency of the workloads is around 50 CPU cycles, while the exclusive-OR operation only takes about one cycle [11].

Using memory access scheduling techniques to exploit row-buffer locality and concurrency is another attractive approach (e.g. [16]). We believe the combination of access scheduling and the permutation-based interleaving scheme can further improve memory performance.

Acknowledgment:

We appreciate the helpful comments from the anonymous referees. We thank Bill Bynum for reading the paper and for his constructive suggestions. This work is supported in part by the National Science Foundation under grants CCR-9400719 and CCR-9812187, and EIA-9977030, by the Air Force Office of Scientific Research under grant AFOSR-95-1-0215, and by Sun Microsystems under grant EDUE-NAFO-980405.

References

[1] D. Burger, J. R. Goodman, and A. Kägi. Memory bandwidth limitations of future microprocessors. In *Proc. of the 23nd Annual International Symposium on Computer Architecture*, pages 78–89, 1996.

[2] D. C. Burger and T. M. Austin. The SimpleScalar Tool Set, Version 2.0. Technical Report CS-TR-1997-1342, University of Wisconsin, Madison, June 1997.

[3] C.-L. Chen and C.-K. Liao. Analysis of vector access performance on skewed interleaved memory. In *Proc. of the 16th Annual International Symposium on Computer Architecture*, pages 387–394, 1989.

[4] Compaq Computer Corp. *Technology for performance: Compaq professional workstation XP1000*, Jan. 1999. White paper (document number ECG050/0199).

[5] V. Cuppu and B. Jacob. Organizational design trade-offs at the DRAM, memory bus, and memory controller level: Initial results. Technical Report UMD-SCA-TR-1999-2, University of Maryland, Nov. 1999.

[6] V. Cuppu, B. Jacob, B. Davis, and T. Mudge. A performance comparison of contemporary DRAM architectures. In *Proc. of the 26th Annual International Symposium on Computer Architecture*, pages 222–233, May 1999.

[7] J. S. Emer and D. W. Clark. A characterization of processor performance in the VAX-11/780. In *Proc. of the 11th Annual International Symposium on Computer Architecture*, pages 301–310, 1984.

[8] Q. S. Gao. The chinese remainder theorem and the prime memory system. In *Proc. of the 20th Annual International Symposium on Computer Architecture*, pages 337–340, May 1993.

[9] D. T. Harper III and J. R. Jump. Performance evaluation of vector accesses in parallel memories using a skewed storage scheme. In *Proc. of the 13th Annual International Symposium on Computer Architecture*, pages 324–328, 1986.

[10] W.-C. Hsu and J. E. Smith. Performance of cached DRAM organizations in vector supercomputers. In *Proc. of the 20th Annual International Symposium on Computer Architecture*, pages 327–336, May 1993.

[11] W. L. Lynch, G. Lauterbach, and J. I. Chamdani. Low load latency through sum-addressed memory (SAM). In *Proc. of the 25th Annual International Symposium on Computer Architecture*, pages 369–379, 1998.

[12] PostgreSQL Inc. *PostgreSQL 6.5*. http://www.postgresql.org.

[13] Rambus Inc. *256/288-Mbit Direct RDRAM*, 2000. http://www.rambus.com/developer/downloads/rdram_256s_0060_10.pdf.

[14] B. R. Rau. Pseudo-randomly interleaved memory. In *Proc. of the 18th Annual International Symposium on Computer Architecture*, pages 74–83, 1991.

[15] B. R. Rau, M. S. Schlansker, and D. W. L. Yen. The CYDRA 5 stride-insensitive memory system. In *Proc. of the 1989 International Conference on Parallel Processing*, volume 1, pages 242–246, 1989.

[16] S. Rixner, W. J. Dally, U. J. Kapasi, P. Mattson, and J. D. Owens. Memory access scheduling. In *Proc. of the 27th Annual International Symposium on Computer Architecture*, pages 128–138, 2000.

[17] T. Sakakibara, K. Kitai, T. Isobe, S. Yazawa, T. Tanaka, Y. Inagami, and Y. Tamaki. Scalable parallel memory architecture with a skew scheme. In *Proc. of the 1993 International Conference on Supercomputing*, pages 157–166, 1993.

[18] A. Seznec and J. Lenfant. Interleaved parallel schemes: Improving memory throughput on supercomputers. In *Proc. of the 19th Annual International Symposium on Computer Architecture*, pages 246–255, 1992.

[19] A. Seznec and J. Lenfant. Odd memory systems may be quite interesting. In *Proc. of the 20th Annual International Symposium on Computer Architecture*, pages 341–350, May 1993.

[20] K. Skadron and D. W. Clark. Design issues and tradeoffs for write buffers. In *Proc. of the 3rd International Symposium on High Performance Computer Architecture*, pages 144–155, Feb. 1997.

[21] G. S. Sohi. High-bandwidth interleaved memories for vector processors - a simulation study. Technical Report CS-TR-1988-790, University of Wisconsin - Madison, Sept. 1988.

[22] S. T. Srinivasan and A. R. Lebeck. Load latency tolerance in dynamically scheduled processors. In *Proceedings of the 31st International Symposium on Microarchitecture*, 1998.

[23] Standard Performance Evaluation Corporation. *SPEC CPU95 Version 1.10*, May 1997.

[24] Transaction Processing Performance Council. *TPC Benchmark C Standard Specification, Revision 3.3.3*, Apr. 1998.

[25] M. Valero, T. Lang, and E. Ayguadé. Conflict-free access of vectors with power-of-two strides. In *Proc. of the 1992 International Conference on Supercomputing*, pages 149–156, 1992.

[26] M. V. Wilkes. The memory gap, Keynote Address. In *Workshop on Solving the Memory Wall Problem*, June 2000.

[27] W. Wong and J.-L. Baer. DRAM on-chip caching. Technical Report UW CSE 97-03-04, University of Washington, Feb. 1997.

[28] J. H. Zurawski, J. E. Murray, and P. J. Lemmon. The design and verification of the AlphaStation 600 5-series workstation. *Digital Technical Journal*, 7(1):89–99, 1995.

Predictor-Directed Stream Buffers

Timothy Sherwood   Suleyman Sair   Brad Calder

Department of Computer Science and Engineering
University of California, San Diego
{sherwood,ssair,calder}@cs.ucsd.edu

Abstract

An effective method for reducing the effect of load latency in modern processors is data prefetching. One form of data prefetching, stream buffers, has been shown to be particularly effective due to its' ability to detect data streams and run ahead of them, prefetching as it goes. Unfortunately, in the past, the applicability of streaming was limited to stride intensive code.

In this paper we propose Predictor-Directed Stream Buffers *(PSB), a scheme in which the stream buffer follows an address prediction stream instead of a fixed stride. In addition, we examine using confidence techniques to guide the allocation and prioritization of stream buffers and their prefetch requests. Our results show for pointer-based applications that PSB provides a 30% speedup on average over no prefetching, and provides an average 10% speedup over using previously proposed stride-based stream buffers for pointer-intensive applications.*

1 Introduction

A great deal of effort has been invested in reducing the impact of cache misses on program performance. As with any other latency, cache miss latency can be tolerated using compile-time techniques such as instruction scheduling, or run-time techniques including out-of-order issue, decoupled execution, or non-blocking loads. It is also possible to reduce the latency of cache misses using multi-level caches, victim caches, and prefetching.

Several approaches have been proposed for prefetching data to reduce or eliminate load latency. These range from inserting compiler-based prefetches to pure hardware-based data prefetching. Compiler-based prefetching annotates load instructions or inserts explicit prefetch instructions to bring data into the cache before it is needed to hide the load latency. They use locality analysis to insert prefetch instructions, showing significant improvements [21]. Hardware-based prefetching can dynamically predict prefetch address streams and predict prefetch addresses that may be hard to find using compiler analysis. Compiler and hardware-based prefetching can be used together, since the compiler can be used to prefetch load instructions for which it can accurately determine locality information, and the hardware prefetcher can be used for those load address patterns not captured. In this paper we focus on a new hardware-based prefetcher.

The focus of our research is improving the performance of data prefetching with stream buffers in the context of a realistic processor design. Stream buffers were originally proposed by Jouppi [19] to prefetch a stream of sequential cache blocks. When a cache miss occurs, the next sequential cache block is allocated into a stream buffer. The stream buffer then prefetches sequential cache blocks from that address, as bandwidth permits, until the buffer is full. As prefetches are used, new data is brought in, keeping the buffer far enough in advance of the data's use so that it can potentially hide the entire latency.

Palacharla and Kessler [22] extended stream buffers by associating a stride with each stream buffer. They examined providing a stride from a table which was indexed by the area of memory being accessed. Farkas et. al. [13] further extended this research by using a PC indexed stride table, which allows for detection of many strides over the same region of memory.

In this paper we propose a new form of stream buffer called the *Predictor-Directed Stream Buffer* (PSB). Instead of associating a fixed stride with each buffer, we use a *predictor* to generate the next address to prefetch. We simulate the use of a hybrid *Stride Filtered Markov* (SFM) predictor to direct stream buffer prefetching and find it is quite adept at finding both complex array access and pointer chasing behavior over a set of pointer intensive benchmarks.

Farkas et. al. [13] show the importance of using allocation filters to prevent the stream buffers from being allocated and deallocated too often and for too many streams, an effect we call *stream thrashing*. We propose a technique based on confidence for eliminating stream thrashing as well as making more effective use of available processor and predictor resources. This is done by using confidence to guide stream buffer allocation and prefetch prioritization.

The rest of the paper is organized as follows. Section 2 describes past address prediction work as it relates to PSBs. In section 3, prior hardware prefetching models are discussed. Section 4 describes our Predictor-Directed Stream Buffer architecture. Simulation methodology and benchmark descriptions can be found in Section 5. Section 6 presents results for our architecture, and our conclusions are summarized in section 7.

2 Address Prediction

To guide hardware-based prefetching, accurate address prediction is needed. In performing this research, we examined using stride-based address prediction, Markov/context address prediction, and correlated address prediction.

2.1 Stride

A *stride* predictor [8, 12] keeps track of not only the last address referenced by a load, but also the difference between the last address of the load and the address before that. This difference is called the stride. The predictor speculates that the new address seen by the load will be the sum of the last value seen and the stride. We chose to use the two-delta stride predictor [12, 28], which only replaces the predicted stride with a new stride if that new stride has been seen twice in a row.

2.2 Context/Markov Predictor

Context [28, 29, 32] and *Markov* [6, 7, 18] predictors are fundamentally similar, in that each predictor bases its prediction on the last values seen. An order k context/Markov predictor uses the k past values to predict the next one. It can only provide a prediction, if the given pattern has been seen and the transition is recorded into a prediction table.

A Markov predictor assumes that the address stream seen in a program can be efficiently modeled by a Markov model. A Markov model is a set of states and transition frequencies where each state has a probability of transition to another. Each transition from address A to B is assigned a weight representing the fraction of As that are followed by a B. The Markov predictor described in [18] is a first order context predictor as it uses only the last address to predict the next one.

Bekerman et. al. [2] propose yet another context-based predictor. For every load, they combine a series of past base addresses (they state that 4 is enough for reasonable accuracy), to generate a history and store it into a first-level table. They use that history as an index into a second level table that stores a predicted *base* address. They then add the load's static offset (which could be stored in the first-level table) with the predicted base address. By using base addresses, a high-level of global correlation is achieved for multiple load instructions accessing different fields in the same object.

In this paper, we only provide results for stride and first order Markov-based prediction. We simulated higher order Markov predictors and the correlation predictor [2], but saw little to no improvement in prediction accuracy and coverage over first order Markov predictor for the programs we examined. This is partially due to the fact that correlated loads lie within the same cache block for the programs we examined. Therefore, correctly predicting the correlated load provides less gains in terms of prefetching, since we perform our predictions and prefetches at the cache block granularity.

3 Hardware Prefetching Models

We classify the prior hardware prefetching research into three models – Fetch Stream Prefetching, Demand-Based Prefetching, and Decoupled Prefetching.

3.1 Fetch Stream Prefetching

The first model follows the branch prediction or fetch stream, predicting and prefetching addresses [9, 16, 10, 4].

Chen and Baer [9] proposed an approach to provide the load prediction early by using a Look-Ahead PC, which can run ahead of the normal instruction fetch engine. The LA-PC is guided by a branch prediction architecture that runs ahead of the fetch engine, and is used to index into an address prediction table to predict data addresses for cache prefetching. Since the LA-PC provided the instruction address stream ahead of the normal fetch engine, they were able to initiate data cache prefetches farther in advanced than if they had used the normal PC, which in turn allowed more of the data cache miss penalty to be masked. The amount of load latency that can be hidden is dependent upon how far the look-ahead PC can get in front of the execution stream.

Reinman et.al. [23] extended the approach of Chen and Baer [9] to instruction prefetching. In their approach, they only have one branch predictor instead of two as in Chen and Baer. This is accomplished by decoupling the branch predictor from the instruction cache with a fetch target queue between them. The queue is used to store fetch block predictions, which are then fed into the instruction cache in a later cycle. The fetch addresses in the queue are used to perform instruction cache prefetching. They recently extended this approach to perform power-efficient instruction prefetching by decoupling the tag component of the instruction cache access from the data component of the cache access [24]. The tag component verifies if an address is in the cache in a separate cycle before the data component access for the instruction lookup. If the fetch address is not found, it is prefetched, while the fetch address is queued up to be consumed by the data component. In this new design, the data component access consumes significantly less power, since only one way of the data component is driven, and the way was determined during the tag access in a prior cycle. They are currently extending this design to fetch stream data cache prefetching.

3.2 Demand-Based Prefetching

The second model can be classified as demand-based prefetching. In this approach an action such as a cache miss or the use of a cache block has to occur for a prefetch to be generated.

An early example of a demand-based prefetching architecture is *Next Line Prefetching* (NLP) by Smith [31], where each cache block was tagged with a bit indicating when the next block should be prefetched. When a block is prefetched its tag bit is set to zero. When the block is accessed during a fetch and the bit is zero, a prefetch of the next sequential block is triggered and the bit is set to one.

Another demand-based prefetching architecture is Shadow Directory Prefetching (SDP) by Charney and Puzak [6]. In SDP, each L2 cache block has a shadow address associated with it. The shadow address points to the cache block accessed right after the corresponding cache block, providing a simple Markov transition. A hit in the L2 cache with a useful shadow entry triggers a prefetch of the shadow address. Alexander and Kedem [1] examined using a similar Markov table, but distributed over the DRAM modules, which are used to prefetch cache blocks from DRAM array into an SRAM buffer.

The last example we will discuss is the Markov prefetcher used by Joseph and Grunwald [18]. When a cache miss occurred, the miss address would index into their Markov prediction table to provide the next set of possible cache addresses that have followed this miss address before. After these addresses are prefetched, the prefetcher stays idle until the next cache miss. They do not use the predicted addresses to re-index into the table to generate more predictions for prefetching.

In order to minimize the load on the bus, prefetch bandwidth is limited by employing *accuracy based adaptivity* [18]. In this scheme, two-bit saturation counters are added to each prediction address. The idea is to remove prefetches that have exhibited poor behavior in the past. When a prefetch is discarded from the prefetch buffer without being used, the corresponding counter is incremented. If the prefetched block is used, then the counter associated with the entry that made the prediction, is decremented. When the sign bit of the counter is set, the relevant entry in the prediction table is disabled. Prefetch requests from disabled entries are tracked so that they can be enabled when they start making correct predictions.

3.3 Decoupled/Stream Prefetching

In this model the prefetcher is loosely decoupled from the instruction fetch stream and can potentially prefetch down multiple predicted streams independent of what the instruction fetch stream is doing.

3.3.1 Decoupled Models

An access decoupled architecture partitions programs into a prefetching instruction stream and an execution instruction stream [15, 3, 17]. As long as the prefetch stream can run ahead of the execution stream, the memory latency can be masked. Roth et. al. [25, 26] has examined both a software and hardware approach for prefetching recursive data structures using a decoupled model. Yang and Lebeck [33] examined an architecture which uses the compiler to create small prefetch kernels of instructions, which are executed in parallel with the original application in a separate prefetch engine.

3.3.2 Stream Buffers

Jouppi introduced *stream buffers* to improve direct mapped cache performance [19]. The stream buffers follow multiple streams prefetching them in parallel and these streams can be completely decoupled from the instruction stream of the processor. They are designed as FIFO buffers that prefetch consecutive cache blocks, starting with the one that missed in the L1 cache. On subsequent misses, the head of the stream buffer is probed. If the reference hits, that block is transferred to the L1 cache.

Palacharla and Kessler [22] suggested two techniques to enhance the effectiveness of stream buffers : *allocation filters* and a *non-unit stride* detection mechanism. The filter prevents a stream buffer from being allocated until two consecutive misses occur for the same stream. Also presented by Palacharla and Kessler is a *minimum delta* non-unit detection scheme. With this scheme, the dynamic stride is determined by the minimum signed difference between the miss address and the past N miss addresses. If this minimum delta is smaller then the L1 block size, then the stride is set to the cache block size with the sign of the minimum delta. Otherwise, the stride is set to the minimum delta.

To implement the non-unit stride detection an address indexed stride table is used. To find the striding behavior the memory is divided up into chunks, and associated with each chunk is a stride. While this approach is quite effective at finding strides, we found that it was uniformly outperformed by the per-load stride detector of Farkas et. al. [13]. Therefore, we only present comparison results of our approach with the PC-based stride prediction stream buffers.

Farkas et. al. [13] made an important contribution by extending this model to use a *PC-based* stride predictor to provide the stride on stream buffer allocation. The PC-stride predictor determines the stride for a load instruction by using the PC to index into a stride address prediction table. This differs from the minimum-delta scheme, since the minimum-delta uses the global history to calculate the stride for a given load. PC-stride predictor uses an associative buffer to record the last miss address for N load instructions, along with their program counter values. Thus, the stride prediction for a stream buffer is based only on the past memory behavior of the load for which the stream buffer was allocated.

Farkas et. al. [14] further enhanced the stream buffer design of Palacharla and Kessler by enforcing the streams being followed by multiple stream buffers to be non-overlapping. This prevented duplication and saved bus bandwidth. Furthermore, instead of the FIFO structure which had been originally proposed by Jouppi, they proposed the use of a fully-associative stream buffer lookup, which we model.

4 Predictor-Directed Stream Buffers

We will now describe our Predictor-directed Stream Buffer (PSB) architecture. The PSB architecture resides on chip and prefetches data from the L2 cache and main memory into the stream buffers. If a prefetch request is not found in the L2, it will service the request from main memory. We concentrate on stream buffers instead of the many other architectures described in the previous section because of their simple yet effective design, their ability to follow a prefetch stream independent of the fetch stream, and the design fits nicely with an on-chip prefetcher to try to hide L2 and main memory latency.

We present an approach that extends the PC indexed stream buffer design of Farkas et. al. [13]. As described in Section 3, the PC index scheme uses a stream buffer which is guided by a static stride, provided at allocation time by a per-PC stride table as shown in Figure 1. This approach can work well for stride-based applications, but the stream buffers do not follow the correct stream for non-stride based load patterns, such as during the traversal of a recursive data structure.

To address this problem, we propose Predictor-Directed Stream Buffers (PSB) as shown in Figure 2. The general idea of a PSB is to use a predictor to generate an address stream for prefetching. The predictor takes as input some prediction information, such as the last address accessed and history information, and then generates a prediction for a given stream buffer. This prediction is then stored back into the stream buffer, and the prediction information in the stream buffer is updated. In this way we can generate prediction n from prediction $n-1$. The base of the recursion is a cache miss which causes a stream buffer allocation.

There are two major parts to PSBs, a per-stream history which is stored with each stream buffer, and a stateless address predictor which is shared between stream buffers. The per-stream history is used to keep data about a particular stream buffer and may be used for a variety of purposes, such as indexing into the address predictor, confidence information, and local stride. The primary service of the per-stream history is to store a current or speculative state which can be fed to the predictor. The prediction from the address prediction table is then used to update the state information in the stream buffer so that a new speculative prediction can be made. It is a key point that the address prediction table is

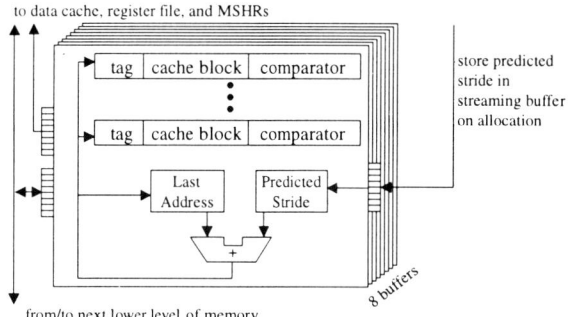

Figure 1: Stride-based Stream Buffer Architecture. Eight stream buffers are shown (overlapping each other). Each stream buffer can hold N cache blocks. When a stream buffer is allocated, it is assigned a predicted stride to use to generate all of its prefetch addresses.

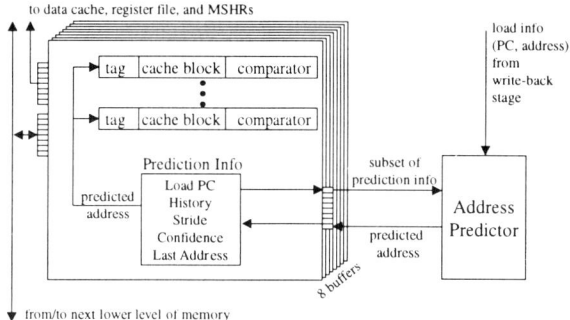

Figure 2: A Predictor-Directed Stream Buffer. We modify the stream buffer so it accesses a separate address prediction table to get its next prefetch address.

not updated when the stream buffer makes a prediction, this step is done separately in the write-back stage when a load has a data cache miss.

This model allows the stream buffer to follow the address prediction stream of any address predictor, whose predictions are more accurate than those of a fixed-stride predictor.

4.1 Predictor-Directed Stream Buffer Implementation

Figure 2 shows the general model of our predictor-directed stream buffer architecture. Each stream buffer holds (1) the PC of the load that caused the stream buffer to be allocated, (2) the last predicted address for the load, and (3) any additional prediction information (e.g., history state or confidence) needed to perform the next address prediction. The stream buffer is on-chip next to the address predictor, which

45

in our case is a stride-filtered Markov predictor.

There are several stages of execution a stream buffer will go through over the course of a program, starting with the allocation of a stream and ending with it's reallocation. We now show the initialization, steady state operation of, and termination of a stream in a stream buffer.

Allocation A stream buffer is allocated, subject to allocation filters (see section 4.3), when a load executes and it misses both in the data cache and the stream buffer. When a load is given a stream buffer, it copies its PC, current address, and any additional prediction information to the stream buffer from the address predictor. This initialization stage is only done once per allocation, and is directed only from predictor to stream buffer, the state of the address predictor is not modified. This copied state will later be used for indexing into the prediction table.

Prediction Each cycle, one stream buffer is chosen to make a prediction using the address predictor, according to priority heuristics described in section 4.4. The information stored in the stream buffer is used to index into the address predictor, returning the next predicted address, and potentially updating the stream buffer's history information. We properly model allowing only a single prediction per cycle to be generated from the predictor. Due to the fact that only one request (miss or prefetch) can be processed by the bus from the L1 to the L2 cache at a time, the predictor was not a bottleneck even with the one prediction per cycle limitation.

Once a stream buffer has been allocated, the stream buffer's history information is updated after each prediction. The address prediction table, as was mentioned earlier, remains unchanged while generating a prediction for a stream buffer. For example, a design such as a context predictor which uses a history of the last N addresses to index into the address predictor would store the history of its last N predictions in the stream buffer, and use this as an index into the address predictor each cycle. The history of the last N addresses stored in the stream buffer is updated after a prediction, *not* the state in the address prediction table. Therefore, the stream buffer maintains its own prediction history information.

Before inserting the prediction into the stream buffer, the stream buffers are searched in parallel for the cache block of the predicted address. This was used by Farkas et. al., [13] to prevent stream buffers from prefetching down overlapping paths. If the prediction is found to be already resident in a buffer entry then the prediction is ignored, no useful prediction is made that cycle, and the stream buffer prediction history information is updated. If prediction is not found in the stream buffer, the prediction is stored in the stream buffer's least recently used entry, and that entry is marked as ready for prefetching. Once all entries have been predicted for a stream buffer, no further entries will be predicted until (1) an entry is cleared during a lookup (it is a hit), or (2) the stream buffer is reallocated.

Prefetching Once an entry has a valid prediction associated with it, it is ready to be prefetched. We only allow prefetches to occur if the L1-L2 bus is free at the start of any given cycle. When the bus is free, a stream buffer with an entry containing a valid un-prefetched prediction is chosen using the priority scheduling algorithms described in section 4.4. The prefetch is then sent to the lower levels of memory and the entry is marked as prefetched and waiting.

Lookup When a load performs a lookup in the L1 data cache, it searches all of the stream buffer entries in parallel for a hit. For our results, we assume the data cache lookup latency is the same as the stream buffer lookup latency. If there is a hit in the stream buffer, and the data is not yet ready in the data cache, the cache block stored in the stream buffer is moved into the data cache. If there is a tag hit in the stream buffer, but the block is not ready in the stream buffer, the tag is moved into a data cache MSHR, and the data cache handles the block when it comes back from memory. For a stream buffer hit, the corresponding stream buffer entry is freed for a new prediction and prefetch.

We will now describe our design using a Stride-Filtered Markov (SFM) address predictor, although any address predictor [2, 18, 28, 29, 32] can be used to guide the predictor-directed stream buffer. We examined several types of predictors (including stride with correlated [2]), but only provide results for a SFM table, as it performed uniformly better.

4.2 Stride-Filtered Markov Predictor

Charney and Reeves [7] and also Joseph and Grunwald [18] introduced *Markov* prefetching, and provided results for a "stride and Markov in series" predictor. We use this predictor to guide our predictor-directed stream buffer, and make a few minor improvements which are described below.

To provide address prediction for the stream buffers we use a *Stride-Filtered Markov* (SFM) predictor. The predictor has a two-delta stride table in front of a Markov prediction table, as shown in Figure 3. In the write-back stage, the load instruction is checked to see if it hit or missed in the L1 data cache. The prediction table is only updated on a miss (i.e. we are predicting the miss stream). In addition, our implementation does not store loads that receive their value forwarded from stores in the prediction table, since we found little benefit from prefetching these loads.

In the write-back stage, the load-PC (for a missed load) is used to index into the stride table. The stride table stores (1) the last address for the load, (2) the last stride for the load, (3) the 2-delta stride, and (4) some confidence information. If the stride calculated by (current miss address - last address) does not match the last stride or 2-delta stride, then the Markov table is updated noting the transition from last address to current address. The last address is stored as

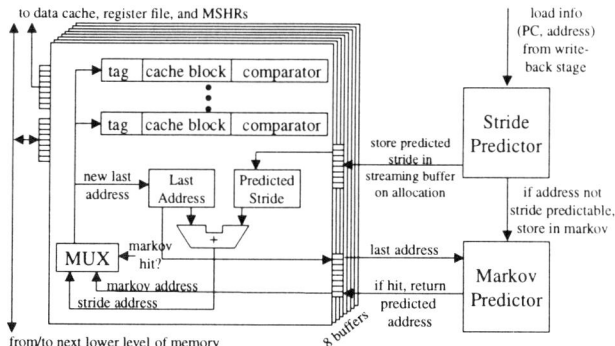

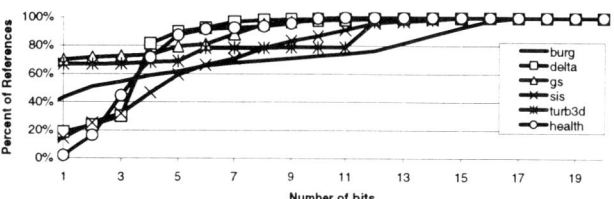

Figure 3: Stride-Filtered Markov Predictor-Directed Stream Buffer Architecture. When a stream buffer is allocated it is assigned a fixed stride from the stride-pc table. To generate the next prefetch address the last address is (1) looked up in the Markov table, and (2) used to calculate a next stride address. If the Markov table hits, then the Markov address is used, otherwise the next stride address is used for the prefetch.

Figure 4: The number of bits to accurately predict cache misses using the Markov Difference Predictor. The y-axis shows the percent of L1 cache misses that could be correctly predicted given the number of bits used for each entry of the markov table shown on the x-axis. The cache miss address is predicted by adding together the address used to index the Markov table with the value stored in the Markov table.

the tag, and the current address as the data entry. Accordingly, when that same last address is seen again, it will get a hit in the Markov table, predicting the next miss address not captured by the stride predictor.

For the SFM predictor examined in this paper, we do not use any history to index into the Markov part of the table, in other words we present results from a first order Markov predictor. We examined using higher order Markov predictors as in [18], but found that it provided little improvement, confirming their results. The only additional information we copy into the stream buffer from the predictor is some confidence information, to guide priority scheduling described below.

In order to reduce the size of the Markov predictor table we store into the table only the difference between consecutive cache miss addresses, rather than the absolute address as is done in prior work. Of course this number can be further reduced by storing this difference as the number of cache blocks rather than at a byte granularity. To calculate the address to prefetch, a stream buffer adds its last missing address to the signed offset contained in the table. The table is still indexed by the last miss as in the standard Markov table. Figure 4 shows how many bits are needed to represent the address difference for all of the miss transitions found in the Markov table. The results show that having 16 bits captures almost all of the transitions. This number could perhaps be further reduced by smart heap memory allocation which could place objects with high temporal locality close to one another. In this paper we use a Markov table with 2K entries, which uses a total of 4Kbytes for the data storage. In addition, the tag size can also be reduced by storing only partial address tags.

4.3 Allocation Filtering

Stream buffer allocation is one of the most important parts of a stream buffer architecture. Since there are only a small number of stream buffers, there is high contention, as every data cache miss could potentially allocate a stream buffer.

Farkas et. al. [13] showed that using *two miss stride filtering* provided good results for a PC-based stream buffer. Two miss filtering only allocates a stream buffer for a load when it misses 2 times in a row, and the last two strides are identical. For our predictor-directed stream buffers we examine two methods for filtering allocation – a general form of two miss filtering, and using our new prediction confidence to guide allocation.

When updating the SFM predictor for a load that misses in the cache, both the PC-based stride table and the address based Markov table are indexed, and potentially updated. Our two-miss allocation filter allows a load to allocate a stream buffer when the load has two cache misses in a row, and both times the load would have been correctly predicted using the stride predictor or the Markov predictor. If this occurs, then it allocates a stream buffer. This modified scheme is our two-miss allocation filter.

The second heuristic we examine uses address prediction confidence to guide stream buffer allocation. Each entry in the PC-based table stores an *accuracy counter*, which is incremented every time the load's update address matches the prediction of the stride or Markov table, and decremented when it does not match. The saturating counter reflects the ability of the predictor being able to predict the load's misses. By separating the confidence counters from the stream buffer we can gauge how well a particular load is performing before we allocate a stream buffer to it. In this way we can avoid stream thrashing. When a stream buffer is allocated it copies the accuracy confidence counter into a *priority counter* in the stream buffer. Maintaining the priority counter is described in more detail in the next section.

On a cache miss, the accuracy confidence counter in the

prediction table is used to guide stream buffer allocation. If the address prediction confidence level of the load is above an allocation threshold, it is allowed to contend for a stream buffer. Our results suggest that a threshold value of 1 is appropriate for our benchmark suite. In addition, a load is only allocated a stream buffer if there is at least one stream buffer whose *priority* confidence counter is less or equal to the *accuracy* confidence counter of the load. If the load's accuracy confidence is lower than all of the stream buffers priority confidence, then a stream buffer will not be allocated for it.

4.4 Stream Buffer Priority

The predictor and bus create a resource constraint, since there are potentially several stream buffers which have empty entries, or have predicted addresses waiting to be prefetched. We examine two approaches for determining which stream buffer should get access to the predictor and L1-L2 bus each cycle.

The first heuristic is *Round-Robin* giving each buffer an equal chance at performing a prediction or prefetch. A pointer is kept to the last stream buffer to perform a prediction and another pointer for the last entry to issue a prefetch. The stream buffers are then sequentially examined in round-robin order, looking for a buffer with an entry in need of prediction or a predicted entry ready to be prefetched.

The second heuristic uses *Priority Counters* to guide which stream buffer gets to perform the next prediction or prefetch. Every time there is a lookup and the stream buffer gets a hit, the priority counter is incremented by a constant value (2 in our implementation). To enable the reuse of stream buffers that had high confidence but outlived their usefulness, after several allocation requests (i.e. data cache misses that also miss in stream buffers) we decrement each stream buffer's priority counter by a value of 1. We found using 10 L1 data cache misses as our aging period provided decent results. When determining which stream buffer gets to use the predictor or perform a prefetch, the stream buffers are examined in the order from highest priority to lowest. If there are several stream buffers that are at the same confidence level, we use an LRU policy to choose the winner. As described in section 4.3 when a stream buffer is allocated, the accuracy confidence is copied into the stream buffer's priority counter. This cuts down the contention time of load that has proven to be predictable.

In addition, as also described in the prior section, the priority counter is used to guide stream buffer allocation when using accuracy confidence to guide allocation. A stream buffer will only be re-allocated for a data cache miss if the load's prediction accuracy confidence is greater than or equal to a stream buffer's priority counter. Therefore, stream buffers that are performing useful prefetches will stay allocated and have a longer lifetime.

Program	Description
health	A hierarchical health-care system simulator taken from the Olden Benchmark suite (input: 3 500).
burg	A program that generates a fast tree parser using BURS technology. It is commonly used to construct optimal instruction selectors for use in compiler code generation. The input used was a grammar that scribes the VAX instruction architecture.
deltablue	A constraint solution system which is implemented in C++, with an abundance of short lived heap objects.
gs	Ghostscript is an implementation of Adobe Systems' PostScript (tm) language. The input run converts a PostScript file into a jpeg.
sis	Synthesis of synchronous and asynchronous circuits (input: simplify). It includes a number of capabilities such as state minimization and optimization. The program has approximately 172,000 lines of source code and a good deal of pointer arithmetic.
turb3d	Simulates isotropic, homogeneous turbulence in a cube with periodic boundary conditions in x,y,z coordinate directions (input: ref).

Table 1: Description of benchmarks used.

4.5 TLB Translation and Prefetching

As we store the virtual effective address of a load in our predictor, we need to translate this to a physical address before we access memory. On a prefetch, we access the data TLB for the translation and perform a replacement if necessary. In essence, this amounts to TLB prefetching [27]. However, we did not observe any benefits or performance losses caused by this approach, as the benchmarks we have used had only a small number TLB misses. The TLB translations could potentially be stored with each stream buffer when the stream buffer is allocated. Then a TLB lookup would only need to be performed when the next virtual prefetch address goes outside the current page boundary.

5 Methodology

The simulator used in this study was derived from the SimpleScalar/Alpha 3.0 tool set [5], a suite of functional and timing simulation tools for the Alpha AXP ISA. The timing simulator executes only user-level instructions, performing a detailed timing simulation of an aggressive 8-way dynamically scheduled microprocessor with two levels of instruction and data cache memory. Simulation is execution-driven, including execution down any speculative path until the detection of a fault, TLB miss, or branch mis-prediction.

To perform our evaluation, we collected results for the programs shown in Table 1. The programs were compiled on a DEC Alpha AXP-21164 processor using the DEC FORTRAN, C and C++ compilers under OSF/1 V4.0 operating system using full compiler optimization (-O4 -ifo). Table 2 shows the number of instructions simulated, L1 data cache miss rate, percent of executed in-

program	#inst (Mill)	%L1 MR	%lds	%sts	IPC	L1-L2 %bus	L2-M %bus
health	33	26.5	36.0	14.2	0.62	38.5	0.5
burg	300	6.5	19.1	18.7	1.91	19.5	4.8
deltablue	96	16.7	28.9	9.9	1.22	39.3	4.1
gs	300	2.0	19.2	6.8	3.5	6.8	0.9
sis	300	3.7	28.7	12.8	1.94	12.2	0.9
turb3d	300	6.5	23.3	16.2	2.54	26.2	13.7

Table 2: Baseline results showing the number of instructions simulated, L1 data cache miss rate, percent of executed instructions that were loads and stores, the IPC for each program, and the percent of cycles the bus was busy from the L1 to L2, and the bus from the L2 to main memory were busy.

structions that were loads and stores, the IPC for each program, and the percent of cycles the bus from the L1 to L2, and the bus from the L2 to main memory were busy (occupied). Turb3d was fast forwarded 1.3 billion instructions [30] before gathering statistics.

5.1 Baseline Architecture

Our baseline simulation configuration models a next generation out-of-order processor microarchitecture. We've selected the parameters to capture underlying trends in microarchitecture design. The processor has a large window of execution; it can fetch up to 8 instructions per cycle. It has a 128 entry re-order buffer with a 64 entry load/store buffer. To compensate for the added complexity of disambiguating loads and stores in a large execution window, we increased the store forward latency to 2 cycles.

To make sure that the prefetching speedups we report are from actual prefetching benefit and not from compensating for a conservative memory disambiguation policy, we implemented perfect store sets [11]. Perfect store sets cause loads to only be dependent on stores which write to the same memory, i.e when they are actually dependent instructions. In this way loads will not be held up by false dependencies making the prefetcher look better. The performance difference between the two schemes is explored in section 6.

In the baseline architecture, there is an 8 cycle minimum branch mis-prediction penalty. The processor has 8 integer ALU units, 4-load/store units, 2-FP adders, 2-integer MULT/DIV, and 2-FP MULT/DIV. The latencies are: ALU 1 cycle, MULT 3 cycles, Integer DIV 12 cycles, FP Adder 2 cycles, FP Mult 4 cycles, and FP DIV 12 cycles. All functional units, except the divide units, are fully pipelined allowing a new instruction to initiate execution each cycle. We use a McFarling gshare predictor [20] to drive our fetch unit. Two predictions can be made per cycle with up to 8 instructions fetched.

We rewrote the memory hierarchy in SimpleScalar to better model bus occupancy, bandwidth, and pipelining of the second level cache and main memory. For the majority of our results, the L1 instruction cache is a 32K 2-way associative cache with 32-byte lines. The baseline results are run with a 32k 4-way associative data cache with 32-byte lines. A 1 Megabyte unified L2 cache is simulated with 64-byte lines. The L2 cache has a latency of 12 cycles, and is pipelined three accesses deep. The main memory has an access time of 120 cycles. The L1 to L2 bus can support up to 8 bytes per processor cycle whereas the L2 to memory bus can support 4 bytes per cycle.

6 Prefetching Performance

This section compares predictor-directed stream buffers to the best performing prior stream buffer approach. This is the pc-based stride stream buffers of Farkas et. al. [13], which was described in section 3. We call their approach *PC-Stride*, where data cache missed loads are kept track of in a 256 entry 4-way associative stride address prediction table. On a miss, the predicted stride is copied into the stream buffer to guide the predictions. We examined using PC stride tables larger than 256 entry, but they provided little to no improvement.

For our PSB architecture, we also use a 256 entry 4-way stride address prediction table to filter stride predictions out of a 2K entry Markov table. We use a differential Markov table as described in section 4.2, where each entry in the Markov table is only 16-bits (total table size of 4Kbytes). The advantage of PSB over PC-Stride is that we can accurately follow non-stride based miss patterns. Results are shown for PSB for all four combinations of the allocation filter and priority scheduler. These are (1) two miss allocation filter with round-robing scheduling (2Miss-RR), (2) two miss allocation filter with priority confidence scheduling (2Miss-Priority), (3) confidence allocation with round-robin scheduling (ConfAlloc-RR), and (4) confidence allocation with priority scheduling (ConfAlloc-Priority). For the accuracy confidence counter stored in our stride table, we used a saturating value of 7, and for the priority confidence counter in the stream buffers we used a saturating confidence value of 12. See Section 4 for the other values used for the accuracy and priority counters.

For both the PC-Stride and the PSB architectures we used 8 stream buffers, each with 4 entries. All stream buffers are checked in parallel on a lookup. In addition, when a stream buffer generates a prediction, all stream buffers are checked to guarantee that the stream buffers do not follow overlapping streams.

For the address predictors we use, we predict the virtual address stream instead of the physical address stream, and we perform TLB translations on those addresses when performing the prefetch. Since we only insert loads into the stride PC-table on a cache miss, we only require a small

256 entry stride PC-table to capture all the critical loads that miss. Finally, we only store and use cache block addresses *not* the full address for both the stride and Markov tables.

Figure 5 shows the speedup over the baseline architecture IPC shown in Table 2 for PC-Stride and our predictor-directed stream buffer configurations. Results are shown for five pointer-based applications, and one stride-based FORTRAN program. We ran several FORTRAN programs, and they all had similar performance to the results shown for turb3d. Since these programs are mostly stride-based, our PSB architectures achieves basically the same performance as the PC-stride architecture, getting benefit only from the addition of confidence and scheduling. For pointer based applications, our results show that predictor-directed stream buffers can achieve significant speedups (17% speedup for deltablue and 18% speedup for burg) over using PC-stride guided stream buffers.

It can be seen in Figure 5 that confidence allocation is very important for burg and sis. The reason why performance degrades for sis when using 2Miss filter allocation for our approach is due to stream thrashing. Using the confidence counters to guide allocation, allows stream buffer allocation to concentrate on highly predictable loads, and avoids replacing stream buffers that are receiving a lot of hits. Stream thrashing is a serious problem for programs with large amounts of missing loads as is the case in both large programs and tight inner loops which are highly software pipelined. Performing loop unrolling and software pipelining increases the number of load instructions in the program, which can degrade the performance of stream buffers. If an architecture has stream buffers, a loop with a hardware predictable reference stream may achieve better performance performing no loop unrolling, and instead use the stream buffers to hide the load latency.

Figure 6 shows the prefetching accuracy for the different configurations examined, where prefetching accuracy is the percentage of all prefetches that were used by the processor. Allowing the stream buffer to follow non-stride predictions can increase the prefetching accuracy by almost a factor of 2 for deltablue when using confidence allocation.

Figure 7 shows the cache miss rates for the baseline and prefetching architectures. We define a cache miss as an access to a cache block which is not currently resident in the cache, i.e. accesses to in-flight data count as cache misses. We have found this tracking of cache misses to be more representative of the system behavior than simply checking the cache tags and MSHRs for a hit.

The total impact of the system can be seen in figure 8 which shows the average load latency for the different benchmarks and techniques. For deltablue, we remove 4 full cycles from the average latency, and 3 cycles for burg. Even a moderate reduction in average latency can produce a significant performance impact and this is reflected in the speedups obtained.

Figure 9 shows the percent of bus utilization for both the bus from the L1 to L2, and the bus from the L2 to main memory. This reveals an interesting characteristic of sis. When confidence is not employed, the prefetcher spends the majority of its time issuing useless prefetch requests to the L2 cache due to stream buffer thrashing. The bus utilization rises by a factor of four and the accuracy drops significantly.

By far the largest consumers of L1 to L2 bandwidth are deltablue, and health, and it is for these programs which stream buffer prioritization scheduling performed the best. The scheduling of prefetches allows the stream buffers that are most likely to hit to use the bandwidth first, allowing these high confidence prefetches to cover more latency. Stream buffer priority scheduling provided an additional speedup of 11% for deltablue when confidence was used in conjunction.

The speedup that we are achieving is due to the hiding of latency associated with capacity problems in the L1 cache. This is shown by figure 10, where we look at the performance for 16K 4-way, 32K 2-way, and 32K 4-way cache. The results show the speedup obtained for the different prefetching techniques over a baseline architecture with the same cache configuration. It can be seen that the speedup obtained is independent of cache size over a reasonable set of configurations.

6.1 Perfect Disambiguation Results

As mentioned earlier, we simulated the effects of perfect load-store disambiguation. The IPC results with and without perfect memory disambiguation for the baseline architecture and our proposed scheme are presented in Figure 11. For no disambiguation (NoDis), a load waits to issue until all prior stores have issued. Perfect store sets [11] provides a decent speedup for the baseline architecture for deltablue and sis. However it yields little improvement in conjunction with prefetching for all programs, except for sis.

7 Summary

We chose to focus on stream buffers because of their ability to follow address streams independent of what the fetch stream is doing. Prior stream buffer architectures were limited to following down a stream using a fixed stride [13], which limits their benefit for commercial pointer-based applications. To go beyond this limit we presented a new stream buffer architecture (Predictor-Directed Stream Buffer) to follow non-stride streams. In addition, we presented a new stream buffer allocation and priority scheduling technique based on confidence.

It should be noted that any address predictor can be used to guide the predicted prefetch stream for our predictor-directed stream buffer. Due to space constraints, we only

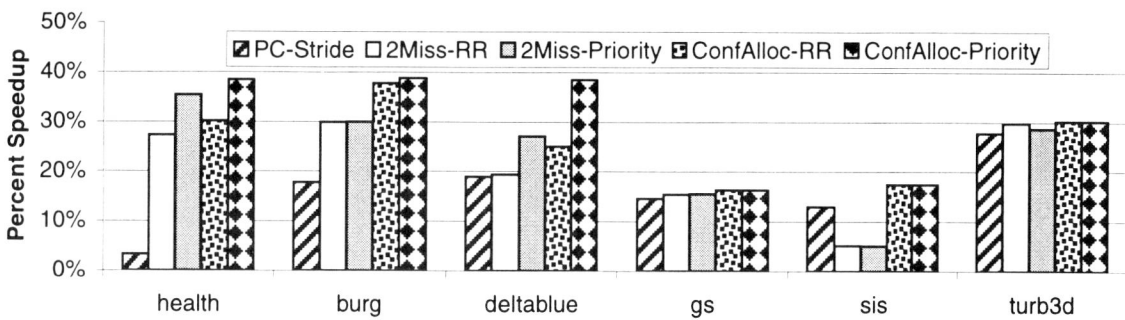

Figure 5: Percent speedup over base using prior PC-stride prefetching and our Predictor-Directed Stream Buffers.

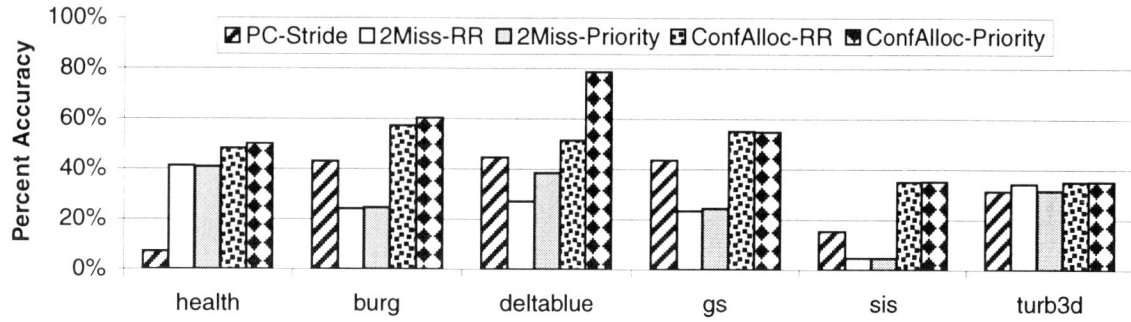

Figure 6: Prefetch accuracy. This is the number of prefetches used divided by the number of prefetches made.

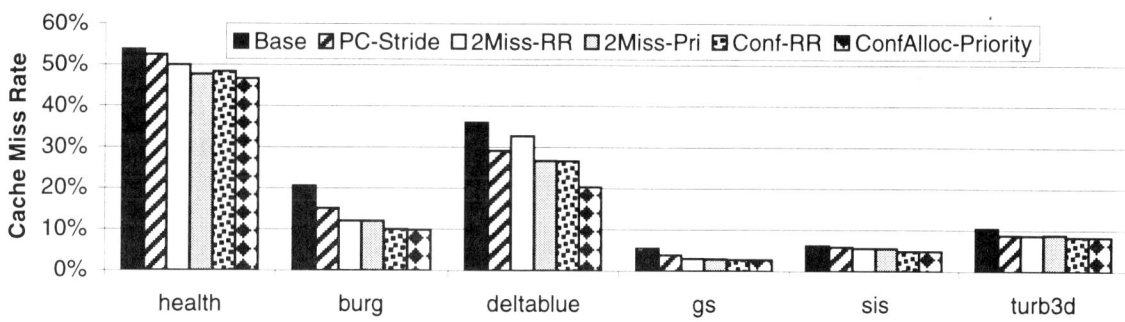

Figure 7: Data cache miss rates (where in-flight cache blocks count as a miss).

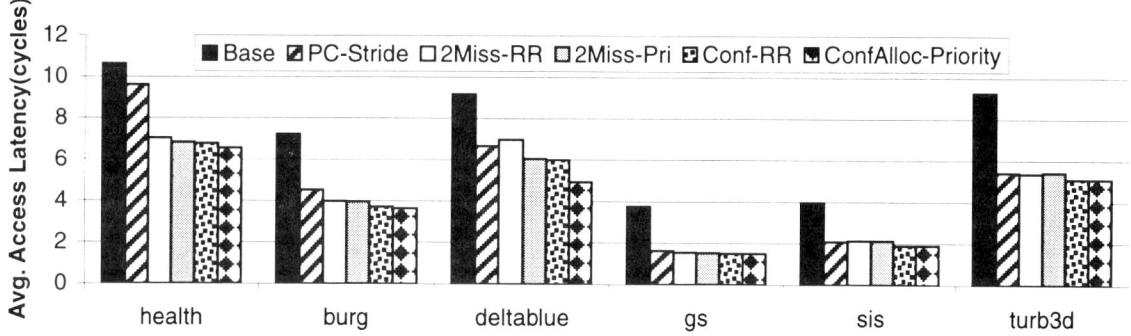

Figure 8: Average latency of a load in cycles for the different architectures.

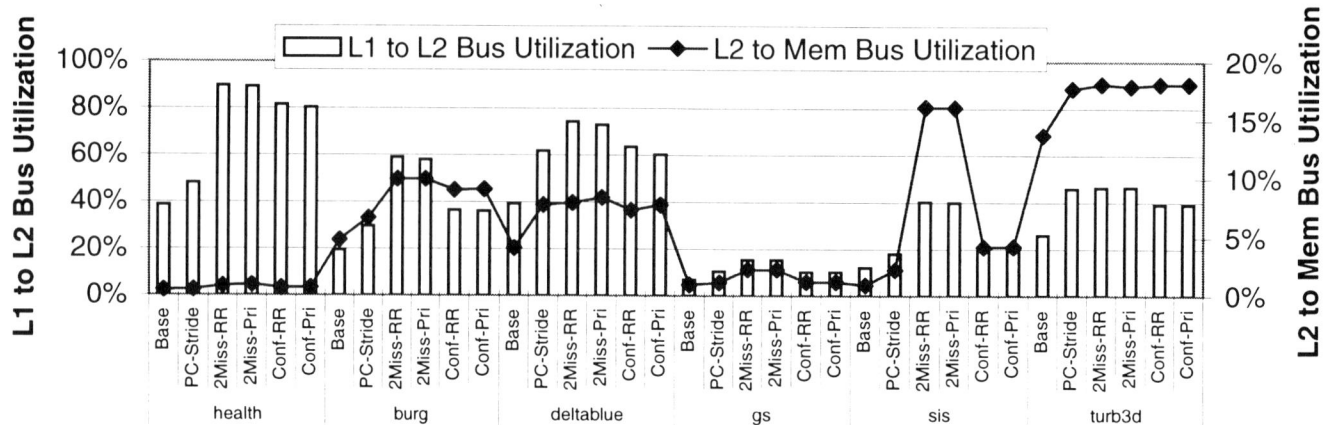

Figure 9: The percent of cycles the bus was busy. The L1-L2 bus utilization is shown with bars using the left axis, and the L2 to Main Memory bus utilization uses the right axis.

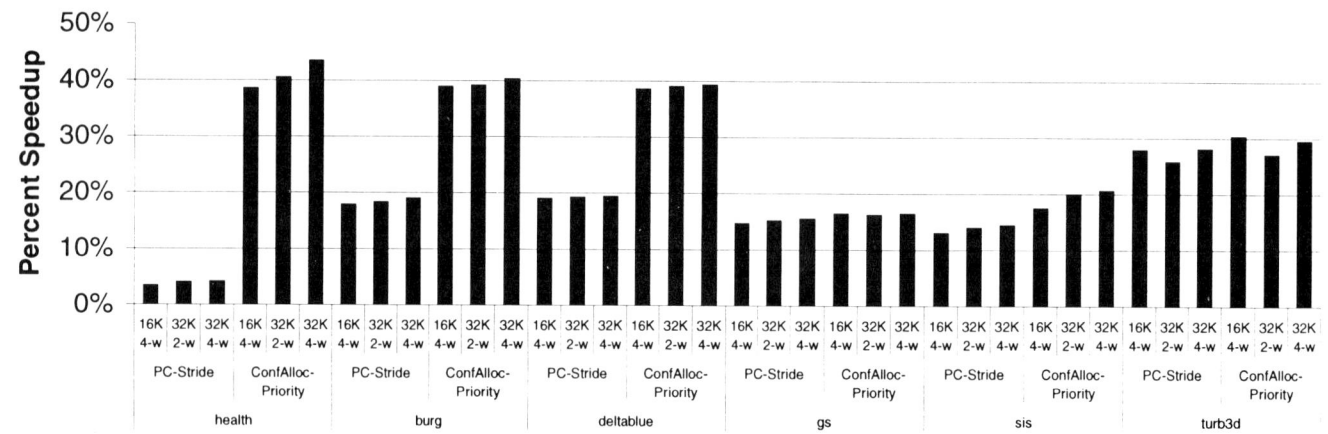

Figure 10: Percent Speedup Varying the Cache Size and Associativity.

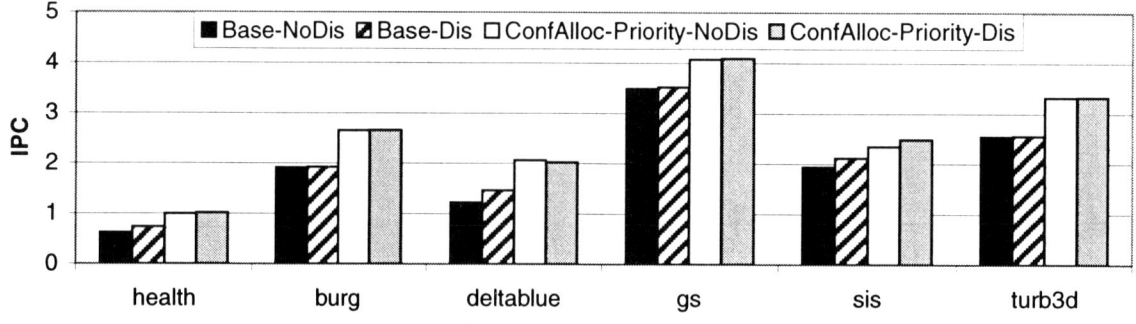

Figure 11: Performance results with (Dis) and without (NoDis) perfect store sets (perfect disambiguation).

presented results for using a stride-filtered Markov address predictor to guide stream buffer prefetching. The Markov predictor was a differential Markov predictor whose data size was only 4Kbytes. We found this predictor to perform better than other recently proposed context [28] and correlated predictors [2] for data prefetching.

For stride-based applications (e.g., FORTRAN programs), predictor-directed stream buffers provided similar performance to stride-based stream buffers. For the 5 pointer-based applications we examined, predictor-directed stream buffers provide a 30% speedup on average over no prefetching, and 10% average speedup over using the best performing prior stream buffer architecture.

Acknowledgments

We would like to thank the anonymous reviewers for providing useful comments on this paper. This work was funded in part by NSF CAREER grant No. CCR-9733278, by DARPA/ITO under contract number DABT63-98-C-0045, and a grant from Compaq Computer Corporation.

References

[1] T. Alexander and G. Kedem. Distributed prefetch-buffer/cache design for high performance memory systems. In *Proceedings of the Second International Symposium on High-Performance Computer Architecture*, February 1996.

[2] M. Bekerman, S. Jourdan, R. Ronen, G. Kirshenboim, L. Rappoport, A. Yoaz, and U Weiser. Correlated load-address predictors. In *26th Annual International Symposium on Computer Architecture*, May 1999.

[3] A. Berrached, L. Coraor, and P. Hulina. A decoupled access/execute architecture for efficient accesss of structured data. In *In the Hawaii International Conference on System Services*, January 1993.

[4] B. Black, B. Mueller, S. Postal, R. Rakvie, N. Utamaphethai, and J. P. Shen. Load execution latency reduction. In *12th International Conference on Supercomputing*, June 1998.

[5] D. C. Burger and T. M. Austin. The simplescalar tool set, version 2.0. Technical Report CS-TR-97-1342, University of Wisconsin, Madison, June 1997.

[6] M.J. Charney and T.R. Puzak. Prefetching and memory system behavior of the spec95 benchmark suite. *IBM Journal of Research and Development*, 41(3), May 1997.

[7] M.J. Charney and A.P. Reeves. Generalized correlation based hardware prefetching. Technical Report EE-CEG-95-1, Cornell University, February 1995.

[8] T-F. Chen and J-L. Baer. Effective hardware-based data prefetching for high performance processors. *IEEE Transactions on Computers*, 5(44):609–623, May 1995.

[9] T.F. Chen and J.L. Baer. Reducing memory latency via non-blocking and prefetching caches. In *Proceedings of the Fourth International Conference on Architectural Support for Programming Languages and Operating Systems (ASPLOS-IV)*, pages 51–61, October 1992.

[10] C. Chi and C. Cheung. Hardware-driven prefetching for pointer data references. In *In the ACM International Conference on Supercomputing*, pages 377–384, June 1998.

[11] G. Chrysos and J. Emer. Memory dependence prediction using store sets. In *25th Annual International Symposium on Computer Architecture*, June 1998.

[12] R. J. Eickemeyer and S. Vassiliadis. A load instruction unit for pipelined processors. *IBM Journal of Research and Development*, 37:547–564, July 1993.

[13] K. Farkas, P. Chow, N. Jouppi, and Z. Vranesic. Memory-system design considerations for dynamically-scheduled processors. In *24th Annual International Symposium on Computer Architecture*, June 1997.

[14] K. Farkas and N. Jouppi. Complexity/performance tradeoffs with non-blocking loads. In *21st Annual International Symposium on Computer Architecture*, pages 211–222, April 1994.

[15] M. Farrens and A.Pleszkun. Implementation of the pipe processor. *IEEE Computer*, January 1991.

[16] J. Gonzalez and A. Gonzalez. Speculative execution via address prediction and data prefetching. In *11th International Conference on Supercomputing*, pages 196–203, July 1997.

[17] G.P. Jones and N.P. Topham. A comparison of data prefetching on an access decoupled and superscalar machine. In *30th International Symposium on Microarchitecture*, December 1997.

[18] D. Joseph and D. Grunwald. Prefetching using markov predictors. In *24th Annual International Symposium on Computer Architecture*, June 1997.

[19] N. Jouppi. Improving direct-mapped cache performance by the addition of a small fully associative cache and prefetch buffers. In *Proceedings of the 17th Annual International Symposium on Computer Architecture*, May 1990.

[20] S. McFarling. Combining branch predictors. Technical Report TN-36, Digital Equipment Corporation, Western Research Lab, June 1993.

[21] T.C. Mowry, M.S. Lam, and A. Gupta. Design and evaluation of a compiler algorithm for prefetching. In *Proceedings of the Fifth International Conference on Architectural Support for Programming Languages and Operating Systems (ASPLOS-V)*, October 1992.

[22] S. Palacharla and R. Kessler. Evaluating stream buffers as secondary cache replacement. In *21st Annual International Symposium on Computer Architecture*, April 1994.

[23] G. Reinman, B. Calder, and T. Austin. Fetch-directed instruction prefetching. In *32nd International Symposium on Microarchitecture*, November 1999.

[24] G. Reinman, B. Calder, and T. Austin. A power efficient speculative fetch architecture. Technical Report UCSD-CS2000-0657, University of California, San Diego, June 2000.

[25] A. Roth, A. Moshovos, and G. Sohi. Dependence based prefetching for linked data structures. In *Eigth International Conference on Architectural Support for Programming Languages and Operating Systems*, October 1998.

[26] A. Roth and G. Sohi. Effective jump-pointer prefetching for linked data structures. In *26th Annual International Symposium on Computer Architecture*, May 1999.

[27] A. Saulsbury, F. Dahlgren, and P. Stenstrom. Recency-based tbl preloading. In *27th Annual International Symposium on Computer Architecture*, June 2000.

[28] Y. Sazeides and J. E. Smith. The predictability of data values. In *30th International Symposium on Microarchitecture*, pages 248–258, December 1997.

[29] Y. Sazeides and J. E. Smith. Modeling program predictability. In *25th Annual International Symposium on Computer Architecture*, June 1998.

[30] T. Sherwood and B. Calder. Time varying behavior of programs. Technical Report UCSD-CS99-630, University of California, San Diego, August 1999.

[31] J. E. Smith and W.-C. Hsu. Prefetching in supercomputer instruction caches. In *Proceedings of Supercomputing*, November 1992.

[32] K. Wang and M. Franklin. Highly accurate data value prediction using hybrid predictors. In *30th International Symposium on Microarchitecture*, December 1997.

[33] C. Yang and A. Lebeck. Push vs. pull: Data movement for linked data structures. In *In the ACM International Conference on Supercomputing*, June 2000.

Superscalar Architecture I

On Pipelining Dynamic Instruction Scheduling Logic

Jared Stark †   Mary D. Brown ‡   Yale N. Patt ‡

Microprocessor Research Labs †
Intel Corporation
jared.w.stark@intel.com

Dept. of Electrical and Computer Engineering ‡
The University of Texas at Austin
{mbrown,patt}@ece.utexas.edu

Abstract

A machine's performance is the product of its IPC (Instructions Per Cycle) and clock frequency. Recently, Palacharla, Jouppi, and Smith [3] warned that the dynamic instruction scheduling logic for current machines performs an atomic operation. Either you sacrifice IPC by pipelining this logic, thereby eliminating its ability to execute dependent instructions in consecutive cycles. Or you sacrifice clock frequency by not pipelining it, performing this atomic operation in a single long cycle. Both alternatives are unacceptable for high performance.

This paper offers a third, acceptable, alternative: pipelined scheduling with speculative wakeup. This technique pipelines the scheduling logic without eliminating its ability to execute dependent instructions in consecutive cycles. With this technique, you sacrifice little IPC, and no clock frequency. Our results show that on the SPECint95 benchmarks, a machine using this technique has an average IPC that is 13% greater than the IPC of a baseline machine that pipelines the scheduling logic but sacrifices the ability to execute dependent instructions in consecutive cycles, and within 2% of the IPC of a conventional machine that uses single cycle scheduling logic.

1. Introduction

To achieve higher levels of performance, processors are being built with deeper pipelines. Over the past twenty years, the number of pipeline stages has grown from 1 (Intel 286), to 5 (Intel486), to 10 (Intel Pentium Pro), to 20 (Intel Willamette) [2, 6]. This growth in pipeline depth will continue as processors attempt to exploit more parallelism.

As pipeline depths grow, operations that had previously taken only a single pipeline stage are pipelined. Recently, Palacharla, Jouppi, and Smith [3] stated: "Wakeup and select together constitute what appears to be an *atomic* operation. That is, if they are divided into multiple pipeline stages, dependent instructions cannot issue in consecutive cycles." They use the word *atomic* here to imply that the entire operation must finish before the wakeup/select operations for dependent instructions can begin. Thus, if dependent instructions are to be executed in consecutive cycles—which is necessary for achieving the highest performance—the scheduling logic performs this operation in one cycle.

This paper demonstrates that this logic can be pipelined without sacrificing the ability to execute dependent instructions in consecutive cycles. It introduces *pipelined scheduling with speculative wakeup*, which pipelines this logic over 2 cycles while still allowing back-to-back execution of dependent instructions. With this technique, deeper pipelines and/or bigger instruction windows can be built. This will allow processors to exploit more parallelism, and therefore, allow processors to achieve higher performance.

The paper describes two implementations of pipelined scheduling with speculative wakeup for a generic dynamically scheduled processor: the budget implementation and the deluxe implementation. The budget model has a lower implementation cost than the deluxe model, but not as great an improvement in performance. The generic processor and these two implementations are examples only. There are many processor microarchitectures, and many possible implementations of pipelined scheduling with speculative wakeup. We could not model all of them. Nevertheless, we hope that by examining these simple examples, microarchitects will be able to implement pipelined scheduling with speculative wakeup on real-world microarchitectures.

The paper then compares the IPC (Instructions Per Cycle) of machines using these two implementations to the IPC of a baseline machine that pipelines the scheduling logic but sacrifices the ability to execute dependent instructions in consecutive cycles. For the 8 SPECint95 benchmarks, the average IPC of the machine using the budget implementation is 12% higher than the IPC of the baseline machine, and the IPC of the machine using the deluxe implementation is 13% higher. This paper also compares the IPC of machines using these two implementations to the IPC of a conventional machine that does not pipeline the scheduling logic. Both machines have IPCs that are within 3% of the IPC of the conventional machine. If the critical path through the scheduling logic limits the cycle time for conventional machines, which is very likely if the scheduling operation is considered an atomic unit, these two implementations of pipelined scheduling with speculative wakeup may allow a significant boost in clock frequency with only a very minor impact on IPC.

This paper is divided into six sections. Section 2 presents background information necessary for understanding this study. Section 3 describes conventional instruction scheduling logic. Section 4 describes pipelined scheduling with speculative wakeup. Section 5 presents the experiments, and Section 6 provides some concluding remarks.

2. Background

This section presents background information necessary for understanding our study. Section 2.1 presents our pipeline model. Section 2.2 introduces some terms. Section 2.3 introduces the scheduling apparatus.

2.1. Pipeline Model

Figure 1 shows the pipeline of a generic dynamically scheduled processor. The pipeline has 7 stages: fetch, decode, rename, wakeup/select, register read, execute/bypass, and commit. Each stage may take more than one cycle. For example, the execute/bypass stage usually takes two or more cycles for loads: one cycle to calculate the load address, and one or more cycles to access the cache.

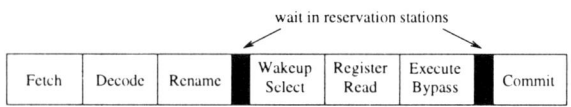

Figure 1. Processor Pipeline

In the fetch stage, instructions are fetched from the instruction cache. They are then decoded and their register operands renamed. Next, they are written into the reservation stations where they wait for their source operands and a functional unit to become available. When this occurs (that is, an instruction wakes up and is selected), the instruction is sent to a functional unit for execution. Its register values are either read from the register file or bypassed from earlier instructions in the pipeline. After it completes execution, it waits in the reservation stations until all earlier instructions have completed execution. After this condition is satisfied, it commits: it updates the architectural state and is deallocated from the reservation stations.[1]

[1] Conventional machines aggressively deallocate reservation stations. We do not consider aggressive deallocation, and simply assume that reservation stations are deallocated at commit.

Note that after an instruction is selected for execution, several cycles pass before it completes execution. During this time, instructions dependent on it may be scheduled (woken up and selected) for execution. These dependent instructions are scheduled optimistically. For example, if they depend on a load, they are scheduled assuming the load hits the cache. If the load misses, the dependent instructions execute—spuriously—without the load result. The dependent instructions must be re-scheduled (and thus, re-executed) once the load result is known.

2.2. Terminology

Figure 2 shows a partial data flow graph. Each node represents an operation. The arrows entering a node represent the values consumed by the operation. The arrow exiting a node represents the value produced by the operation.

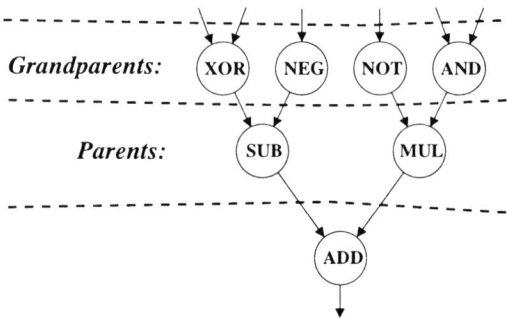

Figure 2. Example Data Flow Graph

The ADD operation consumes the values produced by its *parents*; i. e., the SUB and MUL operations. The ADD's parents consume the values produced by its *grandparents*; i. e., the SUB consumes the values produced by the XOR and NEG operations, and the MUL consumes the values produced by the NOT and AND operations. The reverse relationships also hold: the ADD is the *child* of the SUB and MUL operations; and the *grandchild* of the XOR, NEG, NOT, and AND operations.

2.3. Scheduling Apparatus

Three pieces of logic are needed to perform the dynamic scheduling: rename logic, wakeup logic, and select logic.

The rename logic maps an instruction's architectural register identifiers to physical register identifiers. This eliminates the anti and output register dependencies between instructions. We assume the map is stored in a register file, as described by Palacharla, Jouppi, and Smith [3], and as implemented in the MIPS R10000 [5]. Accessing this register file with an architectural register identifier yields the physical register identifier to which it is mapped.

The wakeup logic is responsible for waking up the instructions that are waiting for their source operands to become available. For conventional scheduling, this is accomplished by monitoring each instruction's parents. For pipelined scheduling with speculative wakeup, it is accomplished by monitoring each instruction's parents *and* grandparents. The wakeup logic is part of the reservation stations. Each reservation station entry (RSE) has wakeup logic that wakes up any instruction stored in it.

The select logic chooses instructions for execution from the pool of ready instructions. We assume each functional unit has a set of dedicated RSEs, as described by Tomasulo [4]. Select logic associated with each functional unit selects the instruction that the functional unit will execute next. The selection is performed by choosing one ready instruction from the functional unit's set of dedicated RSEs.

Figure 3 will be used to further describe the operation of the scheduling apparatus. It shows a microarchitecture that has 8 functional units and 128 RSEs.

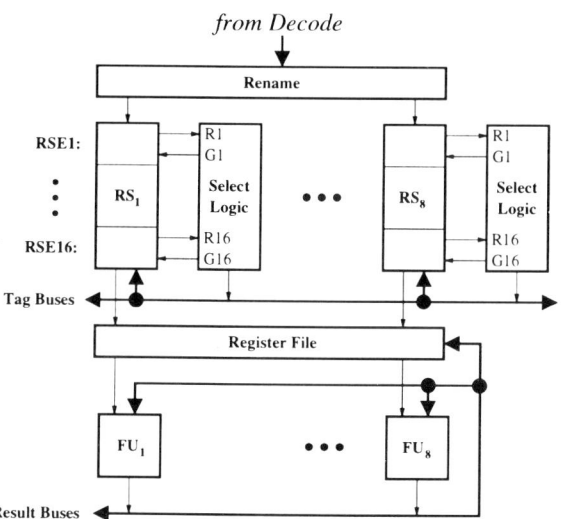

Figure 3. Processor Microarchitecture

Each functional unit has a dedicated set of 16 RSEs, select logic, a tag bus, and a result bus. The select logic chooses the instructions the functional unit executes from the RSEs. After an instruction is chosen, a tag associated with the instruction is broadcast over the tag bus to all 128 RSEs. This tag broadcast signals dependent instructions that the instruction's result will soon be available. After an instruction executes, it broadcasts its result over the result bus to the register file and to any dependent instructions starting execution.

After an instruction is fetched, decoded, and renamed, it is written into a RSE. Each RSE has wakeup logic that monitors the tag buses. For conventional scheduling, when the tags of all the instruction's parents have been broadcast, the RSE asserts its request line. (The request lines are labeled R1–R16.) For pipelined scheduling with speculative wakeup, the RSE asserts its request line, if, for each of the instruction's parents, the parent's tag has been broadcast or all the parent's parents' tags have been broadcast. The select logic for each functional unit monitors the request lines of the functional unit's dedicated set of RSEs, and grants up to one of these requests each cycle. (The grant lines are labeled G1–G16.) After a request is granted, the instruction that generated the request is sent to the functional unit for execution. In addition, the tag for that instruction is broadcast over the tag bus. The instruction either reads its register values from the register file or receives them from instructions just completing execution via bypasses.

3. Conventional Scheduling

Sections 3.1, 3.2, and 3.3 describe the implementations of the rename, wakeup, and select logic for conventional dynamic instruction scheduling. Section 3.4 gives an example of the operation of conventional 1-cycle scheduling, and Section 3.5 gives an example of the operation of conventional scheduling pipelined over 2 cycles.

3.1. Rename Logic

Register renaming performs two primary tasks: allocating physical registers for the destinations of instructions, and obtaining the physical register identifiers for the sources of instructions. An instruction reads the rename map for each architectural source register to obtain the physical register identifier for that source. It also writes the identifier of its allocated physical register into the rename map entry associated with its architectural destination register.

In a superscalar processor, a group of instructions must be renamed at the same time. To detect dependencies between instructions in the same group, the sources of each instruction are compared to the destinations of all previous instructions in the same group. If an instruction's parent is in its group, the identifier of the physical register allocated to the parent overrides the identifier obtained from the rename map. Figure 4 shows the dependency analysis logic for the first three instructions in a group.

3.2. Wakeup Logic

After instructions have been renamed, they wait in reservation stations for their sources to become ready. Each RSE contains information about each of the instruction's sources, such as the physical register identifier (tag) for the source, whether the source is ready, and the number of cycles it takes the producer of the source's value to execute. Figure 5 shows the state information for one RSE. The fields

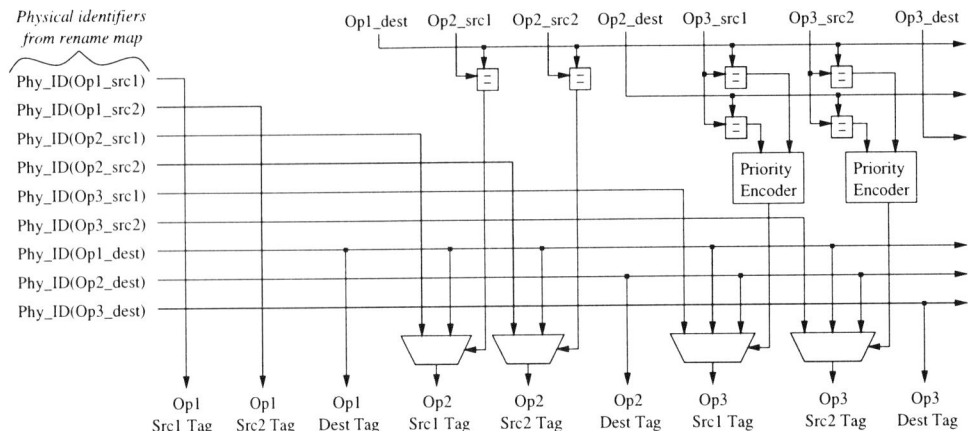

Figure 4. Dependency Analysis Logic for Three Instructions

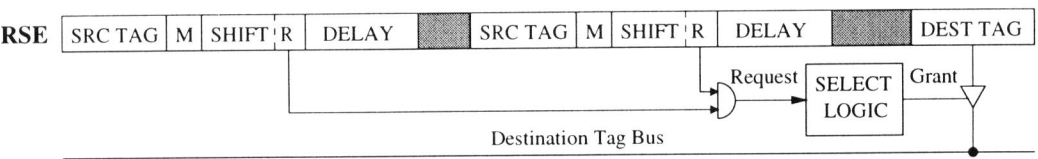

Figure 5. Scheduling Logic for One Reservation Station Entry

labeled SRC TAG contain the tags of the source operands. The R (READY) bit for each source is set if the data for that source is available in the register file or is available for bypass from a functional unit.

In our machine model, instructions broadcast their tags in the same cycle they are selected for execution. Because not all instructions have the same execution latency, the number of cycles between the time their tags are broadcast and the time their results are available is not constant. The DELAY fields are used to handle this variability.[2] For each source, the DELAY field encodes the number of cycles—relative to some base—between when the tag for the source is broadcast and when the associated result is available. We will provide more details shortly about the actual number that is encoded. For the logic implementation described in this paper, this number is encoded as an inverted radix-1 value; e. g., 3 is represented by '1...1000'.

Figure 6 shows the wakeup logic of one source tag for our machine model. It is similar to the MIPS R10000 wakeup logic [5] but has been modified for handling multi-cycle operations. When the destination tag of a parent is broadcast, one of the tag comparators will indicate that a match has occurred, and the M (MATCH) bit will be set. The MATCH bit is a sticky bit that will remain set after the tag match. On a tag match, the SHIFT field is loaded with the value contained in the DELAY field. The SHIFT field is actually contained in an arithmetic right shift register. The MATCH bit is the shift enable for this register. The least significant bit of the SHIFT field is the READY bit mentioned above. After the READY bits for all source operands have been set, the instruction requests execution.

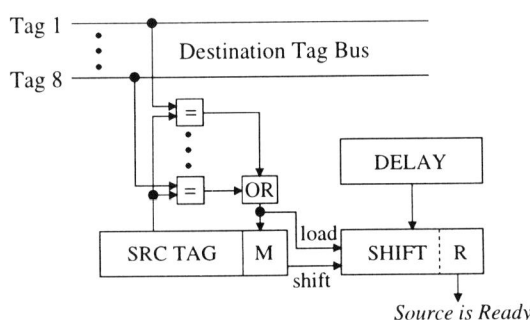

Figure 6. Conventional Wakeup Logic

For a source whose producer has an N-cycle execution latency, the DELAY field contains N-1 zeros in the least significant bits of the field. The remaining bits are all set to 1. This allows the READY bit to be set N-1 cycles after the match. For example, in our model, a load instruction that hits in the data cache takes three cycles to execute. Sup-

---

[2]Alternative solutions exist. For example, if each functional unit only executes instructions that all have the same latency, the tag broadcast can simply be delayed so that it occurs a fixed number of cycles before the result broadcast. This eliminates the need for the DELAY fields. However, if functional units can execute instructions of differing latencies, this solution is unsuitable at high clock frequencies: Multiple pipe stages may need to broadcast tags, rather than just one. Either the pipe stages will need to arbitrate for tag buses, or the number of tag buses will need to be increased.

pose the DELAY field is four bits. The DELAY field for an instruction dependent on a load would contain the value '1100'. When the tag match for the load occurs, this value will be loaded into the SHIFT field, and the MATCH bit will be set. After two more cycles, the SHIFT field will contain the value '1111', and, assuming the load hit in the cache, this source will be ready. For a source operand with a 1-cycle latency, the DELAY field will be '1111'. As soon as there is a tag match, the READY bit will be set, allowing the instruction to request execution.

The value for the DELAY field is obtained from a table in the rename stage. The table also provides values for the MATCH bit and SHIFT field for when the tag for a source is broadcast before the instruction is written into the reservation stations. This table is the analogue of the busy-bit table in the MIPS R10000 [5]. For each physical register, an entry in the table stores its DELAY field, MATCH bit, and SHIFT field. When a destination tag is broadcast, the MATCH bit and SHIFT field of the entry corresponding to the tag is updated just like the MATCH bit and SHIFT field of the wakeup logic for a matching source operand.

During decode, an instruction's execution latency is determined. After the instruction's register operands have been renamed, the table entry corresponding to the instruction's physical destination register is updated. Its DELAY field is set to a value derived from the instruction's execution latency, its MATCH bit is reset, and its SHIFT field is set to 0. Each of the instruction's physical source registers then accesses the table to determine its DELAY field, MATCH bit, and SHIFT field.

3.3. Select Logic

The select logic for each functional unit grants execution to one ready instruction. If more than one instruction requests execution, heuristics may be used for choosing which instruction receives the grant [1]. The inputs to the select logic are the request signals from each of the functional unit's RSEs, plus any additional information needed for scheduling heuristics such as priority information. Implementations of the select logic are discussed elsewhere [3] and will not be covered in this paper. As shown in Figure 5, when both READY bits are set, the instruction requests execution. If the instruction receives a grant, its destination tag is broadcast on the tag bus. The execution grant must also be able to clear the MATCH, SHIFT, and READY fields of the RSE so that the instruction does not re-arbitrate for selection.

3.4. Dependent Instruction Execution

In this implementation of conventional scheduling logic, an instruction wakes up in the last half of a clock cycle, and is potentially selected in the first half of the next clock cycle. Note that the wakeup and selection of the instruction straddles a clock edge. If the instruction is selected, the grant from the select logic gates the instruction's destination tag onto the tag bus, which is then fed to the tag comparators of the wakeup logic. Thus, the tasks of selection, tag broadcast, and wakeup must all occur within in one cycle in order for dependent instructions to wakeup in consecutive cycles.

Figure 7 is an example of the conventional scheduling operation. It shows the pipeline diagram for the execution of the left three instructions of the data flow graph in Figure 2. This schedule assumes each instruction has a 1-cycle latency, and all other parents and grandparents of the ADD are already done. In cycle 1, the READY bit for the XOR's last source is loaded with a 1. In cycle 2, the XOR is selected for execution. Its destination tag is broadcast on the tag bus, and the MATCH, SHIFT, and READY fields of its RSE are cleared so that it does not request execution again. In this same cycle, the SUB matches the tag broadcast by the XOR, and a 1 is loaded into its READY bit. In cycle 3, the SUB is selected, it broadcasts its destination tag, and wakes up the ADD....

Clock:	Cycle 1	Cycle 2	Cycle 3	Cycle 4	Cycle 5	Cycle 6
XOR:	Wakeup	Select/ Broadcast	Reg Read	Execute/ Bypass		
SUB:	Wait	Wakeup	Select/ Broadcast	Reg Read	Execute/ Bypass	
ADD:	Wait	Wait	Wakeup	Select/ Broadcast	Reg Read	Execute/ Bypass

Figure 7. Execution of a Dependency Chain Using 1-Cycle Conventional Scheduling

3.5. Pipelined Conventional Scheduling Logic

To break the conventional scheduling logic into a 2-cycle pipeline, a latch must be added in the path of the select logic, tag broadcast, and wakeup logic. We will assume the execution grant from the select logic is latched. Hence the select logic takes one cycle, and the tag broadcast and wakeup logic take one cycle.

Because a latch has been inserted in what was previously an atomic operation, there is a minimum of 2 cycles between the wakeup of dependent instructions. If a parent instruction has a 1-cycle execution latency, this will create a 1-cycle bubble in the execution of the dependency chain. If the parent takes two or more cycles to execute, the bubble can be avoided by using a different encoding for the DELAY field. For 2-stage pipelined scheduling logic, the DELAY field for any 1-cycle or 2-cycle operation should be encoded as all 1s. For a latency of N (N > 1) cycles, the

Clock:	Cycle 1	Cycle 2	Cycle 3	Cycle 4	Cycle 5	Cycle 6	Cycle 7	Cycle 8	Cycle 9
ADD:	Wakeup	Select	Broadcast/ Reg Read	Execute					
LOAD:	Wait	Wait	Wakeup	Select	Broadcast/ Reg Read	Execute	Execute	Execute	
OR:	Wait	Wait	Wait	Wait	Match Tag	Wakeup	Select	Broadcast/ Reg Read	Execute

Figure 8. Execution of a Dependency Chain Using 2-Cycle Pipelined Conventional Scheduling

DELAY field should contain N-2 zeros in the least significant bits, and the upper bits would be set to 1.

Figure 8 shows an example of executing the dependency chain ADD → LOAD → OR using 2-cycle pipelined scheduling logic. The ADD instruction wakes up in cycle 1 and is selected for execution in cycle 2. The ADD is the parent of the LOAD, and has a 1-cycle latency, so the LOAD's DELAY field is '1111'. In cycle 3, the ADD broadcasts its tag. The LOAD matches, loads its SHIFT field with the contents of the DELAY field, and thus wakes up. The load instruction is selected for execution in cycle 4, and broadcasts its tag in cycle 5. The tag match triggers the OR to set its MATCH bit and load the SHIFT field with the contents of the DELAY field. Since the LOAD is a 3-cycle operation, the contents of the DELAY field for the OR's source would be '1110'. At the end of cycle 6, the value '1111' is shifted into the OR's SHIFT field, and the OR wakes up. In cycle 7, the OR is selected for execution. Note that because the ADD is a 1-cycle operation, there is a 1-cycle bubble between the ADD and the LOAD. However, there is no bubble between the LOAD and the OR since the extra scheduling cycle is hidden by the execution latency of the LOAD.

4. Pipelined Scheduling with Speculative Wakeup

In the last section, we showed that pipelining the conventional scheduling logic introduces pipeline bubbles between dependent instructions. In this section, we show how to pipeline this logic over two cycles without having these bubbles.

Here is a brief overview of this technique: If the parents of an instruction's parent have been selected, then it is likely that the parent will be selected in the following cycle (assuming the parent's parents are 1-cycle operations). Thus, for scheduling logic pipelined over 2 cycles, the child can assume that when the tags of the grandparent pair have been received, the parent is probably being selected for execution and will broadcast its tag in the following cycle. The child can then speculatively wakeup and be selected the cycle after its parent is selected. Because it is not guaranteed that the parent will be selected for execution, the wakeup is only speculative.

Sections 4.1, 4.2, and 4.3 describe implementations of the rename, wakeup, and select logic for this scheduling mechanism. Section 4.4 gives an example of the scheduling operation. Section 4.5.1 discusses an implementation that reduces the amount of logic and state that is kept in the reservation stations. Section 4.5.2 shows that scheduling with speculative wakeup also works for machines that have instruction re-execution.

4.1 Rename Logic

For pipelined scheduling with speculative wakeup, the rename logic is responsible for determining the destination tags of the instruction's grandparents as well as the destination tags of its parents. The grandparents are required for speculative wakeup, which will be described in the next section. At the end of rename, each of the instruction's architectural source register identifiers has been replaced by a parent's destination tag, *and* the set of destination tags of that parent's parents.

To do this, the rename map must be modified. Each map entry is extended so that, in addition to the original physical register identifier, it contains the set of identifiers of the physical registers that are needed to compute the value of the physical register specified by the original identifier. That is, for the instruction that updated the entry, the entry contains the instruction's destination tag, and the set of destination tags of the instruction's parents.

At the beginning of rename, an instruction's architectural source register identifiers are used to index the rename map. Each rename map lookup yields one of the instruction's parent's destination tag, and the set of destination tags of that parent's parents. At the end of rename, the instruction's destination tag is known, and the destination tags of the instruction's parents are known. This information is used to update the map entry whose index is equal to the instruction's architectural destination register identifier.

The dependency analysis logic also needs to be modified. For conventional scheduling, when there is a dependency between two instructions in the group of instructions being renamed, the destination tag of the earlier instruction must be selected as the source tag of the later, dependent instruction. This ensures that the dependent instruction has the correct destination tag for its parent. For pipelined scheduling with speculative wakeup, the logic must also ensure that the dependent instruction has the correct destination tags for that parent's parents. Note that the correct destination tags for that parent's parents are simply the parent's source tags.

To account for this, the set of destination tags for a particular parent's parents is determined by a MUX. An example of one of these MUXes is shown in Figure 9. The MUX in this figure selects the source tags of the third instruction's first parent; i. e., it selects the first two grandparent tags. The inputs to this MUX come from the rename map and the outputs of the MUXes shown in Figure 4. The first input to the MUX is the set of destination tags for the parent's parents that were read from the rename map, and is selected when the parent is not in the group. In Figure 9, this input, labeled Parent_IDs(Op3_src1), comes from the same entry of the rename table as Phy_ID(Op3_src1) shown in Figure 4. The second input to the MUX is the set of source tags for the first instruction in the group, and is selected if the parent is the first instruction in the group. The third input to the MUX is the set of source tags for the second instruction in the group, and is selected if the parent is the second instruction in the group. The control for this MUX is the same as the control used for the MUX to select the third instruction's first source tag shown in Figure 4. Hence, this MUX adds at most one input-to-output delay to the critical path of the rename logic. (The control for the MUX is determined well before the input arrives.)

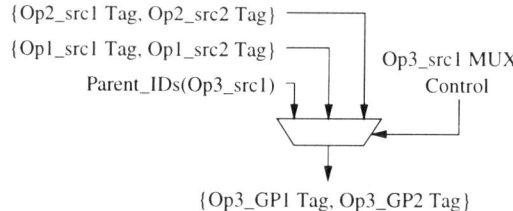

Figure 9. A Grandparent MUX

4.2. Wakeup Logic

The reservation stations contain wakeup logic for parents and grandparents. The wakeup logic for each source is identical to that explained in Section 3.2. As in the conventional 2-cycle pipelined scheduling logic, the DELAY field for each parent contains N-2 zeros in the least significant bits, and ones in the other bits, where N is the execution latency of the parent. The DELAY field for each grandparent contains N-1 zeros in the least significant bits, and ones in the other bits, where N is the latency of the grandparent.

Not all parent and grandparent fields are used for wakeup. If a parent instruction is a multi-cycle operation, then the fields for its parents can be ignored; that is, their RSE fields can be marked invalid. Instead only the tag of the multi-cycle parent will be used. As explained in Section 3.5, there is no pipeline bubble between the execution of a multi-cycle parent and its child for 2-cycle pipelined scheduling logic.

Figure 10 shows how the READY bits for the parent and grandparent tags are used to form the request sent to the select logic. A request is generated when the instruction is speculatively ready. As shown, an instruction is speculatively ready when, for each parent, the parent's parents are ready or the parent is ready.

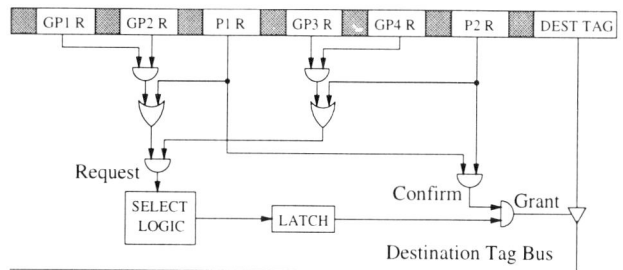

Figure 10. Speculative Wakeup Logic

Although the logic path to the request line shown in this figure has two additional gates compared to the implementation shown in Figure 5, this path could be shortened by taking advantage of the fact that no more than four sources are needed for wakeup. If a parent is a multi-cycle operation, then the RSE field for the parent can be copied into one of the grandparent fields before placing the instruction in the reservation station. In this case, a 4-input AND gate would replace the AND-OR-AND path.

4.3 Select Logic

The request line shown in Figure 10 only indicates that the instruction is speculatively ready, so the confirm line is used to verify that the instruction is ready to execute. The confirm line is only asserted when all of the instruction's parents are ready, and is typically asserted one cycle after the request line. If the request has the highest priority, and the confirm line is asserted, which means the instruction is really (non-speculatively) ready, the request is granted. Otherwise, the request is not granted.

False selection occurs whenever a request is not confirmed. That is, if the request line is asserted, and the confirm line is not asserted one cycle later, false selection occurs. False selection is a performance problem when it prevents a *really* ready instruction from being selected. This only occurs when the request that wasn't confirmed had the highest priority and there were really ready instructions that could have been selected.

For pipelined scheduling with speculative wakeup, an instruction and its parents can assert their request lines at the same time. The machine must guarantee that the parents are eventually selected for execution, otherwise, deadlock can occur. There are many ways to provide this guarantee. The most obvious is to use instruction age to assign selection priorities; i. e., older instructions (instructions that occur earlier in the dynamic instruction stream) have priority over younger instructions. Another is to use a round robin scheme to assign selection priorities.

4.4. Dependent Instruction Execution

To illustrate the operation of pipelined scheduling with speculative wakeup, consider the dependency graph in Figure 11a. All instructions are 1-cycle operations except for the LOAD, which takes 3 cycles. The SUB instruction will wakeup on the tag broadcasts of the OR, XOR, and LOAD instructions since the AND is a 1-cycle operation and the LOAD is a 3-cycle operation. The DELAY field for the SUB's first parent, the AND, will contain the value '1111'. This field will only be used for confirmation after selection has occurred. The DELAY fields for the SUB's first two grandparents, the OR and XOR, will contain the value '1111'. The DELAY field for the SUB's second parent will be encoded as '1110' so that the SUB will delay its wakeup for at least 1 cycle after the tag of the LOAD is broadcast. The last two grandparent fields for the SUB are marked as invalid, since they will not be used.

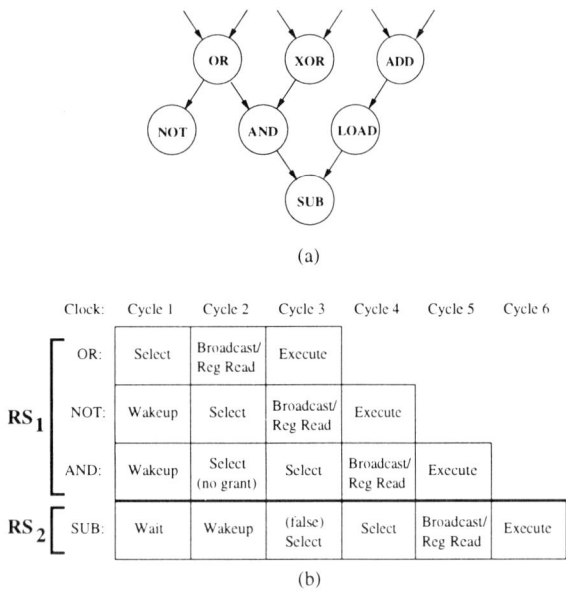

Figure 11. Example of Speculative Wakeup

Figure 11b shows an example of the scheduling operation of this data flow graph when false selection occurs. For this example, assume that the XOR, ADD, and LOAD instructions have already executed by cycle 1. Also assume that all instructions except the SUB are in the same set of reservation stations (designated by RS_1), and the SUB is in a second set (RS_2). (There are no extra delays for broadcasting tags or data between sets of reservation stations in this example.) In cycle 1, the OR is selected for execution and the AND and NOT wakeup on the tag broadcast by the OR's last parent. In cycle 2, the SUB wakes up after matching the tag broadcast by the OR. The AND and NOT both request execution in this cycle, but only the NOT receives an execution grant. The NOT and AND also match the tag broadcast by the OR instruction. In cycle 3, the AND and SUB are both selected for execution. In cycle 4, the AND's selection is confirmed and its tag is broadcast, but the SUB's selection is not confirmed. This false selection may have prevented the selection of another instruction in RS_2 in cycle 3. The SUB requests execution again, and the selection is confirmed in cycle 5.

4.5. Implementation Considerations

4.5.1. Reducing the Cost of the Wakeup Logic. We assume the tag buses running through each RSE set the size of the reservation stations, and that the wakeup logic associated with each RSE can easily be hidden underneath all these wires. If that is not the case, it is possible to reduce the number of tags—and thus, size of the wakeup logic—required to perform pipelined scheduling with speculative wakeup. Two observations are required to understand how this can be done.

The first: An instruction can always wake up using its parent tags. The grandparent tags are only provided for performance reasons. If some (or all) of them are missing, the machine still functions correctly.

The second: An instruction becomes ready for execution only after all its parents' destination tags have been broadcast. If the machine can predict which parent will finish last, it can use only the destination tags of that parent's parents to become speculatively ready. That is, each RSE will have the tags of all the instruction's parents, and, for the parent that was predicted to be last, the tags of its parents. If the prediction is wrong, the machine still functions correctly: the instruction just isn't selected as soon as it could be.

We used a simple scheme to predict the last parent. A 2-bit saturating counter was stored along with each instruction in the instruction cache. When an instruction was fetched, the upper bit of the counter specified whether the first or second parent would finish last. During rename, only the parents of the parent that was predicted to finish last were stored in the grandparent fields. While an instruction was in the reservation stations, it recorded which parent finished last.[3] When the instruction committed, it decremented the

---
[3]Actually, the only time the grandparent fields are used is when the parent has a latency of 1 cycle. The instruction actually recorded which parent with a 1 cycle latency finished last.

counter if the first parent finished last, and incremented it if the second parent finished last.

4.5.2. Operation of Instruction Re-execution. The scheduling logic presented can handle instruction re-execution without any modification. As mentioned in Section 2.1, the child of a load instruction is scheduled assuming the load hits the cache. If the load misses, or if the load is found to have a memory dependency on an earlier store instruction, the load result may be delayed. When this happens, the chain of instructions dependent on the load must be re-scheduled. This is accomplished by rebroadcasting the load's destination tag on the tag bus. When the tag is rebroadcast, all children of the load will rewake since loads are multi-cycle operations. All grandchildren of the load will either rewake immediately, or if the dependent parent is a multi-cycle operation, will rewake after that parent broadcasts its tag. Hence there is never a situation where a dependent of the load is not rewakened.

5. Experiments

To measure the impact of pipelining the scheduling logic, we modeled four machines: a *baseline* machine, which uses conventional scheduling pipelined over 2 cycles; a *budget* and a *deluxe* machine, which use 2-cycle pipelined scheduling with speculative wakeup; and an *ideal* machine, which uses conventional 1-cycle scheduling logic. The budget machine uses RSEs that can hold only two grandparent tags. Last parent prediction is used to select which two. The deluxe machine uses RSEs that can hold all grandparent tags. As mentioned in Section 3.5, the baseline machine only introduces pipeline bubbles when scheduling single-cycle instructions, not when scheduling multi-cycle instructions.

All machines were 8-wide superscalar processors with out-of-order execution, configured as shown in Table 1. They required 2 cycles for fetch, 2 for decode, 2 for rename, 1 for register read, and 1 for commit. The ideal machine required 1 cycle for wakeup/select. The others required 2. The execution latencies are shown in Table 2. An instruction with a 1-cycle execution latency requires a minimum of 10 cycles to progress from the first fetch stage to commit.

The machines were simulated using a cycle-accurate, execution-driven simulator for the Alpha ISA. Figure 12 shows the IPC of the four machines over the SPECint95 benchmarks. The 15% IPC difference between the baseline and ideal machines represents the amount of performance that can be gained by using pipelined scheduling with speculative wakeup. The deluxe machine gains 86% of this difference. On average, the deluxe machine performs 13% better than the baseline machine, and within 2% of the ideal machine. The budget machine performs within 1% of the

Branch Predictor	15-bit gshare, 2048-entry BTB
Instruction Cache	64KB 4-way set associative (pipelined) 2-cycle directory and data store access
Instruction Window	128 RSE (16 for each functional unit)
Execution Width	8 multi-purpose functional units, only four of which support load/store operations
Data Cache	64KB 2-way set associative (pipelined) 2-cycle directory and data store access
Unified L2 Cache	1MB, 8-way, 7-cycle access 2 banks, contention is modeled

Table 1. Machine Configuration

Instruction Class	Latency (Cycles)
integer arithmetic	1
integer multiply	8, pipelined
fp arithmetic	4, pipelined
fp divide	16
loads	1 + dcache latency
all others	1

Table 2. Instruction Class Latencies

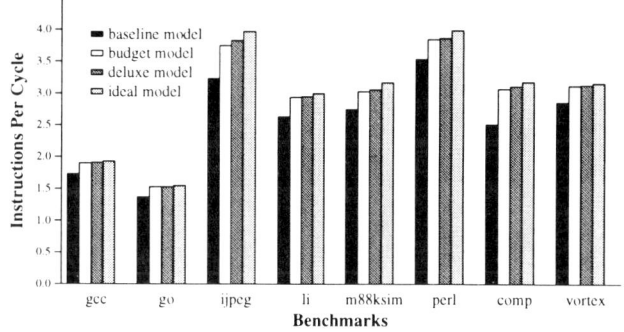

Figure 12. Comparison of the Four Machines

deluxe machine.

The IPC differences between the budget, deluxe, and ideal machines are primarily due to false selections caused by speculative wakeup. False selections only impact IPC if other instructions that were ready to execute were prevented from executing due to a false selection. Figure 13 shows the amount of false selections and scheduling opportunities lost due to false selections for the budget and deluxe machines. This graph shows the fraction of scheduling opportunities in which a selection resulted in: (1) a false selection that prevented a ready instruction from receiving an execution grant, (2) a false selection, but no instructions were ready, and (3) a correct selection. The fourth case—the only other possible case—is when no instructions request execution. The first of each pair of bars (bars with solid colors) show the cycle breakdown for the budget machine. The second of each pair (striped bars) show the breakdown for the deluxe machine. As the graph shows, the selection logic for a given

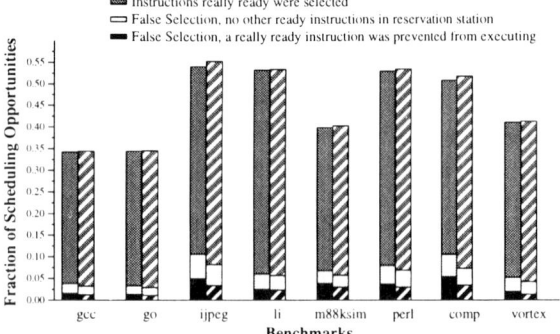

Figure 13. Selection Outcomes

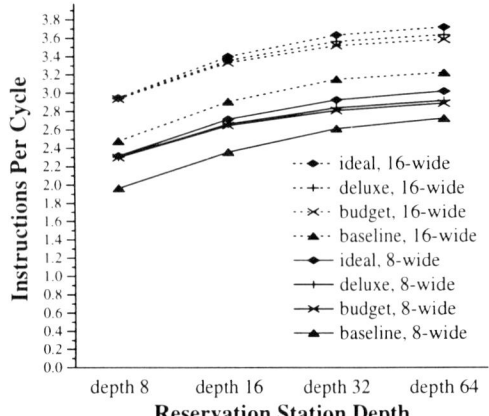

Figure 14. Comparison of the Four Machines for Different Window Sizes

functional unit awarded an execution grant 35% to 55% of the time. A ready instruction was prevented from executing due to a false selection only 1% to 7% of the time. Note that these metrics cannot be compared to IPC since they measure both non-speculative *and speculative* instructions.

The frequency of false selections is quite sensitive to the amount of functional unit contention. Simulations of the four machines using both 8 and 16 functional units and several instruction window sizes were run to demonstrate the effect of this contention on IPC. The simulation parameters of the 16-wide issue machines are similar to those of the 8-wide machines except that 8 of the 16 functional units are capable of executing load and store instructions. Figure 14 shows the harmonic mean of the IPC of the SPECint95 benchmarks for all models using both issue widths when the number of RSEs for *each* functional unit is varied from 8 to 64. The machine model with the most contention for execution resources is the 8-wide machine with a 512-entry instruction window. For this configuration, pipelined scheduling with speculative wakeup gains 65% of the difference between the baseline and ideal machines.

6. Conclusion

This paper demonstrates that the dynamic instruction scheduling logic can be pipelined without sacrificing the ability to execute dependent instructions in consecutive cycles. It introduced pipelined scheduling with speculative wakeup, which pipelines this logic over 2 cycles. This technique significantly reduces the critical path through this logic while having only a minor impact on IPC. If the critical path through this logic limits the processor cycle time, this technique allows microarchitects to build higher performance machines by enabling higher clock frequencies, deeper pipelines, and larger instruction windows.

Acknowledgements

We especially thank Paul Racunas, Jean-Loup Baer, and the anonymous referees for their comments on earlier drafts of this paper. This work was supported in part by Intel, HAL, and IBM. Mary Brown is supported by an IBM Cooperative Graduate Fellowship.

References

[1] M. Butler and Y. Patt, "An investigation of the performance of various dynamic scheduling techniques," in *Proceedings of the 25th Annual ACM/IEEE International Symposium on Microarchitecture*, 1992.

[2] *IA-32 Intel Architecture Software Developer's Manual With Preliminary Willamette Architecture Information Volume 1: Basic Architecture*, Intel Corporation, 2000.

[3] S. Palacharla, N. P. Jouppi, and J. E. Smith, "Complexity-effective superscalar processors," in *Proceedings of the 24th Annual International Symposium on Computer Architecture*, 1997.

[4] R. M. Tomasulo, "An efficient algorithm for exploiting multiple arithmetic units," *IBM Journal of Research and Development*, vol. 11, pp. 25–33, January 1967.

[5] K. C. Yeager, "The MIPS R10000 superscalar microprocessor," *IEEE Micro*, vol. 16, no. 2, pp. 28–41, April 1996.

[6] A. Yu, *Client Architecture for the New Millennium*, Intel Corporation, February 2000. Spring 2000 Intel Developer Forum Keynote Presentation.

The Impact of Delay on the Design of Branch Predictors

Daniel A. Jiménez   Stephen W. Keckler   Calvin Lin

Department of Computer Sciences
The University of Texas at Austin
Austin, TX 78712
{djimenez,skeckler,lin}@cs.utexas.edu

Abstract

Modern microprocessors employ increasingly complicated branch predictors to achieve instruction fetch bandwidth that is sufficient for wide out-of-order execution cores. While existing predictors can still be accessed in a single clock cycle, recent studies show that slower wires and faster clock rates will require multi-cycle access times to large on-chip structures, such as branch prediction tables. Thus, future branch predictors must consider not only area and accuracy, but also delay. This paper explores these tradeoffs in designing branch predictors and shows that increased accuracy alone cannot overcome the penalties in delay that arise with larger predictor structures. We evaluate three schemes for accommodating delay: a caching *approach, an* overriding *approach, and a cascading* lookahead approach. *While we use a common branch predictor,* gshare, *as the prediction component, these schemes can be constructed using most types of predictors.*

1 Introduction

Accurate branch prediction is essential to sustaining high IPC in pipelined microprocessors. Until now, the huge body of branch prediction research has focused on only two dimensions of the problem—area and accuracy—and has found that larger hardware budgets yield higher accuracy for two reasons: They allow longer history lengths, and they reduce *aliasing*, which occurs when two unrelated branches destructively share the same hardware branch prediction resources. Indeed, much of the recent work has focused on methods for reducing aliasing [19, 13, 12, 21, 5]. With growing chip capacities, the focus of the research community on area and accuracy has led to large elaborate predictors, some of which require 16K to 64K byte structures [7].

Recent studies, however, have shown that as feature sizes shrink, larger wire delays and smaller clock cycles will lead to multi-cycle access to large on-chip structures [1]. Thus, future branch predictors will need to consider a third dimension: delay. Figure 1 illustrates the problem of ignoring delay. Using an idealized delay of one cycle to access the pattern history table (PHT), the *gshare* predictor [13] sees improved IPC—due to improved prediction accuracy—as the size of the PHT is increased. By contrast, with an aggressive clock frequency (2GHz) and a realistic delay model for today's 180 nanometer technology, the curve drops off at 1KB where the PHT requires two cycles to access, and IPC drops significantly at 32KB where delay becomes three cycles. This problem will be exacerbated by the smaller process technologies of the future, as shown by the curve for 100nm technology, which drops to 3 cycles 8KB.

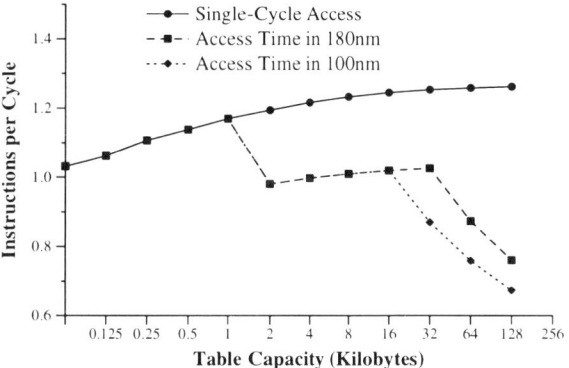

Figure 1: Instruction Throughput versus Capacity for the *gshare* predictor. Using idealized single-cycle access, IPC (and prediction accuracy) increases with increasing pattern history table capacity. Using realistic delay models, IPC drops when the delay is 2 cycles, and falls precipitously when the delay is 3 cycles.

This paper explores the tradeoffs in delay, area, and accuracy for the design of future branch predictors. We examine three approaches for dealing with delay in future process technologies: a two level caching scheme, an *overriding* scheme that allows a first prediction to be overturned by a more accurate second prediction, and a *cascading* lookahead scheme that exploits the time between branches to start reading prediction tables.

Each approach can be implemented with almost any two-level branch predictor as components. We use *gshare* as the basic prediction component because it is well-understood and often used as a standard for comparison. To calibrate our results with existing technology, we also simulate a hybrid predictor similar to that found in the Alpha 21264 [11] microprocessor, and we show how this hybrid predictor scales to future technologies.

This paper makes the following contributions.

- We show that delay in the predictor significantly erodes performance, so future branch prediction work must consider delay in their designs.

- We show that increasing delay to improve accuracy is never a good tradeoff.

- We show that there are approaches to branch prediction that can effectively use large structures with multi-cycle access times.

- We show that the overriding approach performs best and can improve IPC by 10% over *gshare* in 35nm technology at an aggressive clock rate.

This paper is organized as follows. Section 2 describes related work. Section 3 discusses the technological challenges that branch predictors face. Section 4 describes three approaches to dealing with multi-cycle delay, and Section 5 presents experimental results.

2 Related Work

Most recent research in dynamic branch prediction focuses on the two-level scheme of Yeh and Patt [23], which uses two-bit saturating counters to record the history of particular branches or branch patterns. As Sechrest, et al. showed [19], aliasing can limit the accuracy of branch predictors. A variety of techniques for reducing aliasing have been suggested [13, 12, 21, 5], and given sufficiently large predictor tables, many of these two-level achieve similar performance [5].

Lookahead branch prediction, including predicting multiple branches per cycle, has been suggested as a means for predicting branches that have not yet been presented to the predictor. One of the first lookahead branch predictors was proposed by Yeh, et al. [22] as the Multiple Branch Two-Level Adaptive Branch Predictor. This predictor uses the result of the first branch prediction to speculatively update the history register for a second branch prediction. No branch addresses are required since only the global history register is used to access the pattern history tables. Seznec, et al. improve on this idea by enhancing the BTB to enable the predictor to use the address of the current instruction block to perform prediction for the next instruction block [20]. This scheme enables the fetches to multiple blocks to be pipelined. Onder, Xu and Gupta propose a similar scheme in which predictions for an entire branch sequence are made all at once, and instruction fetch can continue unimpeded through the last branch [14].

Driesen and Hölze propose a "cascaded" predictor that dynamically filters easily predicted branches, relieving aliasing effects in the PHT [4]. Our work borrows the idea of cascading, but uses it to alleviate delay. Similarly, Evers describes the use of two PHTs with different history lengths and different access times, and suggests that the slower one can override the other [6]. The Alpha 21264 branch predictor uses the idea of overriding: the branch predictor can override the less accurate instruction cache line predictor, with

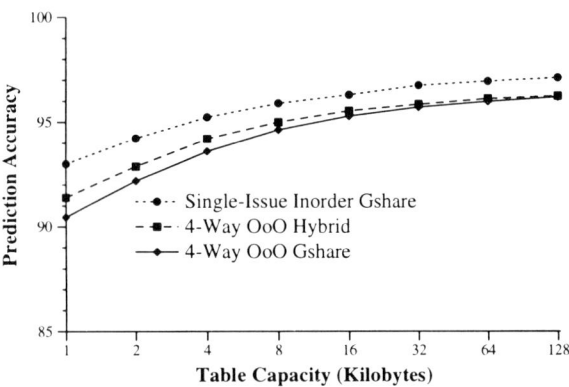

Figure 2: Prediction Accuracy versus Pattern History Table Capacity for our benchmarks. As the capacity increases, so does the prediction accuracy. Accuracy is worse for a 4-way out-of-order machine because the branch history is not always updated in time for the next prediction.

a penalty of a single cycle, as opposed to the seven-cycle branch misprediction penalty [11].

Of course, the real goal in these strategies is to improve instruction fetch bandwidth and preferably take branch prediction off the critical path. Recent research has focused on trace caches as a mechanism to capture a long stream of sequential instructions that can be easily fetched at peak bandwidth [18, 15]. Branch prediction guides the trace selection in the instruction fetch engine, at times predicting multiple branches per cycle. A more radical approach is the Fetch Target Buffer (FTB) proposed by Reinman, et al. [16]. The FTB stores the addresses of predicted blocks of instructions and is designed as a two level cache for fast access and accurate block prediction. Like our study, Reinman, et al. consider technology constraints in the design of the FTB. Frameworks like the FTB can benefit by using delay-sensitive branch prediction strategies as their branch prediction components.

3 Challenges for Branch Prediction

This section discusses the near term technological trends in fabrication technologies that branch predictor designers must confront. We first discuss the tradeoffs between accuracy and delay, explaining why delay is becoming increasingly significant. We then explain why large tables lead to large delays. Together, these observations frame our search for the latency-sensitive predictors that we discuss in the next section.

3.1 Predictor Delay vs. Accuracy

Branch prediction accuracy increases with the amount of memory allocated to the branch prediction table. Figure 2 shows the accuracy of the *gshare* branch predictor on several benchmarks (see Table 2 for a list of the benchmarks used in this study) as the prediction table capacity is increased, both in a sequential in-order machine and a 4-way out-of-order machine simulated with SimpleScalar [2]. The graph also shows the accuracy of a hybrid predictor similar to that in

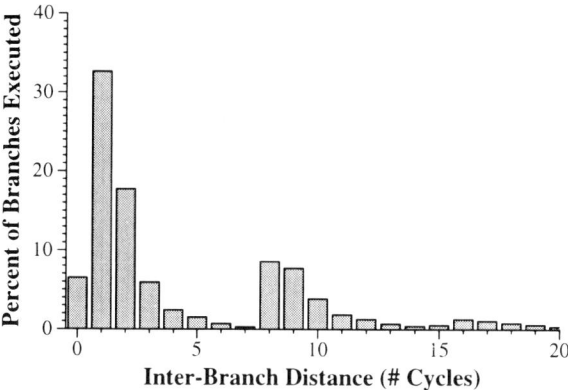

Figure 3: Histogram of average inter-branch latencies, measured in cycles, between prediction requests, for the SPEC 2000 integer benchmarks. Over 60% of the prediction requests occur at least one cycle after the previous request.

the Alpha 21264. We see that wide issue out-of-order execution has an important effect on prediction accuracy, increasing the misprediction rate roughly 25% over the single-issue in-order case because some predictions are demanded before the global pattern history register can be updated with the most recent branch outcomes. This effect also occurs with a single-issue in-order machine, but is much less pronounced since fewer branches can be in flight at the same time.

Similar graphs appear in most recent branch prediction papers. These graphs tacitly imply that branch prediction accuracy, and hence instructions-per-clock (IPC), can be improved by increasing the size of the prediction table. However, larger structures lead to larger access delays; worse, aggressively increasing clock rates (as the marketplace demands) increases the structure access time as measured in clock cycles.

Our studies show that it is almost never worth increasing the delay of a branch predictor for the sake of improved accuracy. For example, Figure 1 shows that as we increase the capacity of the tables in *gshare*, we increase delay and decrease IPC. This effect can be explained with the following equation which roughly approximates the cost C of executing a branch instruction:

$$C = d + (r \times p)$$

where d is the delay of branch predictor, r is the misprediction rate, and p is the misprediction penalty. While the delay d may not always be on the critical path of the pipeline, increasing d will reduce the instruction fetch bandwidth to the execution cores. Because misprediction rates tend to be close to 10%, changes in d have a larger impact than small changes in r.

3.2 Branch Frequency

A program's control behavior is based not only on the predictability of its branches, but also on the branch frequency. If branch prediction is required on every clock cycle, any delay in branch prediction will substantially slow the instruction fetch rate. However, if branches are widely spaced, then

Gate (nm)	16FO4 Clk f_{16} (GHz)	10FO4 Clk f_{10} (GHz)
250	0.70	1.12
180	0.96	1.54
130	1.33	2.13
100	1.74	2.78
70	2.48	3.97
50	3.47	5.55
35	4.96	7.94

Table 1: Projected clock rates using FO4 Clock scaling.

branch prediction latency will have less impact on performance. We use SimpleScalar to measure the average branch frequency in ten SPEC 2000 integer benchmarks on a 4-way out-of-order machine configuration. The results in Figure 3 show that 61% of the branches had at least one unused cycle between predictions. The unused cycles provide additional time to predict future branches.

3.3 Technology Scaling

Branch predictors, like other microarchitecture structures, are affected by two technology scaling trends. At smaller feature sizes, wire delay grows in significance relative to transistor speeds and can affect the latency of the fetch engine and the branch predictor. Furthermore, microprocessor designers continue to aggressively increase the clock rates, outstripping the speed improvements achieved by transistors that have smaller gate lengths in each successive technology [1]. These faster clocks exacerbate the tradeoff between capacity and delay in microprocessor components.

To account for accelerating clock rates, we use a technology independent metric, the *fanout-of-four* (FO4) delay metric, to measure clock period [9]. One FO4 delay is the time for an inverter to drive 4 copies of itself. Reasonable models show that under typical conditions, the FO4 delay, measured in picoseconds, is equal to $360 \times L_{drawn}$, where L_{drawn} is the minimum gate length for a technology, measured in microns. The number of FO4 delays in a clock period is an indicator of the number of levels of logic in a pipeline stage. In this paper, we examine two edges of the clock scaling envelope: f_{10}, which corresponds to a clock period of 10 FO4 delays, and f_{16} corresponding to 16 FO4 delays. Table 1 lists the technologies that we consider in this paper and the clock rates that result from aggressive (f_{10}) and conservative (f_{16}) scaling.

We base our estimates of branch predictor delay on the access time of the memory-oriented structures such as the pattern history table (PHT). To model PHT delay, we use the methodology described by Agarwal, et al. [1], which augments the ECacti cache delay modeling tool [17] with scaled technology parameters. We convert the access time produced by the augmented ECacti model into cycles, according to both the f_{10} and f_{16} clock scaling strategies. As shown in Figure 4, with the aggressive f_{10} clock, only small tables of 1024 entries can be accessed in a single cycle, and at 35nm, only 512 entries can be accessed in one cycle. Accepting a 2 or 3 cycle delay increases the capacity to 16K and 64K entries, respectively. Using the conservative f_{16} clock rate,

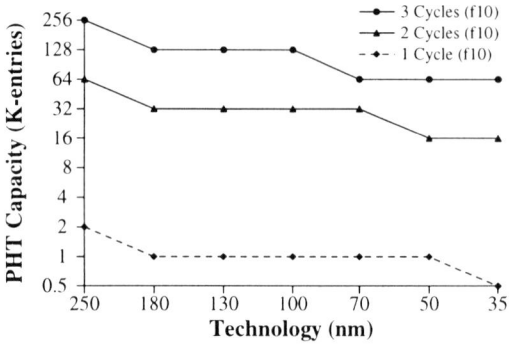 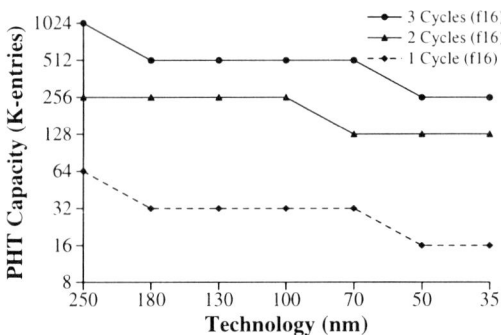

Figure 4: Pattern History Table capacity and access latency across technologies at agressive (f_{10}) and conservative (f_{16}) clock frequencies.

much larger structures can be used, ranging from 16K to 512K, as the access latency grows from 1 to 3 cycles.

As a consequence of technology and clock scaling, the challenge for the microarchitect is to achieve high accuracy in branch predictors whose table sizes are limited. Thus, branch predictors cannot be evaluated solely on prediction accuracy. Latency must be taken into account as the branch predictor will often reside on the critical path for the execution of the program. However, some of the latency of branch prediction can be hidden if spaces between branches can be found. The remainder of this paper examines techniques for achieving high prediction accuracy while minimizing prediction latency for future process technologies.

4 Latency Sensitive Branch Predictors

In this section we describe three ways to configure branch predictors to increase accuracy in the face of increasing latency. These techniques all have a common theme: a small table is used to provide quick prediction, and a large table is used to provide higher accuracy. The techniques are appropriate when standard techniques for branch prediction might exceed one cycle, and are general techniques that can be applied to most prediction algorithms. We assume that the branch target buffer (BTB) is kept at a constant capacity and access time. While this is not realistic because of technology and clock rate impact on BTB capacity, it allows us to focus solely on the scaling of the branch predictor. Similar strategies can be applied to the BTB.

4.1 Caching Prediction Tables

The first strategy to combat the long latency of large branch prediction tables is to build a small cache of branch prediction table entries. This allows us to realize the benefits of reduced aliasing and increased history length without the added latency of the large table, since the cache will work in one cycle. Figure 5 shows the organization of the *gshare* predictor augmented by a cache. The branch history and branch address are hashed using the XOR gate, and the resulting address is sent to both the pattern history table cache (PHTC) and the pattern history table (PHT). The PHT consists of 2-bit saturating counters, with the number of counters equal

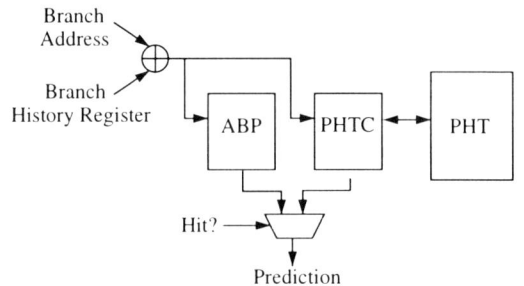

Figure 5: Caching Branch Predictor

to the number of combinations of addresses produced by the hash function. The PHTC caches a subset of those counters in a smaller table that can be accessed more quickly than the PHT. If the correct counter is found in the PHTC, then the prediction can be made immediately. If a miss in the PHTC occurs, then the PHT must be consulted to find the correct saturating counter. Like traditional caches, an entry in the PHTC is replaced with the correct counter from the PHT. When the branch direction is determined during a later stage of the execution pipeline, the counters in the PHT and PHTC are updated to reflect the correct or incorrect prediction of that branch.

If a PHTC miss occurs, the wait for the correct prediction from the PHT will delay instruction fetch and will degrade overall performance. Two alternatives can be used to prevent this additional delay. The prediction produced by the PHTC, albeit for the wrong branch, can be used. We instead build a small auxiliary branch predictor (ABP) that can be accessed at the same time as the PHTC. If the PHTC misses, then the result from the ABP is used. The accuracy of this hybrid-like predictor is a function of the capacities of the subsidiary predictors and the ability of the PHTC to capture the locality of branch instructions.

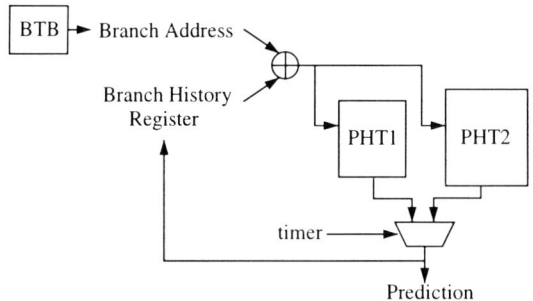

Figure 6: Cascading Branch Predictor

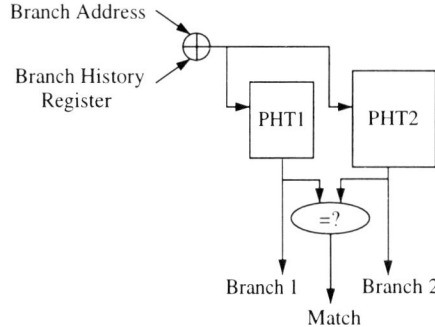

Figure 7: Overriding Branch Predictor

4.2 Cascading Lookahead Branch Prediction

Lookahead branch prediction has been proposed as a mechanism to increase fetch bandwidth by generating addresses for future branches [22, 20]. The same technique can be applied to reduce the impact of longer latency branch predictors. If the branch predictor is not needed on every cycle, then natural spacing between branches can be used to perform a prediction for the next branch that is likely to arrive. Thus, if branches are spaced so that the predictor is accessed only every other cycle, the predictor can have a two cycle latency without introducing additional delay.

The *gshare* predictor can be adapted to look one branch ahead. While *gshare* uses the branch history register and branch address to compute the PHT address, the lookahead predictor uses the predicted history and predicted branch target address. The predicted history is computed by appending the prediction of the most recent branch to the branch history register. The predicted branch target address is taken directly from the BTB as a result of the previous branch prediction. As a consequence, this scheme relies on the accuracy of the BTB. If the prediction can complete before the next branch arrives at the predictor, prediction is instantaneous. However, if the prediction requires multiple cycles (due to a large table) and the next branch arrives before the prediction is complete, the instruction fetch engine stalls.

Cascading lookahead branch prediction implements a series of tables of ascending size and latency. Figure 6 shows a two-level cascading predictor. Like a lookahead predictor, the next prediction is based on the last prediction and the last predicted branch target. Prediction is begun simultaneously on both levels of the cascading predictor. If the latency to the next branch to be predicted is large, then the prediction from the second level table is selected. If the next branch arrives before the second level table can complete its access, then the prediction from the first level table is used.

The combination of a small first level table and a larger second level table can provide high aggregate accuracy with low latency. However, the utility of the larger table depends on its access time and the inter-branch latency. If branches occur extremely frequently, the second level of the cascade will not be used. The cascading design can be trivially extended to more than two levels. Furthermore, hybrid predictors of varying latencies can be incorporated into the cascading strategy. In our description above, the logic to select which prediction to use is based only on the arrival time of the next branch. More complicated selectors could trade off latency versus accuracy by predicting which of many predictions is best for the subsequent branch.

4.3 Overriding Branch Predictor

An overriding branch predictor (Figure 7) provides two predictions. The first prediction comes from a fast PHT (PHT1), and the second prediction comes from a slower, but more accurate PHT (PHT2). When branch prediction is requested, the first prediction is used and acted upon while the second prediction is still being made. If the second prediction differs from the first prediction, the actions taken based on the first prediction are squashed and instructions are fetched using the second prediction; thus, the second predictor overrides the first predictor. For the overriding scheme, we assume that the penalty of restarting an overridden fetch is equal to the delay of PHT2. A similar technique is used in the Alpha 21264, in which the branch predictor, whose results become known only in the second stage of the pipeline, can override the less accurate instruction cache line predictor [11] at the cost of a single stall cycle. We assume the predictor is pipelined such that no branch needs to wait for the completion of a PHT2 lookup for a previous branch.

5 Results and Evaluation

In this section we evaluate the three latency sensitive branch predictors and compare them to *gshare* across a spectrum of process technologies. As displayed in Table 2, we use ten SPEC 2000 integer benchmarks for our simulation. We simulate the different prediction strategies described above using delay estimates at seven process technologies ranging from 250nm to 35nm. We simulate the benchmarks using the SimpleScalar out-of-order simulator and PISA instruction set, configured with parameters similar to those for the Alpha 21264; the simulator is a modified version of the one used by Agarwal et. al. [1]. Each simulation runs for 500 million

Benchmark	Description
164.gzip	LZ77 compression
175.vpr	Place and route for FPGAs
176.gcc	C compiler
181.mcf	Minimum cost network flow solver
197.parser	Natural language processing
253.perlbmk	Perl
254.gap	Computational group theory
255.vortex	Database
256.bzip2	Block-sorting compression
300.twolf	Place and route

Table 2: Subset of the SPEC 2000 integer benchmark suite.

	Capacity (bits)	# entries	Bits/entry	Ports
BTB	48K	512	96	1
Reorder buffer	8K	64	128	8
Issue window	800/320	20	56	8
Integer RF	5K	80	64	10
FP RF	5.6K	72	80	10
L1 I-Cache	512K	1K	512	1
L1 D-Cache	512K	1K	512	2
L2 Cache	16M	16K	1024	2
I-TLB	14K	128	112	1
D-TLB	14K	128	112	2

Table 3: Parameters used for the simulations, similar to the Alpha 21264.

instructions or until the application terminates, whichever comes first. In the simulations, the global pattern history register is updated speculatively and backed up on a mispredict, while updates to the PHTs are done when the updating branch commits.

Since we are focusing solely on the branch predictor, we keep the other structure sizes constant at values shown in Table 3. Our main results use the aggressive f_{10} clock rate, which emphasizes the scaling difficulties of branch predictor structures. We also report results for the more conservative f_{16} clock. Although f_8 was used in the original technology scaling work [1], we choose f_{10} as our aggressive clock rate because our hybrid predictor is unworkable at the f_8 clock rate.

For each process technology, we configure the simulator with the largest branch prediction structures (predictor tables, cache, etc.) reachable at the given number of cycles allocated to branch prediction. The structure sizes are obtained using the modified version of ECacti described in Section 3. For each benchmark we measure IPC, aggregate branch predictor accuracy, and other statistics related to the branch prediction schemes. Aggregate branch prediction performance is computed as the arithmetic mean over the benchmarks. Note that the capacity of each structure is set by its access time, rather than any chip area limitation. With smaller feature sizes, this assumption is fair, as the amount of effective chip area is far larger than is reachable in the number of cycles we consider.

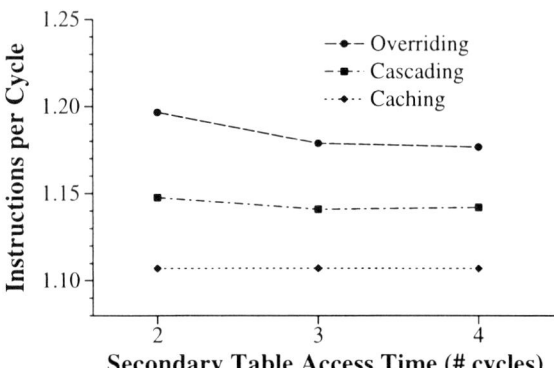

Figure 8: IPC at 100nm for various configurations of primary and secondary structures in the caching, overriding, and cascading predictors at the f_{10} clock rate.

5.1 Predictor Configuration

For each predictor, we consider several configurations of structure capacity and latency in search of the best configuration at each technology generation. Figure 8 shows the results of these experiments for the caching and cascading predictors at 100nm. In the caching predictor, the two structures are the PHTC and the PHT, while in the overriding and cascading predictor the two structures are the PHT1 and PHT2. As the secondary structure access times increase, the resulting IPC is slightly worse for the overriding predictor and slightly better for the cascading predictor. The size of the secondary structure for the caching predictor makes little difference in performance. The rest of our results are reported using the best configurations found for each prediction technique.

Each *gshare* component of the various predictors uses the maximum history length, e.g., if a *gshare* predictor has 1024 entries, then the maximum history length is $log_2 1024 = 10$. Studies have shown that the using the maximum history length does not always yield the best accuracy [13, 8], so we empirically identify the best history length for *gshare* at each hardware budget. We find that, for our PISA instruction set, branch predictor configurations, and benchmarks, the best history length is always the maximum.

In the caching predictor, we varied the latency of the PHT from 2 to 4 cycles, keeping the PHTC at a 1-cycle access time. Note that increasing the latency of each table also increases its capacity.

For the cascading and overriding predictors, we keep access to the primary PHT at one cycle while varying access to the secondary PHT from from 2 to 4 cycles. Increasing the second level (PHT2) latency reduces IPC slightly for the overriding predictor, but increases IPC slightly for the cascading predictor.

The best configurations for the caching predictor at the f_{10} clock rate can be seen in Table 4. The PHTC has an unusually small number of entries compared with the other structures. Unlike a normal cache that has large cache lines, our caching predictor requires many times more tag bits than data bits. The extra wire length involved in accessing the tag

Technology (nm)	ABP Delay	ABP Entries	PHTC Entries	PHT Delay	PHT Entries
250	1	2K	512	2	64K
180	1	1K	256	2	32K
130	1	1K	256	3	128K
100	1	1K	256	4	256K
70	1	1K	256	2	32K
50	1	1K	256	2	16K
35	1	512	128	2	16K

Table 4: The best configurations of the ABP and PHT table sizes, as well as number of PHTC for the caching predictor at each technology for the f_{10} clock rate.

Technology (nm)	PHT1 Delay	PHT1 Entries	PHT2 Delay	PHT2 Entries
250	1	2K	2	64K
180	1	1K	3	128K
130	1	1K	2	32K
100	1	1K	2	32K
70	1	1K	3	64K
50	1	1K	3	64K
35	1	512	2	16K

Table 5: The best configurations of the PHT1 and PHT2 for the cascading and overriding predictors at each technology for the f_{10} clock rate.

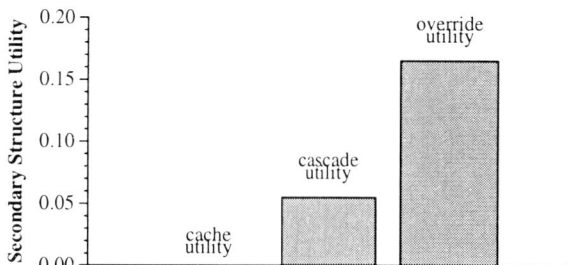

Figure 9: The utility of the secondary structures is highest in the overriding predictor and lowest in the caching predictor.

bits severely restricts the number of cache entries, limiting the effectiveness of this scheme. Other prediction components in which the size of the basic prediction element is large with respect to the number of tag bits, such as the perceptron predictor [10], may be more amenable to a caching scheme.

The best configurations for the cascading predictor at the f_{10} clock rate are shown in Table 5. The best configurations for the overriding predictor are identical to those of the cascading predictor, since the two predictors have much the same architecture and differ only in their policy of when and whether to use the second-level PHT. Indeed, the stream of updates to the PHT1 and PHT2 structures should be the same in both overriding and cascading predictors; the only difference is that the overriding predictor always uses the PHT2 prediction, while the cascading predictor only uses the PHT2 prediction when it has enough time.

The best configurations for each predictor at the more conservative f_{16} clock rate (not shown) allow larger tables and single-cycle access for the hybrid predictor at every technology.

5.2 Structure Usage Rates

The simulations keep statistics on the rate at which the various structures are accessed. To explain the relative performance of each technique, Figure 9 shows the utility of each predictor. These statistics explain the relative performance of each technique. For the caching scheme, the the PHT is accessed for 7.5% of all branches, and this access results in a prediction different from that of the ABP in 0.013% of all branches. This explains why the performance of the caching predictor is so similar to *gshare* by itself: it almost always relys on the ABP, and when it doesn't, the ABP and PHT almost always agree.

For the cascading scheme, the PHT2 structure is used for 45.6% of all branches, and its prediction differs from that of PHT1 for 5.5% of all branches, thus the second level table is useful for only 5.5% of branches.

For the overriding scheme, the frequency with which the predictions of PHT1 and PHT2 disagree, i.e., how often the more accurate predictor is used, is 16.5%, so the overriding scheme is the most useful of the predictors. These results are for 100nm technology; the statistics are similar across all technologies.

5.3 Hybrid Predictor

To demonstrate the effect of delay on predictors more complex than *gshare*, and calibrate our clock estimates with a real-world processor, we simulate a hybrid predictor similar to the branch predictor of the Alpha 21264. We report IPC and accuracy figures for this predictor along with our other results. This predictor maintains both global and local branch history information. The global pattern history register is used to index into a PHT while the branch address is used to index into a table of local histories, which is then used to index another PHT. A choice table is indexed by the global pattern history register. The global branch history is update speculatively, and all other tables are updated when the branch commits. We assume the lookups in the global PHT, local history table, and chooser table are all started at the same time, and the lookup in the local PHT occurs immediately after the local history register becomes available from the local table. The global PHT and chooser table have four times the capacity of the local PHT, and the local PHT and local histories table have the same number of entries.

This predictor closely resembles the Alpha predictor [11] with two exceptions: (1) on the Alpha, the prediction becomes available only in the second pipeline stage, and can override the first-stage line predictor, while our predictor operates in the first pipeline stage; and (2), we allow the capacity of our predictor to vary depending on the access times at

Technology (nm)	Delay	Local Entries	Global Entries
250	1	128	512
180	2	4K	16K
130	2	4K	16K
100	2	4K	16K
70	2	4K	16K
50	2	2K	8K
35	2	2K	8K

Table 6: The best configurations for the hybrid predictor at each technology for the f_{10} clock rate. Beyond 250nm technology, the predictor simply can't work in one cycle because of sequential lookups into the local history table and local PHT, so delay slips to two cycles, with a corresponding increase in table capacities.

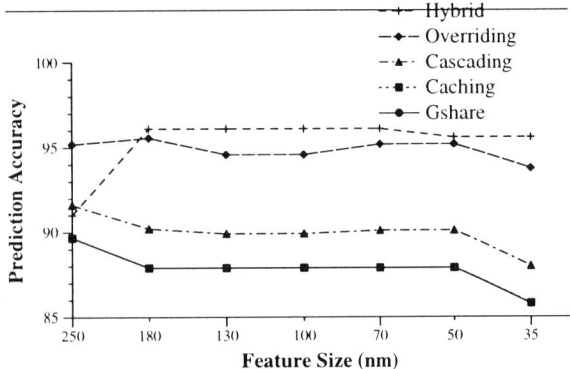

Figure 10: Accuracy vs. Technology for the five prediction strategies at f_{10}. The hybrid predictor is more accurate only because its best configuration consumes two cycles, allowing it to use large table.

the different clock rates and technologies.

The configurations for the hybrid predictor at the f_{10} clock rate are seen in Table 6. Unlike the *gshare*, this hybrid predictor requires two table accesses: first in the table of local histories, and then in the local PHT. Consequently, this hybrid predictor is much more sensitive to delay that prediction schemes that require only a single table access. In fact, at the aggressive f_{10} clock rates, we found that the table sizes are prohibitively small for single cycle predictor access at 180nm and smaller. Our original experiments used an f_8 clock rate, but that resulted in multi-cycle predictor latency at 250nm as well. Finally, using the table sizes of the Alpha 21264 in 250nm technology results in an access time of 1.55 ns, which corresponds to the published clock frequency of the Alpha of approximately 600MHz [11].

5.4 Aggressive Clocking

Figure 10 shows the accuracies of the best configurations of the various predictors at the f_{10} clock rates. As shown in the graph, accuracy tends to decrease with feature sizes, because the prediction table capacities decrease. The accuracy of the overriding predictor increases slightly from 100 to 70nm, since the best configuration for 70nm technology allows the PHT2 to take three cycles, while the best configuration in 100nm allows only two cycles. Likewise, the accuracy of the hybrid predictor increases from 250 to 180nm as the best configuration predicts in two cycles, allowing a larger area to be used. Of the schemes that can provide a prediction in a single cycle, the overriding predictor achieves the highest accuracy because it always uses larger second-level predictor, either because it agrees with or overrides the first-level predictor. The cascading predictor performs worse because it sometimes uses the less accurate first-level predictor, either because there are not enough cycles to use the second-level predictor, or because the branch target from the BTB is incorrectly predicted. Thus this predictor faces the challenge of branch misprediction as well as branch target misprediction. Finally, caching performs less well, not even exceeding the accuracy of a single level *gshare* predictor.

Of course, accuracy is not necessarily indicative of performance, particularly when prediction time is a variable. Figure 11 show the instruction throughput (IPC) for each of the configuration described above. The hybrid predictor, while achieving the best accuracy, reflects the lowest IPC at the smaller technologies, due to the access time increasing to two cycles. The rest of the predictors follow parallel trajectories with performance reflecting the overall accuracy of the predictor. Clearly, the overriding predictor, with it higher accuracy, is best for every process technology at the aggressive f_{10} clock rate.

5.5 Conservative Clocking

Figures 12 and 13 show accuracy and IPC of the same prediction schemes, but with different configurations for the more conservative f_{16} clock rate. At this clock rate, the accuracy of the predictors are very similar, since the first-level PHTs are larger. For instance, the cascading predictor can use a first-level PHT with 64K entries; having a larger second-level PHT2 does little to increase the accuracy of this predictor. Again, overriding achieves the highest accuracy, but the accuracy of hybrid decreases as feature size decreases. At the f_{16} clock rate, the hybrid scheme can be implemented in a single cycle, but the table sizes drop somewhat at 180nm and 35nm, causing a reduction in accuracy. The overall instruction throughput is similar, again reflecting the comparable accuracies of the different schemes.

That the IPC achieved by each scheme at f_{16} is no surprise. When the clock rate is set at a more conservative level, more time is available to all predictors and technology scaling is less critical. However, total performance is the product of the clock rate and the IPC. Thus the question is whether the IPC reduction at f_{10} outweighs the benefits of the faster clock rate. Note from Figures 11 and 13 that the IPC from the overriding scheme at f_{10} is only 3% less than that at the faster clock rate. Combined with a 1.6 times improvement in clock rate, overall performance will improve by using an aggressive clocking strategy. The benefits also exist with the other predictor schemes, but the benefits are somewhat less, due to larger degradation in IPC.

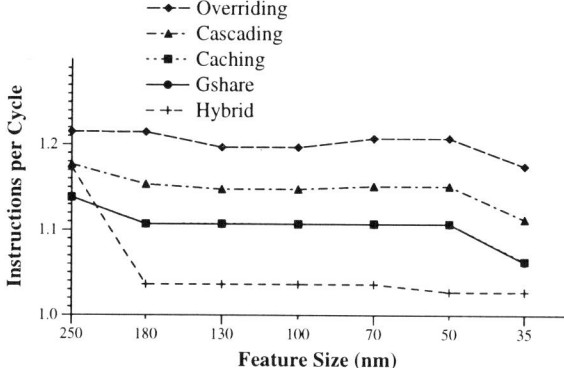

Figure 11: IPC vs. Technology for the five prediction strategies at f_{10}.

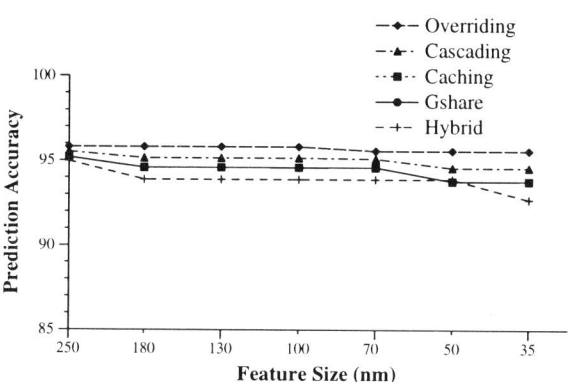

Figure 12: Accuracy vs. Technology for the five prediction strategies at f_{16}.

6 Conclusions

Until now, branch prediction design has focused on accuracy while ignoring delay. We have shown that as wire delays and clock rates increase, branch predictor designs that optimize for accuracy can have a negative impact on overall IPC. Thus, future branch predictor efficacy depends on both *accuracy* and *delay*, and researchers should account for both when reporting branch prediction results. According to our scalable models for branch predictor access time, today's predictors will not be accessible in a single cycle in sub-100nm technologies with aggressive clocking. In deep sub-micron technologies that are latency rather than capacity dominated, a branch predictor's area will become less important than its latency in the critical path.

In this paper we have examined a number of alternative branch predictor architectures and evaluated them in the context of future process technologies. We found that a hybrid predictor is adequate until its latency exceeds one cycle, causing IPC to plummet. The predictor that caches a pattern his-

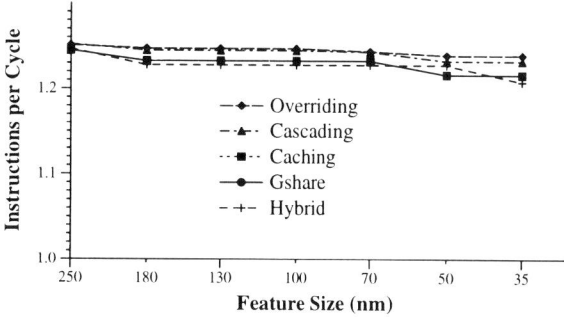

Figure 13: IPC vs. Technology for the five prediction strategies at f_{16}.

tory table (PHT) for *gshare* performs no better than *gshare* by itself. The tags needed to implement a caching scheme requires more bits than the cache itself, and limits both cache capacity and utility. The cascading lookahead predictor that uses the time in between branches to make predictions performs reasonably well at aggressive clock rates. The overriding predictor that allows a slow predictor to cancel the prediction of a faster, but less accurate predictor performs the best in our experiments.

To continue supplying a sufficient number of instructions to the execution core, future microarchitectures must move branch prediction latency off of the critical path. The schemes we present, particularly the cascading and overriding predictors, can be augmented by using something other than *gshare* as the primary or secondary predictor. We believe that the secondary predictor is the ideal place for a more complex and longer latency predictor, as it can be kept off of the critical path. Architectures such as the Fetch Target Buffer [16] are promising because they decouple the fetch engine from the execution engine. Other hardware alternatives include a more efficient branch predictor encoding such as that suggested by Jiménez and Lin [10], or multiple levels of cascaded predictors. The ideas of a cascading predictor and an overriding predictor can be combined, so that a late prediction from a second (or even third) PHT can override an earlier prediction; we believe this idea would outperform the overriding predictor by itself. Finally software may be able to assist further though branch classification [3] or through scheduling that increases the spacing of branches in the instruction stream.

7 Acknowledgements

We thank Vikas Agarwal for providing and modifying ECacti to enable better modeling of predictor structures, and Rajagopalan Desikan for his assistance in modeling predictors in SimpleScalar. We also thank the anonymous referees for their valuable suggestions. This research is supported by an IBM University Partnership Program award, NSF CAREER Grant ACI-9984660, DARPA Contract #F30602-97-1-0150, and ONR grant N00014-99-1-0402.

References

[1] V. Agarwal, M. Hrishikesh, S. W. Keckler, and D. Burger. Clock rate versus IPC: The end of the road for conventional microarchitectures. In *The 27th Annual International Symposium on Computer Architecture*, pages 248–259, June 2000.

[2] D. Burger and T. M. Austin. The simplescalar tool set version 2.0. Technical Report 1342, Computer Sciences Department, University of Wisconsin, June 1997.

[3] P.-Y. Chang and U. Banerjee. Branch classification: a new mechanism for improving branch predictor performance. In *Proceedings of the 27th International Symposium on Microarchitecture*, November 1994.

[4] K. Driesen and U. Hölze. The cascaded predictor: Economical and adaptive branch target prediction. In *Proceedings of the 31th International Symposium on Microarchitecture*, December 1998.

[5] A. Eden and T. Mudge. The YAGS branch prediction scheme. In *Proceedings of the 31st Annual ACM/IEEE International Symposium on Microarchitecture*, November 1998.

[6] M. Evers. *Improving Branch Prediction by Understanding Branch Behavior*. PhD thesis, University of Michigan, Department of Computer Science and Engineering, 2000.

[7] M. Evers, P.-Y. Chang, and Y. N. Patt. Using hybrid branch predictors to improve branch prediction accuracy in the presence of context switches. In *Proceedings of the 23rd International Symposium on Computer Architecture*, May 1996.

[8] M. Evers, S. J. Patel, R. S. Chappell, and Y. N. Patt. An analysis of correlation and predictability: What makes two-level branch predictors work. In *Proceedings of the 25th Annual International Symposium on Computer Architecture*, July 1998.

[9] M. Horowitz, R. Ho, and K. Mai. The future of wires. In *Semiconductor Research Corporation Workshop on Interconnects for Systems on a Chip*, May 1999.

[10] D. A. Jiménez and C. Lin. Dynamic branch prediction with perceptrons. In *Proceedings of the Seventh International Symposium on High Performance Computer Architecture*, January 2001.

[11] R. Kessler. The Alpha 21264 microprocessor. *IEEE Micro*, 19(2):24–36, March/April 1999.

[12] C.-C. Lee, C. Chen, and T. Mudge. The bi-mode branch predictor. In *Proceedings of the 30th Annual International Symposium on Microarchitecture*, November 1997.

[13] S. McFarling. Combining branch predictors. Technical Report TN-36m, Digital Western Research Laboratory, June 1993.

[14] S. Onder, J. Xu, and R. Gupta. Caching and predicting branch sequences for improved fetch effectiveness. In *International Conference on Parallel Architectures and Compilation Techniques*, October 1999.

[15] S. J. Patel, D. H. Friendly, and Y. N. Patt. Critical issues regarding the trace cache fetch mechanism. Technical Report CSE-TR-335-97, Department of Electrical Engineering and Computer Science, The University of Michigan, May 1997.

[16] G. Reinman, T. Austin, and B. Calder. A scalable front-end architecture for fast instruction delivery. In *Proceedings of the 26th International Symposium on Computer Architecture*, May 1999.

[17] G. Reinman and N. Jouppi. Extensions to cacti, 1999. Unpublished document.

[18] E. Rotenberg, S. Bennett, and J. E. Smith. Trace cache: A low latency approach to high bandwidth instruction fetching. In *Proceedings of the 29th International Symposium on Microarchitecture*, December 1996.

[19] S. Sechrest, C.-C. Lee, and T. Mudge. Correlation and aliasing in dynamic branch predictors. In *Proceedings of the 23rd International Symposium on Computer Architecture*, May 1999.

[20] A. Seznec, S. Jourdan, P. Sainrat, and P. Michaud. Multiple-block ahead branch predictors. In *Proceedings of the 7th International Conference on Architectural Support for Programming Languages and Operating Systems*, pages 116–127, October 1996.

[21] E. Sprangle, R. Chappell, M. Alsup, and Y. N. Patt. The Agree predictor: A mechanism for reducing negative branch history interference. In *Proceedings of the 24th International Symposium on Computer Architecture*, June 1997.

[22] T.-Y. Yeh, D. T. Marr, and Y. N. Patt. Increasing the instruction fetch rate via multiple branch prediction and a branch address cache. In *Proceedings of the 7th ACM Conference on Supercomputing*, pages 67–76, July 1993.

[23] T.-Y. Yeh and Y. N. Patt. Two-level adaptive branch prediction. In *Proceedings of the 24th ACM/IEEE International Symposium on Microarchitecture*, November 1991.

Improving BTB Performance in the Presence of DLLs

Stevan Vlaovic, Edward S. Davidson and Gary S. Tyson

Advanced Computer Architecture Lab

The University of Michigan

{vlaovic, davidson, tyson}@eecs.umich.edu

ABSTRACT

Dynamically Linked Libraries (DLLs) promote software modularity, portability, and flexibility and their use has become widespread. In this paper, we characterize the behavior of five applications that make heavy use of DLLs, with a particular focus on the effects of DLLs on Branch Target Buffer (BTB) performance. DLLs aggravate hot set contention in the BTB. Standard software remedies are ineffective because the DLLs are shared, compiled separately, and dynamically linked to applications. We propose a hardware technique, the DLL BTB, that adds a small second buffer to the BTB and dedicates it to storing DLL target addresses. We show that the DLL BTB performance is similar to a BTB with a victim buffer, but the DLL BTB requires no parallel lookups or datapaths between the original BTB and the added buffer.

1.0 Introduction

Use of Dynamically Linked Libraries (DLLs) has become widespread, as they enable software providers to change software incrementally when enhancing functionality and adapting to new systems and platforms. Instead of having one large monolithic binary executable, a smaller kernel executable is used, with specific DLLs loaded at run-time to enable execution in the environment of interest. The use of DLLs is increasing commensurate with the increasing size and complexity of modern applications and environments.

DLLs thus allow for more modularity, flexibility, and portability. For instance, in the Win32 API, the three most important DLLs are KERNEL32.DLL (which consists of functions for managing memory, processes and threads), USER32.DLL (which implements user-interface tasks such as window creation and message sending), and GDI32.DLL (which consists of functions for drawing graphical images and displaying text). In order to change the way an image is displayed involves changing only GDI32.DLL and recompiling its source code. Note that, since DLLs are dynamically linked, finding all of the applications that call GDI32 and statically relinking the library is not required, nor is recompilation of monolithic executables that make use of this modified function. This reduces the number of errors introduced, and makes it easier to update older executables. Portability in Windows NT is accomplished by the Hardware Abstraction Layer, as implemented in HAL.DLL, which has the responsibility of interfacing directly to the hardware. Running Windows on different platforms requires rewriting the hardware abstraction layer, or HAL.DLL, while other DLLs, system software and applications can remain (theoretically) unchanged.

Although the benefits of DLLs on software engineering are clear, their impact on performance is not. DLL-reliant applications have not been as widely studied, are inherently much larger, and have much more complex interaction with the hardware than standard benchmarks used by computer architects. We will show that the use of DLL calls exacerbate contention in the Branch Target Buffer (BTB). Since the libraries are dynamically linked and shared among different processes, standard software remedies do not alleviate contention. We then show how a hardware remedy, the DLL Target Buffer (DTB) - a second buffer added to the BTB that is dedicated to storing DLL call targets - can significantly reduce BTB contention.

Section 2 below discusses some previous results in this area. Section 3 characterizes our target applications, while Section 4 discusses how DLLs affect BTB performance. Section 5 describes the DLL BTB design we propose here to reduce BTB contention. Section 6 discusses the results of our DLL BTB evaluations. Section 7 presents some concluding remarks.

2.0 Related Work

Lee et al. [6] provide some insight into applications that use DLLs by discussing some of their results with Etch, a general purpose tool for rewriting arbitrary Win32 binaries on x86 platforms without requiring modification of the source code. Their study compares some popular desktop applications to some SPECINT95 benchmarks in terms of application characteristics, cache behavior, TLB behavior, and branch prediction accuracy. Even though Etch is limited to user level traces only, some important findings about DLLs are outlined. This work and [7] point to the prominent role of DLLs in Win32 environments.

Numerous studies have emphasized branch prediction [13], with a few targeting the Branch Target Buffer [3,8,9]. [3,9] target statically compiled code, but show that BTB design is important. Perleberg and Smith [8] investigate a hierarchical BTB design, but conclude that it is too expensive for the modest improvement it offers in performance. [9] uses a multilevel BTB, but for the purpose of reducing wire delay.

Calder et al. [2] showed that libraries tend to have similar control flow characteristics across different applications. They then reduced the overall branch misprediction rate by up to 28% by simply linking in a preoptimized library. This work gave insight into indirect branches and their negative impact on performance which led Calder [1] to propose new methods of reducing indirect function call overhead in C++ programs. Earlier, Wall [12] had suggested using hardware to predict the targets of indirect function calls.

In contrast with previous work, our work specifically focuses on dynamically linked object files (DLLs) and the applications that use them. We propose a multilateral [10, 11] BTB design, the DLL BTB, consisting of two buffers: a standard BTB with DLL call targets filtered out called the Filtered BTB, and a smaller dedicated buffer called the DLL Target Buffer (DTB), into which these call targets are placed. We contrast the DLL BTB with another multilateral design, a Victim BTB, where a victim buffer [4] is added to a standard BTB. The DLL BTB achieves similar performance on the target applications with a more straightforward design.

3.0 Five Win32 Applications

Target applications should broadly represent the domain of interest. We have chosen five popular Windows NT applications: *Id's Doom, Microsoft Explorer 5.0, Microsoft Visual Studio 5.0, Netscape 4.0,* and *Winamp 2.5e*. *Doom* is one of the early first-person type combat games and is available as shareware. The run of *Doom* included recording a session of a *Doom* game, and then replaying it on the simulator. *Explorer 5.0* is *Microsoft's* web browser; our input is a set of three .htm pages. The first is the CNN web page, the second is an ESPN web page, and the third is University of Michigan's EECS homepage. *Microsoft Visual Studio 5.0* (Msdev) is a code development environment, with 5.0 being the previous release. Our run of *Visual Studio* involved the compilation of *go* from the SPEC95 benchmark suite. *Netscape 4.0* is another web browser, but a few revisions old. The same web pages that were loaded on *Explorer* were also used for *Netscape*. *Winamp 2.5e* is the latest release of a popular mp3 player; its input was "Cool Down Daddy" by Jellyroll. Table 1 highlights some dynamic characteristics of the applications. Basic Block Size is the average size in instructions over the entire benchmark trace (applications and DLLs).

TABLE 1. Application Trace Characteristics

App.	Insts ($\times 10^6$)	Data Refs ($\times 10^6$)	DLL Calls ($\times 10^6$)	Basic Block Size
Doom	761	510	11.9	7.61
Explorer	408	247	4.03	7.07
Msdev	697	432	14.3	5.36
Netscape	865	500	18.5	7.27
Winamp	935	772	8.77	9.08

In order to see how these applications differ from standard benchmarks with regard to instruction cache miss rate, Figure 1 compares our five applications to that of CPU2000. The average miss rate over all the CPU2000 benchmarks is calculated using the reference input set and a direct mapped cache. As seen from the graphs our applications have poorer instruction cache performance than CPU2000, and hence may be expected to have poorer BTB performance as well. Doom has the highest instruction cache miss rate for small caches; for a 4KB direct mapped cache, it misses nearly 9% of the time. However, when the cache is increased to 256KB, the miss rate nearly disappears. Msdev has a modest miss rate for small instruction cache sizes, but doesn't approach zero as quickly as the other applications. For a 1MB direct mapped instruction cache, Msdev still has a 0.5% miss rate.

Branch predictor performance is quite tightly coupled with BTB performance, since the BTB is accessed and updated on every *predicted* taken branch. In our experiments, we updated the BTB only on each branch that is *actually* taken, which puts only those branch addresses and targets into the BTB that are needed. The more accurate the branch predictor, the better the chance of putting useful data into the BTB. In order to see this effect, we measured the branch prediction accuracy with GAg [13], a global predictor that uses a shared history vector and a two-bit saturating counter per history state. Perleberg and Smith [8] show the correlation between instruction cache performance and BTB performance; essentially, the larger the working set in the instruction cache, the larger the working set of branches that needs to be captured by the BTB.

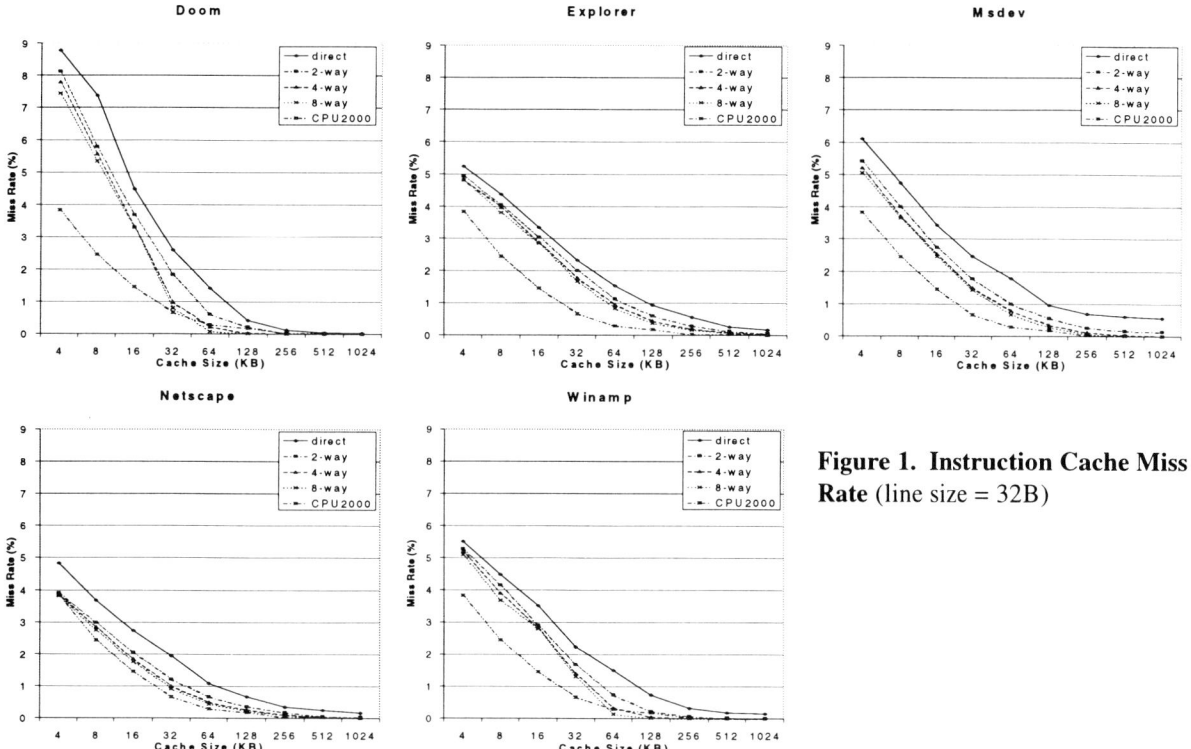

Figure 1. Instruction Cache Miss Rate (line size = 32B)

In Figure 2, the BTB is 1K entry, 4-way with a return address stack of size 8. Since Figure 2 uses the same configuration as our later experiments, we can see that branch prediction accuracy will impact the results presented in Section 6.

In these branch prediction curves, the *direction* line indicates the percentage of time that the branch predictor choses the correct direction. *Address hits* shows the number of times that the branch predictor found an entry with that branch address in the table (but not necessarily with the correct destination). The final curve is the percentage of time that the predictor produced the correct target address (i.e. in this case there would not be any branch penalty in a real processor). Netscape has the most predictable branches, in terms of target addresses, out of all the applications. For a 16K entry GAg predictor, the correct address is delivered nearly 85% of the time. For the same size predictor, Winamp achieves only 60% correct addresses even though the direction prediction accuracy is close to 95% and the address hit ratio is 85%.

4.0 DLL Effects on the BTB

Since it is widely available and in some sense a representation of commonly used applications, the SPEC benchmark suite has generally been used to evaluate new computer architectures. These applications have generally been developed for Unix platforms, and hence do not contain multiple object files that are linked at run-time. This is also true of the latest release, CPU2000. Because of this, they have quite different Branch Target Buffer needs than applications running on Wintel configurations. With a 1K entry, 4-way BTB and perfect branch prediction, the average misses per one thousand instructions is shown in Table 2 for CPU2000, our Win32 applications, and the Win32 applications with DLL calls filtered out.

For example, for indirect branches, a 1K entry, 4-way BTB will miss in the BTB 1.10 times per one thousand instructions for CPU2000, while for our Win32 applications this figure rises to 2.66 times. Note that when the DLL calls are filtered out, the number of misses per one thousand instructions for Indirects falls back close to that of CPU2000. Removing DLL calls had a significant beneficial effect on Calls, reducing the misses per one thousand instructions by 31%. For Conditionals and Unconditionals, there is also a small reduction. The

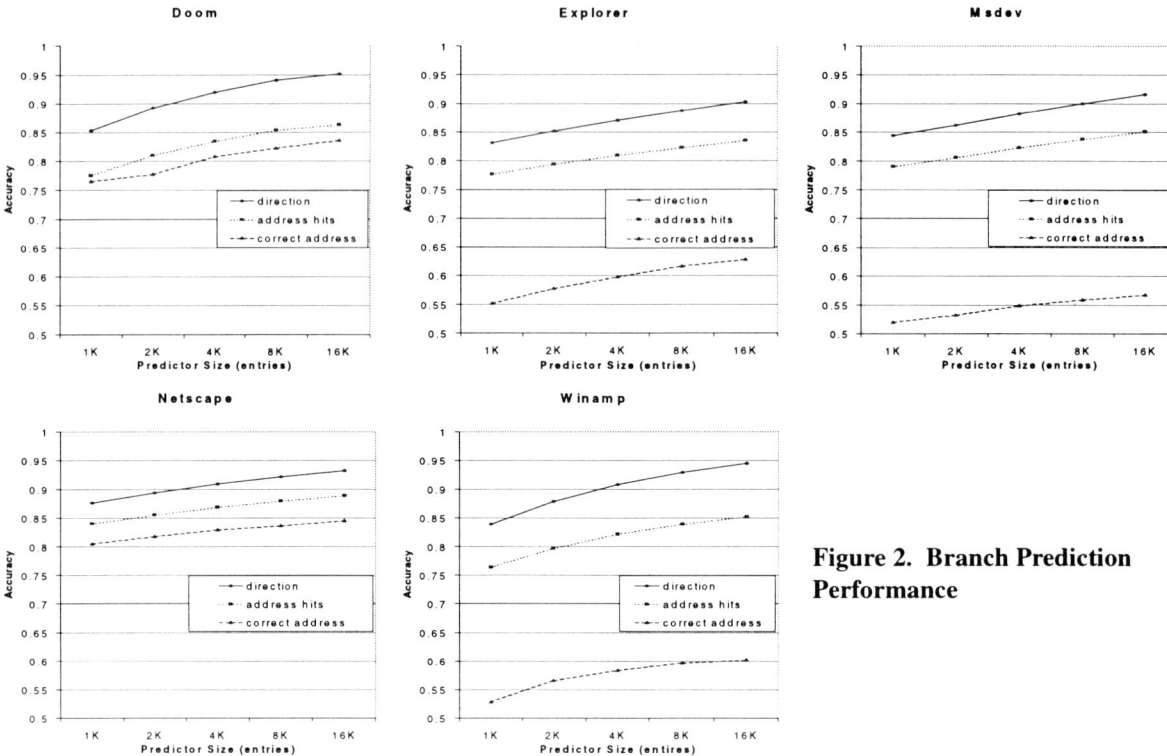

Figure 2. Branch Prediction Performance

results for CPU2000 are averaged over all benchmarks run for 1 billion instructions each.

TABLE 2. Misses per 1000 Instructions in a 1K entry, 4-way BTB (Perfect Branch Prediction)

	CPU2000	Win32	Win32 (no DLL)
indirect	1.10	2.66	1.11
call	1.07	5.22	3.60
conditional	0.73	4.94	4.40
unconditional	1.59	4.90	4.53

4.1 The Windows DLL Linkage

In order to implement DLLs, a number of software mechanisms need to be in place to facilitate multiple binaries. At some point, the actual DLL has to be found and mapped into the process's space. Since DLLs (like regular executables) are just files, the directories on the magnetic media are searched until the appropriate DLL is found. In the Win32 API, a DLL has a preferred location that it maps to; if it doesn't conflict with any previously loaded binary, the loader maps the DLL to that location. Otherwise, it has to be loaded elsewhere, and any absolute addresses contained within the DLL must be corrected to reflect the new location.

Lee et al. [6] provide some insight into why DLL calls are more expensive than statically linked functions:

- DLL calls are implemented as indirect function calls
- DLLs are shared among applications, so improving instruction locality through scheduling is difficult, therefore it is difficult to remap branches to reduce contention for the BTB
- DLLs are aligned on page boundaries which forces the caller and callee to reside in different pages in the address space and contributes to hot set contention in the BTB

Unfortunately, since DLLs must be aligned on page boundaries, it is difficult to reduce the number of conflicts by virtual mapping alone. Alternatively, code layout algorithms can be applied to individual DLLs with self conflicts, and inter-DLL conflicts can be taken into consideration. But because the DLLs are shared between processes, this might reduce the contention only for one process, while increasing it for other processes. We have therefore focused on a hardware remedy for conflict misses in the BTB.

Using our base of a 1K entry, 4-way set associative BTB configuration, we wanted to see what would happen if we filtered DLL calls out of the branch stream. We measured the total number of misses in each BTB set for the entire run and then measured the total number of misses per set with DLL calls removed, i.e the number of misses that would be seen by a Filtered BTB. The differ-

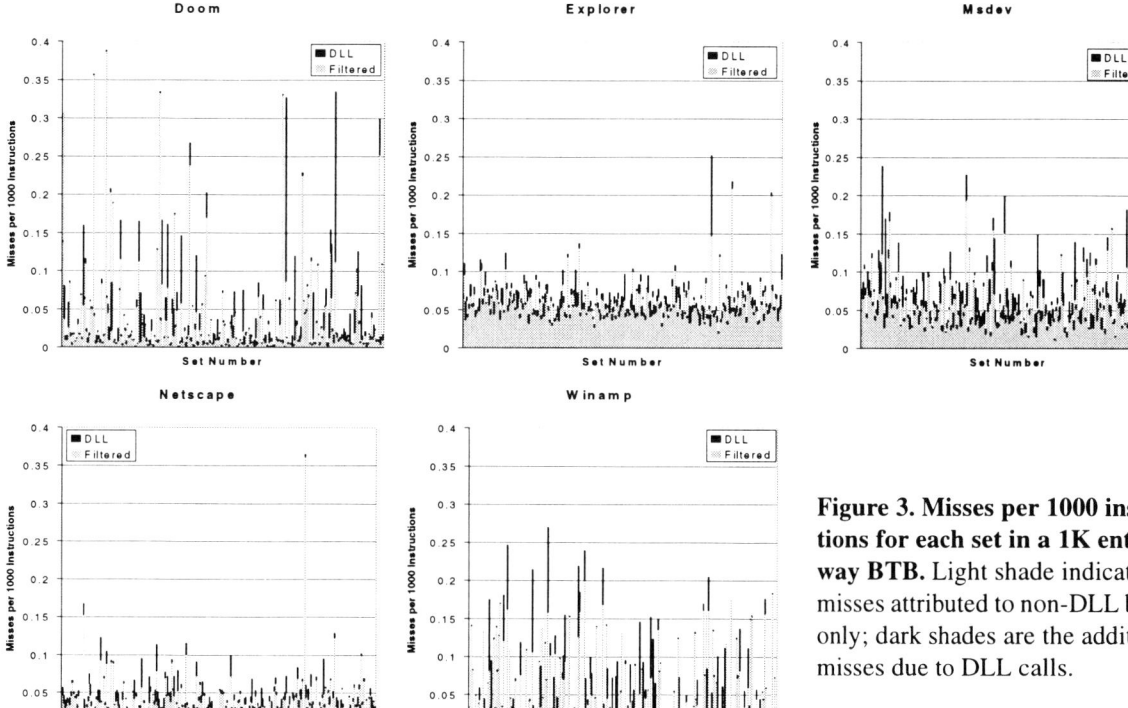

Figure 3. Misses per 1000 instructions for each set in a 1K entry, 4-way BTB. Light shade indicates misses attributed to non-DLL branches only; dark shades are the additional misses due to DLL calls.

ence between these two metrics is a measure of the misses attributed to DLL calls.

This information is shown in Figure 3 for all 5 benchmarks. Many DLL calls are mapped to the same set which creates contention for those sets, seen as a spike on the graph. This shows how DLL calls clearly aggravate hot set contention. Although the behavior of the Filtered BTB is also "spikey", the DLL calls clearly aggravate the problem.

One way to ameliorate these conflicts is to introduce a victim buffer. The victim buffer does help, but since the DLL calls do cause a large percentage of the misses (for relatively few static calls), we will show how reducing the misses for these calls dramatically improves performance.

4.2 DLL Usage

The number of DLL calls will have a direct impact on indirect call overhead. If there are few DLL calls, then the benefit of removing these indirects will be minimal. Lee et al. [6] showed that some applications can spend as much as 50% of their overall running time in DLLs. Unfortunately, they did not measure the actual number of DLL calls or their impact on performance. Their application suite included the standard desktop applications: MSWord, Excel, Netscape, and Photoshop. In this paper we have measured the impact of DLL calls on a more diverse set of applications.

5.0 The DLL BTB

Our general approach to improving BTB performance is to take advantage of the fact that once a DLLs is loaded, the target of a call to it *never* changes; hence DLL calls are fully predictable. DLL calls tend to increase the address predictability percentage, as a simple last-address-seen mechanism in the BTB is sufficient to capture these indirect addresses. However, since DLL calls increase BTB misses considerably, it might be best to remove these easily predictable indirects from the BTB, handle them with some other mechanism and use the BTB to obtain better coverage of other harder to predict target addresses.

An alternative approach is to add a victim buffer [4] to the BTB, which has been proven to reduce hot set conflicts in caches. However, although the victim cache design has been shown to reduce conflicts, it's implementation cost can be excessive. The swaps it requires involve extra datapaths, and both the victim buffer and the BTB have to be searched for every access. Such a Victim BTB should alleviate the hot spot contention due to the clustered DLL call sites.

From Figure 3, we know that much of the hot set contention is due to the additional DLL calls, so we propose a DLL BTB filtering mechanism that performs nearly as well as the Victim BTB without the additional datapath or parallel search requirements.

In the DLL BTB, we assign all DLL call targets to a small fully associative buffer, the DLL Target Buffer (DTB). All other branch targets are entered into the BTB, called the *Filtered* BTB when it is used within a DLL BTB configuration.

Filtering out DLL calls can easily be done at run-time by using the import table of the application. The import table is included at the end of the text segment of every application, and contains the addresses of all imported symbols (functions and variables). DLL calls map indirectly through this table. Since we know the boundary addresses of this table, a simple compare can identify which calls are DLL calls.

The results presented in the next section compare a DLL BTB and a *Victim* BTB with a *Base* BTB. We use a DTB of size 128 entries, which turns out to be a good choice for most of these applications; the Victim buffer is set to the same size. The BTB in the Base and Victim configurations and the filter BTB in the DLL BTB configuration are each 1K entry, 4-way set associative. Each implementation has a 32 entry Return Address Stack (RAS), with the Filtered BTB and the DTB sharing a common RAS. Returns from DLL calls are pushed onto this stack even though DLL call targets are in the DTB.

6.0 Quantitative Results

We have developed a PC simulator based on *Bochs* [5], that models not just the CPU, but the entire target platform in enough detail to support the execution of a complete operating system and the applications that run on it. Currently, we are using out-of-the-box Windows NT 4.0 (Build 1381) as the operating system for our Virtual PC. This simulator runs as a user-level process on a standard PC by modeling the platform components completely in software.

Since Windows NT can execute on the functional simulator, we can study complete commercial applications. This approach allows access to all operating system events in addition to the standard instruction, data, and branch traces of user code. The limitation of this method is that the simulator is only functional, not cycle accurate, which precludes detailed timing analysis. However, our simulator can be used as a front end for more detailed simulations. With our traces we can do workload, memory, and branch prediction studies.

TABLE 3. Taken Control Flow Instructions by Category (per 1000 instructions)

	Doom	Expl.	Msd.	Net.	Win.
ind.	9.97	7.99	15.1	12.7	5.50
ind. calls	8.42	6.20	8.55	10.1	4.00
calls	22.1	21.2	28.9	23.0	14.5
ret.	23.8	22.3	29.0	23.4	15.5
cond.	48.4	39.2	47.0	58.7	53.2
uncon.	36.5	36.0	58.5	34.9	25.8
other	24.3	45.1	52.6	21.3	16.3
total	131	141	187	138	110

Table 3 highlights some of the differences between the five applications by showing the breakdown of the dynamic count of *taken* control instructions of each type. Note that these are all *taken* control instructions. Whereas in a real implementation, we would access the BTB on every *predicted taken* control instruction. If we predict the branch to be taken, and it ends up not being taken, the BTB gets updated with the wrong information. Although with increasingly accurate branch predictors these effects become less important, our results are in effect assuming perfect branch prediction (best-case scenario). The ramifications of how the BTB gets updated can be seen in Figure 2. In these graphs, the BTB remains fixed at 1K entries, but as the predictor size increases, the correct target address generation improves.

In Table 3 and throughout the paper, Calls include both direct calls and Indirect Calls; while Unconditionals include jumps and Returns. DLL calls are implemented as indirect calls. Our applications have significantly more indirect calls than the SPEC95 or CPU2000 benchmarks. A few points are worth noting about Table 3. First, the number of calls and returns are not the same. Some of this discrepancy is due to the nature of the trace, as well as interrupts and exceptions. We started the trace after the system was already up and running, but before we launch the application (this leads to some unbalanced calls and returns). The Other category includes instructions such as LOOP and REP. Based on certain flags, instructions LOOP (loop) and REP (repeat) will stay in the execution core and continue executing (in essence, creating instructions) until the flag condition clears.

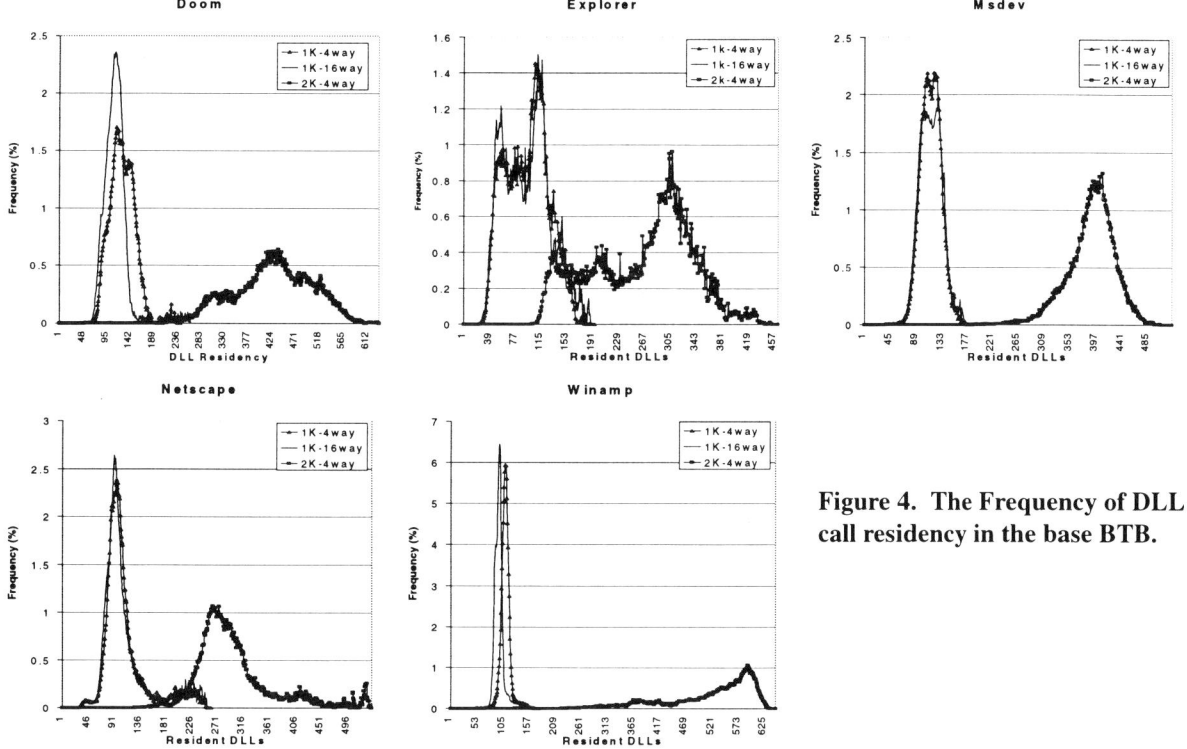

Figure 4. The Frequency of DLL call residency in the base BTB.

6.1 Initial Observations

Of the applications studied, Doom uses DLLs a little less frequently than the others. This is because Doom is not a true 32-bit application, but requires the use of NTVDM.EXE to convert the Win16 calls to Win32 calls.

The Explorer benchmark trace is about half the size of the other benchmark traces. In fact, for the loading of the same three web pages, it took Explorer only 400 million instructions, while Netscape required over 700 million. Although the overall figures are lower, the various ratios are fairly consistent.

The Microsoft Visual C++ environment tends to make liberal use of DLLs, as we see in the following section. Compiling a Win32 application, as opposed to a console application (as *go* was compiled), would have seen an even greater increase in the number of DLLs used by Msdev. Win32 applications require more system support (and hence more DLL calls) to operate.

Finally, Winamp uses the most floating point instructions out of the applications studied. Interestingly, with a 16K entry branch predictor for Winamp, we correctly predict the direction 95% of the time, but correctly predict the right address only 60% of the time. We will see that this drop is due to contention in the 1K entry BTB.

6.2 BTB Residency by Category

To construct Table 4 we simulated a standard size (1K entry, 4-way) Base BTB (B) and a DLL BTB (consisting of a Filtered BTB (F) and a DTB (D)). Table 4 shows a categorization of the accesses to the BTB. The sum of the entries in a column is the total number of BTB accesses per one thousand instructions. The first four rows in the table handle all taken control instructions except DLL calls. The first row represents the total number of times that a non-DLL call hits in both the Base BTB (B) and the Filtered BTB (F) in our DLL BTB. The second row shows the total number of times that a non-DLL branch was found in B but not F. Although intuitively this number should be zero, there are some cases where LRU replaces different entries in the two systems. The third row highlights the additional coverage that the Filtered BTB captures over the Base BTB. The fourth shows taken non-DLL calls that miss in both the Base BTB and the Filtered BTB. The last four rows are analogous to the first four, but handle only DLL calls. For instance, the fifth row shows the total number of times that a DLL call target was found in both the Base BTB (B) and the DTB (D) in our DLL BTB. The seventh row highlights the additional coverage of DLL function calls that our dedicated 128 entry DTB buffer provides. The sixth row gives us insight into whether the 128 entry size is sufficient. For most of the applications, it seems to provide good coverage.

TABLE 4. Likelihood of BTB Residency by Category (per 1000 instructions)

	Doom	Expl.	Msd.	Net.	Win.
$B \cap F$	100.5	114.0	148.7	105.4	86.23
$B \cap \bar{F}$	0.001	0	0.022	0	0
$\bar{B} \cap F$	1.750	0.777	1.356	0.699	1.651
$\bar{B} \cap \bar{F}$	13.44	16.77	16.40	10.43	12.54
$B \cap D$	13.93	7.708	15.48	19.74	6.289
$B \cap \bar{D}$	0.028	0.034	0.080	0.029	0.029
$\bar{B} \cap D$	0.808	0.480	0.532	0.383	1.073
$\bar{B} \cap \bar{D}$	0.838	1.684	4.559	1.317	2.013

For Doom, in Table 4, the Filtered BTB captures only 1.7% of the extra branches whereas the DTB captures 5.6% more DLL function calls. For Msdev, which has the greatest reliance on DLLs, we get a 4% increase in coverage of DLL calls, but only a 0.9% increase in coverage from other branch targets. Since we still miss nearly 30% of all DLL calls with a 128 entry buffer, we might need to use a larger DTB. However, we do capture more DLL calls than the Base BTB. From the instruction cache miss rates in Figure 1, it is clear that Msdev has a larger working set than the other applications. For Netscape, coverage of DLL calls is roughly 93%, which implies that a buffer size of smaller than 128 can be used. Winamp is unique in that the DTB captures 17% more DLL call targets than the standard configuration. For each application, most of these DLL calls actually *pollute* the standard BTB, as seen in Figure 3, and hence we can gain added performance by filtering out these calls.

6.3 DLL Residency

To get a better indicator of coverage, we count the number of DLL calls resident in the base BTB *on every BTB update,* i.e. every taken control flow instruction. Figure 4 shows the frequency distribution of the number of DLL call targets in the BTB over all BTB accesses. This data is shown for each application for three different configurations: the standard 1K entry, 4-way base BTB plus a 1K entry, 16-way and a 2K entry, 4-way configuration for comparison. This information can be used as guide to select the size of the DTB. This curve is a distribution of the number of DLL calls resident in the standard BTB whenever the standard BTB is updated. These curves do not have a bimodal distribution; for every application, the two 1K entry curves end at about the middle of the x-axis.

The DLL residency graph for Explorer shows a wider distribution than for Doom, but the average is close to the same for similar configurations. The varying distribution is due to the shorter instruction trace. Note the higher average of resident DLLs for the 2K entry BTB in which case a larger DTB would definitely be useful. The DLL residency graph for Msdev shows a similar distribution to Doom for the 1K entry sizes, but for the 2K configuration, the average is much higher than for the other benchmarks. On average, nearly 400 DLL calls are resident at any given time. This is almost 15% of the total number of entries. Since DLL calls only comprise 6% of all dynamic taken branches, an average residency of 400 seems excessive. Winamp has the least variance when it comes to the average number of DLL call targets resident in the standard BTB. This would imply that Winamp has one of the smaller instruction footprints, and tends to stay in the same DLLs. As shown in Figure 2, it does have a small instruction footprint.

6.4 DLL BTB Performance

The performance numbers that we present in this section are represented in terms of misses per one thousand instructions. By presenting the data in this fashion, the impact of the hardware optimizations immediately becomes clear. For example, if the penalty to miss in the BTB is 23 cycles and the average instructions per cycle is (IPC) 1.25, saving one miss per one thousand instructions, corresponds to a 23 cycle reduction from 800 to 777 cycles (or about 2.5%). The numbers shown in Table 6 are for the base configuration: a 1K entry, 4-way BTB.

Most of the applications have similar values for the base configuration, except for Msdev. This application has roughly twice as many indirects, and twice as many calls, that miss in the standard BTB. The DLL BTB outperforms the Victim BTB for all of the applications for indirects and indirect calls; however, most of the applications already have low values for these categories. Because this is not true for Msdev, the DLL BTB outperforms the Victim BTB in overall performance (shown in Figure 5).

Generally, the categories with the largest misses per one thousand instructions are Calls and Conditionals. The Victim system has an edge over the DLL BTB throughout these categories, since any hot set contention can be ameliorated by the Victim BTB, whereas only those hot sets caused by DLLs can off-load entries into the DTB.

TABLE 5. Misses Per Instruction (x1000) for 1K entry, 4-way configuration

	Doom			Explorer			Msdev			Netscape			Winamp		
	base	dll	vic	base	dll	vic	base	dll	vic	base	dll	vic	base	dll	vic
ind.	1.41	0.83	1.02	2.45	2.01	2.20	5.86	5.20	5.56	1.63	1.27	1.42	1.95	0.97	1.48
ind. calls	1.30	0.76	0.95	1.70	1.33	1.52	3.68	3.23	3.50	1.09	0.83	0.95	1.73	0.86	1.31
calls	3.84	2.94	2.55	6.11	5.57	5.39	8.16	7.30	7.38	3.63	3.20	3.09	4.36	3.12	2.96
rets	4.21	4.21	4.21	2.48	2.48	2.48	2.64	2.64	2.64	1.35	1.35	1.35	3.42	3.42	3.42
con.	4.72	3.95	2.84	5.15	4.80	4.28	4.50	4.19	4.01	4.46	4.12	3.50	5.85	5.01	3.65
uncond.	5.80	5.47	5.16	4.79	4.64	4.54	6.25	5.93	5.98	2.74	2.60	2.57	4.90	4.64	4.33
oth.	0.69	0.40	0.46	0.45	0.41	0.38	0.43	0.37	0.36	0.24	0.22	0.21	0.45	0.28	0.31

This improvement is an average of 5.3% for calls and 22% for conditionals.

Table 6 shows how the DLL BTB did alleviate some of the hot set contention, and the impact of the number misses per one thousand instructions for the seven categories. To obtain another measure of interference of resources, we measured the average lifetime of a BTB entry. This is measured in terms of the number of instructions, and is done for the Base BTB, the Filtered BTB, and the DTB. These results are shown in Table 6.

Table 6. Average lifetime of a BTB entry (1K 4way)

	Base	Filtered	DTB
Doom	316,198	543,184	333,049
Explorer	67,431	76,072	153,530
Msdev	75,766	93,439	91,674
Netscape	110,163	130,225	199,045
Winamp	715,711	1,346,477	445,162

This table illustrates that, as we would expect, DLL calls have a coarser locality (larger average lifetime) than other branches. The Doom and Winamp applications highlight how much interference can occur between DLL calls and other branches. When DLL calls are removed from the instruction stream (i.e. the Filtered BTB), the lifetime of a BTB entry doubles in these two benchmarks. It is also in these two applications that the most benefit is gained from using the DLL BTB.

To see the effect on overall performance, we deduce the performance analytically. Since we know the total number of instructions and the total number of branches and branch hits, if we fix the IPC and the branch mispredic-

tion penalty, we can calculate the improvement in IPC. Using a Pentium Pro as our model, we fixed the BTB miss penalty to 23 cycles, and our base IPC to be 1.25. Figure 5 shows the overall improvement. This is actually a pessimistic model for our method since a penalty for either swaps of lookups for the Victim BTB is not assigned, and our branch predictor is perfect. For a 16-way BTB for the Winamp application, we actually see around a 10% performance improvement. In most cases, we track the Victim BTB closely; in fact, in the Msdev application the DLL BTB actually surpass the performance of the Victim BTB.

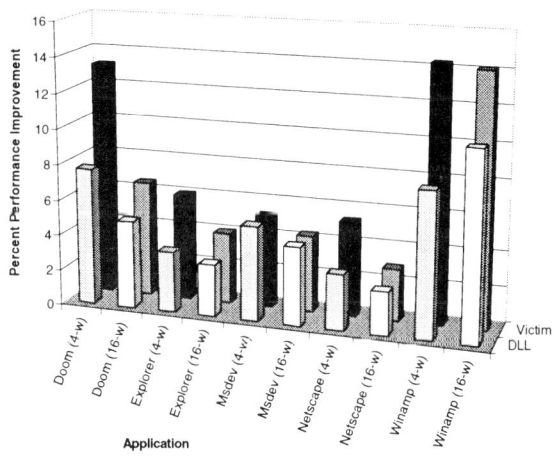

Figure 5. Performance Improvement over the Standard 1K entry System (darker shades 4-way, lighter shades 16-way)

7.0 Concluding Remarks

We have seen that, because of their nature, applications with multiple dynamic object files have different characteristics than their traditional statically linked counterparts. We have highlighted some of these differences in this paper. In one area that they deviate significantly, branch target prediction, we have presented some of the characteristics that can be leveraged to increase performance. Branch target prediction is especially important in today's (and tomorrow's) wide-issue superscalar machines.

The ratio of the number of indirect function calls to direct function calls is much higher in applications that use dynamically loaded libraries. Since these applications have multiple object files, the calling linkage between two functions residing in different object files requires an indirect function call. We have proposed the DLL BTB to separate out these calls and place the targets in a special buffer (DTB) so that they will not interfere with the targets of other types of branches. For a 1K entry Branch Target Buffer, the DLL BTB performs close to that of a Victim BTB for the applications we studied; however, the DLL BTB has the benefit of not requiring the extra datapath that the Victim requires. For larger BTB sizes, our 128 entry DLL target buffer does not improve performance as effectively; our results indicate that a larger DLL target buffer is required in this situation.

Although we primarily looked at one specific microarchitectural resource, the Branch Target Buffer, we can use this work as a jumping off point for other microarchitectural resource usage studies in the presence of multiple object files. Since Win32 applications are different from standard benchmarks and are more widely used in practice, further research tailored to this environment is well justified.

References

[1] B. Calder, D. Grunwald, "Reducing Indirect Function Call Overhead in C++ Programs," *Proceedings of the ACM Principles of Programming Languages,* ACM, 1994.

[2] B. Calder, D. Grunwald, A. Srivastava, "The Predictability of Branches in Libraries," *Proceedings of the 28th International Symposium on Microarchitecture.* pp. 24-34. IEEE, 1995.

[3] P.Chang, E. Hao, Y. Patt, "Target Prediction for Indirect Jumps," *Proceedings of the 24th International Symposium on Computer Architecture*, pp. 274-283, IEEE, 1997.

[4] N. Jouppi, "Improving Direct-Mapped Cache Performance by the Addition of a Small Fully-Associative Cache and Prefetch Buffers," *Proceedings of the 17th International Symposium on Computer Architecture*, pp. 364-373, IEEE, 1990.

[5] K. Lawton, "Welcome to the Bochs x86 PC Emulation Software Home Page!" http://www.bochs.com.

[6] D. C. Lee, P. J. Crowley, J-L Baer, T. E. Anderson, and B. N. Bershad, "Execution Characteristics of Desktop Applications on Windows NT," *Proceedings of the 24th International Symposium on Computer Architecture*, pp. 27-38, IEEE, 1997.

[7] S.E. Perl, R.L. Sites, "Studies of Windows NT Performance Using Dynamic Execution Traces," Digital Systems Research Center Research Report, RR-146, April 1997.

[8] C.H. Perleberg, A.J. Smith, "Branch Target Buffer Design and Optimization," *IEEE Transactions on Computers*, 42(4):396-412, 1993

[9] G. Reinman, T. Austin, B. Calder, "A Scalable Front-End Architecture for Fast Instruction Delivery," *Proceedings of the 26th International Symposium on Computer Architecture*, pp. 234-245, IEEE, 1999.

[10] J. A. Rivers and E. S. Davidson, "Reducing Conflicts in Direct-Mapped Caches with a Temporality-Based Design," *Proceedings of the 1996 International Conference on Parallel Processing*, Vol. I, pp 151-162, August 1996.

[11] E.S. Tam, "Improving Cache Performance via Active Management," Ph.D. Dissertation, University of Michigan, June 1999.

[12] D. Wall, "Predicting Program Behavior Using Real or Estimated Profiles," *Proceedings of the ACM SIGPLAN '91 Conference on Programing Language Design and Implementation*, pp. 59-70, ACM, June 1991.

[13] T. Yeh, "Two-Level adaptive Branch Prediction and Instruction Fetch Mechanisms for High Performance Super-Scalar Processors," Ph.D. Dissertation, University of Michigan, 1993.

Efficient Checker Processor Design

Saugata Chatterjee, Chris Weaver, and Todd Austin

Electrical Engineering and Computer Science Department

University of Michigan

{saugatac,chriswea,austin}@eecs.umich.edu

Abstract

The design and implementation of a modern microprocessor creates many reliability challenges. Designers must verify the correctness of large complex systems and construct implementations that work reliably in varied (and occasionally adverse) operating conditions. In our previous work, we proposed a solution to these problems by adding a simple, easily verifiable checker processor at pipeline retirement. Performance analyses of our initial design were promising, overall slowdowns due to checker processor hazards were less than 3%. However, slowdowns for some outlier programs were larger.

In this paper, we examine closely the operation of the checker processor. We identify the specific reasons why the initial design works well for some programs, but slows others. Our analyses suggest a variety of improvements to the checker processor storage system. Through the addition of a 4k checker cache and eight entry store queue, our optimized design eliminates virtually all core processor slowdowns. Moreover, we develop insights into why the optimized checker processor performs well, insights that suggest it should perform well for any program.

1. Introduction

The enormous complexity of modern microprocessor design presents significant challenges in the verification of these systems. Architects and designers must ensure that designs operate correctly for all possible programs, and they must ensure that this correct functionality is maintained for all (including adverse) operating conditions. If they fail to meet these challenges, the repercussions can destroy profit margins, products, and even companies. In the worse case, failure to meet these challenges could even result in loss of life.

To avoid releasing faulty parts, designers spend considerable effort on functional and electrical verification. Unfortunately, the complexity of modern microprocessors makes this verification process both incomplete and imprecise. The test spaces of stateful design are simply too immense to fully test, necessitating the development of ad hoc test generation and coverage analysis tools to point to where to look for bugs, and when to stop looking. Moreover, the lack of any formality in system definition often leaves verification teams with a hazy definition of correctness. *Formal verification* [8] of a system works to increase test space coverage by proving a design is correct, either through model equivalence or assertion. The approach is significantly more efficient than simulation-based testing as a single proof can verify correctness over large portions of a design's state space. However, complex modern pipelines with imprecise state management, out-of-order execution, and aggressive speculation are too stateful or incomprehensible to permit complete formal verification.

To further complicate verification, new reliability challenges are materializing in deep submicron fabrication technologies (*i.e.* process technologies with minimum feature sizes below 0.25um). Finer feature sizes are generally characterized by increased complexity, more exposure to noise-related faults, and interference from single event radiation (SER). It appears the current advances in verification (*e.g.*, formal verification, model-based test generation) are not keeping pace with these challenges. As a result, design teams are growing larger, development costs are increasing, and time-to-market lengthens. Without significant advances in the quality and speed of verification, the burden of verification will likely slow the rate at which designers can create higher-performance computing devices, a significant source of value in our industry.

1.1. Dynamic Verification

Recently we proposed the use of dynamic verification to reduce the burden of verification in complex microprocessor designs [1,2]. *Dynamic verification* is an online instruction checking technique that stems from the simple observation that *speculative execution is fault tolerant*. Consider for example, a branch predictor that contains a design error, *e.g.*, the predictor array is indexed with the most significant bits of the PC (instead of the least significant PC bits). The resulting design, even though the branch predictor contained a design error, would operate correctly. The only effect on the system would be significantly reduced branch predictor accuracy (many more branch mispredictions) and accordingly reduced system performance. From the point of view of a correctly designed branch predictor check mechanism, a bad prediction from a broken predictor is indistinguishable from a bad prediction from a correct predictor design. Moreover, predictors are not only tolerant of permanent errors (*e.g.*, design errors), but also transient errors (*e.g.*, noise-related faults or natural radiation particle strikes).

Given this observation, the burden of verification in a complex design can be decreased by simply increasing

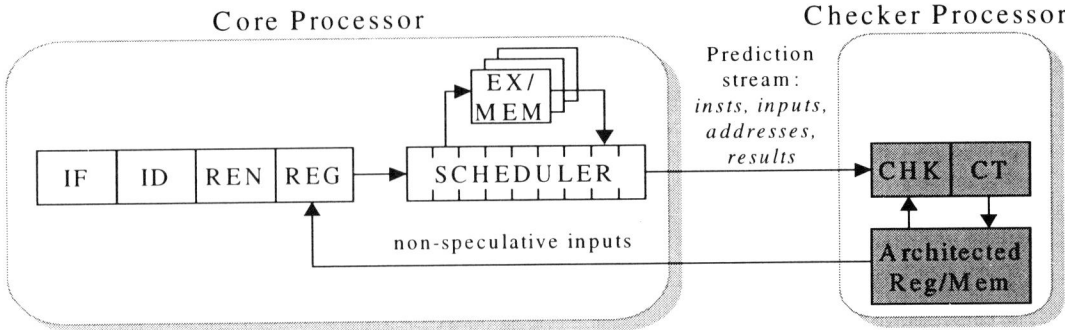

Figure 1. Dynamic Verification Architecture

the degree of speculation. Dynamic verification does this by pushing speculation into all aspects of core program execution, making the architecture fully speculative. In a fully speculative architecture, all processor communication, computation, control and forward progress is speculative. Accordingly, any permanent (*e.g.*, design error, defect, or failure) and transient (*e.g.*, noise-related) faults in this speculation does not impact correctness of the program. Figure 1 illustrates the approach.

To implement dynamic verification, a microprocessor is constructed using two heterogeneous internal processors that execute the same program. The *core processor* is responsible for pre-executing the program to create the *prediction stream*. The prediction stream consists of all executed instructions (delivered in program order) with their input values and any memory addresses referenced. In a baseline design, the core processor is identical in every way to the traditional complex microprocessor core up to (but not including) the retirement stage. In this baseline design, the complex core processor is "predicting" values because it may contain latent bugs that could render these values incorrect.

The *checker processor* follows the core processor, verifying the activities of the core processor by re-executing all program computation in its wake. The checker processor is assumed to be correct since its simple design lends itself to easy verification (including formal verification). The high-quality stream of predictions from the core processor serves to simplify the design of the checker processor and speed its processing. Pre-execution of the program on the complex core processor eliminates all the processing hazards (*e.g.*, branch mispredictions, cache misses, and data dependencies) that slow simple processors and necessitate complex microarchitectures. In the event the core produces a bad prediction value (*e.g.*, due to a design errors), the checker processor will detect the bad value and flush all internal state from the core processor and restart it after the errant instruction. Once restarted, the core processor will resynchronize with the correct state of the machine as it reads register and memory values from non-speculative storage.

The resulting dynamic verification architecture should benefit from a reduced burden of verification, because only the checker needs to be built correctly. The checker processor will fix any errors in core processor computation, reducing the verification of the core to simply the process of locating and fixing *commonly occurring* design errors that could adversely impact system performance. Moreover, the simplicity of the checker processor design (which must be completely correct) lends itself to high-quality functional and electrical verification. In addition, dynamic verification may render other benefits and opportunities in the design of complex microprocessors. A number of promising directions that we are currently exploring (additional details are available in [1,2]) include: reduced time-to-market and design cost, SER and transient fault tolerance, aggressive core circuitry implementations, and reduced core processor complexity.

1.2. Contributions of this Paper

In this paper, we examine in detail the performance of our initial checker processor design. We found that for many programs, slowdowns from the checking process are minimal, but for others (especially floating point codes) slowdowns were non-trivial. We attribute the primary source of these slowdowns to *a)* core processor decoder stalls because of checker processor backpressure at retirement, *b)* storage hazards created as the core and checker processor compete for storage access ports, and *c)* cache misses experienced by the checker pipeline. Our analyses suggest the addition of a dedicated checker processor register file and store queue to relieve any retirement backpressure. Remaining storage hazards and checker processor cache misses are eliminated with the addition of a dedicated checker processor cache. Using the core processor as a (near) oracle prefetcher, a dual ported 4k checker processor cache has virtually no misses and provides sufficient bandwidth for checker processor accesses. The resulting design demonstrates that online instruction checking can be implemented with no slowdowns, and moreover, our results suggest that the checker should perform well for any program.

In Section 2 we give a brief description of the baseline checker processor design. Details pertaining to the pipeline design can be found in [1,2]. Section 3 presents a detailed performance analysis of our initial checker processor design, revealing the specific sources of core processor slowdown. In Section 4, we motivate design changes that eliminate these slowdowns; detailed performance analyses of the optimized design confirm that

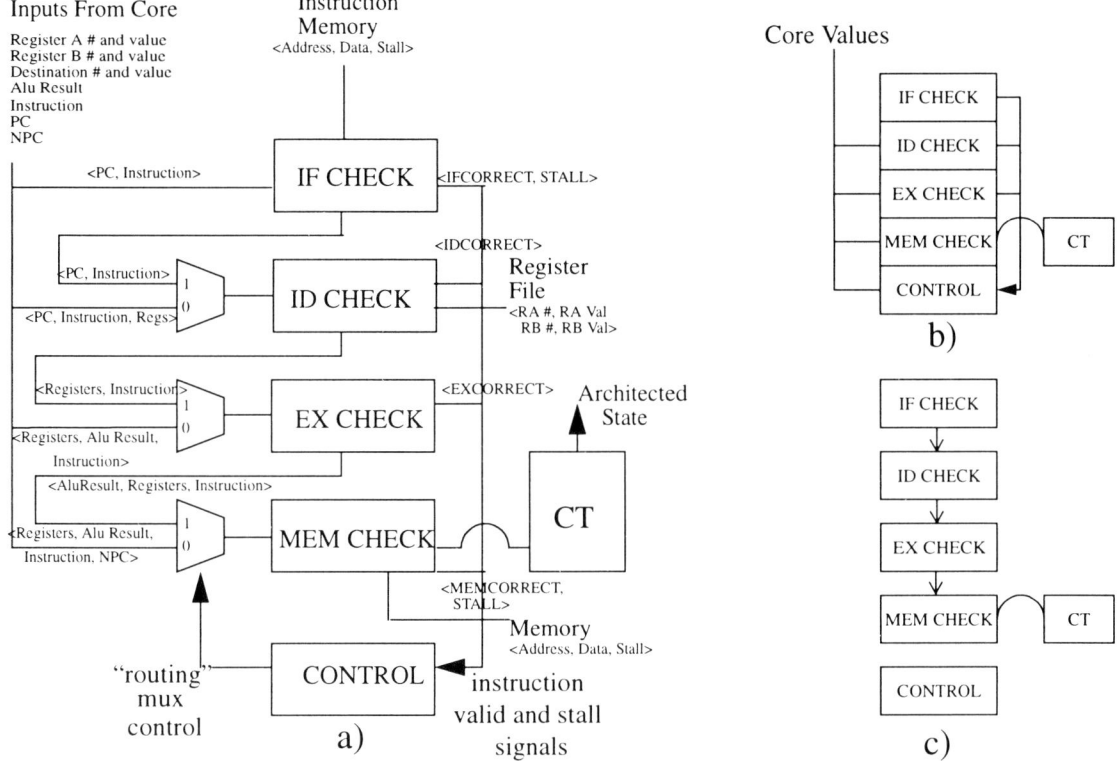

Figure 2. Checker processor pipeline structure for a) a single wide checker processor, b) a checker processor in CHECK mode, and c) a checker processor in RECOVER mode

our enhancements work well. Section 5 details additional related work (not covered in [1,2]). Finally Section 6 summarizes, draws conclusions and discusses future work.

2. Checker Processor Architecture

For dynamic verification to be viable, the checker processor must be simple and fast. It must be simple enough to reduce the overall design verification burden, and fast enough to not slow the core processor. A single-issue two-stage checker processor is illustrated in Figure 2a. The design shown is very general, it can detect and correct any error in core processor computation. Later, we will describe how this design can be simplified if portions of the core processor design are verified to be correct.

Figure 2b show the checker in its normal checking mode. When the core processor retires an instruction, the checker pipeline receives an instruction with core processor predictions. These predictions include the next PC, instruction, instruction inputs, and addresses referenced (for loads and stores). The checker processor ensures the correctness of each component of this transfer by using four parallel stages, each of which verifies a separate component of the prediction stream. Each parallel stage implements a substep of instruction execution and verifies the computed value is identical to that received from the core. If each prediction from the core processor is correct, the result of the current instruction (a register or memory value) as computed by the checker processor is allowed to retire to non-speculative storage in the *commit (CT)* stage of the checker processor.

In the event any prediction information is found to be incorrect, the bad prediction is fixed, the core processor is flushed and restarted, and the core and checker processor pipelines are restarted after the errant instruction. Core flush and restart use the existing branch speculation recovery mechanism contained in all modern high-performance pipelines. As shown in Figure 2b and 2c, the routing MUXes can be configured to form a parallel checker pipeline or a recovery pipeline, respectively.

In recovery mode the pipeline is reconfigured into a serial pipeline, very similar to the classic five-stage pipeline [7]. In this mode, stage computations are sent to the next logical stage in the checker processor pipeline, rather than used simply to verify core predictions. Unlike the classic five-stage pipeline, only one instruction is allowed to enter the recovery pipeline at a time. As such, the recovery pipeline configuration does not require bypass datapaths or complex scheduling logic to detect hazards. Processing performance for a single instruction in recovery mode will be quite poor, but as long as faults are infrequent there will be no perceivable impact on program performance [4]. Once the instruction has retired, the checker processor re-enters normal processing mode and restarts the core processor after the errant instruction. An important aspect of the checker design is that the check and recovery modes use the same checking modules, thereby reducing the area cost of the checker and its design complexity.

Table 1. Benchmarks and baseline statistics

Benchmark	#instr. fwd. (M)	#instr. exec. (M)	% ld exec.	% st. exec.	Base IPC
Compress95	100	250	11.0%	1.0%	1.4303
Crafty00	100	250	32.4%	5.9%	1.4748
Gap00	100	250	25.5%	11.3%	2.2079
Gcc	100	250	25.7%	11.0%	1.2951
Go	100	250	29.3%	8.1%	1.3061
Ijpeg	100	250	18.4%	8.0%	2.6679
Li	100	250	24.3%	11.3%	1.7986
Perl	100	250	23.3%	11.2%	1.2566
Twolf00	100	250	26.3%	8.6%	2.2663
Applu00	100	250	25.9%	10.4%	1.8859
Hydro2d	100	67	23.1%	7.3%	2.2125
Lucas00	100	250	18.4%	0.5%	3.3628
Mesa00	100	250	27.0%	7.3%	2.0450
Tomcatv	0	79	20.1%	7.6%	1.7343
Turb3d	100	250	23.4%	14.9%	2.6035

Pipeline scheduling in the checker processor is trivial. If any checker pipeline is blocked for any reason, all checker processor modules are stalled. This simplifies control of the checker processor and eliminates the need for instruction buffering or complex non-blocking storage interfaces. Since there are no dependencies between instructions in normal processing, checker processor pipeline stalls will only occur during a cache miss or structural (resource) hazard.

The design description given assumes a single wide checker, but we believe that scaling a checker processor is a simple enough task. To make a deeper checker, the separate checker modules simply need to be pipelined deeper. This can be accomplished without adding bypass or complex control because of the minimal inter-pipestage dependencies. To make a wider checker, inter-instruction dependencies must also be verified, but can be done so in parallel with normal instruction checking. Checker scalability will be explored more fully in future work.

3. Performance of the Checker Processor

3.1. Experimental Framework

The simulators used in this study are derived from the SimpleScalar/Alpha 3.0 tool set [5], a suite of functional and timing simulation tools for the Alpha AXP ISA. The timing simulator executes only user-level instructions, performing a detailed timing simulation of an aggressive 4-way dynamically scheduled microprocessor with two levels of instruction and data cache memory. Simulation is execution-driven, including execution down any speculative path until the detection of a fault, TLB miss, or branch misprediction.

To perform our evaluation, we collected results for nine of the SPEC95 benchmarks [14] and six of the SPEC2000 benchmarks. There are nine integer programs and six FP ones. All programs were compiled on a DEC Alpha AXP-21164 processor using the DEC C and Fortran compilers under OSF/1 V4.0 operating system using full compiler optimization (-O4). The six Spec2000 benchmarks were compiled on an Alpha 21264 under OSF/1 V4.0 operating system using at least -O4 optimization. Table 1 shows the benchmarks, the number of instructions that were executed (fast forwarded) before actual simulation began, and the number of instructions simulated for each program (up to 250 million). Also shown are the percentage of dynamic instructions that were loads and stores and the baseline machine IPC.

3.2. Baseline Core Processor Architecture

Our baseline simulation configuration models a future generation out-of-order processor microarchitecture. We've selected the parameters to capture underlying trends in microarchitecture design. The processor has a large window of execution; it can fetch and issue up to 4 instructions per cycle. It has a 256 entry re-order buffer with a 64 entry load/store buffer. Loads can only execute when all prior store addresses are known. In addition, all stores are issued in program order with respect to prior stores. There is an 8 cycle minimum branch misprediction penalty. The processor has 4 integer ALU units, 2-load/store units, 2-FP adders, 1-integer MULT/DIV, and 1-FP MULT/DIV. The latencies are: ALU 1 cycle, MULT 3 cycles, Integer DIV 12 cycles, FP Adder 2 cycles, FP Mult 4 cycles, and FP DIV 12 cycles. All functional units, except the divide units, are fully pipelined allowing a new instruction to initiate execution each cycle.

The processor we simulated has a 16K direct mapped instruction cache and a 16k 4-way set-associative data cache. Both caches have block sizes of 32 bytes. The data cache is write-back, write-allocate, and is non-blocking with 2 ports. The data cache access latency is one cycle (for a total load latency of two cycles). There is a unified second-level 256k 4-way set-associative cache with 32 byte blocks, with a 6 cycle cache hit latency. If there is a second-level cache miss it takes a total of 34 cycles to make the round trip access to main memory. We model the bus latency to main memory with a 10 cycle bus occupancy per request. There is a 32 entry 8-way associative instruction TLB and a 32 entry 8-way associative data TLB, each with a 30 cycle miss penalty.

3.3. Checker Processor Baseline (Shared) Architecture

The checker processor in all experiments is a four instruction wide pipeline that instructions enter when they have completed and are the oldest instruction in the machine that has not yet entered the checker pipeline. Instructions are processed in-order, any instruction that stalls causes later instructions to also stall. In the baseline configuration, the computation pipeline latency is one cycle longer than the functional unit it checks (for the result comparison). It is assumed that there is a computation pipeline for each of the functional units, as a result, no structural hazards are introduced. The baseline communication pipeline takes two cycles unless there are structural hazards in accessing register file and

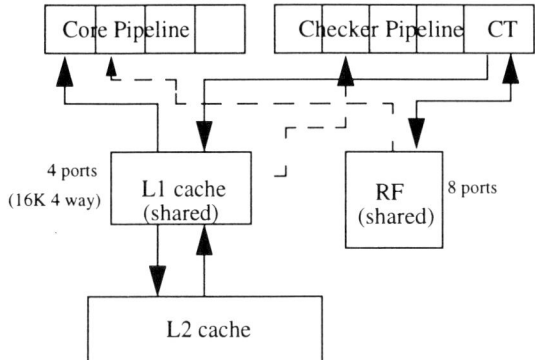

Figure 3. Baseline Checker Processor Architecture

cache ports. In the baseline checker architecture, the storage accesses compete with the core processor for eight architected register file ports and four cache ports, with priority given to the checker accesses. The core processor only accesses the architected register file when an operand is not found in the physical register file (*i.e.*, it is not in flight). Reorder buffer entries are not deallocated until instructions exit the commit stage of the pipeline, after the checker verifies the operation. The watchdog timer countdown is reset to 60 cycles (the round trip latency to memory) whenever an instruction commits.

We omitted the instruction fetch check stage of the checker processor from our experiments. We believe that it is sufficiently straightforward to protect against incorrectly fetched instructions, simply verify correctness of the core processor instruction cache design and protect all instruction storage in the core processor with ECC. As such, there is no need to determine if the instruction has been correctly fetched, the checker processor need only determine if the PC of the fetch was correct.

Our baseline checker processor architecture (Figure 3) is identical to that presented in our previous report [1]. The baseline storage system looks very similar to a traditional microprocessor system with the checker processor inserted just before commit. The core and checker processors share ports to a common architected register file and L1 data cache (possessing eight and two read ports, respectively). The checker has priority while accessing the storage elements, and the core can only access them in a cycle where ports are not fully consumed by checker accesses. When a core instruction is ready for retirement, it is pushed into the checker processor pipeline. During checking, the core processor must continue to hold speculative state resources (e.g., reorder buffer and load/store queue entries) for the instruction being checked. Once checking is complete, the commit stage retires nonspeculative values into the register file and the cache and the core processor may release speculative storage associated with the finished instruction.

In this design, there are three ways the checker processor can slow the progress of the core processor. First, any contention for the ports between the checker and core will lead to core processor stalls. Second, the checker processor pipeline delays the retirement of instructions, forcing the core processor to hold speculative state longer, thus creating backpressure at retirement. If speculative state resources fill, the core processor decoder will stall as it will not be able to allocate re-order buffer and load/store queue resources. Finally, checker processor cache misses stall the entire checker pipeline, which again can lead to increased pressure on core processor speculative state. The checker processor will only experience misses when data referenced by the core processor is replaced before the checker processor is able to re-execute the memory reference.

As can be seen from Table 2 the average slowdown from the fifteen benchmarks was 2.48%. Overall, the slowdown factors are kept mostly in check, however, there was a wide disparity in the performance for a few individual benchmarks. The most notable slowdowns came from the floating point programs *hydro2d* and *tomcatv*, which had slowdowns of roughly 10.5% and 13% respectively. *Hydro2d* also experiences the largest increase in the number of decoder stalls, a leading factor to its poor performance. *Hydro2d* is a very computationally intensive program, which is used to solve hydrodynamically Navier Stokes equations in astrophysics applications. The program is well tuned and it makes quite efficient use of machine resources, such that any backpressure will manifest in the form of slowdowns. Storage access stalls in the core were infrequent; there are two primary reasons for this. First, storage hazards are not created when the core processor accesses physical registers or load/store queue entries. Second, for the integer programs especially, many storage hazards occur during misspeculation and thus do not slow nonspeculative core progress.

There were a non-trivial number of L1 cache misses experienced by the checker processor, especially for the floating point codes. These programs tend to stream through memory, touching cache lines only a few times and then quickly replacing them with other memory contents. Figure 5 graphs the average delay (in cycles) between first execution of an instruction and its final re-execution on the checker pipeline. We term this delay the *slip* of the instruction. *Tomcatv*, which computes fluid dynamics and geometric translations, experienced the worst slowdown in conjunction with the largest increase in L2 accesses. For programs with large slip values, especially the floating point codes, delaying the second check reference to retirement can create a non-trivial number of L1 data cache misses.

4. Increasing Checker Processor Efficiency

4.1. Eliminating Decoder Stalls and Storage Hazards

It is a simple process to eliminate decoder stalls and storage hazards, they are both structural hazards that can be eliminated by simply increasing the number of resources available to the checker processor. In this case, speculative state and storage ports. Figure 4 illustrates our approach to adding these extra resources; we call this design the *FastShared* model. We add a dedi-

Table 2. Analysis of Shared Model Checker Performance

Benchmark	Performance	Stalls							
	Slowdown (Shared Vs. Base)	Decoder		Storage Ports		Cache Misses		L2 Traffic Increase [and incur. %]	
		Base	Shared	Base	Shared	Base	% of Dl1 misses from Shared	Base	Increase in L2 Traffic for shared
compress95	0.01%	0.00%	0.00%	0	0.00%	0	0.00%	0	[0]% -3789 [-0.08%]
crafty00	0.04%	0.26%	0.21%	0	2.17%	0	3.17%	0	[0]% 89472 [0.58%]
gap00	3.91%	19.23%	17.50%	0	2.27%	0	80.30%	0	[0]% 1118312 [19.52%]
gcc	2.00%	1.67%	2.72%	0	0.82%	0	28.20%	0	[0]% 1013148 [6.87%]
go	0.18%	0.28%	0.37%	0	0.83%	0	12.12%	0	[0]% 402933 [3.69%]
ijpeg	1.20%	11.31%	9.14%	0	1.93%	0	14.59%	0	[0]% 142868 [12.83%]
li	0.34%	0.52%	0.49%	0	0.57%	0	6.48%	0	[0]% 255959 [3.67%]
perl	0.95%	0.35%	0.74%	0	0.36%	0	43.76%	0	[0]% 738170 [4.06%]
twolf00	0.05%	4.64%	3.69%	0	1.49%	0	19.15%	0	[0]% 28457 [0.72%]
applu00	0.59%	42.32%	35.37%	0	2.21%	0	6.53%	0	[0]% 318688 [2.54%]
hydro2d	10.47%	34.47%	40.14%	0	1.45%	0	27.06%	0	[0]% 803670 [19.40%]
lucas00	2.59%	0.00%	0.00%	0	2.16%	0	99.96%	0	[0]% 328945 [50.02%]
mesa00	-0.09%	1.95%	2.02%	0	1.93%	0	92.43%	0	[0]% 9639 [0.22%]
tomcatv	12.99%	6.31%	2.02%	0	0.45%	0	52.07%	0	[0]% 1630372 [37.01%]
turb3d	1.93%	28.61%	9.32%	0	2.66%	0	43.23%	0	[0]% 1100773 [34.91%]
AVERAGE	2.48%	10.13%	8.25%	0	1.42%	0	33.40%	0	[0]% 531841 [13.06%]

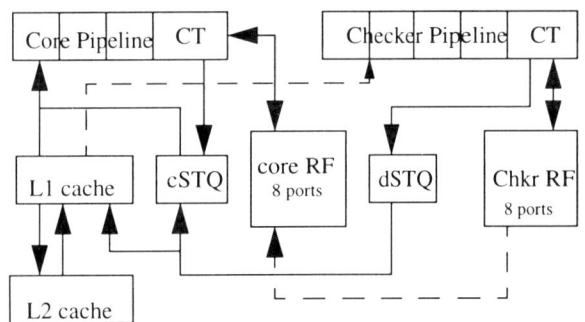

Figure 4. *FastShared* Storage Model
(16K 4way) 4 ports (2 dedicated checker Wr. Ports)

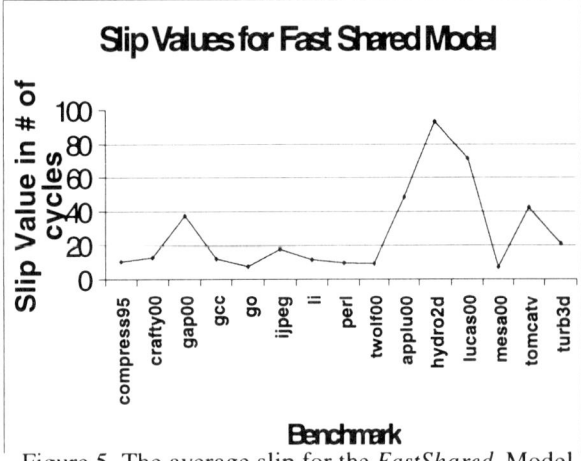

Figure 5. The average slip for the *FastShared* Model

cated checker processor register file, two store queues, and additional ports to the L1 cache (2 total). The split register file permits the core to retire register values (speculatively) into its private register file, thus allowing it to release its internal reorder buffer speculative state at the time instructions are transferred into the checker processor pipeline. The checker processor register file contains truly non-speculative state, if the checker processor detects an error in core processor computation, it must re-synchronize the core processor register file. This can be easily implemented by copying the checker processor register file contents to the core processor register file when faults are declared. The L1 data cache is still shared between the core and checker processors, however, extra ports eliminate storage related stalls.

The core store queue (cSTQ) permits the core processor to release load/store queue entries when instructions pass to the checker processor, thereby further relieving speculative state pressure. The cSTQ holds retired stores until they pass through the checker at which time the space can be reclaimed. Since the checker writes back store values to the shared cache, the cSTQ need not write back the same store values. To ensure a coherent view of speculative memory state, the core processor probes the cSTQ in parallel with the L1 data cache, if any cSTQ entries match the referenced address, the latest value is used in lieu of the L1 data cache value. Checker stores write to the checker STQ (dSTQ). The dSTQ writes to the L1 cache and releases cSTQ and dSTQ entries for the store. When the core executes a load, if it does not hit in the LSQ, the L1 cache and the cSTQ have to be searched in parallel with the latest STQ value overriding L1 cache values. If either the cSTQ or the dSTQ fills up, the corresponding stage stalls until the store at the head of the queue is committed and an entry becomes available. The (dSTQ) serves a similar purpose: to prevent checker pipeline stalls on store write misses, store value are placed into the dSTQ and later written to memory when L1 data cache write ports are available. The space cost for the store queues is minimal - two small queues with eight entries each virtually eliminated all backpressure in the core processor.

Table 3 details the performance of the *FastShared* model. It is quite effective in reducing core processor decoder stalls, in all cases (with the exception of *Applu00*) there are less stalls than in the baseline

Table 3. Analysis of FastShared Model Checker Performance

Benchmark	Performance		Stalls							
	Slowdown (FastShared Vs Base)	Speedup (FastShared Vs Shared)	Decoder		Storage Ports		Cache Misses		L2 Traffic Increase [and incr. %]	
			Shared	FastShared	Shared	FastShared	% of Dl1 misses from Shared	% of Dl1 misses from Fast Shared	Increase in L2 Traffic for shared	Increase in L2 Traffic for Fast-shared
compress95	0.00%	0.01%	0.00%	0.00%	0.00%	0	0.00%	0.00%	-3789 [-0.08%]	2 [0.00%]
crafty00	0.02%	0.02%	0.21%	0.20%	2.17%	0	3.17%	3.17%	89472 [0.58%]	1042317 [6.78%]
gap00	0.01%	0.03%	17.50%	7.68%	2.27%	0	80.30%	80.30%	1118312 [19.52%]	1179802 [20.6%]
gcc	1.25%	0.77%	2.72%	1.19%	0.82%	0	28.20%	29.00%	1013148 [6.87%]	2562353 [17.37%]
go	0.15%	0.03%	0.37%	0.08%	0.83%	0	12.12%	12.12%	402933 [3.69%]	1727555 [15.80%]
ijpeg	0.28%	0.93%	9.14%	8.73%	1.93%	0	14.59%	14.57%	142868 [12.83%]	154662 [13.88%]
li	0.05%	0.30%	0.49%	0.31%	0.57%	0	6.48%	6.49%	255959 [3.67%]	726937 [10.41%]
perl	0.95%	0.01%	0.74%	0.31%	0.36%	0	43.76%	43.76%	738170 [4.06%]	2822083 [15.53%]
twolf00	0.07%	-0.02%	3.69%	3.59%	1.49%	0	19.15%	19.15%	28457 [0.72%]	54349 [1.37%]
applu00	-0.13%	0.73%	35.37%	39.46%	2.21%	0	6.53%	6.53%	318688 [2.54%]	2354622 [18.74%]
hydro2d	10.49%	-0.02%	40.14%	13.77%	1.45%	0	27.06%	27.06%	803670 [19.40%]	806233 [19.46%]
lucas00	2.59%	0.00%	0.00%	0.00%	2.16%	0	99.96%	99.96%	328945 [50.02%]	328945 [50.02%]
mesa00	-0.09%	0.00%	2.02%	2.01%	1.94%	0	92.43%	92.43%	9639 [0.22%]	9933 [0.22%]
tomcatv	12.99%	0.00%	2.02%	0.94%	0.45%	0	52.07%	52.07%	1630372 [37.01%]	1419675 [32.23%]
turb3d	1.74%	0.19%	9.32%	5.14%	2.66%	0	43.23%	43.56%	1100773 [34.91%]	1754036 [55.63%]
AVERAGE	2.03%	0.19%	8.25%	5.56%	1.42%	0	33.40%	35.34%	531841 [13.06%]	1126307 [18.54%]

checker processor configuration. The approach even eliminates stalls that exist in the baseline model due to store write misses, resulting in less decoder stalls for most programs than the baseline experiments without a checker processor. Thus for some programs, *Applu00* and *Mesa00*, there are actually performance gains over the baseline. Storage ports stalls are completely negated by the addition of the additional register file and additional ports to the cache.

Overall, slowdowns improved for some programs, e.g., *GCC* and *Ijpeg*, but worsened for other programs such as *Gap00*. The gain in performance would have been more notable, if this model did not aggravate L1 cache misses. This problem, discussed briefly before in conjunction with *Tomcatv's* slowdown, is the interaction of two working sets on the same cache. If the slip is too large there will be replacements in the cache before a load/store reaches the checker. Thus, the line must be retrieved again from the L2. This causes a large increase in the L2 traffic, which is illustrated in the L2 traffic increase column of the table. The *FastShared* model aggravates this condition by adding a store queue that can increase the lifetime of an instruction in the core before it is checked. Average slip measurements are shown in Figure 5. There is a large correlation between the high slip and low performance in the shared models. The size of the data set and number of memory access are also contributing factors. For example, *Lucas* which has the second highest slip value does not experience a large slowdown because it has comparatively very few data cache misses in the baseline. In other words, there is less conflict for the cache space since each working set is smaller.

4.2. Improving Checker Processor Cache Performance

We can address checker processor L1 cache misses by providing a mechanism by which both core and

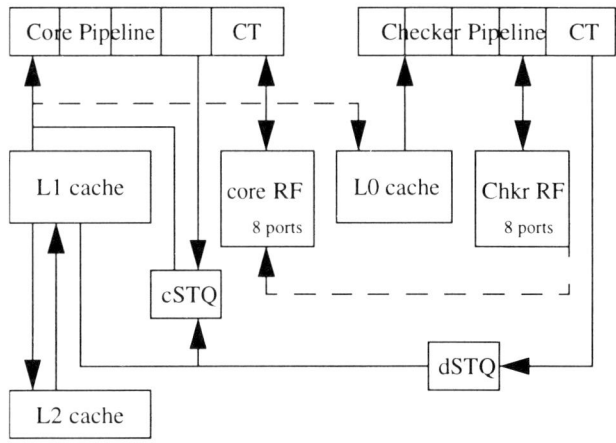

Figure 6. *MiniDiva* Storage Model
Core Cache 16K 4 way 2 rd 2 wr ports
Checker Cache 4K 8 way 4 ports

checker processor data working sets can easily co-exist. The simple approach to this is to split the data cache, giving separate caches to both the checker and the core processors. Figure 6 illustrates the approach, we call this new dynamic verification architecture the *MiniDiva* model.

The *MiniDiva* model extends the *FastShared* model by removing the shared L1 constraint. It provides a small dedicated cache for the checker processor, called the *L0 cache*. The L0 cache is loaded with whatever data is touched by the core processor; *MiniDiva* it taps off the output port of the L1 cache. If the checker processor misses in the L0 cache, it blocks the entire checker pipeline, and the miss is serviced by the core L2 cache. The STQ mechanism and the separate RF are the same as described earlier. When stores commit, they write their

Table 4. Analysis of MiniDiva Model Checker Performance

Benchmark	Performance		Stalls							
			Decoder		Storage Ports		Cache Misses		L2 Traffic Increase [and incr.%]	
	Slowdown (MiniDiva Vs Base)	Speedup (Mini Diva Vs FastShared)	FastShared	Mini Diva	FastShared	Mini Diva	% of Dl1 misses from FastShared	% of Dl1 misses from Mini Diva	Increase in L2 Traffic for Fast shared	Increase in L2 Traffic for Mini Diva
compress95	0.00%	0.00%	0.00%	0.00%	0	0	0.00%	0	2 [0.00%]	9593 [0.20%]
crafty00	0.01%	0.01%	0.20%	0.21%	0	0	3.17%	0	1042317 [6.78%]	819 [0.01%]
gap00	-0.74%	4.81%	7.68%	12.26%	0	0	80.30%	0	1179802 [20.6%]	6293 [0.11%]
gcc	0.02%	1.25%	1.19%	1.65%	0	0	29.00%	0	2562353 [17.37%]	151763 [1.03%]
go	0.00%	0.15%	0.08%	0.22%	0	0	12.13%	0	1727555 [15.80%]	39180 [0.36%]
ijpeg	-0.25%	0.53%	8.73%	10.35%	0	0	14.57%	0	154662 [13.88%]	57265 [5.14%]
li	0.06%	-0.01%	0.31%	0.38%	0	0	6.49%	0	726937 [10.41%]	127888 [1.83%]
perl	0.00%	0.96%	0.31%	0.35%	0	0	43.76%	0	2822083 [15.53%]	65049 [0.36%]
twolf00	0.05%	0.02%	3.59%	3.59%	0	0	19.15%	0	54349 [1.37%]	-191 [-0.01%]
applu00	-1.28%	1.15%	39.46%	40.85%	0	0	6.53%	0	2354622 [18.74%]	3980 [0.03%]
hydro2d	-0.47%	12.23%	13.77%	31.75	0	0	27.06%	0	806233 [19.46%]	75965 [1.83%]
lucas00	0.00%	2.66%	0.00%	0.00%	0	0	99.96%	0	328945 [50.02%]	0 [0.00%]
mesa00	-0.09%	0.00%	2.01%	2.01%	0	0	92.43%	0	9933 [0.22%]	482 [0.01%]
tomcatv	0.20%	14.71%	0.94%	5.87%	0	0	52.07%	0	1419675 [32.23%]	327437 [7.43%]
turb3d	-3.17%	5.00%	5.14%	6.67%	0	0	43.56%	0	1754036 [55.63%]	271265 [8.60%]
AVERAGE	-0.38%	2.90%	5.56%	7.74%	0	0	35.34%	0	1126307 [18.54%]	75786 [1.80%]

result to the L0 cache and the dSTQ. When a free store port is available on the L1 cache, the store in the dSTQ is retired to the L1 cache. If the dSTQ fills the checker processor pipeline stalls until an entry can be written back.

The performance of the *MiniDiva* architecture is summarized in Table 4. Splitting the caches yields almost a 3% improvement over the *FastShared* model. In fact, the *MiniDiva* model even exhibits modest performance gains over the baseline model without a checker processor. We believe that this is due to the cSTQ, which eliminates store writeback misses at commit that can slow the baseline architecture (without a checker processor). This effect is demonstrated in the average decoder stalls percentage which go from 10.13% in the baseline to only 7.74% in the *MiniDiva* model. Second, our data shows that some backpressure may actually cause positive interference in the executing loads and stores. The LSQ and STQ are considered to have infinite bandwidth, thus if a memory access can grab the value it needs from these queues it does not have to reserve a cache port.

The *MiniDiva* model is quite efficient, it eliminates virtually all the checker processor stalls that can slow the core processor, as well as a few core processor stalls. In addition, cache performance improves because the checker processor cache now contains the working set of the checker processor, *i.e.*, loads and stores in the window of core processor execution. With the working set in the L0 cache, core processor activity can no longer displace checker processor working set. A 4k checker cache experiences virtually no misses for any programs. We also looked at slowdowns for a 2k cache, overall slowdown was only 0.77%, but the worst case slowdown rose 4.40% for *Ijpeg*.

While on the surface it may seem adding a second cache is an expensive proposition, there are two mitigating factors. First, the L0 cache eliminates the need for extra ports on the core processor L1 cache, which increases its size and slows its accesses. Second, the cache need only needs to hold the data from when it is first touched in the core until the time it is verified by the checker processor (*i.e.*, slip latency). As such, the *MiniDiva* L0 cache be made very small.

4.3. Eliminating Common Mode L1 failures

In the *MiniDiva* model, the checker processor has its own dedicated L0 data cache. The checker processor register file and L0 and L1 caches hold the architected nonspeculative state of the machine, whereas the core register file holds speculative states. If an error is detected by the checker processor, it rewrites the core register file with values from its own register file. Since the checker processor relies on correct information in the core processor L1 cache, any design errors in this component will manifest as a common failure that could impair correct program execution. For many designs this may not be a significant concern, however, we are currently exploring core processor design strategies, such as self-tuning circuits, that benefit greatly if the core processor L1 cache state is speculative as well.

Figure 7 illustrates an approach to eliminate common mode failures from the core processor L1 cache, we call this design the *SplitDiva* design. There are no STQs present in this design. The core commit stage speculatively commits results to the (speculative) L1 core cache and the core register file. As in the *MiniDiva* model, commits in the core processor are not stalled by the checker processor pipeline. When a fault is detected by the checker processor, it must re-synchronize the core processor L1 with non-speculative storage (*i.e.*, L2 cache state). This process can be easily accomplished by invalidating all core processor L1 cache state. Given that faults are infrequent, the performance implications of this simple (but expensive) approach should be minimal.

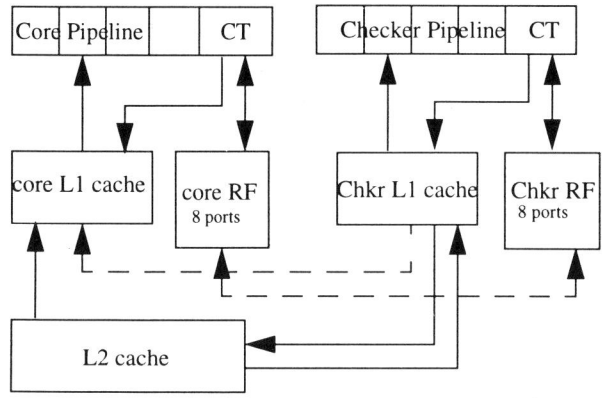

Figure 7. Split Storage Model
Core Cache- (16k 4 way) 2 ports
Checker Cache- (4K 8 way) 4ports

To enable a high hit rate for the checker processor L1 cache, whenever the cache is accessed in the core for loads and stores, the address stream of the reference is sent as a prefetch to the checker processor cache. The checker cache services misses directly from the L2. Thus, there is additional traffic between the checker processor cache and the L2, unlike in the *MiniDiva* model. To minimize L2 traffic increases, lines written from the L2 to the core processor L1 are also immediately placed in the checker processor L1 cache, using a common line bus. In addition, speculative state in the core processor L1 need not be written back to the L2.

An interesting feature of this design is that ECC is no longer needed to protect the core processor L1 cache. Since this state is completely speculative, transient errors due to, for instance, energetic particle strikes will not impair the correct operation of the program. Of course the checker processor L1 cache will require ECC to protect the non-speculative program state. Depending on the size of the checker processor L1 cache and the ECC coding technique, the saving in core processor L1 ECC could go quite far to make up for the area costs of the checker processor and its L1 cache.

Table 5 details the performance of the *SplitDiva* model. Again, the slip between the core and the checker permits memory addresses to be sent as a prefetch stream. Thus stalls in the checker due to cache misses are kept to a minimum. However, unlike the small working set requirements of the *MiniDiva* model, the *SplitDiva* checker processor L1 cache must hold the entire program working set (or as much of it as it can). Fortunately, the core processor address stream presents a very high-quality view of future references well in advance of their use, thus with sufficient L2 cache bandwidth, most checker processor misses can be averted.

Comparing the slowdown of the *SplitDiva* model to the baseline, we notice that this model, with a 4K data cache, has an average slowdown of 1% for all the benchmarks. This is superior to all the storage models discussed so far except the *MiniDiva* model. The *SplitDiva* model, however, offers us greater reliability over all the other storage models, permitting the core L1 cache to be stripped of ECC. This added reliability comes at a cost, though, as can be seen from Table 5.

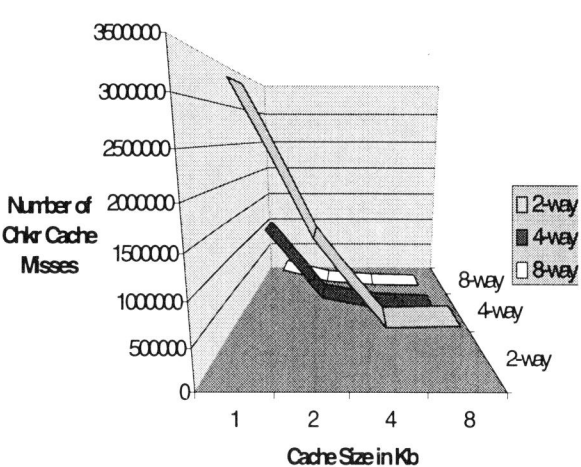

Figure 8. Cache Misses With Respect to Diva cache size and associativity

The *SplitDiva* model has an average slowdown of 1.46% compared to the *MiniDiva* model. The leading factor for this is the increase in L2 traffic for the split model, which is around 75 times that of the *MiniDiva* model.

Figure 8 illustrates the sensitivity of the *SplitDiva* model to checker processor L1 cache geometry. Results are shown for increasing cache sizes and associativity. Clearly, checker processor cache performance is quite good at 4k or higher sizes, and with more associativity (i.e., 4 or 8 way) for even 2k and 1k configurations. However, there is a clear trade-off between cache size and a L2 traffic increases. For the 4-way cache configurations, for example, L2 traffic increases by 86%, 147%, and 245% for decreasing cache sizes of 4k, 2k, and 1k respectively.

4.4. Sensitivity to Other Key Design Parameters

Function Units. To test the *MiniDiva* checker's tolerance for functional units the number of integer ALUs and floating point ALUs was varied. Not surprising, it was found that as the number of ALUs were decreased so did performance. We saw an average slowdown across the fifteen benchmarks of roughly 12% when the number of ALUs were halved from 4 to 2. A subset of the benchmarks was then simulated with only one floating point ALU and one integer ALU in the checker. This subset of three floating point *i.e.*, *Applu00*, *Lucas00* and *Mesa00*, and three integer programs, *i.e.*, *Crafty00*, *Gap00* and *Twolf00*, averaged a 20% slowdown. Clearly, reducing the number of functional units below that of the core execution resources can have significant negative impacts on core processor performance. The number of functional units in the checker must be equal to the core to maintain a good balance with the core commit speed, thereby preventing any slowdowns for efficient programs.

Memory Ports. The versatility of the *MiniDiva* checker was further tested through sensitivity analysis on the

Table 5. Analysis of SplitDiva Model Checker Performance

Benchmark	Performance		Stalls							
			Decoder		Storage Ports		Cache Misses		L2 Traffic Increase [and incr.%]	
	Slowdown (Split Vs Base)	Speedup (Split Vs MiniDiva)	MiniDiva	Split	MiniDiva	Split	% of DI1 misses from MiniDiva	% of DI1 misses from Split	Increase in L2 Traffic for Fast MiniDiva	Increase in L2 Traffic for Split
compress95	0.00%	0.00%	0.00%	0.00%	0	0	0	0	9593 [0.20%]	5251070 [107.5%]
crafty00	0.06%	-0.05%	0.21%	0.31%	0	0	0	0	819 [0.01%]	12461427 [81.0%]
gap00	0.14%	-0.87%	12.26%	20.02%	0	0	0	0	6293 [0.11%]	2816646 [49.17%]
gcc	0.09%	-0.07%	1.65%	1.71%	0	0	0	0	151763 [1.03%]	8861076 [60.07%]
go	-0.01%	0.01%	0.22%	0.27%	0	0	0	0	39180 [0.36%]	13466178 [123%]
ijpeg	0.34%	-0.59%	10.35%	11.69%	0	0	0	0	57265 [5.14%]	1601495 [143.7%]
li	-0.01%	0.06%	0.38%	0.55%	0	0	0	0	127888 [1.83%]	2976652 [42.62%]
perl	-0.01%	0.01%	0.35%	0.39%	0	0	0	0	65049 [0.36%]	11272662 [62.0%]
twolf00	0.01%	0.04%	3.59%	4.76%	0	0	0	0	-191 [-0.01%]	396975 [10.02%]
applu00	0.89%	-2.13%	40.85%	42.97%	0	0	0	0	3980 [0.03%]	19384421 [154%]
hydro2d	7.43%	-7.35%	31.75	38.24%	0	0	0	0	75965 [1.83%]	2143317 [51.74%]
lucas00	6.86%	-6.42%	0.00%	0.00%	0	0	0	0	0 [0.00%]	1973517 [300.1%]
mesa00	0.00%	-0.09%	2.01%	1.96%	0	0	0	0	482 [0.01%]	43803 [0.98%]
tomcatv	0.57%	-0.38%	5.87%	6.94%	0	0	0	0	327437 [7.43%]	627439 [14.24%]
turb3d	1.06%	-4.08%	6.67%	29.91%	0	0	0	0	271265 [8.60%]	2997647 [95.07%]
AVERAGE	1.16%	-1.46%	7.74%	10.65%	0	0	0	0	75786 [1.80%]	5751622 [86.38%]

number of memory ports on the checker processor cache. When the number of memory ports was lowered from 4 to 2 a slowdown of 1.7% was experienced in the benchmarks. A 8.1% slowdown was the result of lowering the memory ports to 1. As is the case for functional unit resources, they should match that of the core to reduce the possibility of core processor slowdown. Slowdowns, however, were mitigated by the dSTQ, is it was able to reduce the impacts of not immediately having more ports available.

Pipedepth. We experimented with increasing the pipeline depth and functional unit depth for the checker pipeline. Similar to earlier presented experiments [1,2], the results were quite encouraging. Increasing the checker pipeline length four-fold (from 2 stages to 8) increased average slowdown for the *MiniDiva* model to only 2.4%, demonstrating that overall the checker processor pipeline is quite tolerant of processing latency. The integer codes were extremely latency tolerant, average slowdown for these programs was only 0.04%. These results suggest that superpipelining the checker processor to scale checker processor bandwidth will likely produce very good results. We are currently exploring this design in detail in conjunction with the implementation of a physical checker processor design.

I-Cache Check. Fetching is a simple operation which can be easily made reliable, using encoding techniques like ECC. Nonetheless, we added a small I-cache (512 entries) to the checker to test performance impacts. The slowdown experienced was less than 1%. High spatial locality in instruction memory and core-driven prefetching eliminated virtually all misses.

Fault Rate. Analysis in our previous work indicated that recovery from faults did not impact performance provided the faults were infrequent enough (less than one every 1000 instructions).

5. Related Work

The related work mentioned here is in addition to those found in [1,2].

Blum and Wasserman discussed checkers with respect to the Pentium Division Bug [4]. In addition to talking about complete checkers, they discussed how a partial checker could be utilized to achieve checking accuracy that was almost perfect. They also postulate that if error rates are kept small enough, correcting procedures can be very time consuming without impacting the performance of the system.

A similar idea of having a simple inorder pipeline that runs in parallel with the main engine is presented by Nakra et al in [9]. In that paper, instructions that already have their operations decoded execute on the simple pipeline upon detection of misprediction in the main engine.

Rotenberg's AR-SMT[11] and more recently Slipstream[13] processors use multiple threads to eliminate hazards and verify correct operation. In Slipstream an advanced stream (A-stream) is used to aid a redundant stream (R-stream) by providing future knowledge to the trailing stream. As a result performance can be increased and the redundancy can be used to detect errors. However this technique does not provide total coverage or resistance to design errors.

Other techniques for obtaining reliability include the redundant hardware approach, as in the IBM S/390 G5 microprocessor [12] and the redundant thread (or SRT) approach. In the SRT approach proposed in [10], redundant threads run concurrently and compare results for fault detection. Performance in SRT processors is improved with one thread prefetching cache misses and branch outcomes for other threads, similar to the prefetching ideas in the *SplitDiva* model.

In a previous study Dundas and Mudge[6] showed that a performance gain was possible, by ignoring cache misses and pre-executing instructions while the processor would normally be stalled. When a cache miss occurred the register file and instruction address would be backed up and the processor would execute in runahead mode. By doing this they were able to generate a fairly accurate prefetch stream. This would in turn warm up the cache and reduce future stalls. A checker processor can use similar techniques, because there is advanced knowledge of the addresses that will be touched by instructions when they enter the checker. A similar mechanism for obtaining prefetches was proposed in an earlier paper by Chen and Baer [3].

6. Conclusions and Future Work

Many reliability challenges confront modern microprocessor designs. Functional design errors and electrical faults can impair the function of a part, rendering it useless. While functional and electrical verification can find most of the design errors, there are many examples of non-trivial bugs that find their way into the field. Concerns for reliability grow in deep submicron fabrication technologies due to increased noise-related failure mechanisms, natural radiation interference, and more challenging verification due to increased design complexity.

To counter these reliability challenges, we previously proposed the use of dynamic verification, a technique that adds a checker processor to the retirement phase of a processor pipeline. If an incorrect instruction is delivered by the core processor, for instance due to a design error or transient fault, the checker processor will fix the errant computation and restart the core processor using the processor's speculation recovery mechanism. Dynamic verification focuses the verification effort into the checker processor, whose simple and flexible design lends itself to high-quality functional and electrical verification.

We presented detailed analyses of a baseline checker processor design identical to the one presented in our initial proposal [1]. We find three factors lead to occasional poor program performance: 1) checker processing latency delays core processor retirement leading to decoder stalls, 2) shared storage resources create competition for storage ports which can force the core processor to delay issuing instructions, and 3) checker processor cache misses occur that also create backpressure on core retirement leading to additional decoder stalls.

To eliminate decoder stalls, we provide a dedicated register file for the checker processor, thereby permitting the core processor to immediately release speculative state resources when instructions enter the checker processor. In addition, a store queue is added to the core processor design , that permits the load/store queue to also release speculative storage when instructions enter the checker pipeline. Checker processor cache misses are eliminated by giving the checker processor its own dedicated data cache. Our approach employs the core processor reference stream as a high-quality prefetch oracle, driving the placement of data into the checker processor cache in advance of any references. We examine two designs, one that draws data from the core processor L1 cache and a more flexible design that draws data directly from the L2 cache. Both designs performed quite well, with 4k 8-way set-associative caches experiencing virtually no misses, however, L2 cache traffic was understandably higher for the latter *SplitDiva* design. Our refined design now exhibits negligible slowdowns for all programs examined, while at the same time keeping checker pipeline and storage costs quite low.

We feel that these results strengthen the case that dynamic verification holds significant promise as a means to address the cost and quality of verification for future microprocessors, while at the same time creating opportunities for faster, cooler, and simpler designs. Currently, we are in the process of better quantifying area, power, and performance aspects of our optimized checker processor design through the development of a physical checker processor design. In conjunction with this effort, we are continuing to refine the checker processor design. Currently, we are exploring strategies to better manage the checker processor cache using advanced prefetching techniques. We are also examining the cost and utility of partial checking mechanism, where reduced functionality checkers are employed. We will report on these results in a future paper.

7. References

[1] T. Austin, "DIVA: A Reliable Substrate for Deep Submicron Microarchitecture Design", In *Micro-32*, Nov 99.

[2] T. Austin, "DIVA: A Dynamic Approach to Microprocessor Verification", *The Journal of Instruction-Level Parallelism Volume 2*, 2000.

[3] J.-L. Baer and T.F Chen, "An effective on-chip preloading scheme to reduce data access penalty", In *Proc. of Supercomputing*, pages 176-186, 1991.

[4] M. Blum and H. Wasserman, "Reflections on the Pentium Division Bug", Intel Corporation, Oct. 1997.

[5] D. C. Burger and T. M. Austin, "The simplescalar tool set, version 2.0", Technical Report CS-TR-97-1342, University of Wisconsin, Madison, June 1997.

[6] J. Dundas and T. Mudge, "Improving data cache performance by pre-executing instructions under a cache miss", *Proc. 1997 Acm Int. Conf. on Supercomputing*, July 1997.

[7] J. Hennessy and D. Patterson, *Computer Architecture: a Quantitative Approach*, Morgan Kaufmann Publishers, Inc. 1996.

[8] W. Hunt, "Microprocessor design verification", *Journal of Automated Reasoning*, 5(4):429-460, Dec. 1989.

[9] T. Nakra, R. Gupta, and M.L. Soffa, "Value Prediction in VLIW Machines", *In ACM/IEEE 26th International Symposium on Computer Architecture*, May 1999.

[10] S. K.Reinhardt and S. S. Mukherjee, "Transient Fault Detection via Simultaneous Multithreading", *In 27th Annual International Symposium on Computer Architecture (ISCA)*, June 2000.

[11] E. Rotenberg, "AR-SMT: A Microarchitectural Approach to Fault Tolerance in Microproessors", *Proceedings of the 29th Fault-Tolerant Computing Symposium*, June 1999.

[12] T.J Slegel et al, "IBM's S/390 G5 Microprocessor Design", *IEEE Micro*, pp 12-23, March/April 1999.

[13] K. Sundaramoorthy, Z. Purser, and E.Rotenberg, "Slipstream Processors: Improving both Performance and Fault Tolerance", *9th International Conference on Architectural Support for Programming Languages and Operating Systems*, Nov. 2000.

[14] SPEC newsletter, Fairfax, Virginia, Sept. 1995.

Compilation

An Integrated Approach to Accelerate Data and Predicate Computations in Hyperblocks

Alexandre Eichenberger
North Carolina State University, Raleigh, NC
alexe@eos.ncsu.edu

Waleed Meleis and Suman Maradani
Northeastern University, Boston, MA
{meleis, smaradan}@ece.neu.edu

Abstract

To exploit increased instruction-level parallelism available in modern processors, we describe the formation and optimization of tracenets, an integrated approach to reducing the length of the critical path in data and predicated computation. By tightly integrating selective path expansion and path optimization within hyperblocks, our algorithm is able to produce highly optimized code without exploring the exponentially large number of paths included in a hyperblock. Our approach extracts more of the implicit predicate correlations in hyperblocks and uses a precise model of predicate correlations to aggressively accelerate data and predicate computations. Experimental results indicate that tracenets can significantly reduce the number of dynamic execution cycles.

1. Introduction

Advances in chip technology and computer microarchitecture have contributed to the increase in instruction level paralielism provided by modern microprocessors, as exemplified by Intel's IA-64 implementation of an Explicitly Parallel Instruction Computing (EPIC) architecture. However, sufficient parallelism to exploit these resources is rarely present in typical applications. Instead, hardware and compiler techniques are used to increase parallelism, including hardware techniques that support speculation and predication and compiler techniques that optimize regions of code such as traces [Fis81], superblocks [Hwu93], and hyperblocks [Ma92].

A successful compiler techniques is superblock scheduling [Hwu93], which selects frequently executed paths in the application and optimizes them under the assumption that each path is mostly executed from start to finish. Increased performance is achieved by overlapping the execution of operations from the consecutive blocks in the superblock and by optimizing the operations more effectively since optimizations are significantly more successful along a single path than in multiple paths of control flow.

However the effectiveness of superblock scheduling is reduced in highly branching code as the probability of executing any given path is reduced. Hyperblock scheduling [Ma92] alleviates this problem by using predicated execution [HD86] to include multiple paths within a single scheduling and optimization region. A hyperblock is formed by applying if-conversion [AKP83][DT93][Ma92], a process that eliminates the branches guarding each included path and guards the operations in each path by a predicate that evaluates to true precisely when the path would have been taken. Predicated operations have side effects only when their guarding predicate is true. Hyperblock scheduling achieves higher performance by eliminating branches and by enabling scheduling and optimizing within a region that covers a larger fraction of the execution time since they include multiple high-frequency paths.

Recent advances in predicated code optimizations reduce the length of the critical path in hyperblocks to increase instruction level parallelism. One technique eliminates the dependences among consecutive branches by moving some branches off trace [SMJ99]. Another technique accelerates the computation of the predicates by systematically restructuring their computation [Aug99]. A third technique eliminates false dependences in a hyperblock by renaming registers and replicating operations [Car99].

In this paper we describe tracenet formation, an integrated approach to reducing the length of the critical path in data and predicated computation. A *tracenet* is a hyperblock containing a network of traces expanded based on reaching values. By tightly integrating selective path expansion and path optimization, our algorithm produces highly optimized code without exploring the exponentially large number of paths in a hyperblock. Selective path expansion expands paths only when optimization opportunities are enabled. Paths that are determined to be infeasible are not considered further. Tracenets accelerate the data computations by increasing the effectiveness of classic optimizations like constant propagation, constant folding, and copy propagation. In addition, tracenets and these optimizations enable the algorithm to extract more of the implicit correlations that exist among predicates of the hyperblock. A precise model of the complete set of possible predicate correlations is used to define invariants which implicitly list all feasible combinations of correlated tests. These invariants allow the algorithm to aggressively minimize predicate computations and generate faster computations of predicate values.

Compared to other path expansion schemes [Car99], our approach targets not only elimination of false dependences but also height reduction along true dependences. Furthermore, while performing more aggressive path expansion, we may expand fewer paths by tightly integrating path expansion with optimizations like constant subexpression elimination that enable us to focus on values rather than on static assignments. Our approach considers the acceleration of data computation needed by predicate compares, extracts implicit correlation among predicates, and uses the predicate correlation data aggressively. These transformations enable the optimization of predicate computations performed by August et al. [Aug99]. While August considers the "implies" and "excludes" relationships among predicates, we classify predicate correlations using a precise model that covers all possible correlations.

The paper is organized as follows. In Section 2, we describe the architectural support for predicated execution. In Section 3, we motivate our approach to accelerating data and predicate computation. In Section 4, we describe the integrated path expansion and optimization algorithm. In Section 5, we present our approach to extraction of predicate correlation and its use in logic minimization. We present measurements in Section 6, compare our approach to related work in Section 7, and conclude in Section 8.

2. Architectural support

PlayDoh is a parameterized processor architecture designed to further research in instruction-level parallelism [KSR94]. Several features are provided to allow a compiler to fully exploit available ILP. The architecture supports both control and data speculation by adding speculative tag bits to each register, and by providing both speculative and non-speculative versions of many operations.

Predicated execution allows an operation to be conditionally executed based on the value of a boolean-valued register. In PlayDoh most operations can be predicated and a varied set of the compare-to-predicate operations that set the value of the predicate registers is provided. The syntax of these operations is:

$$p(<x>), q(<x>) = cond(a,b) ? r.$$

The boolean expression $cond(a,b)$ and the guard predicate r are used to set destination predicates p and q. The final value of p and q depends on the actions specified by $<x>$ and $<y>$, which can be one of un/uc, cn/cc, on/oc, or an/ac.

Inputs		Outputs							
r	cond	un	uc	cn	cc	on	oc	an	ac
0	0	0	0	–	–	–	–	–	–
0	1	0	0	–	–	–	–	–	–
1	0	0	1	0	1	–	1	0	–
1	1	1	0	1	0	1	–	–	0

As a result of a compare-to-predicate operation, either a 1 or 0 is written into a destination predicate, or the destination predicate is left unchanged. These three outcomes (0,1,–) are indicated in the table above. In each case, the first letter of the action specifies the type of predicate setting operation, and the second letter indicates whether the normal or complemented version of the operation is being used.

The unconditional predicate types, un/uc, set the destination predicate equal to the logical conjunction of the expression (or its complement) and the guard predicate. The remaining predicate types leave the destination predicate unchanged if the source predicate equals 0. The OR predicate types, on/oc, set the destination predicate to 1 if the expression (or its complement) is true, and otherwise leave the destination unchanged. This operation can be used to compute the wired-or of a collection of expressions by initially setting the destination to 0, and then applying a compare-to-predicate operation with the same destination to each expression. In a similar way, the AND predicate types, an/ac, can be used to compute the wired-and of a collection of expressions. The conditional predicate types, cn/cc, are identical to the unconditional actions when the guard predicate is true. Otherwise the destination predicate is unchanged.

3. Motivation

Eliminating merge points along frequently executed paths in the control flow graph is critical to enabling aggressive optimization and extraction of instruction-level parallelism. A control merge is a point in the program where two or more execution traces merge. When the merging execution traces have distinct definitions of the same variable, v, the control merge is also called a data merge for variable v. Data merges disable useful optimizations because the compiler cannot determine which code was executed before the control merge. Examples of optimizations disabled by data merges include constant propagation and common subexpression elimination.

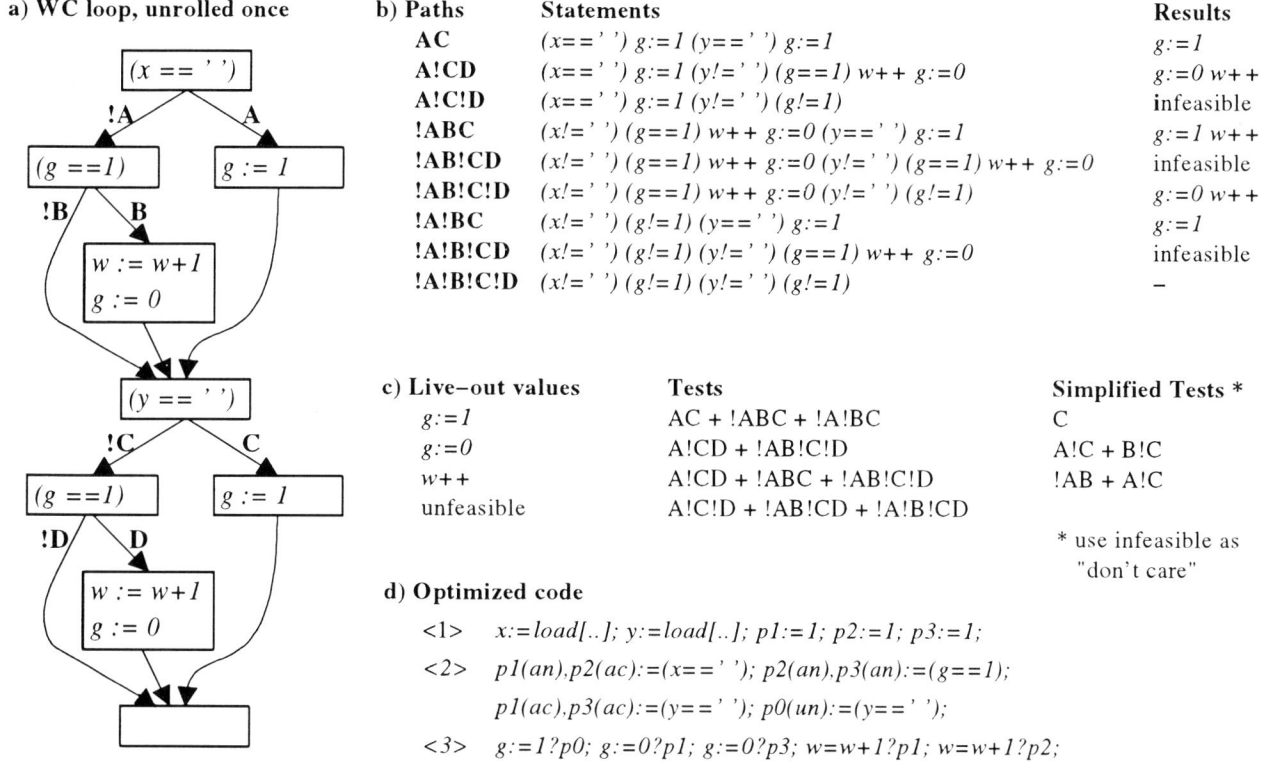

Figure 1. All path optimization of the innermost loop of word count, unrolled once.

Modern scheduling algorithms eliminate data merge points by constructing and optimizing operation traces that do not contain control merges. For example, a superblock includes one path in the control flow and eliminates all data merges within this path. A hyperblock includes multiple paths from the original control flow, eliminates all control merges within the hyperblock, but still includes some data merges that are implicitly present in the predicated code.

Ideally, we would like to have a region that includes multiple predicated paths without any optimization-disabling data merges along its critical paths. This goal can be achieved by fully expanding each path in a region, optimizing each path individually, and recombining any operations that are redundant among the expanded paths. This approach is demonstrated below.

Figure 1 shows the innermost loop of wc, taken from the benchmark suite distributed with Trimaran [Tri99] and simplified for conciseness: we assume here that words are only separated by spaces (not tabs or newlines) and we do not count lines. The variable w contains the current number of words and the variable g is the boolean variable that indicates if the last characters were spaces. Variables x and y contain the characters being analyzed.

In Figure 1a we show the control flow graph for wc after the inner loop has been unrolled once. The graph contains operations on data values, e.g. $w++$ and $g:=0$, and tests that affect the flow of control, e.g. $(g == 1)$ and $(x == '\ ')$. We let boolean variables A, B, C, and D represent the results of the four tests in the code, and the outgoing arcs from each test are either labeled with the appropriate variable or its complement. Figure 1b lists the operations and tests executed on each path. In many cases the sequence of operations performed along a path can be optimized. For example along path AC, one of the two $g := 1$ operations is redundant. On the right side of Figure 1b we show the optimized code for each path. Note three out of nine paths are infeasible since they correspond to inconsistent sequences of operations and test results.

By computing predicates that correspond to each path and predicating the operations that are executed along that path, the optimized paths can be merged into a single code sequence. Further optimization is possible by observing that many of the paths execute identical operations. For example, variable w is incremented along paths $A!CD$, $!ABC$, and $!AB!C!D$. In Figure 1c we show the boolean expressions that correspond to paths that cause each optimized operation to be executed.

We can apply logic minimization techniques to find simplified conditions under which each operation is executed. Certain paths are infeasible and the expressions that correspond to these paths are considered to be don't-cares and can be set to whatever value gives the simplest expression. Using the infeasible paths *A!C!D*, *!AB!CD*, and *!A!B!CD* as don't-cares, the simplified conditions in Figure 1c fully eliminated test *D*, since test *D* is fully determined by *g*'s assignments and tests *A*, *B*, and *C*.

This transformation merges operations that correspond to the same static operation in the original code, such as operation *w++* in the first unrolled iteration that is executed along paths *!ABC* and *!AB!C!D*, as well as operations that correspond to different static operations in the original code, such as operation *w++* in the second unrolled iteration that is executed along path *A!CD*. This transformation preserves the semantics of the code since each instance of *w++* increments the same live-in value of variable *w*.

We show the optimized code in Figure 1d. In cycle 0, variables *x* and *y* are loaded; in cycle 1, the predicate values are computed; and in cycle 2, the data operations are issued with the simplified predicates. Computing *p=!AB+A!C* and executing *w++ ?p* ordinarily takes three cycles on an EPIC architecture. However, we can simultaneously issue one instance of the *w++* operation predicated on *p1=A!C*, and another instance predicated on *p2=!AB*. Since expressions *A!C* and *!AB* are disjoint (i.e. they cannot both be true), at most one instance will execute.

The resulting optimized code executes in 3 cycles for two loop iterations, compared to the 5 cycles obtained with traditional and predicate optimizations. Similarly, unrolling twice yields code that requires 3 cycles (one for loads, one for computing the predicate conditions, and one for executing the operations) while using traditional optimizations gives code that requires 7 cycles.

The drawback of this naive approach is that it individually investigates and optimizes a number of paths that is exponential in the number of tests. In practice it is useful to expand and optimize only a subset of these paths, or subsets of partial paths. Our algorithm generates the same optimized code without generating all paths by (1) tightly integrating path expansion and code optimization to detect infeasible paths and their associated reaching definitions early, and by (2) selectively expanding subsets of paths that generate distinct values to enable optimizations for operations in the critical path. Correlation among predicates is used to detect infeasible paths and reaching definitions as well as to minimize the code defining the predicates.

The first key insight is that we expand paths based on values, not on control flow or original operations. In Figure 1 we saw that variable *w* is incremented along three control paths by two distinct operations in the original control flow graph. If distinguishing between the original and the incremented values of *w* enables useful optimizations, our algorithm would expand two paths: one for the original value and another one for the incremented value. In contrast, a full control path expansion approach would expand all six distinct control paths. Similarly, a static operation path expansion [Car99] would expand three distinct paths: one for the original value of *w*, one for the value of *w* generated by the first increment operation, and one for the value of *w* generated by the second increment operation in the original control flow graph.

The second key insight is that we treat predicate compare operations like regular operations. By expanding paths that compute the values being compared and by optimizing along such paths, we extract more correlation among compares which in turn can lower the overhead to compute and set the predicates. Also, we can break dependences from predicate computation, to regular operation, back to predicate computation, as seen in Figure 1 by the elimination of the data-dependent computation of *D* from the final optimized code.

4. Tracenet formation

We give an overview of the algorithm in Section 4.1, illustrate how it works on the innermost loop from wc in Sections 4.2 and 4.3, and describe the algorithm in detail in Section 4.4.

4.1. Algorithm overview

We propose an algorithm that expands traces in a hyperblock and generates the same optimized code as full path expansion without having to actually consider each path. Paths are expanded as follows. Assume we are processing operation *g:=1* and that we want to distinguish this value of variable *g* from previous values of *g*. To do so, we rename the destination register of the operation, e.g. $g_1:=1$. Each subsequent operation that uses variable *g* may now have to be replicated, with one instance using the register containing the original value of variable *g*, e.g. g_0, and another instance using register g_1. We say that g_1 is a renaming of variable *g*, since g_1 is a distinct register that holds a value originally contained in variable *g*.

The algorithm processes each operation in turn, in program order. Consider that it is currently processing operation *x* which uses variable *v* and defines variable *w*. The algorithm first determines whether more than one register that is a renaming of v reaches operation *x*. If this is the case (e.g. when v_1 and v_2 are two renamings of *v* and when some definitions of v_1 and v_2 reach operation *x*) the algorithm replicates operation *x* to create one instance per renamed register. Replicated operations are added after *x* in the program order and are processed like any of the original operations. When replication occurs, the original operation *x* is removed and the algorithm tries to optimize the replicated operations by exploiting the specific definitions that reach them. After optimization, the algorithm decides whether to rename the destination register of x by evaluating whether renaming generates optimization opportunities along the critical path. Finally, the algorithm records the definitions generated by x and updates the reaching definition data accordingly.

While we replicate and optimize predicate compares as if they were regular operations, we never rename the predicate registers since the computations of the predicates are accelerated separately using an approach similar to the one proposed by August et al [Aug99]. The current value of the predicate registers is analyzed using an approach similar to the one proposed by Johnson and Schlansker [JS96].

(1) p0(un), p1(uc) := (x==' ')
(2) g := 1 ?p0
(3) p2(un) := (g==1) ?p1
(4) w := w+1 ?p2
(5) g := 0 ?p2
(6) p10(un), p11(uc) := (y==' ')
(7) g := 1 ?p10
(8) p12(un) := (g==1) ?p11
(9) w := w+1 ?p12
(10) g := 0 ?p12

Figure 2. Unrolled, if-converted innermost loop from wc.

4.2. Introductory example: expanding path and optimization

Consider the if-converted code in Figure 2 constructed from the control flow graph in Figure 1a. Because all operations are on the critical path, the destination register of each operation will be renamed, provided it generates a new value. Thus, in this example the terms "definition" and "renamed register" are used interchangeably.

The data gathered by our algorithm is shown in Table 1, which reflects the state after processing each operation. The first column contains the original operations that have been processed so far. The second column indicates the symbolic definitions that result from each operation. These include the association of new logical variables with the result of a test, the association of a predicate register with a logical expression, and the assignment of values to definitions. The remaining columns indicate the logical expressions under which each definition reaches the current operation. Reaching definitions for predicate definitions are computed elsewhere [JS96] and are therefore omitted from the table.

The first operation is not replicated and cannot be further optimized. We record in the second column that operation (1) defines a test $(x==' ')$. We let A equal the result of this test. Register $p0$ is equivalent to A and $p1$ is equivalent to the complement of A, as defined by the semantics of the predicate types un and uc described in Section 2. The recording of symbolic definitions for predicate compare operations is similar to the one proposed by Johnson and Schlansker [JS96]. The remaining columns indicate that the original live-in definitions of g and w, g_0 and w_0 respectively, reach this operation unconditionally.

Operation (2) is not replicated and variable g is renamed as g_1. We record in the table the symbolic definition and update the reaching definition expressions. Since operation (2) is predicated on $p0$, which equals A, the definition g_1 is generated under A and the original definition of g is killed under A. The reaching definition expression associated with w_0 is unchanged (as depicted in the table by downward pointing arrows).

Operation (3) is a predicate compare of type un predicated on $p1$. Unconditional predicate compares are atypical because, although they produce a value unconditionally, they read their inputs (g and 1 here) only when their guarding predicate evaluates to true. Of the two available definitions of variable g, g_1 reaching under expression A and g_0 reaching under expression $!A$, only the later is used by operation (3) guarded under expression $!A$. Thus operation (3) can be rewritten as $p2(un):=(g_0==1)?p1$. We record in the second column the new $B\equiv(g_0==1)$ test and the equivalence of $p2$ to $!AB$.

We now consider operations (4)–(7). First, operation $w:=w+1?p2$ generates a renamed register w_1 under expression $!AB$; second, operation $g:=0?p2$ generates a renamed register g_2 under expression $!AB$; and third operation $p10(un),p11(uc):=(y==' ')$ generates a new test labeled $C\equiv(y==' ')$. Consider now the processing of operation (7) which, like operation (2), sets variable g to 1. No replication is required, and common subexpression elimination indicates that the value 1 is already available in the renamed register g_1. Instead of having a new definition of g and/or renaming the variable g again, we regenerate the same symbolic definition $g_1\equiv 1$ but this time under expression C.

The processing of operation (8) is illustrated in Figure 3. Because three definitions of g reach operation (8) in three distinct registers, as shown in Figure 3a, the predicate compare operation is replicated three times. Figure 3b shows each replicated operation guarded by the conjunction of the expression associated with its reaching definition and the original guard of operation (8). Note that an unconditional predicate compare can only be replicated by transforming all but the first replicated operation into or-type predicate compares. In Figure 3c, the constant symbolic definitions are propagated into the replicated operations. Note that the test $(g_0==1)$ was previously assigned the label B. In doing so, we correlate this test with the earlier identical test seen when processing operation (3). Predicate compare operations are evaluated in Figure 3d; the first one sets $p12$ to false,

Original operations	Symbolic definitions	Reaching definition expressions				
		g_0	g_1	g_2	w_0	w_1
(1)*** p0(un),p1(uc):=(x==' ')	A≡(x==' '), p0≡A, p1≡!A	true.	false.	false.	true.	false.
(2) g:=1?p0	g_1≡1	!A	A	↓	↓	↓
(3) p2(un):=(g==1)?p1	B≡(g_0==1), p2≡!AB	↓	↓	↓	↓	↓
(4) w:=w+1?p2	w_1≡w_0+1	↓	↓	↓	A+!B	!AB
(5) g:=0?p2	g_2≡0	!A!B	↓	!AB	↓	↓
(6) p10(un),p11(uc):=(y==' ')	C≡(y==' '), p10≡C, p11≡!C	↓	↓	↓	↓	↓
(7) g:=1?p10	g_1≡1	!A!B!C	A+C	!AB!C	↓	↓
(8) p12(un):=(g==1)?p11	p12≡A!C	↓	↓	↓	↓	↓
(9) w:=w+1?p12	w_1≡w_0+1	↓	↓	↓	!A!B+AC+!BC	!AB+ A!C
(10) g:=0?p12	g_2≡0	!A!B!C	C	A!C+B!C	↓	↓

Table 1. Algorithm state after processing each operation in Figure 2.

the second one sets *p12* to true whenever *A!C* evaluates to true, and the third one never writes anything (i.e. the operation is dead). As a result, *p12* correlates with expression *A!C* as shown in Table 1.

Processing operation (9) does not require replication as only one definition of the variable *w* reaches the operation predicated on expression *A!C*. Note that common subexpression elimination recognizes that w_0+1 has been computed before, and thus no new definition or renamed register is generated. When processing operation (10), common subexpression elimination recognizes that a move of the value zero has been performed before, and this previous definition can be reused.

4.3. Introductory example: code generation

In the case of wc, generating code from Table 1 is straightforward since each reaching definition is either a constant or is a function of the live-in values. The first step is to determine which variable is live-out on the branch, which comes just after operation (10). Here both variables *w* and *g* are live-outs. The next step is to overwrite the original values of *w* and *g* with those of the renamed registers that are reaching the branch. Since the last row of Table 1 indicates the reaching definition expression for each of the renamed register just before the branch, we must overwrite the original value of *w* with the value of w_1 under the expression *!AB+ A!C*. Similarly, we must overwrite the original value of *g* with the value of g_1 under the expression *C* and with the value of g_2 under the expression *A!C+B!C*. Since w_1≡w_0+1, g_1≡1, and g_2≡0, we issue the following code:

w++?(!AB+A!C); g:=1?C; g:= 0?(A!C+B!C) or the code with simpler and faster predicate conditions: w++?(!AB); w++?(A!C); g:= 1?C; g:=0?(A!C); g:=0?(B!C) just as in Figure 1d.

In summary, the algorithm processed each of the operations in the innermost loop of wc, performing an all-path expansion and optimization without having replicated any operations that could not be immediately simplified. It generated one renamed register/definition per value by aggressively using constant propagation and common subexpression elimination. Without tightly integrating such optimization within the path expansion algorithm, the algorithm would have generated many more renamed registers, processed many more replicated operations, and may not have generated such compact code.

4.4. Detailed algorithm

We introduce notation to describe registers in the presence of register renaming. We refer to the inputs and outputs of an operation as uses and defs, respectively. For any two-input/one-output operation we let u_1 and u_2 refer to the first and second uses, respectively, and let d_1 refer to the def. We let $reg(u_1)$ and $reg(u_2)$ be the registers that are used and let $reg(d_1)$ be the register that is defined. We further define $oreg(u_1)$, $oreg(u_2)$, and $oreg(d_1)$ as the registers that are used and defined in the *original* hyperblock, prior to any renaming and replicating. Prior to calling our path expansion algorithm, $oreg(x) = reg(x)$ for any use or def *x* by any operation in the hyperblock. As the algorithm renames registers, $oreg(d_x)$ and $reg(d_x)$ start to differ for each operation *x* that defines a renamed register. Similarly, when an

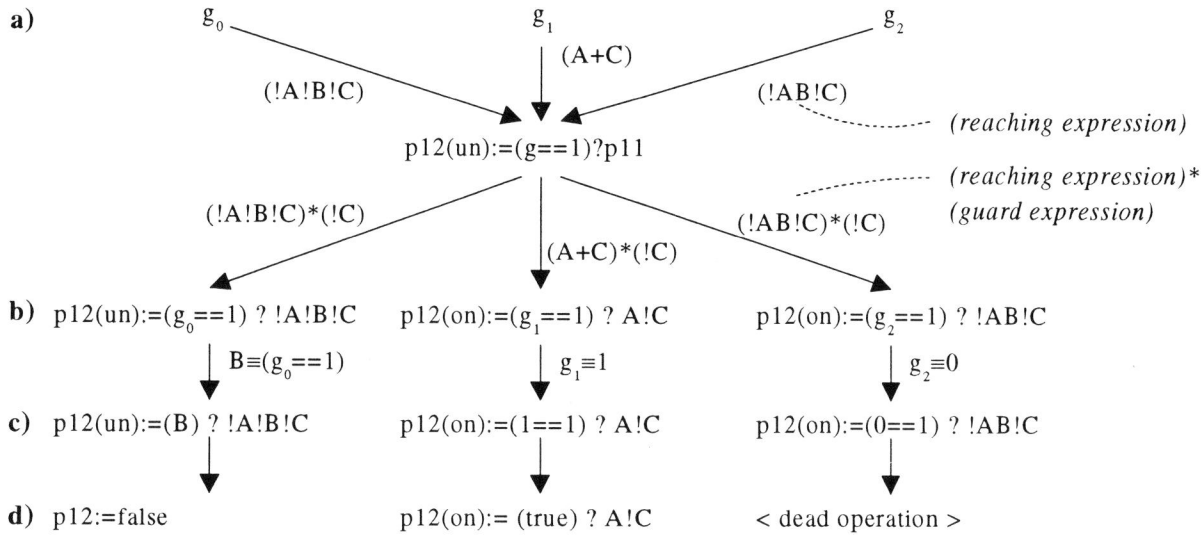

Figure 3. Replication and optimization for operation (8). a) Definitions of *g* that reach operation (8). b) Replicated operations with one instance per reaching definition in a). Replicated operation is predicated on the conjunction of the reaching definition expression and the guard expression of operation (8). c) Replicated operation after constant propagation of its symbolical definitions. d) Replicated operations after constant evaluation of the comparison.

operation is replicated to accommodate defs that reach the operation in renamed register, the replicated operation x is assigned uses u_x with $reg(u_x) \neq oreg(u_x)$. The above definitions are trivially extended to operations with different number of defs and uses.

We further define the expression under which a definition d_x reaches the current operation as $reach\_expr(d_x)$. Expressions are functions of boolean variables, where each boolean variable represents the test of one compare operation. Examples of boolean variables in Section 4.1 are A, B, and C which relate to test $(x ==' ')$, $(g_0==1)$, and $(y==' ')$, respectively. When manipulating expressions, summing is equivalent to oring, multiplying is equivalent to anding, and subtracting is equivalent to taking the difference. Actual expression manipulations are performed in this paper using the Binary Decision Diagrams [Bry86]. We also extend the notion of a reaching definition to registers: the expression under which a register r_x reaches the current operation is defined as $reach\_expr(r_x)$ and is equal to the sum of $reach\_expr(d_y)$ over all definitions d_y such that $reg(d_y) = r_x$. Finally, we let $guard\_expr(op)$ be the expression guarding the execution of *op*.

The algorithm that performs integrated path expansion and optimization is presented in Figure 4. It processes the current operation in three distinct phases. In the first phase, lines (2) through (10), it inspects the reaching definitions to determine whether to replicate the current op. While each operation of the introductory wc example of Section 4.1 used at most one register, the algorithm here handle operations with an arbitrary number of input registers.

In the second phase, lines (11) and (12), the algorithm attempts to simplify the current operation by performing constant propagation, copy propagation, constant folding, and common subexpression elimination. These optimizations are all forward optimizations, and thus fully benefit from any renaming that may have occurred while processing previous operations.

In the third phase, lines (13) through (21), the algorithm proceeds with renaming and analyzing the the side effect generated by the optimized version of the current operation. When the operation sets a predicate, it is analyzed as proposed by Johnson and Schlansker in [JS96] but using Binary Decision Diagrams as internal representation of the predicates and predicate expressions. This analysis is done on the fly since register renaming and optimizations affect the compared registers of predicate compare operations. We also build a predicate correlation database which we describe in more detail in Section 5. No reaching definition analysis is performed on predicate registers as it is done elsewhere [JS96]. For all other operations, the algorithm decides whether to perform register renaming and update the reaching definition expressions, one def at a time.

Some preprocessing is needed to properly handle live-in and live-out values. First, the live-in values are added into the initial reaching definitions under the expression true. Second, we must ensure that the live-out values are maintained in the presence of renaming. We do this by introducing dummy move operations guarded

```
(1)  process(op)
(2)      // phase 1: perform replication if needed
(3)      if op is an original operation then
(4)          for each distinct use of op: u_i do
(5)              rset(u_i) = {reg(d_j) | def d_j reaches u_i and oreg(d_j) = oreg(u_i)}
(6)          for each unique tuple (r_1,..., r_n) where r_1∈rset(u_1),...,r_n∈rset(u_n) do
(7)              expr = reach_expr(r_1)* ... *reach_expr(r_n)
(8)              if (expr*guard_expr(op) ≠ false) then
(9)                  replicate op with renamed uses (r_1,...,r_n) and guarded by expr*guard_expr(op)
(10)         if (replicated some operations) then remove original and return
(11)     // phase 2: apply optimizations on op
(12)     constant propagation, constant folding, common subexpression elimination,...
(13)     // phase 3: perform renaming, predicate analysis, and predicate reaching analysis
(14)     if (op is an operation that sets predicates) then
(15)         analyze op as in PQS [JS96]
(16)     else
(17)         for each def of op: d_i do
(18)             if (beneficial to rename d_i) then reg(d_i) = new reg name
(19)             expr = expr under which def d_i is generated by op
(20)             reach_expr(d_i) += expr
(21)             for each def d_j with oreg(d_i) = oreg(d_j) do reach_expr(d_j) -= expr
(22)     return

(23) tracenet_formation(hyperblock)
(24)     preprocess live-in and live-out
(25)     for each op of hyperblock in program order do process(op)
(26)     optimize live-out and perform speculation
(27)     return
```

Figure 4. Tracenet formation algorithm.

by the same predicate that guards the branch. For example, if variable *v* is live along branch *branch L1 ? p1*, we insert prior to the branch the dummy move operation *v:=v ? p1*. If the variable *v* is renamed while processing the hyperblock, the dummy move will be replicated once per renamed register of *v*. If *v* is renamed twice, as v_1 and v_2, we replicate the original dummy move into *v:=v_1?p1* and *v:=v_2?p1* which precisely gathers the values of variable *v* back into the live-out register. Note that such move operations introduce a one cycle latency penalty, but such copy operations can be removed during the post-processing phase by either performing back-copy propagation or some additional operation replication.

5. Optimization of predicate computation

In this section, we present our approach to minimizing predicate computations, focusing on how to minimize the boolean expressions that define the predicate values. Once the boolean expressions are minimized, the actual generation of predicate compare operations is performed as proposed by August et al. [Aug99] and will not be further discussed here. The extraction of explicit correlation is presented in Section 5.1, the formulating of global predicate invariant is shown in Section 5.2, the minimization of predicate expression using invariant is described in Section 5.3, and additional sources of correlation are explored in Section 5.4

5.1. Extraction of explicitly correlated predicate compares

The wc example in Figure 1 allowed one predicate compare operation to be eliminated from the final optimized code (i.e. test *D* fully correlated with expression *A!C*). In this section, we expand on how predicate correlation is extracted using a more typical example from the inner loop from compress, shown in Figure 5a. The code here is from the output function where a compressed code (variable *c*) is stored in consecutive bytes of an array (variable *a*), depending on the number of interesting bits of data (variable *b*).

While the two branches in Figure 5a are clearly correlated, this correlation is implicit since both branches use different versions of variable *b* (i.e. the first test uses the initial value of *b* and the second test uses a value of *b* which might have been decremented by 8). Because of the dependences from the first test to the decrement operation to the second test, a minimum of 4 cycles are needed to execute this code fragment.

We now show how path expansion enables us to extract explicit correlation from implicitly correlated code. The three operations that contribute to determining the control flow are illustrated in the left column of

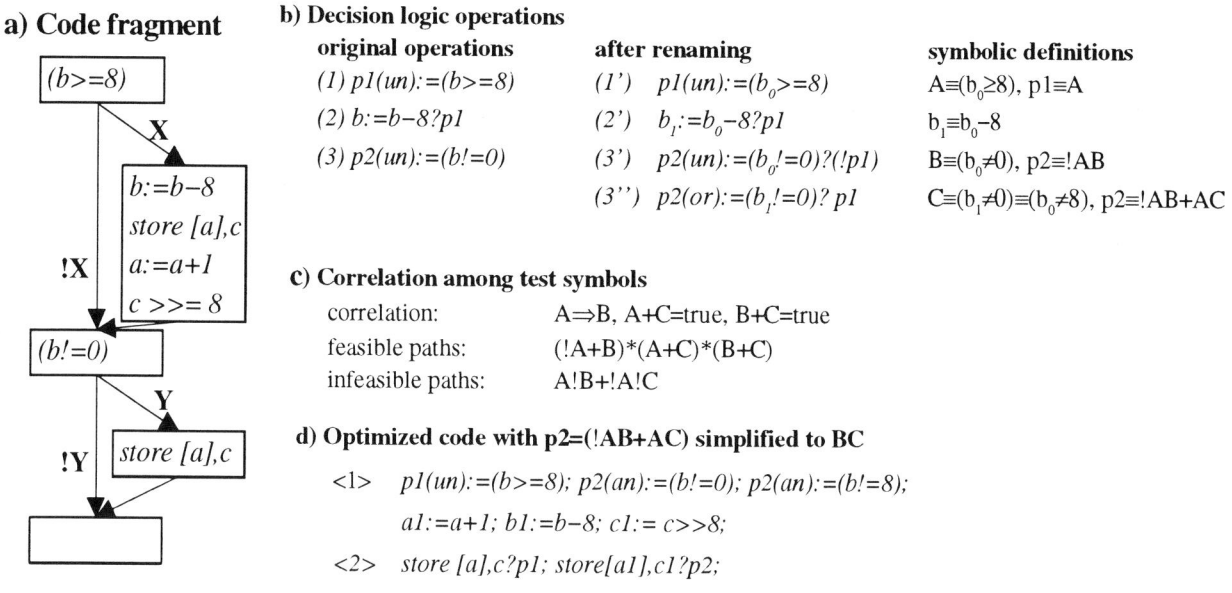

Figure 5. Fragment of the function output called in the inner loop of compress.

Figure 4b. The middle column of Figure 5b depicts the same operations after the renaming of the def register of operation (2) and the replicating of operation (3), with one instance using b_1 under predicate predicate $p1$ and another instance using b_0 under the complement of predicate $p1$. Consider now the symbolic definitions in the left column of Figure 5b. We extract from operation (1') and (3') the tests $A \equiv (b_0 \geq 8)$ and $B \equiv (b_0 \neq 0)$, respectively. We also extract from operation (3'') the test $(b_1 \neq 0)$, which can be rewritten as $C \equiv (b_0 \neq 8)$ by folding the definition $b_1 \equiv b_0 - 8$ into $(b_1 \neq 0)$. As a result, all three tests are a function of the same original value of b. This transforms two implicitly correlated tests into three explicitly correlated tests.

5.2. Gathering correlation data

We expand in this section on the type of correlation data that we gather, expanding on previous work [Aug99]. Consider operation x which uses register r_x and operation y which uses register r_y. We say that both operations *yield the same* value if both operations get the same reaching definitions under the same reaching definition expressions.

In our work, we correlate any two tests that satisfy one of the following criteria.

- Both operations compare one register to one constant, and both uses of their respective registers yield the same value.
- Both operations compare two registers, and the first use by the first operation yields the same value as one of the uses by the second operation and the second use by the first operation yields the same value as the other use by the second operation.

Relation	Logical invariant	Example 1		Example 2	
		test A	test B	test A	test B
A implies B	!A + B	$x > y$	$x \geq y$	$x > 3$	$x > 2$
A and B are a **partition**	$A \oplus B$	$x > y$	$x \leq y$	$x > 3$	$x \leq 3$
A and B are **disjoint**	!(AB)	$x > y$	$x = y$	$x = 3$	$x = 2$
A and B **cover_all**	A+B	$x \geq y$	$x \neq y$	$x > 3$	$x < 7$

Table 2. Four correlation types among tests (*x* and *y* yield the same value for both tests *A* and *B*).

When a pair of compare operations satisfies one of these criteria, the two operations are correlated and their correlation falls into one of the following four types: *imply, partition, disjoint,* and *cover_all*, as described in Table 2. "Imply" means that if the first test is true, the second test must be true; "partition" means that exactly one of the two tests must be true; "disjoint" means that at most one test can be true; "cover_all" means that at least one of the tests must be true.

In general, stronger correlations can be obtained by jointly considering relations of three or more tests. For example, every pair of the (x<y), (x=y), and (x>y) tests are disjoint, but they only form a partition when considering the three of them jointly. Such opportunities can be identified using the "families of comparisons" concept proposed by August et al [Aug99].

While each of the correlation types is useful in some context (e.g. partition and disjoint can eliminate false output dependence, cover_all can determine when a live range is killed, etc.), we use a more systematic representation of these relations. We compute an invariant expression that must be true regardless of the particular outcome of any tests. For example, "A implies B" is the same as stating that $!A+B$ is always true. The second column of Table 2 indicates the logical invariant associated with each of the four correlation types.

Consider our example in Figure 5. Given the $A \equiv (b_0 \geq 8)$, $B \equiv (b_0 \neq 0)$, and $C \equiv (b_0 \neq 8)$ symbolic definitions, we conclude that A implies B, A and C cover_all, and B and C cover_all. The logical invariants associated with the correlations between tests are $(!A+B)$, $(A+C)$, and $(B+C)$, respectively. Each relation must hold regardless of whether A, B, and C are true or false during one execution trace. Thus, we may compute the global invariant as the conjunction of each of the individual logical invariants, i.e. the global invariant is $(!A+B)*(A+C)*(B+C) = AB+!AC$ in Figure 5b.

5.3. Minimizing boolean expressions

To minimize boolean expressions, we proceed as follows. First, we gather all the correlation data and summarize the correlation in a global invariant, say i. In effect, invariant i describes all the feasible ways in which the logical variables representing the tests may be combined. When minimizing an expression f, we only need to compute this expression for the subset of expression f that does not contradict the invariant, i.e. we may minimize only the expression $f*i$.

Conversely, it is acceptable to include some of the infeasible logical variable combinations when minimizing an expression if they enable us to derive a simpler expression. Thus, we may treat the complement of the invariant, $!i$, as don't-cares while minimizing the $f*i$ expression.

For example in Figure 5b, the expression for predicate $p2$ is $(!AB+AC)$, which includes the terms $!AB!C$, $!ABC$, $A!BC$, and ABC. Both the $!AB!C$ and $A!BC$ terms do not intersect with the invariant $AB+!AC$ since the first term contradicts A and C cover_all, and the second term contradicts A implies B. Thus we can minimize the smaller $(!ABC + ABC)$ expression instead of the larger $(!AB+AC)$ expression. Using the complement of invariant $AB+!AC$ as don't-cares, minimizing the expression for $p2$ yields expression BC, which can be computed in one cycle. The final optimized code is shown in Figure 5d: in cycle 1, the predicates are computed and all but the store operations are speculatively executed; and in cycle 2, the two store operations are executed. This contrasts to the 4 cycles that are needed when the correlation between tests are left implicit.

5.4. Additional sources of correlation data and performance asserts

The more correlation data gathered, the more restrictive the global invariant is, and the more concise the minimized expressions will be. So far, correlation data was directly gathered from the tests in the predicate compare operations, but correlation data can be found elsewhere as well.

One source of correlation data is implicitly defined by branches. Consider a branch operation b and its guarding predicate p. Since the code below branch b is executed only if the branch is not taken, we can assume when minimizing predicates that are only used below branch b that the test defining predicate p must be false. Other types correlations may be gathered from the code. When identifying a boolean variable, we can use this information to strengthen correlation data (e.g. if b is a boolean variable, the correlation between tests $(b=0)$ and $(b=1)$ can be strengthened from disjoint to partition). A third source of correlation can be the programmer itself. Defensive programmers often use asserts in their code to catch programming errors. We can provide a similar construct, e.g. termed "passert" for performance assert, to convey more global, program wide invariant to the logic optimizer. Like traditional assert statements, which cause the program to stop when their asserted boolean expression is violated, "passert" statements convey a boolean expression that is guaranteed to be true, or else the correctness of the program becomes irrelevant.

6. Case study

We implemented our algorithms in the Trimaran System [Tri99]. We first added a Binary Decision Diagram [Bry86] predicate representation into the interface of the predicate query system [JS96] to handle complex predicates accurately. We then integrated a two level boolean expression minimization package, Espresso [Bra84], to minimize small expressions optimally and larger expressions heuristically. We also implemented a predicate code generation scheme similar to August et al [Aug99] to generate fast and compact predicate code from the optimized predicate expressions. Our algorithm then uses these components to expand and optimize the paths, simplify predicate expressions, and generate predicated code.

The baseline measurements are obtained by: (1) applying unrolling, traditional optimizations, hyperblock formation, and predicate promotion within Impact [Cha91]; (2) performing program decision logic minimization, scheduling (with speculative execution), and register allocation in Elcor [Rau98]; (3) by simulating the executable within the ReaCT_ILP cycle simulator. The tracenet measurements are obtained by inserting the proposed tracenet formation algorithm before the logic minimization step in Elcor.

machine width	benchmarks		
	wc	129.compress	130.li
16	1.200	1.073	1.087
32	1.500	1.077	1.087
64	1.599	1.077	1.087

Table 3. Dynamic cycle count speedup of tracenet over baseline

The dynamic cycle count speedups of tracenet versus baseline for the full version of wc, 129.compress and 130.li is shown in Table 3 for machines with varying numbers of fully-pipelined general-purpose functional units. Latencies are 1 cycle for ALUs, stores, and branches, 2 cycles for loads, 3 cycles for floats and integer multiplications, and 8 cycles for divisions. At most one branch is scheduled per cycle. Some dynamic effects such as branch mispredictions, cache and TLB misses are not measured to highlight more precisely the effect of the proposed optimizations.

The results indicate that tracenets reduces the number of dynamic cycles for wc, 129.compress, and 130.li by up to 59.9%, 7.7%, and 8.7%, respectively. Note that tracenets currently requires wide machines to achieve good speedup. Manual inspection of the optimized code indicates that some operation replication is not needed for height reduction. Such superfluous replication can be reduced by using a finer model where decisions concerning optimization and replication are made based on a cycle by cycle cost benefit analysis.

7. Conclusions

We have described the creation of tracenets, an extension of hyperblocks that contain a network of expanded traces. Interleaving path expansion with optimization aggressively reduces the length of the critical path and a detailed correlation model reduces the complexity of predicate computations. We are able to extract more implicit predicate correlations that were previously hidden by layers of interacting data and predicate computations. A case study indicates that tracenets can significantly reduce the number of dynamic cycles, e.g. up to 59.9% for wc, 7.7% for 129.compress and 8.7% for 130.li. Future work includes a finer resource and dependence model to guide optimization and renaming decisions during tracenet formations.

Acknowledgments

We thank B. Ramakrishna Rau and the Compiler and Architecture Research Group at HP Labs, Wen-mei W. Hwu and the IMPACT Research Group at the University of Illinois at Urbana-Champaign, and Krishna Palem and the ReaCT-ILP group at the New York University for making their research compiler available.

References

[AKP83] J.R. Allen, K. Kennedy, C. Porterfield, J. Warren. Conversion of control dependences to data dependences, *Conf. Record of POPL-10*, 1983.

[Aug99] D. August et al., The Program Decision Logic Approach to Predicated Execution, *Proc. of the 26th Intl. Symp. on Computer Architecture*, 1999.

[Bra84] R. Brayton et al., Logic Minimization Algorithms for VLSI Synthesis, Kluwer Acad. Pub., 1984.

[Bry86] R.E. Bryant. Graph-Based Algorithms for Boolean Function Manipulation, IEEE Transaction on Computers, C35(8), 1986.

[Car99] L. Carter et al., Predicated Static Single Assignment, in Proceedings of the International Conference on Parallel Architectures and Compilation Techniques, 1999.

[Cha91] P. Chang et al., IMPACT: An Architectural Framework for Multiple-Instruction-Issue Processors, *Proc. 18th Int'l Symp. Computer Architecture*, 1991.

[DT93] J. Dehnert and R. Towle. Compiling for the Cydra-5. *Journal of Supercomputing*, 7(1), 1993

[Fis81] J. Fisher, Trace scheduling: a technique for global microcode compaction, *IEEE Trans. on Comp.*, C-30:478-490, 1981.

[HD86] P. Y. T. Hsu and E. S. Davidson, Highly concurrent scalar processing, in *Proc. 13th Ann. Int'l Symp. Computer Architecture*, 1986.

[Hwu93] W. Hwu et al., The superblock: an effective technique for VLIW and superscalar compilation, *The Journal of Supercomputing*, 1993, 229-248.

[JS96] R. Johnson, M. Schlansker. Analysis techniques for predicated code. *Proc. 29th Ann. IEEE/ACM Intl. Symp. on Microarchitecture*, 1996.

[KSR94] V. Kathail, M. Schlansker, B. R. Rau, HPL PlayDoh Architecture Specification: Version 1.1, Computer Systems Laboratory, *Hewlett Packard Technical Report HPL-93-80(R.1)*, 2000.

[Ma92] S. Mahlke et al., Effective compiler support for predicated execution using the hyperblock, *Proc. of the 25th Intl Symp. on Microarchitecture (MICRO-25)*, pp. 45-54, 1992.

[Ma96] S. A. Mahlke, Exploiting Instruction Level Parallelism In the Presence of Conditional Branches, *Ph.D. Thesis, University of Illinois at Urbana-Champaign*, 1996.

[Rau98] B. R. Rau, V. Kathail, S. Aditya, Machine Description Driven Compilers for EPIC Processors, *Technical Report HPL-98-40, Hewlett-Packard Laboratories*, 1998.

[SMJ99] M. Schlansker, S. Mahlke, R. Johnson. Control CPR: A Branch Height Reduction Optimization For EPIC Architectures. *PLDI*, 1999.

[Tri99] The Trimaran System, www.trimaran.org, 1999.

Accurate and Efficient Predicate Analysis with Binary Decision Diagrams

John W. Sias Wen-mei W. Hwu
Center for Reliable and High-Performance Computing
Department of Electrical and Computer Engineering
University of Illinois
Urbana-Champaign, IL 61801
{sias, hwu}@crhc.uiuc.edu

David I. August
Department of Computer Science
Princeton University
Princeton, NJ 08544
august@cs.princeton.edu

Abstract

Functionality and performance of EPIC architectural features depend on extensive compiler support. Predication, one of these features, promises to reduce control flow overhead and to enhance optimization, provided that compilers can utilize it effectively. Previous work has established the need for accurate, direct predicate analysis and has demonstrated a few useful techniques, but has not provided an efficient, general framework. This paper presents the Predicate Analysis System (PAS), which maps knowledge of predicate and condition relations in general control flow onto a convenient logical substrate, the reduced ordered binary decision diagram. PAS is the first such framework to demonstrate direct, accurate, and efficient analysis of arbitrary condition and predicate define networks in arbitrary control flow.

1. Introduction

The success of EPIC architectures such as IA-64 [1] hinges on the ability of compilers to expose and express instruction-level parallelism. Predication, a key feature of such architectures, improves the efficiency of program control, allows co-execution of instructions from multiple paths, aids in efficient modulo scheduling, and enables other new optimizations. In the *predicated representation*, each operation possesses a Boolean source operand, its *guard predicate*, the value of which determines whether the instruction is executed or nullified. The values of predicates are manipulated by a set of predicate defining instructions. Although *if-conversion*, the process by which branching control is replaced with predicate defining instructions and predicates [2], is typically responsible for most instances of predication, it may also be introduced in hand-written assembly segments or by specialized optimizations (for example, the replacement of Boolean values, originally allocated to general-purpose registers, with predicates). Other work demonstrates the value of a predication-enabling compiler [3, 4, 5, 6, 7, 8].

As the first predicated compilation systems generated predication only by direct if-conversion, analysis systems that could only generate predicate relations from control flow or that could accurately analyze only the forms generated by if-conversion were adequate [5, 9]. Other systems were capable of analyzing arbitrary local use of predication, but relied on potentially expensive symbolic techniques [4]. Two important concerns, however, demand advances in predicate analysis. First, the introduction of predicate optimization techniques [10] and non-if-conversion use of predication pose accuracy, efficiency, and phase ordering problems for existing analysis systems. Second, post-link compilation and re-compilation technologies [11] require accurate analysis and transformation of arbitrary predication. The predicate analysis engine here described supports work in these new areas.

This work presents three chief contributions: First, this technique uses a general Boolean representation framework, the binary decision diagram (BDD), to accommodate arbitrary predicate formulations accurately and efficiently. Second, this mechanism supports analysis of general predication, including loop-carried predication; that is, it is not limited to predication produced by if-conversion. The system is also easily adaptable to new predicate define types, as have become necessary in predicate optimization work. Finally, this mechanism incorporates the analysis of condition relations (i.e. $(\texttt{r1} = 1) \rightarrow (\texttt{r1} > 0)$) into the same efficient framework, enabling both more extensive optimization of predication and the accurate analysis of optimized predicate networks.

2. Support for predicated compilation

The presented system was developed in the context of the IMPACT research compiler, a retargetable instruction-level parallel compiler used extensively in computer architecture research. The IMPACT low-level machine-independent internal representation, Lcode, and the compiler back-end fully incorporate predication. Generation of predicated code in the IMPACT compiler follows the progression shown in Figure 1. Appropriate regions of code are if-

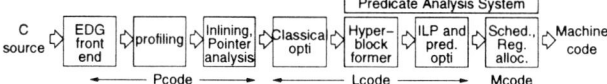

Figure 1: IMPACT predicated code generation path.

Table 1: IMPACT EPIC predicate deposit types.

p_g	C	ut	uf	ot	of	at	af	ct	cf	$\vee$t	$\vee$f	$\wedge$t	$\wedge$f
0	0	0	0	–	–	–	–	–	–	–	1	0	0
0	1	0	0	–	–	–	–	–	–	1	–	0	0
1	0	0	1	–	1	0	–	0	1	1	1	0	–
1	1	1	0	1	–	–	0	1	0	1	1	–	0

converted in the hyperblock formation phase [3]. Following if-conversion, classical optimizations are reapplied in concert with a full suite of ILP optimizations (unrolling, critical path reduction, etc.) and predicate optimizations [10]. Finally, machine-specific code is generated, scheduled, and register-allocated. In this model, the compiler back-end must be able to understand and to use predication effectively.

The IMPACT EPIC model of predication [7] generalizes Hewlett-Packard PD predication support [12] and subsumes IA-64 predication [1]. This model specifies a set of independent single-bit predicate registers, denoted pi, of which p0 is defined as holding the value 1. Each instruction is augmented with a guard predicate. The predicate defining instruction (p_{guard}) p_{dest}_type = src_0 cmp src_1 computes the condition $C = src_0$ cmp src_1 and optionally assigns a value to p_{dest}[1] according to type, C, and the guarding predicate p_{guard}, as shown in Table 1 (a "–" indicates that the destination register is unchanged). The IMPACT EPIC Architecture specifies six deposit types which dictate how the instruction updates its destination. The (U)nconditional, (O)r, (A)nd, and (C)onditional types are as defined in the HP Labs PlayDoh Specification [12] and, under different names, in the IA-64 architecture [1]. The disjunctive and conjunctive types ($\vee$ and $\wedge$) were developed for use in predicate optimization. Although simple if-conversion generates only unconditional and or-type defines with disjoint subexpressions [2], an effective predicate analysis system should support the other types which are useful in optimization of predicate define networks [10, 13] and modulo scheduling.

2.1. Role and scope of predicate analysis

In predicated codes, while the position of an instruction in the control flow graph specifies the *fetch condition* of an instruction, the actual *execution condition* is a function both of the fetch condition and of the guard predicate. A compiler must thus be modified to analyze code containing predication. For example, the traditional notion of instruction dominance "I_1 dom I_2 iff every fetch path from the unique entry node $START$ to I_2 includes I_1 [14]" (expressing fetch dominance, or *fdom*) must be replaced by, "I_1 edom I_2 iff I_1 fdom I_2 and $p_{I_1} \supseteq p_{I_2}$ (p_{I_1} is true whenever p_{I_2} is true)." Predicate analysis provides the compiler with answers to Boolean queries such as "Is $p_{I_1} \supseteq p_{I_2}$?"

As a simple example, Figure 2 shows two code segments which are considered for application of a constant propagation optimization. In Figure 2(a), constant propagation cannot be applied because instruction 2, the assignment to r3, does not dominate instruction 4, the assignment to r4. In Figure 2(c), however, the first definition dominates the second, so the optimization is valid. After if-conversion of (a) into (b) and (c) into (d), which does not alter program semantics, instruction 2 fetch-dominates instruction 4 in both cases. Predicate analysis allows the compiler to distinguish between a legal (d) and an illegal (b) optimization.

While the execution dominance relationship requires a subset query, other relationships such as equivalence, non-intersection, inverse, etc. are desirable for other purposes. The Predicate Analysis System answers these queries for the rest of the compiler. Dataflow analysis is perhaps the primary consumer of predicate relations. Other works [9] address using the predicate analysis results to formulate dataflow algorithms for use in predicated code.

Before considering the database mechanism, it is important to clarify the idea of relational scope. The simplest example that makes this clear is a single if-then-else construct placed in a loop, where the instructions in each side of the construct are controlled by either predicate p1 or predicate p2. These predicates are set as complements in each loop iteration, based on a varying condition. Are p1 and p2 mutually exclusive? When considering a single iteration of the loop, the answer is clearly "yes;" across iterations, however, the answer is "no." Depending on the application of the analysis, one answer or the other may be desired. Since this analysis is based on an single static assignment (SSA) representation (more specifically, gated SSA), we choose to represent the strictest relationships which hold as invariants among static instances of variables. In this example, the static definitions of p1 and p2 are always made together and are always opposite, so we treat them as mutually exclusive. This assertion renders the represented relations useful for instruction-level optimization and scheduling.

3. Previous mechanisms

Three general approaches to predicate analysis have been described previously in the literature, two of which apply to hyperblock code with restricted predicate define types. The first and simplest, the *Predicate Hierarchy Graph (PHG)*, was introduced with the IMPACT hyperblock compilation framework [3]. The PHG relates predicates by keeping

---

[1] In the IMPACT EPIC Predication model, two destination predicates, p_{dest1} and p_{dest2}, may be written in a single instruction using two independently selected semantics. To simplify discussion, predicate defines with two destinations are here conceptually split into two instructions.

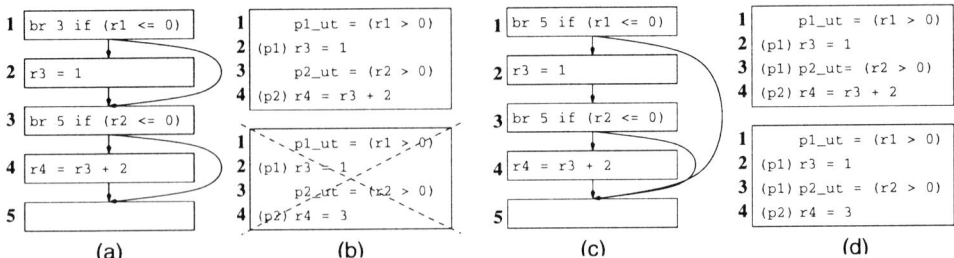

Figure 2: Constant propagation optimization in a predicated region.

track of which predicates guarded the definition of each predicate, or of each component term for OR-type expressions. The PHG thus understands only "genealogical" relationships, and is inaccurate when predicates do not fit neatly into a hierarchical graph. The PHG is unable to represent networks which contain and-type, conjunctive-type, and disjunctive-type predicate defines, precluding direct analysis of code generated by control height reduction optimizations such as those presented in [10] and [13].

A more sophisticated approach, the *Predicate Query System (PQS)* [9], exists within the Hewlett-Packard Elcor framework. The representational mechanism of PQS, the *partition graph*, can describe accurately only those predicate expressions which can be expressed as logical partitions. (p2 and p3 partition p1 iff p1=p2∪p3 and p2∩p3=∅.) This relation is generally satisfied only for unconditional predicate defines and for or-type predicate defines with disjoint terms. Thus, although PQS performs a direct analysis of assembly code containing predication, it can accurately represent only predication conforming to the style of if-conversion. Conservative approximations of relations among other define types have been used in practice; unfortunately, the mechanisms for coping with partition graph inaccuracy introduce the possibility of building for a given set of predicate defining instructions several different partition graphs with varying degrees of accuracy [5]. Thus, while PQS can accurately analyze the example of Figure 3(b) (disregarding condition information), it cannot accurately analyze Figure 3(c). The primary advantages of PAS over PQS, therefore, are its ability to perform fully accurate direct analysis of code utilizing any desired predicate defining semantics, and its ability to incorporate knowledge of condition relations into its logical database.

In the third approach, Eichenberger developed a predicate analysis mechanism for use in register-allocating predicated codes. His mechanism collected logical expressions, termed *P-facts*, which related predicates and, in some cases, related conditions. These *P-facts* were evaluated with respect to each other in a symbolic manipulation environment [4]. Eichenberger's results do not indicate the expense involved in applying this technique. For single-hyperblock analysis, this technique is functionally equivalent to the technique proposed in this paper, but in this work the BDD replaces the symbolic framework, demonstrating the same local accuracy at a low cost. Additionally, this work addresses issues involved in using predication in general control flow, while the techniques of [4] were limited to a single predicated block.

4. The Predicate Analysis System

PAS represents the relationships among predicates defined using the full complement of predicate define types, as well as relations derived from comparison conditions. The following section describes the mapping of conditions and the predicate define network to the underlying binary decision diagram (BDD). BDD naturally describe logical relations in, for example, combinational VLSI circuits; the contribution of PAS is an effective mapping of the predicate analysis problem to this efficient representation.

4.1. Reduced ordered binary decision diagrams

PAS expresses the relations among predicates by defining a set of interrelated Boolean functions. An efficient implementation requires an appropriate representation. In general, a Boolean function $f(x_0, x_1, \ldots, x_n)$ can be represented in a number of forms. The most familiar of these are conjunctive-normal form (sum-of-products or CNF) and disjunctive-normal form (product-of-sums or DNF) forms. Unfortunately, two operations important for predicate analysis, tautology on DNF and satisfiability on CNF, are NP-hard. A different form which is efficient both in tautology and satisfiability is the *if-then-else normal form* (INF) [15]. INF uses only the if-then-else (ITE) operator, where $ITE(x,y,z) \equiv (x \wedge y) \vee (\overline{x} \wedge z)$, to represent Boolean functions. Functions are expressed by recursive decomposition, in the form of a Shannon expansion, using the ITE operator:

$$f(x_0, \ldots, x_n) = x_n f(x_0, \ldots, x_{n-1}, 1) \vee \overline{x_n} f(x_0, \ldots, x_{n-1}, 0)$$
$$\Downarrow ITE(x, y, z) = xy \vee \overline{x}z$$
$$f(x_0, \ldots, x_n) = ITE(x_n, f_1(x_0, \ldots, x_{n-1}), f_0(x_0, \ldots, x_{n-1}))$$

Here, considering the common graph representation, two sub-BDD, f_1 and f_0, are connected as the then- and else-decisions of an ITE node labeled with the variable x_n, and the function f is represented by a reference to this decision node. The whole graph is rooted with the logical constants

0 and 1. A system of INF expressions in which all equal subexpressions are shared is termed a *binary decision diagram* (BDD). A BDD in which all identical *ITE* nodes are shared, in which variables appear in the same order and at most once in any path from root to leaf, and in which no redundant tests are performed is termed a *reduced ordered binary decision diagram* (ROBDD). Such BDD are canonical: each derivation of a particular Boolean function arrives at the same graph representation; that is, any two equal expressions share the same subtree. Certain queries are thus vastly simplified; for example, it is possible to test if two given functions are identical or opposite in constant time. This is useful especially for testing if a function evaluates to the constant 0 or the constant 1. Much work has been done in the development of efficient ROBDD implementations, mostly intended for use in the domain of Boolean logic circuit optimization [15]. BDD have also been applied in software problems, usually in the verification domain.

PAS uses the Colorado University Decision Diagram (CUDD) implementation of ROBDD [16]. CUDD implements "invert" arcs, which can be used instead of "else" arcs to implement the construct:

$$f(x_0, \ldots, x_n) = x_n f_1(x_0, \ldots, x_{n-1}) \vee \overline{x_n f_0(x_0, \ldots, x_{n-1})}$$

Here we observe the same recursive formulation as before, but the formula inverts an existing subgraph (f_0) for use as a subexpression of f without making additional nodes. Represented by an "invert" arc in the graph, this extension allows for constant-time inversion and avoids the addition of extra internal nodes when the complement of an existing subgraph is required. Now only the constant 1 is provided; evaluations to 0 are made via invert-arcs. CUDD ensures canonicity and the optimal reuse of subexpressions by imposing rules on the use of invert-arcs and by using a node hashing table called the *computed-table*, respectively.

Initially, the BDD consists only of the node 1. An interface exists to add new variables to the BDD, each of which is created as a single *ITE* node with a then-arc and an invert-arc to 1. The order of variable definition determines the subsequent order of the variables from root to leaf in each expression path. The BDD is built using the function `ite(f,g,h)`, which builds a subgraph to compute $ITE(f, g, h)$. The function checks to see if the requested node is a terminal case (a constant) or, through a hash, if it already exists in the graph; if so, it is returned immediately. If not, the topmost variable x_t of the existing functions f, g, and h is extracted, and then- and else- sub-BDD are computed (using recursive calls to `ite` which assume $x_t = 1$ and $x_t = 0$, respectively). A new node containing x_t is formed, and the sub-BDD are connected to it, forming the requested function. The `ite` function automatically maintains graph canonicity [17] and operates in time proportional to the size of the resulting function graph.

4.2. Mapping predicate defines to the BDD

Figure 3 shows an example of BDD construction consisting of a single hyperblock. The source code in (a) is translated to the intermediate representation, if-converted and scheduled in (b). Solid lines in the figure indicate the break between cycles in the schedule. Here, predicate analysis informs the scheduler, for example, that the predicates on statements B (p4) and C (p2) are mutually exclusive; thus these instructions may be reordered freely. Although this is obvious in the original control flow graph, the CFG is either lost during if-conversion or may not be available if code is input in a predicated form—hence the need for predicate analysis. Since the logical relations among predicates change infrequently during the compilation process, an efficient approach is to engage in a possibly expensive analysis phase during which a database of relations is built, and from which results may be obtained rapidly.

The code is next subjected to predicate optimization and rescheduled using a predicate analysis of the type described here (Figure 3(c)). One optimization removes the guard predicate on the define that computes p4. This is legal because the logical expression of the predicate guard p3, (r1>-8 && r1<8), is implied by the condition on the instruction, (r1=0). Since the unconditional type define computes the conjunction of the guard with the condition, the guard may safely be eliminated. Like more sophisticated optimizations, this has an effect on the ability of future predicate analyses to determine the relation of predicates p2 and p4. In (b), derivation of predicate expressions alone demonstrates that p4 ∩ p2 = ∅. In (c), however, the predicate analysis needs to examine relations among conditions themselves (and ones more complex than simple recognition of opposites) to reach the same proper conclusion. The following shows how the BDD is constructed to support this analysis.

4.3. Construction of the condition layer

The first step of finding relations among predicates is the definition of relations among condition evaluations. In PAS, these relations are represented together with predicate information in the BDD by providing a set of *condition nodes* [18]. PAS incorporates arbitrary relations within families of conditions based on comparing the same register values, representing, for example, the exclusivity of (r1=1) and (r1=2) while indicating that both are subsets of (r1>0). A family is initially represented as a single interval containing all representable numbers. For each condition that depends on the same register value, the number line is split at the boundaries of the intervals of numbers yielding an evaluation to "true." The number line in Figure 4(a) represents the condition family of r1 in Figure 3. The set of values causing any condition to evaluate to "true" is represented as the union of disjoint intervals. The rela-

```
if (x > -8 && x < 8) {
   stmtA;
   if (x == 0)
      stmtB;
}
else {
   stmtC;
   if (x < 0)
      stmtD;
}
```

(a)

```
             p2_uf = (0=0)
      p1_ut,p2_of = (r1>-8)
(p1)  p3_ut,p2_of = (r1<8)
(p3)  p4_ut = (r1=0)
(p2)  p5_ut = (r1<0)
(p3)  stmtA
(p2)  stmtC
(p4)  stmtB
(p5)  stmtD
```

(b)

```
      p1_ut,p2_uf = (0=0)
      p1_at,p2_of = (r1>-8)
      p1_at,p2_of = (r1<8)
      p4_ut = (r1=0)
      p5_ut = (r1<=-8)
(p1)  stmtA
(p4)  stmtB
(p2)  stmtC
(p5)  stmtD
```

(c)

Figure 3: An example hyperblock: (a) source, (b) if-converted, (c) optimized.

tions among all possible outcomes on this family are represented in the BDD by creating a Boolean space, known as a *finite domain* [19], and assigning all intervals to mutually exclusive and collectively exhaustive expressions. The expressions must be mutually exclusive, as a value can belong to only one interval at a time, and also collectively exhaustive, so that an expression such as "(x>5) || (x<=5)" is recognized as always true.

Figures 4(a) through (d) show the construction of the condition layer for the conditions of Figure 3(c). In this case, the conditions divide the number line into five discrete segments, broken between -8 and -7, -1 and 0, 0 and 1, and 7 and 8. The finite domain technique is applied, using $\lceil \log_2(5) \rceil = 3$ BDD variables to create an eight-element Boolean space $\{(v_2, v_1, v_0) \in (0|1)^3\}$. Since this case requires exactly five elements, we merge the three extra elements to neighbors, forming three two-variable expressions and two three-variable expressions which implement the finite domain. In general, representing i intervals adds $n = \lceil \log_2(i) \rceil$ variables, and generates $2^n - i$ expressions in $n - 1$ variables and $2i - 2^n$ expressions in n variables. This procedure creates the simplest possible finite domain structure for the given number of elements. In the resulting BDD, shown in (a), a segment of the number line is represented by a BDD node; for example, I_0 represents the expression $\overline{v_1}\,\overline{v_0}$ and thus has the equivalent (canonical) BDD expression $\overline{ITE(v_1, 1, ITE(v_0, 1, \overline{1}))}$ as shown. In this and all BDD expressions, the basis variables appear in a fixed order in all paths from root to leaf. The rest of the expressions represented in the BDD are shown in (b), along with a Karnaugh map showing the expressions to be mutually exclusive of each other and collectively exhaustive of the Boolean 3-space, as desired.

Applying the interval composition of the conditions (c), the interval nodes are used together with the ITE operator to compose the condition nodes shown in Figure 4(d). A condition, such as (r1<8), is represented by the disjunction of the interval nodes which represent the set of values resulting in an evaluation to 1. Considering the condition C_0, (r1>-8), we see that $C_0 = I_1 + I_2 + I_3 + I_4$. Thus, $C_0 = v_1'v_0 + v_1 v_0' + v_2' v_1 v_0 + v_2 v_1 v_0 = v_0 + v_1$, represented in the BDD as $ITE(v_1, 1, ITE(v_0, 1, \overline{1}))$. As shown in Figure 4(d), this simplified expression is computed automatically in the BDD as the disjunction representing C_0 is formed, one ITE at a time. At this stage, all relationships among conditions in a family are represented. For example, the expressions for C_0 (r1>-8), $v_0 + v_1$, and C_2 (r1=0), $v_1 v_0'$, show that C_2 implies C_0. This process is described in detail in [18].

4.4. Construction of the predicate layer

The mapping of predicate defines to the BDD is somewhat more straightforward than the mapping of conditions. Consider the acyclic-rendered control flow graph in which all predicates have been given SSA subscripts (as in PQS), and in which all predicate uses are constrained to have a single forward-control-flow-reaching definition (i.e. there exist no predicate ϕ functions). In this form, predicates may not be live around backedges and no predicate use may see definitions from different blocks. The predicate graph is thus constructed in a single topological traversal of the control flow graph by adding at each predicate define a new expression according to Table 2. In the table, $x\,?\,y:z \equiv ITE(x, y, z)$ and $n_{i.j}$ represents the BDD node associated with the predicate p$i.j$ (j represents the SSA subscript). As indicated in the table, a new subgraph representing the defined predicate is generated from previously generated subgraphs representing the predicate source, the previous value of the predicate destination, and the condition. The stated forward-flow constraint guarantees that these expressions are available when they are required.

Returning to the example of Figure 3, we construct the corresponding local relation BDD. A BDD expression has already been defined for each condition used in the generation of predicates, as shown in Figure 4(d). In the following topological traversal, predicate define instruction semantics are applied to generate the form shown in Figure 4(f), which expresses the relations among all predicate definitions. Consider the derivation of the predicate p2. The first assignment (with SSA name p2.0) is an initialization to 0. Thus p2.0 is attached via an invert-arc to 1, as

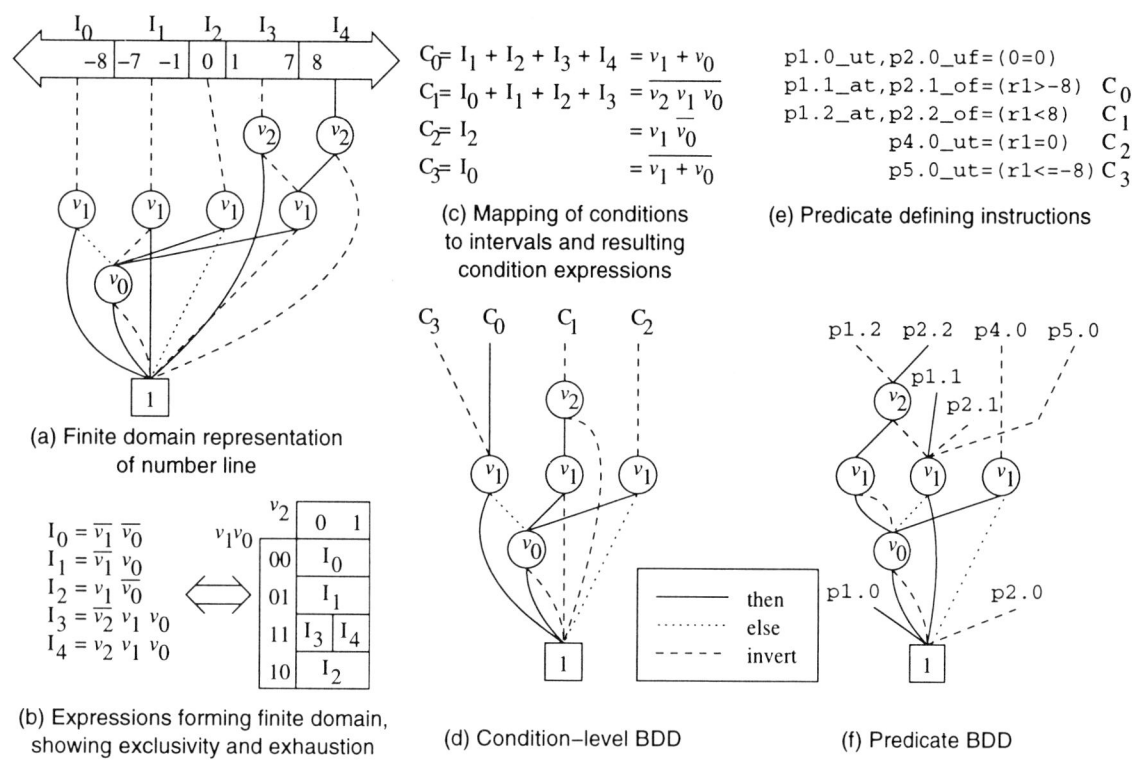

Figure 4: Assembly of Predicate BDD for the example of Figure 3(c).

Table 2: Predicate deposit logic.

SSA pred. def.	ITE Expression
(p_g) $pi.j\_\text{ut} = C$	$n_{i.j} = C?n_g : 0$
(p_g) $pi.j\_\text{uf} = C$	$n_{i.j} = C?0 : n_g$
(p_g) $pi.j\_\text{ot} = C$	$n_{i.j} = C?(n_g?1 : n_{i.j-1}) : n_{i.j-1}$
(p_g) $pi.j\_\text{of} = C$	$n_{i.j} = C?n_{i.j-1} : (n_g?1 : n_{i.j-1})$
(p_g) $pi.j\_\text{at} = C$	$n_{i.j} = n_g?(C?n_{i.j-1} : 0) : n_{i.j-1}$
(p_g) $pi.j\_\text{af} = C$	$n_{i.j} = n_g?(C?0 : n_{i.j-1}) : n_{i.j-1}$
(p_g) $pi.j\_\text{ct} = C$	$n_{i.j} = C?n_g : n_{i.j-1}$
(p_g) $pi.j\_\text{cf} = C$	$n_{i.j} = C?n_{i.j-1} : n_g$
(p_g) $pi.j\_\lor\text{t} = C$	$n_{i.j} = C?1 : (n_g?1 : n_{i.j-1})$
(p_g) $pi.j\_\lor\text{f} = C$	$n_{i.j} = C?(n_g?1 : n_{i.j-1}) : 1$
(p_g) $pi.j\_\land\text{t} = C$	$n_{i.j} = n_g?(C?n_{i.j-1} : 0) : 0$
(p_g) $pi.j\_\land\text{f} = C$	$n_{i.j} = n_g?(C?0 : n_{i.j-1}) : 0$

shown. p2.1 is an or-false-type definition with a constant-true guard predicate and condition C_0. Consulting Table 2, p2.1=$\overline{C_0}$?p2.0:(1?1:p2.0). Since p2.0=0, this degenerate case results in p2.1 being attached via an "invert" arc to the same node as C_0. Finally, by the or-false expression as before, p2.2=$\overline{C_1}$?p2.1:(1?1:p2.1). The two ite calls used in composing this expression compute the node indicated for p2.2. Figure 4(f) shows the BDD after excess condition nodes are freed (once all predicates are computed); thus nodes such as those for C_1 no longer exist in the graph. The CUDD BDD package employs reference counting to ensure that such nodes are removed when no longer required. In a more complex example based on multiple comparison families, several initially independent condition BDD (based on different variables) would be rooted on the same '1' node. During predicate define processing, graphs would be composed of members of the various subtrees, effectively unifying them into one predicate BDD. The resulting BDD expresses relations among all conditions and predicates.

4.5. Handling of general predicate liveness

To simplify discussion, only the analysis of forward-flow, single-definition predication was considered. While this is sufficient for code generated by direct if-conversion, various transformations subsequent to if-conversion, such as hyperblock loop rotation, or other applications of predication can result in more complex forms. This work generalizes predicate analysis to include the remaining forward-flow, multiple-definition and cyclic flow forms. This taxonomy is illustrated in Figure 5. "Forward-multiple" extends upon "forward-single" by allowing control flow merges in the forward acyclic control flow subgraph, and "cyclic" extends further to include flow around loop backedges.

Multiple-definition form. When multiple distinct definitions from different locations in the flow graph reach a given predicate use, the original ϕ-less representation is insufficient. Simply adding ϕ functions and treating these as writes of an unknown value provides a conservative result. Accuracy demands that reaching values be correlated with their paths of origin in a canonical logical value merge.

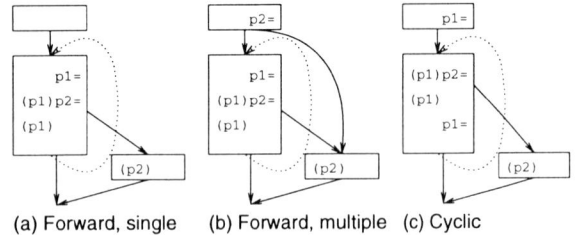

(a) Forward, single (b) Forward, multiple (c) Cyclic

Figure 5: Predicate flow forms.

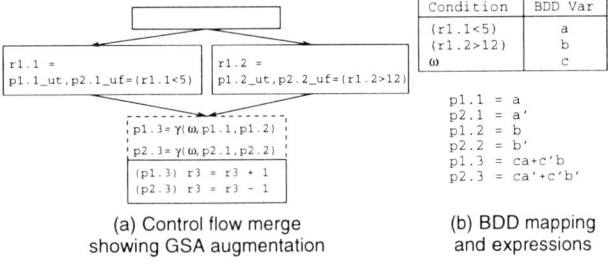

(a) Control flow merge showing GSA augmentation

(b) BDD mapping and expressions

Figure 6: Handling of a control flow merge.

herently acyclic regions [3]). Subsequent transformations, however, may generate flow around backedges. For example, a hyperblock loop may be rotated (as in Figure 5(a) and (c)) to achieve a better instruction schedule, or a Boolean flag initially coded as a variable in a loop by a programmer may be allocated a predicate instead. This transformation, like modulo scheduling, creates predicates whose live ranges cross a backedge.[2] If transformations such as these are to be allowed, a predicate analysis system should be able to accommodate them as well.

In the acyclic case, a topological traversal of the control flow graph ensures that functions needed in predicate definitions are defined at the point of reference, but this no longer holds in the presence of loop-carried dependence. A simple approximation, however, captures relations generated across an arbitrary number of previous iterations of a loop body. In the case of a modulo scheduled loop, this might be equal to the number of modulo stages. In arbitrarily transformed code, this might be some more arbitrary limit, perhaps one previous iteration. We present an extension which allows the BDD form to represent relations that happen to cross loop backedges.

The BDD can be thought of as an efficient symbolic manipulation engine, in which variables allocated to represent unknown inputs can later be rendered irrelevant by further manipulation of expressions or can be used to correlate other values, as in the previous example. We use these properties, combined with μ semantics from GSA, to manage cyclic dependence. The μ function is a special γ function for use at the loop header, at which the analysis must differentiate values from the preheader and the backedge. In $v_{def} = \mu(\omega, v_{\text{preheader}}, v_{\text{backedge}})$ the symbolic variable ω selects either of the two values based on whether execution has come from the preheader or from the loop backedge. While analysis of a use inside the loop body cannot (usually) bind ω to a known logical expression, it can use ω to express useful relations among variables (predicates and registers used in comparisons) that may appear to differ between the first and subsequent loop iterations. The values appearing to the μ function flow along one of two arcs, either from the preheader or from a previous iteration of the loop. Constraints imposed by the effects of a previous iteration on the relations of values flowing around the backedge are expressed in the BDD through a technique called *virtual unrolling*.

As an example, Figure 7(a) shows a loop with a predicate dependence around the backedge. In this case, the loop has been rotated, pushing a define around the backedge and a corresponding initialization into the loop preheader. Clearly, the uses of p1 and p2 are always mutually ex-

Such a merge can be expressed using gated SSA (GSA), a popular representation in parallelizing compilers [20]. Here, gated ϕ functions (γ functions) are inserted for all merges of predicate value. GSA γ functions are of the form $d_3 = \gamma(\omega, d_1, d_2)$, where ω is a logical variable that selects from among the reaching definitions. This is easily incorporated into PAS by treating γ as a new predicate definition type, with the ite expression $n_{d_3} = n_\omega?n_{d_2}:n_{d_1}$. The ω BDD functions can be derived either from the control dependences of surrounding control flow or in a variety of simpler and less expensive ways. Since in this form flow around backedges is still prohibited, a single topological traversal of the acyclic-rendered graph is sufficient to compute the proper graph. Furthermore, control relations need only be encoded to relate those paths which traverse merges of predicate value. Figure 6 shows an example, in which two different sets of definitions for p1 and p2 reach the uses in the bottom block. In this case, however, the predicates are identically related in both cases (always opposites), although the two definitions of each predicate are unrelated. Augmentation of the code for GSA form is shown in the dashed box and with the arrows indicating addition of SSA subscripts. BDD nodes are built for the defines and the γ functions as described; Figure 6(b) shows the resulting BDD expressions. Since the same variable guards both the γ functions, the BDD correctly "correlates" the two pairs of definitions, and the fact that p1 and p2 are always opposites in the bottom block is captured.

Cyclic flow. Only one extension remains: the treatment of predicate value flow around backedges in the control flow graph. Previous approaches, assuming an intra-hyperblock scope, did not require such support (hyperblocks are in-

---

[2]Kernel-only modulo scheduling of a hyperblock loop is actually a simpler special case, in which no cyclic techniques are *required*. They are, however, *applicable*.

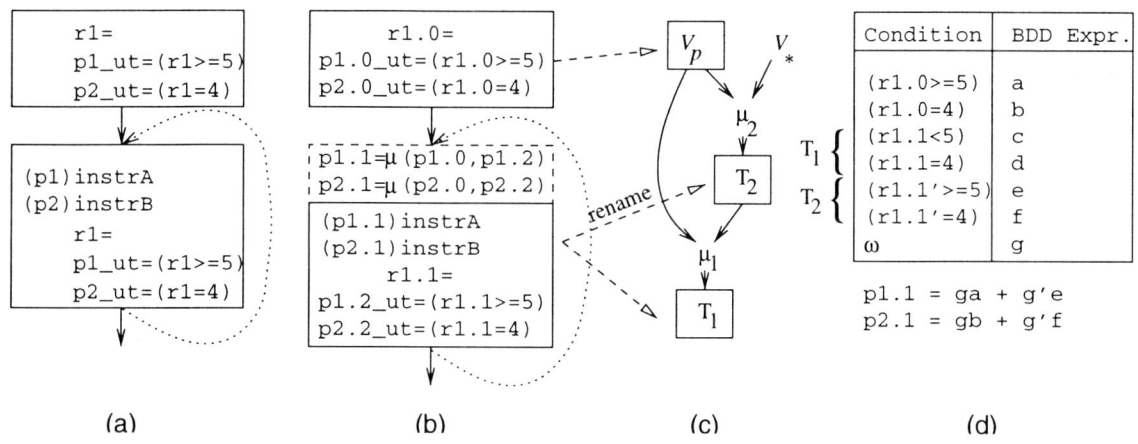

Figure 7: Cyclic predicate flow example.

clusive. Figure 7(b) shows the loop in SSA form. The μ functions share a common free variable ω, as did the γ functions. Suppose we know *a priori* that we can capture all desired relations with one iteration of "look-back" (this will shortly be generalized). When the loop header is encountered, we generate the following (Figure 7(c)): For each predicate pi live in from the backedge, we generate a free variable which we will denote pi^*. These are the predicates annotated in the μ functions; the pi^* versions represent the loop-carried values at the start of the *previous* iteration, about which we know nothing. In Figure 7(c), $V_p = \{\text{p1.0}, \text{p2.0}\}$ and $V_* = \{\text{p1.2}^*, \text{p2.2}^*\}$ denote the sets of values flowing from the loop preheader and from previous iterations, respectively. Now, reasoning that any flow though the backedge must have come through a previous iteration of the loop body, the loop body is "virtually unrolled" and variables are renamed (including ω) as necessary to preserve SSA, creating the copy T_2 (T implies the notion of "transfer function"). The connection among the original loop body (T_1), T_2, and the μ functions is shown in (c). This copy is then processed as normal, generating BDD nodes representing the values flowing from the backedge into the original loop body T_1. These values capture the past iteration's relational information. At this point, both definitions reaching each original μ are available, and the relation graph for the real loop body can easily be computed. Once T_1 is processed, all node handles internal to T_2 are freed, and the garbage collector removes all unnecessary information, as before. In this simple example, since both predicates are unconditionally redefined in each loop iteration, the backedge expressions at μ_1 no longer depend on the free variables pi^*, and the true relations between p1 and p2 are expressed. Figure 7(d) shows the expressions for the predicates of interest; given the exclusivity of a and b and the exclusivity of e and f, encoded in the condition information, p1 and p2 can clearly be identified by the BDD as disjoint. Note that this is the case even though the expressions depend on conditions from a previous iteration (as indicated by the presence of variables related to r1.1').

Virtual unrolling can be performed an arbitrary number of times, depending on the number of iterations of correlation that are required. This could continue until, for example, all pi^* are eliminated from predicate expressions or until some bound is reached. Note that the bound is necessary, since there exist true cyclic dependences for which no amount of look-back will eliminate the pi^*s. This would occur, for example, in a loop containing a predicated or-type predicate define with an initialization outside the loop. (The accurate handling of such recurrences poses a perhaps interesting analysis problem, but lies beyond the scope of this work.) The presence of pi^* variables in an expression, however, does not necessarily preclude determination of logical relations among expressions. Just as the ω variables whose values are not correlated to other variables in the BDD, these free variables serve to "partition the unknown" and to correlate other subexpressions in useful ways.

Figure 8 shows a case in which both predicates and conditions must be treated as live around the backedge. The original code is shown in (a); the effects of virtual unrolling are indicated in (b). After virtual unrolling, the assignment to p2.0 relies on a variable, r1.1, which is given by $\mu(\omega, \text{r1.0}, \text{r1.2}')$; that is, the value used in definition may come from a previous iteration. This is handled in the BDD by taking the two possible condition nodes for r1.1>32, $a = $ r1.0>32 and $b = $ r1.2'>32, and connecting them using the normal semantics for a μ function. The node for p2.0 therefore contains the expression $\omega a + \overline{\omega} b$. On the other hand, p1.1 is the μ merge of two definitions, p1.0 and p1.2'. Supposing $c = $ r1.0<10 and $d = $ r1.2'<10, the expression for p1.1 is $\omega c + \overline{\omega} d$. Here, a and c share a condition family and are disjoint; likewise for b and d. Since the ω variable properly correlates these definitions, p1.1 and p2.0 are correctly recognized by the BDD as disjoint.

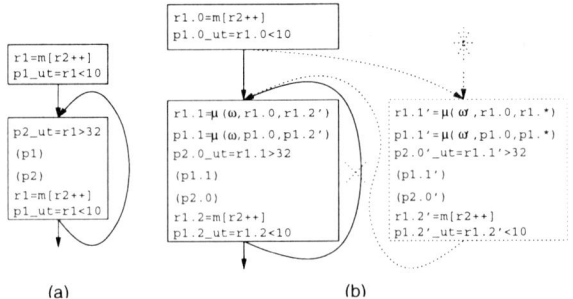

Figure 8: Virtual unrolling. Dotted lines and prime (') marks denote conceptual modifications.

The techniques presented are capable of faithfully representing relations among predicates in the assumed SSA model. The remainder of the paper discusses, first, how the resulting BDD is queried to produce useful results and, second, the efficiency of the approach.

5. Predicate relationship query interface

Following construction of the predicate BDD, PAS provides a query interface for compiler routines to abstract away the details of the BDD implementation. In the IMPACT infrastructure, predicate register operands are tagged with an SSA equivalent that contains a pointer to the representative BDD node. Queries include unary (identity to 1 or 0), binary (subset, intersection, etc.), and multi-predicate (does the disjunction of these predicates subsume another?) functions which reference appropriate nodes in the BDD. Such queries are used to determine, for example, if a predicate is constant-true or constant-false, if dependences should be drawn between two predicated instructions in scheduling, or if code at the end of a block is dead because the expressions for side exit predicates sum to 1.

BDD canonicity guarantees that predicates which are same or opposite are trivially recognized as such (i.e. p1.2 and p2.2 from Figure 4(f)). Other queries are composed using the `ite` function with which the predicate BDD was constructed. For example, the query, "Is p3 a subset of p1.2?" is solved in the BDD by computing q = ite(p3,!p1.2,0) and determining if q = 0, since p3 $\subseteq$ p1.2 if and only the intersection of p3 with the complement of p1.2 is empty. Similar `ite` constructions provide the other query functions. CUDD prevents the accumulation of nodes from retired queries by performing reference counting garbage collection, and employs dynamic programming techniques to eliminate redundant query computations [16].

6. Performance of the PAS

Like all canonical representations of Boolean functions, ROBDD are provably exponential in the worst case. As described earlier, the canonicity of the ROBDD requires a

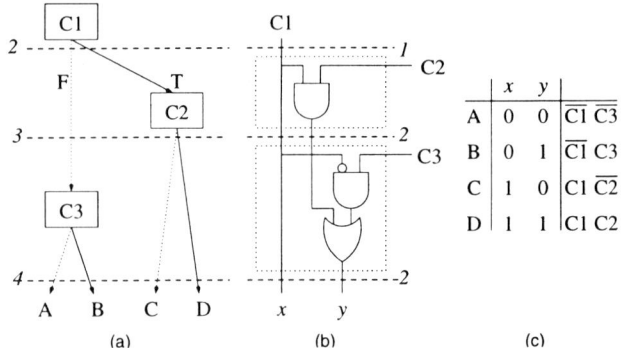

Figure 9: A control flow graph (a), its equivalent circuit (b), and a truth table representing the trajectory.

single fixed ordering of its constituent variables. This ordering has a significant impact on the size of the resulting ROBDD, and many methods of finding the optimal variable ordering for ROBDD have been proposed for various circuits [21, 22]. Unfortunately, variable reordering cannot prevent the representation of some circuits, such as multipliers, from growing exponentially with circuit size [19]. This was a serious point of concern for compiler writers wishing to use a BDD. The following discussion, targeted at this particular application, shows that in the theoretical limit only one very manageable factor leads to exponential growth of the BDD. Furthermore, empirical results are given to demonstrate that this term is not in practice a significant concern.

6.1. Space and Time Complexity of PAS

Since most predication begins as control flow, it follows that the size of the BDD should be related to the complexity of the control flow it replaces. Properties of real programs thus limit the size of the analysis BDD. First, consider using the BDD to represent a control flow graph (CFG). Figure 9 shows a control flow graph and its derived circuit to be represented by the BDD for analysis. Any slice in a topographically sorted control flow graph (with backedges removed) cuts one or more control flow arcs. The relationships among these arcs in such a slice can be represented by the variables of a corresponding slice in an equivalent circuit. For example, in Figure 9, the relationship of the arcs A, B, C, and D can be represented by the two variables x and y, in a manner illustrated by the truth table. Each arc in a slice represents a mutually exclusive execution condition; only one edge in the slice may be selected for each traversal of the graph. Also, at least one arc must be traversed which makes each slice collectively exhaustive with respect to traversals. These properties allow representation by a truth table in which each arc is given one or more rows to cover all rows (collective exhaustion) and in which each row belongs to one and only one arc (mutual exclusion). In our example, A is represented by $(x, y) = (0, 0)$, B by $(0, 1)$, C by $(1, 0)$, and D by $(1, 1)$. The variables x and y have no particular individual meaning, but together encode all possible relationships. As in the finite domain technique, we need no more than $O(\log_2 i)$ variables to represent the arc outcomes for a slice (or the rows in the truth table), where i is the number of arcs in the CFG slice.

The worst-case size of a ROBDD for some ordering is $O(nm2^W)$, where n is the number of input variables, m is the number of output variables, and W is the maximum width of all slices in the circuit being represented [23]. (A fully expanded decision tree for a Boolean function has $O(2^n)$ nodes. At each slice, the BDD can be split into two parts with the first part having W output variables and the second part having W input variables. BDD are at worst a fully expanded decision tree, so the size of the second BDD is $O(2^W)$.) The following discussion will consider the 2^W term as the rest is polynomial.

The exponential term in the size of the ROBDD representing any CFG is 2^W, but W is the maximum of all $O(\log_2 i)$. Therefore, the exponential term becomes $O(2^{\log_2 I})$ or $O(I)$, where I is the maximum control flow graph slice, in the worst case using the ordering provided by the control flow graph. This result is intuitive since the ROBDD and the program's control flow graph both represent the equivalent relations using the ITE structures.

Now, we relate this polynomial upper bound for representing control flow graphs in ROBDD to representing predicated codes. The function computed by the predicate network of a program is identical to the function computed by the control flow graph. The property of canonicity requires that the BDD representing this function is unaffected by the manner in which it is constructed (assuming fixed condition ordering). All predicate networks computing this function are polynomial in the worst case using the ordering provided by the topological sort of the control flow graph.

Loss of the control flow graph does not preclude derivation of an ordering yielding a polynomially-sized BDD. A general method is to apply a register allocation algorithm to the BDD [23]. Other methods such as sifting provide fast and relatively accurate approximations [24]. Alternatively, the compiler could record the order of the conditions before if-conversion. (Note that this is not the same as recording the full CFG.) In practice, the order of the conditions as appearing in even aggressively predicated codes tend to yield good results since in the aggregate a good correspondence exists to the original condition orderings.

The size of the analysis BDD is also influenced by the inclusion of condition relations, which, as we have seen, create fairly full subtrees at a low level of the BDD. Define, as before, *condition family* as the set of conditions whose results are mutually related (non-independent). Define the *live-range* of a condition family in the variable ordering to start at the first condition and end at the last condition in the family. To represent the information encoding all relationships of conditions in the family an additional k variables may be necessary over the family's live range. The size of k for a family is $O(\log_2 r)$, where r is the number of intervals on the previously discussed segmented number line. The size of r can be shown to be to be $O(c)$, where c is the number of conditions in the family, since each condition can create only 0, 1, 2, or 3 new segmented regions on the number line. The size of the BDD with one condition family is at worst polynomial since $O(2^{\log_2 r}) = O(c)$. This can be bounded further by the observation that control flow arcs often encode information redundant with the condition values.

The size of the BDD is guaranteed to remain polynomial for codes with any number of non-overlapping live ranges in the topological sort of the circuit or CFG. In the PAS, condition family live ranges are typically short lived and do not overlap to a large degree since a condition family's live range maps directly to the live range of its defining register (i.e. r1 in r1 < 10 and r1 > 20). The worst case size of the BDD having condition family live ranges that both overlap and participate in the same predicate computations has an exponential term, 2^L, where L is the maximum number of condition families simultaneously live. Again, this is worst case and can be bounded further if control flow encodes redundant information. If the overhead of condition analysis is a concern, the number of overlapping condition families live can be directly controlled by exclusion or by live range splitting. Loss of some precision will occur, though the level of precision will still exceed PHG and PQS. Experimental evaluation shows that the PAS is well behaved in the codes studied without such techniques.

Another contribution of this work is the handling of general predicate liveness. The methods presented to deal with cyclic and multiple-definition forms do not change the upper bound presented here. Virtual unrolling increases the length of the circuit, not the width. The GSA ω simply makes part of the control flow graph relevant to the predicate network.

Once the BDD is built all query functions are performed in polynomial time. Equivalence and inverse queries are constant time. Subset, intersection, and exhaustion are all polynomial in time and space with respect to the size of the functions subject to the query.

6.2. PAS in Practice

To evaluate the performance of the described techniques, the analysis was applied to SPEC CINT95 benchmarks. The benchmarks were compiled aggressively for instruction-level parallelism, with 60% profile-guided selective inlining, formation of very aggressive hyperblock regions, and extensive code transformation and optimization. Instruction scheduling and register allocation were performed. It should be noted that the IMPACT compiler currently does not generate predication making use of the forward-multiple or cyclic schemata, so these techniques are not reflected in these numerical results. Were they to be applied, the results would scale by a linear factor as previously described.

PAS was instrumented to determine the analysis time and maximal BDD size for these benchmarks. Experiments were performed on an HP 9000/785/400 workstation operating at a clock frequency of 400MHz with 1GB RAM. Binary decision diagrams for the final code of all SPEC CINT95 benchmarks were built in 2.4 seconds (excluding the assumed SSA construction time). Especially since the BDD typically needs to be rebuilt only when predicate definition optimizations are performed, the time required for BDD construction is acceptable even in a production environment. To measure query efficiency, all pairs of predicates within each hyperblock were tested for subset, superset, and disjoint relationships. A total of 1,177,491 queries were performed in 3.8 seconds. This rapid query response is due in part to the canonicity of the BDD and in part to memoization techniques applied in CUDD [16]. This result is expected, as the control flow of structured programs results in predicate relationship equations which are relatively small and well-behaved in comparison to the large circuits the BDD is capable of managing.

Figure 10 shows the number of BDD nodes necessary to represent the predicate and condition networks plotted against the number of predicate definitions in each function of each benchmark in SPEC CINT95. In each graph, two types of BDD were built. The first type did not include condition analysis information, while the second type did. Figure 10(a) shows the sizes of the BDD created using the condition variable ordering found in predicated codes aggressively optimized by the IMPACT compiler. Figure 10(b) shows the same graph after an application of sifting was applied to find a better variable ordering [24].

One function was excluded from Figure 10(a) to equalize the scales. This function was *strength_reduce_loop* from *126.gcc*, the sixth largest function in terms of predicate define count (333 predicate defines). With basic condition analysis it required 4995 nodes, fairly typical for functions of this size. However, with family analysis it created 18,529 nodes, the greatest of any function. Despite having 26 two-member, 9 three-member, 2 four-member, and 6 nine-member families this was a growth of only a factor of 3.7 times. With less than 19K nodes, a relatively small number when compared to those seen in many VLSI circuits, the BDD package was able to handle this function very well as indicated by a build time of only 0.11 seconds. Reduction in size through variable sifting reduced the size of this BDD from 18,529 to 4462 nodes.

Experimental results indicated that worst case results for overlapping condition family life-times did not materialize. Exploration of the code revealed that this additional information was often partially redundant or that the cost of overlapping condition live ranges was hidden by the larger predicate network functions. The largest growth factor, computed as (BDD size using families / BDD size using simple conditions), was 4.2 for before sifting and 6.0 afterwards; the average was 1.1 and 1.2 respectively. This may indicate that further analysis may reveal upper bounds more restrictive than those presented in the previous section.

Polynomial, linear, exponential, and power curves were fit to the graphs in Figure 10. In each case, the best fit was a power curve with exponents of between 0.87 to 1.07 and with $0.88 < R^2 < 0.91$ (R^2 approaching 1 indicates higher predictive accuracy). The linear curve shown has $0.41 < R^2 < 0.67$ and the exponential model, $0.55 < R^2 < 0.60$.

7. Conclusions

This paper demonstrated a means of accurately mapping the predicate analysis problem to a powerful and efficient logical substrate, the reduced ordered binary decision diagram (ROBDD). Besides demonstrating a high level of performance, this work extended on previous attempts by incorporating the analysis of predication in general control flow and the analysis of conditions into the same logical framework. Finally, concerns about the growth of the representational medium were addressed. The presented system has the power and flexibility to provide predicate analysis for advanced predicate optimization and recompilation environments.

While control of BDD size is not a practical concern at this point, preliminary results shown here indicate that it may eventually become profitable to study efficient means of achieving near-optimal variable orderings in general predication problems.

Other interesting future work includes the possible extension of the framework to include other types of logical information, perhaps in the form of extensions to the condition analysis framework capable of understanding general arithmetic flow.

Acknowledgments

We thank Professor Farid Najm for suggesting the use of BDD during work on [10] and Professor Sharad Malik for insight which enabled the complexity analysis of PAS. This study was supported in part by a grant from Intel Corporation. John Sias was supported by a National Defense Science and Engineering Fellowship.

References

[1] Intel Corporation, *IA-64 Application Developer's Architecture Guide*, May 1999.

[2] J. C. Park and M. S. Schlansker, "On predicated execution," Tech. Rep. HPL-91-58, Hewlett Packard Laboratories, Palo Alto, CA, May 1991.

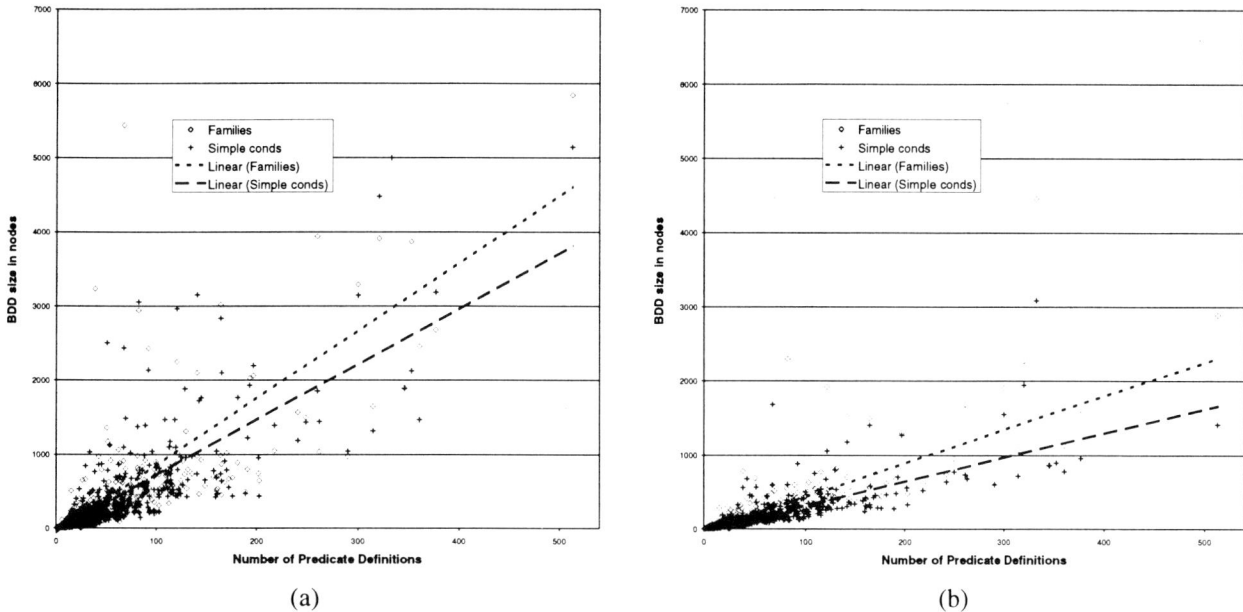

Figure 10: SPEC CINT95 function-level BDD size before (a) and after (b) variable sifting.

[3] S. A. Mahlke, D. C. Lin, W. Y. Chen, R. E. Hank, R. A. Bringmann, and W. W. Hwu, "Effective compiler support for predicated execution using the hyperblock," in *Proceedings of the 25th International Symposium on Microarchitecture*, pp. 45–54, December 1992.

[4] A. E. Eichenberger and E. S. Davidson, "Register allocation for predicated code," in *Proceedings of the 28th Annual International Symposium on Microarchitecture*, pp. 180–191, December 1995.

[5] D. M. Gillies, D. R. Ju, R. Johnson, and M. Schlansker, "Global predicate analysis and its application to register allocation," in *Proceedings of the 29th International Symposium on Microarchitecture*, pp. 114–125, December 1996.

[6] D. I. August, W. W. Hwu, and S. A. Mahlke, "A framework for balancing control flow and predication," in *Proceedings of the 30th Annual International Symposium on Microarchitecture*, pp. 92–103, December 1997.

[7] D. I. August, D. A. Connors, S. A. Mahlke, J. W. Sias, K. M. Crozier, B. Cheng, P. R. Eaton, Q. B. Olaniran, and W. W. Hwu, "Integrated predication and speculative execution in the IMPACT EPIC architecture," in *Proceedings of the 25th International Symposium on Computer Architecture*, pp. 227–237, June 1998.

[8] L. Carter, B. Simon, B. Calder, L. Carter, and J. Ferrante, "Predicated single static assignment," in *Proceedings of the International Conference on Parallel Architectures and Compilation Techniques*, October 1999.

[9] R. Johnson and M. Schlansker, "Analysis techniques for predicated code," in *Proceedings of the 29th International Symposium on Microarchitecture*, pp. 100–113, December 1996.

[10] D. I. August, J. W. Sias, J. Puiatti, S. A. Mahlke, D. A. Connors, K. M. Crozier, and W. W. Hwu, "The program decision logic approach to predicated execution," in *Proceedings of the 26th International Symposium on Computer Architecture*, pp. 208–219, May 1999.

[11] A. Srivastava, "Vulcan," Tech. Rep. TR-99-76, Microsoft Research, September 1999.

[12] V. Kathail, M. S. Schlansker, and B. R. Rau, "HPL PlayDoh architecture specification: Version 1.0," Tech. Rep. HPL-93-80, Hewlett-Packard Laboratories, Palo Alto, CA, February 1994.

[13] M. S. Schlansker, S. A. Mahlke, and R. Johnson, "Control CPR: A branch height reduction optimization for EPIC architectures," in *Proceedings of the ACM SIGPLAN 1999 Conference on Programming Language Design and Implementation*, pp. 155–168, May 1999.

[14] A. Aho, R. Sethi, and J. Ullman, *Compilers: Principles, Techniques, and Tools*. Reading, MA: Addison-Wesley, 1986.

[15] R. E. Bryant, "Graph-based algorithms for Boolean function manipulation," *IEEE Transaction on Computers*, vol. C-35, pp. 677–691, August 1986.

[16] F. Somenzi, "CUDD: Colorado University Decision Diagram package, release 2.30," University of Colorado at Boulder, http://vlsi.colorado.edu/~fabio/CUDD/, 1998.

[17] K. S. Brace, R. R. Rudell, and R. E. Bryant, "Efficent implementation of a BDD package," in *Proc. of the 27th ACM/IEEE Design Automation Conference*, pp. 40–45, January 1990.

[18] J. W. Sias, "Condition awareness support for predicate analysis and optimization," Master's thesis, University of Illinois, Urbana, IL, 1999.

[19] R. E. Bryant, "Symbolic Boolean manipulation with ordered binary decision diagrams," Tech. Rep. CMU-CS-92-160, School of Computer Science, Carnegie Mellon University, Pittsburgh, PA, October 1992.

[20] P. Tu and D. Padua, "Gated SSA-based demand-driven symbolic analysis for parallelizing compilers," in *Conference proceedings of the 1995 International Conference on Supercomputing*, pp. 414–423, 1995.

[21] S. B. Akers, "Binary decision diagrams," *IEEE Transaction on Computers*, vol. C-27, pp. 509–516, June 1978.

[22] S. J. Friedman and K. J. Supowit, "Finding the optimal variable ordering for binary decision diagrams," in *Proc. 24th Annual ACM/IEEE DAC*, pp. 348–355, June 1987.

[23] C. L. Berman, "Circuit width, register allocation, and ordered binary decision diagrams," *IEEE Transactions on Computer-Aided Design*, vol. 10, pp. 1059–1066, August 1991.

[24] R. Rudell, "Dynamic variable ordering for ordered binary decision diagrams," in *Proceedings of the International Conference on Computer-Aided Design*, pp. 42–47, November 1993.

Modulo Scheduling for a Fully-Distributed Clustered VLIW Architecture

Jesús Sánchez and Antonio González

Dept. of Computer Architecture
Universitat Politècnica de Catalunya
Barcelona - SPAIN

E-mail: {fran,antonio}@ac.upc.es

Abstract

Clustering is an approach that many microprocessors are adopting in recent times in order to mitigate the increasing penalties of wire delays. In this work we propose a novel clustered VLIW architecture which has all its resources partitioned among clusters, including the cache memory. A modulo scheduling scheme for this architecture is also proposed. This algorithm takes into account both register and memory inter-cluster communications so that the final schedule results in a cluster assignment that favors cluster locality in cache references and register accesses. It has been evaluated for both 2- and 4-cluster configurations and for differing number and latencies of inter-cluster buses. The proposed algorithm produces schedules with very low communication requirements and outperforms previous cluster-oriented schedulers.

1. Introduction

Technology projections point to wire delays as being one of the main hurdles for improving instruction throughput of future microprocessors [23]. As wire delays grow relative to gate delays and feature sizes shrink, the percentage of on-chip transistors that can be reached in a single cycle will decrease, and microprocessors will become *communication bound* rather than *capacity bound* [1][14].

Techniques to solve this problem at all levels, from applications to technology, will be crucial for performance. Clustering is an effective microarchitectural approach to mitigate the negative effect of wire delays. The main idea is to have a hierarchical organization of the interconnection wires such that units that communicate frequently are interconnected through short and fast wires. On the other hand, units that rarely communicate can use longer and slower wires. In other words, the microarchitecture exploits what we may call *communication locality*. Several commercial microprocessors have adopted this approach, such as the Alpha 21264 [10], which is a superscalar processor, but this trend is even more common for VLIW processors used in the embedded/DSP domain. Examples of the latter are Texas Instrument's TMS320C6000 [24], Equator's MAP1000 [15] and Analog's TigerSharc [8].

Clustering can be applied to different parts of the microarchitecture. Cluster microarchitectures proposed so far, both in the commercial and research arena, distribute the functional units and register files, but the data cache is considered a centralized resource. This centralized organization challenges the scalability of these architectures. Besides, some studies point out that the access time (in number of cycles) to the memory structures is likely to increase with future technologies, even when their capacity is kept constant [1]. This suggests that short latency memory structures should be even smaller than they are today. Because of these two reasons, we believe that a distributed cache memory architecture is key for increasing the performance of future microarchitectures.

In this work we propose a clustered VLIW microarchitecture with a distributed cache memory. This architecture has all the resources distributed: instruction fetch, execute and memory units. It resembles very much a multiprocessor, with the exception that all the clusters progress in a lockstep mode, and inter-cluster register communications are controlled by the compiler by means of certain fields in the ISA. Because of this resemblance we refer to this architecture as a *multiVLIWprocessor*.

The effectiveness of this microarchitecture strongly depends on the ability of the compiler to generate code that balances the workload of the different clusters and result in few inter-cluster communications. In this work we propose a modulo scheduling technique for *multiVLIWprocessors*. The proposed scheduler includes some heuristics for minimizing inter-cluster register communication, based on the information provided by the data dependence graph. Besides, it implements a powerful memory locality analysis based on *Cache Miss Equations* [9], which guides the scheduling of memory instructions with the objective of minimizing inter-cluster memory communications.

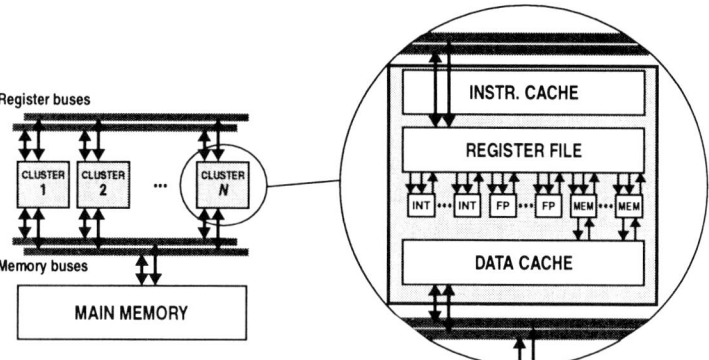

Figure 1. Microarchitectures of a MultiVLIWProcessor

Some previous work related to scheduling of instructions for clustered VLIW architectures can be found in the literature for non-cyclic [6][4][11][18] and cyclic code [17][7][22], but to the best of our knowledge this is the first study that deals with a clustered VLIW architecture that has a distributed data cache.

The rest of this paper is organized as follows. Section 2 describes the architecture of the *multiVLIWprocessor* and some basic background on modulo scheduling. An example that motivates the proposed algorithm is shown in Section 3. In Section 4, the proposed algorithm is described and Section 5 shows performance results obtained for different configurations. Finally, the main conclusions of the work are drawn in Section 6.

2. MultiVLIWProcessors

In this section we first describe the microarchitecture of *multiVLIWprocessors* and then we review some basic concepts of modulo scheduling for the proposed architecture.

2.1. Microarchitecture

Our base architecture (see Figure 1) is composed of several clusters, each one executing a fixed part of each VLIW instruction. All clusters work in lockstep mode, i.e., any stall in one cluster also stalls the other clusters. Every cycle, all clusters fetch their corresponding parts of a new VLIW instruction from their local instruction caches. Each cluster consists of several functional units, a register file and a local data cache memory in addition to the local instruction cache. Functional units can be of three different types: integer arithmetic, floating-point arithmetic or memory access. For the sake of simplicity, we consider that all clusters are homogeneous (i.e., with the same number and type of functional units), but the proposed techniques can be generalized for heterogeneous clusters.

Register values generated by one cluster and needed by another one are communicated through a set of buses that are shared by all clusters (called *register buses*). A value that is put in a register bus can come from either the local register file or the output of a functional unit through a short-circuit. On the other hand, a value that is read from the bus can be stored in a register file, feed a functional unit or both. Thus, instruction register operands can be read from either the local register file or any bus, and instruction results can be written into the register file and to any register bus. All register communication operations are explicitly encoded in the appropriate fields of the VLIW instruction, which are set at compile time. Thus, no additional hardware is needed to manage and arbitrate register buses. The detailed VLIW instruction format is shown in Figure 2. Each instruction for a particular cluster consists of the following fields. An operation for each functional unit in that particular cluster (FUj) and the source (IN BUS) and target (OUT BUS) of the bus (there are as many IN/OUT fields as number of buses). The IN BUS field indicates, if necessary, the register in the local register file in which the value that is in IRV has to be stored. The IRV (*Incoming Register Value*) is a special register in each cluster that latches the value that comes from the bus. The OUT BUS field indicates from which local register a value has to be

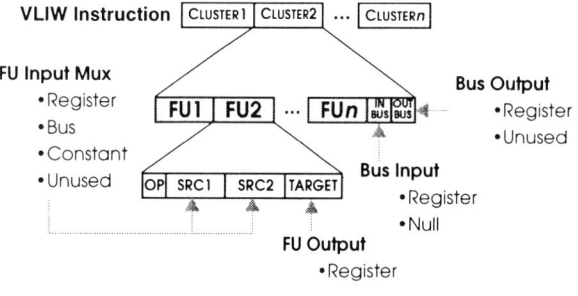

Figure 2. VLIW instruction format

issued to the bus, if any. If the register is being written in that cycle, the data will be bypassed from the output of the corresponding functional unit. Since a bus is a resource shared by all the clusters, when one particular cluster places a data on the bus (OUT BUS), this bus will be busy during the entire bus latency and no other instruction can use it (a bus is considered by the scheduling algorithm as another resource in the reservation table).

Regarding memory accesses, a load/store issued by a cluster first tries its local L1 data cache. If the data is found, the access is satisfied with minimum latency. Otherwise, the hardware tries the cache of the other clusters or, finally, the access is solved by the main memory. Both local memories and main memory are interconnected through one or several buses (that are called *memory buses*). As the cache is physically partitioned among the clusters, coherence among the local caches and the main memory has to be kept. For this reason, a snoopy MSI protocol [5] has been implemented. This protocol is completely transparent to the ISA, and further, both the coherence and the bus arbitration are managed by the hardware. When a memory access misses in its local cache, the miss request is queued in a local MSHR (*Miss information/Status Handling Register*) structure, since the L1 data cache is non-blocking [12]. Then, the access has to compete for a free memory bus in order to access a remote cache or the main memory.

All the dependences with memory operations are dynamically checked, since the scheduler may have considered an optimistic latency for these instructions (i.e., hit in the local cache). If any dependence is not met, the dependent instruction stalls in all clusters until the hazard is resolved.

2.2. Background on Modulo Scheduling

Software pipelining is a very effective technique to statically schedule loops. The most popular scheme to perform software pipelining is called modulo scheduling [20][13]. The two main parameters that statically characterize a modulo scheduled loop are the *initiation interval* (II) and the *stage count* (SC). The former reflects the number of cycles that a kernel iteration takes (assuming no stalls), whereas the latter shows how many iterations are overlapped, and determines the length of the prolog and epilog.

For a clustered VLIW architecture, both II and SC can be affected by inter-cluster register communications. If the communication buses become saturated, a higher II is required. Moreover, communication operations may increase the length of the schedule, and therefore the SC may be increased. Thus, the IPC of a clustered VLIW architecture will be lower than that of an equivalent unified VLIW architecture with the same resources in general. On the other hand, a clustered architecture may reduce the critical delays such as the register file access time and the bypass latency [19], and allow for faster clock rates.

For this paper, which focuses on modulo scheduling for *multiVLIWprocessors*, the number of cycles needed to execute a particular modulo scheduled loop can be modeled through the following expression [21]:

$$NCYCLE_{Total} = NCYCLE_{Compute} + NCYCLE_{Stall}$$

Where $NCYCLE_{Compute}$ represents a fixed number of cycles that depends on the particular static scheduling produced by the compiler. During these cycles the processor is doing useful (or at least scheduled) work. $NCYCLE_{Stall}$ represents the number of cycles where the processor is stalled and depends on several factors as we detail below. The value of $NCYCLE_{Compute}$ can be computed before executing the loop if the number of times the loop is executed (NTIMES) and the number of iterations of each execution (NITER) are known, as shown by the next expression:

$$NCYCLE_{Compute} = NTIMES * ((NITER + SC - 1) * II)$$

The value of $NCYCLE_{Stall}$ cannot be computed statically. It represents the number of stall cycles due to incomplete information managed by the compiler. For instance, some memory instruction latencies may be unknown since the compiler does not know whether they will hit in the first level cache. If the value loaded by a memory instruction feeds another operation (i.e., the latter depends on the former) but the latter was scheduled using an underestimation of the memory latency, it will stall until the memory access is finished. In the assumed microarchitecture, the final latency of a memory instruction depends on three factors:

- Latency of memory accesses, which depends on the memory level that satisfies the access: local cache, remote cache or main memory.
- Number of entries in the MSHR of the lockup-free caches. If there is no available entry for a new miss request, the instruction stalls until there is a free entry.
- Cycles waiting for a free bus and bus latency.

Thus, considering all of these factors, the total latency of a memory access can be represented by this formula:

$$LAT_{MemAccess} = LAT_{Cache} + \\ MISS_{LC} * (NC_{WaitingEntry} + NC_{WaitingBus} + LAT_{MemoryBus} + \\ \max(LAT_{Cache}, MISS_{RC} * LAT_{MainMemory}))$$

Where both $MISS_{LC}$ and $MISS_{RC}$ represent binary values that are 1 if the access misses in local cache and all remote caches respectively, or 0 otherwise. $NC_{WaitingEntry}$ represents the number of cycles that a miss access is wait-

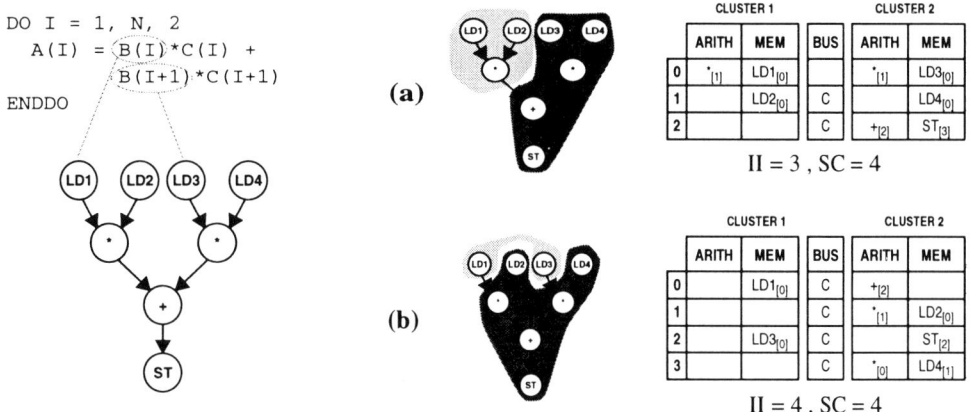

Figure 3. Motivating example

ing for an available entry in the MSHR. $NC_{WaitingBus}$ is the number of cycles that the access is waiting for a free bus. Note that a bus can be also busy for coherence operations and this is taken into account by our simulator. Finally, although we have considered $LAT_{MainMemory}$ as a fixed parameter, in the above expression note that for some references this number could be smaller if an earlier miss has already started loading the relevant cache line. This fact has also been accounted for our simulator.

3. Motivating Example for the Proposed Scheduler

The objective of this study is twofold: first, demonstrate that when the data cache is partitioned among the different clusters, the selection of the cluster where each memory instruction is scheduled is very important and can dramatically affect the final performance of a program (the same holds for register values, but this has already been shown by previous papers). Second, we propose a modulo scheduler that takes into account both register and memory inter-cluster communications.

In this section, we illustrate through an example how the cluster selection can affect the total number of cycles in which a code section is executed. Consider that we want to perform modulo scheduling of a loop whose code and dependence graph are shown in Figure 3. Assume the processor consists of 2 clusters, each one with its local register file and data cache (direct-mapped), and 2 functional units: one for arithmetic operations (with 2-cycle latency) and one for memory operations. There is one inter-register bus with a 2-cycle latency. The latencies for memory accesses are: 2 cycles for a local cache, 2 cycles for a bus transaction and 10 cycles for an access to main memory.

For this loop, the *minimum initiation interval* (mII) for an equivalent unified architecture with the same resources is 3 cycles. The partition and scheduling that minimizes the number of register communications between clusters and, thus, that achieves the same II as the equivalent unified architecture is shown in Figure 3(a). In this figure, the left part represents the partition of the operations between the clusters whereas the right part shows the modulo reservation table obtained after modulo scheduling. Each operation is scheduled in a particular slot and the number in brackets represents the stage at which this operation is scheduled. The usage of the register bus is also shown in this table. Whenever a bus transaction takes place, the corresponding bus time slot is reserved and it is indicated by a C in the reservation table.

Then, the $NCYCLE_{Compute}$ of the resulting loop can be computed as:

$NCYCLE_{Compute(a)} = NTIMES * ((N + 4 - 1) * 3) = NTIMES * (N + 3) * 3$

However, suppose that both arrays B and C are located in memory at a distance that is a multiple of the local cache memory size. This means that we will have ping-pong interferences between LD1 and LD2, and between LD3 and LD4. Thus, the spatial locality exhibited by the four instructions cannot be exploited and the four accesses always miss. The result is that the instruction(s) that consume the memory values suffer many stalls. In the example, the VLIW instruction that contains the multiplications cannot continue its execution until the misses are satisfied. Assuming that we have sufficient memory buses, the number of cycles that the instruction stalls is the latency of a bus transaction plus an access to main memory, since the latency to the local cache was taken into account by the scheduler. Then, the number of stall cycles is:

$$NCYCLE_{Stall(a)} = NTIMES * N * (2+10) = NTIMES * N * 12$$

An alternative scheduling is shown in Figure 3(b). Based on the locality properties previously observed, in this second alternative cluster assignment is selected in order to take advantage of the locality exhibited by memory instructions. For this reason, LD1 and LD3 are scheduled in the same cluster in order to profit from its group reuse, and the same applies for LD2 and LD4 which are scheduled in the other cluster. In this way, ping-pong interferences are removed and we can take advantage of the spatial reuse. However, as we can see in the example, for this case two communications between register values are needed per iteration, and then the II has to be increased from 3 to 4. Thus, $NCYCLE_{Compute}$ is computed as:

$$NCYCLE_{Compute(b)} = NTIMES * ((N + 3 - 1) * 4) = NTIMES * (N + 2) * 4$$

However, the miss rate of LD3 and LD4 is 25% (assuming eight data elements per cache block), and LD1 and LD2 always hit (excepting the first iteration). Thus, the number of stall cycles is:

$$NCYCLE_{Stall(b)} = NTIMES * N * (2*(2+10)* 0.25) = NTIMES * N * 6$$

Then, putting all together, we have that the total number of cycles in both strategies as:

$$NCYCLE_{Total(a)} = NTIMES * (15 * N + 9)$$

$$NCYCLE_{Total(b)} = NTIMES * (10 * N + 8)$$

Therefore, we can conclude that the second strategy, which takes into account both register and memory communications, achieves a schedule that is 1.5 times faster than the original one, which is optimized only for register communications.

4. Register and Memory Communication-Aware Modulo Scheduler

In this section we present a modulo scheduler that tries to minimize both register and memory inter-cluster communications and at the same time balance the workload. We first review a previously proposed scheduler, which is very effective at minimizing register communications, and which we will use as a baseline for comparisons. Then, we present the data locality analysis framework that is used by the scheduler. Finally, the modulo scheduler is described.

4.1. Baseline Algorithm

We use as the baseline algorithm the one proposed in our previous work [22], which was shown to be very effective at minimizing register communications and maximizing the workload balance. In that work, the target architecture was similar to the one proposed in Section 2.1, but in that case all clusters accessed a shared L1 cache. Below, we briefly review the algorithm proposed there. For more details, the interested reader is referred to the original paper [22].

The algorithm employs a unified assign-and-schedule approach, that is, cluster selection and scheduling of operations is done in a single step. The heuristic for selecting a cluster is the number of edges that exit from the dependence subgraph corresponding to all the nodes already scheduled in a particular cluster. This value represents a measure of the number of register communications. An attempt is made to schedule an operation (i.e., a node in the dependence graph) in all the clusters in which there is an available slot. The one chosen is the one in which the best profit from output edges is achieved (that is, the difference between output edges before and after including this operation in the partial schedule). All the operations are scheduled using the same algorithm and following a particular order that is crucial for performance. If an instruction cannot be scheduled (because no issue slot is available, or there are not enough registers, or the register buses are saturated), the II is increased and the whole process is re-started (except the ordering).

4.2. Overview of the Cache Miss Equations

Cache Miss Equations (CME) is an analytical framework to model the cache behavior that is very accurate for codes that make use of scalar variables and affine[1] array references, which is very common in numeric applications. This framework was proposed by Gosh, Martonosi and Malik [9]. CME describes the precise relationship among the iteration space, array sizes, base addresses and cache parameters for a loop nest.

A direct solution of the CME is an NP problem, which makes it infeasible for many practical cases. The problem can basically be stated as counting integer points inside an exponential number of polyhedra. However, Bermudo *et al.* [3] proposed some techniques to speed-up the counting process by exploiting some intrinsic properties of the particular type of polyhedra generated by the CME. Further, Vera *et al.* [25] proposed a sampling scheme in order to estimate the solution by means of confidence intervals.

---

1. An array reference is affine if the expressions that indicate the referenced element in each dimension are linear functions of the loop induction variables.

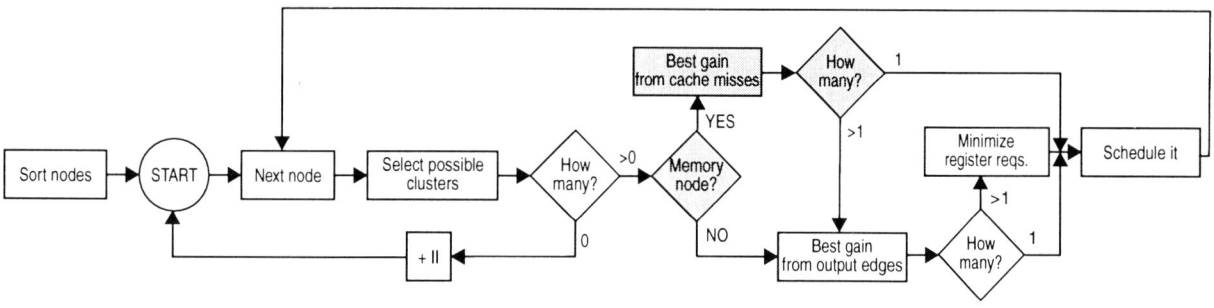

Figure 4. *RCMA* modulo scheduling step by step

These two techniques together drastically reduce the computing time to just about a few seconds per loop for most programs, and then the time required to compute and solve the equations is comparable to the time required by other typical optimizations of the compiler. In this paper, we use this implementation of the CME to estimate the amount of reuse that is exploited by any subset of memory instructions. CME will allow the scheduler to estimate the amount of memory communications among clusters or between clusters and main memory. The scheduler uses this information to guide its scheduling decisions. For instance, given a memory instruction, it is beneficial to schedule it in a cluster where there already are other instructions from which it reuses data (group reuse). On the other hand, it is detrimental to schedule the instruction in a cluster where there already are other instructions that cause many cache conflicts with the current one. CME allow the schedule to quantify the amount of reuse and conflicts among any group of instructions of the same loop nest. CME are used to produce the following statistics:

- The number of misses incurred by a set of memory references for a particular cache configuration (capacity, block size and associativity)
- The miss ratio of a particular memory instruction in this set.

4.3. Scheduler for a Distributed Cache

The proposed algorithm is called *RMCA* (which stands for *Register and Memory Communication-Aware*) modulo scheduling. It is an evolution of the algorithm reviewed in Section 4.1 and its main steps are depicted in Figure 4 (new features are shown in gray boxes). All nodes in the data dependence graph are first sorted according to the criteria used by the original paper [22]. This ordering minimizes the number of nodes that have both predecessors and successors in the set of nodes that precede it in the order. Then, cluster selection and scheduling is performed in a single step following that order. However, there is now a distinction between two types of nodes: (a) memory operations, and (b) non-memory operations. For operations of the latter group, the algorithm does not change. However, when a memory operation is scheduled, a different strategy is used. Instead of choosing the cluster where the gain from output register edges is maximized, the cluster selection depends on the profit from cache misses. In other words, each time a memory operation is scheduled, all clusters are tried, and for each one, the number of cache misses contributed by memory operations scheduled in that cluster, before and after introducing the current operation, is computed through the CME. Then, the cluster(s) where this gain is maximized is chosen. If more than one cluster is optimal with respect to cache misses, the scheduler selects one of them using the same strategy as for non-memory operations. Although the solver of the CME have to be repeatedly invoked, the method is very fast due to the optimizations mentioned in Section 4.2., and the time required by the scheduler is a small percentage of the total compilation time.

This algorithm tries to minimize the number of cache misses, and thus it attempts to minimize the inter-cluster memory communications. However, the latency of these communications can be hidden by scheduling some load instructions using the cache-miss latency (binding prefetching, as proposed in [21]). When a load is scheduled using the cache-miss latency, the operation that consumes the data read by the load will not be stalled because it is scheduled assuming the worst-case latency. However, scheduling instructions using a larger latency can have a negative effect on both register pressure and length of the schedule. On one hand, the lifetime of the load destination register is increased. On the other hand, the II can be increased if this instruction belongs to a recurrence and this increased latency makes the recurrence the most restrictive constraint on the II. Besides, the length of the schedule for a single iteration may increase, which may cause an increase in the SC, which in turn affects the durations of the prologue and epilogue. Therefore, as shown in [21], it may be much more effective to schedule with a miss latency only those loads that are likely to miss. This can be done as long as the latency does not increase the II with respect to the schedule produced when loads are scheduled with a hit latency. Thus, the proposed scheme includes another step: once the target cluster of an instruction is determined, it is scheduled using the cache-miss latency if the miss ratio of this instruction in this particular cluster (considering the partial schedule produced so far) is greater than a certain threshold, and provided that this latency does not increase the II if the operation is in a recurrence. The assumed miss latency is the time to access main memory, that is, $LAT_{Cache} + LAT_{MemoryBus} + LAT_{MainMemory}$ (note that we do not consider the memory bus contention since it is not known at this moment, although it could be estimated).

Note that with this scheme some memory instructions are scheduled with the miss latency even if their miss ratio is lower than 100%. This may happen for instance for instructions with spatial locality. In this case, loop unrolling could be used to generate multiple instances of the same instruction such that one of them always miss and the other always hit [16]. However, we have not considered this optimization in this paper.

5. Performance Results

This section analyzes the performance of the proposed scheduler. The main performance metric that we use is the number of cycles executing instructions of modulo scheduled loops. Note that this metric does not include the effect of clustering on the cycle time, thus, differences observed for different schedulers and the same architecture directly translate into differences in execution time. However, the number of cycles for different architectures should be divided by cycle time to measure differences in execution time. Since we are concerned with differences among alternative schedulers, we prefer not to include the effect of cycle time in our metric, to isolate the effect of the schedulers. A study of the impact of clustering on cycle time can be found elsewhere [19] as well as on energy consumption [26], which is another important factor that can be reduced through clustering.

5.1. Configurations and Benchmarks

The scheduling algorithm has been evaluated for three different configurations of the *multiVLIWprocessor* architecture. These configurations are shown in Table 1. The first configuration is called *Unified* and it is composed of a single cluster with four functional units of each type (integer, floating point and memory) and a unique register file of 64 general-purpose registers.

Resources	Unified	2-cluster	4-cluster
INT / cluster	4	2	1
FP / cluster	4	2	1
MEM / cluster	4	2	1
REGS / cluster	64	32	16

Latencies	INT	FP
MEM	2	2
ARITH	1	3
MUL/ABS	2	6
DIV/SQR/TRG	6	18

Table 1. MultiVLIWProcessor configurations and operation latencies

This configuration represents our baseline. Both the *2-cluster* and *4-cluster* configurations have the register file partitioned (into two and four partitions respectively). The former has 2 functional units of each type and 32 register per cluster and the latter includes 1 functional unit of each type and a register file of 16 registers per cluster. The three configurations are 12-way issue.

For all configurations, the total L1 cache size is 8KB, divided into equal-sizes among the different clusters. This cache capacity is realistic for embedded/DSP processors. For instance, the TI TMS320C6711 has an L1 data cache of 4Kbytes [24]. In our architecture, each local cache is direct-mapped, non-blocking with 10 entries in the MSHR. An access to a local cache is satisfied in 2 cycles, whereas an access to main memory takes 10 cycles. For the clustered configurations we will present results for different number and latency of both register and memory buses.

The modulo scheduling algorithm has been implemented in the ICTINEO compiler [2] and some SPECfp95 benchmarks have been evaluated: *tomcatv, swim, su2cor, hydro2d, mgrid, applu, turb3d* and *apsi*. Note that modulo scheduling is an effective technique for both numeric and multimedia applications, but it is not so effective for applications such as SPECint95 due to the small number of iterations for each loop execution and the abundance of conditionals.

The performance figures shown in this section refer to the modulo scheduling of innermost loops with a number of iterations greater than four. Our measurement shows that code inside such innermost loops represents about 90% of all the executed instructions, so that the statistics for innermost loops are quite representative of the whole program. Only instructions that belong to modulo scheduled loops are taken into account by the simulator. Thus, the programs were run until the first 100 million memory instructions in these loops using the ref input data set.

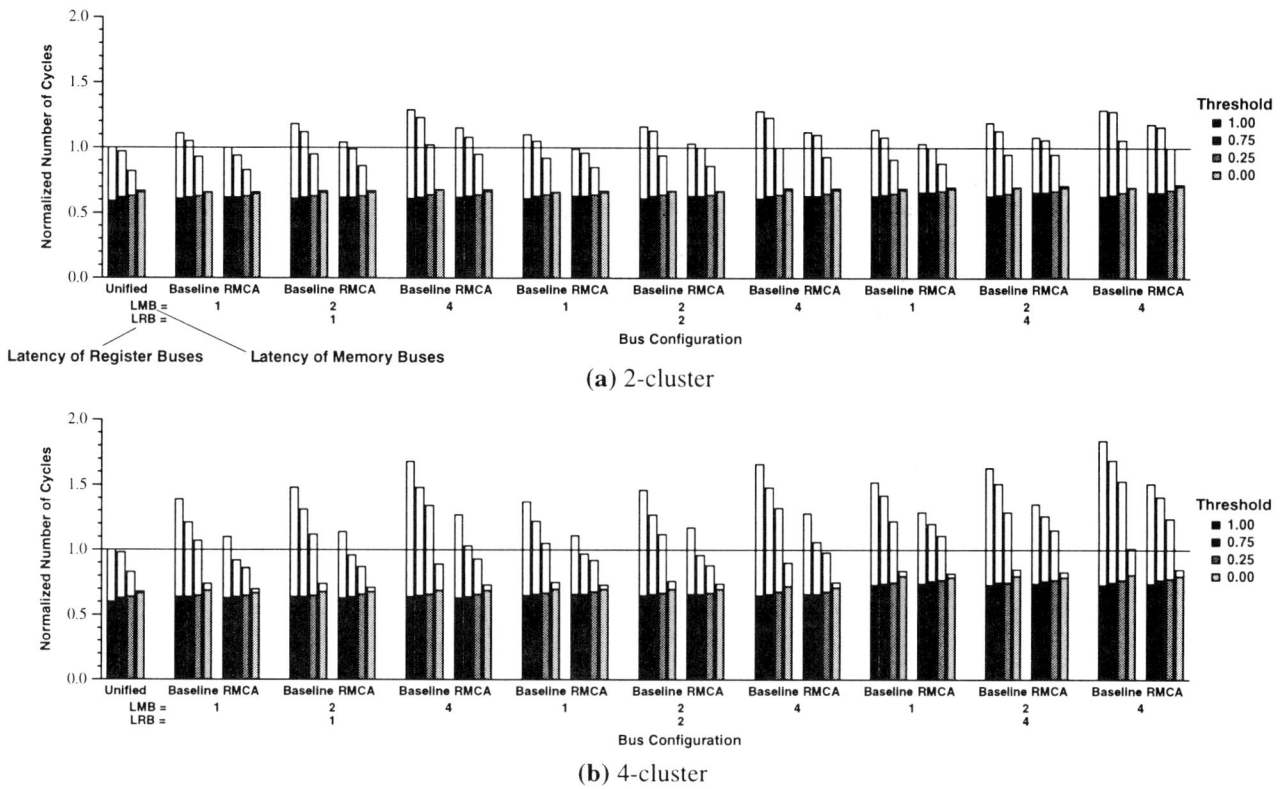

Figure 5. Results obtained for an unbounded number of buses (averaged for all benchmarks)

5.2. An Unbounded Number of Buses

Before considering realistic configurations, we have evaluated an architecture with an unbounded number of buses to test the performance of the proposed algorithm under extreme situations where bus bandwidth in not a problem. The remaining parameters of the architecture are those listed in Section 5.1 and the latency of the buses is parametrized. Figure 5 shows the normalized number of cycles averaged for all benchmarks, for 2 and 4 clusters and the different latencies considered. The first set of four bars represents the results for the unified configuration. The rest represent the results for the clustered configuration for different latencies of register buses (LRB - *Latency of Register Buses*) and memory buses (LMB - *Latency of Memory Buses*). For the different sets, we have evaluated two different schedulers:

- The baseline scheduler outlined in Section 4.1, which is very effective at minimizing register communications.
- The proposed algorithm, that takes into account both register and memory communications, which is labeled as *RMCA*.

Each set of four bars represents the results obtained for different values of the cache miss threshold (from 1.00 to 0.00) that determines whether a load is attempted to be scheduled with a miss latency. Note that threshold 1.00 represents the traditional scheme, that is, using always the cache-hit latency for memory operations. On the other hand, threshold 0.00 is most similar to the one proposed in [21], where all operations that do not cause an increment in the II (due to recurrences) are scheduled using the cache-miss latency. The only difference is the locality analysis employed, which is more powerful in this paper. Each bar is split into two parts: the compute time (or $NCYCLE_{Compute}$) is the black/grey part, whereas the stall time (or $NCYCLE_{Stall}$) is the white one.

From these graphs we can see that for all configurations (number of clusters, latencies and thresholds) the scheme that takes into account memory communication (*RMCA*) outperforms the one that ignores this feature (*Baseline*). As expected, for smaller values of the threshold the compute time increases (since it may increase both the II due to register requirements, and the SC due to an increase in the length of the schedule) but the stall time decreases. Note that with a threshold of 0.00 the stall time is almost zero for all configurations and the number of cycles for the *multiVLIWprocessor* are comparable to those of the unified configuration. We can also observe that for small thresholds (0.25 or 0.00) both *Baseline* and *RMCA*

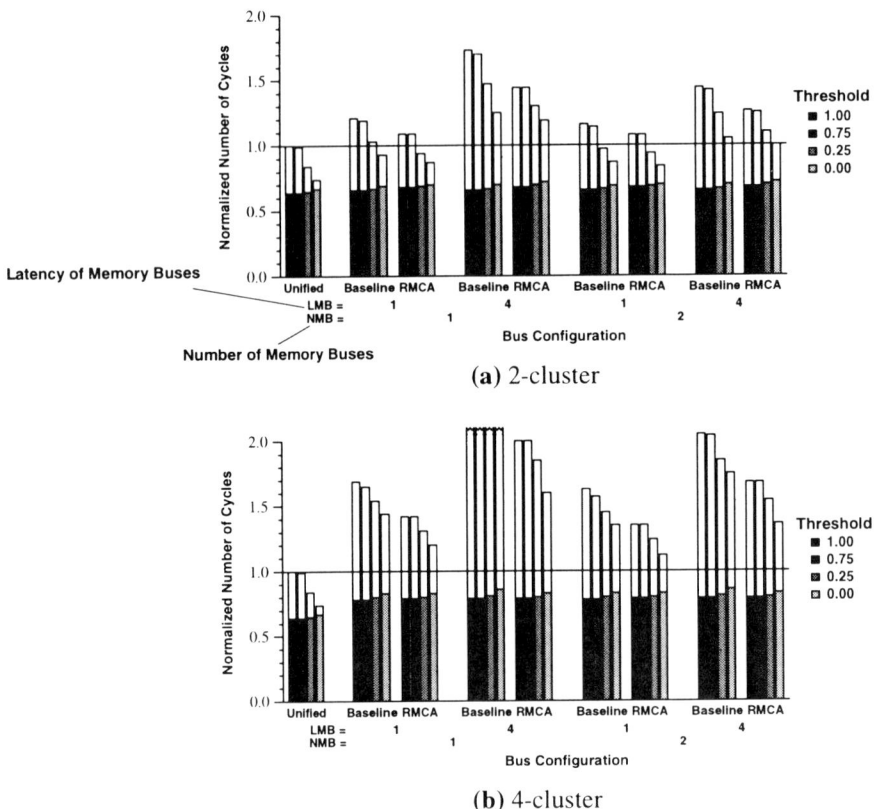

Figure 5. Results obtained when the number of buses is limited (averaged for all benchmarks)

strategies achieve similar performance, since the latency of cache misses is hidden by scheduling loads with the cache-miss latency. Nevertheless, note that for an unbounded number of buses the time waiting for a free bus ($NC_{Waiting\text{-}Bus}$) is zero, and hence, if the latency is hidden, the number of misses has no effect. However, as we will see in next section, when the number of memory buses is limited, the difference between both schemes will be notable, since the schedules produced by the *RMCA* scheme require much less communications.

5.3. Evaluation of Realistic Configurations

We have shown the potential benefits that can be achieved when memory communication are taken into account by the scheduler. In this section we study the results when a realistic inter-cluster communication network is considered.

We have evaluated configurations with a fixed number and latency of register buses (2 buses with 1-cycle latency) and for a different number and latency of memory buses. In Figure 6 we can see the results for both 2 and 4 clusters. Each set of four bars has the same meaning as in the previous section. The first set represents the results for the uni-

fied configuration. The rest are the averaged results for the different strategies (*Baseline* and *RMCA*) for 1 and 2 buses (NMB - *Number of Memory Buses*) and 1 and 4 cycles of latency (LMB - *Latency of Memory Buses*). We can observe in these graphs that, as in the unbounded study, the *RMCA* strategy outperforms the *Baseline* for all configurations. However now, for small values of the threshold, the difference between both strategies is more remarkable, mainly for 4 clusters. For the most effective threshold (0.00), the *RMCA* scheme outperforms the baseline scheduler by about 5% for 2 clusters and 20% for 4 clusters. We have observed that the reason for this difference is the time spent waiting for an available bus in order to initiate a communication. When the number of memory buses is unbounded this value is zero, because there is always an available bus. However, when the number of buses is limited, reducing the number of misses is also important since lesser the number local cache misses, lesser the number of accesses competing for a free bus time slot.

6. Conclusions

In this work we have proposed a novel microarchitecture called *multiVLIWprocessor*, which has a fully-distributed clustered VLIW organization. The main novelty of this architecture with respect to previous proposals for clustered VLIW processors is the distributed data cache, which introduces new challenges to the instruction scheduler.

In this paper we have also presented a modulo scheduler designed for this particular architecture. This scheduler, by means of a powerful locality analysis based on the *Cache Miss Equations* and an analysis of the register data dependence graph, generates codes with very low inter-cluster communication requirements. We have also shown that the proposed scheduler outperforms previous schemes that just focused on register communications.

Acknowledgements

This work has been supported by the Spanish Ministry of Education under contract CICYT-TIC 511/98 and the ESPRIT Project MHAOTEU (EP24942).

References

[1] V. Agarwal, M.S. Hrishikesh, S.W. Keckler and D. Burger, "Clock Rate versus IPC: The End of the Road For Conventional Microarchitectures", in *Procs. of the 27th. Int. Symp. on Computer Architecture*, pp. 248-259, June 2000

[2] E. Ayguadé, C. Barrado, A. González, J. Labarta, D. López, S. Moreno, D. Padua, F. Reig, Q. Riera and M. Valero, "Ictineo: a Tool for Research on ILP", in *Supercomputing'96 (SC'96)*, Research Exhibit "Polaris at Work", 1996

[3] N. Bermudo, X. Vera, A. González and J. Llosa, "An Efficient Solver for Cache Miss Equations", in *Procs. of Int. Symp. on Performance Analysis and System Software*, April 2000

[4] A. Capitanio, D. Dytt and A. Nicolau, "Partitioned Register Files for VLIWs: A Preliminary Analysis of Tradeoffs", in *Procs. of 25th. Int. Symp. on Microarchitecture*, pp. 192-300, 1992

[5] D. Culler and J.P. Singh, "Parallel Computer Architecture. A Hardware/Software Approach", *Morgan Kaufmann Publishers, Inc.*, 1999

[6] J. R. Ellis, "Bulldog: A Compiler for VLIW Architectures", *MIT Press*, pp. 180-184, 1986

[7] M.M. Fernandes, J. Llosa and N. Topham, "Distributed Modulo Scheduling", in *Procs. of Int. Symp. on High-Performance Computer Architecture*, pp. 130-134, Jan. 1999

[8] J. Fridman and Zvi Greefield, "The TigerSharc DSP Architecture", *IEEE Micro*, pp. 66-76, Jan-Feb. 2000

[9] S. Ghosh, M. Martonosi and S. Malik, "Cache Miss Equations: an Analytical Representation of Cache Misses", in *Procs. of Int. Conf. on Supercomputing (ICS'97)*, pp. 317-324, July 1997

[10] L. Gwennap, "Digital 21264 Sets New Standard", *Microprocessor Report*, 10(14), Oct. 1996

[11] S. Jang, S. Carr, P. Sweany and D. Kuras, "A Code Generation Framework for VLIW Architectures with Partitioned Register Banks", in *Procs. of 3rd. Int. Conf. on Massively Parallel Computing Systems*, April 1998

[12] D. Kroft," Lockup-Free Instruction Fetch/Prefetch Cache Organization", in *Procs. 8th Int. Symp. on Computer Architecture*, pp. 81-87, 1981

[13] M. Lam, "Software pipelining: An Effective scheduling technique for VLIW Machines", in *Procs. on Conf. on Programming Languages and Implementation Design*, pp. 258-267, June 1993

[14] D. Matzke, "Will Physical Scalability Sabotage Performance Gains", *IEEE Computer, Vol. 30, No. 9*, pp. 37-39, Sept. 1997

[15] "MAP1000 unfolds at Equator", *Microprocessor Report, 12(16)*, Dec. 1998

[16] T.C. Mowry, M.S. Lam and A. Gupta, "Design and Evaluation of a Compiler Algorithm for Prefetching", in *Procs. of the 5th. Ann. Symp. on Programming Languages and Operating Systems (ASPLOS-V)*, pp.62-73, Oct. 1992

[17] E. Nystrom and A. E. Eichenberger, "Effective Cluster Assingment for Modulo Scheduling", in *Procs. of 31th. Int. Symp. on Microarchitecture*, pp. 103-114, 1998

[18] E. Özer, S. Banerjia and T.M. Conte, "Unified Assign and Schedule: A New Approach to Scheduling for Clustered Register File Microarchitectures", in *Procs. of 31st Int. Symp. on Microarchitecture*, pp. 308-315, Nov. 1998

[19] S. Palacharla, N.P. Jouppi, and J.E. Smith, "Complexity-Effective Superscalar Processors", in *Procs. of the 24th. Int. Symp. on Computer Architecture*, pp. 1-13, June 1997

[20] B.R. Rau and C.D. Glaeser, "Some Scheduling Techniques and an Easily Schedulable Horizontal Architecture for High Performance Scientific Computing", in *Procs. on the 14th Ann. Workshop on Microprogramming*, pp. 183-198, Oct. 1981

[21] J. Sánchez and A. González, "Cache Sensitive Modulo Scheduling", in *Procs. of 30th. Int. Symp. on Microarchitecture*, pp. 338-348, Dec. 1997

[22] J. Sánchez and A. González, "The Effectiveness of Loop Unrolling for Modulo Scheduling in Clustered VLIW Architectures", in *Procs. of the 29th. Int. Conf. on Parallel Processing*, pp. 555-562, Aug. 2000

[23] Semiconductor Industry Association, "The National Technology Roadmap for Semiconductors: Technology Needs", 1997

[24] Texas Instruments Inc., "TMS320C62x/67x CPU and Instruction Set Reference Guide", 1998

[25] X. Vera, J. Llosa, A. González and C. Ciuraneta, "A Fast Implementation of Cache Miss Equations", in *Procs. of the 8th. Int. Workshop on Compilers for Parallel Computers*, pp. 319-326, Jan. 2000

[26] V.V. Zyuban, "Low-Power High-Performance Superscalar Architectures", *PhD Thesis, Dept. of Computer Science and Engineering, University of Notre Dame*, Jan. 2000

Accelerator Architecture

Two-level Hierarchical Register File Organization for VLIW Processors

Javier Zalamea, Josep Llosa, Eduard Ayguadé and Mateo Valero *
Departament d'Arquitectura de Computadors (UPC)
Universitat Politècnica de Catalunya
{jzalamea,josepll,eduard,mateo}@ac.upc.es

Abstract

High-performance microprocessors are currently designed to exploit the inherent instruction level parallelism (ILP) available in most applications. The techniques used in their design and the aggressive scheduling techniques used to exploit this ILP tend to increase the register requirements of the loops. If more registers than those available in the architecture are required, some actions (such as spill code insertion) have to be applied to reduce this pressure, at the expense of some performance degradation. This degradation could be avoided if a high–capacity register file were included without causing a negative impact on the cycle time of the processor.

In this paper we propose a two-level hierarchical register file organization for VLIW architectures that combines high capacity and low access time. For the configuration proposed in this paper, the new organization achieves a speed–up of 10–14% over a monolithic organization with 64 registers; it is obtained with a 43% (40%) reduction in area (peak power dissipation). Compared to a monolithic file with 32 registers, the speed–up is as much as 38% with just a 14% (4%) increase in area (peak power dissipation).

1. Introduction

Current high-performance microprocessors use hardware and software techniques to exploit the instruction level parallelism (ILP) available in applications. Their architecture makes use of deep pipelines in an attempt to reduce the cycle time and simultaneous issue of operations in order to increase the number of instructions executed per cycle. It is expected that future designs will make extensive use of both techniques. Therefore, new processor organizations and compiler techniques are required to effectively exploit this potential parallelism.

The proper scheduling of instructions plays a critical role in the final performance. This scheduling is done at run–time in out–of–order superscalar processors (with the aid of the compiler which performs extensive code scheduling to facilitate the dynamic detection of parallelism). However, in Very Long Instruction Word (VLIW) architectures the scheduling of instructions is done at compilation time. The static nature of VLIW schedules requires good compilation techniques that effectively exploit the ILP available in programs [4, 12, 20].

Loops are the main time consuming part of numerical programs. Software pipelining [5, 14] is a loop scheduling technique that extracts parallelism from loops by overlapping operations from various consecutive iterations. Modulo scheduling [8, 22] is a class of software pipelining algorithms which has been incorporated in many production compilers. In a modulo scheduled loop, the *Initiation Interval* (*II*) is the number of cycles between the initiation of successive iterations. For a loop, the lower the *II* the higher the number of operations executed per cycle. For example, Figure 1 shows the average number of floating point computations performed per cycle[1] for different processor configurations *GPxMy-REGz* (x being the number of general–purpose floating–point functional units, y the number of memory ports, and z the number of registers in the register file). Notice that, in general, increasing the number of resources results in an increase in the performance achieved. For each loop and processor configuration, the *II* is bounded either by recurrences in the dependence graph or by resource constraints in the target architecture. For instance, increasing the number of functional units by a given amount may not result in the same increase of performance because of the loops which are limited by either recurrences or by other resources.

The drawback of aggressive scheduling techniques such as modulo scheduling is their high register requirements

---

*This work has been supported by the Ministry of Education of Spain under contract TIC 98/511 and by CEPBA (European Center for Parallelism of Barcelona). Javier Zalamea is granted by the Agencia Española de Cooperación Internacional.

[1]Assuming the experimental workbench (set of loops, modulo scheduler, ...) described in Section 2.

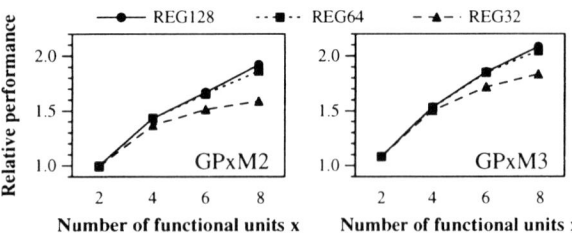

Figure 1. Average number of floating point computations performed per cycle for processor configuration *GPxMy-REGz*, relative to *GP2M2-REG32*.

[17] compared to less aggressive and less effective scheduling techniques. In addition, the use of aggressive processor configurations tends to increase the number of registers required by software pipelined loops. For this reason, many proposals have focused on minimizing the register requirements of modulo scheduling [9, 11, 18]. However, despite these techniques, many registers are still required. For instance, for one of the above mentioned processor configurations (*GP6M2*), the dashed line in Figure 2 shows the percentage of loops that can be scheduled with a specific number of registers using a register–conscious modulo scheduler. The solid line in the same figure shows the percentage of cycles spent in the execution of these loops. Notice that although less than 15% of the loops require more than 32 registers (and even less require more than 64 registers), they represent close to 40% of the total execution time. Other optimizations applied to loops (such as unrolling, common subexpression elimination, back substitution, ... [17]), techniques oriented towards hiding the negative effects of cache misses (such as prefetching [2] or blocking), breaking the data dependences (such as data speculation) or breaking the control dependence flow (predication, control speculation) increase even more the register requirements.

When a loop requires more registers than available, register pressure must be decreased by either increasing the *II* or by adding spill code (i.e. temporarily storing values in memory and freeing, for several cycles, the registers used). These two alternatives degrade performance at the expense of alleviating the high register demand. The evaluation performed in [16] shows that reducing the execution rate tends to generate worse schedules than spilling variables. New heuristics for register spilling have been proposed and proven to be very effective [28]. In any case, the performance degradation is still significant and could be avoided if additional capacity were provided in the register file.

The organization and management of the register file has been a subject of research in the past. The main idea behind all this research is to trade off aspects related to storage capacity, area, cycle time and power dissipation of the register file. The monolithic register file organization traditionally used in the design of microprocessors does not scale well when the register requirements and the number of ports required to access it are high. In this paper we present an alternative design for the register file of future aggressive VLIW processors that tries to combine high capacity and high number of ports with low access time. The higher capacity reduces spill code and allows the application of aggressive software prefetching techniques.

This paper is organized as follows: Section 2 presents the framework used to evaluate the performance of our proposal. Section 3 studies the behavior of software pipelined loops for different configurations of the VLIW processor in which the number of registers in the register file, the memory bandwidth and the latency are varied. From this study, which includes the effect of the cycle time of the processor, the necessity for an alternative design of the register file is foreseen. Section 4 proposes the use of a two–level hierarchical organization; cycle time, area and peak power dissipation are the metrics used to compare the proposal with other monolithic register file organizations. Section 5 describes alternative designs proposed in the literature. Section 6 evaluates the proposal, assuming both an ideal memory system (always hits in the cache) and a real memory environment. Finally, Section 7 concludes the paper and presents some future work.

2. Evaluation framework

The proposal presented in this paper is validated using the framework described in this section. A workbench composed of all the loops from the Perfect Club benchmark [1] that are suitable for software pipelining is considered representative of the loops in numerical applications. A total of 1258 loops, that represent about 80% of the total execution time of the benchmark have been scheduled using HRMS (Hypernode Reduction Modulo Scheduling) [18], a register–conscious pipeliner. HRMS generates near–optimal schedules with minimum register requirements. If the schedule generated by HRMS does not fit into the available number of registers, an iterative process is started in which the register requirements are progressively reduced. This process combines the two techniques mentioned above (i.e. increase of the *II* and the insertion of spill code) [28].

The evaluation framework includes a set of statically scheduled VLIW configurations *GPxMy–REGz* already defined as follows: *x* is the number of general–purpose floating–point functional units, *y* is the number of memory ports (number of load/store units) and *z* is the number of

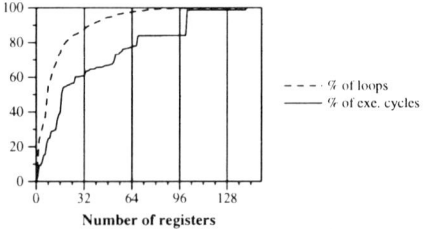

Figure 2. Register requirements for *GP6M2*.

registers in the register file. In all configurations, the latencies of operations performed in the functional units are: 4 cycles for addition and multiplication, 17 cycles for division and 30 cycles for square root. All operations are fully pipelined except for division and square root. In this paper, we focus our study and experimental evaluation on aggressive processor configurations which could be implemented in a near future and which result in a reasonable efficiency (see Figure 1): $x=6$, $y=\{2,3\}$ and $z=\{16,32,64,128\}$.

The memory is designed around a multi–ported memory system (y ports) with a $L1$–cache of 32 Kb and 32 bytes line size. The $L1$–cache is lockup–free and allows up to 8 pending memory accesses. Hit latency for load operations is 2 cycles. Write operations take one cycle to complete. Miss latency is assumed to be in the range 4–32 cycles.

The performance metrics used in the evaluation are: execution cycles (directly obtained from the II and the number of iterations of the loops), memory traffic (including spill code), and execution time (where the access time of the register file is considered). The evaluation also compares the area occupied by the register file organization. Aspects related to power dissipation are briefly considered in this paper. All figures are given relative to a baseline configuration $GP6M2$–$REG128$.

In order to estimate access time, area and power dissipation for the different register file configurations, we use the model described in [23] targeted at a CMOS process with a minimum drawn gate length of $0.18\mu m$. These figures depend on the number of registers, the number of access ports (which is in turn determined by the number of functional units x and memory ports y), and the clock frequency. For instance, for $GP6M2$–$REGz$, the number of ports is: 14 read ports (2 for each functional unit and 2 for the memory) and 8 write ports (one for each functional unit and 2 for the memory). Since the register file is the main centralized structure in a VLIW architecture, it can be assumed that the cycle time of future processors will be determined by the access time to the register file. For instance, Table 1 shows the cycle time, area and peak power dissipation for the set of monolithic register file organizations considered in this paper. Cycle time is given in nanoseconds, area is given in millions of λ^2 and power is given in watts. Also, all are given relative to the baseline configuration.

3. Register requirements for VLIW schedules

The register requirements of software pipelined loops increase with the aggressiveness of the processor configuration and the latencies of the functional units and memory used. Techniques that try to hide the long latency of cache misses (like prefetching) also increase the register requirements. In this section we analyze the behavior, in an ideal memory system, of the workload considered in this paper when varying the capacity of the register file, the number of ports to memory and the latency of memory.

3.1. Register file size

For a particular VLIW architecture, the number of registers available in the register file may constrain the maximum performance that software pipelined loops may attain. For a loop, if its register requirements are larger than the size of the register file, spill code is required in order to reduce this pressure. Spill code increases memory traffic and therefore may reduce performance (increase of the II due to a saturation of the memory ports).

Figure 3 shows the behavior of our benchmark set for the 4 register file configurations considered. When the size of the register file is increased, the number of cycles needed to execute the loop and the memory traffic are reduced. This is due to the reduction of the spill code. For instance, configuration $GP6M2$–$REG16$ needs 1.6 times more cycles than $GP6M2$–$REG128$. Similarly, $GP6M2$–$REG16$ generates about 2.3 times more memory traffic than $GP6M2$–$REG128$. However, the execution time plot (Figure 3.c) shows a direct trade–off between the register file size and the actual performance. This plot is obtained by multiplying the values in Figure 3.a by the cycle time of each register file (Table 1). Notice that $GP6M2$–$REG128$ results in the best performance in terms of number of cycles. However, the high access time of its register file results in a clear degradation of the execution time. In terms of execution time, $GP6M2$–$REG32$ performs best in our workbench.

	Cycle time	Area	Power
Reg	ηs (relat.)	$\lambda^2 * 10^6$ (relat.)	W (relat.)
GP6M2			
128	1.651 (1.000)	5.325 (1.000)	10.409 (1.00)
64	1.451 (0.879)	2.662 (0.500)	6.030 (0.58)
32	1.280 (0.775)	1.331 (0.250)	3.504 (0.34)
16	1.130 (0.685)	0.666 (0.125)	2.054 (0.20)
GP6M3			
128	1.687 (1.022)	6.193 (1.163)	12.435 (1.19)
64	1.479 (0.896)	3.097 (0.582)	7.222 (0.69)
32	1.303 (0.789)	1.548 (0.291)	4.203 (0.40)
16	1.149 (0.695)	0.774 (0.145)	2.466 (0.24)

Table 1. Cycle time, area and power dissipation for some register file configurations: absolute and relative to a baseline configuration $GP6M2$–$REG128$.

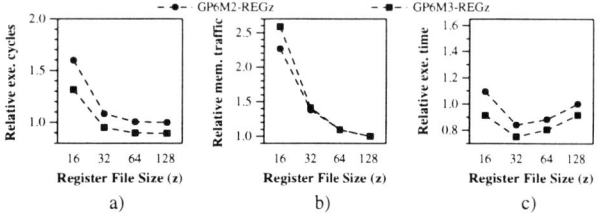

Figure 3. Behavior for several register file configurations relative to the baseline $GP6M2$–$REG128$.

3.2. Memory ports

Increasing the number of ports to memory makes the architecture more aggressive in terms of achievable ILP. This clearly benefits memory bounded loops (i.e. loops limited by the number of memory ports). Furthermore, having an additional memory port also gives more opportunities to schedule spill operations which are needed when the register requirements are higher than the actual register file size.

Having an additional memory port does not contribute to a high increase in the access time of the register file. As shown in Table 1, the gap between the two register file configurations with the same size is not significant (close to 2%). Moreover, the additional memory port complicates the design of the memory hierarchy (with an increase in the memory latency, the area and the power consumption); however, this aspect is not considered in our evaluation.

The two independent plots in Figure 3 show the behavior for *GP6M2–REGz* and *GP6M3–REGz* on the benchmark set. Notice that adding one memory port reduces both the number of cycles required to execute the loops and the actual execution time. The memory traffic is higher because more ILP is exploited, more spill is required and therefore more pressure is put on the memory ports. However, the differences tend to reduce as the register file size increases (due to the reduction in spill code). For instance, the additional memory port produces a speed–up of 19% in a configuration with 16 registers and 12% in a configuration with 32 registers.

In conclusion, the designer of a VLIW microarchitecture would like to obtain the IPC reported by a configuration with a large number of registers (e.g. *GP6Mx–REG128*) and with the cycle time of configurations with a low number of registers (e.g. *GP6Mx–REG16*). In this paper we present an alternative design for the register file that tries to achieve both things. However, before going into detail, we analyze the influence of the memory latency in performance and register requirements.

3.3. Memory latency

In this subsection we analyze the effect of the memory latency on register pressure. A range of values between 2 and 32 cycles is considered. Although very high values may seem unrealistic for the first level of cache, they are included in our analysis for the following reasons. First, technology trends indicate that the gap between the processor cycle time and the cache hit latency will increase; therefore, considering memory latencies in the range of 4–8 cycles should be possible in the near future. Second, some current designs are proposed so that certain instructions (e.g. floating point) bypass the first level of cache; in this case, observed latencies in the range of 8–16 cycles are reasonable. And third, previous research has shown that scheduling load operations with miss latency (i.e. with the second–level hit latency) may produce better schedules than scheduling them with hit latency [24]. Scheduling load operations with their hit latency generates a valid schedule that forces the processor to stall the execution of a whole long instruction whenever a cache miss occurs on it. Binding prefetching (also known as early prefetching) consists in scheduling load operations assuming their cache miss latency. This ensures that data will always be available when needed. However this early availability increases the lifetime of values brought from memory and, as a consequence, the register pressure.

Figure 4 shows the behavior for different values of the memory latency. First of all, notice that some of the plots do not have values for all the latency values. When the memory latency increases, our software pipeliner fails to find a valid schedule for some of the loops: the register pressure is so high that the addition of spill code does not effectively reduce it (in fact, the register requirements of the spill instructions can not be absorbed by the registers available). These loops have to be scheduled using a non–pipelined scheduler and for this reason, have not been considered.

Second, notice that the execution cycles increase with the memory latency. This is due to the additional register pressure caused by the load instructions and to the increase in the latency of critical recurrences (i.e. cycles in the dependence graph that limit the *II*) which includes at least one memory operation.

Finally, the trade–off between IPC and cycle time is also noticeable in Figure 4. For small values of the memory latency (e.g. 2 or 4 cycles), the *GP6M2–REG32* register file performs best. This conclusion is applicable to systems in which the processor/memory gap is small and use schedulers that consider hit latency for memory instructions. For latency values in the range 8 to 16 cycles (e.g. future systems with a high processor/memory gap or when using schedulers that apply binding prefetching), configuration *GP6M2–REG64* is able to better trade–off IPC and cycle time. Configuration *GP6M2–REG128* become interesting when we consider very high values of the memory latency (i.e. when considering binding prefetching and future technologies that lead to a high processor/memory gap).

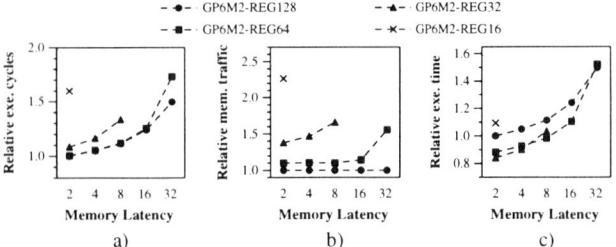

Figure 4. Behavior for different values of memory latency relative to the baseline *GP6M2–REG128*.

4. New register file organization

In the previous section we concluded that a register file with a high number of registers and a large number of access ports is required in order to effectively exploit ILP. However, the cycle time obtained from the access time to the register file easily offsets the gains obtained in terms of instructions executed per cycle.

In order to have a register file organization with a large number of ports and a low access time, this paper proposes a two-level hierarchical register file organization, as shown in Figure 5.a. The first level, named *R1*, has a small capacity but a high number of ports (in order to feed all the functional units); this will permit a design with a small access time. The second level, named *R2*, has a higher capacity in order to avoid the degradation that might be caused by the small capacity of *R1*, to reduce the necessity of spill and to improve the performance through the use of binding prefetching. This level interacts with *R1* and with the first level of cache memory; *R2* is not directly accessible by the functional units so it has a small number of ports. This level will be designed so as to have as many registers as possible without penalizing the access time determined by *R1*.

The main drawback of the two-level register file organization is the increase in the latency observed between memory and functional units and the increase in the number of instructions in the program. In this organization, a memory *load* operation brings data to *R2*, so that an extra number of cycles is required in order to move data from *R2* to *R1*. The same happens in a *store* operation which requires a first move from *R1* to *R2* followed by the memory access. This extra latency increases the *II* when a loop has a critical recurrence including at least one memory operation.

In a VLIW processor, this movement between *R1* and *R2* is controlled by the compiler. Two new operations are needed to move data between register file levels: *loadR* and *storeR*. The compiler inserts a *loadR* after the original *load* operation. Similarly, the compiler inserts a *storeR* operation before the original *store* operation. The compiler can also move data between levels in order to spill values when the pressure in *R1* is higher than its capacity.

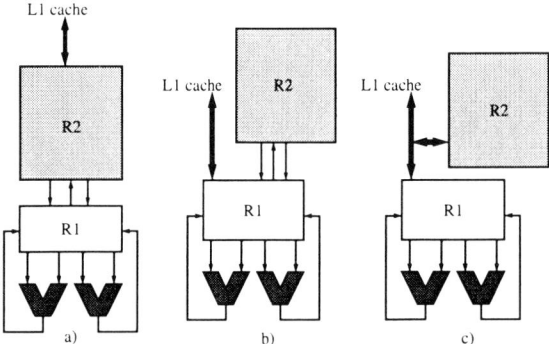

Figure 5. a) Two-level hierarchical register file; b) and c) two alternative CCM organizations.

The explicit management of these data movements requires modifications in the algorithm used for register allocation and spilling. The proposed algorithm first allocates registers in *R1* using the wands-only strategy with end-fit and adjacency ordering [21]. If there are not enough registers in *R1*, spill code between *R1* and *R2* is inserted. Spill code is added using the techniques proposed in [28] and using only the *loadR* and *storeR* instructions. Once the register allocation and spill is completed for *R1*, the algorithm proceeds with *R2*. In *R2* the algorithm has to fit the registers required by data brought from the memory as well as the registers required by the spill of *R1*. Register allocation and spilling is performed using the same techniques as for *R1*. Notice that this spill code temporarily stores values in memory; however, the high capacity of our register file organization reduces the necessity for this.

4.1. Design issues

In a two-level hierarchical register file there are three parameters that influence the final performance (without varying other parameters such as the number of functional units and memory ports). These parameters are: a) number of registers in *R1*, b) number of read and write ports between *R1* and *R2* and c) number of registers in *R2*. We assume that the number of registers in each level is a power of two.

In order to find the most appropriate value for *R1*, 3 possible configurations have been explored (8, 16, and 32):

- For the 8 registers configuration, there are so few registers that our software pipeliner fails to schedule many of the benchmark loops due to the high number of functional units available in the architecture evaluated; although possible schedules could be found, they would have very high values for the *II*.

- For the 16 registers configuration, the software pipeliner is able to schedule all the loops in the benchmark set. This therefore is the minimum size that should be considered.

- For the 32 registers configuration, the software pipeliner is also able to schedule all the loops. However, its access time is slightly higher than the access time of a monolithic 32 register file. Moreover, even assuming an infinite number of ports and an unlimited number of registers in the second level, the performance (in number of cycles) is worse than the performance of the monolithic design with 32 registers.

Therefore, 16 registers have been included in *R1* because this allows the schedule of all the loops and has a competitive cycle time compared to the design with 32 registers which achieved the best execution time with small memory latencies (Figures 3.c).

In order to determine the number of read and write ports between *R1* and *R2*, we have first assumed that *R1* has 16 registers, the number of ports between *R1* and *R2* is unlimited and that *R2* has also an unlimited number of registers. Figure 6 shows the cumulative distribution of loops that require, on average, a specific number (e.g. a loop that requires 4 read ports in cycle 0, 2 in cycle 1 and 0 in cycle 2 requires, on average, 2 ports per cycle). For instance, 80% of the loops require an average of 2 load ports at most. Since software pipelining tries to saturate all the resources available, it is sufficient to have as many ports as the maximum average required to schedule all the loops. In Figure 6, it should be noted that the scheduler never uses more than 2 store ports and 4 load ports.

The parameters decided at this point, together with the number of functional units, determine the access time to *R1*. The upper part of Table 2 estimates this. The capacity of *R2* is selected as the maximum capacity with an access time smaller than (or equal to) the access time of *R1*. This means that the number of cycles to execute *loadR* and *storeR* operations is one cycle. Notice that we could use more registers in *R2* and schedule these move operations with the appropriate latency. The lower half of Table 2 shows an estimate of the access time for *R2* with 64 and 128 registers. From these figures, 64 registers in *R2* fulfills the requirements (although using 128 registers would only increase the cycle time by 2% but would require more area and power). Moreover, we have experimentally proven that with 64 registers, the spill to memory is negligible.

In summary, the two-level hierarchical register file organization proposed in this paper (named *TWO16*) has the following parameters: 16 registers in the first level *R1*; 64 registers in the second level *R2*; 2 store ports from *R1* to *R2*; and 4 load ports from *R2* to *R1*.

4.2. Register file area and power dissipation

In this subsection we estimate the area and power dissipation for the register file configuration proposed in this section and compare it with that of a monolithic organization. The model described in [23] is used to compute these figures for a monolithic register file (see Table 1 for configurations *REG16*, *REG32*, *REG64*, and *REG128*). For the two-level organization, we assume that they are computed as the sum of the individual figures for *R1* and *R2*.

Table 2 shows the area estimated for configuration *TWO16*. Notice that in the monolithic organization, the area of $REGz$ is linear with z because all of them have the same number of ports. The area of *R1* in configuration *TWO16* is the same as *REG16* with 3 memory ports; the area of *R2* is smaller than the area of *REG64* because it has less access ports. From these area estimations, we conclude that *TWO16* is 14% larger than *REG32* and 43% smaller than *REG64* in processor configuration *GP6M2*.

Regarding power dissipation, the model in [23] gives the dissipation per access to the register file. The peak power dissipation is computed multiplying this value by the maximum number of accesses per cycle that the register file supports. From these estimations, we conclude that the power dissipation of *TWO16* is 4% greater than *REG32* and 40% less than *REG64* in processor configuration *GP6M2*. A complete evaluation of power consumption is necessary in order to perform an accurate comparison of both organizations. In this evaluation, the power consumption of other parts of the system should be considered, such as the instruction and data caches. For instance, notice that the traffic with the data cache is reduced (due to the reduction of spill operations) and therefore its power consumption is, too. However, the number of accesses (and their width) to the instruction cache is increased (due to the the higher values of the *II* and the extra length of the instruction). This evaluation is part of our current work.

5. Related register file organizations

The organization and management of the register file has been a subject of research in the past. The main idea behind all this research is to strike a compromise between the parameters related to storage capacity, area, access time and power dissipation of the register file. As we have concluded in Section 3, the single monolithic register file which has been traditionally used in microprocessors does not scale well when the register requirements are high, i.e. when using either aggressive processor configurations or instruction scheduling algorithms such as software pipelining. Recently, [23] developed a taxonomy of register architectures and evaluated it for media and signal processors with a large number of arithmetical units.

Size	Ports	Cycle time	Area	Power
R1	R/W	ηs (relat.)	$\lambda^2 * 10^6$ (relat.)	W (relat.)
16	14/10	1.1489 (0.695)	0.774 (0.145)	2.818 (0.270)
R2	R/W	ηs (relat.)	$\lambda^2 * 10^6$ (relat.)	W (relat.)
64	6/4	1.0205 (0.618)	0.745 (0.140)	0.840 (0.081)
128	6/4	1.1735 (0.711)	1.491 (0.280)	1.648 (0.158)
TWO16		1.1489 (0.695)	1.519 (0.285)	3.658 (0.351)

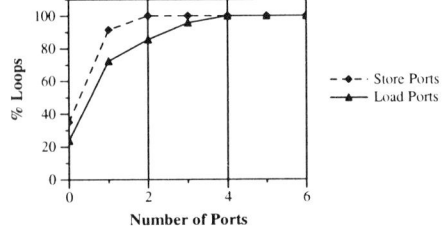

Figure 6. Analysis of requirements: number of read and write ports between *R1* and *R2*.

Table 2. Access time, area and power for *R1* and *R2* in the two-level register file organization (absolute and relative to the baseline configuration *GP6M2-REG128*).

5.1. One–level (distributed/partitioned) register file organization

Some proposals for alternative register file organizations focus on the use of multiple register banks so as to reduce the number of ports needed by each register bank. Register banks can be used to replicate the available registers: fully replicated as in some current out–of–order microprocessors [13, 27] or partially replicated for VLIW processors [15]. Register banks can also be used to distribute the total number of registers [3, 10]. The partition limits the connectivity between register banks and functional units thus creating a set of clusters; different topologies can be used to connect clusters (global shared buses [3] or rings [10]).

Other proposals do not restrict the connectivity between the register banks and the functional units. Banks may be designed with different characteristics or purposes. For instance, [19] proposed to reduce the number of registers required in the main register bank by adding a second port–limited bank (called the sack) with only one read port and one write port. Each bank tries to capture values with different locality properties.

5.2. Hierarchical register file organization

The hierarchical organization of the register file is not new. In these organizations not all banks can directly feed the functional units and/or memory. The level close to the functional units can be designed with less capacity and therefore, small access time. For instance, the CRAY–1 [25] included, for the scalar functional units, two independent banks (one for addresses and another for data) each with a two–level organization: the lower level (close to the functional units) had 8 registers and the upper level had 64 registers able to do block transfers with the memory. The upper level had no connection with the functional units; both register files were connected to the main memory. The upper level was used by the compiler to optimize data locality.

In a different context, [26] proposed the hierarchical design of a register file. Their register file had 1024 registers in three levels: "close" level with 5 registers, "middle" level with 59 registers and "distant" level with 960 registers. In this hierarchy, the latency to access a given register level is less when closer to the functional units.

In parallel with the work presented in this paper, a caching mechanism for the register file in dynamically scheduled processors has been proposed [7]. The organization is hierarchical and the allocation of values to registers is performed at runtime. The mechanism is transparent to the compiler and acts as a cache for the register file.

5.3. Local memory for spill code

A register file organization oriented towards capturing spill code in DSP processors is proposed in [6]. The small (and fast) local memory, which is available in some of these processors, is used as a holding place for spilled values. They called it CCM (compiler–controlled memory). The CCM does not share the address space with the cache memory. Spilling to the CCM removes spill traffic from the path to main memory and eliminates the cache pollution introduced by spill operations. Their proposal was evaluated in a simple machine model that issued one instruction per cycle. In order to do a more realistic comparison with our proposal, Section 6.1 evaluates their performance with our machine configurations, our scheduler and benchmarks.

Figure 5 shows two possible implementations for the CCM proposal. Figure 5.b shows an implementation in which the buses connecting $R1$ to $R2$ and memory are independent. In this case, memory and spill operations can be scheduled in the same cycle. However, the access time to the register file is increased due to the additional ports. For this implementation, two configurations are evaluated with 16 registers in $R1$: $CCMind(16-6)$ with 4 write and 2 read ports and $CCMind(16-3)$ with 2 write and 1 read ports.

Figure 5.c shows an alternative implementation in which the $R2$ and memory are accessed through the same bus (shared bus). In this case the number of ports is not increased and therefore the cycle time is not affected. However, the modulo scheduler has more constraints in order to schedule memory and spill operations because they require the same resource. For this implementation, two configurations are evaluated: $CCMsh(16)$ and $CCMsh(32)$ with 16 and 32 registers in $R1$, respectively.

Table 3 shows the cycle time estimated for the 4 different configurations assumed for the CCM. We have considered that the $R2$ does not limit the cycle time and is large enough to ensure that all the spill traffic is kept in $R2$.

6. Performance evaluation

This section evaluates the performance of the hierarchical register file organization $TWO16$ and compares it with two monolithic designs $REG32$ and $REG64$. First, the evaluation is carried out assuming an ideal memory system (i.e. always hit in the cache); the performance of $TWO16$ is also compared with the performance for two possible implementations of the CCM organization [6]. Finally, the evaluation is carried out assuming a real memory system.

Configuration	Size R1	Ports Read	Ports Write	Cycle time ηs (relat.)
$CCMind(16-6)$	16	20	14	1.1844 (0.717)
$CCMind(16-3)$	16	19	12	1.1580 (0.701)
$CCMsh(32)$	32	18	10	1.2805 (0.775)
$CCMsh(16)$	16	18	10	1.1304 (0.685)

Table 3. Access time for a set of CCM register file implementations.

6.1. Ideal memory system

Figure 7.a shows the execution cycles spent in the loops for the three possible configurations. Notice that *TWO16* always requires more cycles to execute the benchmark set than *REG64*. Compared to *REG32*, *TWO16* requires less execution cycles when the latency to memory is higher than 4 cycles. This is due to the extra cycles needed to move data to/from memory and the small capacity of the first level *R1*. Figure 7.b shows that *TWO16* practically absorbs all the memory traffic incurred by spill operations.

Figure 7.c shows the relative execution time when the cycle time is factored in. Notice that *TWO16* outperforms both *REG32* and *REG64* configurations for all memory latencies. For low latencies (2 cycles) *TWO16* is 6% (11%) faster than the *REG32* (*REG64*) configuration. However if the memory latency is larger the speed–up increases. For instance, for 8 cycles of latency, *TWO16* shows a speed–up of 18% compared to *REG32*; for 32 cycles of latency the speed–up is 22% compared to *REG64*.

The low cycle time achieved by the hierarchical configuration makes it very competitive even assuming systems with the monolithic register file and more ports with the memory system. Figure 7.d–f shows the results when configuration *GP6M3* is considered. Notice that, in terms of relative execution time, configuration *REG32* is better only if the memory latency is small (2 cycles); for higher latencies, *TWO16* performs slightly better (4%) than *REG64* with less ports in the memory hierarchy. Moreover, notice that the scheduler always finds a possible software pipelined schedule for all the values of memory latency (it is not able to do so for *REG32* when the memory latency is higher than 8 and for *REG64* when the latency is higher than 16.

For the four configurations of the CCM proposal previously defined, we have repeated the simulations and their results are shown in Figure 8. The plot for memory traffic has

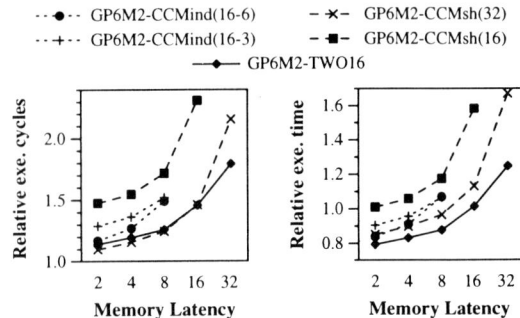

Figure 8. Behavior of some alternative implementations of CCM compared to *TWO16*.

been eliminated because it always remains constant (i.e. all configurations completely eliminate spill to memory). Notice that, in terms of number of execution cycles, the register file organization proposed in this paper performs better than the two *CCMind* configurations evaluated, much better than *CCMsh* with 16 registers in *R1* and similar to *CCMsh* with 32 registers in *R1* (up to 16 cycles). In terms of execution time, the performance achieved by the proposal in this paper is always higher and less sensitive to cache miss latency.

6.2. Real memory system and binding prefetching

In this section we analyze the behavior of the proposed register file organization in a real memory environment. As mentioned in Section 2, hit latency for load operations is 2 cycles and miss latency may have three possible values: low (10 ηs), medium (20 ηs) and high (40 ηs). Cache–miss latencies in cycles are computed assuming the corresponding cycle time for each configuration of the register file. For example, Table 4 shows the cache miss latency in cycles for the *GP6M2* configuration.

The evaluation breaks down the total number of cycles and execution time into two components: useful (i.e. when the processor is doing useful work) and stall (i.e. when the processor is blocked waiting for a cache miss to complete the access). All performance figures in this section are relative to the number of useful cycles of configuration *GP6M2–REG32* with small cache–miss latency.

The modulo scheduler used in our experimental framework can assume either hit latency to schedule memory load operations or apply binding prefetching. Scheduling with hit latency minimizes the register pressure and theoretically increases performance. This generates a valid schedule that stalls the processor whenever a cache miss occurs or when-

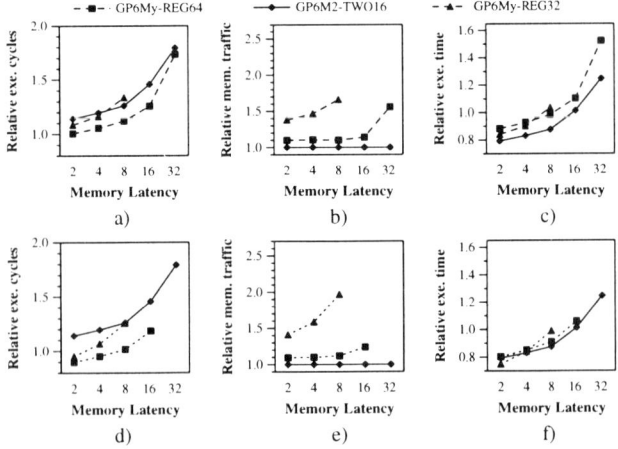

Figure 7. Behavior of *GP6M2–REG32/64* (first row), *GP6M3–REG32/64* (second row) and *GP6M2–TWO16*, all of them relative to *GP6M2–REG128*.

Configuration	Cycle time	Cache–miss latency		
	ηs	Small	Medium	High
GP6M2–REG32	1.2805	8	16	32
GP6M2–REG64	1.4513	7	14	28
GP6M2–TWO16	1.1489	9	18	35

Table 4. Cycle time and cache–miss latencies for 32, 64 and two–level register files.

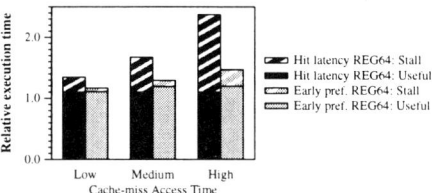

Figure 9. Execution time when scheduling loops using hit latency or selective binding prefetching.

ever a dependent instruction needs the datum brought from memory (in case of lockup–free caches). Binding prefetching can be used to tolerate the latency of these cache misses [2]. Binding prefetching consists in scheduling the *load* instructions assuming cache miss latency. Binding prefetching does not increase memory traffic but increases register pressure, as shown in Section 3.3. However, the higher capacity of the proposed *TWO16* organization allows us to apply aggressive prefetching techniques.

In this paper we use a selective binding prefetching approach. The algorithm assumes that those load operations included in recurrences as well as spill load operations are scheduled assuming hit latency. All other load operations are scheduled assuming miss latency. Those loops which execute a small number of iterations are also scheduled assuming hit latency for all their memory load operations (in order to avoid long prologues and epilogues in the software pipelined code). For instance, Figure 9 compares the performance of configuration *GP6M2-REG64* when loops in our benchmark set are scheduled either assuming hit latency or when applying selective binding prefetching. Notice that binding prefetching generates schedules that noticeably reduce the execution time (for instance, up to 40%). With binding prefetching, the number of useful cycles is increased and the number of stall cycles reduced; notice that stall cycles are not completely eliminated due to the misses that may happen in recurrences and in short loops.

Assuming that binding prefetching always results in better schedules, we proceed with a comparison of the monolithic and two–level register organizations. Figure 10.a shows the execution cycles relative to the useful cycles of the *REG32* configuration. Notice that *GP6M2–REG64* requires less cycles to execute than its *TWO16* counterpart. However, the influence of the cycle time offsets this result in favor of the two–level organization, as shown in Figure 10.b. For instance, *TWO16* reduces the execution time of *REG64* in a range of 10–14%. Compared to *REG32*, the reduction in execution time is as much as 38%.

7 Conclusions

High-performance microprocessors are currently designed to exploit the inherent ILP available in most applications. The techniques used in their design and the aggressive scheduling techniques tend to increase the register requirements of the loops. If more registers than those available in the architecture are required, some actions are required to reduce this pressure, at the expense of a performance degradation.

The monolithic register file design that has traditionally been used to interconnect functional units and provide short–term storage does not scale well when the architecture becomes aggressive, which is the current trend in the design of high–performance microprocessors. Cycle time, area and power consumption are the factors that limit its performance and usability. These limit the size of the register file and therefore introduce some degradation because of the addition of spill code. This degradation could be avoided if high–capacity register file organizations could be included in VLIW designs, but without having a negative impact on the cycle time, area and power of the processor.

In this paper we have proposed a two–level hierarchical register file organization that combines high capacity and low access time. For the configurations and workload evaluated, the best register file configuration consists of 16 registers in the first level and 64 registers in the second level. The high capacity of the register organization reduces the amount of register spilling and therefore its additional memory traffic. It also allows the use of more aggressive prefetching techniques to hide the negative effect of high miss latencies. The proposed organization achieves a cycle time 2% greater than a monolithic register file configuration with 16 registers. For one of the processor configurations and workload evaluated in this paper, this new organization reduces the execution time by 10–14% when compared to a monolithic organization with 64 registers; this speed–up is obtained with a 43% reduction in area. Compared to a monolithic organization with 32 registers, the reduction in execution time is up to 38% with a 14% increase in area.

In addition, the new organization requires much less peak power (40%) than a monolithic organization with 64 registers and slightly more (4%) than 32 registers. We estimate that this small difference in peak power will result in

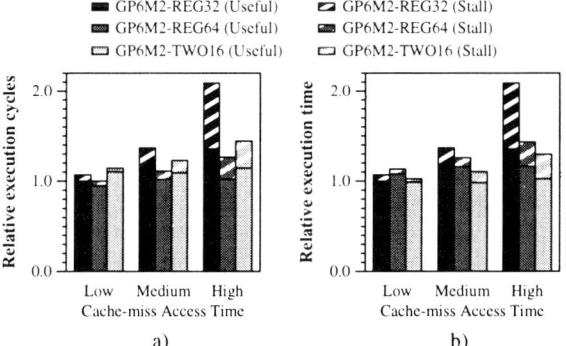

Figure 10. Performance evaluation for configuration *GP6M2* with three different configurations for the register file: *REG32*, *REG64* and *TWO16*.

less energy consumption because of less memory accesses caused by spill code. However, the additional instruction accesses may reduce this advantage. Further research is required to accurately evaluate energy consumption.

In some way, the hierarchical organization proposal in this paper could be defined as a functional clustering in which one cluster is composed of the functional units and a small register file with a large number of ports. The second cluster is composed of the memory units and a higher register file with the less ports. We are currently extending this idea in order to have multiple clusters for the functional units with smaller register files.

References

[1] M. Berry, D. Chen, P. Koss, and D. Kuck. The Perfect Club benchmarks: Effective performance evaluation of supercomputers. Technical Report 827, Center for Supercomputing Research and Development, November 1988.

[2] D. Callahan, K. Kennedy, and A. Porterfield. Software prefetching. In *Proc Fourth Int. Conf. on Architectural Support for Programming Languages and Operating Systems (ASPLOS-IV)*, pages 40–52, April 1991.

[3] A. Capitanio, N. Dutt, and A. Nicolau. Partitioned register files for VLIWs: A preliminary analysis of tradeoffs. In *MICRO25*, pages 292–300, 1992.

[4] P. Chang, S. Mahlke, W. Chen, N. Warter, and W. Hwu. IMPACT: An architectural framework for multiple-instruction-issue processors. In *Proc., 18th Internat. Symp. on Computer Architecture*, pages 266–275, 1991.

[5] A. Charlesworth. An approach to scientific array processing: The architectural design of the AP120B/FPS-164 family. *Computer*, 14(9):18–27, 1981.

[6] K. D. Cooper and T. Harvey. Compiler–controlled memory. In *Proc., Eighth Internat. Conf. on Architectural Support for Programming Languages and Operating Systems*, pages 100–104, October 1998.

[7] J. Cruz, A. Gonzalez, M. Valero, and N. Topham. Multiple-banked register file architectures. In *Proc., 27th Annual Internat. Symp. on Computer Architecture*, June 2000.

[8] J. Dehnert and R. Towle. Compiling for the Cydra 5. *The Journal of Supercomputing*, 7(1/2):181–228, May 1993.

[9] A. Eichenberger and E. Davidson. Stage scheduling: A technique to reduce the register requirements of a modulo schedule. In *Proc. of the 28th Annual Int. Symp. on Microarchitecture (MICRO-28)*, pages 338–349, November 1995.

[10] M. Fernandes, J. Llosa, and N. Topham. Partitioned schedules for clustered vliw architectures. In *Proc., 12th International Parallel Processing Symposium and 9th Symposium on Parallel and Distributed Processing (IPPS/SPDP'1998)*, pages 386–391, March 1998.

[11] R. Huff. Lifetime-sensitive modulo scheduling. In *Proc. of the 6th Conference on Programming Language, Design and Implementation*, pages 258–267, 1993.

[12] W. Hwu, S. Mahlke, W. Chen, P. Chang, N. Warter, R. Bringmann, R. Ouellette, R. Hank, T. Kiyohara, G. Haab, J. Holm, and D. Lavery. The superblock: An effective technique for VLIW and superscalar compilation. *Journal of Supercomputing*, 7(1/2):229–248, 1993.

[13] R. Kessler. The Alpha 21264 microprocessor. *IEEE Micro*, 19(2):24–36, March 1999.

[14] M. Lam. Software pipelining: An effective scheduling technique for VLIW machines. In *Proceedings of the SIGPLAN'88 Conference on Programming Language Design and Implementation*, pages 318–328, June 1988.

[15] J. Llosa, M. Valero, and E. Ayguadé. Non-consistent dual register files to reduce register pressure. In *1st Symposium on High Performance Computer Architecture*, pages 22–31, January 1995.

[16] J. Llosa, M. Valero, and E. Ayguadé. Heuristics for register-constrained software pipelining. In *Proc. of the 29th Annual Int. Symp. on Microarchitecture (MICRO-29)*, pages 250–261, December 1996.

[17] J. Llosa, M. Valero, and E. Ayguadé. Quantitative evaluation of register pressure on software pipelined loops. *International Journal of Parallel Programming*, 26(2):121–142, April 1998.

[18] J. Llosa, M. Valero, E. Ayguadé, and A. González. Hypernode reduction modulo scheduling. In *Proc. of the 28th Annual Int. Symp. on Microarchitecture (MICRO-28)*, pages 350–360, November 1995.

[19] J. Llosa, M. Valero, J. Fortes, and E. Ayguadé. Using Sacks to organize register files in VLIW machines. In *CONPAR 94 - VAPP VI*, September 1994.

[20] B. Rau and J. A. Fisher. Instruction-level parallel processing: History, overview and perspective. *Journal of Supercomputing*, 7(1/2):9–50, July 1993.

[21] B. Rau, M. Lee, P. Tirumalai, and P. Schlansker. Register allocation for software pipelined loops. In *Proc. of the ACM SIGPLAN'92 Conference on Programming Language Design and Implementation*, pages 283–299, June 1992.

[22] B. R. Rau. Iterative modulo scheduling: An algorithm for software pipelining loops. In *Proc. of the 27th Annual International Symposium on Microarchitecture*, pages 63–74, November 1994.

[23] S. Rixner, W. Dally, B. Khailany, P. Mattson, U. Kapasi, and J. Owens. Register organization for media processing. In *Proc., 6th High-Performance Computer Architecture (HPCA-6)*, pages 375–386, January 2000.

[24] J. Sanchez and A. Gonzalez. Cache sensitive modulo scheduling. In *Procs. of the 30th Annual Int. Symp. on Microarchitecture (MICRO-30)*, pages 338–348, December 1997.

[25] D. Siewiorek, C. Bell, and A. Newell. *Computer Structures: Principles and Examples*. MacGraw-Hill, Pittsbutgh, Pennsylvania., 1982.

[26] J. Swensen and Y. Patt. Hierarchical registers for scientific computers. In *International Conference on Supercomputing*, pages 346–353, July 1988.

[27] S. White and S. Dhawan. POWER2: Next generation of the RISC System/6000 family. In *IBM RISC System/6000 Technology: Volume II*. IBM Corporation, 1993.

[28] J. Zalamea, J. Llosa, E. Ayguadé, and M. Valero. Improved spill code generation for software pipelined loops. In *Procs. of the Programming Languages Design and Implementation (PLDI'00)*, June 2000.

PipeRench Implementation of the Instruction Path Coprocessor

Yuan Chou, Pazhani Pillai, Herman Schmit, John Paul Shen
Department of Electrical and Computer Engineering
Carnegie Mellon University
Pittsburgh, PA 15213
{yuanchou,pillai,herman,shen}@ece.cmu.edu

Abstract

This paper demonstrates how an Instruction Path Coprocessor (I-COP) can be efficiently implemented using the PipeRench reconfigurable architecture. An I-COP is a programmable on-chip coprocessor that operates on the core processor's instructions to transform them into a new format that can be more efficiently executed. The I-COP can be used to implement many sophisticated hardware code modification techniques. We show how four specific techniques can be mapped to the PipeRench pipelined computation model. The experimental results show that a PipeRench I-COP used to perform trace construction and trace optimizations for a trace cache fill unit not only achieves good performance gains but can potentially be implemented in less than 10 mm^2 (assuming 0.18 micron technology) or approximately 3% of the die area of a current high-end microprocessor. We believe these results demonstrate the usefulness and feasibility of the I-COP concept.

1 Introduction

1.1 Dynamic Code Modification

Spurred by relentless progress in VLSI design and fabrication, hardware design is evolving at a rapid pace and increasingly sophisticated microarchitectures are being implemented. On the other hand, software is changing much more slowly. One reason is the existence of a large installed base of legacy code that is too expensive to be replaced or recompiled. Another reason is that the deployment of new highly optimizing compilers usually lags behind the deployment of new microarchitectures. The end result is the increasing incompatibility between the compiler-produced object code and the most efficient implementations of fast execution cores that must execute these object code.

One recently proposed approach to solve this problem is to add hardware in the microarchitecture to dynamically modify the object code into an internal format that can be more efficiently processed by fast execution cores. We refer to this general approach as *hardware code modification*. For example, the Intel P6 [1] decoders translate the x86 instructions into an internal format called uops that are then executed by the execution core. Another example is the trace cache [2], which rearranges the ordering of instructions so that frequently executed sequences of instructions are stored in contiguous locations. The trace cache can reduce the complexity of instruction fetching and decoding. There are also proposals to optimize these traces [9][10] before loading them into the trace cache. Recently, there is a proposal to perform run-time program re-layout in hardware [25]. We believe that in the quest for ever higher performance, increasingly sophisticated hardware code modification techniques will be needed in the future.

An *Instruction Path Coprocessor* (I-COP), proposed in [3], is a programmable on-chip coprocessor that allows these hardware code modifications to be implemented in software much like microcode. An I-COP is analogous to a datapath coprocessor, except that it operates on the core processor's *instructions* themselves. The programmable nature of an I-COP affords several advantages. First, complex code modifications that are difficult to implement directly in hardwired logic may be more easily implemented in I-COP code. Second, it allows many code modification techniques to be implemented using the same engine, each of which can be selectively and adaptively invoked at run-time. Third, it allows specialization of microprocessors with the use of different I-COP code or even different I-COP implementations. Fourth, it makes it possible to modify and upgrade the machine simply by changing I-COP code without changing the hardware. We believe an I-COP can potentially be a valuable addition to the microarchitect's toolbox.

In evaluating the feasibility of the I-COP concept, [3]

showed that an I-COP programmed to implement trace construction and trace optimizations achieves good performance. The longer latency (as compared to hardwired logic) that the programmable I-COP takes to perform the code modifications had little impact on performance because the I-COP is located at the back-end of the core processor and because of the frequent reuse of the modified code. The prototype I-COP proposed consists of two VLIWs each with four general function units. Such an I-COP implementation can require a significant amount of chip area.

This paper proposes a novel and much more efficient I-COP implementation using a reconfigurable architecture called PipeRench [4]. In such an implementation, I-COP programs are actually *configuration bits* that are downloaded to the reconfigurable fabric at run-time. After configuration, the fabric becomes a hardware design that implements the desired computation. What distinguishes PipeRench from other reconfigurable fabrics is that it supports very fast reconfiguration as well as a virtualization technique called *pipeline reconfiguration*, which allows a large logical design to be implemented on a small piece of hardware through rapid configuration of that hardware. This virtualization enables smaller I-COP implementations, and also allows complex I-COP programs to be written without the concern that they may not fit within the size of the reconfigurable fabric.

It was shown in [4] that the PipeRench reconfigurable fabric provides significant performance benefits for an application that exhibits one or more of the following features:

1. It operates on bit-widths that are different from a processor's basic word size.
2. Its data dependencies allow multiple function units to operate in parallel.
3. It is composed of a series of basic operations that can be combined into one specialized operation.
4. It can be pipelined.
5. Constant propagation can be performed, reducing the complexity of the operations.
6. The input values are reused many times within the computation.

The results in [3] suggest that the potential I-COP applications exhibit many of these features. For example, the data bit-widths in the I-COP applications are odd and varied. There is also abundant parallelism in these I-COP programs, thus allowing multiple functional units to operate in parallel. In addition, large portions of these programs are composed of basic operations that can be combined into specialized operations. In this paper, we show how hardware code modifications can be mapped to the PipeRench pipelined computation model and that the PipeRench I-COP achieves good performance. Furthermore, we demonstrate that a PipeRench I-COP can be implemented at very reasonable hardware cost, and in so doing, further validate the usefulness of the I-COP concept.

The rest of this paper is organized as follows. Section 2 familiarizes the reader with the I-COP concept and the PipeRench reconfigurable architecture. Section 3 describes our PipeRench I-COP design and how I-COP applications are implemented in this design. Section 4 presents the results of our exploration of the PipeRench design space as well as die-area estimates of selected designs. Section 5 concludes this paper.

2 Background

2.1 Instruction Path Coprocessors

An I-COP is a programmable coprocessor that operates on the core processor's instructions to transform them into a new format that can be more efficiently processed by fast execution cores. These transformations can involve the ordering of instructions, the type of instructions (e.g. from the original instruction to a sequence of simpler instructions) and even the instruction set (e.g. from the original ISA to a new ISA tailored to the microarchitecture).

2.1.1 Interface With Core Processor

The I-COP is located on the same chip as the core processor and runs concurrently with the core processor. In order not to negatively impact the core processor's cycle time, it is situated at the core processor's back-end and interacts primarily with the core processor's completion/retirement stage. The I-COP requires minimal explicit control by the core processor and rarely stalls the core processor. Figure 1 shows the interface between the I-COP and the core processor.

An I-COP should be able to access non-architected entities of the core processor, such as instruction and data caches, trace cache, branch and value predictor tables etc. Where such accesses are allowed, careful considerations are made to ensure that they do not affect the core processor's critical timing paths.

In order for the I-COP to intelligently invoke the appropriate I-COP code based on application characteristics, the core processor has built-in monitors to track its currently executing application's behavior. The I-COP can either poll these monitors or the I-COP can be interrupt-driven. In the latter case, when the monitors exceed or dip below threshold levels, they interrupt the I-COP and cause it to vector to specific I-COP routines.

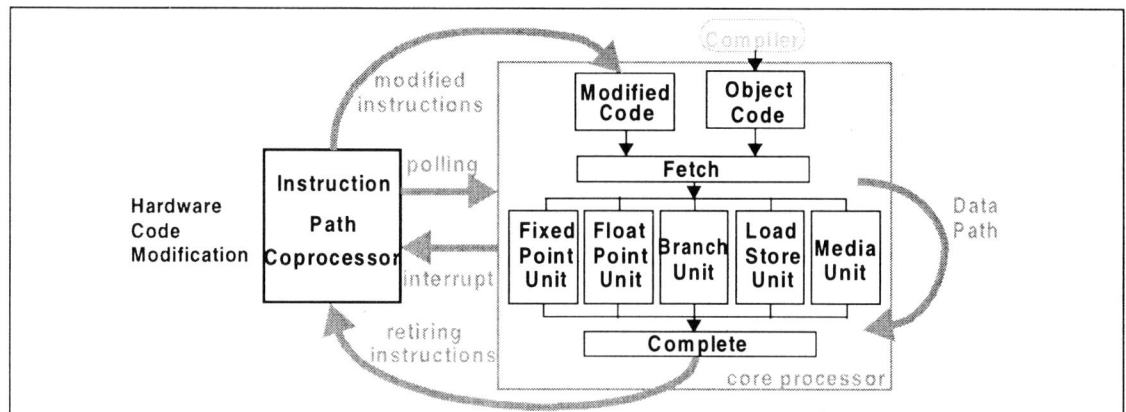

Figure 1. Interface between I-COP and core processor.

2.1.2 Initial Implementation

The initial I-COP implementation [3] was based on conventional CPU design and comprised of one or more VLIW engines (called slices) operating in parallel. For the I-COP applications studied, two VLIW slices with four general functional units each represented a good cost-performance trade-off. The VLIW organization was chosen to minimize hardware complexity, since I-COP programs are relatively small and can easily be statically scheduled. All the slices share a common data memory. Since an I-COP replaces hardwired designs with a programmable engine, slow-down can be expected. To ensure adequate performance, parallelisms in I-COP programs were exploited; instruction-level parallelism was exploited within a VLIW slice and task-level parallelism was exploited across VLIW slices.

The instruction set for the I-COP VLIW slices consisted of 22 instructions. The core of the instruction set was a simple integer-based load/store architecture. In addition, ten specialized instructions were provided to facilitate writing efficient I-COP programs. The most important of these are powerful (and complex) pattern matching instructions to enable regular expression recognition to be performed quickly. Predication support as well as branch delay slots were also provided to eliminate the need for branch prediction. More details about this implementation can be found in [3].

The experimental results showed that this initial I-COP implementation achieved good performance for the I-COP applications studied. However, the drawback is that it requires a significant amount of hardware and can potentially consume sizable chip area.

2.2 PipeRench

PipeRench [4] is a reconfigurable fabric that supports the computational model shown in Figure 2. In this model, a computation on a data stream is expressed as a linearly interconnected set of S pipeline stages, where every stage is a function of the registered output of the previous stage and the registered output of the current stage. Many media and embedded computational kernels can be mapped to this model with many pipeline stages, which allows for high clock speeds and high throughputs. The small amount of feedback allows for efficient implementation. Many instruction transformation techniques can also be mapped to this model. In most instruction transformations, the particular transformations initiated by any instruction only affect subsequent instructions, which fits the limited feedback model.

Assuming that new inputs arrive every cycle, an implementation of this pipeline will require S stages. In PipeRench, the technique of pipeline reconfiguration [5] is used to support the cases when the input stream has an arrival rate, or throughput T, which is less than one every cycle. In this case, S physical stages cannot be kept busy. Alternatively the technique is also useful when the cost of S stages is prohibitive. The technique is illustrated in Figure 3, where the number of stages in the application, S, is five and the number of physical pipeline stages P, is three. As the figure shows, the configuration of stages happens concurrently with the execution of other stages.

Using pipeline reconfiguration, the relationship between S, P and T is given by $T = max\left(\frac{P}{S}, 1\right)$. If $P \geq S$ and the input streams consist of a set of N words, the entire

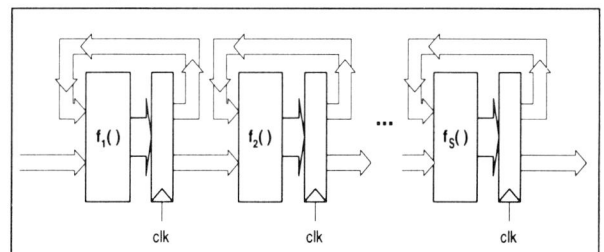

Figure 2. PipeRench computation model.

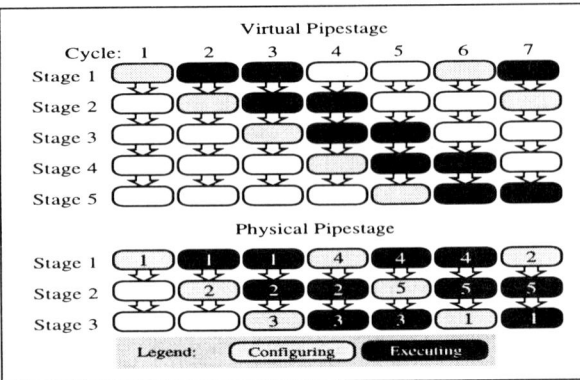

Figure 3. PipeRench pipeline reconfiguration.

computation will have a latency of $N+S$ cycles. If $P < S$, then virtualization is necessary, and the computation will take $S \left\lceil \frac{N}{P} \right\rceil + P$ cycles to complete. In the rest of this paper, we use the term *virtual stripes* to refer to the pipeline stages required by the application and the term *physical stripes* to refer to the physical pipeline stages available. As any virtual stripe can be mapped to any physical stripe, all the physical stripes must have the same functionality and interconnect.

The current architecture of PipeRench is optimized by evaluating a set of media-centric applications and is illustrated in Figure 4. Each physical stripe consists of sixteen ALUs (labelled PEs), which are each eight bits wide, connected with a byte-wise crossbar and an elaborate set of shift registers. The ALUs are capable of all possible bit-wise functions on two operands, as well as addition, subtraction and multiplexing. Each of the ALUs also contains an eight entry register file which is pipelined to provide pipeline interconnect to downstream pipeline stages. State values (those feeding back in Figure 2) can only be stored in one specific register in the register file. An input and output bus moves operands on and off the execution fabric.

A physical design of this architecture has been completed in 0.35 micron and 0.18 micron process technologies. In 0.18 micron, a single physical stripe consumes 1.03 sq mm of silicon area, and operates at over 200MHz. Some small additional chip area is required for storage of configuration information and state that needs to be held during virtualization. This is a very conservative design, with static CMOS circuits and fabricated in an ASIC process. We expect considerable headroom in improving both die area and clock speed.

PipeRench applications are written in the *Dataflow Intermediate Language* (DIL), which is a single-assignment language with C operators and a type system that allows the bit-width of variables to be specified. The DIL compiler [6] converts the source into a dataflow graph, decomposes this graph into the native operators of the architecture and places and routes the operators on the PipeRench fabric. The output of the compiler is a set of *configuration bits* (actually divided into a number of subsets, one subset per virtual stripe) that are used to configure the physical stripes at run-time.

2.3 PipeRench I-COP Advantages

In addition to being area-efficient, which we will demonstrate in Section 4.3, the PipeRench I-COP implementation also offers a number of other advantages. The PipeRench architecture allows the designer to easily trade off the size of the reconfigurable fabric with other parts of the microarchitecture to optimize the overall design. Since the DIL code for the I-COP applications do not even need to be modified, changes to the number of physical stripes can be made very late in the design cycle. Moreover, when the same microarchitecture is implemented in the next process generation, the designer has the option of increasing the number of physical stripes available to increase performance. Since physical stripes in the reconfigurable fabric are identical, this can be accomplished with minimum redesign. The designer can also choose to upgrade the resident I-COP programs to further enhance performance. All in all, the PipeRench I-COP allows the designer to improve the performance of the core processor with minimal logic and circuit redesign.

The PipeRench I-COP also retains the other I-COP advantages like allowing complex hardware code modification techniques to be implemented as I-COP code and allowing many hardware code modifications to be implemented using the same engine, each of which can be selectively and adaptively invoked at run-time. In addition, the PipeRench I-COP makes it especially easy to specialize the core processor by varying the size of the reconfigurable fabric to achieve different performance goals and support different levels of complexity in the I-COP programs.

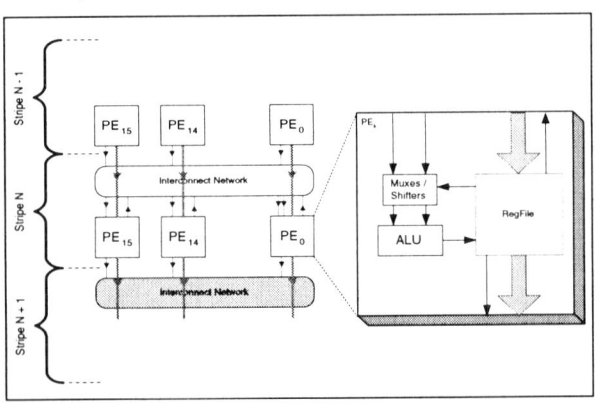

Figure 4. PipeRench Architecture.

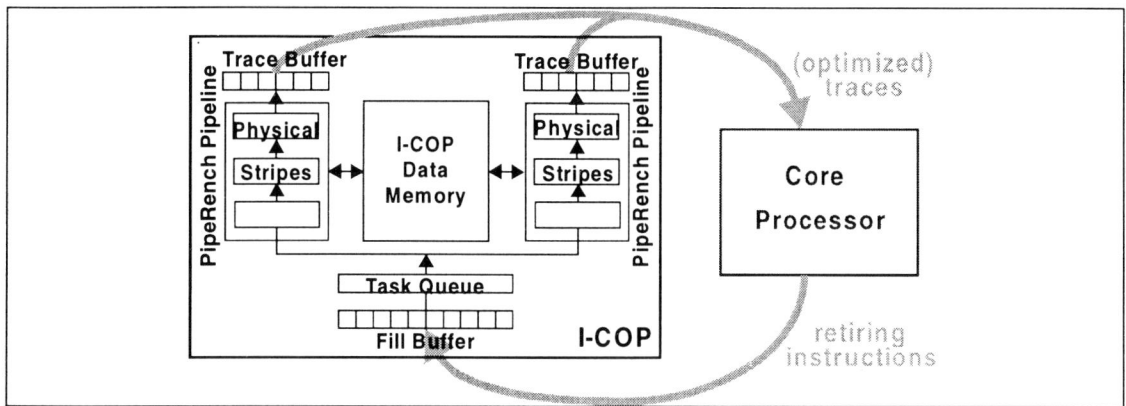

Figure 5. PipeRench I-COP implementation.

3 PipeRench I-COP Implementation

In this section, we describe the design of the PipeRench I-COP. In order to assess its performance and die area requirements, we study how it can implement four specific hardware code modification techniques: namely trace construction, register move trace optimization, stride data prefetch trace optimization, and linked data structure prefetch trace optimization. These are the same techniques implemented in the earlier study [3] and therefore allows us to compare the PipeRench and VLIW implementations in terms of performance and area efficiency. In Section 3.2, we describe how these four code modification techniques are implemented on the PipeRench I-COP as DIL programs. We anticipate that in the future, many other advanced code modifications will be mapped to the PipeRench I-COP computation model.

3.1 PipeRench I-COP Design

The PipeRench I-COP implementation comprises of one or more PipeRench pipelines (each consisting of one or more physical stripes) operating in parallel. A PipeRench pipeline constructs and optimizes traces by treating the retiring instructions from the core processor as *streaming input data*. The outputs of each PipeRench pipeline are written to its local *trace buffer*, which acts as temporary storage to hold a trace as it is being constructed. When a trace is fully constructed, it is copied from the trace buffer to the trace cache. A PipeRench I-COP implementation with two pipelines is shown in Figure 5. The fill buffer collects the retiring instructions from the core processor, and the task queue distributes them to the PipeRench pipelines. When the fill buffer is full, instructions are dropped at basic block boundaries. If a PipeRench pipeline has sufficient physical stripes to match the number of virtual stripes required by the I-COP applications, it accepts one fill buffer instruction per cycle as input and writes one instruction to the trace buffer per cycle as output. Otherwise, the physical stripes are time multiplexed and the throughput of trace processing will be less than one instruction per cycle. In Section 4, we evaluate the performance impact of varying the number of Pipe-Rench pipelines and the number of physical stripes per pipeline.

3.2 Implementing Code Modifications Using PipeRench

To implement code modifications on the PipeRench I-COP, they are first mapped to the PipeRench computation model described in Section 2.2. They are then written in the DIL language and compiled by the DIL compiler to produce the configuration bits used to configure the physical stripes of the PipeRench I-COP at run-time.

3.2.1 Trace Construction

The trace cache [2][7][8] stores frequently executed sequences of instructions in physically contiguous storage locations, thus allowing high bandwidth instruction fetch without multiple cache ports nor instruction alignment logic. This dynamic regrouping of instructions is performed by a hardware structure called the *fill unit* which is located at the back-end of the machine. A trace comprises not only of regrouped instructions but also the outcomes of the branches in the trace, the exit addresses of the trace (to facilitate partial matching [7]) and the type of the last instruction in the trace.

In our I-COP implementation, logic associated with the fill buffer examines its first 16 entries and determines the end of a new trace. It then copies those instructions from the fill buffer to the I-COP memory and inserts a task into the task queue. Whenever a PipeRench pipeline is free, it picks up a task from the front of the task queue and treating the fill buffer instructions in I-COP memory as streaming input, processes one instruction in the trace at a time and outputs the processed instructions to the trace buffer (see Figure 6). In the case of branch instructions, the PipeRench pipeline also outputs the branch outcome and

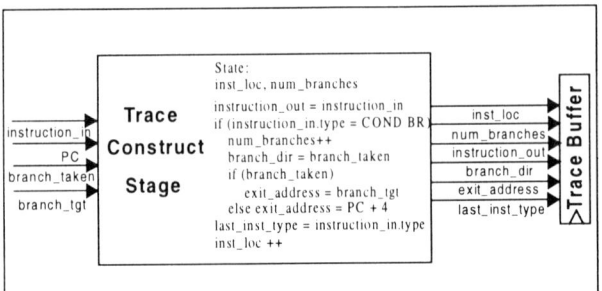

Figure 6. Trace construction using PipeRench.

exit address associated with that branch to the trace buffer. When the trace is fully constructed, the trace cache inside the core processor is read to check if there is an existing trace with the same starting PC. The new trace is written to the trace cache as long as it is not a subset of an existing trace. The PipeRench pipeline is then ready to pick up a new task. Based on the reconfigurable fabric's resource constraints (16 8-bit ALUs per stripe), the DIL compiler maps the trace construction logic to 11 virtual stripes. More details on the PipeRench implementation of trace construction and the other code modification techniques can be found in [26].

3.2.2 Register Move Trace Optimization

Beyond basic trace construction, the I-COP can perform optimizations on traces to achieve additional performance. Recently, there have been proposals for various trace optimizations [9][10]. The register move optimization [9] is one such example. In this optimization, instructions within a trace which move a value from one register to another register without modifying it are marked as *explicit move* instructions by the fill unit. Examples of such instructions are:

ADD Ra <- Rb + 0

SHIFT Ra <- Rb << 0

Instead of using execution resources to execute these instructions, their output registers are renamed to the same physical registers (or operand tags depending on the register renaming scheme used) as their input registers. Aside from saving execution resources, this also enables dependent instructions to execute earlier. The register renaming logic is modified to handle such explicit moves. A slight complication is that the input registers of dependent instructions within the same trace have to be substituted with the input register of the *explicit move* instruction.

In our PipeRench I-COP implementation shown in Figure 7, the register move optimization is performed after trace construction and before the trace is written from the trace buffer to the trace cache. Because this optimization is fairly expensive, it is not applied the first time a trace is

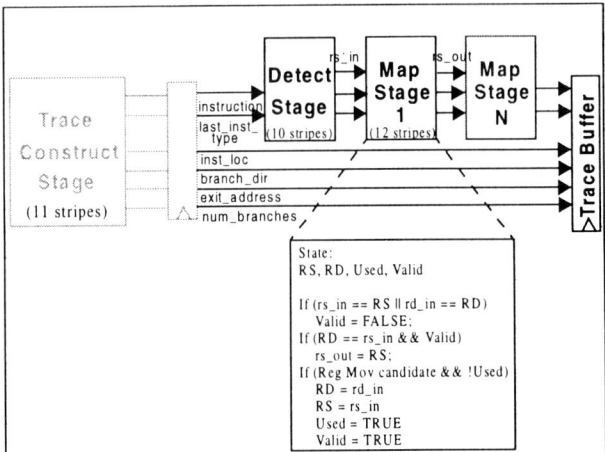

Figure 7. Register move optimization using PipeRench.

written into the trace cache. It is only applied to a trace that is found to be already in the trace cache and has been accessed x number of times. We found $x = 5$ to be a good choice. Also, a trace is only optimized if it contains more than one conditional branch, since we assume the compiler already performs this optimization within a basic block. The input to the optimization is a stream of instructions from the result of trace construction and the output is a stream of optimized instructions that are written to the trace buffer. For every input instruction, two operations have to be performed. First, it must be determined if this instruction is a candidate for the optimization and if so, its type should be changed to that of an *explicit move*. Second, one or both of its source operand specifiers (i.e. register numbers) must be modified if that operand is dependent on an earlier register move candidate in the trace.

The first operation is essentially combinational logic and is performed by the Detect Stage shown in Figure 7. The DIL compiler produces a design of this stage that requires 10 virtual stripes.

The second operation is accomplished by keeping a set of mappings, labelled as the Mapping Stages in Figure 7. Each stage stores four values:

* a **valid** flag
* a 5-bit value **RD** which represents a register that is being mapped
* another 5-bit value **RS** which represents the register to which **RD** gets mapped
* a single bit, called the **used** flag, which is set if this stage has a valid mapping or ever had a valid mapping

At the beginning of each new trace, all of the stages are set to **invalid** and **unused**. When an instruction enters a stage, if the stage is **valid** and if a source register of the incoming instruction (rs_in) matches **RD**, then that source register will be renamed (rs_out) to **RS**. If the incoming instruction is a register move candidate and the stage is **unused**, and if this instruction's mapping has not yet been stored, then the stage will be marked as **used** and **valid**. The source and destination of the instruction (rs_in and rd_in) will be stored in **RS** and **RD** respectively. A one bit flag will be sent to downstream stages indicating that the mapping for this instruction has already been stored.

If an instruction reaches a stage in which the destination of the instruction (rd_in) matches either **RD** or **RS**, the stage will be set to **invalid**. However, the stage will remain marked as **used**, since it previously had a valid mapping in it. This prevents future register move candidates from storing their mappings ahead (in stage order) of an already stored mapping and ensures that older mappings in the trace always appear earlier in stage order. This in turn ensures that when a new register move candidate stores its mapping, its source register will have already been correctly renamed. Each instruction only needs to pass through the pipeline just once, thus enabling a throughput of one instruction per cycle.

For a simple example of how this design works (it can also handle all the complex cases), consider the following example of a trace with just three instructions:

ADD r2 <- r1 + 0 *(1)*

ADD r4 <- r3 + r2 *(2)*

ADD r2 <- r10 + r11 *(3)*

Instruction *1* is eligible for the optimization and will create the mapping (**RD** = 2, **RS** = 1). Instruction *2* is not eligible for the optimization but one of its source operands matches the stored mapping (**RD** = 2, **RS** = 1) and so the instruction is transformed to ADD r4 <- r3 + r1. Instruction *3* is also not eligible for the optimization and since its destination matches the stored mapping (**RD** = 2, **RS** = 1), the mapping is invalidated.

The DIL compiler produces a design that requires 12 virtual stripes for each Map Stage. In our simulations, we found that having just one set of mapping (i.e. only one *explicit move* is allowed in a trace) achieves most of the performance gains of this trace optimization. This means this trace optimization takes a total of 10 + 12 = 22 virtual stripes in addition to the 11 virtual stripes for trace construction.

3.2.3 Stride Prefetch Trace Optimization

The stride prefetching scheme we implement in the I-COP is based closely on the hardware scheme proposed by Chen and Baer [11]. The basic idea is to record the effective addresses of loads as they are executed, compute the latest stride by comparing this address to the last effective address generated by the same static load, and update a 2-bit state machine. Depending on the resulting state of the state machine, a prefetch request may be generated. All this information is recorded in a table called the Reference Prediction Table (RPT) stored in the I-COP data memory. Whenever a load is encountered during the construction of a trace, the 512-entry RPT is consulted to determine if it has a consistent stride. If so, a prefetch instruction is inserted in the trace before it is written to the trace cache. The prefetch instruction is only inserted if there is an empty slot in that particular trace cache line. This optimization is performed after trace construction and before the trace is written from the trace buffer to the trace cache. The input to the optimization is a stream of instructions from the result of trace construction and the output is a stream of the same instructions plus possibly one or more prefetch instructions. The DIL compiler produces a design that requires 14 virtual stripes.

3.2.4 LDS Prefetch Trace Optimization

Linked data structures (LDS) include linked lists, trees and graphs etc., where individual nodes are dynamically allocated from the heap and linked together through pointers to form the overall structure. The LDS prefetching we implement is based on that proposed by Roth et al. [12]. In this scheme, the goal is to correlate pairs of loads like the following, where the result of the first load is used as the base address for the second load:

LOAD r2<- M[0(r1)]

LOAD r3<- M[8(r2)]

After the correlation is established, whenever the first load is executed, a prefetch can be issued for the second load to hide the potential cache miss latency. Correlations are established by actual values rather than by symbolic means, with the help of two tables stored in the I-COP data memory: the 256-entry Potential Producer Window (PPW) and the 512-entry Correlation Table (CT). Whenever a load is encountered during the construction of a trace, it updates the PPW and CT. It also searches the CT and if it is found to be a producer, a prefetch instruction is inserted as part of the trace before the trace is written to the trace cache. The DIL compiler produces a design that requires 9 virtual stripes.

3.2.5 Comparison With VLIW-based I-COP

Table 1 compares the number of virtual stripes required by the PipeRench I-COP programs to the number of operations and cycles needed by the VLIW-based I-COP for the same programs. For the PipeRench I-COP, the number of cycles required to execute the program depends on the number of physical stripes available and is governed by the equations in Section 2.2. In Section 4.2, we study the performance impact of varying the number of physical stripes.

I-COP Application	Virtual Stripes	VLIW ops	VLIW cycles
Trace construction	11	50	18
Register move trace optimization	22	423	106
Stride prefetch trace optimization	14	130	33
LDS prefetch trace optimization	9	86	22

Table 1: Comparison between PipeRench and VLIW-based I-COP implementations.

4 Experimental Results

4.1 Simulation Methodology

Our performance simulator is built around Digital's ATOM tool [13] and uses the Alpha ISA [14]. Although it is trace-driven, it models the resource contention (but not cache effects) due to instructions on the mispredicted path.

The organization of the core processor is as follows. The trace cache contains 128KB of instructions (2048 lines of 16 instructions) and is 4-way set associative. Partial matching is implemented. The branch predictor is as described in [7]. It is an adaptation of the *gshare* predictor, and makes 3 predictions per cycle. We assume a perfect return address stack which is used to predict subroutine returns. The L1 instruction cache is 16KB and direct-mapped, with a 14 cycle miss latency. Because of the low instruction cache miss rates, an L2 instruction cache is not modeled.

Functional Units	Units	Latency
Simple Integer	8	1
Complex Integer	4	4
Load/Store	4	2/1
Branch	4	1
Floating-Point Add/Multiply	4	3
Floating-Point Divide	4	11(sp), 15(dp)

Table 2: Core processor execution resources.

The front-end pipeline of the core processor, from fetch to dispatch, is four stages deep. Instructions are dispatched to a 512 entry centralized instruction window and are allowed to issue out-of-order. Perfect memory disambiguation is assumed. The functional unit mix and their execution latencies are shown in Table 2; all functional units are fully pipelined. The L1 data cache is 16KB and direct-mapped and the miss latency to the L2 data cache (assumed off chip) is 14 cycles. The L2 data cache is 256KB and 2-way set associative, with a miss latency to main memory of 75 cycles. In our data prefetching experiments, prefetched data are brought into a 64 entry fully-associative prefetch buffer. The PipeRench I-COP model is integrated with the core processor's simulator and is simulated in detail at the machine cycle level.

Seven SPECint95 benchmarks [15] and three pointer-intensive Olden benchmarks [16] are used. Their input sets and dynamic instruction counts are shown in Table 3. The benchmarks are compiled using the default optimization flags of the SPEC distribution and are run to completion.

Benchmark	Input Set	Inst Count
compress	10000 e 2231	54M
ijpeg	tinyrose.ppm	89M
m88ksim	dhry2tiny.lit	99M
go	5 9	78M
gcc	-O genoutput.i	106M
li	queens 6	56M
perl	trainscrabbl	47M
health	5 levels, 500 iters	176M
perimeter	4K x 4K image	43M
treeadd	1024K nodes	98M

Table 3: Benchmark characteristics

4.2 Performance Data

In this section, we show the performance of the core processor under different PipeRench I-COP organizations. In particular, we vary the number of physical stripes per PipeRench pipeline as well as the number of PipeRench pipelines. Since the reconfigurable fabric may have to be clocked at a slower clock speed than the core processor, we show two sets of results. The first assumes the reconfigurable fabric is clocked at the same speed as the core processor while the second assumes it is clocked at half the speed.

While evaluating the different design points of the design space, it is helpful to bear in mind that each physical stripe in a 0.18 micron process occupies 1.03 sq mm of silicon area (approximately 1/300th the area of a 300 sq mm die used in current high-end microprocessors).

4.2.1 Trace Construction

Figure 8 shows the performance of the core processor with its I-COP implemented in different PipeRench organizations for trace construction. In particular, we vary the number of PipeRench pipelines as well as the number of physical stripes per pipeline. The upper graph assumes that the PipeRench I-COP runs at the same speed as the core processor while the lower graph assumes that it runs at half the speed. In both graphs, the y axis shows the harmonic mean of the IPCs of the seven SPECint95 benchmarks and the x axis represents the total number of physical stripes. The sets of data points on each graph represent varying the number of PipeRench pipelines. The number of physical stripes per pipeline can be derived by dividing the total number of physical stripes by the number of pipelines. For

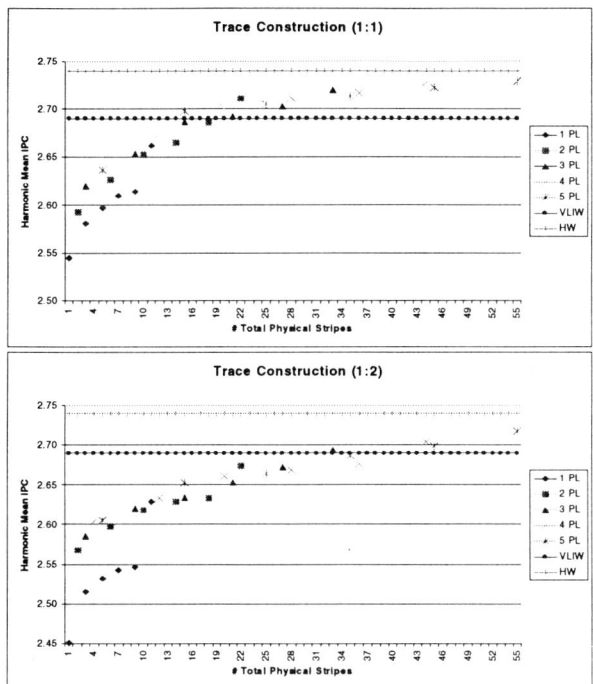

Figure 8. Trace construction performance.

example, the data point [2 pipelines (PL), 14 total physical stripes] implies there are seven physical stripes per PipeRench pipeline. For comparison, the performance of the VLIW-based I-COP (labeled VLIW) as well as a hardwired trace cache fill unit (labeled HW) are also shown.

The throughput at which the I-COP constructs traces is directly proportional to the total number of physical stripes available, while the latency of trace construction is inversely proportional to it. When the throughput of trace construction is reduced, more instructions are dropped from the fill buffer since the I-COP is not able to keep up with the rate at which instructions are retired by the core processor. However, because of the frequent reuse of previously constructed traces, these dropped instructions do not adversely affect overall performance. Moreover, because the I-COP is located at the back end of the core processor, longer latencies in trace construction also do not seriously affect performance. Therefore, there is diminishing returns in performance as the total number of physical stripes is increased.

Given a fixed total number of physical stripes (and throughput), performance varies slightly depending on the exact PipeRench organization. This is due to several factors. First, the latency of trace construction has a ceiling function (see Section 2.2) that produces discontinuities. In particular, 11 physical stripes per pipeline results in particularly good performance because the average trace length is approximately 11 instructions. Second, the number of PipeRench pipelines affects trace selection because instructions are dropped from the fill buffer at a different timing. When there are more pipelines, there will be a longer series of contiguous traces followed by a larger number of dropped instructions. When there are fewer pipelines, there will be a shorter series of contiguous traces followed by a smaller number of dropped instructions. The former situation is more desirable than the latter, so in general, for a given number of total physical stripes, it is better to have more pipelines and fewer physical stripes per pipeline.

For a particular performance level (i.e. fixed value on y axis), the most desirable PipeRench I-COP organization is the one with the least total number of physical stripes. For example, if we want to match the performance of the VLIW I-COP implementation, the design point [3 pipelines, 15 total physical stripes] is the best organization when the clock speed of the PipeRench I-COP matches the clock speed of the core processor. When the clock speed is half that of the core processor, the design point [3 pipelines, 33 total physical stripes] is the best organization.

4.2.2 Register Move Trace Optimization

Figure 9 shows the performance of different PipeRench organizations when the register move optimization is applied in addition to basic trace construction.

The graphs in Figure 9 are organized in a similar fashion to those in Figure 8. Because the PipeRench I-COP is efficient in implementing this optimization (22 virtual stripes in addition to 11 virtual stripes for basic trace construction; in contrast, the VLIW requires 423 instructions in addition to 50 instructions for basic trace construction), fewer total physical stripes are needed to match the VLIW implementation. When the PipeRench I-COP runs at the same speed as the core processor, the [4 pipelines, 12 total physical stripes] organization matches the performance of the VLIW I-COP. When it runs at half the speed, the [5 pipelines, 25 total physical stripes] organization accomplishes the same goal.

From the results, we also observe that when compared to basic trace construction, given the same PipeRench I-COP organization, applying this optimization improves performance. For example, the harmonic mean IPC of the I-COP organization [3 pipelines, 15 total physical stripes] (assuming I-COP and core processor run at the same clock speed) increases from 2.69 to 2.72. Although these performance improvements are modest, no additional I-COP hardware was required; only the I-COP code, i.e. the PipeRench *configuration bits,* are changed.

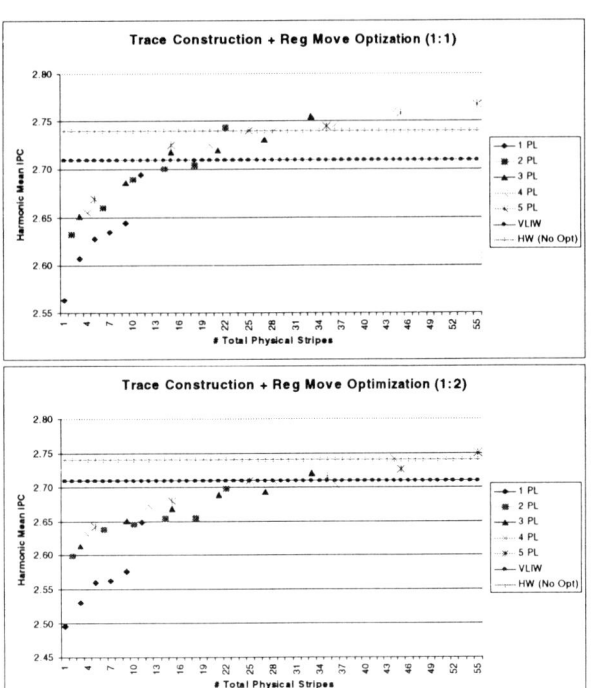

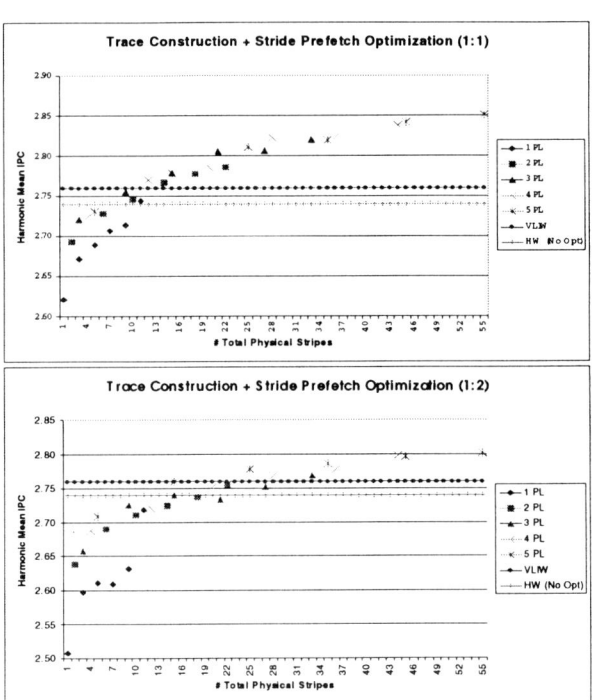

Figure 9. Register move optimization performance.

Figure 10. Stride prefetch performance.

4.2.3 Stride Prefetch Trace Optimization

Figure 10 shows the performance of different PipeRench organizations when the stride data prefetch optimization is applied in addition to basic trace construction. This optimization is applied to all traces. The results are clearly superior to those in Figure 8, demonstrating the advantage of an I-COP in being able to improve core processor performance by modifying I-COP code and without changing the I-COP hardware. The PipeRench I-COP is efficient in implementing this optimization, requiring only a [3 pipelines, 9 total physical stripes] organization to match the VLIW I-COP when it is running at the same clock speed as the core processor. When it is running at half the speed, a [5 pipelines, 15 total physical stripes] organization is required. Note also that these I-COP organizations also handily exceed the performance of the hardwired trace cache fill unit performing trace construction with no trace optimization (labeled HW (No Opt) in Figure 10).

4.2.4 LDS Prefetch Trace Optimization

Figure 11 shows the performance of a PipeRench I-COP running at the same clock speed as the core processor when the LDS data prefetch optimization is applied. Because the IPC performance of the *health* benchmark is an order of magnitude lower than those of the other two Olden benchmarks, we avoid using the harmonic mean of their IPCs. Instead, the performance of each benchmark is shown separately. The I-COP organization shown is the same one that matches the performance of the VLIW I-COP for the stride data prefetch optimization, i.e. 3 pipelines, 9 total physical stripes. We observe that a small PipeRench I-COP is able to match the performance of the VLIW I-COP. The performance of this PipeRench I-COP also exceeds that of the hardwired trace cache fill unit with no trace optimization by a considerable margin.

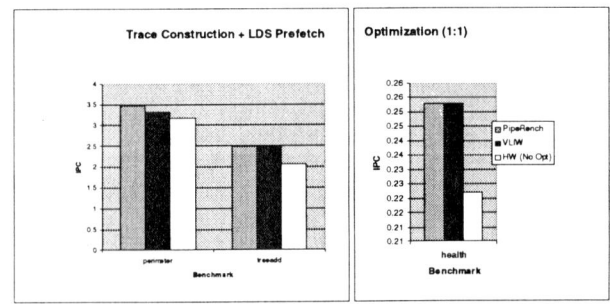

Figure 11. LDS prefetch performance (1:1 clock speed).

Figure 12 is similar to Figure 11 except that the results shown are for an I-COP that runs at half the clock speed of the core processor. The I-COP organization shown is the same one that matches the performance of the VLIW I-COP for the stride data prefetch optimization, i.e. 5 pipelines, 15 total physical stripes. Again, we observe that a small PipeRench I-COP is able to match the performance of the VLIW I-COP.

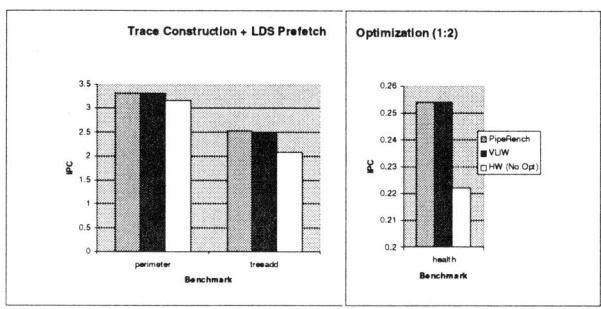

Figure 12. LDS prefetch performance (1:2 clock speed).

4.2.5 Estimated Area of PipeRench I-COP

To match or exceed the VLIW I-COP performance for trace construction and all three trace optimizations, and assuming that the PipeRench I-COP is only able to run at half the speed of the core processor, the estimated die area of the PipeRench I-COP (33 total physical stripes) fabricated in a 0.18 micron process is 33 x 1.03 = 34 sq mm. To put this in perspective, Table 4 shows the estimated die

Component	% of die	Process (u)	Area (mm²)	Area scaled for 0.18 u
IBM G6 [17]	FPU	7.1	0.22	15.3	10.2
Transmeta 3120 [18]	FPU	12.3	0.22	9.5	6.3
UltraSparc-2i [19]	FPU	12.0	0.29	18.0	6.9
AMD K6 [20]	FPU	14.3	0.35	23.1	6.1
NEC MP98 [21]	64KB cache	8.0	0.15	9.1	13.1
NEC Cache SRAM [22]	512K cache	100.0	0.25	132.0	68.4

Table 4: Die areas of microarchitecture structures.

areas of other microarchitecture structures in the same process. The PipeRench I-COP is roughly equivalent in area to 256KB of fast SRAM, or about 11% of the die area of a current high-end microprocessor. If the I-COP is able to run at the same speed as the core processor, the die area required drops to approximately 15 x 1.03 = 15 sq mm, or roughly equivalent to 128KB of fast SRAM, or about 5% of the die area.

As noted in Section 2.2, these area estimates are likely to be conservative due to the conservative circuit design and fabrication process assumed. Also, the DIL compiler achieves relatively low utilization of PipeRench resources because of its fast and greedy approach to placement and routing, as illustrated in Table 5. The percentage resource utilization numbers are obtained by dividing the total number of native PipeRench operations in the application by the total number of ALUs available in a design with the resultant number of physical stripes. Significant performance improvements can easily be obtained by optimizing the PipeRench architecture, circuit design and compiler for I-COP applications.

I-COP Application	Resources Utilized Per Stripe
Trace construction	54%
Register move trace optimization	55%
Stride prefetch trace optimization	70%
LDS prefetch trace optimization	56%

Table 5: Utilization of PipeRench fabric resources.

If one is willing to trade off a little performance (2.6% lower for trace construction, 1.8% for the register move trace optimization, 1.1% lower for stride prefetch trace optimization), and assuming the PipeRench I-COP is only able to run at half the speed of the core processor, one can implement the [3 pipelines, 9 total physical stripes] I-COP in 9 x 1.03 = 9.27 sq mm, which is roughly equivalent in area to 64KB of fast SRAM, or 3% of the die area of a current high-end microprocessor. In future fabrication processes (0.13 micron and beyond), the I-COP will occupy an even smaller fraction of the available die area.

5 Conclusions and Future Work

In this paper, we have described an efficient means of implementing an I-COP by using the PipeRench reconfigurable architecture. We also show how hardware code modifications can be mapped to the PipeRench pipelined computation model. In our experimental evaluation, we found that a PipeRench I-COP used to perform trace construction and trace optimizations for a trace cache fill unit not only achieves good performance but can be implemented in less than 11% of the area of a current high-end microprocessor. If one is willing to trade off only a little performance, this figure can be reduced to 3% or lower. We believe that this demonstrates that an I-COP can be implemented in a reasonable amount of chip area.

In addition to being area-efficient, the PipeRench I-COP implementation also allows the designer to easily trade off the size of the reconfigurable fabric with other parts of the microarchitecture to maximize overall performance. As the PipeRench configuration bits do not need to be modified, this trade-off can be changed very late in the design cycle. The PipeRench I-COP implementation is also highly scalable. As I-COP programs become more complex or more I-COP programs need to be run concurrently, the number of physical stripes in the reconfigurable fabric can be increased with minimal design effort.

In conclusion, we believe that we have demonstrated the I-COP concept to be useful and feasible. With the need for increasingly sophisticated hardware code modification techniques, we believe that an I-COP is a potentially powerful tool in the microarchitect's arsenal. We also believe that hardware code modification techniques enabled by the I-COP can be synergistically combined with software runtime code optimization techniques to further improve the performance of future high performance microprocessors.

Our current research focuses on studying other I-COP applications like using an I-COP to perform run-time trace scheduling [23] and completion-time branch prediction in the context of a trace cache [24]. We also plan to study the interface between the I-COP and the core processor in greater detail, and in particular how the core processor can selectively and adaptively invoke the appropriate I-COP programs based on application behavior. Finally, we hope that the demonstrated feasibility of the I-COP concept will serve to stimulate further research into advanced hardware code modification techniques.

Acknowledgment

PipeRench development was primarily sponsored by DARPA, under contract DABT 63-96-C-0083. This work benefited from machines donated by Intel, and was also supported in part by ONR (N00014-97-1-0701, N00014-96-1-0928) and in part by Intel Corp.

References

[1] Linley Gwennap, "Intel's P6 Uses Decoupled Superscalar Design," in Microprocessor Report, Vol. 9, Issue 2, February 1995.

[2] E. Rotenberg, S. Bennett and J. Smith, "Trace Cache: a Low Latency Approach to High Bandwidth Instruction Fetching," in Proc. of 29th International Symposium on Microarchitecture, 1996.

[3] Y. Chou and J. Shen, "Instruction Path Coprocessors," in Proc. of 27th International Symposium on Computer Architecture, June 2000.

[4] S. Goldstein et al., "PipeRench: A Coprocessor for Streaming Multimedia Acceleration," in Proc. of 26th International Symposium on Computer Architecture, May 1999.

[5] H. Schmit, "Incremental Reconfiguration for Pipelined Applications," in Proc. of Workshop on FPGAs for Custom Computing Machines, April 1997.

[6] M. Budiu and S. Goldstein, "Fast Compilation for Pipelined Reconfigurable Fabrics," in Proc. of 7th International Symposium on Field Programmable Gate Arrays, February 1999.

[7] S. Patel, D. Friendly and Y. Patt, "Critical Issues Regarding the Trace Cache Fetch Mechanism," Technical Report CSE-TR-335-97, University of Michigan, May 1997.

[8] B. Black, B. Rychlik and J. Shen, "The Block-based Trace Cache," in Proc. of 26th International Symposium on Computer Architecture, May 1999.

[9] D. Friendly, S. Patel and Y. Patt, "Putting the Fill Unit to Work: Dynamic Optimizations for Trace Cache Microprocessors", in Proc. of 31st International Symposium on Microarchitecture, 1998.

[10] Q. Jacobson and J. Smith, "Instruction Pre-Processing in Trace Processors", in Proc. of 5th International Symposium on High Performance Computer Architecture, 1999.

[11] T. Chen and J. Baer, "Effective Hardware-Based Data Prefetching for High-Performance Processors", IEEE Transactions on Computers, Vol. 44, No. 5, 1995.

[12] A. Roth and G. Sohi, "Effective Jump-Pointer Prefetching for Linked Data Structures", in Proc. of 26th International Symposium on Computer Architecture, 1999.

[13] A. Srivastava and A. Eustace, "ATOM: A System for Building Customized Program Analysis Tools," in Proc. of SIGPLAN Conference on Programming Language Design and Implementation, 1994.

[14] Alpha Architecture Handbook, Digital Equipment Corporation, 1992.

[15] http://www.spec.org

[16] A. Rogers, M. Carlisle, J. Reppy and L. Hendren, "Supporting Dynamic Data Structures on Distributed Memory Machines", ACM Transactions on Programming Languages and Systems, 17(2), March 1995.

[17] K. Diefendorff, "Processors Penetrate Gigahertz Territory," Microprocessor Report, Vol. 14, Archive 2, February 2000.

[18] T. Halfhill, "Transmeta Breaks x86 Low-Power Barrier," Microprocessor Report, Vol. 14, Archive 2, February 2000.

[19] "Low-Cost UltraSPARC-2i Appears," Microprocessor Report, Vol. 12, No. 1, January 26, 1998.

[20] D. Draper et al., "Circuit Techniques in a 266 MHz MMX-enabled Processor," IEEE Journal of Solid State Circuits, Vol. 32, No. 11, November 1997.

[21] P. Glaskowsky, "NEC Decants Merlot," Microprocessor Report, Vol. 14, Archive 3, March 2000.

[22] H. Nambu et al., "1.8-ns Access, 550-MHz, 4.5-Mb CMOS SRAM," Vol. 33, No. 11, IEEE Journal of Solid State Circuits, Vol. 33, No. 11, November 1998.

[23] R. Nair and M. Hopkins, "Exploiting Instruction Level Parallelism in Processors by Caching Scheduled Groups," in Proc. of 24th International Symposium on Computer Architecture, June 1997.

[24] R. Rakvic, B. Black and J. Shen, "Completion Time Multiple Branch Prediction for Enhancing Trace Cache Performance," in Proc. of 27th International Symposium on Computer Architecture, June 2000.

[25] M. Merton et. al, "A Hardware Mechanism for Dynamic Extraction and Relayout of Program Hot Spots," in Proc. of 27th International Symposium on Computer Architecture, June 2000.

[26] P. Pillai, "The Instruction Path Coprocessor Implemented on the PipeRench Fabric," CMuART Tech. Report, Carnegie Mellon Univ., 2000.

Efficient Conditional Operations for Data-parallel Architectures

Ujval J. Kapasi, William J. Dally, Scott Rixner, Peter R. Mattson, John D. Owens, Brucek Khailany

Computer Systems Laboratory
Stanford University
Stanford, CA 94305
{ujk, billd, rixner, pmattson, jowens, khailany}@cva.stanford.edu

Abstract

Many data-parallel applications, including emerging media applications, have regular structures that can easily be expressed as a series of arithmetic kernels operating on data streams. Data-parallel architectures are designed to exploit this regularity by performing the same operation on many data elements concurrently. However, applications containing data-dependent control constructs perform poorly on these architectures. Conditional streams convert these constructs into data-dependent data movement. This allows data-parallel architectures to efficiently execute applications with data-dependent control flow. Essentially, conditional streams extend the range of applications that a data-parallel architecture can execute efficiently. For example, polygon rendering speeds up by a factor of 1.8 with the use of conditional streams.

1. Introduction

Many applications contain abundant data-parallelism, particularly emerging media applications such as graphics and video, image, and signal processing. Data-parallel architectures, such as vector [2][11][15][16], SIMD [3][12], and stream [9] processors, are well suited to extracting this data parallelism, achieving very high levels of performance. They utilize partitioned register files and reduced control overhead in order to support 10s to 100s of ALUs efficiently on a single chip [10]. The applicability of these architectures to current workloads is reflected by the recent emergence of SIMD ISA extensions, such as VIS [14] and MMX [8], as well as vector microprocessors [1][5][17]. However, strictly data-parallel machines are limited to executing applications that are largely free of data-dependent control constructs. Data-dependent control is typically handled by using select operations that leave computing resources idle or by using the memory system to reorder data. Either approach results in significant degradations of efficiency.

This paper introduces the concept of *conditional streams*, which extends the application range of data-parallel architectures by converting data-dependent control into data-dependent data routing. A data-parallel machine with conditional stream support more efficiently executes applications that would otherwise require data-dependent control. For instance, polygon rendering achieves a speedup of 1.8x when conditional streams are applied to it.

Many data-parallel applications have regular structures that can be represented as a series of computation *kernels* operating on data *streams* [9]. For example, consider the kernel in Figure 1 (pseudocode is provided in Figure 4), which converts pixels from the RGB color space to the YUV color space, as might be done as part of a video coding application [4]. This kernel consumes a single input stream of pixels in RGB, performs a set of identical calculations in parallel across a set of SIMD processing elements, and produces a single output stream of converted YUV pixels. In the *stream programming model*, applications are composed of a series of such kernels that consume data streams produced by previous kernels and generate data streams for use by subsequent kernels.

Figure 2(a) illustrates one type of data-dependent control, an *if* statement, that cannot be efficiently executed on a data-parallel machine. This code gets an input element, *x*, from the input stream (*in*) and applies one of two functions to it based on whether *x* is positive or negative. It then sends the result for negative inputs to one output stream (*a*), and the result for positive inputs to a different output stream (*b*).

Figure 1: Kernel and streams example

The research described in this paper was supported by the Defense Advanced Research Projects Agency under ARPA order E254 and monitored by the Army Intelligence Center under contract DABT63-96-C-0037. Several of the authors are also supported by National Science Foundation and/or Stanford Graduate Fellowships.

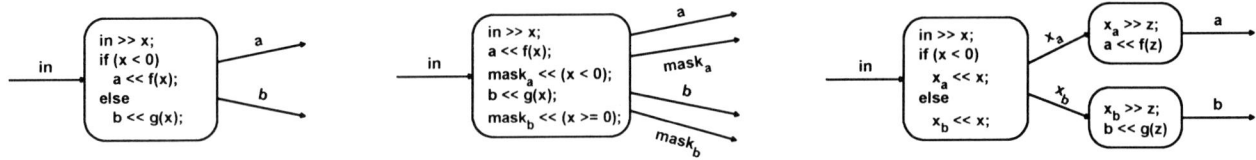

(a) original code (b) SIMD without conditional streams (c) SIMD with conditional streams

Figure 2: *If-then-else* statement on a SIMD machine

On a data-parallel machine, where every processing element executes the same code, this example kernel would typically be implemented using mask streams as illustrated in Figure 2(b). For each input element, both outputs are calculated and associated mask streams are generated to indicate which elements of each output stream are valid. This approach leads to three significant inefficiencies. First, every processing element executes both f and g on every data value of *in*. Second, twice as much output data is generated than is necessary since there is an entry in both streams, *a* and *b*, for every element of *in*, and this will require more storage.[1] Finally, either the execution time of subsequent kernels that must scan over this unneeded data increases, or explicit memory or communication operations are required to compress the result streams so that all elements are valid.

Alternatively, a machine with conditional streams first separates the input stream to avoid computing unneeded results as illustrated in Figure 2(c). The first kernel performs a *conditional output* operation passing negative elements of the input stream (*in*) to one output stream (x_a) and positive elements of the input stream to another output stream (x_b). The kernel at the upper right of Figure 2(c) then applies function f to stream x_a, generating a dense output stream *a* in which every element is valid. Similarly, the lower right kernel applies g to the positive elements of *in* producing the dense output stream *b*. The conditional output operation allows the data-dependent control of Figure 2(a) to be converted to data-dependent routing. As a result, there is no wasted computation, the output streams contain only valid elements, and no subsequent memory or communication operations are needed to compact the resulting streams.

The remainder of this paper develops the concept of conditional streams in more detail. Section 2 lays the groundwork for conditional streams by describing data-parallel architectures and the stream programming model. Section 3 discusses conditional streams and presents several situations where they can be applied. Section 4 discusses the microarchitectural additions required to implement conditional stream functionality in hardware, as well as how to implement a software solution. The evaluation methodology used to gather results is described in Section 5, including a description of a processor implementing the conditional stream mechanism. The evaluation results and discussion are in Section 6. Finally, Section 7 describes related work.

2. Background

Figure 3 shows a block diagram of a SIMD stream processor. The processor is organized into n partitions, each containing a processing element (PE) and a local memory. The local memories collectively form a stream register file (SRF) that is distributed across the partitions. Data streams are stored in this SRF as they are forwarded from one computation kernel to the next. All processing elements must be identical and may contain several functional units and local register files for temporary results. The n partitions are controlled by a single shared controller that broadcasts identical instructions to all of the processing elements and identical addresses to all of the local memories. This architecture is efficient for two main reasons: 1) the shared controller reduces control overhead; and 2) the partitioned organization exploits locality to provide high data bandwidth.

Applications targeted for a stream processor are written using the *stream programming model*, which structures applications as a series of kernels that operate on streams of data records. Each kernel consumes data records in sequence from its input streams and generates data records in sequence to its output streams. Kernels are restricted to accessing only their internal local variables, the head records of input streams, and the tail records of output streams. They cannot make arbitrary memory references.

Figure 4 shows the pseudocode for the simple kernel *RGB_2_YUV* presented in the Introduction and contains a graphical depiction of its execution on a stream processor with four SIMD partitions. The dotted lines across the figure show how data and processing are allocated across the partitions. On the first iteration of the loop, PE0 through PE3 access the input stream (*rgb*) and fetch RGB_0 through RGB_3 from their associated SRF banks. Each record access is atomic in that a PE must receive all the components of a particular record. The RGB pixels are then converted to YUV_0 through YUV_3 concurrently within the four PEs, and these computed values are sent to SRF0 through SRF3. Each subsequent loop iteration will process

---

[1] The data in streams *a* and *b* could technically be stored in one stream, but the output of the following kernels would still require twice as much storage.

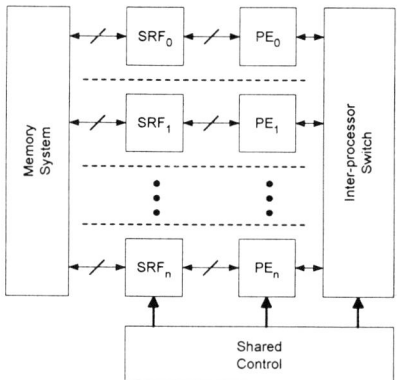

Figure 3: Stream Processor Architecture

four pixels in the same manner. In practice, kernels can be much more complicated. They often contain considerable computation, interaction among stream elements, and multiple input streams and output streams that are consumed and produced at different rates. However, *RGB_2_YUV* is representative of most streaming kernels in that it loops over the data records of its input stream, performs some computation on each record, and produces successive values of its output stream. This code structure can be seen in Figure 4.

A SIMD processor efficiently executes perfectly data-parallel code, such as the *RGB_2_YUV* kernel, because every PE contributes useful computation every cycle. However, other computations require data-dependent control flow. Though, even if the data in each PE requires different types of processing, the PEs still must execute the same code since they share a single controller. Thus, data-dependent conditionals present a challenge. A simple example of such a computation, an *if statement*, is presented in the Introduction. In the following section, more complicated and realistic examples of data-dependent processing will be discussed. Furthermore, the concept of conditional streams will be introduced as a mechanism that can extend the efficiency and range of applications that can be executed on SIMD processors.

3. Conditional Streams

A *conditional stream* is a data stream that is accessed conditionally based on a case value local to a PE. Conditional access allows arbitrary stream expansion and stream compression in space (across hardware partitions) and time (across loop iterations). As will be shown, this property allows efficient execution of applications with data-dependent control on a SIMD architecture.

Figure 5 shows the data movement performed by a conditional input stream operating on a SIMD machine with four partitions. The dotted lines separate data and hardware associated with each partition. Each PE

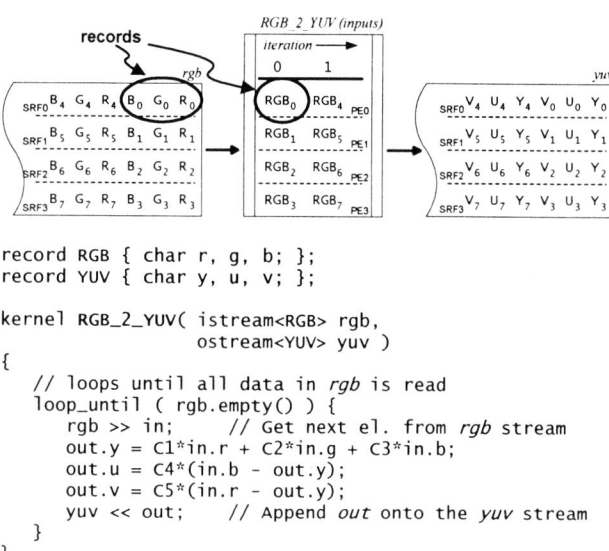

```
record RGB { char r, g, b; };
record YUV { char y, u, v; };

kernel RGB_2_YUV( istream<RGB> rgb,
                  ostream<YUV> yuv )
{
    // loops until all data in rgb is read
    loop_until ( rgb.empty() ) {
        rgb >> in;      // Get next el. from rgb stream
        out.y = C1*in.r + C2*in.g + C3*in.b;
        out.u = C4*(in.b - out.y);
        out.v = C5*(in.r - out.y);
        yuv << out;     // Append out onto the yuv stream
    }
}
```

Figure 4: RGB_2_YUV kernel

independently decides whether to read a record from the conditional input stream each iteration based upon values from the *case* stream. On cycle 0, only PE0 and PE2 have a TRUE case value. Thus, the first two elements of the stream, the values *A* and *B*, are transferred to these PEs. The data value *B* is transferred from SRF1 to PE2, requiring communication across the partitions. (Section 4 discusses how the interprocessor switch is used to do this.) During the second iteration, PEs 1, 2, and 3 read from the input stream, receiving data values *C*, *D*, and *E* from SRFs 2, 3, and 0 respectively. Each PE that reads a value from the input stream receives the next value in sequence regardless of which SRF that value is located in. In effect, the stream is expanded in space (across hardware partitions) and in time (across loop iterations) according to the values in the case stream. In contrast, a conventional SIMD machine can only decide on each loop iteration whether or not all PEs should collectively read the next four values from the stream. On these machines, cross-partition communication requires cycling data through the memory system or coordinating communication through the interprocessor switch with software.

The programmer has access to conditional stream functionality via the simple primitive used in Line 6 of the code in Figure 5. This primitive can be used in a variety of modes to enable SIMD processors to efficiently execute applications with data-dependent control. All of the following modes can be classified as space-time expansions or compressions of data streams:

- *switch* — uses conditional output to compress
  In this mode, data is routed into one or more streams such that each stream will consist of homogeneous data. This guarantees that even though different control flow

```
1   kernel example( istream<bool> case,        // An input stream to this kernel
2                   cistream<int> input_stream ) // A conditional input stream to this kernel
3   {
4       loop_until ( case.empty() ) {
5           case >> sel;                        // sel determines which PEs will access the stream
6           input_stream(sel) >> data;          // A PE receives an element of the stream only if sel
7       }                                       //   is true in that PE
8   }
```

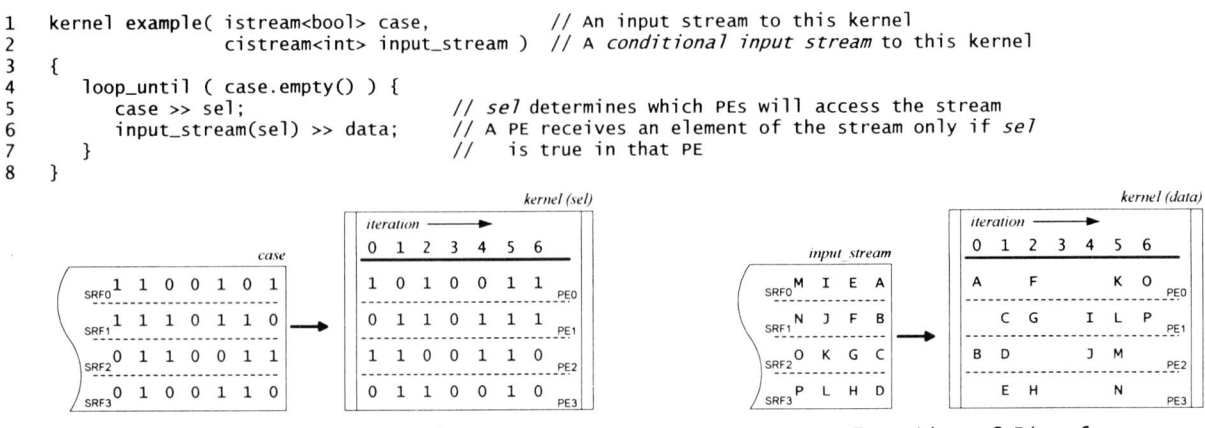

Figure 5: Conditional input stream execution with four PEs. Note that the convention adopted here is that the elements in a stream are ordered from top to bottom then right to left, and that time in a kernel goes from left to right.

and different computations may be required to process each of these resulting streams, every data element within a particular stream can be processed identically.

- *combine* — uses conditional input to expand
  Conditional input streams are used in this mode to combine two or more input streams into one output stream. The relative rates at which the input streams are processed are usually data-dependent.

- *load-balance* — uses conditional input to expand and conditional output to compress
  When the results of a computation require a variable (data-dependent) amount of time to generate, conditional streams can be used in this mode. A PE reads data from an input stream only when it is ready to start processing new data and writes to an output stream only when a valid result has been generated.

3.1. Conditional Switching

Figure 6(a) illustrates an example application snippet that reads a stream of values, filters out values that are greater than four, performs a non-trivial computation on the remaining values, and outputs the result. Without conditional streams, the kernel, *filter_process*, must produce a mask stream as shown in the figure. Each PE must perform the computation and write a result every loop iteration, even if it operates on a data element that is to be filtered out. A separate output stream, *mask*, indicates which elements of the *processed* stream are valid. When run on a SIMD machine, this code is inefficient in three ways. First, the function *compute* will be evaluated for all input elements, valid or invalid. Second, the invalid entries in the output stream will decrease the duty factor of subsequent kernels. Further filtering may exponentially decrease that duty factor until the stream is explicitly compressed through the main memory or inter-processor switch. Third, the final stream will occupy more space than necessary in the register file since it contains many unnecessary invalid values.

A SIMD processor with conditional streams performs the same function using two kernels as shown in Figure 6(b). When executing the first kernel, *filter*, each PE performs the test on its input element and conditionally outputs the element to an intermediate stream, *filtered*, which is now compressed, containing only valid data. In the second kernel, *process*, each PE reads a datum from the *filtered* stream, performs the computation, and appends the result to the output stream. There is no unnecessary computation as the PEs operate only on valid data, and there is no reduction in duty factor downstream because the output stream contains only valid data. In practice, the filtering operation can often be appended to the end of a previous computation kernel, eliminating the need for an additional kernel and its associated overhead.

Conditional switching is applicable to *case statement* types of data-dependent control where the computation and output performed for a data element is dependent on the value of the data element. For example, different computation may be performed depending on the state of finite elements or the type of geometry primitives. This application of conditional streams is especially useful when a rare case, such as an exception, requires a lot of processing. Normally, most PEs would idle while the exception case is processed. Conditional switching extracts only these exception cases to be dealt with independently. This works well if ordering is not important; otherwise, a separate mask stream can be generated and used to restore order at a later stage.

3.2. Conditional Combining

Figure 7 shows an example kernel, *interleave*, that produces an ordered stream (*out*) from two input streams

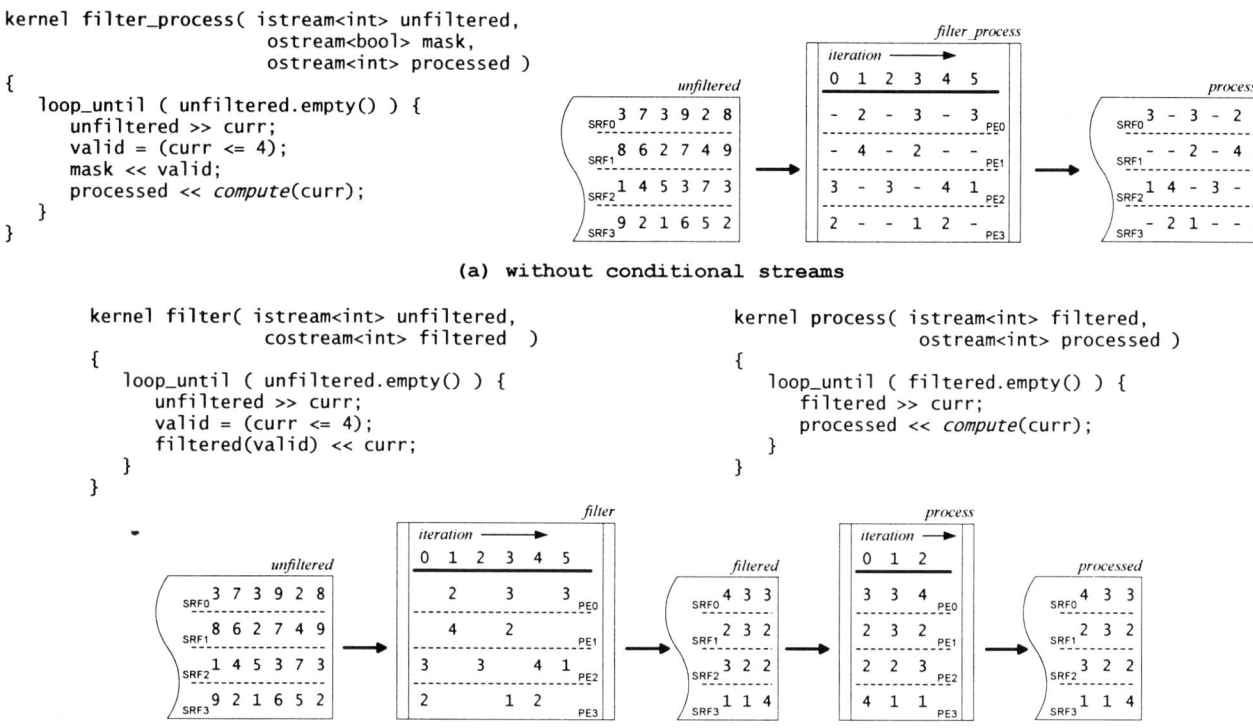

Figure 6: Kernel pseudocode for the filter/process operation (*compute(x) = x*)

```
kernel interleave( istream<bool> case,
                   int addrA, int addrB,
                   ostream<unsigned int> loadIdx )
{
  loop_until ( case.empty() ) {
    case >> sel;

    // ACnt = # of PEs below you in which sel==1
    // BCnt =       "     "    "    "   "  sel==0
    // Note: PE_i is 'below' PE_j if (i < j)
    ACnt = numBelow(sel);  BCnt = MY_ID - ACnt;
    myAddr = sel ? (ACnt + addrA) : (BCnt + addrB);

    // numA calc. by broadcasting highest PE's val
    numA = broadcast(NUM_PE-1, ACnt + (sel ? 1 : 0) );
    addrA += numA;  addrB += NUM_PE - numA;

    loadIdx << myAddr;
  }
}
```
            (a) without conditional streams

```
kernel interleave(istream<bool> case,
                  cistream<int> inA,
                  cistream<int> inB,
                  ostream<int> out )
{
  // assume case.len == inA.len + inB.len
  loop_until ( case.empty() ) {
    case >> sel;
    inA(sel) >> a;
    inB(!sel) >> b;
    out << (sel ? a : b);
  }
}
```
            (b) with conditional streams

Figure 7: The *interleave* operation

and a third stream of case values. Each case value specifies from which input stream the next element of the output stream should originate: from *inA* if the case value is true, from *inB* otherwise. The code in Figure 7(a), which does not employ conditional streams, uses the values in the stream *case* to generate an index stream (*loadIdx*) that will be used to gather the elements of *inA* and *inB* from main memory. The index stream is generated by keeping explicit track of the running address of streams *inA* and *inB* in variables *addrA* and *addrB* respectively. After the index stream is complete, the output stream is generated by storing the *inA* and *inB* streams to memory and then performing an indexed load using the addresses in the index stream (not shown). As in this example, the PEs in a traditional SIMD processor cannot arbitrarily control the consumption rate of an input stream without a memory operation. Since the consumption rates of the two input streams are not known *a priori* for the *interleave* operation, the PEs can only control the expansion of the *inA* and *inB* streams indirectly via the indices in *loadIdx*.

The code in Figure 7(b), which employs conditional combining, eliminates the extra memory operations and the explicit operations required for the address calculations. Based on the case value *sel*, each PE simply requests a value from the appropriate stream and appends it to the output stream. Essentially, the conditional input stream correctly expands the data to the PEs so that the

```
kernel process( istream<int> in,
                ostream<bool> mask
                ostream<int> processed )
{
    loop_until ( in.empty() ) {
        in >> curr;
        // loop ends when (curr <= 0) in all PEs
        loop_until (curr <= 0) {
            mask << (curr > 0);
            processed << curr--;
        }
    }
}
```

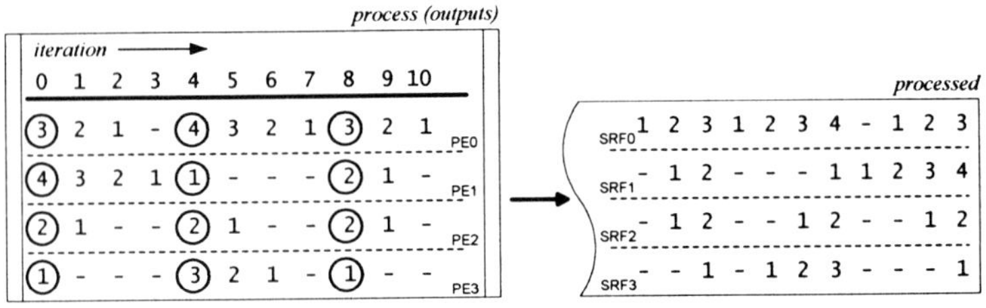

(a) without conditional streams

```
// uses conditional input stream to load balance
kernel process( cistream<int> in,
                ostream<int> processed )
{
    in(TRUE) >> curr;
    loop_until ( in.empty() ) {
        processed << curr--;
        // curr only updated if (curr == 0)
        in(curr == 0) >> curr;
    }
    // process final elements, if necessary
    cleanup();
}
```

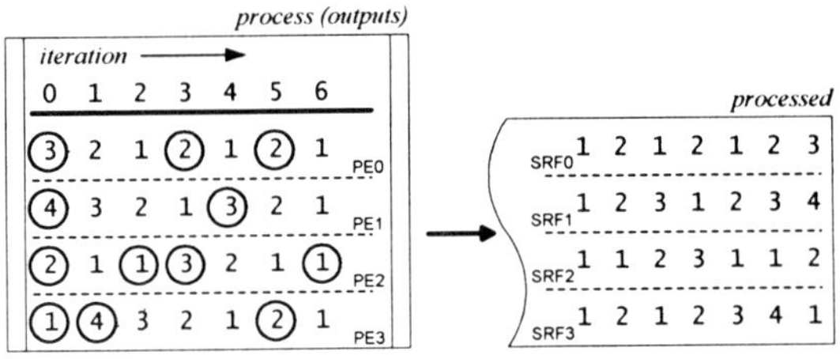

(b) with conditional streams

Figure 8: Pseudocode illustrating conditional streams used in the *load-balancing* mode

actual data can be interleaved while executing the kernel, obviating the need for extra memory transfers.

3.3. Conditional Load-Balancing

Load-imbalance often occurs on SIMD processors when PEs with short computations idle while one or more PEs with long computations perform additional iterations. Furthermore, the idle PEs may also generate NULL outputs during these idle cycles. Figure 8 illustrates how conditional streams can eliminate both the idle cycles and NULL outputs due to load-imbalance. For each input *curr* from the input stream, the kernels in the figure output the sequence of numbers {*curr, curr-1, ... , 1*}. The figure also shows the sequencing of the input and output streams during kernel execution.

Figure 8(a) illustrates an implementation without conditional streams. Two nested loops are used; data is read from the input stream by the outer loop, while the inner loop iterates until every PE completes processing its element. PEs with smaller values of *curr* finish earlier but are forced by the SIMD control to continue executing loop iterations and generating NULL outputs.

Figure 8(b) shows the same kernel using conditional input for load-balancing. This code only requires a single loop. On each iteration of the loop each PE generates an output value and reads a new element from the input stream only if it has completed processing the previous element, (i.e., if *curr* == 0). Thus, as soon as a PE finishes processing a data element, it requests and receives another one. The PEs perform neither idle iterations nor generate NULL outputs. PEs only remain idle when the input stream has been exhausted and while other PEs finish processing their final elements.

A concrete example is provided in the figure, where a circle around a datum indicates the cycle it was received by the PE. PE3 only needs 1 iteration to process the data element it initially receives. Since conditional stream access is not used in the code in Figure 8(a), PE3 must continue executing, outputting NULLs until the PE with the largest value of *curr* is finished three loop iterations later. The result is an output stream containing several NULLs. Figure 8(b) shows PE3 processing a new data element in the second iteration using a conditional input operation. As the variance of the processing times for the data elements increases, the savings provided by conditional load balancing improves. However, the order of the outputs produced with conditional load-balancing differs from that produced with the traditional implementation, neither of which are the same order as would result from a strictly serial implementation. In this example, if the order of the outputs was a concern, a sort would be performed on the output data (assuming additional ordering information was carried through the kernel). This issue, as it pertains to a polygon rendering pipeline, is discussed further in Section 6.3.

4. Microarchitecture

Implementing conditional streams requires both buffering and inter-partition communication of stream elements. The register file in the stream architecture presented in Section 3 operates under SIMD control; that is, each PE accesses the same location within its own

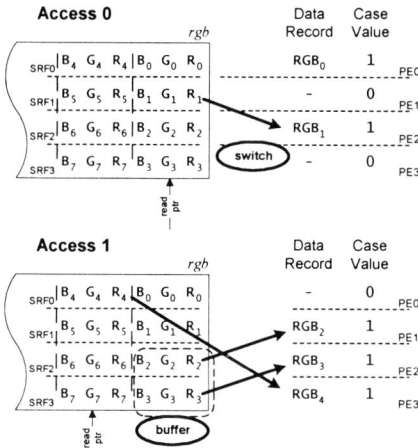

Figure 9: Sample conditional input access sequence

register file partition. Also, every PE can only read from its associated register file partition. Conditional streams require additional functionality, as shown in Figure 9. The figure shows two conditional stream accesses to an input stream of RGB data records and indicates the communication and buffering needed.

The figure shows that the data record RGB_1 is required by PE2 but is located in the register file partition associated with PE1. Therefore, the value must be communicated over the interprocessor switch. The second access in Figure 9 requires reading the first record of certain register file partitions (RGB_2 and RGB_3) and the second record in another partition (RGB_4). RGB_2 and RGB_3 must be buffered in order to provide the necessary data.

Figure 10 illustrates how a small buffer that is indexed using a local pointer in each PE in concert with an interprocessor switch can be used to implement conditional stream operations. Figure 10(a) illustrates the usage of the register file, buffer, and switch for a sequence of three conditional input operations.

Figure 10(b) shows the five steps required for the first access of Figure 10(a). First, the case values are examined to determine which PEs require input data. Second, control signals are generated for the switch, buffer, and register file by the shared controller (only shown in the top diagram in Figure 10(b)) to be used in the next three steps. Next, the appropriate buffer entry in each PE is accessed. For this first access, both values come from the right-hand side of the buffer. In step four, the data read from the buffer is communicated through the switch to the requesting PEs. Finally, if one side of the buffer has been completely emptied by the operation, as occurs after the second access, the empty side of the buffer is refilled by reading the next stream elements from the register file.

The controller determines whether or not to read new data values into the buffer, from which side of the buffer each PE should read, and the switch configuration. For example, the first access in Figure 10(a) only reads two values from right-hand side buffer entries, hence new values are not required. Then, when the second access reads three values and empties the right-hand side entries in the buffer, the controller causes four new values to be read from the input stream and written into these empty entries in the buffers. Since both data values for the first access are in right-hand side entries in the buffer, all read addresses are identical. However, the second access requires data values which reside in different sides of the buffer in the PEs. To account for this, the controller sets the read addresses of the buffer differently in each PE.

Dealing with output conditional streams, with the final values of input and output conditional streams, and with record lengths greater than one are all relatively straightfoward. Output streams are supported by sending data in the opposite direction. Data flows from the PEs through the switch into the buffer and eventually into the register file. At the end of an input stream, there may not be enough data in the buffers to satisfy all requests. An extra value, not shown in the figure, must be generated by the controller indicating to each PE whether or not valid data was received. An output conditional stream may not have received enough data to fill the final buffer entries. A user supplied NULL must be used to fill those empty entries if necessary. Finally, note that the accesses depicted in Figure 10 are for non-record data types. In order to keep transfers of records atomic, entries in the buffer in each PE are allocated for each record component, and steps 3-5 in Figure 10(b) must be iterated for each record component.

The implementation discussed so far requires a change only to the shared controller depicted in Figure 3. However, conditional streams can also be implemented without any dedicated control, assuming that a switch and a method for executing a hardware select (to perform the buffering) are available in each PE. In this case, the controller's functionality can be completely duplicated in software by storing the necessary conditional stream state, albeit redundantly in some cases, in every PE. The case values are broadcast over the switch, and each PE uses this information in conjunction with the stream state it has stored to determine which of the two buffer entries to read from. The switch permutation is calculated by the PEs and used to route the data from the buffer through the switch as before. Finally, since the access to the input stream for new data and the write into the buffer are either performed by every PE or by none at all, they can be enclosed in a branch. The code within the branch is only executed by every PE once all the entries in one of the two buffer sides have been emptied. This software approach is less efficient than the above hardware support, and will be explored further in Section 6.

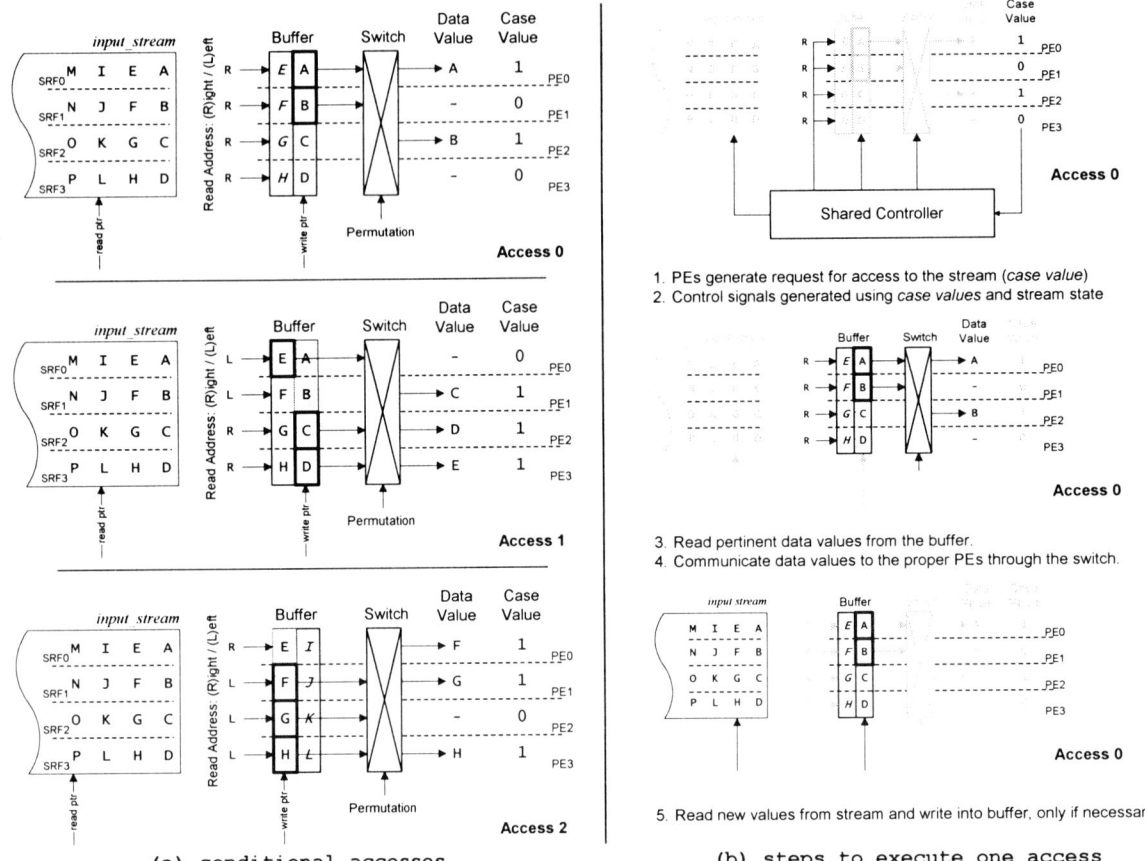

Figure 10: Buffer and switch usage and control for a conditional input stream. In (a), locations in the buffer that are being read are in bold outlined boxes, and values which have already been read are in grayed boxes. Italicized entries indicate values which were written into the buffer by the previous access (or that were just initialized).

5. Experimental Setup

To evaluate the performance advantages of conditional streams, a set of benchmarks was executed on a cycle-accurate simulator of the Imagine Stream Processor [9]. Imagine is similar in concept to the generic SIMD stream processor shown in Figure 3. Each processing element contains six 32-bit arithmetic units (three adders, two multipliers, and a divider) interconnected via a distributed register file structure, as shown in Figure 11. Each processing element has a communication unit which interfaces that processing element to the inter-PE switch. Imagine contains eight identical PEs controlled by a single microcontroller that broadcasts instructions. The only control flow operation supported by the microcontroller is a loop. Loop termination can be controlled by the value of a boolean in all of the PEs, by a counter, or by exhausting an input stream in the stream register file (SRF).

Data-dependent conditionals represent a programming challenge on typical SIMD machines that contain no control flow instructions other than loops. Imagine provides three mechanisms for dealing with data dependent conditionals: the select operation, a register offset addressable scratch-pad memory, and hardware conditional streams. The select operation can execute on any arithmetic unit in a single cycle. Based on a boolean value, the output of the select operation is set to the value of either its left or right input, similar to the C "?:" operator. Each PE in Imagine contains a 256 entry scratch-pad memory that is addressed by using a common base address, supplied by the microcontroller, added to an offset computed locally in each PE. This allows each PE to reference different locations inside its local scratch-pad, simplifying functions such as adaptive histogramming or matrix transposition. Conditional streams on Imagine are implemented as described in Section 4. The scratch-pad memories in the PEs are used as the buffer storage and the communication units provide the interface to the interprocessor switch in order to shuffle data records between hardware partitions for conditional stream accesses. When used for conditional streams, both of these units execute special instructions that supply the indices to the scratch-pads and the communication pattern directly from the conditional stream hardware. Every conditional

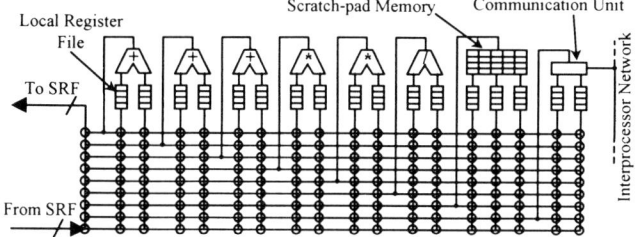

Figure 11: Processing element of Imagine

stream access requires a read from and a write to the scratch-pad memories, a communication, and a stream access. All four of these operations take one cycle each on Imagine. Additional cycles are required to generate the control signals from the case values; two cycles for conditional input streams and one cycle for conditional output streams. When implemented in software, 26 and 51 extra operations are required for each conditional input and output access respectively (for record lengths of one).

Each of the eight processing elements in Imagine has access to a 16KB bank of the stream register file. The eight banks of the SRF are connected to a streaming memory system that supplies a peak bandwidth of 4GB/s to off-chip double data rate SDRAM. Imagine is expected to operate at 500MHz, yielding a peak computation rate of 20GFLOPS and a peak SRF bandwidth of 32GB/s.

6. Results and Discussion

The performance of three configurations are evaluated: TRADITIONAL, a stream processor without conditional stream support; HARDWARE, a stream processor with hardware conditional stream support; and SOFTWARE, a stream processor with only software support for conditional stream accesses. These configurations are evaluated on two microbenchmarks based on the examples of Section 3. Two realistic applications are also considered: merge sort and polygon rendering.

6.1. Microbenchmarks

Figure 12 shows the results of running the *conditional switching* microbenchmark, which is largely based on the example illustrated in Figure 6. The graph shows the execution time as the number of arithmetic operations in the function *compute* increases from 10 to 100 for the three implementations. Since filtering would most likely occur at the end of another kernel in a real application, an additional 30 arithmetic operations are performed before the filtering in order to simulate a more realistic workload. This processing occurs in the kernel *filter_process* for TRADITIONAL and in *filter* for the other two. Results are shown for a 256 element data set where 0%, 50%, and 100% of the data elements are valid. TRADITIONAL executes for the maximum number of cycles regardless of how many elements are valid because it uses a mask stream. Hence the TRADITIONAL curves in all three graphs are identical. The 0% percent curves show maximum performance gains possible with conditional streams for this benchmark. Since the stream of compressed valid values in the conditional stream implementations will be empty for the 0% case, execution time is constant regardless of how long it takes to process valid values. Finally, the 100% curves show the overhead of each of the conditional stream methods. Most of the overhead in HARDWARE is due to splitting the computation into two kernels. SOFTWARE has additional overhead since operations are added to the inner loop of the *filter* kernel for emulating conditional stream accesses. Despite this overhead, SOFTWARE still offers better performance than TRADITIONAL when handling infrequent cases that require large amounts of processing. Finally, HARDWARE and SOFTWARE are initially flat in the 50% and 100% curves because 20 operations are not enough to completely fill the branch delay slots in a minimum length loop on Imagine.

The other microbenchmark, *load-balance*, is based on the example presented in Section 3.3, except instead of a trivial decrement each iteration, 60 and 100 arithmetic operations per output element are simulated. The results are in Figure 13 for 10 different input datasets that consist of 256 randomly generated elements. Within a dataset, the number of outputs produced when processing its elements is uniformly distributed with a mean of 10. The x-axis of the graph is the standard deviation of the number of outputs produced by the elements within a dataset. The total number of outputs generated by each dataset differ by less than 1%. Each dataset will thus require roughly the same number of cycles to execute in the ideally load-balanced case.

Both conditional streams implementations offer similar performance regardless of the standard deviation in the processing time for each dataset. In contrast, TRADITIONAL incurs a synchronization penalty between elements, thus requiring more time as the standard deviation of the dataset increases. The results for the dataset with a standard deviation of zero indicate that the overhead of dealing with load-imbalance is larger in TRADITIONAL than in HARDWARE. The overhead in TRADITIONAL is due to synchronizing the PEs, while the overhead in HARDWARE is due to extra control, buffering, and communication required for conditional streams.

6.2. Merge Sort

The first application considered is a merge sort, which sorts two smaller pre-sorted streams into one larger combined sorted stream, and which can be used as a building block for a larger full sort. Merge sort is an

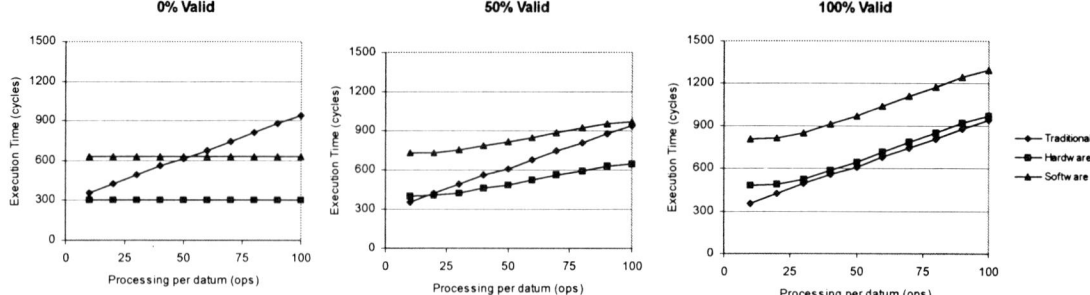

Figure 12: Conditional switching microbenchmark results

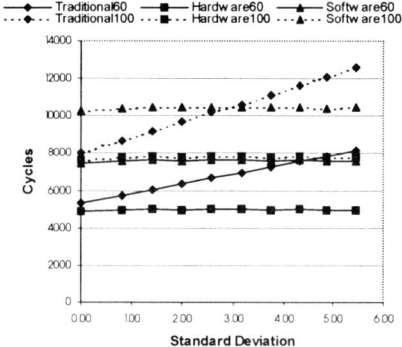

Figure 13: Conditional load-balance microbenchmark results

important example because it cannot be implemented in any reasonable fashion on a stream processor without conditional streams. This is because the rate of expansion of the two input streams must be determined while analyzing the data in the two streams. A stream of case values cannot be generated separately as in the *interleave* example of Section 3.2, because the two input streams would have to be expanded in order to generate the case stream, which was the initial problem.

Conditional streams, though, do allow an elegant solution on a stream processor. Initially, each of the n PEs reads one element from each input stream ($2n$ elements total). Software coordinates PE communication in order to determine the smallest n elements out of the $2n$ elements read. These elements are then rearranged in increasing order and output. Each PE then reads data from an input stream only if the value it previously read from that stream was small enough to be sent to the output stream. Now, the situation is the same as the initial case, and this process repeats until both streams are exhausted.

By allowing the expansion of the input streams to occur between the PE array and the register file instead of in the memory system, a merge sort can be efficiently implemented on a stream processor with a straightforward kernel. Without this ability, either a full sort or an algorithm with multiple passes is required.

6.3. Polygon Rendering

A typical polygon rendering pipeline [6] was implemented on the TRADITIONAL and HARDWARE configurations. The pipeline has three stages: geometry, rasterization, and composition. The application is strip-mined such that batches of triangles are loaded into the SRF and carried through the whole pipeline together. The batch size was chosen to be as large as possible while still allowing all temporary data to fit fully in the SRF without requiring memory spills. This size was 192 triangles for HARDWARE and 40 triangles for TRADITIONAL.

The geometry portion of the pipeline, which is perfectly data-parallel, transforms a stream of triangles from model space to screen space and performs lighting calculations. The rasterization stage generates spans from triangles, and then rasterizes each span to produce several fragments. At this point, a hash kernel separates out the fragments within the stream which are at a unique screen location from those that fall on the same screen location as another fragment within the batch.

A z-comparison test is performed on the stream of unique fragments using the old z-buffer values, and the fragments that pass are used to update the z- and frame-buffers. The stream of conflicting fragments is then sorted according to screen location to ensure all fragments at the same screen location are near each other in the stream. This allows the rest of the fragment composition stage to easily handle these exception cases. The fastest sort methods in this particular situation are a full merge sort for HARDWARE and a bitonic sort for TRADITIONAL. A complete description of the implementation on Imagine can be found in [7].

Note that the hash and sort are required because the application does not process one triangle at a time. Instead it amortizes control and memory access overheads over a whole stream of triangles (a batch). Also, the application requires that all fragments must be composited in the same order as the originating triangles in the source data. Since both implementations in the rasterization stage can potentially reorder the data in a way that violates this requirement, a small overhead is incurred. In particular, each triangle is assigned an ID that is carried through the pipeline until the sort, where it is used as a secondary sort key. However, note that HARDWARE does not incur any additonal penalty over TRADITIONAL. While the hash kernel splits all fragments into two streams, these two streams do not need to be composited in order or together. Also, the sort is required for the conflicting fragments for both configurations, not just HARDWARE.

Finally, intermediate streams in the TRADITIONAL configuration may contain invalid values. For example, one particular kernel marks all backward facing triangles as invalid. Also, the rasterization kernels produce invalid output as some PEs idle waiting for others to finish processing taller triangles or wider spans. These invalid values affect the duty factor of kernels later in the pipeline. To mitigate this, streams are compressed through memory at opportune points in the pipeline. These streams are stored using a mask, so that the stream will reside in a compressed form in memory, and will return to the SRF via a regular load operation. The final z-buffer and frame-buffer stores are also predicated so that only those fragments passing the z-test will generate writes to external memory.

Table 1: Polygon Rendering Results

Configuration	Batch Size (Triangles)	Execution (Cycles)	Mem. Accesses
TRADITIONAL	40	1,068,777	348,992
HARDWARE	40	836,881	131,080
HARDWARE	192	583,457	131,488
HARDWARE4	192	593,049	131,488

Table 1 shows the results of running the application on the two configurations. Comparing the results for a batch size of 40 on both configurations shows a speedup of 1.3x when using conditional streams. Two factors are responsible for this speedup. First, conditional streams increase the duty factor of PEs by using conditional switching and load-balancing. Second, TRADITIONAL has to periodically make extra memory references to compress streams that are diluted with NULLs.

The largest batch size TRADITIONAL can process without spilling any intermediate streams to memory is 40 triangles. In comparison, HARDWARE can process 192 triangles per batch since all streams are compressed while in the SRF. This reduces overhead incurred for loop prologues and epilogues. Since kernels are usually heavily software pipelined, this overhead can be significant, and a larger batch size considerably reduces the execution time of the application. For this scene a 1.8x speedup over TRADITIONAL was achieved.

The final configuration evaluated was HARDWARE4. This configuration has an inter-processor switch that is pipelined, but that has a latency four times that of the switch in the HARDWARE configuration. In all other respects it is similar to HARDWARE. The switch latency may increase as the number of PEs increase, and this may affect the performance of applications that use conditional streams since all data in a conditional stream is routed through the switch. However, this increase in switch latency has minimal effect on performance for this application, showing only a 9.8% slowdown when the latency is increased by a factor of four.

7. Related Work

A common approach to handling conditionals, as found in the early Solomon machine [12] and other data-parallel architectures, is to idle some PEs while others compute. Many vector processors, such as the Cray-1 [11] and the VPP500 [15], take a similar approach. On almost all vector processors, the only way to compress or expand a vector is through gather/scatter instructions that cycle data through memory. A notable exception is the NEC SX Supercomputer [16], which provides vector register-register compress and expand instructions. While these instruction don't actually touch any memory locations, they still occupy the global register file port(s), as well as the memory system port(s) and switch, potentially interfering with other critical memory loads and stores.

Smith, et al. provide a good summary of support for conditionals on vector processors to date and also conclude that solutions whose performance depends on the fraction of valid values in a vector (*density-time*) are preferred to those whose performance depends simply on the length of the vector (*VL-time*) [13]. For example, register-register primitives allow *density-time* processing. They, however, propose a new density-time solution that modifies the register file ports. Their implementation increments the vector register address to point to the next valid input entry based on the VM (a vector mask register). Memory addresses are also adjusted, requiring a multiplier for strided accesses. In addition, limited load-balancing is possible with their approach.

Conditional streams also achieve *density-time* processing. However, conditional streams are applicable to a larger variety of situations, such as merge sorting and optimal load-balancing. Also, in contrast, conditional streams use global register file bandwidth and storage more efficiently since streams diluted with invalid entries are never stored in the global register file.

8. Conclusions

Data-parallel architectures effectively exploit the parallelism in applications expressed in the stream programming model. However, data-dependent control constructs reduce efficiency as they do not map well to these architectures. Conditional streams are a mechanism to convert these control constructs into data-dependent data routing, and can result in significant speedups on media processing applications such as polygon rendering.

Data-dependent control flow requires each PE to perform different operations on its data, which is not possible with SIMD control. Instead, conditional streams convert control decisions into routing decisions. Data streams are transferred to and from (expanded and compressed) the PEs in such a way that all PEs execute the same control flow while still computing useful data. This functionality is exposed to the programmer by allowing stream accesses to be conditional upon a case value local to each PE. This simple abstraction compresses and expands data streams for the three modes presented in this paper: conditional switching, conditional combining, and conditional load-balancing. All of these modes replace data-dependent control constructs with the expansion or compression of data streams without additional memory accesses.

Conditional streams may be used in other modes of operation and are applicable to data-parallel applications with data-dependent control. The concept of conditional streams can also be implemented in software on existing SIMD architectures, but the full performance advantage is realized with additional hardware control. Existing infrastructure, such as the interprocessor switch, is leveraged to reduce the amount of additional hardware required. Hardware-based conditional streams on the Imagine stream processor enable a 1.8x speedup on a polygon rendering application. Furthermore, conditional streams enable efficient merge sorting, which is not possible otherwise.

Performance advantages of SIMD machines can often be offset by their inability to execute data-dependent control flow on many applications. Conditional streams extend the range and efficiency of applications possible on data-parallel architectures. The range of problems for which conditional streams are applicable can be expanded by further investigation of other modes of operation. Also, this paper presented an hardware implementation on the Imagine stream processor. Implementations on other architectures and configurations will potentially require different tradeoffs on how to leverage already existing hardware in order to get the best overall application performance.

Acknowledgements

The authors would like to thank Brian Towles for his help with the experiments, as well as all the other Imagine project members for their contributions to this paper and the project. Finally, we would like to thank everyone who read early drafts of the paper for providing helpful and insightful comments.

References

[1] ESPASA, ROGER, VALERO, MATEO, AND SMITH, JAMES E. Vector Architectures: Past, Present and Future. In *Proceedings of the 1998 International Conference on Supercomputing*, pp. 425-432.

[2] HENNESSY, JOHN L., AND PATTERSON, DAVID A. *Computer Architecture: A Quantitative Approach*, Appendix B, Morgan Kaufmann Publishers, Inc: San Francisco, California, 1996.

[3] HWANG, KAI. *Advanced Computer Architecture: Parallelism, Scalability, Programmability*, Chapter 8, McGraw-Hill, Inc: New York, New York, 1993.

[4] JACK, KEITH. *Video Demystified: A Handbook for the Digital Engineer*, LLH Technology Publishing: Eagle Rock, Virginia, 1996.

[5] LEE, CORINNA G., AND STOODLEY, MARK G. Simple Vector Microprocessors for Multimedia Applications. In *Proceedings of the 31st International Symposium on Microarchitecture* (November, 1998), pp. 25-36.

[6] OPENGL ARCHITECTURE REVIEW BOARD. OpenGL Reference Manual: the Official Reference Document to OpenGL, Version 1.1, Addison-Wesley Developers Press, Reading, Massachusetts, 1997.

[7] OWENS, JOHN D., ET AL. Polygon Rendering on a Stream Architecture. *2000 SIGGRAPH / Eurographics Workshop on Graphics Hardware* (August 2000), pp 23-32.

[8] PELEG, ALEX AND WEISER, URI. MMX Technology Extension to the Intel Architecture. In *IEEE Micro* (August, 1996), pp. 42-50.

[9] RIXNER, SCOTT, ET AL. A Bandwidth-Efficient Architecture for Media Processing. In *Proceedings of the 31st International Symposium on Microarchitecture* (November, 1998), pp. 3-13.

[10] RIXNER, SCOTT, ET AL. Register Organization for Media Processing. In *Proceedings of the Sixth International Symposium on High-Performance Computer Architecture* (January, 2000), pp. 375-387.

[11] RUSSELL, RICHARD M. The Cray-1 Computer System. In *Communications of the ACM* (January 1978), pp. 63-72.

[12] SLOTNICK, DANIEL L., ET AL. The Solomon Computer. In *Proceedings of the Fall Joint Computer Conference* (1962), pp. 97-107.

[13] SMITH, J. E., FAANES, GREG, AND SUGUMAR, RABIN. Vector Instruction Set Support for Conditional Operations. In *Proceedings International Symposium on Computer Architecture* (June, 2000), pp. 260-269.

[14] TREMBLAY, MARC, ET AL. VIS Speeds New Media Processing. In *IEEE Micro* (August, 1996), pp. 10-20.

[15] UTSUMI, TERUO, ET AL. Architecture of the VPP500 Parallel Supercomputer. In *Proceedings of the Conference on Supercomputing* (November 1994), pp. 478-487.

[16] WATANABE, T., ET AL. The Supercomputer SX System: An Overview. In *Proceedings of the Second International Conference on Supercomputing* (November, 1987), pp. 51-56.

[17] WAWRZYNEK, JOHN, ET AL. Spert-II: A Vector Microprocessor System. In *IEEE Computer (March, 1996)*, pp. 79-86.

Flexible Hardware Acceleration for Multimedia Oriented Microprocessors

F. Vermeulen *, L. Nachtergaele, F. Catthoor ‡, D. Verkest, H. De Man ‡,

IMEC, Kapeldreef 75, Leuven, Belgium.
* *also Ph.D. student at the Katholieke Univ. Leuven*
‡ *also Professor at the Katholieke Univ. Leuven*

Abstract

The execution of multimedia applications on a microprocessor greatly benefits from hardware acceleration, both in terms of speed and energy consumption. While the basic functionality implemented in these accelerators remains constant over different product versions, small changes are still often required. With the proposed architecture and protocol, the accelerator hardware has the performance and cost benefits of a hardwired solution, while featuring all the flexibility needed in practice. From a user point of view, the entire application is still programmable.

1. Introduction

To make the design of large systems-on-chip feasible, a tremendous increase in design productivity will be necessary. One of the keys to heavily increase current design productivity is design reuse at the level of system components. A product generation is subject to evolving standards, bug fixes, and changes in user requirements. These small modifications require flexibility in functionality and interfaces. However, when choosing an implementation platform, flexibility is to be traded off against speed and energy consumption. We can accelerate the (flexible) software solution with a (high performance) hardware implementation. But to cope with small and local design changes, we are forced to redesign the hardware or to switch all functionality back to the microprocessor.

The architecture we propose combines an instruction-set processor with custom processor acceleration in a way that offers flexibility at a lower cost than in current software and hardware-software architectures. We implement the functionality on a performance efficient custom hardware solution and we enable the instruction-set processor to take over control at any point during the execution, realizing full flexibility. A novel protocol allows for fine-grain synchronization, which is needed since it is not known in advance when the hardware realization will have to be substituted by a new functionality on the flexible (programmable or reconfigurable) component. This fine-grain synchronization is realized with a control-flow inspection mechanism and an interrupt mechanism. This is the key difference with related work. The overhead in the control switch is minimized thanks to a specific memory organization scheme, where all necessary data is available in shared memory. The performance of the resulting architecture is, even after implementing design changes, of the order of the original custom solution, while flexibility is comparable to a software or field programmable solution. This contrasts with a hardware coprocessor approach, where the coprocessor would become unusable because of design changes, requiring a full redesign or a costly software implementation.

The opportunity window for the proposed solution is in applications that benefit from the custom hardware implementation for power and speed reasons, and where a feasibility study shows a margin on the performance specifications (either in a new design or in a reuse library component). This opportunity window exists because of the orders of magnitude performance gap between custom hardware solutions and an instruction-set or reconfigurable processor implementation. Even when the performance after design changes becomes a few times worse than the original implementation, this still significantly outperforms a complete software or even a fully reconfigurable platform based solution. The proposed architecture leverages the performance margin to efficiently accommodate future design modifications.

For example, we present in Section 5 a custom hardware component (an IDCT) consuming originally 7.8 mW and which we would like to reuse in a new design, but which requires small modifications in the new context. Our approach enables this reuse at a power consumption of 10.5 mW, which in many cases will also satisfy the specifications (which cannot be said for the 122 mW pure software implementation). Any part of the functionality can be adapted, but the performance penalties incurred when implementing some functionality in software which was formerly implemented in hardware, limit the total amount of modifications to around 10% code change. In practice, this is adequate to cope with changes in standards, user requirements, and bug fixes.

In this paper, we focus on the protocol and architecture concepts. The impact on hardware-software design methodology has been addressed in [1].

2. Related work

In design reuse, flexibility at the stage of hardware design can be provided through parameterizable component designs. Flexibility after hardware fabrication can be provided by programmable hardware (e.g. instruction-set processors) and reconfigurable hardware (e.g. field programmable logic).

Instruction-set processors are more and more being customized with dedicated instructions, data types and memory architectures [2, 3, 4]. This is supported by retargetable and memory optimizing compilers [5, 6, 7, 8]. The trade-off is here between fine-grain software control (instruction control overhead) and associated data access bottleneck (overhead from register–register operation), and accelerators implementing complex operations. In this conventional "co-processor" solution the switching granularity between the two platforms is too large, which limits flexibility. Design changes may make the (re)use of the accelerator hardware impossible. In the presented architecture, the hardware is not running as a slave of the instruction-set processor, but both have synchronized master controllers. This allows one to further reduce the data transfer and instruction control bottleneck, beyond the arithmetic bottleneck.

To obtain a highly efficient implementation especially for data-intensive applications, the data access mechanisms of the accelerator hardware also need careful integration with the instruction-set processor memory architecture. Compared to our architecture, which also has this memory architecture integration, the accelerator hardware solution shows a higher design cost and nearly no flexibility.

To make custom hardware solutions more flexible, reconfigurable computing architectures ranging from general purpose FPGAs [9, 10, 11] to application specific reconfigurable architectures are proposed. General purpose reconfigurable logic suffers from a performance penalty (area, power, clock frequency). This penalty can be reduced in dedicated reconfigurable architectures with custom designed subblocks (e.g. [12]) and in the case of multimedia applications, a specific memory architecture [13, 14, 15]. In order to guarantee the flexibility that will be necessary in the application, a large design-for-reuse investment is then needed.

The architecture we propose in this paper combines a custom hardware solution with an instruction-set processor or field programmable solution in a novel way. It introduces an alternative new range of cost efficient implementations between the pure hardware and pure software implementations.

3. Flexible hybrid architecture

A well-known performance difference exists between the different target technologies (application-specific or reconfigurable technology) and processor architectures (custom or instruction-set processor). Important factors in this difference are the matching of application and architecture on the aspects of data types and arithmetic, memory hierarchy, and exploitation of parallelism. To be able to reuse an optimized hardware accelerator, even when small functional changes are necessary, we introduce our novel protocol between the accelerator hardware and the microprocessor. This allows to move any changed functionality onto the microprocessor at reuse time (providing that less than about 10% of the functionality is changed), enabling, from a user point of view, full programmability (see Fig. 1).

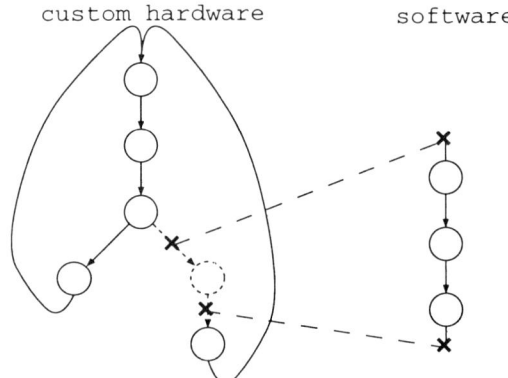

Figure 1. CDFG of original custom hardware functionality, with one part (dotted lines) replaced by a CDFG implemented in software. The crosses represent the context switching, occurring at a point which is not fully predefined when the chip is processed.

The two unique aspects of the proposed architecture that explain its cost efficiency compared to conventional solutions, are the fine granularity control switch and the low overhead context switch. Both aspects are discussed in the next paragraphs.

To obtain negligible power overhead when the custom hardware is performing its original functionality, both the custom and the instruction set processor run as master controllers. This allows for selective power-down of processors, using conventional low-power techniques [16]. Power-down modes are typically already present in embedded pro-

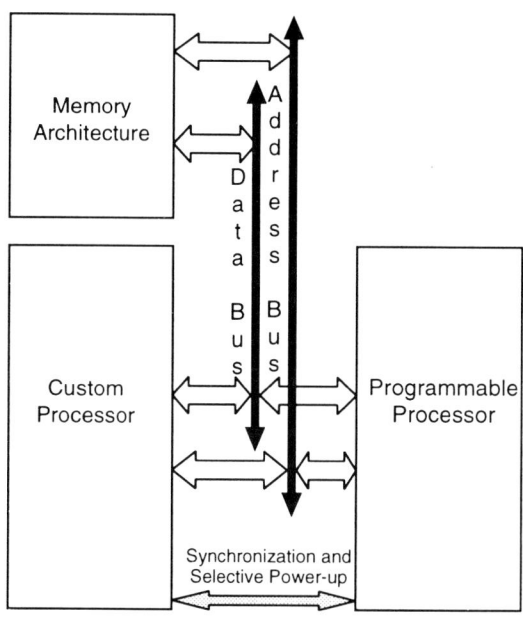

Figure 2. Proposed flexible architecture.

cessors and memory systems, so they are no extra cost of this architecture. The hardware controller is modified to allow for a flexible interrupt by the instruction-set processor using the protocol explained in the next section. This allows for fine-gain control (needed for flexibility), without the permanent instruction control overhead present in an instruction-set processor.

At the moment of the control switch between the custom and the instruction-set processor, also a context switch has to happen. The context switch is usually the most expensive aspect, since copying data between custom and instruction-set processor memory space (message passing) involves a large speed and power penalty. Therefore the proposed architecture exhibits a partly shared memory architecture between the custom and instruction-set processors (see Fig. 2). During the custom processor design, we remove memory system bottlenecks by a data transfer and storage exploration [17], which allows us to implement this memory sharing without redesign and with only a limited overhead in terms of energy consumption.

We require the context to be in the shared memory at the moment of the potential control switch points. This limits the number of switching points in the hardware control flow. A coarse granularity in functional parts that can be moved to the software processor, potentially results in a larger overhead, since also unchanged functionality will have to be implemented in software.

A first solution is a larger sharing of memory hierarchy, i.e. not only main memory, but also part of the intermediate and potentially even the most accessed local storage. This is a trade-off between design time spent at design-for-reuse time and flexibility.

An alternative solution is to provide extra data copies to shared memory blocks. Enabling more switching point with this technique involves a trade-off between flexibility and performance: an initial power penalty is incurred, but the incremental power penalty for design changes is smaller when more switching points are available. The design effort for providing extra data copies is limited.

4. Protocol for flexible interrupt

In the proposed architecture, both the custom and instruction-set processor run as master controllers. However, the instruction-set processor is tightly synchronized with the custom processor and can interrupt the latter at carefully selected states. This is realized through the protocol presented in this section.

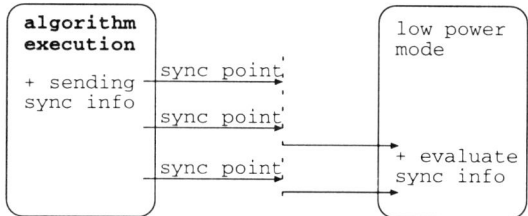

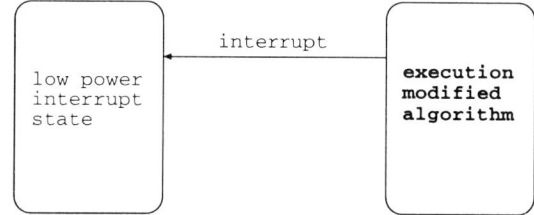

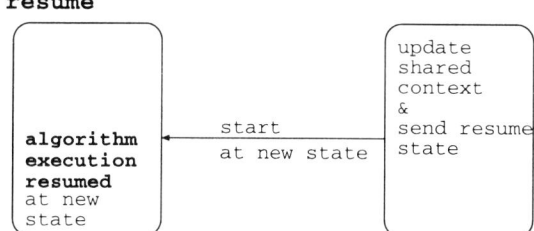

Figure 3. Phases of the control communication protocol between custom and instruction-set processor.

In the first phase of the protocol (Fig. 3), the custom

processor is processing on the data and its master controller communicates state information to the software processor. This communication can be minimized to a very large extent. Only the path taken in relevant data-dependent branches has to be communicated (these are synchronization points as in Fig. 4). The real-time software is designed at the time of reuse and tracks the relevant custom processor state information. The processor only needs to evaluate the state information necessary to determine whether the custom processor needs to be interrupted (e.g. bug fix for only one operating mode) and the exact moment when to interrupt the processor. This means that the instruction-set processor, which can be in low power mode or be executing another task, only needs a coarse grain polling of the synchronization information and often information on many branches can be evaluated in a single operation. For this reason, an interrupt approach at the instruction-set processor side (as in a conventional "coprocessor") would be a much more compute-intensive task than the proposed polling approach. This further reduces the synchronization overhead between hardware and software (which is in this architecture already much lower than in conventional architectures.)

An efficient implementation for the protocol would be for the custom processor to directly write the bit encoding of the branch to part of a special register of the instruction-set processor (called the synchronization register). The hardware can write the bits of this register as in a circular buffer, allowing the instruction-set processor to read the outcome of multiple branches in a single read and allowing a larger time window for the synchronization. The real-time software can track the custom processor state information by polling the synchronization register.

The second phase of the protocol is entered when the functionality on the custom processor has to be interrupted. The software will set up the environment in the instruction-set processor to be able to execute the changed functionality and will then, at the appropriate moment, signal an interrupt to the custom processor. Note that also here there actually is a time window in which the interrupt signal can be sent, since the custom processor only acts on an interrupt at the defined switching points. The deadline for an interrupt signal will be earlier than the switching state if the hardware is pipelined or runs at a higher clock speed.

Finally, after executing the modified code, the instruction-set processor clears the interrupt and notifies the custom hardware of the state in the original control flow at which to resume operation. At this point, the software must have restored the (now adapted) context in shared memory for the custom processor to operate on.

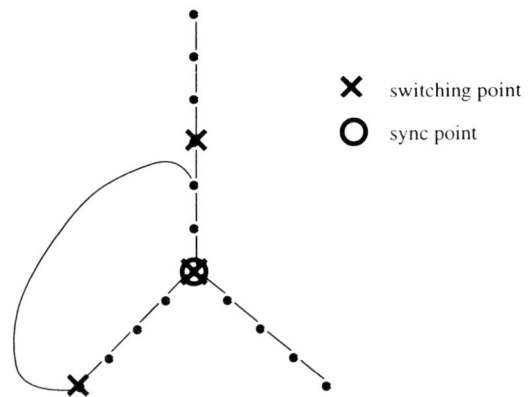

Figure 4. Example state transition graph, with annotated switching and synchronization points.

5. Demonstrators

To evaluate the relevance and feasibility of the methodology in real-life designs, components were taken from different application domains: video compression, wireless communication and ADSL (Asymmetric Digital Subscriber Line) modem.

In the most simple instance of the proposed architecture (Fig. 5), the original hardware has a single external memory. The added instruction-set processor chosen was an ARM7 [18]. The ARM was chosen as a power efficient small embedded processor with tool support (compiler, simulator, ...). The ARM should be regarded as one instance of a class of embedded processors (present in a reuse library), from which an optimal solution is selected. A more dedicated ASIP (application specific instruction-set processor) can have a better performance on specific applications and can also have dedicated support for the synchronization protocol through specific instructions and registers. However, it requires more design effort to derive initially, so a trade-off is involved. Also a reconfigurable architecture can be considered for the flexible processor component.

5.1. IDCT component

In the H.263 video conferencing block coding standard, a block-based encoding/decoding of image frames is performed to exploit spatial and temporal redundancy. The inverse discrete cosine transform (IDCT) operates on 8-by-8 blocks. The software has been compiled using the ARM compiler and power was evaluated using the average power figure of 1.6 mW/MHz [18]. Hardware executing the algorithm is synthesized and its power is evaluated on the resulting netlist. We cosimulated the custom hardware at

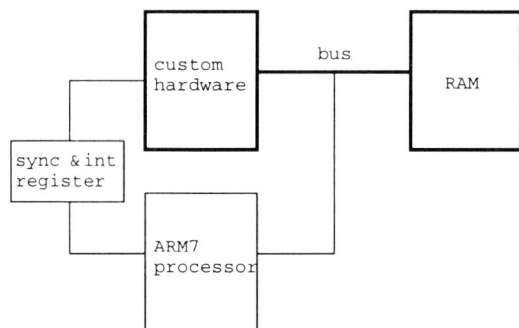

Figure 5. Simple instance of proposed flexible architecture (with original architecture in bold).

gate-level and the ARM cycle-accurate model. In all our experiments we normalized towards execution speed (all implementations run the algorithm in real-time).

For a standard image size IDCT implemented in custom hardware in a $.35\mu$ technology, energy consumption is 7.8 mW and area 2.8 mm^2. The real-time pure software solution needs 122 mW and 20.5 mm^2 (which is still optimistic, since the implemented algorithm matched the ARM processor rather well).

The finite state machine (FSM) description of the IDCT controller has been adapted according to the presented protocol (Fig. 6). This means:

- adding a write to the external synchronization register (read by the instruction-set processor) at synchronization points in the control flow. In this specific case, the loop counter is written at the end of the loop body.

- reading the external interrupt register (written by the instruction-set processor) at synchronization points and jump to the interrupt state.

- adding an interrupt state. It polls the interrupt register. When the interrupt flag is cleared, the controller resumes execution at the state (e.g. loop counter) specified in the interrupt register.

The necessary adaptations were done at the behavioral specification level, as a post-processing step on an existing soft IP component [19], so the design effort is very limited.

We have found that, synthesized for the same speed, only a limited area (1%) and energy consumption (4%) increase results from adding the protocol control to the custom solution. In typical cases, software execution is much slower than hardware execution. To compensate for this, we will need a performance margin on the hardware. For example if software is 10 times slower than real-time and we want to be able move 5% of functionality, we need hardware that is two times faster than real-time to obtain a real-time implementation. Synthesizing for faster than real-time speed (10 MHz instead of 4.28 MHz) added 8% to the area and 1% to the energy consumption (providing that the memory system could accommodate the higher speed).

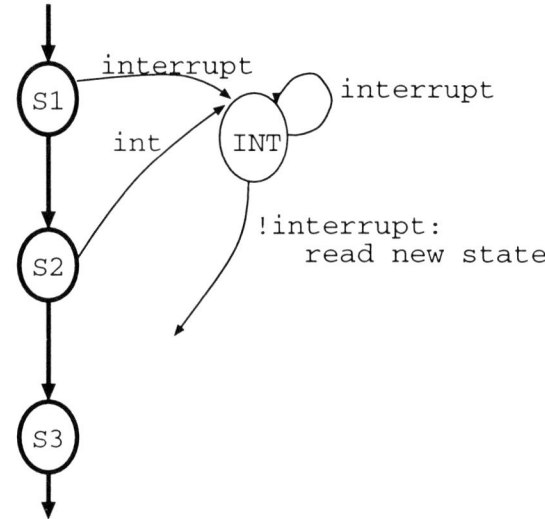

Figure 6. Custom hardware controller adapted to support the proposed protocol (original state transition diagram in bold).

Starting point for the software development at reuse time, is that the hardware behavior is fixed and hence fully known. Synchronizing to the exact point of interruption is done through cycle counting and reading of the synchronization register. To cope with custom hardware that runs much faster than the instruction-set processor, the software may have to prepare the interrupt signal many cycles before the actual interrupt point. The low power goal is realized by powering down most of the instruction-set processor when the hardware is active. Since the ARM is implemented as static logic, we can stop the clock for a number of cycles, by adding an external counter. It is clear that an ASIP designed for this purpose would have special logic and instructions to support even lower power operation during synchronization.

The final architecture has an area of 23 mm^2 which is approximately the combined area of the custom and instruction-set processor, except for the shared memory hierarchy. The power consumption is now 8.1 mW when none of the functionality is moved to the instruction-set processor. When active, the processor adds a proportional share of 116 mW to this. The extra instructions to move control between custom and instruction-set processor form a fixed cost, which is most of the time negligible with respect to the functional instructions.

Figure 7 shows the evolution of power consumption as a function of the fraction of changed functionality (counted in ARM cycles compared to the cycle count of a complete software implementation). For example, if we change the specification for the corner block calculation (2% of the calculations), the power increases from 7.8 mW to 10.5 mW, which is still acceptable (which is not the case for the 122 mW pure software implementation) and would not legitimate the major design cost (in engineering hours and time-to-market) that would be incurred if the hardware were re-designed.

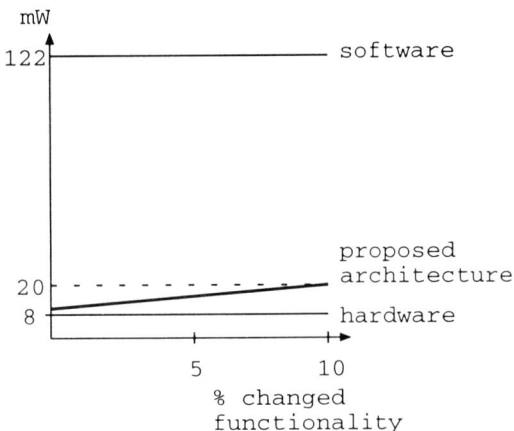

Figure 7. IDCT energy consumption as function of fraction changed functionality, evaluated for conventional and proposed architecture.

Apart from the off-the-shelf instruction-set processor, three other alternatives to provide a flexible implementation platform were evaluated: an implementation on reconfigurable hardware, a DSP implementation and an ASIP implementation (see Table 1). The design was compiled on a Xilinx Virtex XCV600 FPGA and power has been estimated with Xilinx Virtex Power Estimator 1.5. The DSP is a TI TMS320C6701. The power has been obtained by multiplying cycle counts with power figures from the C6000 Power Consumption Summary [20].

Between ASICs and general purpose instruction-set processors, a large range of ASIP instruction-set architectures can be designed, where flexibility and design time are spent to gain performance. W. Dougherty [21] et al. have found a factor 3 power increase going from an ASIC to a minimal ASIP for a FIR filter. We have made an estimation of a best-case power consumption in an ASIP based on the power attribution in a StrongARM [22] low power processor and assuming the best case of same datapath and internal memory energy as the custom hardware and only considering the instruction and memory management overhead. Energy consumption figures are summarized in Table 1. An indication of the (re)design cost is given to stress the design reuse trade-offs involved.

5.2. FFT component

In wireless Local Area Networks (LAN's) based on Orthogonal Frequency Division Multiplexing (OFDM) the Fast Fourier Transform (FFT) is a crucial component, which is also a major contributor in cost. As shown in [23], an FFT can gain significantly from an optimized data storage organization, which explains the factor 41 in power difference found with respect to the instruction-set processor implementation of this 64-point 16-bit FFT. This clearly motivates the proposed solution for flexible reusable components. The proposed architecture including memory has three times the area of the original custom component. But this area penalty is here traded off against power/speed and flexibility. The energy saving compared to a full software solution is again significant. If for example a simple windowing operation has to be added to the FFT, an (extrapolated) instruction-set implementation would require 7.8 W, against 0.3 W for the solution with our hybrid architecture.

5.3. Reed-Solomon component

A third reusable component on which we have evaluated the proposed architecture is a Reed-Solomon forward error correcting code as found in ADSL modems. This application benefits even more from a specific memory architecture and from bit-level operations. That explains the 305 times larger power and 6 times larger area in a pure ARM implementation. Note that in this demonstrator, the large power penalty incurred in an instruction-set processor implementation seems to limit the applicability of our approach, since moving only a few percent of the functionality to software causes a power increase of an order of magnitude. However, this can easily be solved by adding an appropriate ASIP instead of the ARM.

6. Conclusion

We have proposed a novel hybrid processor architecture that allows to implement functionality on a custom hardware accelerator without losing the flexibility of a software implementation. The synchronization protocol ensures a low power overhead from the instruction-set processor when the custom hardware is performing the original functionality of the IP component and yet it allows for a fine granularity control switch.

The opportunity window for this approach is in designs that have a margin on the performance specifications, which

Implementation	Power (mW)	Area (mm²)	Maximum clock speed (MHz)	Clock speed for RT execution (MHz)	(Re)design cost
custom hardware	7.8	2.8	10	4.3	very high
proposed arch.	10.5	23.3	10	5.2	moderate
ASIP	16.1	17.8	10	4.3	high
FPGA	67	–	–	–	moderate
software ARM	122	20.5	59	52.8	moderate
software DSP	159	–	150	21.1	moderate

Table 1. Energy consumption, area, maximum clock speed, clock speed needed for real-time execution, and (re)design cost for different implementations of IDCT, after 2% functionality change.

the proposed architecture efficiently uses to accommodate small design modifications.

The energy consumption claims have been evaluated on several realistic designs. A modified IDCT example shows a 12 times lower power dissipation for an implementation on our platform, compared to a pure software implementation. The design changes are entirely made in software, avoiding an expensive hardware redesign.

References

[1] F.Vermeulen, F.Catthoor, D.Verkest, H.De Man, "Extended Design Reuse Trade-Offs in Hardware-Software Architecture Mapping," *Intl. Wshop on Hardware/Software Codesign 2000,* pp.103-107, San Diego, CA, May 2000.

[2] http://www.tensilica.com/.

[3] http://www.carmeldsp.com/.

[4] P.Panda, N.Dutt, A.Nicolau, "Data Cache Sizing for Embedded Processor Applications," *Design Automation and Test in Europe Conf,* Paris, France, pp.925-926, Feb. 1998.

[5] S.Adve, D.Burger, R.Eigenmann, A.Rawsthorne, M.Smith, C.Gebotys, M.Kandemir, D.Lilja, A.Choudhary, J.Fang, P.Yew, "Changing Interaction of Compiler and Architecture," *IEEE Computer,* Vol.30, No.12, pp. 51-58, Dec. 1997.

[6] E.Torrie, M.Martonosi, C.Tseng, M.Hall, "Characterizing the Memory Behavior of Compiler-Parallelized Applications," *IEEE Trans. on Parallel and Distributed Systems,* Vol.7, No.12, pp.1224-1236, Dec. 1996.

[7] D.Truong, F.Bodin, A.Seznec, "Improving Cache Behavior of Dynamically Allocated Data Structures," *Int. Conf. on Parallel Architectures and Compilation Techniques,* Los Alamitos, CA, pp.322-329, 1998.

[8] Target Compiler Technologies NV, *http://www.retarget.com/.*

[9] A.DeHon, J.Wawrzynek, "Reconfigurable Computing: What, Why, and Implications for Design Automation," *Proc. of Design Automation Conf.,* New Orleans, LA, pp.610-615, Jun. 1999.

[10] G.Borriello, C.Ebeling, S.Hauck, S.Burns, "The Triptych FPGA Architecture," *IEEE Trans. on VLSI Systems,* Vol.3, No.4, pp.491-501, Dec. 1995.

[11] F.Vahid, T.Givargis, "The Case for a Configure-and-Execute Paradigm," *7th Int. Workshop on HW/SW Co-Design,* Rome, Italy, pp. 59-63, May 1999.

[12] D.C.Cronquist, P.Franklin, S.G.Berg, C.Ebeling, "Specifying and compiling applications for RaPiD," *IEEE Symp. on FPGAs for Custom Computing Machines,* Los Alamitos, CA, pp. 116-25, 1998.

[13] H.Schmitt, D.Thomas, "Synthesis of Application-Specific Memory Designs," *IEEE Trans. on VLSI Systems,* Vol.5, No.1, pp.101-111, Mar. 1997.

[14] P.Lippens, J.van Meerbergen, W.Verhaegh, "Allocation of Multiport Memories for Hierarchical Data Streams," *Proc. of IEEE/ACM Int. Conf. on Comp.-Aided Design,* Santa Clara, CA, pp. 728-735, Nov. 1993.

[15] S.Bakshi, D.Gajski, "A Memory Selection Algorithm for High Performance Pipelines," *Proc. of the European Design Automation Conf,* Brighton, Great Britain, Sep. 1995.

[16] "Low power CMOS design," (eds. A.Chandrakasan, R.Brodersen), *IEEE Press,* 1998.

[17] F.Catthoor, S.Wuytack, E.De Greef, F.Franssen, L.Nachtergaele, H.De Man, "System-level transformations for low power data transfer and storage," in paper collection on "Low power CMOS design" (eds. A.Chandrakasan, R.Brodersen), *IEEE Press,* pp.609-618, 1998.

[18] Advanced RISC Machines, Ltd, *http://www.arm.com/Pro+Peripherals/Cores/ARM7TDMI/*

[19] VSI Alliance, "VSI Alliance Architecture Document," *VSI Alliance,* 1.0 edition, 1997.

[20] Texas Instruments, "TMS320C6000 Power Consumption Summary - Application Report SPRA486B," *http://www-s.ti.com/sc/psheets/spra486b/spra486b.pdf*

[21] W.Dougherty, D.Pursley, D.Thomas, "Instruction Subsetting: Trading Power for Programmability," *IEEE Wshop on VLSI 1998,* Los Alamitos, CA, pp.42-47, 1998.

[22] J.Montanaro et al, "A 160-MHz, 32-b, 0.5W CMOS RISC Microprocessor," *IEEE Journal of Solid-State Circuits,* vol.31, no.11, pp.1703-14, Nov. 1996.

[23] F.Vermeulen, F.Catthoor, D.Verkest, H.De Man, "Formalized Three-Layer System-Level Model and Reuse Methodology for Embedded Data-Dominated Applications", *IEEE Trans. on VLSI Systems,* Vol.8, No.2, pp.207-216, Apr. 2000.

Low-Power Design

Very Low Power Pipelines using Significance Compression

Ramon Canal[†], Antonio González[†] and James E. Smith[‡]

[†]Departament d´Arquitectura de Computadors
Universitat Politècnica de Catalunya - Barcelona
{rcanal,antonio}@ac.upc.es

[‡]Department of Electrical and Computing Eng.
University of Wisconsin-Madison
jes@ece.wisc.edu

Abstract

Data, addresses, and instructions are compressed by maintaining only significant bytes with two or three extension bits *appended to indicate the significant byte positions. This* significance compression *method is integrated into a 5-stage pipeline, with the extension bits flowing down the pipeline to enable pipeline operations only for the significant bytes. Consequently register, logic, and cache activity (and dynamic power) are substantially reduced.*

An initial trace-driven study shows reduction in activity of approximately 30-40% for each pipeline stage. Several pipeline organizations are studied. A byte serial pipeline is the simplest implementation, but suffers a CPI (cycles per instruction) increase of 79% compared with a conventional 32-bit pipeline. Widening certain pipeline stages in order to balance processing bandwidth leads to an implementation with a CPI 24% higher than the baseline 32-bit design. Finally, full-width pipeline stages with operand gating achieve a CPI within 2-6% of the baseline 32-bit pipeline.

1. Introduction

There are many microprocessor applications, typically battery-powered embedded applications, where energy consumption is the most critical design constraint. In these applications, where performance is less of a concern, relatively simple RISC-like pipelines are often used [8][10]. A variety of circuit and microarchitecture techniques are employed to conserve energy when the processor is operating, and power-down "sleep" modes are invoked when the processor is not in use. In current CMOS technology, most energy consumption occurs when transistor switching or memory access activity takes place [3]. Therefore, in this paper we focus on reducing dynamic energy consumption. Dynamic energy consumption is proportional to the switching activity, as well as the load capacitance and the square of the supply voltage. Thus, an important energy conservation technique is to reduce switching activity by "gating off" portions of logic and memory that are not being used.

Recently [1] it was proposed that rather than basing logic gating decisions entirely on *operation* types, certain *operand* values could also be used to gate off portions of execution units. In particular, arithmetic involving short-precision operands only needs to be performed on the (relatively few) numerically significant bits. Operands containing insignificant bits (typically leading zeros or ones) can yield simpler computations or can be used to avoid computations altogether. Note that this operand-based gating targets a different source of energy consumption than operation-based gating, and both operation- and operand-based gating techniques can be used concurrently.

We generalize the notion of operand gating to all stages of the pipeline as a way of reducing switching activity and hence, dynamic energy consumption. The key principle is the use of a small number of *extension bits* appended to all data and instructions residing in the caches, registers, and functional units. In Fig. 1, the extension bits are shown along the bottom of a basic pipeline. These bits correspond to portions of the datapath, and they flow through the pipeline to gate-off unneeded energy-consuming activity at each stage, including pipeline latching activity. New extension bit values are generated only when there is a cache line filled from main memory (although they could also be maintained in memory) and when new data values are produced via the ALU. The points where extension bits are generated are indicated in Fig. 1 by circled "G"s.

For the instruction caches, extension bits allow a simple form of compression targeted at reducing instruction fetch activity, rather than reducing the number of bits in the program's footprint. For other datapath elements, they enable a form of compression where memory structures actively load and store only useful (significant) operand bytes. For arithmetic and logical operations, the extension bits enable operand gating techniques similar to those proposed in [1].

Given that only significant bytes require datapath operations and storage, pipeline hardware can be simplified by using byte-serial implementations, where the datapath width may be as narrow as one byte, and a pipeline stage is used repeatedly for the required number of significant bytes. Although there are many alternative implementations with different degrees of parallelism, they all have some serialization in the pipeline. In particular, low-order byte(s) and extension bits are first accessed and/or operated on; then additional bytes may be accessed and/or operated on if necessary. We describe and evaluate several pipeline implementations of this type.

When compared with a conventional 32-bit pipeline, significance compression can reduce activity by 30-40% for each pipeline stage. The simplest implementation (byte-serial) suffers a CPI (cycles per instruction) increase of 79% but wider pipelines incur a performance loss as little as 2-6%.

The paper is organized as follows. Section 2 presents several techniques to reduce the activity at each stage of the pipeline. The experimental framework is described in section 3. Sections 4, 5, and 6 present implementations with differing levels of complexity and performance. Finally, section 7 contains a summary and conclusions.

2. Techniques for Reducing Activity Levels

In this section, we develop methods for reducing memory and logic activity for each pipeline stage. Because activity in

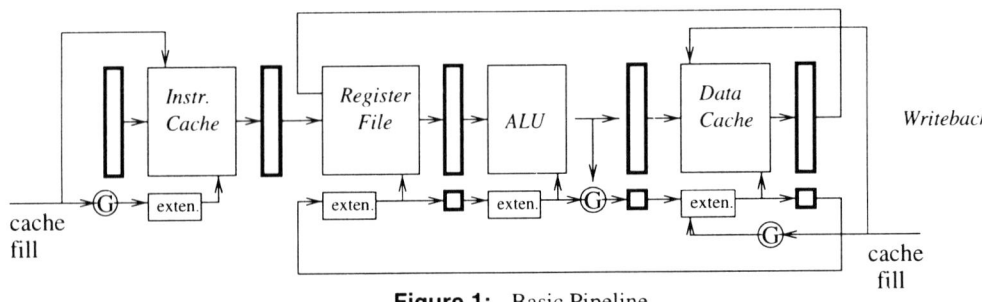

Figure 1: Basic Pipeline

the simple pipeline depends primarily on data values and instructions, we first undertake a trace-driven study to determine the required activity for each of the major pipeline operations. Then, in later sections, we propose and study pipelined implementations that come close to achieving the minimum "required" activity levels.

This work is based on a simple 5-stage pipeline with in-order issue as is often used for low power embedded applications. We consider the 32-bit MIPS instruction set architecture (ISA) and focus on integer instructions and benchmarks -- commonly used in the low power domain.

2. 1. Data Representation

The basic technique for representing data is to tightly compress data bits that do not hold significant data. For example, a small two's complement integer has only a few numerically significant low-order bits and a number of numerically insignificant higher order bits (all zeros or all ones).

In principle, one could consider significance at bit-level granularity, i.e. store and operate on exactly the numerically significant bits and no more. However, implementations are likely to be simpler and more efficient overall if a coarser granularity is used. Consequently, we primarily consider byte granularities and focus on the significant bytes rather than bits. Byte granularity is rather arbitrarily chosen, but it seems to be a good compromise of implementation complexity and activity savings. For comparison we also provide some results for halfword (16-bit) granularities. In general, one could consider non-power-of-two bit sequences and dividing words into sequences of different lengths, but this remains for future study. Because the lowest order data byte is very often significant, we will always represent and operate on the low order byte. Then we will use a very small number of bits (2 or 3) to indicate the significance of the other 3 bytes (of a word).

A simple encoding is to add two extra *extension bits* to encode the total number of bytes that are merely sign extensions. For example, the 32-bit number 00 00 00 04 (in hexadecimal) can be encoded as - - - 04 : 11. This is a mixed hexadecimal/binary notation that uses hexadecimal for significant (represented) bytes, a dash for the insignificant (non-represented) bytes, and a binary pattern after the colon for the values of the extension bits. In the above example, the only significant byte is 04 with three sign extension bytes, so the extension bits encode a binary three. This simple method also works for two's complement negative numbers if it is assumed that the high order significant bit of the most significant data byte is extended. For example, the number FF FF F5 04 can be represented as - - F5 04: 10. I.e.

it has two significant bytes, and the most significant bit of these two bytes is extended to fill out the full 32-bit number. This encoding works well and has an overhead of two bits per 32-bit word (about 6 percent).

After inspecting commonly occurring data/address patterns, it is apparent that there are other, easily compressible values. In these cases there are some "internal" bytes that are all zeros or all ones, and these bytes are in a sense insignificant (slightly abusing the meaning of "significance"). An important case occurs for memory addresses in upper memory. These addresses often have nonzero upper bits, nonzero lower bits, but zero bits in between. For example, the data segment base of our experimental framework (see section 3) is set at address 10 00 00 00, thus a variable may be located at address 10 00 00 09.

To handle these cases, we propose a scheme with three extension bits (approx. 9% overhead). In this scheme, the extension bits apply on a per-byte basis. Each extension bit corresponds to one of the upper three data bytes (as before, the least significant byte is always fully represented). If an extension bit is set to one, it indicates that the previous byte position is sign extended; if the extension bit is zero, it indicates the corresponding byte is significant. Consequently, the earlier example 10 00 00 09 is represented as 10 - - 09: 011. As a more complex example, FF E7 00 04 is represented as - E7 - 04 : 101

The three-bit extension scheme allows for eight different patterns of significant/insignificant bytes (assuming the low order byte is always significant). We performed a study with the Mediabench benchmarks [6] to determine the relative frequency of occurrence of each (see section 3 for more details of the experimental framework). Table 1 lists the results. In the table, the notation "sess" indicates that the first, third, and fourth bytes are all significant and that the second byte is the sign extension of the third. The data show that the four most common cases include about 94% of operand values, and these four cases are the same as those that can be encoded with the two extension bit format described earlier. This suggests a trade-off between the two- and three-bit schemes. The former reduces the overhead from 9% to 6% whereas the latter may potentially reduce activity for about 6% more operands. We chose to study the 3-bit scheme, although one could reasonably argue that the 2-bit scheme is better due to simplicity and overhead advantages; in any case, the performance results are likely to be very similar for both schemes.

Table 1 also indicates the high level of compression that is possible. About 60 percent of the data values used in the

Table 1: Frequency of significant byte patterns

Cases	Register values	Ld/St values	Overall values	Acc.
eees	61.8	45.7	61.0	61.0
eess	13.3	20.3	13.6	74.6
ssss	12.3	17.6	12.6	87.2
esss	7.1	12.2	7.4	94.6
sses	1.8	0.3	1.8	96.4
sess	1.6	2.9	1.6	97.9
eses	1.4	0.8	1.4	99.2
sees	0.8	0.3	0.8	100

Table 2: Activity and latency estimates for PC updating

number of bits per block	Activity (bits operated on)	Latency (cycles)
1	2.0000	2.0000
2	2.6667	1.3333
3	3.4286	1.1429
4	4.2667	1.0667
5	5.1613	1.0323
6	6.0952	1.0159
7	7.0551	1.0079
8	8.0314	1.0039

pipeline have only one significant byte and 75 percent have at most two. In the following subsections, we consider each stage of the instruction pipeline and describe ways that activity can be reduced via appended extension bits.

2.2. PC Increment

Incrementing the PC is at the very beginning of the pipeline. When incrementing the program counter, we do not literally append extension bits to the operands. One of the operands is always +1 (the PC is word resolution), so it is known to have only one significant bit. The PC, on the other hand, is held to full 30-bit precision. The PC increment is performed byte-serially to reduce activity. In particular, we first increment only the low order byte. If a carry out is produced, the next byte is incremented on the next cycle, etc. If a carry out is not produced at any stage, no additional byte additions need to be done.

This method very often saves adder and PC latching activity for higher order bytes, but it can lead to some performance loss in the uncommon cases when there is a carry beyond the low order byte, and instruction fetch is temporarily stalled while additional byte additions are performed. A brief analysis sheds some light on this trade-off. In general, one can consider a block-serial implementation where the block size is not necessarily a byte. The size of the block determines the performance and the activity savings. Performance is maximized by the biggest block size (i.e. 30 bits), but the activity savings are null. On the other hand, a smaller block may have a slightly lower performance but may produce significant activity savings.

If the block size is N bits, and we assume that at a random point in time all instruction addresses have the same probability, then we can calculate the probability that i stages (each of size N) are required to compute PC+1, and based on this probability, we can then compute the average number of bits operated on (Activity) and the average number of cycles to compute a PC (Latency).

Table 2 shows the Activity and Latency statistics for values of N ranging from 1 to 8. Higher values of N are not interesting because they hardly improve performance, and activity increases significantly. Minimum activity is achieved for $N=1$, but this incurs a 1-cycle penalty per instruction on average (as expected). $N=5$ may be a good trade-off because activity is reduced by 83%, and performance is degraded by just 3%. Finally, $N=8$ provides negligible degradation in performance with an activity reduction of 73.2%. In section 2.9 we validate these analytical figures with an empirical analysis. As indicated above, we assume a block size of 8 bits for the PC increment.

2.3. Instruction Cache

To save instruction cache activity, instruction words are stored in a permuted form. The goal is to reduce the number of instruction bytes that have to be read, written, and latched. This objective is somewhat related to the more common instruction compression techniques [4,5,12,13,18] that attempt to store more instructions in a given amount of memory. In our case, each instruction is still allocated a full word in the instruction cache. However, not all bits have to be read/written/latched each time an instruction is placed in the cache or is fetched. Simple permutation-based compression schemes are important because the energy consumption of the decompression task should not offset the benefits of reducing the number of bits to be processed. Permutation methods of this type are likely to be specific to the ISA, and we consider methods that work well for the MIPS ISA. While the exact methods may not extend entirely to other ISAs, similar methods are likely to be applicable –at least for RISC ISAs.

Although we considered a number of methods, two basic schemes seem to work well for the MIPS ISA and probably provide a significant majority of the benefit that can be achieved. First of all, we observe that the MIPS ISA very often uses one of two formats[1] [11]:

- R-format: A 6-bit opcode, three 5-bit register fields, a shift amount field, and a 6-bit function code.
- I-format: A 6-bit opcode, two 5-bit register fields, and a 16-bit immediate value.

In the R-format, the number of significant instruction bits can frequently be reduced to three bytes by recoding the six-bit function field so that the most common eight cases use three bits of the field with zeros in the other three bits. For these eight common cases, only three instruction bytes must be fetched and latched. In the other less common cases, all four instruction bytes must be fetched. Shifts that use the shift amount field do not use the first register field (*rs*), so the fields can be permuted by moving the shift amount (*shamt*) into what is normally the *rs* field.

The permutation for R-format consists of shuffling bits in a minor way and re-encoding the function bits. Figs. 2a and 2b show the permutations for the R-format instructions. The function field is split into two 3-bit fields, f1 and f2, as noted above. To determine which function re-encoding to use, we first traced the Mediabench benchmarks and counted the dynamic frequency of each of the function codes. The results are in Table 3. Thus, the most common eight function codes are recoded to 6-bit encodings, where the last three

---
[1] There is a third format (J-format), but it only accounts for 2.2% of the executed instructions in the Mediabench.

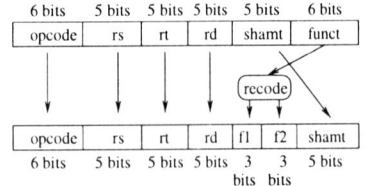
a) First permutation for R-format inst.

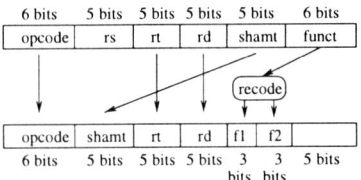
b) Second permutation for R-format inst.

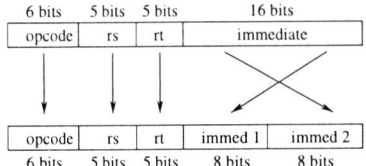
c) Permutation for the I-format instructions

Figure 2: Permutations for the different instruction formats

bits are all zeros (and do not have to be fetched). All the other function code patterns are mapped to the remaining six bit patterns. From the table we see that 86.7% of all the R-format instructions require three bytes when modified in this manner.

For the I-format, we simply note that often eight or fewer immediate bits are actually significant, and in these cases three instruction bytes are again adequate. Fig. 2c shows the permutation for the I-format instructions. For I-format instructions we also traced the benchmarks and determined the sizes of the immediate values. It was found that 59.1% of all instructions use immediate values and 80% of these immediates require only eight bits.

Although there are a few cases where it can be done, we do not attempt to reduce the number of fetched instruction bytes to fewer than three. Consequently, we add a single "extension" bit to the instruction word portion of the instruction cache. This bit indicates whether three or four bytes should be fetched and latched. Note that only one bit is used and it serves multiple purposes depending on the actual 6-bit opcode. For typical R-format opcodes it indicates that the low order three function bits (field $f2$) are zeros. For the shift amount R-format opcodes, it also moves the *shamt* field, and for I-format opcodes it indicates an 8-bit immediate.

Overall, in the Mediabench suite a total of 36.9% of instructions are R-format that use the function field; 4.1% are R-format but the function field is not used; 56.9% are I-format, and 2.2% are J-format. Combining this with the immediate and function code frequency statistics, the average number of bytes fetched and latched per instruction is 3.17 bytes (3.29 if we include the extension bit). This represents a savings of about 20% (at an overhead of 3% for the extra bit per word). There is also additional overhead during instruction cache fill for permuting/modifying the instruction bits, but this is a relatively small amount of additional activity, assuming a reasonable instruction cache miss rate. Finally, note that the order of the rearranged instruction bytes is chosen so that the bytes needed earlier in the pipeline are toward the most significant end. This enables better performance for implementations (to be given later) that read instruction bytes serially. For example, after an implementation fetches the first two bytes, there is enough information to perform the initial opcode decode and register

Table 3: Dynamic frequency of function codes

Opcode	Percentage	Cumulative
ADDU	36.0	36.0
SLL	16.2	52.2
SRA	9.1	61.3
SLT	8.2	69.5
SUBU	8.2	77.7
SLTU	3.3	81.0
XOR	3.1	84.1
MFLO	2.7	86.8
Others	2.5 .. 0.0	100

read operations. The other bytes give the immediate bits, a result register field, and/or ALU function bits that are not needed until later in the pipeline

2. 4. Register File Access

For the register file, extension bits as described in Section 2.1 are used. When the register file is accessed, first the low order data byte and the extension bits are read. Depending on the values of the extension bits, additional register bytes may be read during subsequent clock cycle(s). In a study of the Mediabench suite described below, we determined that the extension bits result in large register file activity savings. On average, the number of bits that are read is reduced by 47%.

To implement the single-bank, 32-bit register file of the baseline configuration and each of the 8-bit register banks required by the pipelines proposed in this work, different layouts can be used. In particular, the physical arrangement of the data array of each bank has a significant impact on the performance of the register file. Splitting the data array into multiple arrays, either horizontally or vertically, or widening the number of bits per word line has a significant impact on the access time as shown by Wada, Rajan and Przybylski [17], as well as power consumption. The layout that minimizes access time may not be optimal with respect to power consumption. Computing the optimal layout in terms of power consumption or finding the best trade-off between access time and consumption is an interesting work but it is beyond the scope of this paper. In the following discussions, we assume that each bank is implemented through a single array (i.e., 32 word lines of 32 bits each for the 32-bit baseline configuration, and 32 word lines of 8 bits each for the proposed pipelines).

Under these assumptions, note that even in the worst case when all 32 bits are required, the multiple access do not necessarily increase energy consumption. The word line consumption of each single access is reduced by a factor of about four, since every bank is about one fourth the width and thus, word lines are about one fourth as long. Bit line consumption is reduced by about four, since the number of bit lines in each bank is reduced by a factor of four. Sense amplifier consumption is also reduced by a factor of four for each access, since the number of sense amplifiers matches the number of bit lines. Thus, four accesses result in approximately the same word line, bit line and sense amplifier energy consumption as the 32-bit bank file.

2.5. ALU Operations

ALU operations are performed using only the numerically significant register bytes and the extension bits as input operands. The ALU produces significant result bytes as well as the extension bits that go with them.

ALU operations are performed in a byte-serial fashion. Because additions/subtractions, memory instructions, and branches all require an addition, and they collectively account for 70.7% of the executed instructions in the Mediabench suite, this operation is the most critical one to be implemented efficiently. For each byte position, there are three major cases, depending on which of the operands have significant byte(s) in the position being added.

- Case 1: Both bytes are significant. In this case, the byte addition must be performed.
- Case 2: Only one of the operands has a significant byte. If the non-significant byte is zeros (ones) and the carry-in from the preceding byte is zero (one), the result byte will be equal to the significant byte. If the non-significant byte is zeros (ones) and the carry-in is one (zero), the result byte is the significant byte plus one (minus one). In all these cases one could simplify logic, for example by bypassing the addition. However, we do not include these potential optimizations in activity statistics.
- Case 3: Neither of the operands has a significant byte in the position being added. Consider the addition of two bytes, $C_i = A_i + B_i$, where A_i and B_i are both sign extensions of their preceding bytes, A_{i-1} and B_{i-1}. There is a general rule with some exceptions. The general rule is that the result byte C_i is not significant, and the result is computed simply by setting the extension bits of the result because C_i will also be a sign extension of C_{i-1}. In the exceptional cases, the ALU must generate a full byte value. Table 4 lists all exceptions to the general rule.

To understand the exceptions to the general rule of case 3, consider the example where A_{i-1}=00000001, B_{i-1}=01111111; A_i and B_i are both sign extensions (i.e. they are equal to zero). Then the addition of $A_i + B_i$ will obviously be zero, but because byte C_{i-1} has a one in its most significant bit, C_i is not the sign extension of C_{i-1}. In this case, the processor has to generate the full byte value, although the addition is not actually necessary.

Finally, note that in some cases a result byte may not be significant although the two source operand bytes are significant (e.g. 3 + -3 = 0). To handle these cases, there is simple logic that examines each result byte and generates extension

Table 4: Cases in which byte C_i has to be generated

Values of A_{i-1} and B_{i-1} (the order is not significant)		Extra conditions
00xxxxxx	01xxxxxx	5th bit produces carry
01xxxxxx	01xxxxxx	-
11xxxxxx	10xxxxxx	5th bit produces carry
10xxxxxx	10xxxxxx	-
00xxxxxx	11xxxxxx	5th bit produces carry
01xxxxxx	10xxxxxx	5th bit produces carry

bits accordingly. This logic basically checks whether all bits of a byte and the most significant bit of the previous byte have the same value. It then sets the extension bits for the result accordingly.

Another common ALU operation that can be optimized is the comparison, which represents the 6.9% of the instructions in our benchmarks. In this case, the normal byte processing order can be reversed, with the computation starting at the most significant byte and finishing with the least significant one. However, as soon as the two compared bytes are different, no more bytes must be computed, even for comparisons of the type greater-than or less-than.

This reversal of access order can be implemented with different levels of complexity depending on the particular processor design. For instance, for the byte-serial implementation described in section 4, the reversal is easily implemented since this design has a single byte-wide register file and a byte-wide ALU. In other cases such as the byte-parallel skewed implementation described in section 6, the order reversal is more complex and may require an additional register port for avoiding structural hazards.

Finally, bit-wise logical operations, which represent 4.2% of the instructions in our benchmarks, can also be byte-pipelined. In this case, whenever two bytes are sign extensions, the result will also be a sign extension. Note that other optimizations are feasible when just one of the operands is a sign extension, but we have not considered them. For instance, *A AND 0 = 0*, *A AND -1 = A*, etc. As shown below in Section 2.9, extension bits result in an average reduction of the ALU activity of 33% for Mediabench.

2.6. Data Cache Operation

The data cache holds data in a manner similar to the register file. I.e. extension bits are appended to each data word and only the bytes containing significant data are read and written. The address bytes may also be formed sequentially, beginning with the low order byte. This means that the cache index will be computed before the tag bits, and that the tag bits may be formed as part of multiple byte additions.

Consequently, the tag comparison may be done in two sections as the tag bits become available. If the lower order tag bits do not match the cache tags, then an "early miss" can be signaled, and the higher order address and cache tag bits do not have to be formed and compared, resulting in reduced activity. However, because the miss rate is often relatively low, the activity saving is likely to be insignificant.

There is similar activity for cache writes; the extension bits for the store data are read from the register file and written alongside the data. For cache fills, the extension bits must be generated as data is brought from memory

Table 5: Activity reduction (%) for datapath operations (8 bit)

Benchmark	Fetch	RF read	RF writes	ALU	D-cache data	D-cache tag	PC increment	Latches
cjpeg	17.3	46.0	41.7	30.3	39.6	0.2	73.3	40.4
djpeg	19.4	41.1	37.1	22.7	39.9	0.1	73.3	36.6
epicdec	19.1	45.1	35.2	30.0	20.3	0.1	73.3	39.7
epicenc	20.6	42.5	46.7	42.0	0.9	0.0	73.3	46.7
g721dec	19.3	50.5	47.3	39.6	43.9	1.9	73.3	45.4
g721enc	19.3	50.7	46.9	39.7	44.5	1.0	73.3	45.4
gs	13.6	47.7	47.2	35.5	39.9	1.3	73.3	42.4
gsmdec	17.4	45.7	40.3	33.1	38.1	0.2	73.3	41.0
gsmenc	19.0	45.1	35.4	31.7	13.0	0.7	73.3	39.9
mesamipmap	16.2	37.5	30.5	19.4	12.4	3.6	73.3	32.9
mesaosdemo	15.6	33.7	26.9	15.2	19.0	0.5	73.3	30.2
mesatexgen	16.8	40.5	36.7	23.2	12.3	1.9	73.3	35.6
mpeg2dec	17.0	43.7	38.9	28.3	36.1	0.4	73.3	38.9
mpeg2enc	20.9	47.0	48.7	32.2	30.2	0.0	73.3	42.6
pgpdec	19.0	38.9	29.8	20.5	25.0	2.8	73.2	34.3
pgpenc	18.0	39.7	34.2	25.3	30.6	0.0	73.3	36.0
rasta	16.6	43.9	38.3	27.2	12.2	2.8	73.3	38.0
rawcaudio	20.0	71.7	69.2	67.6	57.4	0.0	73.3	67.4
rawdaudio	20.0	71.7	69.2	67.6	57.4	0.0	73.3	65.4
AVG	18.2	46.5	42.1	33.2	30.1	0.9	73.3	42.2

Table 6: Activity reduction (%) for datapath operations (16 bit)

Benchmark	Fetch	RF read	RF writes	ALU	D-cache data	D-cache tag	PC increment	Latches
AVG	18.2	35.9	30.3	22.1	23.4	0	46.7	34.9

(although the extension bit concept could also be maintained in main memory). We show below in Section 2.9 that the above techniques reduce the activity on the data cache by 31% for the data array and 1% for the tag array.

2.7. Register Write Back

During the register write-back stage, only bytes holding significant values have to be written into the register file. The extension bits also have to be stored. For ALU data, the bits are generated as described above in Section 2.5. For memory data, the extension bits read from the data cache are used. We show below in Section 2.9 that extension bits result in an average reduction of 42% in register file write activity.

2.8. Pipeline latches

Significant energy is consumed in pipeline latches [16], not just the major datapath elements. The extension bits are used for gating the pipeline latches in the normal way [9,14]. Only the PC bytes that change require latch activity. Based on extension bits, only significant register, ALU and cache bits need to be latched. Hence, activity savings in the datapath elements is reflected directly in activity savings in the pipeline latches immediately following the datapath elements. Furthermore, clock signals can be gated at the byte level, threby reducing clock activity.

Latch activity depends on the particular implementation. The lowest latch activity is achieved by the implementations with fewer pipe stages. This is the case for instance of the byte-serial implementation described in section 4. In this case, we show in the next section that the latch activity can be reduced on average by 42%.

2.9. Activity performance

To determine the activity savings for the techniques described above, we performed a trace driven simulation of the Mediabench [6]. Only byte activity indicated by the extension bits was performed. Table 5 provides the overall results for byte granularity, and for comparison, Table 6 contains average results for halfword granularity significance compression. The tables show percent activity savings.

The byte-serial PC increment operation saves 73% activity, because the great majority of the time, only the least significant byte is changed, as predicted by the analysis in Section 2.2. I-cache activity saving is 18%, and is quite uniform across all benchmarks. On average 47% of the Register read activity is saved, with individual benchmarks saving from 34% to 72%. ALU activity saving averages 33% (ranging from 15% to 68%) and data cache activity saves an average of 30% (ranging from 1% to 57%). The data cache activity is measured for data fills, reads and writes. The average saving on the data bank is 31% (ranging from 1% to 57%) whereas the saving for the tag bank is negligible. Register writeback saving is on average 42% (ranging from 30% to 69%). Finally, for implementations where the number of stages is not increased beyond the basic 5-stage pipeline, the latch activity is reduced by 42% on average and between 30% and 67% for individual benchmarks.

The 16-bit serial savings remain substantial (Table 6), but are somewhat less than the byte serial activity savings, as expected. The primary advantage of the 16-bit granularity is in implementation simplicity and in performance, as will be shown in the next section.

Holding and maintaining the extension bits adds an overhead of 9% when three bits are used, and the PC increment and fetch stages have much less overhead.

The bottom line is that the net overall activity savings (and therefore the overall energy savings) can be substantial. Major savings are possible in each of the pipeline stages. Finally, note that these results are for a 32 bit architecture; if

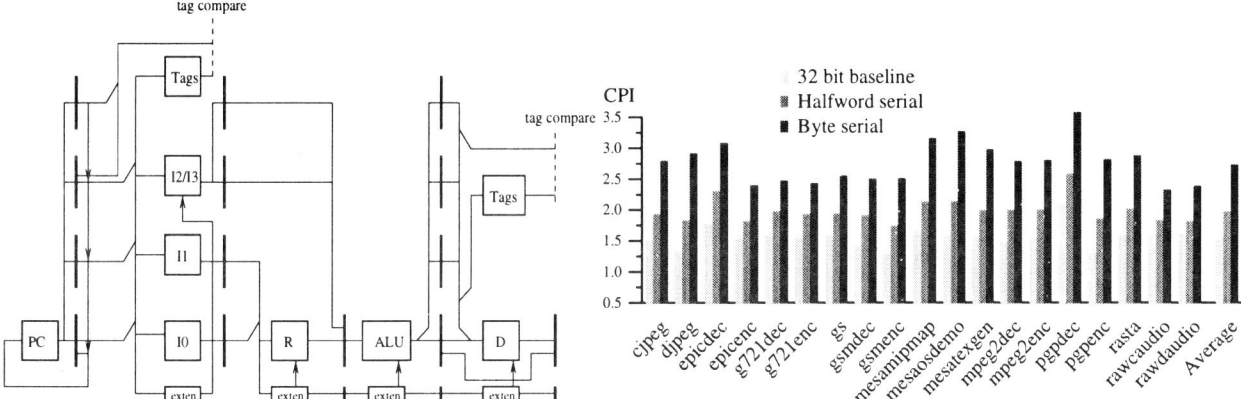

Figure 3: Byte-serial implementation

Figure 4: Performance of the byte-serial implementation

a 64-bit ISA were to be used (as in [1]), the savings will likely be much greater.

3. Experimental Framework

We developed a simulator for several proposed pipeline implementations using some components of the SimpleScalar toolset, primarily the instruction interpreter and the TLB and cache simulators. In all cases we assumed an in-order issue processor, with the following microarchitecture parameters:

- First level split instruction and data cache: 8 KB, direct-mapped, 32-byte line, 1-cycle hit time.
- Second level unified cache: 64 KB, 4-way., 32-byte line, 6-cycle hit, 30-cycle miss.
- I-TLB: 16 entries, 4-way, 1-cycle hit, 30-cycle miss.
- D-TLB: 32 entries, 4-way, 1-cycle hit, 30-cycle miss.

The processor does not perform any type of branch prediction, thus every branch stalls the fetch stage until the branch is resolved in the ALU stage. This is in keeping with some very low power embedded processors, although the trend is toward implementing branch prediction. The implications of branch prediction will be the subject of future study.

We used the Mediabench benchmark suite [6], which were compiled with the gcc compiler with "-O3 -finline-functions -funroll-loops" optimization flags into a MIPS-like ISA. As a baseline for comparison we use a conventional 32-bit wide processor, with 5 pipeline stages: Instruction Fetch, Decode and Register Read, Execute, Memory, and Write Back.

4. Byte-Serial Implementation

Having established potential activity reductions that can be achieved (and therefore energy reductions), we now consider implementations that attempt to achieve these levels while providing good performance. Implementations will differ in total hardware resources although they may not necessarily differ in circuit activity.

First, we consider a simple *byte-serial* implementation that has a one byte wide data path. If more than one data/address byte is needed at a given stage, then that pipeline stage will be used sequentially for multiple cycles. While later sequential data bytes are being processed, however, earlier bytes can proceed up the pipeline. For example, if it is necessary to read 3 bytes from the register file, first the low order byte is read and passed on to the EX stage, then while the next byte is being accessed, the EX unit can perform on the first data byte and pass it to the data cache stage.

Fig. 3 shows the byte-serial implementation. In this microarchitecture there is a single register file bank (R), a single ALU, and a single data cache bank, all one-byte wide. Inter-stage latches are provided to store values on a byte basis and only the significant bytes are required to be latched. In addition, the extension bits must flow through the pipeline and a three bit latch is provided between some stages for this purpose. The ALU stage includes a special unit that operates on extension bits as described in Section 2. 5. There is one byte-wide PC increment unit that operates serially and three instruction cache banks that are accessed in the first stage along with the extension bit. Then, if the extension bit indicates that it is needed, the instruction remains in this stage for one more cycle while one of the banks is accessed again. Using a three byte wide instruction cache stage is a departure from the strictly byte serial implementation. This decision was made to avoid excessive stalls while reading instructions; otherwise, every instruction would incur at least two stall cycles because the minimum number of bytes per compressed instruction is three.

Fig. 4 shows the performance of the byte-serial implementation, expressed as cycles per instruction (CPI). For comparison, the CPI of a baseline 32-bit wide implementation is also shown. For most programs, the performance of the byte-serial implementation is significantly lower than that of the 32-bit processor. CPI is increased by 79% on average, although activity (and energy) is reduced by 30-40% for most of the pipeline functions (Table 5).

If the pipeline is widened to 16-bits, the average CPI becomes 1.96, which is just 29% higher than that of the byte-wide implementation, but the activity savings are lower (around 20-30% for most of the pipeline functions). Note that the relative performance of the pipelined schemes is quite uniform across all the benchmarks.

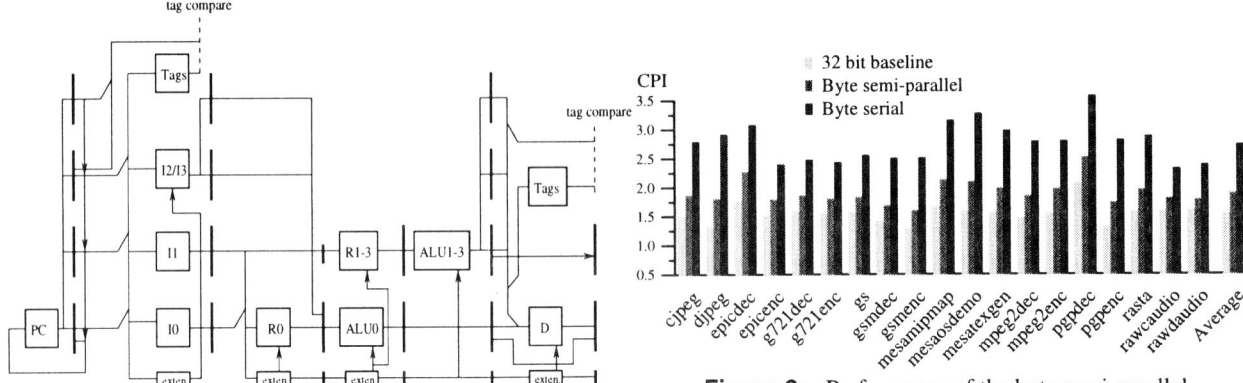

Figure 5: Byte semi-parallel implementation

Figure 6: Performance of the byte semi-parallel microarchitecture

5. Semi-Parallel Implementations.

The byte-serial implementation achieves significant activity reduction, but at the cost of substantial performance losses with respect to the baseline 32-bit pipeline. For some applications, energy savings may be much more important than performance, and this may represent a good design point. There may be other applications, however, where performance is more important, and performance losses should be reduced. We now consider methods that retain low activity levels, but use additional hardware to improve performance.

The principle is to improve performance by adding additional byte-wide datapath elements at the various pipeline stages. For example, the register file can be constructed of two byte-wide files (rather than one) and produce a full data word in 2 cycles instead of 4. Similarly, multiple byte-wide ALUs can be used to increase throughput in the execute stage.

Adding these units does not necessarily increase circuit and memory access activity, however, because not all the units have to be enabled every cycle. For example, if a data item has only one significant byte, then a register access can be performed for one byte of a two byte wide register file, while the other byte is disabled. Similarly, if the source operands of an addition only have two significant bytes, these bytes will be operated in two of the ALUs while the others will be disabled.

Finally, the numbers of byte-wide units in each of pipeline stages do not have to be the same. That is, the number of byte ALUs or memories can be established to permit balanced processing bandwidths among the pipe stages. To determine how many parallel units and memories should be used, we first undertook a bottleneck study of the byte-serial implementation to see where the major stalls occur. We observed that in the byte-serial architecture the ALU is the most important bottleneck, 72% of the stalls were caused by structural hazards in the EX stage. Thus, increasing the bandwidth of the ALU stage is the most effective approach to increase performance. To quantify how much bandwidth is required in each stage, we did the following simple analysis.

Consider each of the major pipeline stages. First, the study in Section 2.3 shows that an instruction requires about 3.2 bytes to be fetched on average. The ALU operates on an average of 2.7 bytes, but since the maximum CPI is 1.5 (32-bit baseline processor), the activity of the ALU will not be higher than 2.7/1.5 = 1.8 bytes/cycle on average. Next, around one third of instructions access memory, and each access is 2.8 bytes wide on average. Thus, less than one byte per cycle is accessed on average. Based on this study, we determined that a good balance is achieved with an instruction cache three bytes wide, a register file and ALU 2 bytes wide, and data cache one byte wide.

An implementation for this configuration is shown in Fig. 5 and is referred to as *byte semi-parallel*. The instruction cache essentially contains three byte-wide banks and works as in the byte-serial implementation.

The register access stage is skewed with the low order byte being accessed first together with the extension bits. In the next stage the low order byte is operated on, and at the same time another register byte is read if needed according to the extension bits. If there is more than one additional byte the instruction uses this stage for multiple cycles. The next stage performs the ALU operation on the additional bytes and is used for as many cycles as the previous stage. The following stage performs the data cache access (if needed). It first reads/writes the low order byte, the tags, and the extension bits and, according to the latter, the instruction uses this stage sequentially for multiple cycles until all data are read/written. Finally, the last stage writes the result into the register file. It first writes the low order byte, the extension bits and one additional byte if needed. If more than one additional byte must be written, this stage is used for multiple cycles.

Fig. 6 shows the CPI of this microarchitecture along with that of the 32-bit baseline processor and the byte-serial implementation. On average, the CPI is 24% higher than the 32-bit baseline processor. We observe that the performance is much closer to the 32-bit implementation than the byte-serial implementation while all the activity savings are retained except for a few additional latches.

6. Fully Parallel Implementations

The above still loses some performance – bottlenecks cannot be perfectly balanced all the time because of bursty behavior that most programs exhibit. So, we consider pipelines with maximum (4 bytes) parallelism at each stage, and use oper-

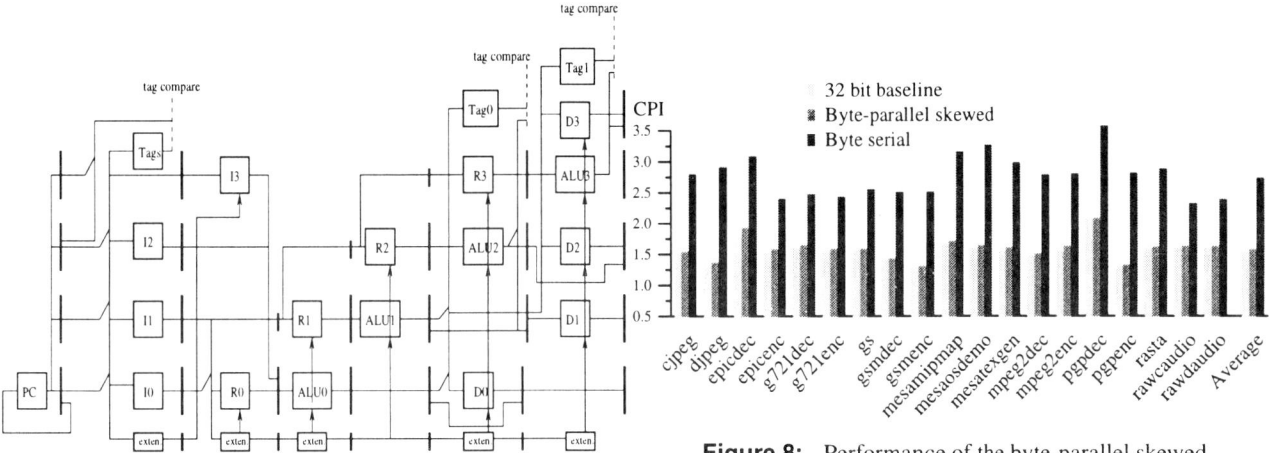

Figure 7: Byte-parallel skewed microarchitecture

Figure 8: Performance of the byte-parallel skewed microarchitecutre

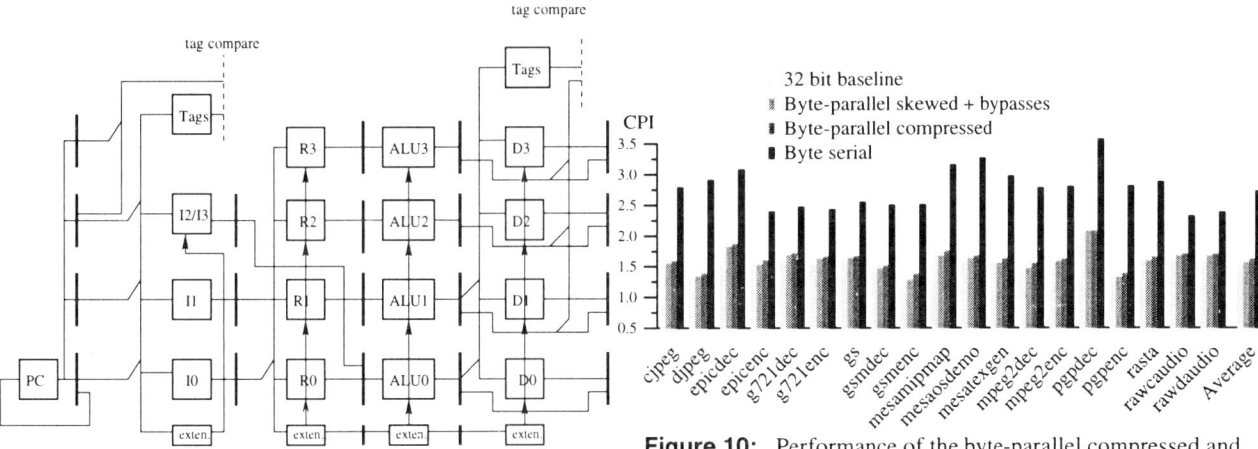

Figure 9: Byte-parallel compressed pipeline

Figure 10: Performance of the byte-parallel compressed and skewed + bypasses microarchitecture

and gating to enable only those datapath bytes that are needed. This requires a skewing of stages in a similar way to the semi-parallel implementation described in the previous section. A block diagram of a portion of the microarchitecture, which is referred to as byte-parallel skewed, is depicted in Fig. 7.

This pipeline is optimized for the long data case, i.e. where the pipeline keeps flowing even if each operand is a full 4 bytes. No stage is used more than once (except for the PC computation in very few cases). Although the activity of the functional units is the same as that of the byte-pipelined and semi-parallel implementation, the longer pipeline of the byte-parallel skewed implementation implies more latch activity and more backward bypasses. The performance of this microarchitecture is shown in Fig. 8. We can observe that the CPI is very close to that of the 32-bit baseline processor for all programs in which case the byte serial implementation would be a very good design choice.

Another alternative is a "compressed" parallel pipeline implementation (see Fig. 9). In this case, the pipeline consists of the original 5 stages. Each instruction spends one cycle in the Ifetch stage to read 3 bytes and an additional one if a fourth byte is needed. Then it moves on to the second stage where it reads the low order byte and the extension bits. If more bytes are needed, the instruction spends one more cycle in the same stage to read all of them in parallel. Then the instruction moves on to the ALU stage where it executes in a single cycle, using only the functional units that operate on significant bytes. Then it moves on to the memory stage where it reads first the low order byte and the extension bits, and if needed, it spends an additional cycle to read all the remaining bytes. If it is a store, all the significant bytes along with the extension bits are written in a single cycle. Finally, all significant bytes and the extension bits are written into the register file in a single cycle.

This design works well for short data because the pipeline length is kept minimal and this reduces the branch penalty and the number of backward bypasses. Furthermore, functional unit and latch activity is kept minimal (equal to the byte-serial implementation). However, full-width (32-bit) data operations suffer stalls in some stages, which result in performance losses when compared with the full parallel implementation. Performance is shown in Fig. 10. The CPI increase compared with the 32-bit baseline processor is 6% on average, which is quite close to the performance of the byte parallel skewed configuration.

We can get the best of both (performance wise) by putting forwarding paths into the byte-parallel skewed pipeline. In this way, when a short operand is encountered, it can skip the stages where no operation is performed. This reduces the latch activity to the same level as that of the byte-serial implementation, and at the same time the effective pipeline length is shortened, which reduces the branch penalty. However, the number of backward bypasses is the same as that of the byte-parallel skewed implementation.

The performance of this architecture is also shown in Fig. 10. Now performance is very close to the baseline 32-bit processor (the CPI is only 2% higher on average) while the activity is reduced around 30-40% for most of the stages. A disadvantage, however, is that this design has rather complicated control and many data paths (for forwarding) -a more detailed analysis is required and will be a subject of future study.

7. Summary and Conclusions

The significant bytes of instructions, addresses, and data values essentially determine a minimal activity level that is required for executing a program. For a simple pipeline design, we showed that this level is typically 30-40% lower than for a conventional 32-bit wide pipeline. Every stage of the pipeline shows significant activity savings (and therefore energy savings).

We proposed a number of pipeline implementations that attempt to achieve these low activity levels while providing a reasonable level of performance. The byte-serial pipeline is very simple hardware-wise, but increases CPI by 79%. For some very low power applications, this may be an acceptable performance level, in which case the byte-serial implementation would be a very good design choice. We should also point out that the narrower data path may result in a faster clock, which will reduce performance loss, but this was not considered in this paper.

For higher performance, the pipeline stages can be widened. A rough analysis indicates that three bytes of instruction fetch, two bytes of register access and ALU, and one byte of data cache might provide a good balance of bandwidths. For this configuration, the CPI is 24% higher than that of the full width baseline design. Activities are still at their reduced levels, and this design may provide a very good design point for many very low power applications.

Finally, we considered designs with a four byte wide datapath at each stage. Operand gating is retained for reducing activity, but under ideal conditions throughput is no longer restricted. These designs can come very close in performance to the baseline 32-bit design while again retaining reduced activity levels. The disadvantage of these schemes is an increased latch activity, or additional forwarding paths or more complex control. We believe that these may be a very important class of implementations however, because of their high performance levels, and they deserve additional study.

Note also that different designs may imply a variation in the load capacitance, which also affects dynamic energy consumption. In particular, a narrower data-path may shorten some wires and thus reduce its capacitance. This paper focused on pointing out the potential of these architectures to reduce pipeline activity. The final quantification of energy requires a further detailed circuit-level analysis of the implementations.

Acknowledgements

This work was supported by the IBM University Partnership Program, the CICYT project TIC 98-0511. We would like to thank Jaime Moreno and George Cai for many insightful comments on this work. Ramon Canal would like to thank his fellow PBCs for their patience and precious help.

References

[1] D. Brooks and M. Martonosi, "Dynamically Exploiting Narrow Width Operands to Improve Porcessor Power and Performance", in Proc. of 5th. Int. Symp. on High- Perf. Comp. Arch., 1999.

[2] D. Burger, T.M. Austin, S. Bennett, "Evaluating Future Microprocessors: The SimpleScalar Tool Set", Technical Report CS-TR-96-1308, University of Wisconsin- Madison.

[3] G. Cai and C.H. Lim, "Architectural Level Power/Performance Optimization and Dynamic Power Estimation", in the Cool Chips tutorial of the 32nd Int. Symp. on Microarchitecture 1999.

[4] K.D. Kissell, "MIPS16: High-density MIPS for the Embedded Market", SGI MIPS group, 1997.

[5] M. Kozuch and A. Wolfe, "Compression of Embedded Systems Programs", in Proc. of the Int. Conf. on Computer Design, 1994

[6] C. Lee, M. Potkonjak and W. H. Mangione-Smith, "Mediabench: A Tool for Evaluating and Synthesizing Multimedia and Communications Systems", in Proc. of the 30th Int. Symp. on Microarch., Dec. 1997, pp. 330-335.

[7] C.R Lefurgy, E.M Piccininni and Trevor N Mudge, "Evaluation of a High Performance Code Compression Method", in Proc. of the 32nd Int. Symp. on Microarchitecture 1999.

[8] J. Montanaro and et al. "A 160-MHz, 32-b, 0.5 W CMOS RISC Microprocessor", Digital Tech. J'rnal, v.9. Dec, 1997.

[9] E. Musoll, "Predicting the usefulness of a block result: a micro-architectural technique for high-performance low-power processors", in Proc. of the 32nd Int. Symp. on Microarchitecture 1999.

[10] "PowerPC 405CR User Manual", IBM/Motorola, 6/2000.

[11] C. Price, "MIPS IV Instruction Set", MIPS Tech. Inc, 1995.

[12] J. Turley, "Thumb Squeezes Arm Code Size", Microprocessor Report, vol 9. n. 4, March 1995.

[13] J. Turley, "PowerPC Adopts Code Compression", Microprocessor Report, October 1998.

[14] S. Manne, A. Klauser and D. Grunwald, "Pipeline Gating: Speculation Control for Energy Reduction", in Proc. of the 25th Int. Symp on Comp. Arch. ,June 1998, pp.132-141.

[15] T.Sato and I. Arita, "Table Size Reduction for Data Value Predictors by Exploiting Narrow Width Values", in Proc. of the 2000 Int. Conf. on Supercomp., May 2000, pp.196-205.

[16] N. Vijaykrishnan, M. Kandemir, M.J. Irwin, S.H. Kim and W. Ye, " Energy-Driven Integrated Hardware-Software Optimizations Using SimplePower", in Proc. of the 27th Int. Symp on Comp. Architecture, 2000, pp. 95-106.

[17] T. Wada, S. Rajan and S. Przybylski, "An Analytical Access Time Model for On-Chip Cache Memories", IEEE Journal of Solid-State Circuits, v.27, n. 8, pp. 1147-1156, Aug. 1992

[18] A. Wolfe and A. Channin, "Executing Compressed Programs on an Embedded RISC Architecture", in Proc. of the 19th Int. Symp. on Microarchitecture, 1992.

A Static Power Model for Architects

J. Adam Butts and Gurindar S. Sohi
Computer Science Department
University of Wisconsin-Madison
`{butts,sohi}@cs.wisc.edu`

Abstract

Static power dissipation due to transistor leakage constitutes an increasing fraction of the total power in modern semiconductor technologies. Current technology trends indicate that the contribution will increase rapidly, reaching one half of total power dissipation within three process generations. Developing power efficient products will require consideration of static power in the earliest phases of design, including architecture and microarchitecture definition. We propose a simple equation for estimating static power consumption at the architectural level:

$P_{static} = V_{CC} \cdot N \cdot k_{design} \cdot \hat{I}_{leak}$, *where V_{CC} is the supply voltage, N is the number of transistors, k_{design} is a design dependent parameter, and $\hat{I}_{leak}$ is a technology dependent parameter. This model enables high-level reasoning about the likely static power demands of alternative microarchitectures. Reasonably accurate values for the factors within the equation may be obtained directly from the high-level designs or by straightforward scaling arguments. The factors within the equation also suggest opportunities for static power optimization, including reducing the total number of devices, partitioning the design to allow for lower supply voltages or slower, less leaky transistors, turning off unused devices, favoring certain design styles, and favoring high bandwidth over low latency. Speculation is also examined as a means to employ slower transistors without a significant performance penalty.*

1. Introduction

Power consumption has become an important consideration in modern microprocessor design. The problem is exacerbated in multiprocessor systems such as servers in which multiple processors are in close proximity. Increasing the power dissipation much beyond current levels will result in disproportionate increases in cost as current power delivery and heat removal systems reach limits. Mobile and embedded microprocessors are also power constrained. While maximization of battery life is an obvious goal, heat removal is an important problem as well. The increasing role of power dissipation as a performance limiter has led to the consideration of power in the early stages of the design process. Traditionally the responsibility of circuit designers, power dissipation has become more important to architects as the ability of circuit techniques to control it have been rendered insufficient. The availability of simple estimation methods and the spread of simulators which provide power dissipation data have enabled power dissipation to influence high level design decisions.

Architectural efforts to control power dissipation have been directed primarily at the dynamic component of power dissipation. Dynamic power is the result of switching and is ideally the only mode of power dissipation in CMOS circuitry. It constitutes the major component of total power dissipation in today's technologies. Dynamic power dissipation is described by the familiar $P_{dyn} = CV_{CC}^2 f$ where C is the capacitance of switching nodes (roughly proportional to the number of switching devices), V_{CC} is the supply voltage, and f is the effective operating frequency (frequency times activity factor). In order to limit dynamic power dissipation, techniques such as clock gating [12, 31, 32], cache sub-banking [28], and eliminating needless computation [5, 19] have been employed. The goal of each of these techniques is to reduce the number or frequency of switching devices (attacking C or f, respectively). Optimization of the supply voltage to minimize the power/performance ratio is also performed, but this process is seldom influenced by architects.

As transistors become smaller and faster, another mode of power dissipation has become important. This is static power dissipation, or the power due to leakage current in the absence of any switching activity. Technology scaling is increasing both the absolute and relative contribution of static power dissipation. Static power dissipation is equal to the product of the supply voltage and the leakage current. While the rate of reduction of supply voltage is decreasing, leakage current is increasing exponentially.

The increasing contribution of static power is clearly evident even in today's designs. Consider two implementations of Intel's Pentium III processor manufactured on Intel's 0.18 μm process, the Pentium III 1.0 GHz B and the Pentium III 1.13 GHz [13]. The Intel datasheet lists the maximum core power dissipation of the 1.0 GHz part at 33.0 watts and the deep sleep (i.e., static) power dissipation at 3.74 watts. The 1.13 GHz processor has a total power dissipation of 41.4 watts and a static power dissipation of 5.40 watts. While the total power has increased by only 25%, the static power has increased by 44% and comprises 13% of the total power dissipation. The active power dissipation of the processor core varies significantly depending on the workload while the static power dissipation is almost constant. The datasheet values represent peak power dissipation values; therefore, static power is even a larger percentage of the total power dissipation on average.

Figure 1 shows the increases in static and dynamic power for Intel's past few technologies [34]. Projecting these trends forward, static power dissipation will equal dynamic power dissipation within a few generations. Higher order effects unimportant today and aggressive dynamic power optimizations could cause the static and dynamic power contributions to become equal in as little as two generations. Thus, it is important for architects to be aware of how they may control static power dissipation in future technologies.

The causes of leakage current are complex and far removed from the realm of architecture. Yet as static power dissipation becomes comparable to dynamic power dissipation, architects will be called upon to consider it in making design decisions. The purpose of this paper is to provide architects with a means

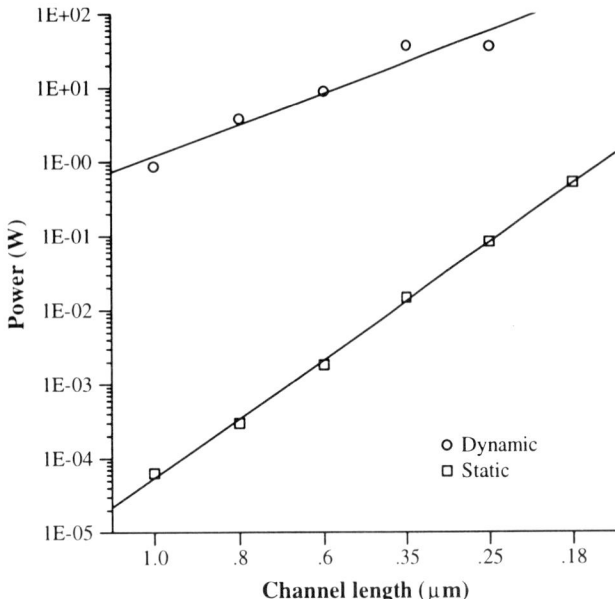

Figure 1. Trends in dynamic and static power dissipation showing increasing contribution of static power (from Thompson, et. al. [34])

of estimating static power and some general techniques for limiting it. We propose a simple four parameter model useful at the architectural level: $P_{static} = V_{CC} \cdot N \cdot k_{design} \cdot \hat{I}_{leak}$. The model parameters are summarized in Table 1. Overall static power consumption may be reduced by reducing any of the parameters. The table lists some general techniques applicable to reducing each parameter.

The level of abstraction in the model is appropriate for its application by architects. Each of the parameters is amenable to estimation at the architectural level (either based on the design or the expected target technology). A more detailed model would require accuracy in technology and design parameters that would not be available at an early stage in the design process. Furthermore, absolute accuracy is not as important as relative accuracy when making design tradeoffs. Finally, the model suggests different means of addressing static power early in the design process. Some may claim that architects have no control over static power because of its strong dependence on technology and circuit optimization (which does not typically involve architects). While lower level optimizations more directly affect the final static power dissipation, awareness of the issue during the architectural definition can result in an architecture better suited to later optimization.

We proceed with a brief review of semiconductor technology. Next, we motivate the increasing importance of static power with a discussion of trends in transistor scaling. The static power model above is then derived and the characteristics of each of the model parameters are discussed in detail. Finally, the model is used to motivate some general architectural-level techniques for addressing static power dissipation.

2. CMOS Technology Review

We start with a review of the basic terminology and operation of the silicon field-effect transistor. Silicon CMOS (Complementary Metal Oxide Semiconductor) has emerged as the dominant semiconductor technology for high performance microprocessors. Relative to other semiconductor technologies, silicon CMOS is cheaper, is more easily processed and scaled, and has a higher performance/power ratio. This section describes the important features of MOS transistors and introduces terminology used throughout the remainder of the paper. Readers familiar with this material are encouraged to skip to Section 3, while those desiring more detail may find it in any of several readily available texts from which this review was distilled [23, 30, 37].

A MOS transistor is a four terminal semiconductor device that can function as a switch or an amplifier (Figure 2). By convention, all terminal voltages are measured with respect to the source node. The gate voltage is symbolized by V_{gs}, the drain voltage by V_{ds} and the body voltage by V_{bs}. In digital circuit design, the transistor is usually used as a switch. Current flow between the source and drain terminals is controlled by the voltage at the gate terminal. The gate is electrically isolated from the rest of the device by a thin insulating layer (silicon dioxide for silicon devices). The gate influences the device via the elec-

Table 1. Summary of static power model parameters

Parameter	Description	Scaling behavior	Reducing
V_{CC}	Power supply voltage	Decreases by 30 % per process generation	• Multiple supply voltage domains • Increase IPC to allow lower clock frequency (allowing V_{CC} reduction) at same performance
N	Number of transistors in design	Increases by 100 % per process generation	• Reduce functionality (e.g., removing special purpose circuitry) • Use circuit style requiring fewer transistors for same functionality
k_{design}	Empirically determined parameter representing the characteristics of an average device	Approximately constant	• Use efficient circuit style • Reduce clock frequency to allow more complex (high fan-in) logic
$\hat{I}_{leak}$	Technology parameter describing the per device subthreshold leakage	Highly dependent on aggressiveness of V_T (threshold voltage) scaling	• Partition design into frequency domains allowing use of less aggressive (lower leakage) devices in some domains

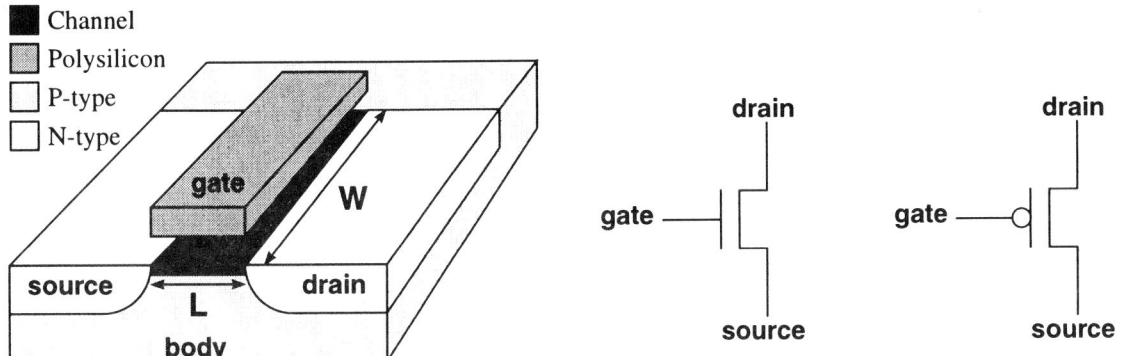

Figure 2. MOS transistor cross-section (N-type) and schematic symbols (N-type and P-type)

tric field resulting from different gate biases. Thus, the transistor is designated a Field Effect Transistor or FET.

The primary function of the body terminal is to ensure isolation of the source and drain. Impurities are added (a process called doping) to the source, drain, and body regions. The source and drain regions are doped to the opposite type as the body (N- or P-type), creating junctions through which current (ideally) can not flow. Under the influence of the gate, the type of the region at the surface of the silicon between the source and drain (called the channel) can be reversed, forming a current path between the source and drain. Since the gate is electrically insulated from the rest of the device, a transistor gate appears as a capacitor to its driving circuitry. Ideally, once the gate capacitor is charged (or discharged) to its desired state, no current is required to maintain that state; therefore, no power is consumed. The threshold voltage of the transistor (symbolized by V_T) is the voltage required at the gate (relative to the source) to turn on the transistor. It is a complicated function of the device dimensions and exact doping profiles of the transistor. N- and P- type transistors differ in the doping of the source, drain, and body regions (the Complementary in CMOS).

Most device parameters (e.g., doping profiles and oxide thickness) are fixed by the particular technology to which a design is targeted. In most cases circuit designers are limited to specifying the device dimensions (W and L) to specify the relative strengths of the devices. Some technologies provide devices with different threshold voltages as well. These technologies are referred to as MTCMOS (multi-threshold CMOS). Alternatively, the threshold voltage may be controlled by applying different voltages to the body terminal. Thus, the design parameters include the lateral device dimensions and sometimes the threshold voltage.

Power consumption in CMOS circuitry is classified as either dynamic or static (Figure 3). Dynamic power dissipation occurs during state changes (i.e., when devices are switching). It is primarily due to the charging of the capacitive load associated with the output wiring and the gates of subsequent transistors (C dV/dt). A smaller component of dynamic power arises from the short-circuit current that flows momentarily while the complementary devices in a gate are simultaneously conducting during an output state change. Static power dissipation is a result of the various leakage modes of the MOS transistor. While there are many different leakage modes, the most important leakage mechanism in modern submicron channel length technologies is subthreshold leakage [15]. Subthreshold leakage is current that flows between the source and drain even when the transistor is off (i.e., the voltage at the gate is below the threshold voltage).

3. Technology Scaling

To allow for higher clock frequencies and more devices on a chip, technologies are scaled every few years [27]. Device engineers performing the scaling must develop transistors years in advance of when they will be manufacturable. Using Moore's law as a guide, they target a 30% decrease in linear dimensions resulting in a 50% area reduction versus the prior generation. Simultaneously, the smaller dimensions allow for a speed increase of 25-30%. The primary constraint on device scaling is the process technology (e.g., lithography). Another important constraint is reliability. Many reliability parameters are functions of the electric fields that exist within the device. Permanent damage to the transistor may result if certain electric fields are exceeded. This has led to a scaling methodology known as constant field (sometimes called ideal) scaling [9].

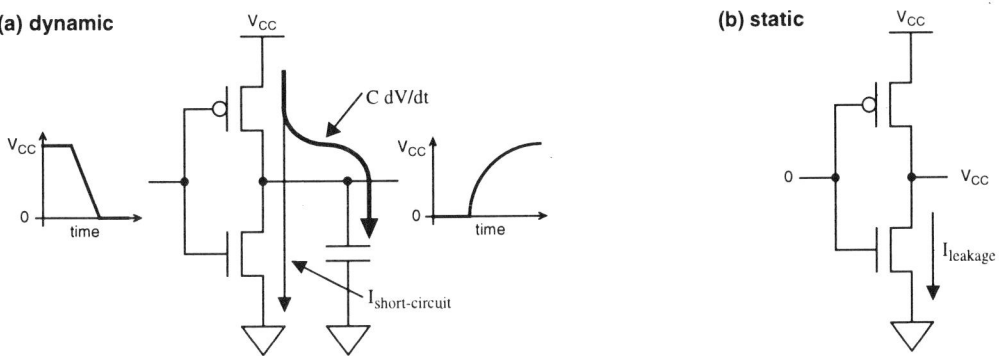

Figure 3. (a) Dynamic and (b) static power dissipation mechanisms in CMOS technologies

Constant field scaling reduces the supply voltage by the same factor as device dimensions in order to keep the electric fields the same across technology generations. This has the added benefit of addressing dynamic power dissipation (which is proportional to the square of the supply voltage). With the physical dimensions and supply voltage determined, device designers adjust other parameters (e.g., doping profiles) to maximize the performance of the device within the specified constraints. While actual technologies have not adhered strictly to constant-field scaling [7], it is illustrative of the general trends and problems associated with scaling.

Due to the complexities of device simulation, it is not practical to simulate even small circuits at the level of detail required by device engineers. Therefore, device engineers attempt to optimize simple delay metrics to arrive at a device design. These metrics may be calculated from the detailed simulation of a single transistor. After confirming the performance with actual fabricated test devices, parameters are derived for a device model that can be used in subsequent circuit-level simulations. One common delay metric used is shown in Equation 1. C_{gate} is the gate capacitance of a transistor per unit width (at a specified channel length), V_{CC} is the supply voltage, and I_{Dsat} is the maximum (saturation) drain current that can flow through a transistor (per unit width). Derived from the differential equation describing the charging of a capacitor, this metric measures the approximate time required to charge the gate capacitance of one transistor by another transistor.

$$t = \frac{C_{gate} \cdot V_{CC}}{I_{Dsat}} \quad \text{(Eq. 1)}$$

Consider the behavior of the delay metric of Equation 1 under constant field scaling. The supply voltage (V_{CC}) is reduced by some factor S. Therefore to reduce delay by the same factor, it is sufficient to keep the ratio C_{gate} / I_{Dsat} constant. C_{gate} is proportional to the channel length and inversely proportional to the oxide thickness. Since both of these dimensions are reduced by S, C_{gate} stays constant. Thus, to achieve the expected performance improvement (delay reduction), the drive current I_{Dsat} must remain constant under scaling. In modern technologies, I_{Dsat} is a complicated function of many parameters including $V_{CC} - V_T$, C_{gate}, and L (the channel length).

The quantity $V_{CC} - V_T$ is referred to as the gate overdrive; it is the maximum voltage that may be applied to a transistor's gate beyond that required to turn on the transistor. I_{Dsat} is proportional to a small power (between 1 and 2) of $V_{CC} - V_T$ [26]. Recalling that V_{CC} is being decreased by S, the reduction in gate overdrive reduces I_{Dsat} by a factor larger than S. While other factors increase the drive current as devices are scaled (primarily L), these are insufficient to obtain the expected delay reduction at a constant V_T in deep submicron CMOS technologies. Therefore, V_T has also been reduced (see Figure 4). Performance goals and a desire to decrease V_{CC} further (to address dynamic power) have also driven the reduction in threshold voltage.

It is this continuing reduction of V_T that is causing static power to become increasingly important. Subthreshold leakage current increases exponentially as threshold voltage decreases [12]:

$$I_{Dsub} = k \cdot e^{\frac{-q \cdot V_T}{a \cdot k_B \cdot T}} \quad \text{(Eq. 2)}$$

where q and k_B are physical constants, a and k are device parameters, and T is the absolute temperature. The above relationship is depicted in Figure 5 (V_T is taken to be the gate voltage at 1 µA/µm drain current). Note that the leakage current at a fixed threshold voltage also increases exponentially with temperature.

Static power is equal to the product of the supply voltage and I_{Dsub}. The exponential increase in I_{Dsub} causes the static power to increase rapidly despite supply voltage scaling. The relative contribution of static power is also growing. Dynamic power increases linearly with the capacitance being switched (increas-

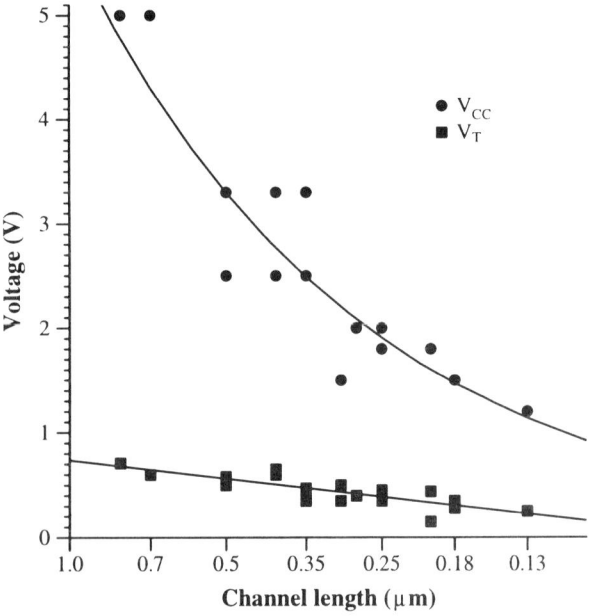

Figure 4. V_{CC} and V_T scaling showing reduction in gate overdrive ($V_{CC} - V_T$) (from data published in IEDM and ISSCC from 1990-2000)

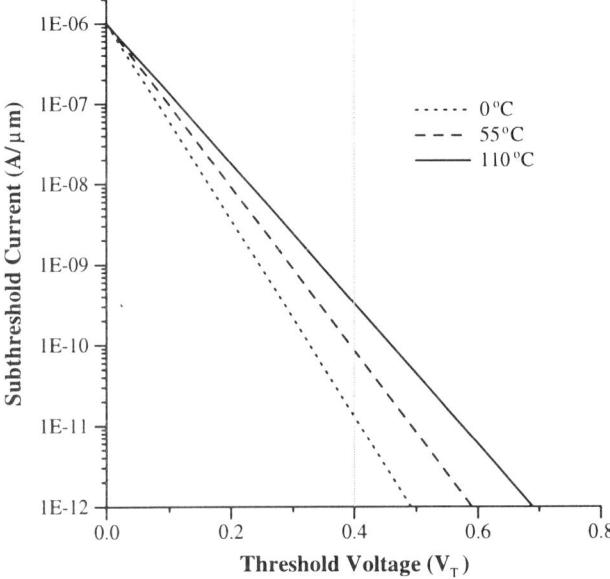

Figure 5. Effect of threshold voltage and temperature on subthreshold current

ing as the number of devices is increased) and the switching frequency (increasing as delay is reduced), but decreases with the square of the supply voltage. Thus, it is increasing much more slowly than static power (refer to Figure 1). As the primary component of power consumption today, dynamic power is being aggressively attacked in all phases of the design process to ensure that it does not restrict performance. Focusing on limiting dynamic power further increases the relative importance of static power.

4. A Static Power Model

While accurate power models are important for simulation, it is desirable to have a simple formula to allow for high-level consideration of the power characteristics of alternative designs. The absolute accuracy of such a formula is not nearly as important as the relative accuracy since the architect will generally be uninterested in determining the exact number of watts used by a particular design. In this section, we will present a formula that is a useful high-level model of static power consumption. Each of the model parameters discussed in detail with emphasis on how it scales and how it may be estimated.

4.1. Model Derivation

In this section, we derive the static power model presented in the introduction. The dearth of publicly available data on leading-edge microprocessors makes it difficult to compare the model's results with actual data. Thus, a top-down, intuitive derivation would be almost impossible to validate. Therefore, we chose a bottom-up derivation based on a widely accepted single-device model. It should be noted that successful application of the model does not depend on the material in this section. Instead, the derivation is presented to make explicit the simplifying assumptions necessary to arrive at a high-level model from the detailed device-level equation.

We begin with the BSIM3v3.2 MOSFET transistor model equation for subthreshold drain current I_{Dsub} [17]:

$$I_{Dsub} = I_{s0} \cdot \left(1 - e^{\frac{-V_{ds}}{v_t}}\right) \cdot e^{\frac{V_{gs} - V_T - V_{off}}{n \cdot v_t}} \quad \text{(Eq. 3)}$$

V_{off} is an empirically determined model parameter, v_t is a physical parameter proportional to temperature, and n is derived from a host of other model and device parameters. I_{s0} is dependent on the transistor geometry and may be written as $I_{s0}' \cdot W / L$. For single devices in the normal "off" state, $V_{ds} = V_{CC}$ and $V_{gs} = 0$. Substituting these biases into Equation 3, the factor in parenthesis becomes 1 (since $V_{ds} = V_{CC} \gg v_t$), and the last factor may be split into a product of exponents:

$$I_{Dsub} = \left(\frac{W}{L}\right) \cdot I_{s0}' \cdot e^{\frac{-V_{off}}{n \cdot v_t}} \cdot e^{\frac{-V_T}{n \cdot v_t}} \quad \text{(Eq. 4)}$$

$$= \left(\frac{W}{L}\right) \cdot k_{tech} \cdot e^{\frac{-V_T}{n \cdot v_t}}$$

$$= \left(\frac{W}{L}\right) \cdot k_{tech} \cdot 10^{\frac{-V_T}{S_t}}$$

where $k_{tech} = I_{s0}' \cdot exp(-V_{off} / (n \cdot v_t))$ and $S_t = 2.303 \cdot n \cdot v_t$. S_t is referred to as the subthreshold swing parameter. It is a measure of how effectively a transistor shuts off and is equal to the inverse slope of $log(I_D)$ vs. V_{gs} (in mV/decade) for $V_{gs} < V_T$. Although the channel length (L) appears explicitly in the equation, it should be noted that k_{tech} and S_t still have a complicated dependence on channel length. W is actually the dimension of interest since nearly every device is drawn at the minimum allowed L. Since L may be considered fixed, k_{tech} and S_t will be invariant for almost all of the devices in a given technology. The ratio of the two dimensions (the aspect ratio) was not included in k_{tech} since it depends on the design in which the transistor is used and not the technology.

Equation 4 applies to an isolated off transistor. This level of detail is inappropriate for reasoning at the architectural level. Therefore, we assume certain statistical properties about large numbers of devices to generalize the equation. Specifically, we assume that the distribution of transistor geometries (described by the aspect ratio) is the same across large groups of transistors employed in the same type of circuitry. The latter qualification is very important. Consider the transistors used in a cache array versus those employed in datapath logic: the cache transistors will be the minimum possible size to achieve high density, while the datapath transistors will be sized to operate at the best possible speed.

The circuit type also influences the proportion of the transistors which are switched off (f_{off}). In the absence of DC current paths (chains of on transistors between V_{CC} and ground), it is the off transistors which will determine the leakage current. In full static CMOS, half of the transistors should be off at any given time. However, other types of logic (e.g., domino, pass gate, or memory array) will have different leakage characteristics.

In addition to device geometries, the stacking factor of transistors is also dependent on the circuit type. Stacked transistors are those that are connected in series drain to source (Figure 6). The leakage current through each transistor in a stack must be equal; furthermore, the voltage drop across the entire stack can not exceed V_{CC}. Provided more than one transistor in the stack is off, the V_{ds} for the off transistors will be $< V_{CC}$. Thus, the leakage current is reduced by the $1 - e^{\frac{-V_{ds}}{v_t}}$ term in Equation 3. For a stack of four transistors, the reduction in leakage can be up to a factor of 20 [14]. Stacked transistors also have a non-zero body bias (potential difference between the source and body nodes) which affects I_{Dsub} through the variables n and V_T. We define a design dependent parameter k_{stack} that is the average leakage due to different stacking factors weighted by the portion of devices in the circuit with each stacking factor relative to the leakage of a single device. It is always less than one and will be lower in circuit types with higher average stacking factors (e.g., circuits with high fan-in gates).

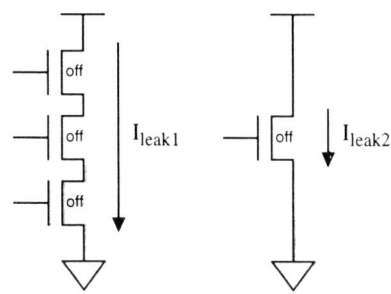

Figure 6. Leakage in stacked transistors ($I_{leak1} \ll I_{leak2}$)

While we have introduced the attributes of the design that affect leakage individually, they are not actually separable. Stacked transistors, for example, are generally drawn with a larger aspect ratio to make up for the reduced drive capability of stacked devices over a single device. Also, stacking factor only reduces leakage when more than one device in the stack is off. Thus, f_{off} and k_{stack} are not independent either. Because these factors are not separable, we combine them into a single circuit-dependent constant k_{design} as follows. Summing the subthreshold current given by Equation 4 for a group of N transistors, we derive:

$$I_{leakage} = \sum_i^N I_{Dsub_i} = N \cdot \overline{I_{Dsub}} \quad \text{(Eq. 5)}$$

$$= N \cdot f\left[\left(\frac{W}{L}\right), f_{off}, k_{stack}\right] \cdot k_{tech} \cdot 10^{\frac{-V_T}{S_t}}$$

$$= N \cdot k_{design} \cdot k_{tech} \cdot 10^{\frac{-V_T}{S_t}}$$

for a group of transistors with the same technology parameters. Barred parameters represent average values over all of the transistors. At this point, we note that the difference in leakage characteristics (quantified in Equation 5 by k_{tech}, V_T, and S_t) between N- and P-type MOSFET's is highly dependent on the specific technology. Provided they are similar for the two types of transistors, both types may be modeled simultaneously. In this case, k_{design} also incorporates the ratio between the two types of devices. If the devices differ significantly in the magnitude of k_{tech}, V_T or S_t, the model must be applied separately to the two groups of devices as shown in Equation 6 (where f_N is the fraction of N-type MOSFET's and the technology parameters are subscripted with the device type to which they apply). For the remainder of the paper, we assume the first case applies.

$$I_{leakage} = N \cdot \left[f_N \cdot k_{designN} \cdot k_{techN} \cdot 10^{\frac{-V_{TN}}{S_{tN}}} + \right. \quad \text{(Eq. 6)}$$

$$\left. (1 - f_N) \cdot k_{designP} \cdot k_{techP} \cdot 10^{\frac{-V_{TP}}{S_{tP}}} \right]$$

Given that power dissipation is the product of the potential difference (voltage) and the current flowing through that difference, the total static power is given by:

$$P_{static} = V_{CC} \cdot N \cdot k_{design} \cdot k_{tech} \cdot 10^{\frac{-V_T}{S_t}} \quad \text{(Eq. 7)}$$

Equation 7 specifies three technology dependent parameters (k_{tech}, S_t, and V_T) that may be combined into a single technology constant $\hat{I}_{leak}$:

$$P_{static} = V_{CC} \cdot N \cdot k_{design} \cdot \hat{I}_{leak} \quad \text{(Eq. 8)}$$

where $\hat{I}_{leak}$ is the normalized leakage current (the right hand side of Equation 4 without W/L). Because of its simplicity, this variation is likely to be applied for high-level reasoning. Also, the interdependence of the technology parameters makes this model more appropriate than one where the technology parameters are seemingly independent. For MTCMOS technologies, for example, using different values of $\hat{I}_{leak}$, rather than different values of V_T for fixed k_{tech} and S_t, will be more accurate. We choose to emphasize the more detailed model of Equation 7 in the next section to underscore the nature and magnitude of the impact of the technology parameters (especially the threshold voltage) on static power.

While formulas similar to Equation 7 appear in the device literature [21, 25], they fail to differentiate the design and technology contributions to the leakage power; instead, an average per device leakage is a parameter. Such a broad parameter is impossible to estimate at any level in the design process: architects can not be expected to reason with actual leakage values during design studies, and device and process engineers can not guess about the high-level applications of various groups of devices. By separating the contributions of architectural application (design) and device physics (technology) the individual parameters can be better estimated.

4.2. Model Parameters

The parameters of the static power model of Equation 7 may be divided into two groups. The technology parameters are derived from measurements or simulations of individual devices. These parameters all appear in Equation 4 for the subthreshold leakage of a single device and are bundled into $\hat{I}_{leak}$ in Equation 8. They are all dependent on a host of lower-level process parameters (e.g., oxide thickness and doping profiles) in complex ways. The design dependent parameters (V_{CC}, N, and k_{design}) apply to groups of devices interconnected in a specific design style. Within certain constraints, they are independent of the process technology and may be varied independently. In this section, we examine each parameter in detail, focusing on relevant constraints and the determination and scaling of parameter values.

k_{tech} and S_t are relatively unimportant for high level applications of the model. Both parameters are likely to be bundled into $\hat{I}_{leak}$ along with V_T for practical applications of the model. For relative comparisons between designs targeting the same technology, the value of k_{tech} is immaterial; however, the value of k_{tech} will differ for the different threshold devices in MTCMOS technologies. The difference is easily predictable and can be estimated accurately when the threshold voltages themselves are known. S_t can potentially have a large impact on leakage current via the exponential relationship between the two. The two primary determinants of S_t are oxide thickness and temperature. Temperature control is a function of system-level design and can not be used to differentiate designs. Technologies providing multiple oxide thicknesses are not common; therefore, S_t is nearly the same for the alternate devices available in MTCMOS technologies. The scaling of oxide thickness has been slowly decreasing the magnitude of S_t over time. The minimum S_t is set by thermodynamic considerations and is about 60 mV/decade at room temperature [30]. Historical data shows that S_t is between about 80 and 100 mV/decade; SOI (silicon on insulator) technologies can more closely approach the ideal value [38].

The most important of the technology parameters is the threshold voltage V_T. It is the scaling of the threshold voltage (Figure 4) that is causing static power to become a concern. The tremendous (exponential) impact of a higher threshold voltage on static power has motivated the spread of MTCMOS technologies. At the cost of additional design and process complexity, these technologies provide devices differing in speed and leakage characteristics. Today's MTCMOS technologies provide only two options. The low-threshold voltage device provides a small speed benefit (~10%) for a large increase in subthreshold leakage (~4×) [34]. Although V_T is a technology parameter, MTCMOS enables (crude) tuning of device characteristics to the requirements of a particular circuit.

Although V_{CC} is categorized as a design parameter, it is heavily constrained by the technology. The electric fields that occur in the transistors are directly proportional to V_{CC}; therefore, reliability limits often provide an upper bound on the supply voltage. Also, certain analog circuitry found within microprocessors (e.g., cache array sense amplifiers) requires a minimum V_{CC} to operate correctly. The reason that V_{CC} is classified as a design parameter is that it is adjusted late in the design cycle (after working chips are available) to achieve the maximum performance. Its value is made as high as possible while maintaining acceptable reliability parameters and power consumption. V_{CC} partitioning (using different supply voltages for different circuits within the chip) is also a design technique that influences this parameter. It is currently used to allow for a higher voltage for off-chip communications than used in the core. This allows the power consumption to be lowered, but complicates the design due to the required voltage translation circuitry. For this reason, finer granularity voltage partitioning is not suitable to further lower power consumption.

Under constant field scaling, V_{CC} should be reduced approximately 30% per generation. While this trend was followed in the initial reductions of supply voltage from 5 V, the emphasis on high performance has resulted in V_{CC} scaling more slowly recently than the scaling model would suggest (Figure 4) [7, 33]. The latest technology projections from the SIA forecast a continuation of this trend for the performance market [27]. In the mobile and embedded markets, the increasing pressure to limit power consumption will cause V_{CC} scaling to return to the constant-field scenario. Although V_{CC} projections for a target technology are available early in the design process, the exact value of V_{CC} is unimportant since (like k_{tech}) its value is not needed to compare alternative designs in a given technology.

The number of transistors (represented by N) is the simplest of the design variables. At the architectural level it must often be estimated since circuit designs are not yet available. Presuming a circuit with known functionality has been designed in the past, a reasonably accurate estimate may be obtained with little effort. Estimation methods are especially useful for comparison of architectural alternatives that may not reach the circuit design phase. N is only constrained by the functionality required of the circuit and the available area in which to implement it. For a given functionality, the number of transistors should be constant across generations. With more transistors available, however, overhead is likely to increase as testability and performance monitoring features are added to more circuits. Increasing clock frequency also can impact device overhead as fewer gates may be placed between latches.

The remaining design parameter k_{design} encompasses the distribution of device types (N- and P-type), geometries (W and L), states (on vs. off), and stacking factors that are characteristic of a certain circuit type (see Section 4.1). Identifying more circuit types leads to better accuracy (as the aggregate properties of circuits in a more precise class are more similar), but requires additional effort both in determining k_{design} values and in applying the model. Example circuit types appropriate for architecture-level applications include logic (e.g., datapath circuitry), static RAM array, and associative array. Derivation of k_{design} for a particular circuit design style is performed by devising a small, representative circuit for each style. Circuit simulation is then performed to obtain total leakage current (an

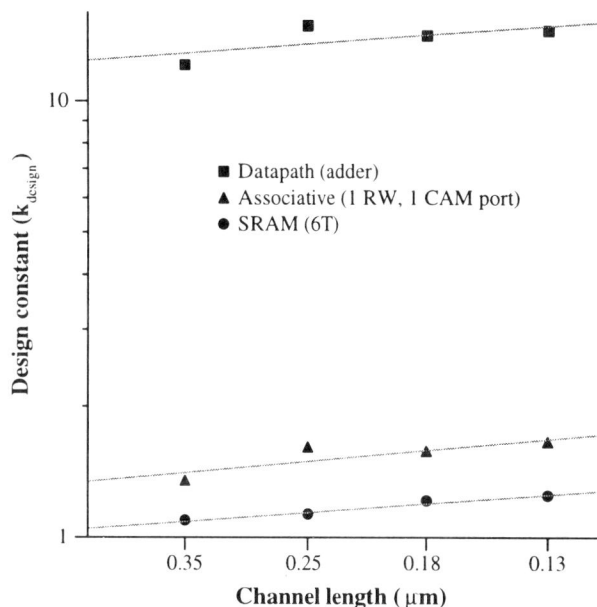

Figure 7. Technology impact on k_{design} parameters for different circuit styles

average over several states should be used). k_{design} is then calculated using the static power model (Equation 7) with the technology parameters used during the simulation. Figure 7 presents k_{design} values for the three example design styles derived from simulation of several different technologies.

The data in Figure 7 were derived using actual transistor models and process parameters from Intel. Cells representing each sample design style were selected from the Pentium III design database and simulated together with two reference transistors (N- and P-type). All transistor dimensions were scaled appropriately for each technology prior to simulation. The leakage current of the reference transistors was averaged and divided by the aspect ratio to obtain a normalized leakage parameter $\hat{I}_{leak}$ for each technology. Each circuit's leakage current was divided by $\hat{I}_{leak} \cdot N$ to obtain the k_{design} values. The resulting values show only a slight increase over four technology generations. The values for the 0.35 μm process are systematically lower than the other values; this is the result of a different transistor model required for simulation of that technology.

Table 2 contains k_{design} values for the circuit types in Figure 7 as well as those for two additional circuit types (obtained by hand analysis of the corresponding circuits). The table also lists the number of transistors (N) used in the reference circuit for calculating the k_{design} values and notes about the specific circuits and adjustments to k_{design}. For example, an 8-bit, 4-input multiplexor would have 32 transistors (2 / bit / input * 8 bits * 4 inputs) and a k_{design} of 4.3 (1.9 + 1.2 for the third input + 1.2 for the fourth input). Static CMOS logic has two complementary (N- and P-type) transistors for each gate input. The k_{design} value varies depending on the speed and fan-out of the particular logic. Note that the median value for static logic in Table 2 is lower than that for the adder in Figure 7. The value in the table is more representative of average logic than the value for the aggressive adder used for the scaling study.

Table 2. k_{design} values

Circuit	N	k_{design}	Notes
D Flip-flop	22 / bit	1.4	Edge-triggered FF
D Latch	10 / bit	2.0	Transparent latch
2-input mux	2 / bit / input	1.9	+1.2 / input over 2
6T RAM cell	6 / bit	1.2	1 RW port
CAM cell	13 / bit	1.7	1 RW, 1 CAM
Static logic	2 / gate input	11	Depends on speed, load (± 3)

Recall that the average device geometry was incorporated into k_{design} in the form of the aspect ratio W / L. Being the ratio of two dimensions, device aspect ratios ideally do not change under scaling. The value of including these parameters as a ratio into the design constant (instead of the technology constant) is now apparent. Because the aspect ratio is independent of technology, k_{design} values (once derived) are valid for projecting static power requirements in other technologies.

5. Reducing Static Power

The model for static power presented in the previous section suggests different ways in which static power may be controlled: reducing any factor in the equation will reduce the power requirement. Thus, the static power may be lowered by reducing the supply voltage (lower V_{CC}), using fewer devices (lower N), using a more power efficient design style (lower k_{design}), or using slower devices (higher V_T, lower $\hat{I}_{leak}$). Depending on the method employed, any of these options may require performance to be sacrificed to realize power savings. We will discuss architectural applications of each of these options in this section. We conclude the section with a discussion of likely applications of speculation to power-efficient architectures.

5.1. Reducing the Supply Voltage

The supply voltage is not typically thought of as an architecturally controllable parameter. However, the nature of the architecture influences the supply voltage optimization which occurs at the end of the design cycle. Architects can enable lower supply voltages by making performance less sensitive to latency. Circuits with less strict latency requirements can operate at a lower clock frequency and supply voltage. By partitioning the circuit into several domains operating at different supply voltages, both static and dynamic power savings are possible. Modern microprocessors already use this technique to allow for a higher voltage for off-chip communication than is used in the core. Level shifter circuits are required for communications between voltage domains. The partitioning should take into account the extra delay incurred in crossing domain boundaries.

To reduce the supply voltage for the entire chip without partitioning, the global clock frequency must be reduced. Architectures which emphasize high IPC over high clock frequencies to achieve performance are superior in power characteristics provided the added complexity does not erase the gains through increased device count. The point at which an

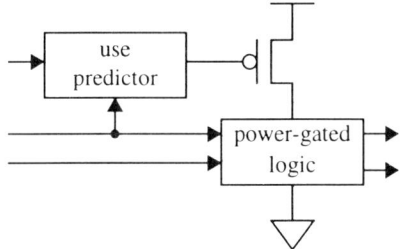

Figure 8. Power gating: gated logic receives power only when PMOS switching device is active

architecture falls on the frequency-IPC scale directly influences the domain in which the supply voltage may be adjusted.

5.2. Reducing the Number of Devices

One obvious technique that may be employed to reduce static power is to reduce the total number of devices. Finding opportunities to reduce the device count enough to impact power dissipation without decreasing performance or functionality is difficult, however. Normal design practices eliminate obvious redundancy. Furthermore, a large number of devices must be removed to have a noticeable impact. Thus, units with replication make obvious targets. Cache size, number of functional units, and issue/retire bandwidth may all be reduced with varying degrees of difficulty and performance impact. If power optimization is a goal from the beginning, effort spent balancing the processor's resources reduces unnecessary replication by allocating fewer overall devices only where they are most needed. Another beneficial task for architects would be to equalize utilization: bursty operation requires a high maximum throughput to attain a given performance level. Equalizing resource requirements over time results in a lower total resource requirement for a given performance. Each of these approaches is appropriate for study at the architectural level.

Another method to reduce N without actually removing devices is to turn them off when they are unused. Power gating is analogous to clock gating: the supply voltage (rather than the clock) of some functional unit is switched on only when the unit is required. Additional circuitry is added to determine the need for the unit. This circuitry may monitor inputs to the switched unit or use other available signals (Figure 8). The gated circuitry will not dissipate any power when turned off. However, this must be balanced against the power dissipated by the gating circuitry and the power switching device itself. The power switching device must be large enough (W) to handle the average supply current of the circuit while in operation. If the device has a high enough threshold voltage, its leakage power can be lower than that of the gated circuit (which may use lower thresholds to be fast during operation). However, the addition of a gating device can result in reduced performance and noise margins [24, 36].

The major problem with power gating is the latency between when the signal to turn a unit on arrives and when the unit is ready to operate. Due to the huge capacitance on the power supply nodes in a unit, several clock cycles will be needed to allow the power supply to reach its operating level[†]. There are two alternatives which may apply regarding this latency. If the functional unit is required very rarely or is not on the critical computation path, it may not significantly impact performance to stall until the unit is ready. Alternatively, the requirement for a unit may be predicted far enough in advance for the unit to be ready when it is required.

Predicting the need for a functional unit raises the question of what kinds of microarchitectural events can be predicted accurately in advance. One obvious choice is the use of floating point functionality. Some operating systems already track the use of floating point hardware by applications to avoid saving the floating point registers on context switches when unnecessary [20]. Thus, the floating point hardware may be switched at the same granularity as context switches. Portions of the cache may also be turned off provided the working set of the application fits in a subset of the cache [22]. Other opportunities include decode logic for rare or privileged instructions, interrupt logic (a timer interrupt, usually the most frequent interrupt, at 100Hz occurs only every 10 million clock cycles at 1GHz), or logic to handle certain rare exceptions. Architectural study is ideal for determining the impact of increased startup latencies and the feasibility of prediction.

5.3. Using More Efficient Circuits

The design factors comprising k_{design} offer few opportunities for static power reduction directly. Architects may not think directly about the distribution of device geometries or stacking factors; however, the requirements of the microarchitecture ultimately determine the type of circuitry which can be used for its implementation. For example, targeting higher IPC at a lower clock frequency allows for more logic between pipeline latches; power savings are realized by allowing the use of more complex gates with larger average stacking factors.

The k_{design} values in Table 2 suggest some additional ways of employing power-efficient circuits. Wide multiplexors should be avoided as they have a cost which grows super-linearly with the number of inputs. A tri-state bus with multiple drivers can accomplish the same function with lower total leakage (tri-state drivers have stacked devices where pass-gate multiplexors do not). Associative arrays are approximately three times leakier (including the larger number of transistors) than simple random-access memories. Implementing pseudo-associativity using hashing may be appropriate depending on the exact requirements of the microarchitecture.

5.4. Using Multiple Threshold Voltages

Technologies which provide multiple threshold voltages allow for an even better tradeoff between static power and performance. By using slower transistors, the leakage current may be reduced significantly. Note that it is not sufficient to simply clock a regular device more slowly, since this does not affect the subthreshold leakage. The transistor must actually be *slower*.

Different transistor speeds may be used in different ways. One method would be to employ the fast devices only along critical timing paths. Although algorithms have been proposed to automatically perform this task [29, 36], a concern is that automated modification of path delays could result in races. A second technique involves determining which functional units require the lowest latencies and allocating the budget of fast, leaky devices to these units only. To reduce dynamic power consumption, at least one announced product divides core logic into clock domains of different frequencies [18]. Limited partitioning has occurred ever since core frequencies exceeded bus frequencies.

Partitioning enables one to use a device speed appropriate to the particular clock domain in which the device is to be located. Architects are best suited to determine which functionality belongs in which clock domain and what particular method of interdomain communication should be used. This partitioning allows for optimization of both static and dynamic power consumption.

Threshold voltage may also be adjusted by applying a voltage to the body node of a transistor to reverse bias the source-body junction. By raising the threshold voltage, this technique also results in slower devices. The ideal use of such a technique would be to apply the body bias only when the circuitry is unused and return to normal conditions when the circuit is required. The very high resistance of transistor body nodes results in a similar problem as in power gating, but of a much higher magnitude: establishing or removing a body bias will require a long time due to the high resistance of the body nodes of MOSFET's. Therefore, functional units that have long idle periods and startups that can be accurately predicted with architectural state are most appropriate for these techniques.

5.5. Power Reduction with Speculation

Speculation can be an important tool for architects when designing power-efficient architectures. Specifically, it provides a means of using slower devices without proportionally impacting performance. The performance critical speculation circuitry employs fast devices, while the slower devices are used to verify the speculative results. The additional latency is incurred only when the speculation is incorrect. In some cases, the circuitry to perform the speculation is simple and very few of the power-hungry fast devices are required. The verification circuitry may use higher-threshold devices, use a lower supply voltage, run at a lower clock frequency, or some combination resulting in both static and dynamic power savings over a fast, non-speculative solution at little performance cost. An architecture such as DIVA [2] in which a slow checker augments a fast, highly speculative core could directly benefit from intelligent partitioning based on device speed requirements.

As a more specific example, consider data speculation on L1 cache accesses. Such speculation is already implemented on Intel's Willamette for performance reasons [10]. L1 cache accesses are on the critical execution path for load instructions. Recognizing that the majority of such accesses hit in the cache, it is reasonable to speculatively assume that any data retrieved from a direct-mapped cache is correct prior to checking the tags. The cache tags and tag match logic may then be implemented with slower, more efficient circuitry. Mis-speculation detection suffers from an increased latency implied by the slower circuitry. Performance is only impacted in the event of an L1 cache miss. Without speculation, the tags and matching logic would have to be fast to avoid a significant performance penalty. The potential power savings depends on the exact cache behavior, the amount of logic that was moved off of the critical path, and the amount of additional logic required to recover from mis-speculation.

Another application of speculation was referred to briefly in Section 5.2 in the context of predicting when certain circuitry will be needed. It may be hard to determine when certain functional units are required and when they may be shut off to save power. Instead of choosing to leave these units on constantly, it may be more appropriate to speculatively power-down such functional units. Provided the speculation accuracy is reasonable, a large decrease in power consumption would incur only a small performance penalty. Mis-speculation would be visible as increased latency of the functional unit. In architectures which are power-limited (the peak performance is limited by power

---

† The switching device must supply current corresponding to the average power dissipation. Consider a circuit representing 1% of a chip that dissipates 150 W at 1.5 V. The device must conduct 1 A of average current. Assuming a decoupling capacitance of 500 nF for the entire chip, the supply node capacitance of the switched unit will be approximately 5 nF. Charging 5 nF to 1.5 V with 1 A takes approximately (Equation 1): (5 nF)(1.5 V) / (1 A) = 7.5 ns or 7.5 cycles at 1 GHz.

considerations), such techniques could actually allow for higher performance.

6. Related Work

Prior work on power modeling of power dissipation at the architectural level has been focused almost entirely on dynamic power. The oft quoted $P_{dyn} = CV_{CC}^2 f$ is easily derived by consideration of a loaded inverter (see for example [37]). This metric is often used to compare the dynamic power requirements of alternative designs. A survey of more detailed power modeling tools was compiled by Blaauw, *et. al.* [4]. Several researchers have reported modifying performance simulators to provide power estimates as well [6, 35].

Reducing power consumption in microprocessors is the subject of active research. These works tend to focus on caches because of the large potential gains and ease of modeling [1, 3, 16, 28]. Dynamic power reduction in more irregular structures is demonstrated by efficiency based arguments wherein the amount of switching or needless work is reduced [5, 11, 19, 32]. Static power has been addressed in recent work by Powell, *et. al.* [22] which combines circuit and architectural techniques to reduce the power consumption in a processor's cache. The cache miss rate is used to determine the working set size of the application relative to that of the cache. Power is then removed from the unused portions of the cache via a gating transistor.

The device and circuits communities have been concerned with increasing static power for several generations. Besides numerous publications of specific technologies with improved leakage characteristics (e.g., MTCMOS), several reviews have focussed on leakage current as an important concern in future technologies. Keshavarzi, *et. al.* present the various leakage modes of the MOS transistor and identify subthreshold leakage as the dominant one [15]. De and Borkar project leakage power growing 5× per generation and conclude that power dissipation and delivery will be the main barrier to future scaling [8].

7. Conclusion

Static power dissipation due primarily to subthreshold leakage will become an important component of overall power dissipation. Technology trends are reducing the transistor threshold voltage to achieve performance target. While dynamic power is partially offset by the reduction in supply voltage that occurs during scaling, static power is increasing exponentially as the threshold voltage is decreased. Static power will likely contribute as much to total power as dynamic power in as little as two technology generations unless architects consider it as important as dynamic power when making design tradeoffs.

Modeling static power consumption at the architectural level is possible using a relatively simple equation (Equation 7). The equation combines technology-based factors (k_{tech}, V_T, and S_t) with design-dependent parameters (V_{CC}, N, and k_{design}). A simpler version of the model combines the technology parameters into a single constant $\hat{I}_{leak}$. Each of the parameters is readily obtainable by projecting technology trends or performing simple simulations. The model provides a useful level of abstraction for application at an early stage in the design process. Low-level detail is sacrificed for ease of application. Secondly, the relative accuracy of model predictions does not require precise values of technology parameters which may not be available. Finally, the model illuminates various approaches for reducing the static power dissipation.

Reducing the number of devices used is a straightforward approach when the performance loss may be controlled or mitigated by other factors. Turning off unused devices is another way to control power consumption although the long restart latency must be considered. It may be possible to predict some events far enough in advance to hide this latency. Partitioning the design into blocks based on the latency requirements can enable per-block supply voltage tuning or the selective use of high threshold devices. High threshold (i.e., slower) devices are inherently less leaky and reduce power requirements. Technologies that provide multiple threshold devices are already available and will become commonplace.

One useful application of slower devices is to the logic used to check the correctness of speculation. This decouples the increased latency of the slower logic from overall performance since the slower logic is on the critical execution path only during mis-speculation recovery. By using fewer fast devices to generate the speculative result than would be required to generate the actual result, static power savings are achieved.

Many of the techniques described to limit static power dissipation have the side effect of controlling dynamic power dissipation as well. Reducing the number of devices (N) directly reduces the switching capacitance (C) which affects dynamic power. In the absence of clock gating, power gating has a similar effect since only powered devices contribute to the switching capacitance. Using lower supply voltages in less critical logic blocks also reduces dynamic power. Finally, because the switching frequency f is limited by the device performance (V_T), reducing the frequency wherever possible also benefits dynamic power. In contrast, techniques for reducing dynamic power dissipation (e.g., clock gating) do not generally improve static power dissipation. Considering only dynamic power dissipation can actually lead to choosing a microarchitecture with higher total power dissipation (e.g., one that uses fast, leaky devices to achieve high-throughput when latency is not critical).

Architects are in a position to affect the power requirements of their designs. Given the ability to reason about power, the architect can factor that information in when making trade-offs between alternative designs. Due to the long design cycle, architects must be considering power dissipation now to deliver products which are not unduly constrained by power.

Acknowledgements

The authors would like to thank Intel Corp. for allowing use of their simulation infrastructure. Richard Green and Jeff Smith of Intel provided comments and advice which were extremely helpful. Finally, the authors thank the referees for their reviews.

This work was supported in part by National Science Foundation grants MIP-9505853 and CCR-9900584, donations from Intel Corp. and Sun Microsystems, and the University of Wisconsin Graduate School. Adam Butts is supported by a fellowship from the Fannie and John Hertz Foundation.

References

[1] D. Albonesi. Selective Cache Ways: On-Demand Cache Resource Allocation. In *Proceedings of the 32nd International Symposium on Microarchitecture*, November 1999. pp. 248-259.

[2] T. Austin. DIVA: A Reliable Substrate for Deep Submicron Microarchitecture Design. In *Proceedings of the 32nd International Symposium on Microarchitecture*, November 1999. pp. 196-207.

[3] R. Bahar, G. Albera, and S. Manne. Power and Performance Tradeoffs Using Various Caching Strategies. In *Proceedings of the International Symposium on Low Power Electronics and Design*, 1998. pp. 64-69.

[4] D. Blaauw, A. Dharchoudhury, R. Panda, S. Sirichotiyakul, C. Oh, and T. Edwards. Emerging Power Management Tools for Processor Design. In *Proceedings of the International Symposium on Low Power Electronics and Design*, 1998. pp. 143-148.

[5] D. Brooks and M. Martonosi. Dynamically Exploiting Narrow Width Operands to Improve Processor Power and Performance. In *Proceedings of the 5th International Symposium on High-Performance Computer Architecture*, January 1999. pp. 13-22.

[6] D. Brooks, V. Tiwari, and M. Martonosi. Wattch: A Framework for Architectural-Level Power Analysis and Optimizations. In *Proceedings of the 27th International Symposium on Computer Architecture*, June 2000. pp. 83-94.

[7] B. Davari. CMOS Technology Scaling, 0.1 µm and Beyond. In *Proceedings of the International Electron Devices Meeting*, 1996. pp. 555-558.

[8] V. De and S. Borkar. Technology and Design Challenges for Low Power and High Performance. In *Proceedings of the International Symposium on Low Power Electronics and Design*, 1999. pp. 163-168.

[9] R. Dennard, F. Gaensslen, H. Yu, V. Rideout, E. Bassous, and A. LeBlanc. Design of Ion-Implanted MOSFET's with Very Small Physical Dimensions. *IEEE Journal of Solid-State Circuits*, 9(5), October 1974. pp. 256-268.

[10] P. Glaskowsky. Pentium 4 (Partially) Previewed. *Microprocessor Report*, August 28, 2000.

[11] R. Gonzalez and M. Horowitz. Energy Dissipation in General Purpose Microprocessors. *IEEE Journal of Solid-State Circuits*, 31(9), September 1996. pp. 1277-1284.

[12] M. Horowitz, T. Indermaur, and R. Gonzalez. Low-Power Digital Design. In *Proceedings of the 1994 IEEE Symposium on Low Power Electronics*. pp. 8-11.

[13] Intel Corporation. *Pentium III Processor for the SC242 at 450 MHz to 1.13 GHz Datasheet*. pp. 26-30.

[14] M. Johnson, D. Somasekhar, and K. Roy. Models and Algorithms for Bounds on Leakage in CMOS Circuits. *IEEE Trans. on Computer-Aided Design of Integrated Circuits and Systems*, 18(6), June 1999. pp. 714-725.

[15] A. Keshavarzi, K. Roy, and C. Hawkins. Intrinsic Leakage in Low Power Deep Submicron CMOS ICs. In *Proceedings of the IEEE International Test Conference*, 1997. pp. 146-155.

[16] J. Kin, M. Gupta, and W. Mangione-Smith. The Filter Cache: An Energy Efficient Memory Structure. In *Proceedings of the 30th International Symposium on Microarchitecture*, December 1997. pp. 184-193.

[17] P. Ko, J. Huang, Z. Liu, and C. Hu. BSIM3 for Analog and Digital Circuit Simulation. In *Proceedings of the IEEE Symposium on VLSI Technology CAD*, January 1993. pp. 400-429.

[18] K. Krewell. Quicktake: Willamette Revealed. *Microprocessor Report*, February 2000. p. 19.

[19] S. Manne, A. Klauser, and D. Grunwald. Pipeline Gating: Speculation Control for Energy Reduction. In *Proceedings of the 25th International Symposium on Computer Architecture*, June 1998. pp. 132-141.

[20] H. Massalin and C. Pu. Threads and Input/Output in the Synthesis Kernel. In *Proceedings of the 12th Symposium on Operating Systems Principles*, December 1989. pp. 191-201.

[21] E. Nowak. Ultimate CMOS ULSI Performance. In *Proceedings of the International Electron Devices Meeting*, 1993. pp. 115-118.

[22] M. Powell, S. Yang, B. Falsafi, K. Roy, T. Vijaykumar. Gated-V_{DD}: A Circuit Technique to Reduce Leakage in Deep-Submicron Cache Memories. In the *Proceedings of the International Symposium on Low Power Electronics and Design*, July 2000. pp. 90-95.

[23] J. Rabaey. *Digital Integrated Circuits: A Design Perspective*. Prentice-Hall, 1995.

[24] K. Roy. Leakage Power Reduction in Low-Voltage CMOS Design. In *Proceedings of the IEEE International Conference on Circuits and Systems*, 1998. pp. 167-173.

[25] T. Sakurai, H. Kawaguchi, and T. Kuroda. Low-Power CMOS Design through V_{TH} Control and Low-Swing Circuits. In *Proceedings of the International Symposium on Low Power Electronics and Design*, 1997. pp. 1-6.

[26] T. Sakurai and A. Newton. Alpha-Power Law MOSFET Model and its Applications to CMOS Inverter Delay and Other Formulas. *IEEE Journal of Solid-State Circuits*, 25(4), April 1990. pp. 584-594.

[27] Semiconductor Industry Association. *International Technology Roadmap for Semiconductors*, 1999 edition. Austin, TX: SEMATECH, 1999.

[28] C. Su and A. Despain. Cache Designs for Energy Efficiency. In *Proceedings of the 28th Annual Hawaii International Conference on System Sciences*, 1995. pp. 306-315.

[29] V. Sundararajan and K. Parhi. Low Power Synthesis of Dual Threshold Voltage CMOS VLSI Circuits. In *Proceedings of the International Symposium on Low Power Electronics and Design*, 1999. pp. 139-144.

[30] S. Sze. *Physics of Semiconductor Devices, 2nd. Ed.* John Wiley and Sons, 1981.

[31] V. Tiwari, R. Donnelly, S. Malik, and R. Gonzalez. Dynamic Power Management for Microprocessors: A Case Study. In *Proceedings of the 10th International Conference on VLSI Design*, 1997. pp. 185-192.

[32] V. Tiwari, D. Singh, S. Rajgopal, G. Mehta, R. Patel, F. Baez. Reducing Power in High-Performance Microprocessors. In *Proceedings of the Design Automation Conference*, 1998. pp. 732-737.

[33] Y. Taur and E. Nowak. CMOS Devices Below 0.1 µm: How High Will Performance Go? In *Proceedings of the International Electron Devices Meeting*, 1997. pp. 215-218.

[34] S. Thompson, P. Packan, and M. Bohr. MOS Scaling: Transistor Challenges for the 21st Century. *Intel Technology Journal*, Q3 1998.

[35] N. Vijaykrishnan, M. Kandemir, M. Irwin, H. Kim, and W. Ye. Energy-Driven Integrated Hardware-Software Optimizations Using SimplePower. In *Proceedings of the 27th International Symposium on Computer Architecture*, June 2000. pp. 95-106.

[36] Q. Wang and S. Vrudhula. Static Power Optimization of Deep Submicron CMOS Circuits for Dual V_T Technology. In *Proceedings of the International Conference on Computer-Aided Design*, 1998. pp. 490-496.

[37] N. Weste and K. Eshraghian. *Principles of CMOS VLSI Design: A Systems Perspective, 2nd. Ed.* Addison-Wesley, 1993.

[38] D. Wouters, J. Colinge, H. Maes. Subthreshold Slope in Thin-Film SOI MOSFET's. *IEEE Transactions on Electron Devices*, 37(9), September 1990. pp. 2022-2033.

A Framework for Dynamic Energy Efficiency and Temperature Management*

Michael Huang, **Jose Renau**, **Seung-Moon Yoo**, and **Josep Torrellas**
Department of Computer Science
University of Illinois at Urbana-Champaign
http://iacoma.cs.uiuc.edu

ABSTRACT

While technology is delivering increasingly sophisticated and powerful chip designs, it is also imposing alarmingly high energy requirements on the chips. One way to address this problem is to manage the energy dynamically. Unfortunately, current dynamic schemes for energy management are relatively limited. In addition, they manage energy either for energy efficiency or for temperature control, but not for both simultaneously.

In this paper, we design and evaluate for the first time an energy-management framework that tackles both energy efficiency and temperature control in a unified manner. We call this general approach Dynamic Energy Efficiency and Temperature Management (DEETM). Our framework combines many energy-management techniques and can activate them individually or in groups in a fine-grained manner according to a given policy. The goal of the framework is two-fold: maximize energy savings without extending application execution time beyond a given tolerable limit, and guarantee that the temperature remains below a given limit while minimizing any resulting slowdown. The framework successfully meets these goals. For example, it delivers a 40% energy reduction with only a 10% application slowdown.

1 INTRODUCTION

Continuous technical advances are fueling the trend toward more sophisticated and powerful chip designs. Such designs, including high-end microprocessors, chip multiprocessors, systems on a chip, and other advanced embedded systems are quickly increasing their functionality and clock rates. Unfortunately, they are also increasing their energy consumption requirements alarmingly.

One way to address this problem is to manage the energy consumed in the chips. There are two main aims of energy management: to ensure that the energy is used efficiently and to guarantee that power consumption is never so high that the chip reaches dangerous temperature levels.

Efficient energy use is desirable in all systems. However, it is critical in portable devices, where battery energy is limited. It is also an important way to reduce cost in systems that have periods of idle time, also called slack [25]. Slack appears not only in interactive and real-time systems; it also occurs in general-purpose environments like web servers or routers with high-end processors where the performance is often bottlenecked by the network.

Likewise, curbing high power consumption to limit high temperatures is useful in all systems. It enables lower-cost packaging and cooling systems for the chips. It also makes the chip more reliable. Finally, it may enable a more aggressive design or a higher clock speed.

To address these two issues, namely energy efficiency and temperature control, many low-power architectural techniques have been proposed and implemented. For example, they include putting the system in sleep mode [28]; scaling the voltage and/or frequency [11, 13, 25]; switching contexts to a job that consumes less power [27]; reconfiguring hardware structures [1]; gating pipeline signals, for example to control speculation [5, 23]; throttling the instruction cache [28]; clock optimizations, including multiple clocks and clock gating [10]; better signal encoding [10]; low power memory design techniques [15] like bank partitioning or divided word line; low power cache design techniques like cache block buffering [33], sub-banking [9, 30], or filter caches [20]; and TLB optimizations [17].

While most of these techniques are likely to be useful for the upcoming, energy-consuming chips, we feel that their effectiveness can be enhanced. To start with, while some of these techniques have been used adaptively [1, 8, 5, 23, 25, 27], many others have been designed to be always active. In reality, for many of the latter, it would be advantageous to turn them on and off dynamically, based on the requirements of the application and the environmental conditions. They could enable useful energy-performance tradeoffs.

In addition, most of these techniques were proposed to work independently of each other. If we combined many of them in a single framework that can activate and deactivate them individually or in groups according to a given policy, the resulting system could be both more powerful and more flexible.

Finally, proposed dynamic approaches have targeted either energy efficiency [1, 8, 23, 25] or temperature control [5, 27] but not both simultaneously. If a multi-technique framework can combine support for both aspects, it can become a fairly complete approach to energy management.

The general approach of dynamically managing energy for both energy efficiency and temperature control we call *Dynamic Energy Efficiency and Temperature Management (DEETM)*. The contribution of this paper is the design and evaluation for the first time of one such DEETM framework. Our framework supports a combination of energy-management techniques. It is implemented with a combination of software and hardware for fine-grained energy management. The framework has two goals: (i) maximize the

---
*This work was supported in part by the National Science Foundation under grants NSF Young Investigator Award MIP-9457436, MIP-9619351, and CCR-9970488, DARPA Contract DABT63-95-C-0097, and gifts from IBM and Intel.

savings of energy in the chip without extending the execution time of the application beyond a given tolerable limit, and (ii) guarantee that the temperature of the chip remains below a given limit while minimizing any resulting slowdown. In our evaluation, we show that the framework satisfies these goals. For example, it delivers a 40% energy reduction with only a 10% application slowdown.

This paper is organized as follows: Section 2 presents the design and implementation of our framework for DEETM; Section 3 discusses how we evaluate it; Section 4 evaluates the framework; and Section 5 presents related work.

2 A FRAMEWORK FOR DEETM

In this section, we describe our framework for DEETM: its main ideas (Section 2.1), the algorithm used (Section 2.2), the software interface (Section 2.3), some related issues (Section 2.4), and the techniques included in the framework (Section 2.5).

2.1 Main Ideas

Advanced chips can benefit from a dynamic framework that manages energy in a fine-grained manner to accomplish two goals. The first one is *temperature control*: guaranteeing that the temperature of the chip remains below a given limit while minimizing any slowdown. The second goal is *energy efficiency control*: maximizing the savings of energy in the chip without extending the execution of the application beyond a tolerable limit.

For the framework to be versatile, it should include multiple techniques for energy management. Different techniques may target the energy consumption in different components of the chip, for example processor cores, I-caches, D-caches, or DRAM arrays. They may, instead, target the same component but do so with a different energy-performance tradeoff. In such an environment, the framework can dynamically activate the techniques individually, concurrently, gradually with a priority order, or even in a mutually exclusive manner.

As initial support for the framework, we assume that the chip contains a distributed thermal sensor along the lines of the PowerPC [28] and a counter with the number of instructions executed. In addition, it contains two registers, *MaxTemp* and *MaxSlowdn*, which are set in software with the maximum temperature allowed and the maximum job slowdown that can be tolerated, respectively.

2.2 Algorithm Description

Our framework includes two algorithms: a temperature-limiting one called *Thermal* and an energy-saving one called *Slack*. They try to satisfy the first and second goals discussed above, respectively. These algorithms control the activation of a set of energy-management techniques.

At any given time, the set of techniques that are active is called the *Current Set*. These techniques may have been selected by the Thermal or by the Slack algorithm. The set of techniques that are selected by the Thermal algorithm is called the *Thermal Set*.

The two algorithms work as follows. When the Thermal algorithm runs, it compares the current temperature to the temperature limit. Depending on the result, it may add or subtract one technique to or from the Thermal Set. When the Slack algorithm runs, it first deactivates the Current Set to measure the baseline IPC value of the application. Then, it activates the Thermal Set and possibly additional techniques until the new IPC shows that the tolerable slack is used up.

To adapt to changing conditions, these algorithms run periodically. The period between runs we call *Macrocycle*. Since the two algorithms do not need to have the same period, we define a thermal macrocycle and a slack macrocycle (Figure 1-(a)).

The thermal macrocycle should be set roughly to the time taken by the thermal sensor to detect a change in temperature after a technique is activated. Since heat transfer occurs at the ms level [31], the thermal macrocycle has to be of the order of a few ms, possibly 1-15 ms. If the macrocycle is too short, the Thermal algorithm will overreact, since there is not enough time to feel the effect of any newly activated technique. However, if it is too long, we risk damaging the chip with a temperature that is over the limit for too long. The appropriate length of the macrocycle is different in each system. It depends on the heat dissipation characteristics of the chip and the sophistication of the distributed thermal sensor.

Selecting the slack macrocycle is not as delicate. However, since the Slack algorithm decides what fraction of the time to activate each technique for, based solely on the IPC at the beginning of the macrocycle, we need to pay attention to two issues. First, the macrocycle should be short enough not to miss significant changes in application behavior. Otherwise, the resulting slowdown may be very different than initially expected. In practice, a macrocycle of the order of a few ms, possibly 1-15 ms, is appropriate.

The second issue is that slack macrocycles should all have the same duration and not be cut off short. The reason is that, when the Slack algorithm runs, its calculations use the expected duration of the macrocycle to decide the length of time to activate each technique for. Cutting the macrocycle short makes such calculations inaccurate. We will see later how we address this issue.

In the following, we describe the two algorithms in detail. Note that both algorithms want to deliver large energy reductions without excessive slowdowns. Consequently, they prefer techniques that minimize the product of the energy consumed by the application times the execution time (*energy-delay product* [10]). As a result, both algorithms pick the techniques to activate in the same order. Such order follows a ranking set up by the OS or application based on the expected energy-delay product impact of each technique.

Thermal Algorithm

The Thermal algorithm is typically implemented as an interrupt handler in the OS. Alternatively, it could be implemented in hardware. The algorithm is shown in Figure 1-(b). If the thermal sensor indicates a temperature higher than *MaxTemp*, the next highest-priority technique not yet in the Thermal Set is added to it. Otherwise, if it indicates a temperature lower than a low-threshold value *MinTemp*, the lowest-priority technique in the Thermal Set is removed.

If we have added a new technique to the Thermal Set, before leaving the algorithm, we set the Current Set to the maximum of Current and Thermal Sets. This is done to ensure that the new technique is immediately active. If a technique was removed from the Thermal Set, however, it cannot be removed from the Current Set until the Slack algorithm runs.

MinTemp is set to minimize instability. A sophisticated design can keep a different *MinTemp* for each of the techniques. To choose the appropriate *MinTemp* for a given technique, we can use past profiles to estimate the temperature reduction that the technique delivers under usual conditions. Then, we set *MinTemp* to slightly less than *MaxTemp* minus the average value of such a temperature reduction. With this approach,

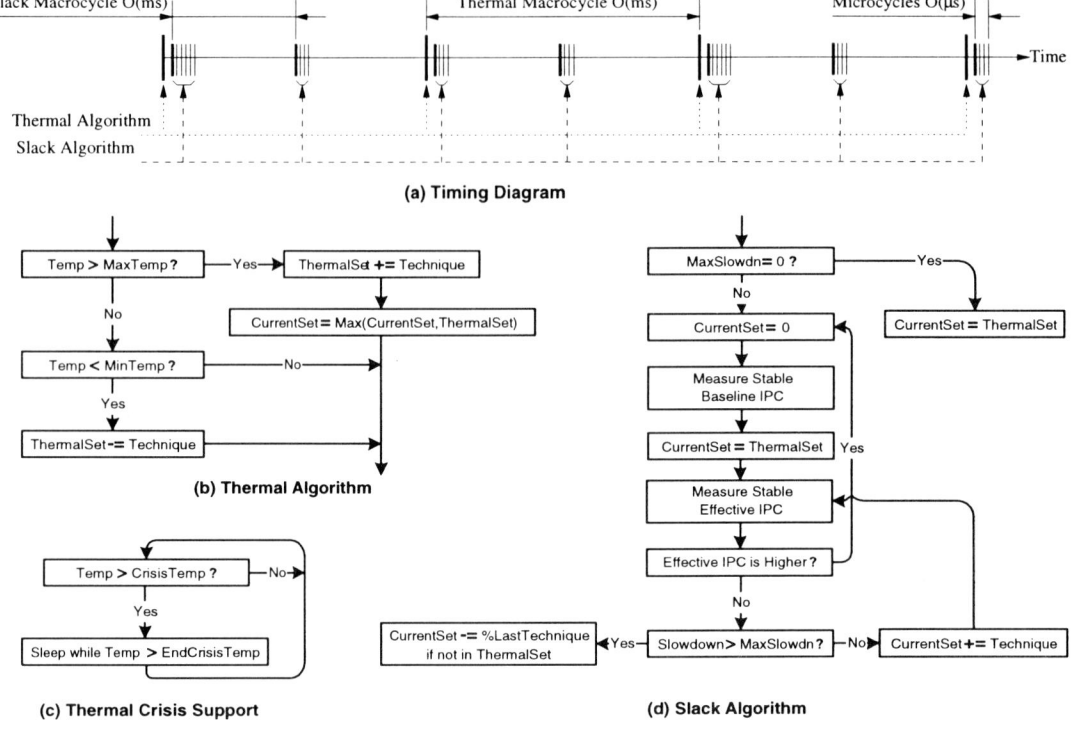

Figure 1: Algorithms used in our framework.

we minimize the chances that the deactivation of a technique brings us back to over *MaxTemp*.

Note that, in some cases, we may not be able to prevent the temperature from rising over the limit. For example, such a situation may be caused by a virus. For this reason, the chip must include support for a thermal crisis. One possible such support is shown in Figure 1-(c): if the temperature reaches a *CrisisTemp* temperature, the hardware unconditionally sets the system to sleep until the temperature is safely lower than *CrisisTemp*.

Slack Algorithm

The Slack algorithm is implemented in hardware instead of as an OS routine. The reason is that, every time that it runs, it needs to repeatedly measure the number of instructions executed by the application at μs-level intervals. After several such measurements in the background, the algorithm makes the decision. These intervals we call *Microcycles* (Figure 1-(a)). We will see that, for higher accuracy, a microcycle is of the order of a few μs.

The Slack algorithm is shown in Figure 1-(d). If no slowdown can be tolerated, the Current Set is simply set to the Thermal Set. Otherwise, the Current Set is deactivated so that the hardware can measure the stable baseline IPC of the application. To compute the IPC, the hardware reads at microcycle intervals the counter of instructions executed. It may take several readings until a reasonably stable IPC is obtained. Note that by deactivating all techniques for several μs we do not risk a dangerous temperature surge because the time is too short.

We then set the Current Set to the Thermal Set and, to find out the resulting slowdown, calculate the new *effective* IPC. The new effective IPC is the new measured IPC plus a correction if the Thermal Set includes techniques that change the clock frequency.

With this new effective IPC, we can compare the slowdown caused by setting the Current Set to the Thermal one, to the maximum tolerable slowdown (*MaxSlowdn*). If *MaxSlowdn* is higher, we augment the Current Set with the next highest-priority technique not yet in it and again measure the effective IPC. This process is repeated until the application slowdown is equal to or higher than *MaxSlowdn*. If the slowdown is higher than *MaxSlowdn*, the last technique that has been added to the Current Set is marked as active for only a fraction of the Slack macrocycle, such that the final slowdown ends up being no higher than *MaxSlowdn*. The only exception is when this last technique added belongs to the Thermal Set, in which case, it cannot be deactivated. Finally, when we reach this point, the algorithm exits.

Every time that we go through the loop of adding a new technique to the Current Set, the hardware may need to take several measurements spaced one microcycle apart, until a stable IPC is obtained. Unfortunately, it is possible that, at the same time, the application also goes through a change in its regime that induces a change in IPC. In this case, to avoid confusing our algorithm, we proceed as follows. If the effective IPC suddenly becomes higher after activating a technique, it is clear that the regime changed. If we pressed on with more techniques until we reached the original target IPC, we would be slowing down the application beyond the tolerable limit. Consequently, as shown in Figure 1-(d), we stop the algorithm and restart it from the beginning.

If, instead, the regime change is in the opposite direction, our algorithm will not notice it: we will assume that the technique just activated is solely responsible for the large IPC reduction. However, this is fine. Our algorithm will end up producing a conservative solution: in the final system, the true slowdown relative to the baseline execution will be less than it could be tolerated. Consequently, the end user is not negatively affected.

Note that some of the techniques used may have non-trivial activation delays. Such is the case, for example, for voltage-frequency scaling, which takes 10-20 μs to activate or deactivate [11]. Such delays, however, are negligible compared to the duration of a macrocycle. For example, if a slack macrocycle takes 2 ms, activating and deactivating voltage-frequency scaling takes only about 2% of the macrocycle. Furthermore, because the impact of voltage-frequency scaling on the IPC is fairly predictable, we do not need to deactivate it at every beginning of a macrocycle to estimate the baseline IPC. This fact further reduces overhead.

Finally, since both the Thermal and the Slack algorithms may update the Current Set, we need to prevent inconsistencies. To this end, and also to ensure that slack macrocycles are not cut off short, we propose the following timing (Figure 1-(a)). We choose the slack macrocycle so that a thermal one contains several slack macrocycles plus a few μs. After the OS has executed the Thermal algorithm and is about to return execution to user mode, it sets the hardware to trigger the next run of the Slack algorithm in a few μs. We set this delay so that, when the Slack algorithm finally runs, it finds the user application in a warmed-up state. From then on, the Slack algorithm runs periodically, always in the background. Finally, when an interrupt triggers the Thermal algorithm again, the first action of the OS is to temporarily disable the hardware that triggers the Slack algorithm. If it so happens that the Slack algorithm was running at the time, this action stops it and automatically sets the Current Set to the Thermal Set.

2.3 Software Interface

The *MaxTemp* and *MaxSlowdn* registers presented above are part of our framework's software interface. In addition, for each energy-management technique, the interface contains a register with the relative priority of activation of the technique (Figure 2). All registers are set by the OS, although *MaxSlowdn* can also be set by the application. With this support, our algorithms can decide what techniques to include at any time in the Current Set.

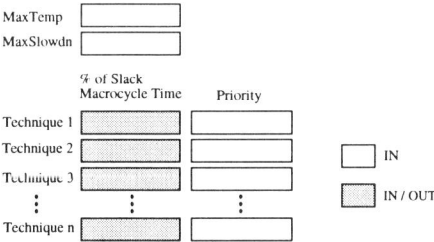

Figure 2: Software interface of our framework.

However, the OS should also have a means to directly overwrite the decisions taken by our default algorithms. This capability can be useful when the OS has specific information on the performance or energy characteristics of the application that is running. Such information may be available from a profile of the application.

One way to extend the interface is to allow the OS to overwrite the decisions of the algorithms as shown in Figure 2. We add one input/output register for each technique in the framework. For a given technique, the register indicates the fraction of the slack macrocycle for which the technique is activated. While these registers are automatically set by the Slack algorithm as it adds techniques to the Current Set, they can also be overwritten by the OS.

2.4 Related Issues

Two important related issues are whether to implement the algorithms in hardware or in software, and whether to make the decisions in a centralized or distributed manner in the chip. We consider these issues next.

2.4.1 Hardware vs Software Implementation

The Thermal algorithm is implemented as an OS interrupt handler. While the Slack algorithm could also be implemented in software, we choose to implement it in hardware. This is in contrast to related algorithms proposed in the literature that exploit system idleness in software [4, 25].

A software implementation of the Slack algorithm would certainly be sufficient if we restricted our work to a certain class of energy-management techniques or to a certain class of applications. Specifically, suppose that we restricted our techniques to those that induce predictable slowdowns like voltage-frequency scaling. In this case, the OS can simply activate the technique for the time duration that will induce the desired slowdown.

Likewise, software might be enough if we restricted the applications to those that, by repeating certain high-level operations, easily tell how fast they are executing. For example, consider video streaming applications. Their speed can be easily monitored by recording the number of frames per unit of time that are being processed. It is easy for the OS to know what is the slowdown caused by a certain energy-management technique by simply checking the new frame rate. There is no need to measure the IPC.

However, we want our Slack algorithm to deliver accurate solutions for all classes of techniques and applications. To see why it requires a hardware implementation, recall that the Slack algorithm repeatedly measures the IPC of the application. While software can support measurements at ms-level intervals, only a hardware solution can support measurements at μs-level intervals. In practice, we need a hardware solution only if the behavior of the application changes significantly at ms-level intervals while staying relatively uniform at μs-level intervals.

We have evidence that μs-level measurements are beneficial in our applications. To understand why, consider a loop. In general, IPC measurements at μs-level intervals will yield fairly uniform values, irrespective of the duration of the loop, as long as 1 μs includes a few iterations. However, IPC measurements at ms-level intervals will yield uniform values only if the loop lasts for many ms. In our applications, much of the code appears to exhibit more uniformity at μs-level intervals than at ms-level intervals. Consequently, we set the interval between measurements (microcycle) to a few μs and, therefore, implement the Slack algorithm in hardware.

2.4.2 Distribution vs Centralization

We now consider how to apply our framework to chips with multiple processor cores. Ideally, we would like to run the framework in a distributed manner. Each processor would have its own framework, running algorithms that read local sensors and make decisions on what techniques to activate locally. This approach is appealing because, potentially, each processor may be running a very different application.

In practice, while some energy-management techniques like those that modify the cache hierarchy can be easily controlled on a per-processor basis, other techniques are best controlled for the whole chip. Consider, for example, voltage-frequency scaling. Using a different voltage and frequency in each processor neighborhood introduces complexity and makes communication between the processors trickier.

One possible alternative is to use per-processor frameworks to run the algorithms and then, after a global synchronization step, make a global decision. However, such an approach is likely to suffer from synchronization overhead.

The approach that we take is to run the algorithm in a centralized manner. Signals from the different processor neighborhoods bring information from the distributed sensors to a central framework module. The module feeds the highest temperature and the sum of all the instructions executed to a centralized algorithm. While this approach requires a more careful timing design, it simplifies the decision-making process.

2.5 Energy Management Techniques

The different energy-management techniques in the framework will target different components of the chip and impact the energy, execution time (delay), and energy-delay product of applications differently. In this section, we select a few, representative techniques to include in the prototype framework that will be evaluated in Section 4.

All the techniques that we select reduce the average power consumption at the expense of slowing down the application. However, while some techniques reduce the total energy consumed in the application run, others do not. Consequently, the techniques in the first group may or may not decrease the energy-delay product, while those in the second group always increase it.

Among the techniques in the first group, we include: sub-banked data caches [9, 30], filter instruction caches [20], voltage-frequency scaling [11, 13], and reduced memory voltage [16]. In each of these cases, when the technique is activated, the system goes from a default configuration to a lower-energy, lower-performance one. These techniques can be used for both the Thermal and Slack algorithms.

Among the techniques in the second group, we include slowing down data cache hits and putting the processor to light sleep. These techniques simply introduce extra delay to reduce the average power. Due to their energy inefficiency, we will try to keep them out of our Thermal and Slack algorithms. However, they may contribute to the thermal crisis support.

We now briefly describe these techniques, while a more detailed description can be found in [36]. The values used for their parameters are listed in Section 3.1. Our framework can be easily extended to include other techniques.

Sub-Banked Data Cache

With cache sub-banking, a cache access activates only part of the cache line selected instead of the whole line [9, 30]. To support sub-banking, the cache is augmented with additional decoding logic and transmission gates. When sub-banking is not activated, this logic adds negligible delay to the cache access time.

When sub-banking is activated, a cache access consumes less energy. This is because the number of activated bit lines and sense amplifiers is reduced. However, the presence of the extra decoding logic and transmission gates tends to increase the cache access time. Consequently, cache hits consume less energy but are slower. The energy consumption and speed of cache misses are unaffected.

Filter Instruction Cache

The on-chip I-memories that supply instructions to the processors in an embedded chip are often designed with high-performance SRAM to ensure that their latency is minimal. They are also large, to hold the whole program. As a result, each access to them, while fast, consumes significant energy.

To address this problem, a small I-cache can be placed between the I-memory and the processor. Accesses to this cache are not faster in number of cycles than accesses to the already fast I-memory. However, they consume much less energy. As a result, this cache works somewhat like a filter cache [20].

If this filter cache is deactivated, all fetches go directly to memory, enabling a fast yet energy-consuming system. If, instead, the cache is activated, hits in the cache take the same time but consume much less energy. Misses, however, force the fetch to go to memory, adding up additional latency and energy consumption. Overall, with the cache activated, the system is likely to be slower but consume less energy.

An alternative design could be to eliminate the filter cache and add sub-banking to the I-memory. In such a design, however, accesses to an I-memory sub-bank could suffer one extra cycle of latency. The result is likely to be a slower system than the one with the filter cache.

Voltage-Frequency Scaling

Reducing both the voltage and the frequency of the chip is a well-known technique [11, 13]. Dynamic energy is proportional to the square of the supply voltage, while dynamic power is proportional to the frequency and to the square of the voltage. To apply this technique, we simply reduce linearly the voltage and frequency of the whole chip to V_{dd_low} and f_{low}. This change works for the linear section of the scaling curve.

Reduced Memory Voltage

We lower the voltage of only the DRAM array to V_{mem_low}. This can be done by changing the reference voltage used in an on-chip voltage converter according to the outputs of a detector [16]. Voltage changes have to be managed carefully because they induce non-linear changes to transistor characteristics. In this technique, to scale down other parameters as we scale down the voltage, we use circuit simulations. In addition, during the low-power mode, we also change the DRAM refresh intervals. The procedure that we use is outlined in [36].

Slowing Down Data Cache Hits

This technique progressively reduces the number of outstanding data loads and stores that a processor can have and, later, increases the latency of cache hits. More specifically, the number of allowed outstanding accesses is progressively halved. Once we reach 1 load and 1 store, we progressively increase the cache hit latency one cycle at a time. When this technique is to be deactivated, we undo these changes in reverse order.

Light Sleep Mode

In this technique, we put the processor in a light sleep mode for a period of time. We do not turn off the PLL, clock distribution, or DLLs to minimize any wake-up penalty. We simply gate the clock at the output of the DLLs. Since, by default, we were already clock-gating all the units not used, this technique cannot save much energy. In fact, because we are keeping the PLL, DLLs, and clock distribution lines on while slowing down the application, this technique ends up increasing the energy consumed. However, it reduces the average power consumed in the system.

3 EVALUATION ENVIRONMENT

We evaluate an implementation of our adaptive framework on top of an advanced chip with multiple superscalar cores and DRAM banks. We use detailed software simulations at the architectural level. The simulations are performed using

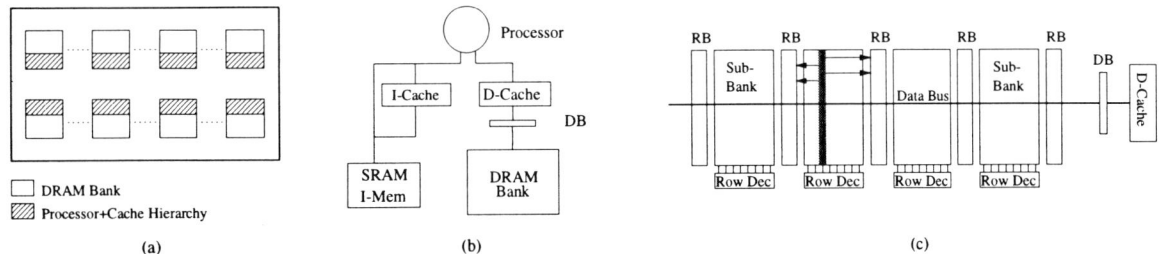

Figure 3: Chip architecture modeled: overview of the chip (a), per-processor memory hierarchy (b), and per-processor DRAM bank organization (c). In the charts, *RB*, *DB*, and *Row Dec* stand for row buffer, data buffer, and row decoder, respectively.

Processor	D-Cache	I-Cache	I-Memory	Data Buffer	Row Buffer	DRAM Sub-Bank
2-issue in-order at 800 MHz	Size: 8 KB	Size: 128 inst.	Size: 8 KB	Number: 1	Number: 5	Number: 4
BR Penalty: 2 cycles	Assoc: 2	Assoc: 1	Line: 4 inst.	Size: 256 b	Size: 1 KB	Num Cols: 4096
Int,Ld/St,FP Units: 2,1,0	Line: 32 B	Line: 4 inst.	RTrip: 1.25 ns	Bus: 256 b	Bus: 256 b	Num Rows: 512
Pending Ld,St: 2,2	RTrip: 1.25 ns	RTrip: 1.25 ns		RTrip: 3.75 ns	RTrip: 7.5 ns	RTrip: 15 ns

Table 1: Parameters for a single memory bank and processor pair. In the table, *BR* and *RTrip* stand for branch and contention-free round-trip latency from the processor, respectively.

Technique	Label	Parameter Value
Sub-banked data cache	*SubBank*	Cache hit if no sub-banking: RTrip = 1.25 ns, E = 222.8 pJ Cache hit if sub-banking: RTrip = 2.50 ns, E = 69.1 pJ
Filter instruction cache	*IFilter*	I-mem access: RTrip = 1.25 ns, E/inst = 51.6 pJ I-cache hit: RTrip = 1.25 ns, E/inst = 15.4 pJ I-cache miss + I-mem access: RTrip = 2.5 ns, E/inst = 67.0 pJ
Voltage-freq. scaling	*VoltFreq*	V_{dd_low} = 1.44 V, f_{low} = 640 MHz, overhead of any scaling = 10 μs
Reduced memory voltage	*MemVolt*	V_{dd} = 1.8 V: RB access (RTrip = 7.5 ns, E = 500.1 pJ), DRAM access (RTrip = 15 ns, E = 3702.2 pJ) V_{dd} = 1.2 V: RB access (RTrip = 7.5 ns, E = 500.1 pJ), DRAM access (RTrip = 21.25 ns, E = 2634.6 pJ)
Slowing D-cache hits	*SloHit*	–
Light sleep mode	*Sleep*	–

Table 2: Values of the parameters used in our energy-management techniques. In the table, *E*, *RB*, and *RTrip* stand for energy, row buffer, and contention-free round-trip latency from the processor, respectively.

a MINT-based [32] execution-driven simulation system [21] that models all the components of the chip, including the superscalar processors. The simulator includes energy consumption models. In the following, we describe the architecture modeled, how we estimate the energy consumed, the applications executed, and the metrics used.

3.1 Architecture Modeled

As an example of an advanced chip, we model a processor-in-memory chip with 64 simple processors cycling at 800 MHz and 64 Mbytes of DRAM. The target technology is IBM's 0.18 μm Blue Logic SA-27E ASIC [12] with some expected improvements in DRAM density [36]. The default voltage is 1.8 V.

The chip is modeled after a *FlexRAM* chip [19]. Processors are 2-issue wide and statically scheduled. Each processor is associated with a 1-Mbyte DRAM bank. A processor can directly access its own DRAM bank as well as the DRAM of its left and right neighbors. Such support allows communication between the processors, effectively connecting them in a ring. In addition, as in *FlexRAM*, the chip contains an on-chip controller that executes the serial sections of the application, including initialization, broadcast, and reduction operations [19]. The controller's contribution to the execution of our applications constitutes on average only 8% of the time, and is mostly limited to the initialization and ending parts of the application. For these reasons and because most chip resources are very underutilized when the controller runs, we do not include the controller's contribution in our evaluation.

Figure 3 shows the architecture of the chip. In the figure, Chart (a) gives an overview of the chip, while Chart (b) shows the memory hierarchy of each processor in the chip and Chart (c) shows the organization of each DRAM bank into sub-banks. Table 1 shows the most important architectural parameters for a single memory bank and processor pair.

Table 2 shows the values for the parameters of the energy-management techniques included in our framework. The energy values used will be justified in the next section. The values of some other framework parameters are as follows. Changing the memory voltage with *MemVolt* is assumed to have negligible overhead. Both the thermal and the slack macrocycles are set to 1 ms, while the microcycle is set to 1 μs. To avoid instability in the Thermal algorithm, we set a different *MinTemp* for each technique, as shown in Section 3.4. Finally, every time that we execute the Thermal algorithm, we charge 200 cycles to account for the overhead of the execution in the OS.

3.2 Estimating the Energy Consumed

To estimate the energy consumed in the chip, we have applied scaling-down theory to data on existing devices reported in the literature, as well as used several techniques and formulas reported in the literature [3, 30, 18, 24, 34, 35]. A detailed discussion of the methods that we have followed can be found in [36]. In this section, we give an overview of how we estimate the energy consumed in the processor cores, memory hierarchies, and clocks. We also discuss how we validated the models.

Processor Cores

Each core is a 32-bit 2-issue processor with a DLX-like pipeline. It supports a simplified version of the MIPS ISA with only 28 16-bit instructions [19]. We take the data from [35] and, by applying general scaling theory and considering technology trends, we estimate the average energy consumed in the register file, branch unit, ALU, and the other modules of the processor. Then, we can estimate the energy consumed by each type of instruction by adding up the energy of all the modules used by that particular instruction type. We assume perfect clock gating inside the processor code. With this approach, for example, we estimate that an add, a branch, and a multiply instruction consume an average of 56.1, 34.8, and 251.2 pJ, respectively.

Memory Hierarchies

To compute the energy consumed in the memory hierarchy, we use popular models [30, 18]. We classify memory hierarchy accesses based on what level of the hierarchy they reach, and depending on whether they are reads, writes, or dirty line displacements. Then, we compute the average energy consumed by one access of each class. This is done by dividing the access into simple operations. For example, a read that hits in the row buffer is divided into a cache tag check, a read hit in the row buffer, and a line fill into the cache. Finally, to compute the overall energy in the memory hierarchy, we multiply the number of accesses of each class times the corresponding energy per access in the class, and then accumulate the contribution of all classes. As an example, Table 3 shows the average energy consumed by a read and a write access to different levels of the hierarchy.

Level of the Hierarchy	Rd Energy (pJ)	Wr Energy (pJ)
D-cache	222.8	246.3
I-mem (per instr)	51.6	56.8
Row buffer	500.1	2740.6
DRAM bank	3702.2	3286.2

Table 3: Average energy consumption per access.

Clocks & Other

The clocking system includes 1 main PLL and 16 distributed local DLLs [29]. The clock network is laid out in the chip using an H-tree structure to minimize skew. To estimate the overall energy of the clocking system, we estimate and add the contributions of several components, namely PLL, DLLs, buffers, and distribution lines. Such contributions are estimated based on [3] and on capacitance models. Overall, the estimated average energy per cycle is 957.5 pJ. This figure does not include the energy for the clock inside the processor cores. The latter is included in the computation for the cores. Further details can be found in [36].

Validation

We validate our energy estimates with several experiments. We report on two of them here. In the first validation, we examine our cache model. We compare our energy estimates to those generated with the CACTI v2 models [34]. Since CACTI uses a relatively old sense amplifier model, we change it to a more aggressive one. The comparison shows that our estimates of energy consumption in the data cache and CACTI's are only 9% different [36].

In a second validation, we focus on the relative energy consumption of the I-cache, D-cache, clock, and processor core. Such a relative breakdown of energy for the Strong ARM processor is available from [24]. We compute the corresponding estimates for one of our processors plus its associated caches and share of the clock. While there are some differences between the two architectures, getting a similar breakdown is reassuring. The comparison shows that the contribution of each of the components does not differ by more than an absolute 6% between the two systems [36].

3.3 Applications Executed

For the experiments, we use 6 applications that are suitable to the integer-based processor-in-memory chip considered: they access a large memory size, are very parallel, and are integer based. They come from several industrial sources. We have parallelized each application into 64 threads by hand.

Table 4 lists the applications and their characteristics. They include the domains of data mining, neural networks, protein matching, multimedia, and image compression. Each application runs for several billions of instructions. Appendix A gives more information on each application.

3.4 Metrics Used

We characterize an application run with four metrics: performance (measured with total execution time, also called *delay*), average power consumption, total energy consumption, and product of energy times execution time (energy-delay product [10]). We will strive for a low energy-delay product, since it implies a good balance between high speed and low energy consumption.

In some experiments, we need to estimate chip temperature. However, our models only use energy and power metrics. We currently do not have a thermal model that, taking into account the chip package and cooling support, translates sustained power dissipation into chip temperature.

It is known, however, that heat transfers occur at the ms level [31]. As a result, it has been suggested to use the average power dissipated over many cycles as a proxy for temperature [5]. We follow this approach and use a metric called $Power^*$ as a proxy for chip temperature. At a given time, $Power^*$ is 0.75 times the average power consumed by the chip in the last millisecond plus 0.25 times the value of $Power^*$ a millisecond ago. While clearly not perfect, this recursive definition tries to approximate the behavior of temperature. Using this metric, the proxy for *MinTemp* for *VoltFreq*, *SubBank*, and *IFilter* is set to 45%, 75%, and 78%, respectively of the proxy for *MaxTemp*.

4 EVALUATING THE FRAMEWORK

To assess our DEETM framework, we evaluate three issues: the management of multiple energy-management techniques (Section 4.1), the Thermal algorithm (Section 4.2), and the Slack algorithm (Section 4.3).

4.1 Technique Analysis & Comparison

Given a DEETM framework with multiple techniques, the first question to ask is what combination of techniques should it apply and in what order. We now answer this question for our framework.

Comparing Individual Techniques

We start by comparing the individual techniques with the following experiment for each application. We execute the application without activating any technique and record the average power dissipated P_{orig} (last column of Table 4). Then, for each technique, we perform four runs dynamically activating the technique with different intensities. The inten-

Appl.	What It Does	Problem Size	D-Cache Hit Rate	Average Power(W)
GTree	Data mining: tree generation	5 MB database, 77.9 K records, 29 attributes/record	0.507	10.2
DTree	Data mining: tree deployment	1.5 MB database, 17.4 K records, 29 attributes/record	0.986	10.8
BSOM	BSOM neural network	2 K entries, 104 dimensions, 2 iterations, 16-node network, 832 KB database	0.947	15.5
BLAST	BLAST protein matching	12.3 K sequences, 4.1 MB total, 1 query of 317 bytes	0.969	8.7
Mpeg	MPEG-2 motion estimation	1 1024x256-pixel frame plus a reference frame. Total 512 KB	0.999	11.3
FIC	Fractal image compressor	1 512x512-pixel image, 4 512x512-pixel internal data structure. Total 2 MB	0.978	6.1

Table 4: Applications executed.

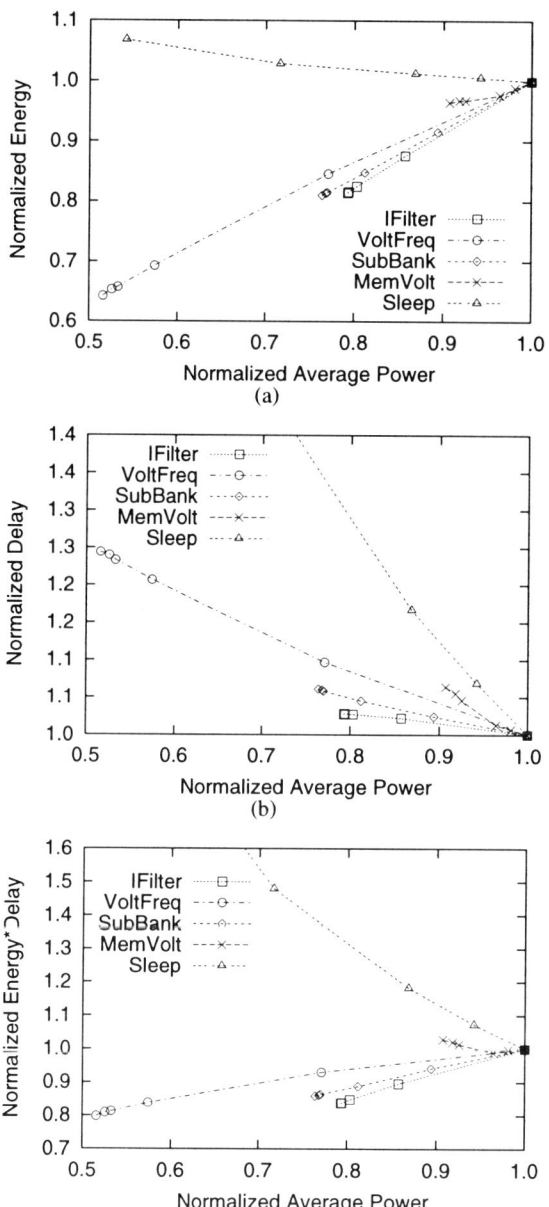

Figure 4: Impact of dynamically applying each individual energy-management technique: total energy consumed by the applications (a), their execution time (b), and their energy-delay product (c). The data is normalized to a run with no active technique and then averaged out across all applications.

sity is regulated with a power threshold: if the power in the last microcycle was over the threshold, the technique gets activated; the technique is deactivated when the power in the last microcycle was such that the technique could be deactivated without going over the threshold again. We set the thresholds to $1.2 \times P_{orig}$, $1.0 \times P_{orig}$, $0.8 \times P_{orig}$, and $0.6 \times P_{orig}$. Finally, we perform an experiment activating the technique for the whole run.

Figure 4 shows the results. The results of each run have been normalized to the run with no active technique for the same application, and then averaged out across all applications. The figure shows the resulting average power consumed in the run (X axes) against the total energy consumed (Chart (a)), execution time (Chart (b), where execution time is labeled *Delay*), and energy-delay product (Chart (c)). Since *SloHit* has a behavior very similar to *Sleep*, we do not show *SloHit* to simplify the charts.

The figure shows that the behavior of *Sleep* is different from the others as the average power decreases. *Sleep* does not reduce the energy (Chart (a)), substantially slows down the applications (Chart (b)) and, as a result, increases the energy-delay product significantly (Chart (c)). Consequently, due to its inefficiency, we only use it as the last resort in a thermal crisis.

The other four techniques (*IFilter*, *SubBank*, *VoltFreq*, and *MemVolt*) decrease the energy consumed by the chip (Chart (a)) and, while they still slow down the application (Chart (b)), they manage to reduce the energy-delay product or keep it roughly constant (Chart (c)). They differ significantly, however, in the slope of their curves and in the maximum power reduction that they can deliver. The maximum reduction is delivered when they are applied statically. This situation corresponds to the leftmost point of each curve.

To compare these four techniques to each other, we examine Chart (c). Recall that we want to minimize the energy-delay products. Under this requirement, the chart tells us what is the best technique to apply individually, and how to rank the techniques in case we want to apply them in a combined manner.

If we want to apply a single technique, we should choose the one that, for the desired average power reduction, delivers the lowest energy-delay product. For example, for power reductions that are less than 20%, *IFilter* is the best. *SubBank* is the best if we want reductions between 20 and 25%, while *VoltFreq* is the best for reductions larger than 25%. From this data, we can see that *IFilter* and *SubBank* are good but limited. Since their scope is only memory system accesses, they deliver modest power reductions.

If, instead, we want to rank the techniques for a possible combined application of them, what matters is not the absolute power reduction but the slope of the curves. Specifically, we approximate each curve with a straight line and record the slope of the line. The techniques with the highest positive slopes should be given the highest priority. Consequently, in our framework, the order of application of the techniques, irrespective of the power reduction desired, should be *IFilter*, then *SubBank*, then *VoltFreq*, and so on.

Note that, for our techniques, the shape of the curves makes it possible to reasonably approximate each curve with a single straight line. This may not be true, however, in other scenarios, where we would need different straight lines in different segments of a given curve. In this case, the ranking of techniques would not be as straightforward: it would depend on the power reduction desired.

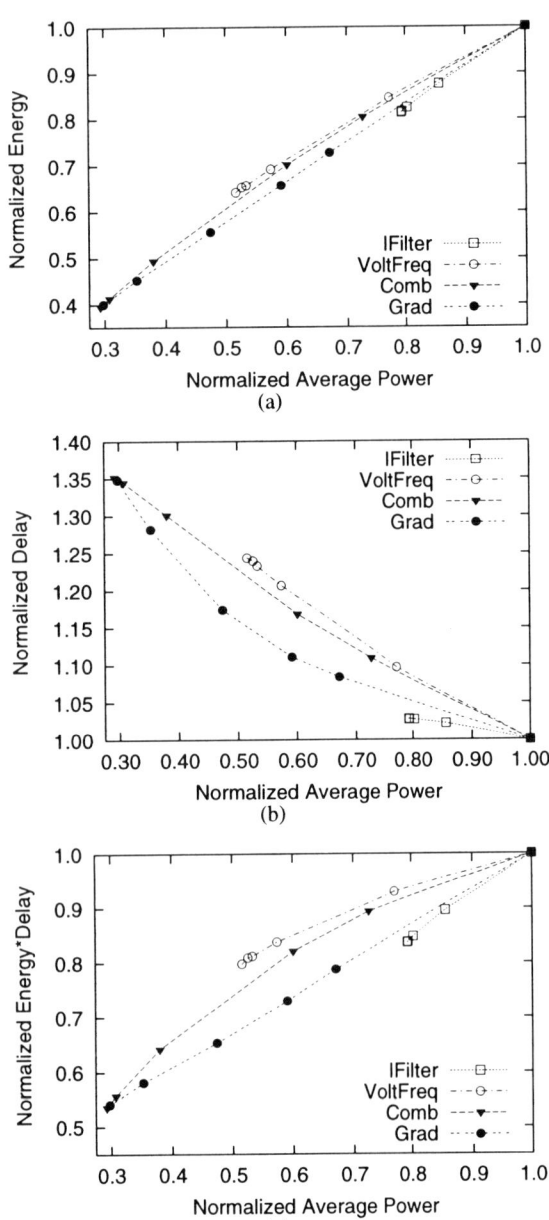

Figure 5: Impact of dynamically applying a combination of energy-management techniques: total energy consumed by the applications (a), their execution time (b), and their energy-delay product (c). The data is organized as in Figure 4.

Another complication occurs if the slope of a curve changes when the technique is combined with other techniques. While we have observed this effect in our framework, it does not change the ranking of techniques listed above.

Finally, we note that *MemVolt* reduces neither the average power much nor the energy-delay product. It is, therefore, unattractive. Its scope for impact is limited to applications with many cache misses. Unfortunately, even in this case, we find that it works poorly because the slower DRAM becomes a contention bottleneck that slows down the application (Chart (b)).

Applying Combined Schemes

To see the potential of our framework, we combine the three most effective techniques, namely *IFilter*, *SubBank*, and *VoltFreq*, into a single scheme. We consider two different schemes: *Comb* activates and deactivates the three techniques simultaneously, while *Grad* activates and deactivates them gradually. *Grad* uses the ranking selected before: it activates *IFilter* first; if more power or energy reduction is needed, it activates *SubBank*; if more is needed, it activates *VoltFreq*. When the techniques must be deactivated, it follows the reverse order.

Figure 5 shows the results of repeating the experiments of Figure 4 for *Comb* and *Grad*. For reference purposes, the figure also includes the curves for *VoltFreq* and *IFilter* from Figure 4. Note, however, that the axes have been expanded relative to Figure 4.

We can see from Figure 5 that, for modest power reductions, the effectiveness of *Comb* is between that of *VoltFreq* and *IFilter*. Specifically, Chart (c) shows that, for a given power reduction, the energy-delay product of *Comb* is between that of *VoltFreq* and *IFilter*. Consequently, *Comb* works well. In addition, *Comb* can deliver much higher power reductions than the individual techniques: if *Comb* is statically applied, it can reduce the average power by up to 70%. As a result, the final energy-delay product obtained in Chart (c) is also much lower than for the individual techniques.

As can be seen in the figure, however, *Grad* is better. Chart (c) shows that, for modest power reductions, this scheme delivers energy-delay products that are nearly as low as *IFilter*, the best of the three techniques. This is because, for this range of reductions, *Grad* is largely *IFilter*. When larger reductions are desired, *Grad* starts using the less optimal techniques. Finally, as we approach large reductions, it gets closer to *Comb*. In all cases except static application, however, *Grad* has a lower energy-delay product than *Comb* (Chart (c)).

These results form the rationale behind our choice of Thermal and Slack algorithms in Section 2.2: a gradual, priority-ordered application of techniques that reduce the energy-delay product. Consequently, we implement the Slack and Thermal algorithms with *Grad*. In addition, as part of the Thermal algorithm, we keep one additional technique ready for activation in case of a thermal crisis. Such a technique, which must be able to reduce the average power consumed as much as needed, is chosen to be *Sleep*.

Variation Across Applications

Finally, we note that, although different applications behave differently, the schemes chosen for our adaptive framework work well across all applications. For lack of space, we only briefly discuss the two individual applications that diverge the most from the average: *GTree* and *DTree*. *GTree* has a high data cache miss rate (Table 4), which causes *SubBank* to have relatively less impact. *DTree*, on the other hand, has relatively more I-cache misses, which causes *IFilter* to be less effective. Overall, however, it can be shown that *Grad* is very effective: it reduces the energy-delay product significantly, while enabling large reductions in average power.

4.2 Evaluating the Thermal Algorithm

The goal of the Thermal algorithm is to keep the temperature of the chip lower than *MaxTemp*, while minimizing any resulting application slowdown. In addition, under no condition should the temperature surpass *CrisisTemp*. As indicated before, we use *Grad* and, if *CrisisTemp* is reached, we activate *Sleep*. We call the resulting scheme *Grad+Sleep*.

To show that *Grad+Sleep* is effective, we demonstrate that, given different *MaxTemp* temperature limits, it effectively keeps the chip temperature below *MaxTemp* practically all the time, while slowing down the execution only modestly. Recall that, as stated in Section 3.4, we use $Power^*$ as a proxy for temperature.

In Figure 6, we show the results of applying *Grad+Sleep* under different $Power^*$ limits. These limits are proxies for *MaxTemp*. For each application, the limits considered are $1.2 \times P_{orig}$, $1.0 \times P_{orig}$, $0.8 \times P_{orig}$, and $0.6 \times P_{orig}$, where P_{orig} is the original average power of the application (last column of Table 4). To get an idea of the absolute values of these limits, if we average them out across all the applications, we get 12.5, 10.4, 8.3, and 6.3 W, respectively. The crisis $Power^*$ is set sufficiently high such that it is never reached. As usual, the data is normalized to the original conditions of the application and then averaged out across all applications.

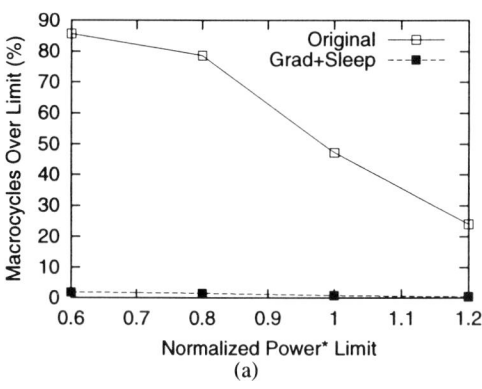

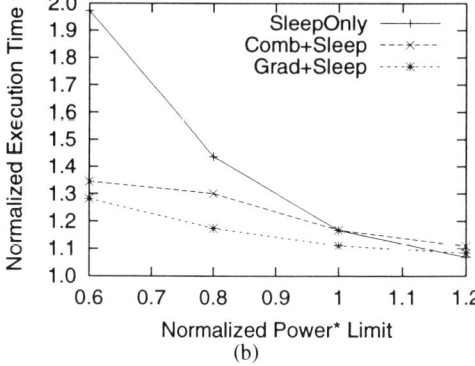

Figure 6: Impact of enforcing different $Power^*$ limits in the chip: fraction of thermal macrocycles over the $Power^*$ limit (a) and resulting execution time of the applications (b). These limits are proxies for *MaxTemp*.

Figure 6-(a) shows the fraction of thermal macrocycles where $Power^*$ is above the limit before we activate our framework (*Original*) and after (*Grad+Sleep*). The chart shows that, irrespective of how low we set the limit to, our framework keeps $Power^*$ below it for practically all the time. This is true even after setting the limit to 0.6 times the average power in the chip before activating the framework, which is the leftmost point of the chart. Such a limit places 85% of the *Original* macrocycles over the limit.

Figure 6-(b) shows the resulting execution time of the applications after activating the framework. If we focus on the *Grad+Sleep* curve, we see that, for modest limits, the scheme induces minimal slowdowns. For example, after setting the limit to 1.2 times the original average power, our framework only slows down the applications, on average, by 8%.

Overall, from the previous two discussions, we see that the goal of the Thermal algorithm is realized. For comparison purposes, however, Figure 6-(b) also shows the impact of using less efficient schemes. *Comb+Sleep* uses *Comb* instead of *Grad*. *SleepOnly* simply uses the *Sleep* technique when $Power^*$ surpasses the limit. More specifically, when a thermal macrocycle records a $Power^*$ higher than the limit, the fraction of non-sleeping cycles in the next macrocycle is decreased proportionally to how much $Power^*$ was over the limit. This scheme is, therefore, self-regulating. From the figure, we see that such schemes induce higher slowdowns than *Grad+Sleep*. *SleepOnly* is especially inefficient for relatively low $Power^*$ limits. However, it works well for the highest limit because it is being applied in a fine-grained manner.

4.3 Evaluating the Slack Algorithm

The goal of the Slack algorithm is to save as much energy as possible without extending the execution of the application beyond a given tolerable slack. As indicated before, we implement the algorithm with *Grad*. To show that our framework is effective, we demonstrate that, given different slack sizes, *Grad* delivers large energy savings without slowing down the job noticeably more than tolerable.

In Figure 7, the framework is tested with different slack sizes, specified as a percentage of the original execution time of the application. As usual, the data is normalized to the original conditions of the application and then averaged out across all applications.

Figure 7-(a) shows the resulting energy consumed by the applications for different slack sizes. The chart shows that *Grad* delivers large energy savings by exploiting even small slacks. For example, if the applications are allowed to exploit a 10% slack, they consume only 60% of the original energy; if they are given a 30% slack, they consume only 40%.

To put the effectiveness of *Grad* in perspective, the chart also shows the curves for $E \times D = constant$ and $E \times D^2 = constant$. As a reference, the voltage-frequency scaling technique [11, 13] often falls in between the $E \times D$ and $E \times D^2$ curves. Indeed, if the scaling of voltage and frequency is linear, since energy is proportional to the square of the voltage and delay is inversely proportional to the frequency, $E \times D^2$ remains constant. In practice, the scaling deviates from linear behavior and we move toward the $E \times D$ curve. Overall, from the distance between these curves and *Grad*, we can see that our framework is very effective, especially with small slacks.

Figure 7-(b) shows the fraction of the tolerable slack that is used up by our framework. We see that, for modest-sized slacks, *Grad* tends to deviate little from using the maximum tolerable slack. Any under- or over-utilization is limited to about 2% of the slack. As the slack increases over 35% of the execution time, the applications cannot use it all, even when all the techniques in *Grad* are in full operation. As a result, part of the slack is wasted. Overall, we see that the goal of the Slack algorithm is realized: *Grad* delivers large energy reductions by exploiting even small slacks.

To gain insight into any possible improvements over *Grad*, Figures 7-(a) and 7-(b) also show the behavior of an ideal scheme that we call *Oracle*. At any given microcycle in the execution, *Oracle* applies the combination of *IFilter*, *SubBank*, and *VoltFreq* that best furthers the goal of the Slack algorithm. Since *Oracle* is based on perfect knowledge of the future, it should have, for a given slack, the lowest energy curve in Chart (a). In some cases, however, *Grad* reduces the energy slightly more than *Oracle*. This is because, due to imperfect prediction of the future, *Grad* sometimes goes slightly over the tolerable slack in Chart (b). Overall, however, the charts show that there is not much difference between the *Oracle* and *Grad* curves, which suggests that *Grad* is very competitive.

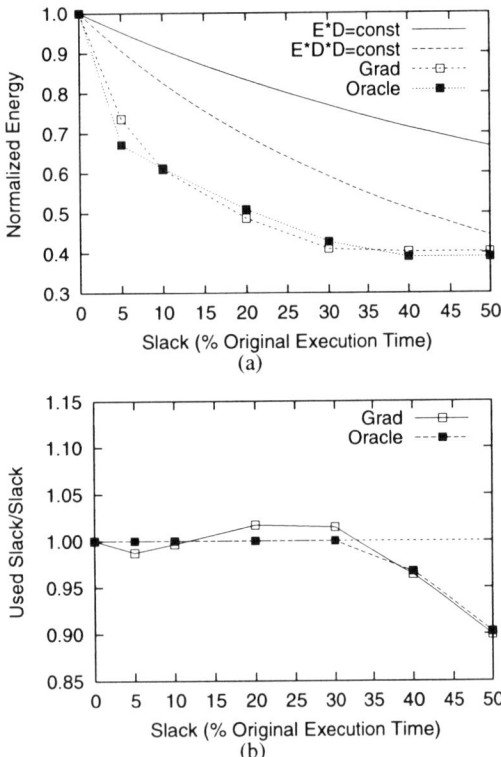

Figure 7: Effect of exploiting different execution slacks: resulting energy consumed by the applications (a) and fraction of the slack that is used up (b).

5 RELATED WORK

Of all the techniques and systems listed in Section 1, the work most related to ours is the one on dynamic systems for chip-level energy management. These systems can be classified into three groups. The first one targets temperature control, for example through context switching to jobs that consume less power [27] or through speculation control [5]. The second group targets energy efficiency without compromising performance, for instance through speculation control [23] or through reconfigurability [1]. A final group targets energy efficiency by exploiting slack and, therefore, slowing down the system. This is done, for example, through voltage and frequency scaling [25] or through switching to less aggressive instruction issue and speculation support [8]. Our work is different in two ways: we target both energy efficiency and temperature control, and we combine many techniques in a unified dynamic framework.

Recently, dynamic application of voltage and frequency scaling or various sleep modes have become popular among microprocessors [11, 13].

A related approach is that of ACPI (Advanced Configuration and Power Interface), an open industry specification that defines an interface for the OS to activate low-power modes [14]. Our work differs from ACPI in two ways. First, in ACPI, any decision and control of power modes is done by the OS. In our framework, the decision and control is best done with a combination of software and hardware, which enables finer-grained energy management. Second, current ACPI releases are only concerned with various sleeping modes, while we combine techniques that trade energy for performance.

ACPI and other OS-driven approaches have been used at the system level to save energy dynamically. For example, it is feasible to save energy by dynamically shutting down unused modules of the system like hard disks or the LAN [4]. Alternatively, the savings can come from dynamically reducing the quality of service to the application [7].

6 CONCLUSIONS AND FUTURE WORK

To address the problem of high energy consumption in current and upcoming chips, several schemes for dynamic energy management have recently been proposed. However, such schemes are still relatively limited and, in addition, tend to tackle only one of the two aspects of energy management: either energy efficiency or temperature control. To address these limitations, this paper has proposed a framework for Dynamic Energy Efficiency and Temperature Management (DEETM). The framework addresses the two aspects of energy management in a unified form. In addition, it combines a suite of energy-management techniques that can be activated individually or in groups according to a given policy.

The evaluation has shown that our framework is very effective, especially when the tolerable slowdowns and temperature limits are modest. In these scenarios, dynamic application of the most fitting techniques in the suite is most cost-effective: temperature limits are enforced with small slowdowns and large energy savings are delivered by exploiting small slacks. For example, the framework delivers a 40% energy reduction with only a 10% application slowdown. Overall, we feel that it makes sense for future advanced chips to include a DEETM framework like ours that combines multiple techniques.

As part of our ongoing work, we are trying to improve our DEETM framework by adding more techniques to it. We can then quantify the complementarity of and the overlap between different techniques.

Another approach that we are exploring is the potential of profiling. We can profile an application and, depending on what are its main energy and performance bottlenecks, tailor the activation of the techniques. Experience with the *Oracle* scheme in Section 4.3, however, suggests that little more can be done for the techniques and applications considered. However, other techniques and applications may behave differently. Finally, we are examining how to tailor the framework for different classes of chips, namely high-end microprocessors, chip multiprocessors, and different types of systems on a chip.

REFERENCES

[1] D. Albonesi. Dynamic IPC/Clock Rate Optimization. In *International Symposium on Computer Architecture*, pages 282–292, July 1998.

[2] S. Altschul, W. Gish, W. Miller, E. Myers, and D. Lipman. Basic Local Alignment Search Tool. *Journal of Molecular Biology*, 215(3):403–410, October 1990.

[3] J. Alvarez et al. A Wide-Bandwidth Low-Voltage PLL for PowerPC Microprocessors. *IEEE Journal on Solid-State Circuits*, 30(4):383–391, April 1995.

[4] L. Benini et al. Monitoring System Activity for OS-Directed Dynamic Power Management. In *International Symposium on Low Power Electronics and Design*, pages 185–190, August 1998.

[5] D. Brooks and M. Martonosi. Adaptive Thermal Management for High-Performance Microprocessors. In *Workshop on Complexity Effective Design*, June 2000.

[6] Y. Fisher. *Fractal Image Compression: Theory and Application*. Springer Verlag, 1995.

[7] J. Flinn and M. Satyanarayanan. Energy-Aware Adaptation for Mobile Applications. In *Symposium on Operating Systems Principles*, pages 48–63, December 1999.

[8] S. Ghiasi, J. Casmira, and D. Grunwald. Using IPC Variation in Workloads with Externally Specified Rates to Reduce Power Consumption. In *Workshop on Complexity-Effective Design*, June 2000.

[9] K. Ghose and M. Kamble. Reducing Power in Superscalar Processor Caches Using Subbanking, Multiple Line Buffers and Bit-Line Segmentation. In *International Symposium on Low Power Electronics and Design*, pages 70–75, August 1999.

[10] R. Gonzalez and M. Horowitz. Energy Dissipation In General Purpose Microprocessors. *IEEE Journal on Solid-State Circuits*, 31(4):1277–1284, September 1996.

[11] T. Halfhill. Transmeta Breaks x86 Low-Power Barrier. *Microprocessor Report*, 14(2):1,9–18, February 2000.

[12] IBM Microelectronics. Blue Logic SA-27E ASIC. http://www.chips.ibm. com/news/1999/sa27e/sa27e.pdf, February 1999.

[13] Intel. *Pentium III Processor Mobile Module: Mobile Module Connector 2 (MMC-2) Featuring Intel SpeedStep Technology*, 2000.

[14] Intel, Microsoft and Toshiba. *Advanced Configuration and Power Interface Specification*, 1999.

[15] K. Itoh. Low Power Memory Design. In *Low Power Design Methodologies*, pages 201–251. Kluwer Academic Publisher, 1996.

[16] K. Itoh et al. An Experimental 1Mb DRAM with On-Chip Voltage Limiter. In *ISSCC Digest of Technical Papers*, pages 84–85, February 1981.

[17] T. Juan, T. Lang, and J. Navarro. Reducing TLB Power Requirements. In *International Symposium on Low Power Electronics and Design*, pages 196–201, August 1997.

[18] M. Kamble and K. Ghose. Analytical Energy Dissipation Models for Low Power Caches. In *International Symposium on Low Power Electronics and Design*, pages 143–148, August 1997.

[19] Y. Kang, W. Huang, S. Yoo, D. Keen, Z. Ge, V. Lam, P. Pattnaik, and J. Torrellas. FlexRAM: Toward an Advanced Intelligent Memory System. In *International Conference on Computer Design*, pages 192–201, October 1999.

[20] J. Kin, M. Gupta, and W. Mangione-Smith. The Filter Cache: An Energy Efficient Memory Structure. *International Symposium on Microarchitecture*, pages 184–193, December 1997.

[21] V. Krishnan and J. Torrellas. An Execution-Driven Framework for Fast and Accurate Simulation of Superscalar Processors. In *International Conference on Parallel Architectures and Compilation Techniques*, pages 286–293, October 1998.

[22] R. Lawrence, G. Almasi, and H. Rushmeier. A Scalable Parallel Algorithm for Self-Organizing Maps with Applications to Sparse Data Mining Problems. Technical report, IBM, January 1998.

[23] S. Manne, A. Klauser, and D. Grunwald. Pipeline Gating: Speculation Control for Energy Reduction. In *International Symposium on Computer Architecture*, pages 132–141, July 1998.

[24] J. Montanaro et al. A 160-MHz, 32-b, 0.5-W CMOS RISC Microprocessor. *IEEE Journal Solid State Circuits*, 31(11):1703–1714, November 1996.

[25] T. Pering, T. Burd, and R. Brodersen. The Simulation and Evaluation of Dynamic Voltage Scaling Algorithms. In *International Symposium on Low Power Electronics and Design*, pages 76–81, August 1998.

[26] J. Quinlan. *C4.5 - Programs for Machine Learning*. Morgan Kaufmann, 1993.

[27] E. Rohou and M. Smith. Dynamically Managing Processor Temperature and Power. In *2nd Workshop on Feedback-Directed Optimization*, November 1999.

[28] H. Sanchez et al. Thermal Management System for High Performance PowerPC Microprocessor. In *IEEE Computer Society International Conference*, pages 325–330, February 1997.

[29] S. Sidiropoulos and M. Horowitz. A Semidigital Dual Delay-Locked Loop. *IEEE Journal on Solid-state Circuits*, 32(11):1683–1692, November 1997.

[30] C-L. Su and A. Despain. Cache Design Trade-offs for Power and Performance Optimization: A Case Study. In *International Symposium on Low Power Electronics and Design*, pages 63–68, April 1995.

[31] C-H. Tsai. *Temperature-Aware VLSI Design and Analysis*. PhD thesis, Department of Electrical and Computer Engineering, University of Illinois at Urbana-Champaign, May 2000.

[32] J. Veenstra and R. Fowler. MINT: A Front End for Efficient Simulation of Shared-Memory Multiprocessors. In *Second International Workshop on Modeling, Analysis, and Simulation of Computer and Telecommunication Systems*, pages 201–207, January 1994.

[33] N. Vijaykrishnan et al. Energy-Driven Integrated Hardware-Software Optimizations Using SimplePower. In *International Symposium on Computer Architecture*, pages 95–106, June 2000.

[34] S. Wilton and N. Jouppi. CACTI: An Enhanced Cache Access and Cycle Time Model. *IEEE Journal on Solid-State Circuits*, 31(5):677–688, May 1996.

[35] N. Yeung. et al. The Design of a 55SPECint92 RISC Processor under 2W. *ISSCC Digest of Technical Papers*, pages 206–207, February 1994.

[36] S-M. Yoo, J. Renau, M. Huang, and J. Torrellas. FlexRAM Architecture Design Parameters. Technical Report CSRD-1584, Department of Computer Science, University of Illinois at Urbana-Champaign, October 2000. http://iacoma.cs.uiuc.edu/flexram/publications.html.

APPENDIX A: APPLICATIONS USED

This appendix describes the applications used. In the following, we use P.Mem to refer to the on-chip controller in the FlexRAM chip that executes the serial sections of the applications. More information on the applications can be found in [19].

GTree is a data mining application that generates a decision tree given a collection of records that we want to classify [26]. The records are distributed across the processors. The P.Mem decides what attributes to use to split the tree and tells the processors what branch they should examine. The processors process their records.

DTree uses the tree generated in *GTree* to classify a database of records [26]. Each processor has a copy of the decision tree and a portion of the database. Each processor processes its local records sequentially. At the end of the execution, the results are accumulated by P.Mem.

BSOM is a neural network that classifies data [22]. Each processor processes a portion of the input. Then, all processors synchronize, a summary of the partial results is combined and re-distributed, and the process begins again. While the original application used floating point, we have converted the application into fixed point to run on our simulated chip.

BLAST is a protein matching application [2]. The goal is to match an amino acid sequence sample against a large database of proteins. Each processor keeps a portion of the database and tries to match the sample against it. Finally, P.Mem gathers the results.

Mpeg performs MPEG-2 motion estimation. The reference image and the working image are distributed across the processors. Each 8x8 block in the working image is compared against the reference image.

FIC is a fractal image compression application that encodes an image using a scheme with a quad tree partition [6]. Each processor has a portion of the image and some calculated characteristics, and performs a local transformation to its portion of the image. The application may have significant load imbalance.

Dynamic Zero Compression for Cache Energy Reduction

Luis Villa,[*] Michael Zhang, and Krste Asanović
MIT Laboratory for Computer Science, Cambridge, MA 02139
{luisv | rzhang | krste}@lcs.mit.edu

Abstract

Dynamic Zero Compression reduces the energy required for cache accesses by only writing and reading a single bit for every zero-valued byte. This energy-conscious compression is invisible to software and is handled with additional circuitry embedded inside the cache RAM arrays and the CPU. The additional circuitry imposes a cache area overhead of 9% and a read latency overhead of around two FO4 gate delays. Simulation results show that we can reduce total data cache energy by around 26% and instruction cache energy by around 10% for SPECint95 and Media-Bench benchmarks. We also describe the use of an instruction recoding technique that increases instruction cache energy savings to 18%.

1 Introduction

Cache accesses consume a significant fraction (30–60% [7, 11]) of total energy dissipation in modern processors. A large portion of cache energy is dissipated in driving the bitlines, which are heavily loaded with multiple storage cells, and so most cache energy reduction techniques have concentrated on reducing bitline energy. One approach is to reduce the bitline capacitance switched on each access, by using a combination of sub-banking, segmented bitlines, and hierarchical bitlines [6]. Another complementary approach is to limit the voltage swing on the bitlines during a read access by pulsing word line drivers [1, 5].

In this paper, we introduce a novel technique for cache energy reduction, *dynamic zero compression* (DZC), which exploits the prevalence of zero bytes stored in the cache. DZC adds an additional *zero indicator bit* (ZIB) to each cache byte that indicates whether the byte contains all zero bits. On a read access, we prevent bitline discharge by disabling the local word line for each byte when the ZIB is set. If the ZIB is clear, the eight data bits are read normally. On a write access, only the ZIB is written if the byte is zero, otherwise both the data bits and the ZIB are written. The ZIB is also used to disable bus drivers connecting the CPU datapath with the cache sub-banks to further reduce cache access energy.

Our initial simulations revealed that over 70% of the bits that are read from or written to the data cache are zeros. Previous work has shown how to exploit this asymmetry in the distribution of ones and zeros to reduce energy for storage arrays with single-ended read bitlines. A single-ended read bitline is typically precharged high and conditionally discharged based on the stored data bit. Register files are often built with single-ended read ports to reduce total wiring cost. The register file bit cell can be modified so that reading a zero on any port causes no bitline discharge, resulting in a savings of 27% of total register file energy [10]. Chang et. al. [12] describe another scheme for ROMs and small RAMs with single-ended bitlines that conditionally inverts stored words to reduce the total number of bitline discharges, and achieves an average of 30% energy reduction for a RAM array.

For larger SRAM array designs, differential bitlines are preferred over single-ended bitlines because they provide greater noise immunity and faster sensing. In a differential design, one of the two bitlines must be discharged for each access regardless of the stored data value. The energy penalty for reads can be reduced by employing a pulsed-word-line technique to turn off the word lines when a sufficient voltage differential has developed on the bitlines [1, 5]. Writes to an SRAM are also usually performed differentially but typically require a full voltage swing on the bitlines and hence consume considerably more energy than low-voltage-swing reads.

Our DZC technique allows us to retain the benefit of differential bitlines while taking advantage of the asymmetric distribution of 1's and 0's to reduce energy dissipation. Instead of treating each bit independently, we group multiple bits together and attach an extra zero indicator bit to indicate when the whole bit field is zero. This scheme also allows us to save energy on write accesses as well as reads since we only write the ZIB rather than the whole bit field. We similarly make use of the ZIB to reduce energy when driving the data bus between the processor and cache.

Several other techniques have been proposed that also

---

[*]On leave from the Centro de Innovación y Desarrollo Tecnológico en Cómputo, Instituto Politécnico Nacional - México D.F.

Benchmark Name	Instructions Executed (millions)			Symbol		Description
compress{test}	28			`comp`		An in-memory version of a common UNIX utility
li{test}	1,120			`li`		xlisp interpreter
ijpeg{test}	577			`jpeg`		JPEG 24-bit image compression standard
go{test}	17,280			`go`		An internationally ranked go-playing program
vortex{test}	10,058			`vor`		An object oriented database
m88ksim{test}	519			`m88k`		Motorola 88100 microprocessor simulator program
gcc{test}	1,497			`gcc`		Based on the GNU C compiler version 2.5.3
perl{test}	369			`perl`		A Perl Interpreter
adpcm	*enc*: 17	*dec*: 13		*enc*:`ade`	*dec*:`add`	A speech compression and decompression program
epic	*enc*: 3,417	*dec*: 176		*enc*:`epe`	*dec*:`epd`	An image data compression utility in C
g721	*enc*: 134	*dec*:1,620		*enc*:`g7e`	*dec*:`g7d`	Adaptive differential PCM voice compression
mpeg2	*enc*:14,432	*dec*:9,724		*enc*:`mpe`	*dec*:`mpd`	A player for MPEG video
pegwit	*enc*: 33	*dec*: 18		*enc*:`pee`	*dec*:`ped`	A program for public key encryption and decryption

Table 1: Benchmarks and descriptions. Each benchmark from the MediaBench Suite has two separate programs: encoding and decoding.

exploit the prevalence of zero values in data streams. Dynamic ALU width adjustment [3] exploits the zeros present in the high order bits of machine words to switch off portions of the ALU, and RAM compression schemes (e.g., [2]) exploit the large number of zero values created by the operating system clearing memory pages prior to allocating them to a new process.

The rest of this paper is structured as follows. Section 2 presents motivation and simulation results for the data cache which reveal that compressing zeros at the byte granularity gives the optimal energy reduction ratio for our benchmark set. Section 3 presents an overview of the structure of a conventional cache array and describes the necessary circuitry changes to implement the DZC technique. It also analyzes the energy consumption in both the conventional cache and the DZC cache. Section 4 presents the resulting data cache energy reduction for our benchmarks. Section 5 shows the energy savings from using DZC on the instruction cache. It then describes how we can use a recoding scheme for MIPS RISC instructions to increase the number of zero bytes, thus increasing the energy savings. Section 6 concludes the paper.

2 Data Cache Accesses

In this section, we present the distribution of zero values in data cache accesses and show how to maximize the energy savings with minimal area overhead. All our simulation numbers are for SPECint95 [4] and the integer programs from MediaBench [8] programs compiled with `gcc` version 2.7.0 for a MIPS-II-compatible processor using optimization level `-O3` and linked with a version of the `newlib` standard C library. We have extended our MIPS processor simulator to gather statistics on the presence of zero values in cache accesses. Refer to Table 1 for our benchmark workload.

We conducted a study to see how various granularities of zero compression would affect the possible energy savings. Figure 1 shows the reduction in bitline swings observed when we apply zero compression to various sized bit fields for read accesses (write accesses have a similar pattern). We show results for 32-bit, 16-bit, 8-bit, and 4-bit groups, where the figures include the bitline swings of the additional ZIBs in each group. We see that the 8-bit grouping gives the greatest savings overall. The 32-bit grouping actually increases the total number of bitline swings for the `pee` and `ped` benchmarks because there are insufficient zero words to compensate for the additional ZIB accesses required on every word. Adopting a word or half word granularity would be difficult for a processor that allowed stores to individual bytes, while a 4-bit granularity would almost double the RAM area overhead. Thus, we will only consider the byte granularity design for the data cache.

3 Cache Circuit Design

In this section we present the circuitry we have developed for the DZC caching scheme. We first briefly discuss the design of a conventional low-power cache and each component of its energy dissipation. We then present the necessary circuit changes required to implement the DZC technique and discuss the effect of the circuit changes on area and delay.

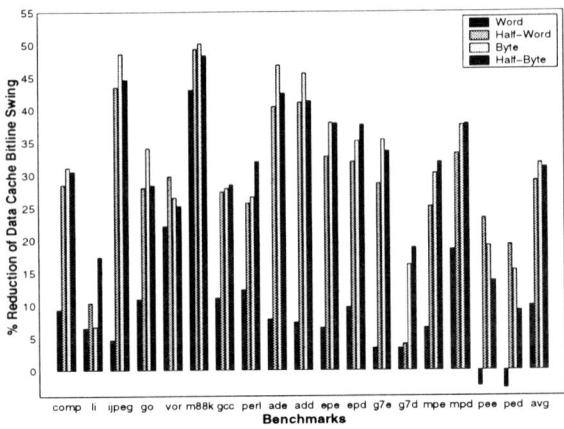

Figure 1: Reduction in the number of bitline swings for read accesses when applying dynamic zero compression to various sized bit fields.

	Read		Write	
	(pJ)	(%)	(pJ)	(%)
Total	44.4	100.0	99.1	100.0
Decoder	5.5	12.4	5.5	5.5
word lines	1.1	2.5	1.1	1.1
Tag bitlines and sense-amp	3.0	6.2	3.0	3.0
Data bitlines and sense-amp	14.5	32.7	69.2	69.9
I/O buses	12.1	27.3	12.1	12.2
Other	8.4	18.9	8.4	8.5

Table 2: Breakdown of energy consumption for 32-bit accesses in base line cache design.

3.1 Baseline Cache Design

We have implemented a low-power 16 KB cache in a TSMC 0.25 μm CMOS process with a nominal 2.5 V supply. The cache is direct mapped and is structured as eight sub-banks of 2 KB each. Tags for each sub-bank are kept in a separate RAM array of 24 bits for each of the 64 cache lines. Figure 2 shows a 2 KB sub-bank. All bitlines are shielded between power and ground rails to minimize capacitive coupling. On any memory access, only the appropriate sub-bank is enabled. Each sub-bank is organized as 128 rows of 128 bits. Each cache line is 32 bytes long, and is held in two consecutive rows of the sub-bank. We reduce the number of active bitlines with local word lines that enable only the required 32-bit segment of any row on any CPU access; we only enable all 128 bit columns during cache refills. In addition, a self-timed circuit is used to limit the voltage swing of bitlines during read accesses by pulsing the word lines [1, 5]; this reduces bitline swing to around 15% of full rail. The CPU to cache interface is a 32-bit bus, while the CPU datapath contains the circuitry to align and sign-extend appropriate bytes for a byte or half-word load, and also the logic to align byte or halfword store data on to the appropriate bytes within the 32-bit bus for stores. The bus employs pulsed differential low-voltage swing drivers to reduce data I/O energy.

Energy consumption figures for the baseline cache design were obtained from HSpice simulations of extracted layout. Table 2 shows a breakdown of the cache energy consumption for 32-bit reads and writes. Writes take over twice the energy of reads primarily because of the greater energy expended in driving the bitlines full swing. Most energy is dissipated in the bitlines and the I/O drivers, which are areas where we expect to obtain savings with the DZC scheme. We next show how we can change the cache circuitry to implement DZC.

3.2 Circuit Modifications

The primary modification to the cache circuitry is to add the zero indicator bit for each byte in the cache as shown in Figure 3. On a write to the cache, we need to check whether the eight data bits are all zero, and if so, we write only the ZIB and disable the write of the eight data bits. If the byte is not zero, we clear the ZIB and write the eight data bits normally. On a read, we want to disable the word line for each byte to avoid swinging the bitlines, thus we add local byte word line gating circuitry controlled by the ZIB. We also add control logic into the drivers connecting cache sub-banks to the CPU to avoid driving the I/O busses for zero bytes. The following sections explain each circuit modification in detail.

3.2.1 CPU Zero-Detect and Store Bus Drivers

During a cache write, the CPU detects whether each byte is zero. If so, it disables the store data bus drivers and

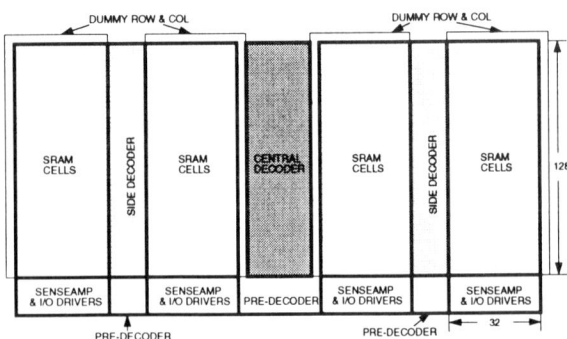

Figure 2: Structure of one 2 KB cache sub-bank.

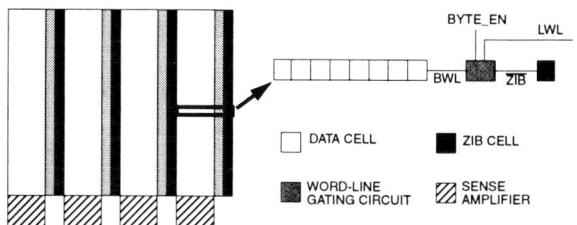

Figure 3: Organization for one 32-bit wide segment of a cache with DZC.

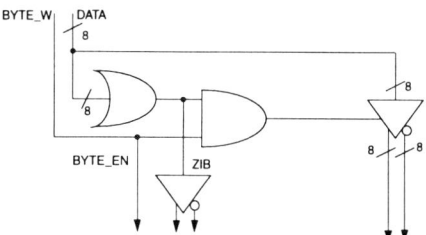

Figure 4: CPU store data driver.

only sends a one on the ZIB bus to the cache, otherwise, it enables the store data drivers and sends a zero for the ZIB. The circuit change for write access is shown in Figure 4. If the byte is not zero, it enables the tristate drivers to drive the data onto the bus. The CPU also emits the usual byte write (BYTE_W) enables for each byte. At the cache side, the byte write enables are combined with the ZIB bit to control whether the eight data bits are written (BYTE_EN).

3.2.2 Word Line Gating Circuitry

Extra word line gating circuitry is used to disable the byte word line when reading or writing zero bytes. Figure 5 shows the modified byte word line gating circuitry. On a cache write access, the cache determines whether to enable the writing of a byte based on the byte write enable signal, BYTE_EN, and the local word line, LWL. If BYTE_EN and the local word line LWL are both asserted, the byte level word line BWL will be asserted.

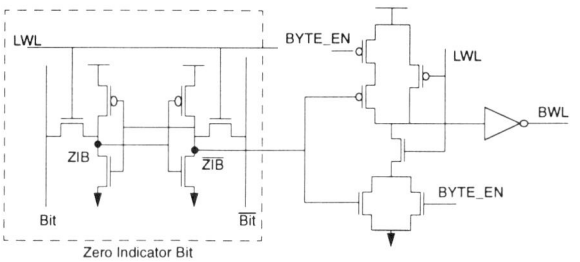

Figure 5: Modified byte word line gating circuit for DZC scheme.

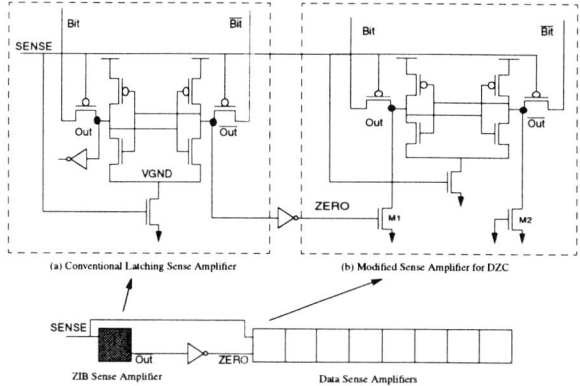

Figure 6: (a) Conventional Senseamp, only used for ZIB. (b) Modified Senseamp for DZC Scheme, used for data bits. The dummy inverter at node Out in (a) is only used for capacitance balancing.

On a cache read access, the byte level word line will be turned on only if the byte is not zero, which is indicated by the ZIB storage output. The CPU keeps BYTE_EN low during a read cycle. The word line gating circuitry adds little delay to read accesses because we have simply replaced the usual per 32-bit word gating circuitry with per 8-bit byte gating circuitry and resized buffers in the new fanout tree.

3.2.3 Sense Amplifier Modification

Our baseline senseamp design is a conventional latching sense amplifier with isolated bitlines as shown in the dotted box (a) in Figure 6. While not sensing, nodes Out and $\overline{\text{Out}}$ follow the values of Bit and $\overline{\text{Bit}}$. When the SENSE signal is asserted, it turns off the p-type transistors connecting Bit to Out and $\overline{\text{Bit}}$ to $\overline{\text{Out}}$ and grounds VGND. If there is a small voltage differential between Nodes Out and $\overline{\text{Out}}$, the inverter pair will amplify this differential to a full rail-to-rail signal.

The word line gating circuitry disables bitline discharge for a read of a zero byte. To avoid having the senseamp hang and burn static current, or swing due to threshold voltage mismatches or noise, we add two n-type transistors (M1 and M2) to the senseamps of the data bits to force them towards zero if ZIB is set. The modifications to the senseamp are shown in the dotted box (b) in Figure 6. The zero transistors are only used here to force a known state on the senseamp; the resulting zero value is not driven to the CPU and is not on any critical path. Shown in Figure 6, the zero transistors of the data bit senseamps are driven from the conventional senseamp used for the ZIB. The ZIB and data bits are read at the same time, i.e., they share the same sense signal. The data bits will not discharge the bitlines

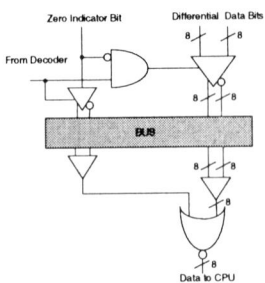

Figure 7: Cache I/O Driver

for a zero byte. If the byte is not zero, the ZERO signal from the ZIB senseamp will stay low, and the data bit senseamps behave exactly the same as the original one and sense the non-zero data byte. If the byte is zero, the ZIB senseamp will assert the ZERO signal to push the data bit senseamps into a stable zero state. Transistor M2 balances the capacitances at the differential nodes $\overline{\text{Out}}$ and Out. Note that for a non-zero byte, the sensing time will only increase slightly due to the additional capacitive load of the drains of the zeroing transistors.

3.2.4 Cache Read Drivers

The circuit change for read access is shown in Figure 7. On the cache side, the ZIB controls the tristate enables for the data bus drivers. The ZIB begins set and conditionally clears after sensing. If it is cleared, we enable the bus drivers in the cache, otherwise they remain tristated. When the data is received in the CPU datapath, a bank of NOR gates produces a zero byte in the case of a set ZIB, or allows the data byte to propagate through if the ZIB is clear.

3.3 Energy Breakdown in DZC Cache

In order to obtain energy consumption figures, we again used HSpice simulation results from extracted DZC cache layout. In the DZC cache the energy consumption can be separated into two major components. First, there is a fixed cost that all accesses must incur regardless of data patterns, caused by the peripheral circuitry including decoders and the self-timing circuitry. The second component, caused by the discharging of the bitlines and I/O buses, varies according to the data patterns. Table 3 shows the energy consumption figures for the DZC cache. The energy figures are lumped into the read or write energy for either a zero byte or a non-zero byte. As expected, writes give much larger savings than reads, because of the greater energy used to swing the bitlines full rail.

	Read (pJ)	Write (pJ)
Zero Byte	5.0	6.7
Non-Zero Byte	11.4	26.9

Table 3: Breakdown of energy consumption for DZC cache design for zero byte or non-zero byte.

3.4 Area and Delay Overhead

Most area overhead is introduced by the ZIBs; there is very little area overhead in the senseamps and word line gating circuitry. The changes in the I/O bus drivers also add insignificant area. In total for the entire cache, the extra circuitry imposes around a 9% area overhead.

We consider read and write delay overhead separately. For a cache write access, write data is usually held in a pipeline buffer for a cycle while the cache tags are checked. The zero check can occur while the write data is waiting in the buffer and hence we expect no visible delay penalty.

For reads, the ZIB is read out in parallel with all the data bits. On the cache side, the data bits are delayed by the need to gate their tristate enables with the zero bit which adds around one FO4 gate delay. On the CPU side, a NOR gate is necessary to reconstruct zeros when the ZIB is set. In total, we estimate that DZC will add around two FO4 gate delays on a read access. The performance impact of this additional read latency depends on the degree of pipelining in the machine and on the amount of instruction-level parallelism present in the code. As a pessimistic example, for a classic RISC five-stage pipeline with an aggressive 16 FO4 delay clock cycle, the two gate delays could be spread over the two cycles of memory instruction execution (address calculation plus cache access) to give an overall cycle time penalty of under 7%. In practice, the machine pipeline structure or cache size might be modified so as not to incur as large a cycle time penalty.

4 Data Cache Results

Figure 8 presents the energy savings for the data cache using dynamic zero compression. The energy savings vary from around 12% for li to close to 40% for m88ksim, with an average of 26%. The energy reduction is less than the average bitline swing reduction of around 33% shown in Figure 1 because of the fixed peripheral circuit costs.

5 RISC Instruction Cache Results

In this section, we first present the energy savings for instruction caching using DZC, then we show how we

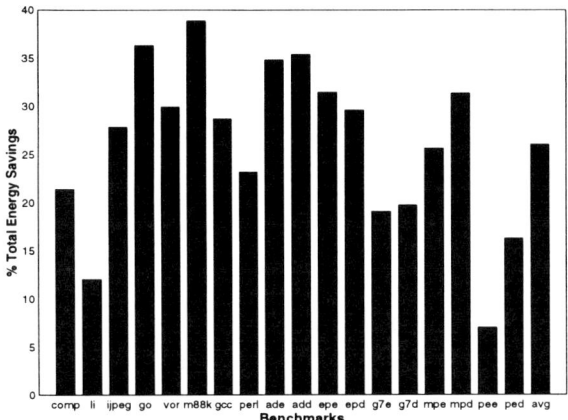

Figure 8: Data cache energy reduction obtained with dynamic zero compression.

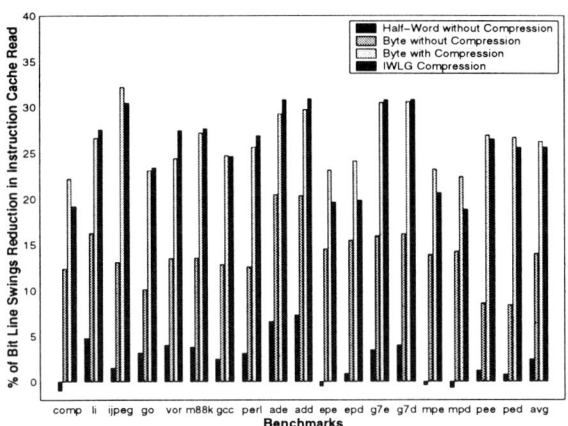

Figure 9: Bitline swing reduction in instruction fetch.

can employ an instruction recoding technique [9] to obtain greater savings in the instruction cache.

The first two bars in each column of Figure 9 show the bitline swing reduction for read accesses with half-word and byte granularities. It is clear that byte granularity gives larger savings, with an average of 15% reduction in bitline swings.

Energy savings are directly proportional to the percentage of zero-valued bytes in cache accesses. To increase the percentage of zero bits, we also experimented with an instruction recoding technique for the MIPS instruction set, previously presented in [9]. This technique compresses commonly used MIPS instructions into fewer bits. For example, many ALU operations use the same register for one source and the destination, and so can be compressed into a two-address form. Another example is that many branches compare against zero and have short offsets, and so can be compressed from the MIPS form which includes a large 16-bit offset and allows comparisons between any two arbitrary registers. The compressed form of these instructions still occupy a full 32-bit slot plus additional encoding bits in the instruction cache, but all unused bits are packed to the low end of the instruction word and set to zero. The instruction recoding takes place at cache refill. The instruction fetch stage is unchanged because the instructions are still addressed as fixed-size units, but instruction decode must be expanded to handle the larger number of instruction types.

The results for instruction word line gating (IWLG) presented in [9] assumed that the instruction word line could be segmented at arbitrary bit positions to disable bitline swings from the unused zero bits. It was found that the greatest reduction in bitline swings was achieved with the 32 instruction bits grouped into three fields of 16 bits, 7 bits, and 9 bits, used to hold three compressed instruction sizes of 16, 23, and 32 bits. The upper 16-bit field is designed to always contain the opcode and the source register specifiers and is never gated so that there is no additional read latency. This scheme allows full speed instruction decode and register access. The remaining 16 bits emerge with some delay, but only contain immediate values or destination register specifiers and hence are not in the decode stage critical path. The bitline swing reduction for the IWLG technique averages around 26%, shown as the last bar in each column in Figure 9.

Although the IWLG scheme gives a large bit swing reduction with effectively no fetch delay penalty, it requires a custom word line gating circuit that prevents using the same cache RAM arrays to store byte-addressed data. A small addition to the DZC compressor circuit allows the same cache RAM array to hold either compressed instructions or data. The modified DZC scheme adds an instruction compressor that is used on cache refills and which employs instruction sizes of 16 bits, 24 bits, and 32 bits to match the byte granularity of word line gating. The DZC instruction recoding scheme changes the meaning of the ZIBs of the two lower bytes to indicate whether the byte is used in the instruction instead of whether the byte is zero-valued. Notice that there exist instances where the byte is used in the instruction but is actually zero-valued, causing bitline swings for zero bytes.

The bitline reduction for the DZC instruction compression scheme is shown as the third bar of each column in Figure 9 and is actually slightly larger than the IWLG scheme at 27%. The DZC achieves slightly greater savings on average because it can compress zero bytes in the top 16 bits of each instruction while the IWLG scheme avoids gating these bits to avoid any read delay.

We experimented with all three different designs, a DZC

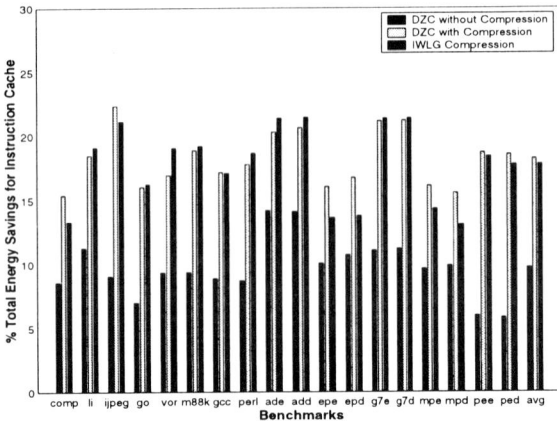

Figure 10: Energy savings in instruction fetch.

cache without instruction compression, DZC cache with instruction compression, and the IWLG cache with custom wordline gating. The energy savings are summarized in Figure 10. The DZC cache without compression averages 10% saving. The optimized IWLG cache achieves energy savings of 17.8%. The DZC cache with instruction compression achieves a slightly greater energy saving of 18.2%.

The DZC cache without compression would be suitable for a unified primary cache system. The IWLG scheme is appropriate for systems with a dedicated instruction cache, as it gives large energy savings and no fetch delay. The DZC compressed cache is suitable for systems with a single cache system that can be variably partitioned between primary instruction and data cache.

6 Conclusion

We proposed a dynamic zero compression technique to reduce cache energy by taking advantage of the high occurrence of zero-valued bytes in the cache. This technique uses a small amount of additional hardware embedded in the RAM array to detect and eliminate the reading and writing of zero bytes. Simulation results show a 26% energy reduction on data cache accesses and 10% on instruction cache accesses when applied to a low-power cache design with sub-banking and low-swing bitlines. The area overhead is about 9% and the latency overhead is around two gate delays. For partitionable primary caches, instruction cache savings can be improved to 18% by using an instruction recoding scheme.

Although this paper has concentrated on the energy savings possible in the primary caches, the zero indicator bits can be propagated throughout the lower levels of the memory hierarchy to provide additional energy savings in memory access and bus transfers.

7 Acknowledgments

Thanks to members of the MIT SCALE and RAW groups and the anonymous reviewers for feedback and comments on earlier drafts of this paper. This work was partly funded by DARPA PAC/C award F30602-00-2-0562 and by a Instituto Politécnico Nacional COFAA grant.

References

[1] B. Amrutur and M. Horowitz. Techniques to reduce power in fast wide memories. In *Symposium on Low Power Electronics*, volume 1, pages 92–93, October 1994.

[2] C. Benveniste, P. Franaszek, and J. Robinson. Cache-memory interfaces in compressed memory systems. In *Solving the Memory Wall Problem Workshop, ISCA-27*, Vancouver, Canada, June 2000.

[3] D. Brooks and M. Martonosi. Dynamically exploiting narrow width operands to improve processor power and performance. In *HPCA-5*, January 1999.

[4] Standard Performance Evaluation Corporation. Spec95, 1995. http://www.spec.org

[5] S. Santhanam *et. al.* A low-cost, 300-MHz, RISC CPU with attached media processor. *IEEE Journal of Solid-State Circuits*, 33(11):1829–1838, November 1998.

[6] K. Ghose and M. B. Kamble. Reducing power in superscalar processor caches using subbanking, multiple line buffers and bit-line segmentation. In *Symposium on Low Power Electronics*, pages 70–75, August 1999.

[7] R. Gonzalez and M. Horowitz. Energy dissipation in general purpose microprocessors. *IEEE Journal of Solid State Circuits*, 31(9):1277–1284, September 1996.

[8] C. Lee, M. Potkanjak, and W. Mangione-Smith. Mediabench: A tool for evaluating and synthesizing multimedia and communication systems. In *Micro-30*, North Carolina, December 1997.

[9] M. Panich. Reducing instruction cache energy using gated wordlines. Master's thesis, Massachusetts Institute of Technology, August 1999.

[10] J. Tseng and K. Asanović. Energy-efficient register access. In *Proc. XIII Symposium on Integrated Circuits and Systems Design*, Manaus, Brazil, September 2000.

[11] N. Vijaykrishnan, M. Kandemir, M. J. Irwin, H. S. Kim, and W. Ye. Energy-driven integrated hardware-software optimization using SimplePower. In *ISCA-27*, Vancouver, Canada, June 2000.

[12] B.-I. Park Y.-S. Chang and C.-M. Kyung. Conforming inverted data store for low power memory. In *ISLPED*, pages 91–93, August 1999.

Memory Hierarchy II

Register Integration: A Simple and Efficient Implementation of Squash Reuse

Amir Roth and Gurindar S. Sohi
Computer Sciences Department, University of Wisconsin - Madison
{amir, sohi}@cs.wisc.edu

Abstract

Register integration (or simply integration) is a mechanism for incorporating speculative results directly into a sequential execution using data-dependence relationships. In this paper, we use integration to implement squash reuse, the salvaging of instruction results that were needlessly discarded during the course of sequential recovery from a control- or data- mis-speculation.

To implement integration, we first allow the results of squashed instructions to remain in the physical register file past mis-speculation recovery. As the processor re-traces portions of the squashed path, integration logic examines each instruction as it is being renamed. Using an auxiliary table, this circuit searches the physical register file for the physical register belonging to the corresponding squashed instance of the instruction. If this register is found, integration succeeds and the squashed result is re-validated by a simple update of the rename table. Once integrated, an instruction is complete and may bypass the out-of-order core of the machine entirely. Integration reduces contention for queuing and execution resources, collapses dependent chains of instructions and accelerates the resolution of branches. It achieves this using only rename-table manipulations; no additional values are read from or written to the physical registers.

Our preliminary evaluation shows that a minimal integration configuration can provide performance improvements of up to 8% when applied to current-generation micro-architectures and up to 11.5% when applied to more aggressive micro-architectures. Integration also reduces the amount of wasteful speculation in the machine, cutting the number of instructions executed by up to 15% and the number of instructions fetched along mis-speculated paths by as much as 6%.

1 Introduction

Modern microprocessors rely heavily on *speculative execution* to achieve performance. Sequential processors (ones that execute sequential programs) speculate on both control and data, executing instructions before all of their input dependences are known with certainty. Successful speculation improves performance by sparing the speculated instructions the wait of having their execution context verified. On the other hand, unsuccessful speculation, or *mis-speculation*, hurts performance by forcing the processor to *recover* to some prior non-speculative state and start over. This paper presents *register integration*, a mechanism for overcoming an inherent inefficiency in conventional sequential mis-speculation recovery.

The inefficiency we speak of is born of a basic antagonistic combination found in sequential programs. While a sequential program is composed of many *locally independent computations*, the *state* of the program is only defined sequentially at dynamic instruction boundaries. Since mis-speculation recovery is defined in terms of this sequential state, a mis-speculation in one computation inadvertently but necessarily causes valid work from sequentially younger computations to be aborted, or *squashed*, and re-executed. Register integration can be used to perform *squash reuse* [2, 18], to salvage the results of squashed computations that are in fact control- and data- independent of the particular mis-speculation event that precipitated the recovery action.

Many processors implement speculation using a level of indirection that maps the architectural register name space to a larger physical register storage space. The larger physical space allows multiple versions of each architectural location (all but one of which is speculative) to simultaneously co-exist. Successful speculation involves the promotion of newer mappings to non-speculative status; mis-speculation recovery restores prior mappings and recycles the speculative storage. Integration is motivated by the observation that only restoration of previous mappings is required for correct recovery. If the speculative values are left intact past a recovery event, then should the processor re-trace part of the squashed path and discover that some of the instructions were useful after all, only the corresponding mappings will need to be restored; the values themselves will already exist and will not need to be re-computed.

The matching of squashed results with re-traced instructions is accomplished using a second mapping into the physical register file, the *Integration Table (IT)*. The IT differs from the sequential mapping (*map table*) in a fundamental way. The map table describes the contents of the physical registers in a transient, sequentially dependent way from the point of view of the architectural registers. In contrast, the IT describes the contents of the physical registers in a persistent, order-independent way that reflects the operations and dataflow relationships used to create the values they contain. While an instruction is being register-renamed, the IT is used to search the physical register file for a physical register that holds the result of a previous squashed instance of the same instruction. If a register is found such that its creating instruction instance had the same physical register inputs as the currently renamed instance, then the currently-renamed instruction is "recognized" as having been previously executed and squashed. The instruction is *integrated* by setting the sequential mapping for its output to point to the physical register allocated during the initial (squashed) execution. The integrated instruction is complete for all intents and purposes; it can commit as soon as the retirement algorithm allows.

Integration has many advantages. Obviously, it reduces consumption of and contention for execution resources. It also collapses data-dependent chains of instructions: a data-dependent chain of dependent instructions cannot be executed in a single cycle, but a completed chain of instructions may be integrated in a single cycle. Integrated branch instructions are resolved immediately, and should these be mis-predicted branches the mis-prediction penalty and subsequent demand on the fetch engine are also reduced. From an engineering standpoint, integration is simple to implement. It is unambiguously correct, involves no explicit verification and does not require additional data paths to either read or write any values into the physical registers. In general, integration involves modifications only to the register renaming stage in the processor; the rest of the pipeline is oblivious to its existence.

Our initial experiments show that a minimal integration configuration can achieve speedups of up to 8% on a representative current-generation microarchitecture. We estimate that the speedup increases to up to 11.5% for more aggressive microarchitectures. Integration also reduces the level of wasteful speculation in a processor, cutting the number of instructions fetched along mis-speculated paths by as much as 6% and the number of instructions executed by 15%.

The rest of the paper is organized as follows. The next section presents the basic integration algorithm and argues for its correctness properties. Section 3 addresses some issues involved in the implementation of integration. In section 4 we evaluate integration using cycle-level simulation. Section 5 discusses related work. Section 6 presents our conclusions.

2 Integration

In this work, we use integration to implement squash reuse, the salvaging of results that were unnecessarily discarded during the process of sequential mis-speculation recovery. In this section, we discuss the basic integration algorithm and describe the principles that allow it to accomplish its goal in a straightforward way. We specifically address the integration of load instructions, which requires additional attention.

2.1 Basic Algorithm

During the course of processing, the program's dataflow graph, in the form of the results of its individual instructions, is stored in the physical register file. At any point in the program, the "active" vertices (results) of this graph are available through a set of mappings that maps architectural register names to physical register locations and their values. New portions of the dataflow graph can only be attached to these "active" vertices. As each instruction is added to the graph, a physical register to hold its value is allocated and mapped to the architectural output. Each instruction is annotated with both the physical register holding its value and the prior physical register mapping of the same architectural location. Recovery entails backtracking over a portion of the program, restoring the previous mapping of each instruction's output while recycling the storage for the squashed result.

Integration exploits the observation that mis-speculation recovery is obligated only to restore some prior sequential mapping into the physical register file. That the results associated with the discarded mappings are also recycled during recovery is an implementation convenience; leaving them intact past the mis-speculation does not impact correctness (of course, they must be recycled eventually lest the processor "leak" away all physical registers). Assuming the results are kept, let us consider the point immediately after the completion of a recovery sequence. Just at this point, all squashed instructions are, in principle, still "attached" to the current state (dependence graph) of the program as defined by the register mapping. The inputs of the oldest squashed instructions are found in this mapping. The fact that the inputs are valid validates the outputs, which are themselves inputs of younger squashed instructions, and so on. Integration is the process of transitively recognizing this validity, instruction by instruction. For every instruction sequenced by the processor, the integration logic looks for the result of a squashed instruction that had the same input mappings. If one is found, the corresponding physical register is "un-squashed" or "pulled back into the sequential flow" simply by setting the sequential mapping to point to it. This action re-validates the physical register mapping, and makes the input mappings of squashed instructions that depend on it valid, allowing them to be subsequently integrated. Notice that this same mechanism naturally avoids the re-use of instructions whose data inputs have been invalidated. As the processor sequences instructions from paths different than the squashed one, the results of these instructions create mappings to new physical registers not found in the squashed dataflow graph. These new mappings effectively "detach" those portions of the squashed dataflow graph that depend on the corresponding architectural name, and prevent them from being integrated.

Integration of a result requires locating a squashed instance of the corresponding instruction with input physical registers identical to those of the current instance being renamed. To facilitate this search, integration relies on the *Integration Table (IT)*, an auxiliary structure that indexes and tags squashed results using instruction identity and input mapping information. Each entry in the IT corresponds to a squashed instruction instance and contains that instruction's PC and the physical registers used for that instance's inputs and output. The IT also contains three fields whose purpose will be made clear later: *Jump-Target* which is meaningful only for control instructions, and *Memory-Address* and *Memory-Value* fields which are meaningful only for loads and stores.

We illustrate the basic algorithm using an example. Figure 1 shows a short program fragment with four variables X,Y,Z and W each allocated to a different logical register. For each dynamic instruction, we show the instruction preceded by its PC, the state of the Map and Integration Tables immediately after the renaming of the instruction and descriptions of the actions taking place during sequential processing and in the IT. The shaded boxes and circled markers highlight the handling of instruction A5. The program undergoes three processing phases. In the first, instructions A1 through A8 are renamed and executed; a new physical register is allocated to each newly created result (marker 2). The second phase begins after all the instructions have completed execution when a branch mis-prediction is detected at instruction A3. Instructions A8, A7, A6, A5 and A4 are recovered in reverse order and the original mappings for their output registers are restored (marker 3). However, instead of recycling the physical registers, each result is entered into the IT and tagged with the instruction PC and physical register inputs used to create it (marker 4). Integration comes into play in the final phase. Having recovered from the mis-prediction, the sequential processor resumes fetching at the re-convergent point beginning at A5. We follow the renaming and potential integration of each instruction carefully.

Intuitively, the re-traced instance of A5 *should* be integrated since removing A4 did not change the value of Y. Indeed, when A5 is renamed for a second time Y is mapped to 51 (marker 5), the same mapping it had during A5's original, squashed execution (marker 1). Properly, the IT contains an entry for an instance of A5 with input physical register 51 (marker 6). By comparing PC/input-register tuples from the dynamic instruction and map table with the corresponding IT tuples (marker 7 with 8, marker 5 with 6), we determine that integration can take place. The act itself consists of setting the output mapping of A5 to the physical register originally allocated for it, 53 (marker 9). The IT entry is removed so that the register will not be integrated by another instruction.

When A6 is renamed for the second time, it finds its input X mapped to register 50. Changing the path has removed A4 and changed the value of X with respect to A6, invalidating it. This invalidation is naturally reflected in the IT, as no entry for A6 with an input of 50 is found. The A6 IT entry has 52 as its input; 52 was created by A4, which was squashed and *not retraced*. Without a match, the instruction is left in the IT until it is evicted. A new physical register, 57, is allocated to the current instance of A6.

Recall, when we integrated A5, we entered its output (53) into the map table. That action set the stage for A7, an instruction that depends on A5, to be integrated now. The squashed version of A7 was executed with input register 53, the output of the squashed A5. When A7 is re-traced, its input is again 53 thanks to the integration of A5. A7 is integrated in exactly the same manner that A5 was.

The final instruction in the group, A8, should not be integrated since it depends on A6, which was itself not integrated. Such indeed is the case. When A6 was *not integrated*, a new mapping (57) was created for X. This new mapping prevents A8 from being integrated, much like the removal of A4 changed the mapping that prevented A6 from being integrated.

In a four wide super-scalar machine, the integration decision on these four instructions can be made in parallel. How this is done is the subject of a future section. However, the example demonstrated the four possible cases for super-scalar integration: basic integration of an instruction (A5), basic non-integration of an instruction (A6), the integration of an instruction that depends on an integrated instruction (A7), and the non-integration of an instruction that depends on a non-integrated instruction (A8).

2.2 Integrating Loads

An integrated instruction can be thought of as having two executions: a *physical execution* where the instruction is actually executed and then squashed, and an *architectural execution* in which the integrated instruction is supposed to execute but doesn't actually do so. For most types of instructions, the algorithm we have shown so far is perfectly safe. The combination of operation and valid input values, denoted by PC and physical registers respectively, guarantees that the results of the physical execution are identical to those that would be produced in the architectural execution, allowing the former to be substituted for the latter. Loads are the exception. The integration of a particular load is not guaranteed to be safe because a conflicting store may have executed between the load's physical and architectural executions. A load that is either blindly integrated despite such a store conflict or that experiences a post-integration conflict is termed *mis-integrated*. Mis-integrations jeopardize correctness.

Loads present a problem because physical register names are not sufficient to detect load/store collisions. There are two ways to ensure that mis-integrated loads are not allowed to retire. The first is to re-execute all integrated loads and treat a change in the output value as a mis-speculation. The second is to store data addresses (and potentially values) with loads in the IT and use stores to invalidate matching loads. The first

Insn Action	Dynamic Insn	Map Table				Integration Table				IT Action
		X	Y	Z	W	PC	I1	I2	O	
Rename/Alloc	A1: X = 0;	50	47	48	49					No Match
Rename/Alloc	A2: Y = 1;	50	51	48	49					No Match
Rename/Alloc	A3: if (Z == 0)	50	51	48	49					No Match
Rename/Alloc	A4: X - 1;	52	51	48	49					No Match
Rename/Alloc	**A5: Y++;**	52	53	48	49					No Match
Rename/Alloc	A6: X++;	54	53	48	49					No Match
Rename/Alloc	A7: W = Y * Y;	54	53	48	55					No Match
Rename/Alloc	A8: Z = X * Y;	54	53	56	55					No Match
Recover	A8: Z = X * Y;	54	53	48	55	A8	54	53	56	Enter
Recover	A7: W = Y * Y;	54	53	48	49	A7	53	53	55	Enter
Recover	A6: X++;	52	53	48	49	A6	52		54	Enter
Recover	**A5: Y++;**	52	51	48	49	A5	51		53	**Enter**
Recover	A4: X = 1;	50	51	48	49	A4	50		52	Enter
Rename/Integrate	**A5: Y++;**	50	53	48	49	A5	51		53	**Match/Remove**
Rename/Alloc	A6: X++;	57	53	48	49	A6	52		54	No Match/Leave
Rename/Integrate	A7: W = Y * Y;	57	53	48	55	A7	53	53	55	Match/Remove
Rename/Alloc	A8: Z = X * Y;	57	53	58	55	A8	54	53	56	No Match/Leave

FIGURE 1. A Working Example of Integration. Shows the three-phase processing of a series of instructions. The three phases are: (i) initial execution (ii) recovery and (iii) squashed-path re-execution. The shaded quantities and circled markers highlight the actions surrounding instruction A5.

method uses a simple IT but reduces the positive impact of successful integration, forcing integrated loads to consume execution bandwidth. The second increases the potential impact of successful integration, but complicates the IT somewhat. Our framework models store invalidations.

3 Implementation Aspects

In this section we discuss several implementation aspects of integration including all modifications that must be made to the base microarchitecture, the integration circuit itself, and the mechanism that ensures the safe integration of loads.

3.1 Base Micro-architecture Requirements

Integration is not a technique that can be applied to all speculative microarchitectures. Its implementation requires that the base microarchitecture allow speculative results to remain intact past a mis-speculation recovery action and support the out-of-order allocation and freeing of speculative storage.

These requirements disqualify many current microarchitectures. In-order speculative microarchitectures like Sun's UltraSparc-III that use working (future) register files indexed by architectural register number both disallow arbitrary assignments of physical results to architectural names and overwrite the mis-speculated instructions results during recovery. Intel's P6 [10] core processors and HAL's SPARC64 V [7] keep speculative results in the re-order buffer, preventing their preservation past a mis-speculation recovery. IBM's Power [19] processors and (we believe) AMD's K7 [5] have physical register files separate from the re-order buffer, but also have an architectural register file and require that physical registers be allocated and freed in-order. Microarchitectures with physical register models that *can* support integration are the out-of-order Alpha processors starting with the 21264 [11], those of MIPS beginning with the R10000 [21], and (we believe) Intel's Pentium 4 NetBurst microarchitecture [9].

3.2 A Micro-architecture with Integration

We now examine a microarchitecture that includes integration and comment on changes in the flow of instructions through the modified pipeline. A pipeline with integration is shown in Figure 2(a); the structural modifications and new register tag and data paths are in bold. We work from the back of the pipeline to the front, explaining how instructions become candidates for integration before dealing with the flow of integrated instructions. A later subsection is dedicated to explaining the integration circuit itself in detail.

Since integration deals with salvaging the results of squashed instructions, the most natural time to insert instructions into the IT is during mis-speculation recovery. Implementation of IT insertion is straightforward for micro-architectures that implement recovery using serial rollback. Most microarchitectures, however, including the Alpha 21264 [11] and MIPS R10000 [21], implement recovery as a monolithic copy from a checkpoint. IT insertion is slightly more involved in this case, but its particulars do not affect integration performance. For clarity, we explain the process as serial.

One important qualification to the IT entry procedure is the exclusion of all instructions that have not completed execution. The reasoning behind this decision is that it is the integration of *completed* instructions that contributes most to performance. Integration provides two main performance benefits: it allows instructions to bypass the issue engine and it collapses dependent chains of instructions. Neither of these benefits applies to instructions that have not issued and only the first applies to instructions that have issued but not completed. However, the number of instructions likely to be integrated while in this post-issue/pre-completion state is small, and in return for forfeiting them, we simplify the handling of integrated instructions by assuming that all integrated instructions are complete. Faulting instructions are also excluded from the IT, since faults may have side effects that would need to be reproduced on integration.

One of the principles of integration is that it allows speculative physical registers to "survive" recovery. This means that during recovery output registers of instructions that are entered into the IT are not reclaimed and added to the free list as usual. However, we must be explicit about who is responsible for eventually freeing the registers of instructions that *are* in the IT, so that these registers are not "leaked". The policy is actually quite straightforward. The IT assumes responsibility for the physical registers of its entries. If an entry is evicted without having been integrated, it physical register is added to the free list. Conversely, if an entry *is* integrated, responsibility for the register returns to the re-order buffer, which handles it in the usual way. One caveat is that the IT entry of an integrated instruction must be cleared so that no other sequential instruction will attempt to get ownership of the corresponding register (the output of two simultaneously active instructions may not be allocated to the same physical register). Notice, the change of ownership mechanism also allows the same instruction to be repeatedly squashed and integrated.

The next subsection describes the integration related modifications to the register renaming logic. Here, we describe what happens to an instruction after it has been integrated which, having decided that only completed instructions can be integrated, is not much. An integrated instruction is entered into the re-order buffer marked as completed and the integrated physical register is set as its "current mapping". Integrated loads (and stores) are allocated load (or store) queue entries that are filled using the IT *Memory-Address* and *Memory-Value* fields and marked as completed. These entries, too, are ordinary. Finally, if the integrated instruction is a branch, the resolution and potential recovery sequences are started immediately using the *Jump-Target* IT field as a recovery address. The integrated instruction can bypass the out-of-order execution core; it does not need to be allocated to a reservation station, scheduled, executed, or written back.

3.3 Integration Circuit

The most delicate piece of the integration mechanism is the integration circuit itself. The integration circuit examines each dynamic instruction and decides whether or not that instruction may be integrated. Of course, it must do so for multiple, potentially dependent instructions in parallel. In this section, we describe one possible implementation of this logic and its complexity. We begin with a scalar description of the circuit, before proceeding to the super-scalar case.

Scalar register renaming occurs in two logical steps. First, an instruction's logical inputs are renamed to physical outputs using lookups in the map table. Second, its logical output is allocated a new physical register and this new logical-to-physical mapping is entered into the sequential map table, allowing future instructions that need the value to obtain their inputs from the correct location. We call the two stages *input routing* and *output allocation*, respectively. Integration adds a piece called *output selection* in which the output mapping must be chosen between a newly allocated physical register and a physical register obtained from an IT entry. The output selection circuit occurs *logically after* the input routing circuit since the integration test must compare the input physical registers of the sequential instance with those in the IT entry. However, the scalar implementation of integration can be thought of as occurring in one of two ways. In the first, output selection is implemented serially after input routing with the integration table indexed by instruction PC *and* input physical registers. In the second, output selection is split into *IT lookup*, which happens in parallel with input routing, and an *integration test*, which occurs logically after it. In this organization, shown in Figure 2(b), the IT is indexed by *PC only* and the physical register numbers are used to match tags. Both schemes likely require pipelining register renaming into at least two stages.

The merits of each implementation are open to debate in the scalar realm, but in a super-scalar environment only the second is viable. While the first scheme interleaves and serializes the input routing and output selection decisions that must be made for each instruction, the PC-only indexed scheme permits a parallel prefix implementation similar to the one used to superscalarize conventional register renaming. Let us review conventional super-scalar renaming. Super-scalar renaming is more complex than scalar renaming because its input routing decisions must reflect intra-group dependences. To do so, dependency-check logic acts in parallel with output allocation. This logic compares the logical input of each instruction in the group with the logical output of each previous in-group instruction; a match overrides the initial input routing retrieved from the map table and routes the input to the appropriate newly allocated physical register. For example, in a group of four two-input, one-output instructions each of the second instruction's inputs has to be compared with the first instruction's output, each of the third instruction's inputs has to be compared with the outputs of the first two instructions and each of the fourth instruction's inputs has to be compared with the outputs of the first three instructions. The total number of comparisons for this case is 12 and in general $I * N(N-1)/2$, with I the number of inputs per instruction and N, the super-scalar width or the number of parallel renaming operations. In general, the depth of the circuit is linear with N and the number of comparisons grows as N^2.

In addition to the conventional dependence-check circuit that compares logical registers, integration requires that we implement output selection and any corrections it might imply for input routing for subsequent instructions. Recall, for the scalar integration test we compared each IT entry input with the corresponding register retrieved from the map table. In the super-scalar case, we must also compare it to the physical register outputs for all integration candidates of all prior instructions in the group. Note, we do not have to compare the candidate inputs with the newly allocated physical registers corresponding to each prior instruction: the situation in which an instruction is dependent on a prior instruction in the group and is integrated while the prior instruction is not is obviously impossible. Nevertheless, although the priority encoding depth of the circuit is still N, the superscalar width, the number of physical register comparisons now grows with both N and the number of possible IT matches, M. The precise formula is $I * (((N(N-1)/2)M + N) * M)$; the growth of the function is IN^2M^2. The complexity of the circuit is very close to that of register renaming for a direct-mapped IT, but diverges for higher-associativity implementations. For instance, a four-wide machine with a direct-mapped IT requires 20 physical register comparisons to implement integration. The same machine with a 2-way IT needs 64 comparisons. Just for scale, an 8-wide machine with a 4-way IT requires 960 com-

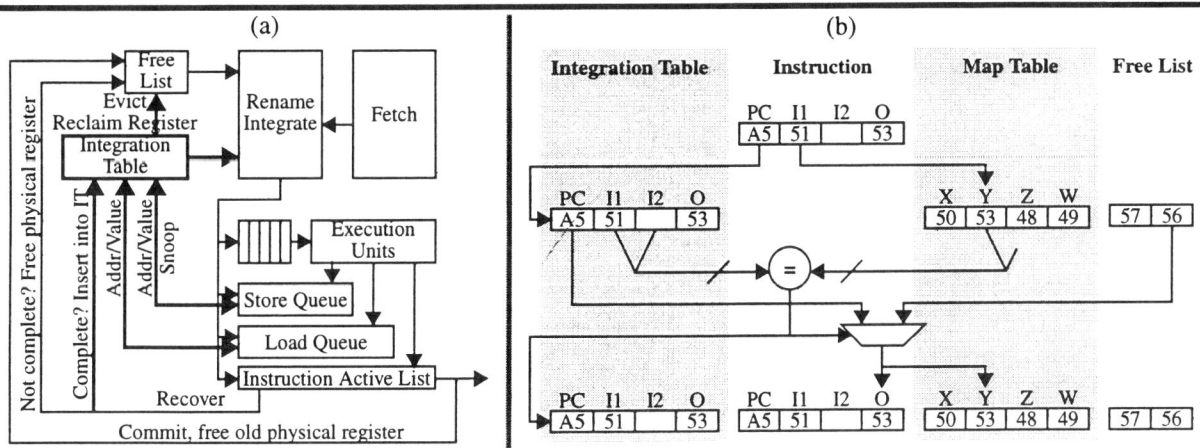

FIGURE 2. Implementation Aspects. *(a) A micro-architecture with integration. Integration-specific modifications in bold. In addition to the actual integration table (IT) and modified rename logic, there are additional paths from the instruction ordering buffer (ROB) to the IT that are used during recovery, a path from the IT to the free list, and paths between the IT and the load and store queues. (b) Scalar, PC-indexed integration circuit. A scalar integration circuit in which the IT and map table are accessed in parallel. An extension of this circuit implements super-scalar integration. The diagram traces the IT, map table and free list, as well as the instruction itself through the two steps of integration-enabled register renaming. At the top of the figure, the instruction shown is raw and the structures are as they appear before the instruction is renamed. At the bottom, the instruction is renamed and the structures reflect that fact.*

parisons! Certainly, a highly associative integration circuit is challenging to build. In the evaluation section, we quantify the performance impact of higher associativity.

We should mention here that some of the complexity of the integration circuit may be moved off-line into the IT itself. For instance, the IT could internally perform the intra-group dependence checks and store groups of dependent instructions in a kind of "trace" that can be integrated using $I*N*M$ comparisons. However, IT management becomes much more complex in this case, and there is the added problem of choosing the grouping of instructions into traces. An investigation of such optimizations is outside the scope of this work.

3.4 Safe Load Integration via Store Invalidation

When first presenting integration, we remarked that special support must be provided to ensure that loads that have been invalidated by intervening stores are removed from integration consideration. At the very least, the mis-integration should be detected so that alternative corrective action can be taken. Mis-integration detection and avoidance are implemented using a simple extension to the processor's basic load speculation mechanism. Processors that support *load speculation* (advancing loads past incomplete stores) detect store/load ordering violations as follows. The load and store queues contain address and value fields. Completed stores check their address and value against address/value pairs of *younger* previously completed loads. An address overlap coupled with a value mismatch signals a memory ordering violation which is handled by replaying the load in some way.

The solution handles two cases. The mis-integration detection case covers conflicts with stores that complete *after* the load has been integrated. Mis-integration detection is implemented naturally by the native load speculation mechanism. Recall, loads are entered into the IT along with their address and value fields from the load queue. When they are integrated, these fields are *restored to* the load queue. To a completing store, therefore, an integrated load looks just like any other completed load and conflicts are handled in the usual way. Mis-integration avoidance targets conflicts with stores that complete *before* a load is integrated. To implement avoidance, we simply extend the store-invalidation procedure to include IT loads. The IT essentially "snoops" completed stores, matching their address/value pairs with the Memory-Address/Memory-Value pairs of IT loads. An address match/value mismatch causes the invalidation of the corresponding load, preventing it from being integrated. Detection and avoidance can also be implemented using purely address-based criteria.

Our results show that most mis-integrations are avoided. Those that aren't, while not impacting correctness, can degrade performance as they are equivalent to normal load or value mis-speculations. Our performance evaluation section will measure the prevalence of mis-integration.

3.5 Handling Data Mis-Speculations

The discussion of load integration brings up an important note regarding integration and the way it must deal with instructions squashed due to data mis-speculations like speculative memory-ordering violations [14, 22] and value mis-speculations [12]. Specifically, for micro-architectures like the Alpha 21264 [11], in which data mis-speculations are handled by squashing, integration must be careful not to confuse a value mis-speculated instruction and its dependent instructions with correctly executed squashed instructions. IT entries that correspond to data mis-speculated results must not be integrated. One broad solution to this problem would be to not enter squashed instructions into the IT during recovery from these kinds of mis-speculations. However, this solution is too harsh since it prevents the correctly executed instructions that were lost during recovery from being salvaged. An effective trick is to enter all completed instructions *except* for the value mis-speculated instruction *itself* into the IT. This omission effectively "detaches" all dependent instructions from possible integration, while leaving all independent instructions intact.

There is an interesting interaction between integration and another technique for salvaging work lost to a data mis-speculation, *selective squashing* [8, 12, 15, 16]. In selective squashing, instructions are kept in reservation stations until retirement allowing them to simply re-issue as data mis-speculations are resolved. If selective squashing *is* implemented, integration is not "activated" during data mis-speculations since the instructions are not squashed and re-fetched. Integration, on the other hand, still handles control mis-speculation squashes which, quite conveniently, cannot be handled by selective squashing. Integration and selective squashing complement each other nicely. However, we do not explore their interaction experimentally; our simulations model full squashing for all mis-speculations.

3.6 Setting the Size of the Physical Register File

A final implementation note concerns the size of the IT and its relationship to the total size of the physical register file. To avoid resource stalls, the number of physical registers should be equal to the maximum number of values (both architectural and speculative) that can be "in play" at any time. For a speculative machine this is equal to the number of architected registers plus the maximum number of renamed in-flight instructions (the size of the re-order buffer). Now, the IT is simply a mechanism for keeping physical registers "in circulation" for longer periods of time; values in the IT are still considered "in play". Consequently, to avoid resource stalls in a micro-architecture with integration, the size of the physical register file should be equal to the number of architected registers plus the size of the re-order buffer *plus* the size of the IT. In our simulated configurations, we use this formula to ensure that the machine never stalls for lack of a free physical register.

4 Performance Evaluation

We evaluate the potential performance impact of integration using cycle-level simulation. We present a full set of results for one specific design meant to represent a potential current-generation (or very near future) microprocessor. We then briefly look at two dimensions in the IT design space, size and associativity. To be fair, we quantify the adverse performance effects of any additional pipeline stages required by integration. Finally, we try to project integration's impact on more aggressive future-generation microarchitectures.

4.1 Experimental Framework

We evaluate integration using the SPEC2000 integer benchmark suite. The programs are compiled for the Alpha EV6 architecture by the Digital UNIX V4 `cc` compiler with optimizations `-O3 -fast`. We use the test datasets for reporting performance for all benchmarks except *perlbmk*. There we are forced to use the training set because the test set contains fork and exec calls that our simulation environment does not support. Where multiple test data sets are given we use the longer running one, specifically *place* for *vpr* and *kajiya* for *eon*. We simulate all programs in their entirety.

The simulation environment is built on top of the SimpleScalar 3.0 [1] Alpha toolkit. The cycle-level simulator models an out-of-order machine similar in organization to an unclustered Alpha 21264 [11] with nominal stages fetch, register rename and dispatch, schedule, execute, writeback and commit. The out-of-order scheduling logic speculates loads aggressively, issuing them even in the presence of prior stores with unavailable addresses. A mis-speculation causes the load and all downstream instructions to be squashed and re-fetched. Our model does not include a dependence-speculation mechanism that may reduce the incidence of memory-ordering violations [3, 14, 22]. However, we don't believe that the inclusion of such a mechanism would take away a significant portion of the impact of integration, since most integration candidates are produced by control mis-speculation. The recovery mechanism itself is modeled as serial with bandwidth equal to commit. Recovery stalls renaming, but execution and retirement from the head of the machine may continue. We model a memory system with non-blocking caches, finite write-buffers and miss-status holding registers (MSHR), and cycle accurate bus utilization. Table 1 shows the simulation parameters in detail. IT configuration is specified inline with the respective presentation of results. The Alpha has 64 architectural registers; the number of physical registers for a given configuration is therefore always set to be 64 + ROB size + IT size.

4.2 Base Configuration Results

Table 2, which is split into two for readability, shows the performance impact of integration using a 256-entry direct-mapped IT on the configuration described above. Data is presented in four main parts. The first two characterize the performance of the base and modified system in terms of instructions fetched and executed, branch mis-predictions and branch mis-prediction resolution latency, and total memory-ordering violations. These numbers give a feel for the degree of mis-speculation in each program and its causes. Comparing these groups of numbers pair-wise gives an idea of the overall effect of integration on speculative (mis-speculative) processor activity. The next two parts measure the activity and effectiveness of integration using more direct metrics. We report absolute counts of instructions integrated, loads integrated, and mis-predicted branches integrated (and ostensibly, immediately resolved).

The shaded at the bottom computes the characteristic and performance metrics of integration and its impact on performance. The *contribution rate* is the number of instructions integrated as a percentage of the total number of instructions committed; it is the amount of work integration contributes to the architectural execution of the program. The *salvage rate* is number of instructions integrated as a percentage of squashed (and completed) instructions and measures the rate at which integration candidates are harvested. The contribution and salvage rates measure both a program's inherent suitability for integration *and* our mechanism's ability to capture integration candidates. The final three metrics measure the percentage of instructions fetched, instructions executed and total execution time saved by integration.

The performance figures show that integration is equally effective on all benchmarks. On some, like *gzip*, *vpr*, *crafty* and *twolf*, it cuts execution time by upwards of 5%. On others, it achieves speedups of less than 1%. To explain this behavior we appeal to the structure of the programs and to the contribution and salvage rates, which help correlate this structure with suitability for integration. There are some programs that for structural reasons simply cannot take advantage of integration. One possibility is that the programs have few squash-causing branch mis-predictions and memory-ordering violations. Another is that branch mis-predictions are present but that the code within the conditional arms is so long that the processor does not have time to fetch and execute the re-convergent region before the branch is resolved. Finally, if the re-convergent region *is* reachable along the mis-speculated path, it is possible that it contains no data-independent instructions, the ones that can later be integrated.

How do the benchmarks break down according to these criteria? *Bzip2*, for instance, encounters branch mis-predictions

Front-End	Symmetric 16K-entry combined 10-bit history gshare and 2-bit predictors. 2K entry, 4-way associative BTB, 32 entry return-address-stack. 3-cycle fetch. 32-entry instruction buffer. Up to 8 instructions from two cache blocks fetched per cycle. A maximum of one taken branch per cycle. 8-wide single-cycle decode. Direct, unconditional jump mis-predictions recovered at decode.
Issue Mechanism	8-way superscalar out-of-order speculative issue with a maximum of 128 instructions or 64 loads or 32 stores in flight. 2-cycle schedule/register read. Loads speculatively issue in the presence of earlier stores with unknown addresses. The load and subsequent instructions are squashed and re-fetched on a memory ordering violation. Recovery from all forms of mis-speculation is serial with a bandwidth of 8 instructions per cycle. Recovery stalls register renaming, but execution of unrecovered instructions may proceed in parallel. Store to load bypass takes 2 cycles. Memory and control instructions have the highest scheduling priority. Priority within a group is determined by age.
Memory System	32KB, 32B lines, 2-way associative, 1-cycle access L1 instruction cache. 64KB, 32B lines, 2-way associative, 2-cycle access, L1 data cache. A maximum of 16 outstanding load misses. 16-entry store buffer. 16-entry ITLB, 32-entry DTLB with 30-cycle hardware miss handling. Shared 1MB, 64B line, 4-way associative, 12 cycle access L2 cache. 70-cycle memory latency. 32B bus to L2 cache clocked at processor frequency. 16B bus to memory clocked at 1/3 processor frequency. Cycle level bus utilization modeled.
Functional Units (latency)	8 INT ALU (1), 2 INT mult/div (3/20), 3 FP add (2), 1 FP mult/div (4/24), 4 load/store (2). The FP adders and all multipliers are fully pipelined.

TABLE 1. Simulated machine configuration.

infrequently (fewer than once every 400 instructions). It falls under the first category. *Bzip2*'s salvage rate is close to 40%, but it *executes* so few instructions along mis-speculated paths as compared to other programs that the overall pool of integration candidates is small. The second two categories are somewhat more difficult to distinguish from one another, but five of the other benchmarks: *gcc, mcf, parser, perlbmk* and *gap* fall into them. These programs incur branch mis-predictions or memory ordering violations every 100 instructions or so (or more frequently), execute (and squash) somewhat more instructions than they commit, yet permit the successful integration of only around 20% of squashed instructions. *Vortex* is a strange case. It executes many instructions along squashed paths but, since many squashes are due to load mis-speculation, integrates only a relatively low percentage of them. Performance gain is achieved because many of the integrated instructions are mispredicted branches. The four benchmarks we mentioned at the top execute a lot of work along mis-speculated paths and integrate that work at a high rate. These programs benefit the most from integration. Other factors that contribute to the observed impact of integration but are difficult to quantify directly are the parallelism in the high-integration regions and the extent to which the integrated instructions help collapse dependence chains.

		gzip	vpr	gcc	mcf	crafty	parser
Committed instructions (M)		3367.27	1566.70	2015.64	259.63	4264.78	4203.56
Base	Fetched instructions (M)	5555.67	3667.92	3816.01	527.87	8080.35	7515.99
	Executed instructions (M)	4114.58	2069.79	2327.15	292.49	5158.60	4854.72
	Mispredicted branches (M)	16.61	20.48	22.93	2.54	38.80	38.08
	Misprediction resolution lat. (c)	29.72	18.41	16.85	33.37	21.48	20.78
	Mis-speculated loads (M)	2.50	0.00	0.20	0.01	1.35	0.14
Base + IT	Fetched instructions (M)	5376.16	3424.83	3709.65	509.96	7659.44	7374.33
	Executed instructions (M)	3481.16	1774.06	2133.07	271.98	4649.16	4582.10
	Mispredicted branches (M)	15.91	20.90	22.97	2.54	38.84	38.05
	Misprediction resolution lat. (c)	27.56	15.66	15.86	31.96	19.27	20.15
	Mis-speculated loads (M)	3.29	0.59	0.36	0.02	1.41	0.20
Integrated instructions (M)		640.70	249.35	167.73	15.85	450.31	274.49
Integrated loads (M)		177.12	90.69	55.60	3.28	200.29	78.19
Integrated mispredicted branches (M)		0.78	0.59	0.17	0.01	0.53	0.54
Integrated/committed (%) (contrib.)		19.0	15.9	8.3	6.1	10.6	6.5
Integrated/squashed (%) (salvage)		61.9	46.7	29.1	24.0	45.3	28.3
Fetched insns saved (%)		3.2	6.6	2.8	3.7	5.2	1.9
Executed insns saved (%)		15.4	15.3	8.3	7.0	9.9	5.6
Execution time saved (%)		4.8	8.1	2.0	1.1	5.2	1.1

		eon	perlbmk	gap	vortex	bzip2	twolf
Committed instructions (M)		458.29	27684.23	1169.58	9808.12	8822.14	258.73
Base	Fetched instructions (M)	987.32	51890.55	1738.94	17977.94	10694.62	530.94
	Executed instructions (M)	554.43	30300.91	1227.20	11673.81	9067.05	295.94
	Mispredicted branches (M)	4.34	261.86	9.80	34.98	24.40	2.89
	Misprediction resolution lat. (c)	14.32	60.65	24.82	12.41	19.56	16.56
	Mis-speculated loads (M)	3.92	13.66	0.15	43.15	0.16	0.32
Base + IT	Fetched instructions (M)	957.22	51341.83	1722.18	17111.10	10638.29	505.40
	Executed instructions (M)	501.30	28964.36	1186.67	9919.20	8917.34	268.77
	Mispredicted branches (M)	4.31	262.07	9.87	33.85	24.49	2.89
	Misprediction resolution lat. (c)	13.56	59.88	24.35	10.36	19.10	14.98
	Mis-speculated loads (M)	3.74	13.56	0.18	40.14	0.52	0.32
Integrated instructions (M)		41.35	1308.39	3.80	157.36	132.05	22.35
Integrated loads (M)		12.37	435.56	1.04	34.93	44.27	8.38
Integrated mispredicted branches (M)		0.30	7.67	0.02	11.73	0.27	0.27
Integrated/committed (%) (contrib.)		9.0	4.7	0.3	1.6	1.5	8.6
Integrated/squashed (%) (salvage)		44.8	22.4	22.4	7.3	33.4	41.4
Fetched instructions saved (%)		3.1	1.1	1.0	4.8	0.5	4.8
Executed instructions saved (%)		9.6	4.4	3.3	15.1	1.7	9.2
Execution time saved (%)		3.0	0.9	0.4	3.1	0.4	5.6

TABLE 2. Detailed Performance Impact of Adding a Direct-Mapped, 256-entry IT to a Current Generation Microarchitecture. Raw quantities are listed in millions of events (M) or cycles (c).

To a first order, integration is primarily a technique for reducing the number of instructions executed in a program. To that end it is fairly successful, reducing the consumption of execution bandwidth by 1% to 15%. However, a rather striking trend is the incredibly strong correlation between the performance of integration and its second order effect, reducing the number of instructions fetched, which it does at rates that vary from close to nil to near 7%. Integration is a technique that operates at decode/rename time. It is is therefore unable to eliminate the latency and bandwidth of fetch from the cost of an integrated instruction. Integration frees up execution bandwidth for new instructions, but does not directly free up more fetch bandwidth to fetch those new instructions (it actually can, but only indirectly via the accelerated resolution of mispredicted branches). As a result, the reduced consumption of execution bandwidth generally leaves bubbles and open slots in the execution pipelines. Actual performance gain is more closely related to the number of instructions eliminated from processing completely.

One opportunity for integration to do harm is by precipitating squashes through mis-integrations. However, our figures show that although memory-ordering squashes are sometimes increased with integration, the number of introduced squashes is small in comparison with the number of loads integrated. On the whole, integration *reduces* the amount of mis-speculation activity in the processor, cutting down the number of instructions fetched and (to a lesser degree) executed. This fact suggests two interesting applications for integration. The first is as a dynamic power and energy reduction technique [13]. This use, of course, requires that the power characteristics of integration itself be acceptable, something that has not yet been investigated. The second application is in a simultaneous multithreading (SMT) processor [6, 20], where several narrow front-ends share a large out-of-order execution engine. This could be an ideal environment for integration, which would reduce contention in the back end, and would require only (replicated) narrow, low-complexity integration circuits.

4.3 Impact of Table Size and Associativity

Two important parameters in the design of the IT are its size and associativity. Since the IT always contains the *most recently squashed* instructions, its size determines the degree to which it can salvage work from *older* squashed regions. If the IT is too small, older squashed instructions would be evicted before they could be integrated. However, an overly large IT is also undesirable since it implies an overly large (and overly slow) physical register file.

The effect of IT size on the performance impact of integration is shown in Figure 3(a). The trends certainly support our program-structure explanation for the bimodal nature of integration, as each group of benchmarks responds differently to changes in IT size. Those benchmarks that fail to benefit from integration for structural reasons do so consistently, regardless of IT size. More integration resources do not change the fact that the product of program and machine does not produce many valid integration candidates. On the other hand, programs whose structure does allow them to support integration, can draw additional benefit from additional integration resources. In general, however, a very large IT is not necessary. A significant fraction of the benefit can be achieved with a small IT that can buffer the squashed results from the last mis-speculated region. For this set of programs and our machine configuration, 256 entries (enough space to buffer instructions from between 4 to 8 mis-speculated regions) appears to be sufficient. The corresponding number of physical registers is 448.

The associativity of the IT has two different uses that impact performance in two ways. From the standard viewpoint, associativity is a mechanism for more efficient management of collisions in the IT. Specific to the integration circuit, however, associativity can also determine the number of squashed instances of the same static instruction that are simultaneously considered for integration. Although the first use does not

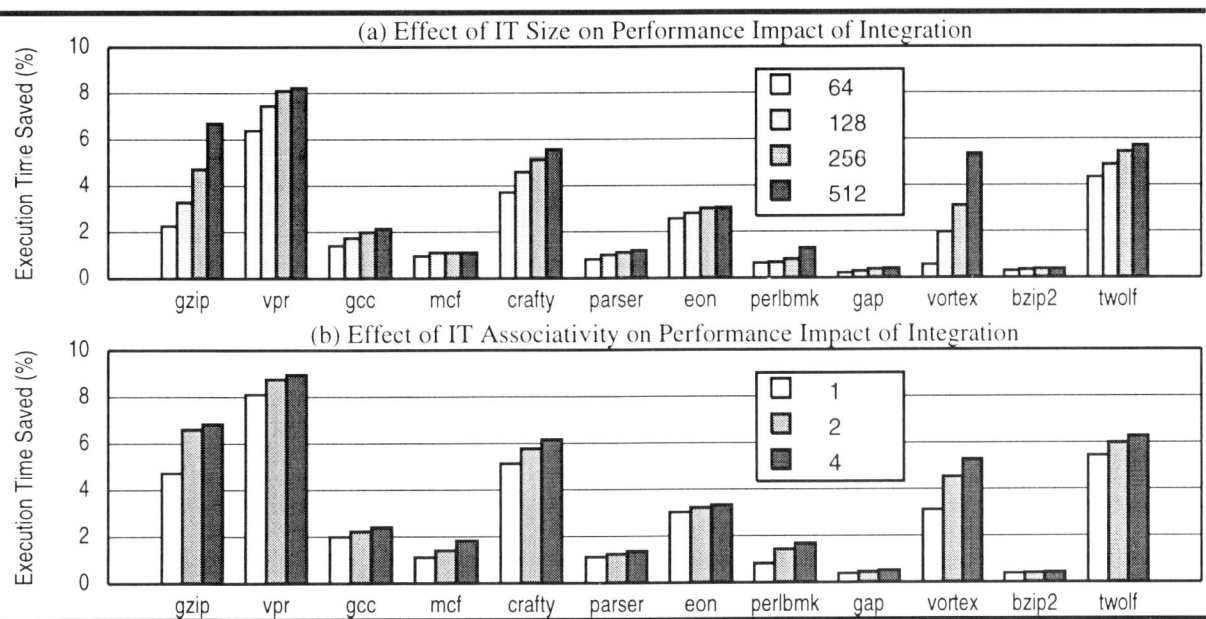

FIGURE 3. Effect of IT Size and Associativity on Performance Impact of Integration. *Percentage of execution time saved using (a) a direct-mapped IT of four sizes: 64, 128, 256 and 512. (the corresponding physical register file sizes are 256, 320, 448 and 704) and (b) a 256-entry IT with associativities 1, 2 and 4.*

necessarily imply the second, we use associativity to quantify both IT eviction policy and integration circuit complexity in order to simplify the discussion. The impact of IT associativity on integration performance is shown in Figure 3(b). The trends are similar to those observed when changing the size of the IT; the bimodal effect is still present for the same program-structural reasons. The trends are much less pronounced, however. Except for in the cases of *gzip* and *vortex*, there is little benefit to having anything more complex than a direct-mapped IT that supplies a single integration candidate per instruction. That higher associativities that would overly complicate the integration circuit are unnecessary is good news indeed.

4.4 Impact of Increased Pipelining

Earlier we mentioned that an implementation of integration *may* require register renaming to be pipelined into two stages. Such an increase in pipeline depth will erode some of the performance gained by integration, and potentially induce absolute slow-downs for programs that did not originally benefit from integration and would now be forced to pay for its implementation. The increased number of physical registers may also require adding additional register read/schedule cycles.

The impact of increased pipelining for both register renaming and register read is shown in Figure 4(a). Integration-induced increased pipelining does mitigate the performance impact of integration, even producing slow-downs for those benchmarks which integration does not help. The dominant effect is an increase in the branch resolution latency which cuts integration's fetch savings. There is an interesting interplay between increased pipelining and integration. On one hand, it lengthens the branch resolution latency, increasing the number of instructions that can be executed along mis-speculated paths. On the other, it slows down the execution of *all* instructions, reducing the completion rate of squashed instructions. The overall effect on the number of integration candidates and integrations is small.

Although the effects of pipeline depth increases take away some of integration's performance, such increases are by no means mandatory. The access times of large physical register files can be controlled using techniques like replication [11, 19] or banking [4] and while integration probably requires two-stage register renaming, it should not add stages to already pipelined renaming implementations.

4.5 Impact of Base Microarchitecture

One final piece of data we would like to provide is an estimate of the impact of integration for more aggressive microarchitectures. To model a microarchitecture that hopefully represents a next-generation microprocessor, we begin with the organization of our basic 8-way machine. We double the re-ordering capability by doubling the sizes of the instruction and memory ordering buffers; the number of physical registers is increased accordingly. In the memory system, we double the size of the L2 cache to 2 MB and increase the number of simultaneously outstanding misses to 16. To simulate a faster clock, we deepen the pipeline to 5-cycle fetch, 3-cycle decode/rename and 4-cycle register read, lengthen cache array access time to 3 cycles, and slow raw memory access time and the memory bus by 50%. In Figure 4(b), we compare the speedups achieved by our baseline integration configuration (a direct-mapped 256-entry IT) when applied to both the current-generation and next-generation microarchitectures.

One trend that is noticeable by its novelty is that, unlike increasing IT size or associativity, a more aggressive microarchitecture *does* increase the impact of integration on programs that do not benefit from it in a more conservative implementation. The reason for this is that a more speculative machine *changes the structural behavior* of the program. Larger re-order buffers that provide more room for speculation and a deeper pipeline that increases the time it takes to discover and resolve branch mis-predictions combine to raise the total number of instructions executed along mis-speculated

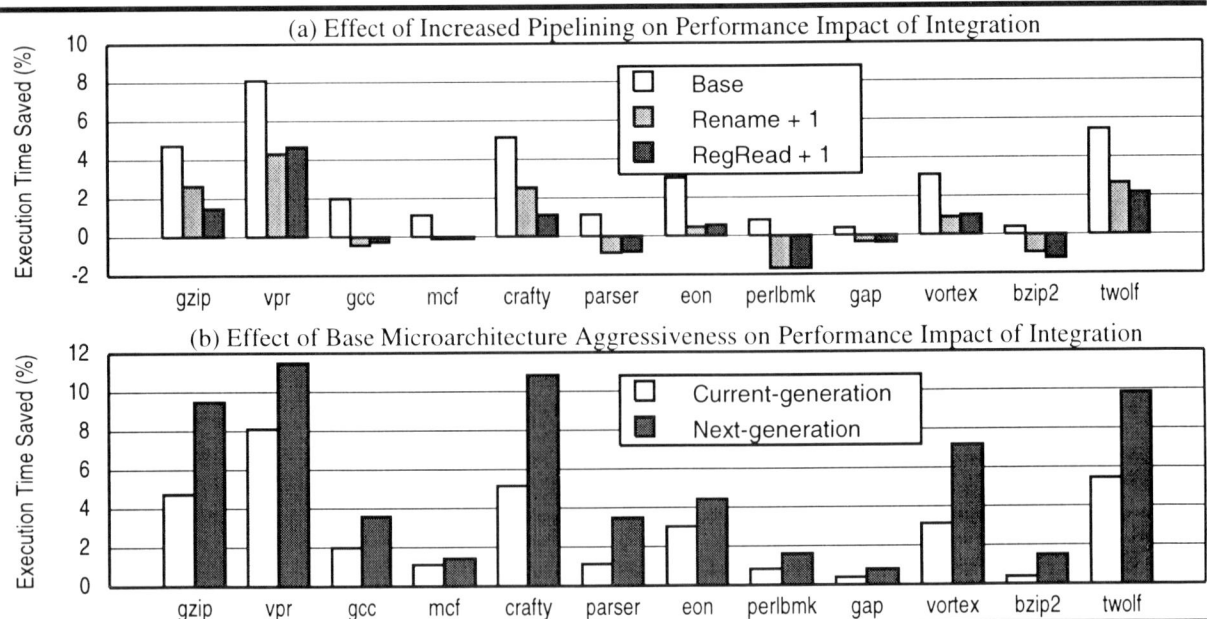

FIGURE 4. Effect of Increased Pipelining and a More Aggressive Base Microarchitecture on Performance Impact of Integration. Execution time saved using a direct-mapped 256-entry IT for (a) our base microarchitecutre with integration-deepend pipeline and (b) a more aggressive base microarchitecture.

paths. That increases the number of potential integration candidates and, in turn, successful integrations. For example, a larger machine can mis-speculate longer along a conditional arm and is more likely to reach (and squash) the re-convergent region along the mis-speculated path. Our results indicate that between 5% and 50% *more* instructions are integrated in the more aggressive, more-speculative configuration.

The relative increase in the effectiveness of integration is probably larger than a simple increase in integrated instructions can account for. As the graph shows, integration is 50% to 120% more effective in reducing execution time in the aggressive configuration than in the base configuration. Absolute performance improvements for the next-generation micro-architecture are close to or over 10% for several benchmarks. The reason for this boost is that in the more aggressive, more deeply pipelined implementation, the benefit of each integrated instruction is also relatively higher. Specifically, the longer register-read times make integration's ability to collapse dependent chains of instructions more important. The *absolute* importance of instant branch mis-prediction resolution is also increased by longer register-read times. However, the *relative* impact of this effect is somewhat mitigated because the depth of the front end increases as well.

5 Related Work

The term *squash reuse* was introduced to describe one of the tasks performed by *Instruction Reuse (IR)* [18]. IR is a table-based technique for avoiding the execution of an instruction that has been previously executed with the same inputs. In addition to squash reuse, in which the reused value comes from the same instance of the instruction that has merely been squashed, IR implements *general reuse*, in which the reused value comes from a different (not necessarily squashed) previous instance that just happens to have the same input operands. Integration implements only squash reuse because it requires that the value already exist in the register file and that the physical register inputs of the squashed instruction match exactly with the inputs of the instruction it will "replace". IR lifts these constraints by storing the squashed *value* inside the lookup table (which is called a *reuse buffer* or *RB*) and writing it into the register file when reuse is detected and by basing the reuse criterion itself is on *instance-independent architectural quantities* like values or logical register names, rather than *instance-dependent micro-architectural* ones like physical register numbers. IR is very applicable, it can exploit general reuse and be implemented on any microarchitecture, but has a somewhat complex implementation. A value-based reuse test implies the need to read registers, which not only complicates the register file, but also moves IR further back in the pipeline, reducing its impact. An architectural-name-based reuse test removes the need to read registers but requires an explicit dependence-tracking scheme within the RB so as not to become too conservative. Both IR forms require additional write data-paths into the register file. In integration, the reused values are already stored in physical registers so no additional register data-paths to read or write any values are required. At the same time, the physical-register-based nature of the reuse test implements dependence-tracking naturally.

The *Dynamic Control Independence (DCI)* [2] buffer is another result salvage mechanism that operates in a centralized window environment. The DCI buffer is a shadow re-order buffer whose contents persist past mis-speculation events that invalidate the architectural buffer (this is a familiar theme). Shadow buffer tags and results can be re-used if the instruction proves to be control- and data- independent. Control independent instructions are found by associatively searching the squashed region of the shadow buffer; their data-independent nature is checked using an architectural-name-based invalidation scheme. The DCI buffer is essentially an architectural-name-based implementation of squash re-use similar to IR that uses a shadow re-order buffer rather than an RB.

We have already alluded to the interplay between integration and *selective squashing* [8, 12, 15, 16], which allows instruction instances to execute multiple times "in-place" before retirement. Selective squashing is an effective way of dealing with data mis-speculations, in which the correct instructions are already in the machine. Selective squashing allows the penalty of squash and re-fetch to be avoided at the cost of keeping instructions in the reservation-station longer and increasing reservation-station contention. Selective squashing, however, cannot salvage work lost to control mis-speculation. Integration and selective squashing are duals. Both techniques salvage instructions by keeping around information for longer than is conventionally required, physical registers for integration and reservation stations for selective squashing. However, while selective squashing actively picks out instructions dependent on the mis-speculation, integration waits for all squashed instructions to be re-processed then picks out the ones that were actually mis-speculation independent.

6 Conclusions and Future Work

We present register integration (or just *integration*), a technique for salvaging valid results that have been unavoidably lost due to the sequential nature of speculation and mis-speculation recovery. Integration is a discipline that allows speculative results to remain in the physical register file past recovery events with the hope that they were independent of the mis-speculation in question and can be used once the particulars of that mis-speculation have been resolved. Integration logic is implemented as a modification to conventional register renaming that recognizes the validity of squashed results using their data-dependences and spares the processor from having to re-execute the corresponding instructions.

Our initial evaluation shows that integration has the potential for noticeable performance improvements of up to 8% at configurations representative of current-generation processors and up to 11.5% for more aggressive, more speculative, more-deeply pipelined next-generation configurations. These speedups are achieved through a combination of reduction in the consumption of execution and fetch bandwidths, the collapsing of dependent instruction chains, and the acceleration of branch resolution. Our numbers indicate that programs typically are able to reuse between 20% and 60% of all squashed instructions that have completed execution prior to squashing, representing between 1% and 19% of committed instructions.

Perhaps more important than integration's performance characteristics, are its mis-speculation reduction characteristics. In addition to improving performance, integration reduces the overall level of wasted work performed by the processor. It reduces the number of instructions executed by re-using squashed computations and its acceleration of branch resolution reduces the number of instructions fetched along mis-speculated paths. According to our results, the number of instruction fetches saved can reach 6% and the number of instruction executions saved, 15%. Both of these numbers grow relatively as the underlying micro-architecture becomes more aggressive. These characteristics make integration an interesting candidate for reducing dynamic-power and energy and also suggest its use in reducing resource contention in simultaneously multi-threaded (SMT) processors.

The implementation of integration is simple, requiring only an integration table (IT), a small cache-like structure with limited content-addressable capabilities and an integration circuit, which is added to the register renaming logic. No changes to either the fetch or execution engines themselves are necessary and integration does not require the reading or writing of any register values, only map table manipulations are used. The performance improvements we present are all achievable with the minimal complexity implementation of integration.

Future work in the area of integration includes a more thorough evaluation of the IT design space, experiments with more varied benchmarks, and a more detailed investigation into the interaction of different micro-architectural parameters with integration. A study of the high-level characteristics of programs that draw benefit from integration is also interesting. We have mentioned possibility for interesting synergy between integration and selective squashing; that possibility needs further investigation. The power aspects of integration and its potential use as a power-reduction technique are also subjects of open research.

The most interesting future direction for integration lies in its ability to support new speculation models. As we have presented it, integration is a mechanism that can re-impose lost sequential semantics on a set of instructions using only their data-dependences. The real power of integration, however, may be in its ability to impose such semantics on a set of instructions that were *not executed sequentially in the first place*. Integration enables a new form of speculation, *data-driven speculation*, in which speculative execution proceeds along statically annotated data-dependence arcs with no regards to sequencing. Integration is used subsequently to sequence the results into a control-driven sequential form required by the architectural interface. In fact, integration was invented during the course of our investigation into a new form of speculative multithreading called *speculative data-driven multithreading (DDMT)* [17].

Acknowledgements

This work was supported in part by National Science Foundation grants MIP-9505853 and CCR-9900584, donations from Intel Corp. and Sun Microsystems, the University of Wisconsin Graduate School and an Intel Ph.D Fellowship. The authors thank the anonymous referees for their reviews.

References

[1] D. Burger and T. Austin. The SimpleScalar Tool Set, Version 2.0. Technical Report CS-TR-97-1342, University of Wisconsin-Madison, Jun. 1997.

[2] Y. Chou, J. Fung, and J. Shen. Reducing Branch Misprediction Penalties via Dynamic Control Independence Detection. In *Proc. 1999 International Conference on Supercomputing*, pages 109–118, Jun. 1999.

[3] G. Chrysos and J. Emer. Memory Dependence Prediction using Store Sets. In *Proc. 25th International Symposium on Computer Architecture*, pages 142–153, Jun. 1998.

[4] J.-L. Cruz, A. Gonzalez, M. Valero, and N. Topham. Multiple-Banked Register File Architectures. In *Proc. 27th Annual International Symposium on Computer Architecture*, pages 316–325, Jun. 2000.

[5] K. Diefendorf. K7 Challenges Intel. *Microprocessor Report*, 12(14), Nov. 1998.

[6] K. Diefendorf. Compaq Chooses SMT for Alpha. *Microprocessor Report*, 13(16), Dec. 1999.

[7] K. Diefendorf. HAL Makes SPARCS Fly. *Microprocessor Report*, 13(5), Nov. 1999.

[8] M. Franklin. *The Multiscalar Architecture*. PhD thesis, University of Wisconsin-Madison, Madison, WI 53706, Nov. 1993.

[9] P. Glaskowsky. Pentium 4 (Partially) Previewed. *Microprocessor Report*, 14(8), Aug. 2000.

[10] L. Gwenapp. Intel's P6 Uses Decoupled Superscalar Design. *Microprocessor Report*, 9(2), Feb. 1995.

[11] R. Kessler. The Alpha 21264 Microprocessor. *IEEE Micro*, 19(2), Mar./Apr. 1999.

[12] M. Lipasti. *Value Locality and Speculative Execution*. PhD thesis, Department of Electrical and Computer Engineering, Carnegie-Mellon University, May 1997.

[13] S. Manne, A. Klauser, and D. Grunwald. Pipeline Gating: Speculation Control for Energy Reduction. In *Proc. 25th Annual International Symposium on Computer Architecture*, pages 132–141, Jun. 1998.

[14] A. Moshovos and G. Sohi. Memory Dependence Speculation Tradeoffs in Centralized, Continuous-Window Superscalar Processors. In *Proc. 6th Annual International Symposium on High-Performance Computer Architecture*, pages 301–312, Feb. 2000.

[15] E. Rotenberg, Q. Jacobson, Y. Sazeides, and J. Smith. Trace Processors. In *Proc. 30th International Symposium on Microarchitecture*, pages 138–148, Dec. 1997.

[16] E. Rotenberg and J. Smith. Control Independence in Trace Processors. In *Proc. 32nd International Symposium on Microarchitecture*, pages 4–15, Nov. 1999.

[17] A. Roth and G. Sohi. Speculative Data-Driven Multithreading. In *Proc. 7th International Symposium on High-Performance Computer Architecture (to appear)*, Jan. 2001.

[18] A. Sodani and G. S. Sohi. Dynamic Instruction Reuse. In *Proc. 24th International Symposium on Computer Architecture*, pages 194–205, Jun 1997.

[19] P. Song. IBM's Power3 to Replace P2SC. *Microprocessor Report*, 11(15), Nov. 1997.

[20] D. M. Tullsen, S. J. Eggers, and H. M. Levy. Simultaneous Multithreading: Maximizing On-Chip Parallelism. In *Proc. 22nd International Symposium on Computer Architecture*, pages 392–403, Jun. 1995.

[21] K. Yeager. The MIPS R10000 Superscalar Microprocessor. *IEEE Micro*, Apr. 1996.

[22] A. Yoaz, M. Erez, R. Ronen, and S. Jourdan. Speculation Techniques for Improving Load-Related Instruction Scheduling. In *Proc. 26th Annual International Symposium on Computer Architecture*, pages 42–53, May 1999.

The Store-Load Address Table and Speculative Register Promotion

Matthew Postiff, David Greene and Trevor Mudge
Advanced Computer Architecture Laboratory, University of Michigan
1301 Beal Ave., Ann Arbor, MI 48109-2122
{postiffm, greened, tnm}@eecs.umich.edu

Abstract

Register promotion is an optimization that allocates a value to a register for a region of its lifetime where it is provably not aliased. Conventional compiler analysis cannot always prove that a value is free of aliases, and thus promotion cannot always be applied. This paper proposes a new hardware structure, the store-load address table (SLAT), which watches both load and store instructions to see if they conflict with entries loaded into the SLAT by explicit software mapping instructions. One use of the SLAT is to allow values to be promoted to registers when they cannot be proven to be promotable by conventional compiler analysis. We call this new optimization speculative register promotion. Using this technique, a value can be promoted to a register and aliased loads and stores to that value's home memory location are caught and the proper fixup is performed. This paper will: a) describe the SLAT hardware and software; b) demonstrate that conventional register promotion is often inhibited by static compiler analysis; c) describe the speculative register promotion optimization; and d) quantify the performance increases possible when a SLAT is used. Our results show that for certain benchmarks, up to 35% of loads and 15% of stores can potentially be eliminated by using the SLAT.

1. Introduction

Register allocation is an important compiler optimization for high-performance computing. Access to data stored in machine registers avoids using the memory subsystem, which is generally much slower than the processor. Register promotion allows scalar values to be allocated to registers for regions of their lifetime where the compiler can prove that there are no aliases for the value [3, 4, 5]. The value is *promoted* to a register for that region by a load instruction at the top of the region. When the region is finished, the value is *demoted* back to memory. The region can be either a loop or a function body in this work, though promotion can be performed on any program region. The benefit is that the value is loaded once at the start of the region and stored once at the end, and all other accesses to it during the region are from a register allocated to the value by the compiler.

Unfortunately, imprecise aliasing information and separate compilation conspire to limit the types and amount of data that can be safely allocated to registers. To allow a relaxation of the compiler's conservative nature, we introduce the *store-load address table (SLAT)* and investigate its use in enabling more effective register allocation. We also introduce a new compiler transformation called *speculative register promotion*, which makes use of the SLAT, and evaluate the performance gains it can provide.

The SLAT and speculative register promotion introduce several new opportunities for register allocation. Figure 1 shows the combinations that we consider in this paper. Figure 1(a) is conventional register allocation as done by most compilers. Figure 1(b) shows the result of register promotion, which requires more sophisticated compiler alias analysis. (Throughout the paper we use the term *alias* somewhat loosely to include all possible references to data though mechanisms other than its primary name, including ambiguous pointers and side-effects.) Figure 1(c) requires further compiler support because in order to prove that the global can be allocated to a register for its entire lifetime requires that the whole program be analyzed at once. This allows the compiler to make the determination that the variable global is only ever used through its name, and never through a pointer. Previous work has examined this optimization [17, 21].

Figure 1(d) shows another example using default register allocation. This time the loop contains a function call, which means that conventional promotion (with separate compilation of functions) cannot be sure that foo() does not access the global variable. Thus global cannot be promoted to a register. Figure 1(e) shows how the SLAT allows promotion to occur anyway. The compiler promotes global as in normal register promotion but uses special opcodes to inform the hardware that the promotion is speculative. Finally, link-time global allocation can be done even under separate compilation when the SLAT is used to protect the global variable. In this case, the mapping operation occurs at the start of the program–say at the top of main()–and is not shown in the figure. Table 1 gives a summary of these allocation strategies.

The remainder of this paper is organized as follows. Section 2 describes the logical organization of the SLAT. Section 3 introduces the speculative register promotion transformation. In Section 4 we describe our experimental setup, while

```
while () {                  ld r5, global              while () {
  ld r5, global             while () {                   add r32, r32, 1
  add r5, r5, 1               add r5, r5, 1            }
  st global, r5             }
}                           st global, r5
```

    (a) Original source   (b) Register promotion   (c) Link-time global allocation

```
while () {                  map r5, global             while () {
  ld r5, global             while () {                   add r32, r32, 1
  add r5, r5, 1               add r5, r5, 1              foo();
  st global, r5               foo();                   }
  foo();                    }
}                           unmap r5, global
```

    (d) Original source   (e) SLAT-based promotion   (f) SLAT-based link-time
                                                                                                                                                 global allocation

Figure 1. The results of using different register allocation strategies. (a) The original source code, in a combination of C and assembler notation. It uses the default strategy for allocation, which does not allocate the global to a register. (b) Register promotion moves the load and store outside of the loop. (c) After application of link-time global variable allocation, each occurrence of global is replaced with r32 and unnecessary copies are removed. (d) Another snippet of source code, which includes a function call, rendering the global not promotable by conventional means. (e) The SLAT allows the promotion to occur in spite of the function call. (f) Link-time global variable allocation can also be performed with help from the SLAT even when separate compilation is used.

our experimental results are analyzed in Section 5. Section 6 describes previous work in the areas of memory disambiguation and register allocation. Finally, we discuss our conclusions and directions for future work in Section 7.

2. The Store-Load Address Table (SLAT)

The store-load address table (SLAT) is a hardware structure that allows the compiler to relax some of the conservative assumptions made due to imprecise analysis of memory communication. Logically, the SLAT is a table where each entry contains a logical register number, memory address and some information flags for bookkeeping. Speculative register promotion uses the SLAT to associate a memory address with a register. All references to this address will be forwarded to the register file as long as the address is mapped in the SLAT. Thus, the SLAT is indexed associatively by address.

Special machine instructions are used by the compiler to manage the SLAT. To initialize a speculative promotion, a special map instruction is used. This instruction includes a memory address and a register number. A SLAT entry is created, indicating that the data at the given memory address resides in the given register. A load from memory is also executed to place the desired data in the register. Likewise, an unmap instruction removes an association from the SLAT, sending the data in the register to the memory. The map and unmap operations are essentially just special load and store operations.

After a map instruction has associated a memory address with a register, every subsequent memory operation examines the SLAT, comparing its address operand with those in the SLAT. When a match (conflict) is detected in the SLAT, the memory operation is redirected to the register file. A load retrieves its value from the SLAT-mapped register instead of from memory; a store uses the mapped register as its destination instead of memory. An unmap instruction at the bottom of the promotion region handles storing the updated register out to memory.

Since the SLAT allows register allocation of potentially aliased variables (including globals that may be used by callee functions) whose scopes may exceed that of a single function, special handling is necessary to close the "gap" between function-scoped machine registers and registers containing mapped data. One example of this problem occurs at function call boundaries. On entry to the callee, all callee-save registers used by the function are first spilled to the stack to preserve existing values for the caller. These registers are restored upon function exit. If one of these callee-save registers is mapped in by the SLAT, the spill instruction must be dynamically modified to store the data to the "home" memory location of the data (the global storage or stack location for an aliased local variable). This home address is available in the SLAT entry for the register being spilled. A reload operation likewise must be modified to load from the home location. These operations require two new memory instructions: spill and reload. These are store and load instructions with special opcodes to indicate their function (saving and restoring of callee-save registers). These instructions must examine the SLAT to see if the referenced register is mapped. Thus the SLAT is also indexed directly by register number. We classify such registers as *callee-update*, analogous to callee-save, because their val-

Allocation Strategy	What is Allocated	Region in Register File	Is Whole-Program Information Used?
(a, d) Default	Unaliased local scalars including compiler temporaries.	Local	No.
(b) Register Promotion	Aliased local scalars or global scalars aliased or not. In either case, they are promoted for regions where they are provably unaliased.	Local	Can be used to enhance alias analysis so that extra candidates can be proven safe to promote.
(c) Link-time global allocation	Unaliased global scalars.	Global	Required.
(e) SLAT-based promotion	Aliased local scalars or global scalars. SLAT allows allocation even in aliased regions.	Mappable	Can be used to reduce number of SLAT promotions necessary.
(f) SLAT-based link-time global allocation	Aliased and unaliased global scalars.	Mappable	Can be used to reduce number of SLAT promotions necessary.

Table 1. Various strategies for allocating registers. In our usage, "aliased" means that the variable's address has been taken somewhere in the program or it could be referenced through a function-call side effect. The register file regions are conceptual divisions of the registers into groups based on their function. The "local" region of the register file is the region used for local variables in the function. The global region contains global variables for their entire lifetime. The mappable region contains mapped (speculatively promoted variables). In our experiments, the local and mappable regions are the same. The letters in column 1 correspond to the labels in Figure 1.

ues are automatically updated by any memory accesses in the callee function.

Because the `reload` instruction must have access to the home memory address for the data, the processor must keep every SLAT entry that is created until an `unmap` deallocates it. Moreover, an address can be mapped to multiple registers or a single register can be re-mapped to a new address. These cases are simplified by the fact that only one mapping is active for a particular function. The compiler can guarantee that no address or register is mapped twice in the same region. It can do this because it only speculatively promotes directly-named scalar variables.

There are several strategies for dealing with these situations. One possibility is to have a large SLAT with a hardware-controlled overflow spill mechanism, similar to that used in the C-machine stack cache [24]. Another possibility is to require compiler management of the SLAT. Instructions to save and restore SLAT entries can be generated in the same way instructions to save and restore callee-save registers are generated. Our simulations assume an infinite-sized SLAT so that we may evaluate its performance potential.

In addition to callee-save spills and reloads, spill and reload operations are necessary to deal with excessive register pressure within a function. Speculative register promotion can increase the amount of this spilling. Since the spilling effectively negates the benefit of register promotion the compiler may simply reverse the promotion if spilling occurs. Memory access size and overlap must also be considered in the SLAT; the compiler can restrict promotions to ease this problem.

3. Speculative Register Promotion Using the SLAT

This section outlines how the SLAT can be used to allow speculative register promotion. Preliminary exploration into the limitations on static register promotion indicated that a significant number of memory operations cannot be promoted due to ambiguous or unseen memory accesses through function calls. This will be quantified later in the paper. To address this problem, we consider a new optimization called *speculative register promotion* which uses the SLAT to allow promotions in these situations. It does this by providing a fallback mechanism in the case that the promotion was too aggressive, i.e. that there was a conflict where the promoted value was not synchronized with its value in memory. When this occurs, the hardware can provide the current value.

As we saw in Section 2, the SLAT is tailored to solve this problem because the hardware compares each load and store address against those stored in the SLAT. Once a value is promoted to a register with a `map` instruction, it can be used or defined several times before a conflicting memory load appears. Since the value in memory could be out of date with respect to the value promoted to the register, both load and store operations have to be examined to see if they are attempting to access the value that was promoted to a register.

The register promoter in our C compiler, MIRV, can promote global scalar variables, aliased local scalar variables, large constants, indirect pointer references (we call these *dereferences*), and direct and indirect structure references. It

Instruction	Action
map reg, addr	Add an entry to the SLAT. If there is a pre-existing mapping for the address in the SLAT, the data is forwarded from the previous register to the register currently being mapped. Otherwise, the data is loaded from memory.
unmap reg, addr	Remove an entry from the SLAT. If there is a previously mapped but unspilled entry, store the data from reg to the previously mapped register.
spill	If the register contains a value that was placed there by a previous map instruction, spill the value to the mapped address (home location) instead of the address specified to the stack spill location.
reload	If the previous SLAT on the SLAT stack has a mapping for this register, reload the value from its mapped address. Otherwise, reload from the specified location on the stack.
load	If any entry in the SLAT stack maps the load address, and has not been spilled, then copy from the mapped register to the load's destination register. Increment slatLoadConflicts.
store	If any entry in the SLAT stack maps the store address, and has not been spilled, then copy from the store source register to the register indicated in the SLAT entry. This implements the "callee update" register convention (a modification of "callee save". Increment slatStoreConflicts.
call	Push a new SLAT onto the SLAT stack.
return	Pop current SLAT from SLAT stack.

Table 2. Description of the actions that take place at various points in the SLAT simulator.

can do so over loops or whole functions. The algorithm is described in detail elsewhere [17]. Speculative register promotion was a simple augmentation to the existing promoter. Any directly-named value (global or local) which is not promoted because of aliases can be promoted speculatively (based on simple selection heuristics). This is accomplished by emitting a promoting load (map) and demoting store (unmap) at the boundaries of the region, with additional information indicating these are speculative promotion operations. The backend of the compiler passes this through via annotation bits in the instruction encoding and the simulator treats the map/unmap operation as described in Table 2. Since global and aliased data can reside in registers, the compiler was also restricted from certain kinds of code motion around those accesses.

4. Experimental Setup

All the benchmarks used in this study were compiled with the MIRV C compiler. The compiler takes a list of optimizations to run on the code as well as the number of registers that are available on the architecture. We ran variants of the SPEC training inputs in order to keep simulation time reasonable. Our baseline timing simulator is the default sim-outorder configuration. A description of MIRV, our compilation methodology, and benchmark inputs is presented in the technical report of [12].

All simulations were done using the SimpleScalar 3.0/PISA simulation toolset [10]. We have modified the toolset (simulators, assembler, and disassembler) to support up to 256 registers. Registers 0-31 are used as defined in the MIPS System V ABI [11] in order to maintain compatibility with pre-compiled libraries. Registers 32-255 are used either as additional registers for global variables or additional registers for local caller/callee save variables.

A modified version of sim-profile was used to simulate the behavior of a program compiled to use the SLAT. The simulator implements an infinite-sized SLAT with ideal replacement. Table 2 shows the actions that are taken at various instructions in the program. While the simulator is idealized and is not particular to an implementation, it allows us to see the potential benefits of the SLAT. Later work will address specific implementation issues.

5. Experimental Evaluation

This section presents our experimental results. Section 5.1 discusses the performance improvements possible with conventional register promotion and shows how it is limited in its applicability. Section 5.2 shows the performance improvement that can be obtained when values can be promoted speculatively.

5.1. Register Promotion

Previous work showed the performance of basic register promotion in the MIRV compiler [17]. That work found that register promotion improves performance from 5% to 15% on some benchmarks. Other benchmarks perform worse with reg-

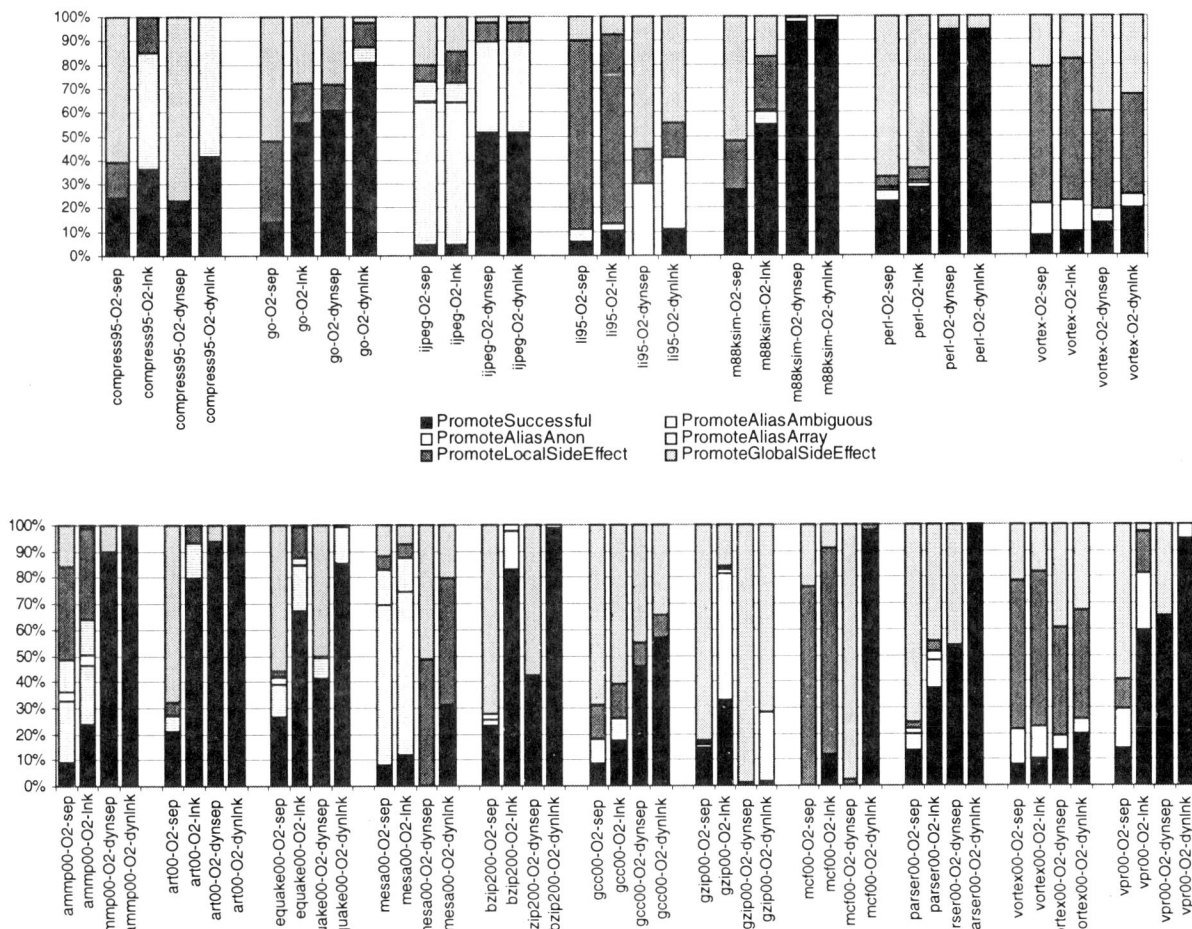

Figure 2. The reasons that scalar candidates could not be promoted. The bars shows the breakdown of reasons that promotion could not occur. All compilations use -O2 optimization. The first bar is separate compilation of modules with no interprocedural alias analysis. The second bar has interprocedural side-effect analysis information annotated at each function call site for improved alias analysis precision. This increased information in turn increases the number of candidates that are provably safe to promote. The percentages shown for these first two bars are percentages of scalar promotion candidates. The third and fourth bars are analogous except that they estimate loss in performance by weighting the counts by dynamic frequency of access to the candidate variables. The legend is explained in Table 3. These numbers are based on compile-time estimates and unlike later figures are only indicative of trends.

ister promotion. This is due to extra register pressure caused by the promotion, which introduces spilling code.

The somewhat lackluster results for many benchmarks led us to evaluate the reasons why promotion is not performing well. The graph in Figure 2 shows statistics kept by the compiler which demonstrate that promotion is often limited by aliasing and side-effects. The figure shows each benchmark (along the X axis) in four different configurations. The first configuration is -O2 with separate compilation of the program's files. The compiler produces the least detailed alias information in this case. The second configuration is similar except that a simple interprocedural side-effect analysis is used to improve the precision of alias analysis at function call sites. This increases the precision of the alias analysis and allows the compiler to determine that more values are safe to promote. For these two bars, the percentages indicate the number of *static* references that fall into each category.

The third and fourth bars are similar to the first and second except that they estimate the effect of the un-promoted values by weighting each value by the number of load and store executions that would have been saved in a training run of the benchmark if the value had been promoted. Thus the percentages on the Y-axis change meaning for the third and fourth bar, because they indicate the estimated percentage of *dynamic* references that fall into each category.

The bars are divided into portions showing the reason that a promotion could not occur. The legend of the graphs are explained in Table 3. The last two categories–local and global side effects–are of interest in this paper because the SLAT can aid the compiler in promoting those references to registers.

Legend Entry	Explanation
Successful	The transformation was not restricted.
AliasAmbiguous	A possible manipulation of some data through a pointer prevented the transformation. In other words, there is a pointer that *might* point to something the restricts the transformation, but the compiler does not know for sure.
AliasAnon	A manipulation of code involving dynamically allocated memory was restricted by some other possible manipulation of dynamic memory.
AliasArray	A transformation involving an array was restricted by some other use of the array. Because MIRV does not track individual array elements, any reference to an array element is considered to reference the entire array.
GlobalSideEffect	A manipulation of code involving a global variable was prevented by a function call. Usually this is because a function is assumed to define and use all global variables when it is called. If, however, the compiler is performing whole-program analysis, this means that the called function references the global variable somewhere in its body, or in the body of some function further down the call chain.
LocalSideEffect	A possible manipulation of some data through a pointer passed to a function prevented the transformation. In other words, a pointer argument to the call might point to a local variable. The compiler must assume that variable is both used and defined by the call, preventing transformations across the call site.

Table 3. An explanation of the legend in Figure 2.

For example, for the compress95-sep bar, about 25% of static references were promoted. About 15% of values were not promotable because of local side effects, and about 60% of values were not promoted because of a global side effect. Local and global side effects are due to function call sites within the promotion region.

Overall, it is evident that of all promotion candidates, only 20% to 30% of potential promotions are actually performed. Some outliers, such as `li` have almost no promotable values, and some have a large portion of candidates that are promotable. More advanced alias analysis (shown in the second bar of each group) increases the number of promotion successes by 20% in many cases. Still, 20% to 50% of promotion candidates are not promotable using the side-effect analysis.

For the non-promotable candidates, the primary reason is side effects due to function calls (both local and global side effects). This implies that any mechanism that allows promotion in such regions will have to handle call sites very well.

The dynamic estimates in the third and fourth bars of the graphs in Figure 2 show slightly different results because the frequency count of loop bodies is taken into consideration when weighting the effect of a successful or missed promotion. The results are very benchmark dependent, sometimes showing that the static estimate was good, as is the case with `vortex` and `art`. In many cases the dynamic estimate shows that the missed promotion opportunities were not significant factors in performance.

There are a significant number of promotion opportunities that are missed because of poor alias analysis. This observation led us to develop speculative register promotion, which is evaluated below.

5.2. Speculative Register Promotion using the SLAT

The main shortcoming of register promotion is the number of cases where promotion cannot happen because of aliasing. In this section, we evaluate the performance benefits possible from allowing more promotion via the SLAT.

5.2.1. Loop and Function Promotion. Table 4 shows the improvements possible with the SLAT. The first two numeric columns show improvement possible on top of MIRV at -O2 optimization, which includes only loop-level promotion. The numbers were collected by modifying the register promoter in MIRV to annotate the candidates that could not be promoted. Each such candidate variable reference (load or store) was annotated and each occurrence was counted during the simulation. The numbers in the table are the percentage of all load and store instructions that were thus annotated, meaning that if we had "perfect" register promotion, all of these loads and stores would have been transformed by the compiler into register references. Note that these percentages are different than shown in Figure 2 because those percentages are only of promotion candidates, not *all* load and store operations. One other caveat with regard to these numbers is that they are overly conservative because they count store operations that may not be necessary because the promoted variable is not actually defined in the promotion region. Therefore, several of the

Category	Benchmark	mirvcc -O2		mirvcc -O2 with function level promotion	
		Reduction in Loads %	Reduction in Stores %	Reduction in Loads %	Reduction in Stores %
SPECint95	compress	18.9	12.8	36.6	14.2
	gcc	1.3	-2.7	1.6	-5.5
	go	1.3	-1.8	1.9	-5.2
	ijpeg	0.3	-0.4	0.3	-0.4
	li	6.5	2.2	8.1	2.6
	m88ksim	0.8	0.0	3.8	-0.2
	perl	0.0	0.0	1.5	-0.1
	vortex	-1.7	-3.1	-1.1	-5.8
SPECfp2000	ammp	4.6	-0.1	4.7	-0.1
	art	13.6	12.2	13.6	12.2
	equake	4.6	-0.1	4.7	-0.1
	mesa	0.5	0.0	0.5	0.0
SPECint2000	bzip	5.3	-0.4	7.3	-1.4
	gcc	2.0	-2.5	2.3	-5.0
	gzip	24.2	12.2	31.4	18.1
	mcf	6.8	1.2	6.9	1.2
	parser	14.0	-0.5	16.9	0.5
	vortex	-1.7	-3.1	-1.1	-5.8
	vpr	7.8	-4.4	13.2	-6.3

Table 4. Reductions in dynamic loads and stores possible for missed promotion candidates with the SLAT. The baseline in columns 3 and 4 is compiled with loop-level register promotion The baseline in columns 5 and 6 is compiled with loop- and then with function-level promotion. The percentages give the number of loads and stores that could be removed if the promotion could take advantage of the SLAT.

"improvements" in store instruction counts are actually negative, indicating that more stores were counted after the optimization than before. The actual performance will be better than these numbers show.

Even with those caveats, the compress, art, gzip, parser, and vpr benchmarks all exhibit significant potential for improvement for both load and store instructions–with 10% to 20% reductions possible in several cases. This substantiates our earlier conclusion that conventional promotion is unable to take advantage of many opportunities. The other results are not very significant, which is not a surprise since this optimization is very dependent on the benchmark.

The third and fourth numeric columns show what happens when loops *and* functions are considered as regions. If a variable can be promoted in a loop, it is done first. Then, if the variable is still profitably promotable over the whole function body, this transformation is made. The result is that function-promoted variables are loaded once at the top of the function and stored once before the function exits, and all other references are to a register instead of to memory. Function-level promotion increases the number of candidate loads and stores for the promoter to examine and we see a corresponding increase in the number of loads and stores that could have been eliminated with speculative promotion, but that were not removed because of aliasing problems. In this case, what has happened is that the pool of promotion candidates has been enlarged by examining the whole function body, but very few of those additional candidates are actually promoted. We verified this by comparing the overall performance of function-level promotion with the base -O2 configuration. There was not any significant difference (less than 1% for all benchmarks). This indicates that while function-level promotion found more candidates it wanted to promote, it could not promote most of them due to aliasing concerns. The SLAT is effective in allowing these promotions to occur.

5.2.2. Whole-Program Global Variable Promotion.

Previous work demonstrates that link-time allocation of global variables to registers is an important performance optimization [17, 21]. The previous work has only considered "unaliased" global variables, i.e. those whose addresses are not taken anywhere in the program. The SLAT could further improve the performance of link-time global variable allocation by allowing global variables whose addresses are taken to reside in registers for their entire lifetime. If an enregistered global variable is accessed through a pointer, the SLAT will correctly redirect the memory operation to the register file.

Experiments showed that most benchmarks are not generally improved by such a scheme. This result indicates that most global variables (or at least the important ones) do not have their address taken. This is intuitive, since the global variables are directly accessible and thus need not be used through a level of indirection. This is still promising for the SLAT, however, in a separate compilation environment. In such an environment, the compiler cannot determine which globals are aliased and which are not because modules are not visible as in our link-time, whole-program allocation scheme. Therefore, the SLAT can allow us to approach the good performance of link-time global variable allocation (as in [17]) without needing to compile the whole program as a single unit.

5.2.3. SLAT Size Considerations. The next question we examine is how many entries the SLAT needs to achieve the performance improvements above. The simulator keeps track of the current number of SLAT entries in use and also tracks the high water mark of this number, which indicates the most SLAT entries that would ever be in use concurrently. The high water mark results are presented in Table 5. Except for li and vortex, none of the benchmarks require more than 50 SLAT entries to speculatively promote all aliased variables. These two benchmarks are exceptional because of their deep function call chains (li is a recursive descent program). Most benchmarks require less than 30 entries. This indicates that the SLAT should be effective while still very small in size. This is important since the SLAT must be fully associative. As described in the caption of the table, the third column is for loop-based register promotion, while the fourth column adds function-level promotion to the normal loop based promotion. Function-level promotion produces more candidates in the function bodies and, as we found earlier, not many of those are promotable because of alias problems. Thus the number of SLAT entries required to accommodate function level promotion is higher than for loop-level promotion–by a large margin in some benchmarks.

These numbers double-count any overlap that occurs because a variable gets allocated to the SLAT more than once. This can happen for global variables promoted in two different functions which are active at the same time on the procedure call stack. Overlap can also happen if a variable is promoted over a loop region and then the function promoter decides to promote it over the whole function body. If we corrected for this effect, the values in the graph would be even lower, meaning that an even smaller SLAT will provide the benefits we seek from speculative register promotion.

We also tracked the variation in the required size of the SLAT over the benchmark run. The resulting distribution (not included in this paper) showed that 90% of the *instructions* were executed under conditions requiring about 1/2 to 3/4 of the maximum number of SLAT entries to capture most of the benchmark's execution. This gives a tighter bound on the required size of the SLAT, although it does still count duplicates.

At this point it may be questioned why the SLAT would ever need more entries than there are architected registers. This is a valid question because at most only one aliased variable can be allocated to a given register at any given time, so the most active SLAT entries would be equal to the number of registers. However, at any given time, there are more values alive than there are registers because there are multiple functions "alive" on the procedure linkage stack. Each function could have promoted several values. While these values are not in the registers (they have been spilled out by the calling convention) they are nonetheless active in the sense that they will be coming back into registers when the procedure stack unwinds as functions are completed. Some sort of SLAT management (similar to callee/caller save registers) would allow the SLAT to be limited in size but we do not consider that in detail in this work.

Category	Benchmark	SLAT Entries Actually Required	
		-O2	-O2 with function promotion
SPECint95	compress	7	19
	ijpeg	23	27
	m88ksim	11	37
	perl	10	26
SPECfp2000	ammp	2	11
	art	11	19
	equake	16	36
	mesa	4	5
SPECint2000	bzip	23	32
	gzip	11	25
	mcf	5	7
	parser	26	44
	vpr	10	16

Table 5. Summary of SLAT utilization for select benchmarks. The third and fourth columns show the maximum number of SLAT entries ever used concurrently in the benchmark, not accounting for duplicates. The third column (mirvcc -O2) is for register promotion over loop bodies. The fourth column adds promotion over whole function bodies.

5.2.4. Other Considerations. When a load or store finds that its operand is mapped by the SLAT, a conflict has occurred and fixup needs to be performed to retrieve the latest value (on a load) or update the mapped register (on a store). Our simulations showed that for compress, gzip, and parser, this happened roughly 2%, 3%, and 5% of memory operations. The rest of the benchmarks were well under 1%.

6. Background and Related Work

This section reports on a number of proposals that combine software and hardware approaches to disambiguation, allocation, and scheduling.

Several previous proposals have discussed methods to allow register allocation for aliased variables. CRegs solves the aliasing problem by associating address tags with each register [18, 19, 20]. These tags are checked against loads and stores to keep the registers and memory consistent. On a store, an associative lookup must update all copies of the data in the CReg array. Variable forwarding was proposed as an improvement to CRegs [22]. This technique allows the elimination of compiler alias analysis, simplifying the software side of the problem but complicating the hardware because a value can be mapped to any registers in the register file. Chiueh proposed an improvement on both CRegs and variable forwarding [23]. Aliased data items are kept in the memory hierarchy (data cache) and accessed indirectly through registers. The registers contain the address of the value and the compiler specifies a bit on each operand in the instruction to direct the hardware to use that register indirectly.

The weakness of CRegs is that writes must associatively update several registers. The SLAT does not require this associative write-update to the register file because the compiler guarantees that only one copy of the data is mapped to a register within a function. This vastly simplifies register access compared to CRegs.

Nicolau proposed a purely software disambiguation technique where a load could be scheduled ahead of potentially dependent stores [2]. This technique is called runtime disambiguation because the hardware checks conditions at runtime to determine if a conflict has occurred.

The Memory Conflict Buffer (MCB) is designed as an extension of Nicolau's runtime disambiguation. It allows the compiler to avoid emitting explicit (software) checks of address operands [8, 9]. Instead, addresses that need to be protected are communicated to the hardware by special load operations and then special check operations ask the hardware whether a conflict has occurred for the given address. Hardware does the address comparisons instead of software. Like for runtime disambiguation, the goal is to perform code scheduling in the presence of ambiguous memory operations.

The SLAT is different from the MCB in that it must retain information across function calls to be effective–as was shown, this is important because many aliases are due to assumed side effects of function calls, so that SLAT must handle function calls elegantly. The information stored in the MCB is not valid across function calls [8].

The IA64 architecture provides hardware support for compiler-directed data speculation through use of an Advanced Load Address Table (ALAT) [12]. It allows static scheduling of loads and dependent instructions above potentially aliased stores. The compiler is responsible for emitting check and fixup code for the (hopefully rare) event that a conflict occurs.

The SLAT is different than the ALAT in a number of respects. The most notable difference is that the hardware must compare not only store addresses to all SLAT entries (as with the ALAT), but in addition it must compare all load addresses as well. This is because the most current value for the memory location could be housed in a register and any loads that access that memory location need to receive the current value. The ALAT cannot provide this functionality because the hardware only checks the addresses of store instructions with the entries in the ALAT.

Another difference is that the SLAT must retain all the information ever entered into it whereas ALAT entries can be replaced because of overflow, conflicts, or context switches. This is because the ALAT requires an explicit check instruction to determine if the fixup code needs to be run. If an entry is missing from the ALAT, the check instruction runs the fixup code. Thus the ALAT is "safe" even when it loses information. On the other hand, if the SLAT "loses" an entry, load and store instructions could be executed without detection of conflicts, which would produce incorrect program output.

Another difference between the SLAT and ALAT is that SLAT fixup is not initiated at the point of transformation but at the point where the conflict occurs. For the ALAT, fixup is always initiated at the point of the original load (which has been converted to a check load). For the SLAT, since the correct data is in a register, the hardware can forward the data for a load from the register or for a store to the register.

Transmeta Corporation recently introduced a line of processors that is designed to run unmodified x86 programs using dynamic binary translation [1, 6]. Capability similar to the ALAT is provided by special hardware and instructions to allow load and store reordering. Two instructions are necessary for this: `load-and-protect` (`ldp`) and `store-under-alias-mask` (`stam`). The `ldp` instruction "protects" a memory region. The `stam` instruction then checks if it would store to a previously protected region. If it would, it traps so that fixup can be performed. The main purpose of this system is to allow Transmeta's code morphing software to allocate stack variables to host registers.

The SLAT differs from this approach in that it is designed for a static compilation environment, hardware corrects conflicts instead of taking an exception, and memory does not necessarily need to be kept up to date since the latest value is in the register.

7. Conclusions

This paper has described the design of the store-load address table, its use in a new optimization we call speculative register promotion, and the reductions in load and store operations possible when using this optimization. We began by showing that register promotion was often limited by compiler alias analysis. The number of loads and stores can be significantly reduced for several of the benchmarks with the addition of a SLAT and speculative register promotion–up to 35% reduction in loads and 15% reduction in stores. Applying the SLAT to link-time global variable allocation does not produce much benefit for most benchmarks. It is more important in this case to note that the SLAT effectively allows link-time allocation even in the face of separate compilation, so that the SLAT can achieve most or all of the benefit of link-time allocation while doing so in a separate compilation environment. Finally, we showed that the SLAT can be modestly sized and achieve the benefits reported here.

There are several important avenues of future work. In addition to providing more detailed performance numbers, we will investigate strategies for determining when the compiler should use the SLAT. We will also address specific SLAT hardware implementation issues as well as compiler management of the SLAT storage. Future work will also include investigating other ways the hardware can help the compiler do aggressive, potentially unsafe operations.

Acknowledgments

This work was supported by DARPA grant DABT63-97-C-0047. The authors are supported on a University of Michigan Rackham Graduate School Predoctoral Fellowship and an Intel Fellowship. Simulations were performed on computers donated through the Intel Education 2000 Grant. Our thanks are also due to the anonymous reviewers who helped us improve the quality of this work.

References

[1] Alexander Klaiber. The Technology Behind Crusoe^{TM} Processors. Transmeta Corporation. January 2000.

[2] Alexandru Nicolau. Run-Time Disambiguation: Comping with Statically Unpredictable Dependencies. IEEE Transactions Computers, Vol. 38 No. 5, pp. 663-678. May, 1989.

[3] Keith Cooper and John Lu. Register Promotion in C Programs. Proc. ACM SIGPLAN Conf. Programming Language Design and Implementation (PLDI-97), pp. 308-319, June, 1997.

[4] A. V. S. Sastry and Roy D. C. Ju. A New Algorithm for Scalar Register Promotion Based on SSA Form. Proc. ACM SIGPLAN'98 Conf. Programming Language Design and Implementation (PLDI), pp. 15-25, , 1998.

[5] Raymond Lo, Fred Chow, Robert Kennedy, Shin-Ming Liu and Peng Tu. Register Promotion by Sparse Partial Redundancy Elimination of Loads and Stores. Proc. ACM SIGPLAN'98 Conf. Programming Language Design and Implementation (PLDI), pp. 26-37, , 1998.

[6] Malcom J. Wing and Edmund J. Kelly, Transmeta Corporation. Method and apparatus for aliasing memory data in an advanced microprocessor. United States Patent 5926832. http://www.patents.ibm.com.

[7] David Bernstein, Martin E. Hopkins, and Michael Rodeh, International Business Machines Corporation. Speculative Load Instruction Rescheduler for a Compiler Which Moves Load Instructions Across Basic Block Boundaries While Avoiding Program Exceptions. United States Patent 5526499. http://www.patents.ibm.com.

[8] David M. Gallagher, William Y. Chen, Scott A. Mahlke, John C. Gyllenhaal and Wen-mei W. Hwu. Dynamic memory disambiguation using the memory conflict buffer. ACM SIGPLAN Notices, Vol. 29 No. 11, pp. 183-193. Nov. 1994.

[9] Tokuzo Kiyohara, Wen-mei W. Hwu; William Chen, Matsushita Electric Industrial Co., Ltd., and The Board of Trustees of the University of Illinois. Memory conflict buffer for achieving memory disambiguation in compile-time code schedule. United States Patent 5694577. http://www.patents.ibm.com.

[10] Douglas C. Burger and Todd M. Austin. The SimpleScalar Tool Set, Version 2.0. University of Wisconsin, Madison Tech. Report. June, 1997.

[11] UNIX System Laboratories Inc. System V Application Binary Interface: MIPS Processor Supplement. Unix Press/Prentice Hall, Englewood Cliffs, New Jersey, 1991.

[12] Matthew Postiff, David Greene, Charles Lefurgy, Dave Helder, Trevor Mudge. The MIRV SimpleScalar/PISA Compiler. University of Michigan CSE Technical Report CSE-TR-421-00. http://www.eecs.umich.edu/mirv.

[13] Intel IA-64 Application Developer's Architecture Guide. May 1999. Order Number: 245188-001.

[14] H. Roland Kenner, Alan Karp, and William Chen, Institute for the Develoment of Emerging Architecture, L.L.C. Method and apparatus for implementing check instructions that allow for the reuse of memory conflict information if no memory conflict occurs. United States Patent 5903749. http://www.patents.ibm.com.

[15] Robert Yung and Neil C. Wilhelm. Caching Processor General Registers. Intl. Conf. Computer Design, pp. 307-312, Oct, 1995.

[16] Robert Yung and Neil C. Wilhelm. Caching Processor General Registers. Sun Microsystems Laboratories Tech. Report. June, 1995.

[17] Matthew Postiff, David Greene, and Trevor Mudge. Exploiting Large Register Files in General Purpose Code. University of Michigan Technical Report CSE-TR-434-00. http://www.eecs.umich.edu/mirv.

[18] H. Dietz and C.-H. Chi. CRegs: A New Kind of Memory for Referencing Arrays and Pointers. Proc., Supercomputing '88: November 14--18, 1988, Orlando, Florida, pp. 360-367, Jan, 1988.

[19] S. Nowakowski and M. T. O'Keefe. A CRegs Implementation Study Based on the MIPS-X RISC Processor. Intl. Conf. Computer Design, VLSI in Computers and Processors, pp. 558-563, Oct, 1992.

[20] Peter Dahl and Matthew O'Keefe. Reducing Memory Traffic with CRegs. Proc. 27th Intl. Symp. Microarchitecture, pp. 100-104, Nov, 1994.

[21] David W. Wall. Global Register Allocation at Link Time. Proc. SIGPLAN'86 Symp. Compiler Construction, pp. 264-275, July, 1986.

[22] B. Heggy and M. L. Soffa. Architectural Support for Register Allocation in the Presence of Aliasing. Proc., Supercomputing '90: November 12--16, 1990, New York Hilton at Rockefeller Center, New York, New York, pp. 730-739, Feb, 1990.

[23] T.-C. Chiueh. An Integrated Memory Management Scheme for Dynamic Alias Resolution. Proc., Supercomputing '91: Albuquerque, New Mexico, November 18-22, 1991, pp. 682-691, Aug. 1991.

[24] David R. Ditzel and H. R. McLellan. Register Allocation for Free: The C Machine Stack Cache. Proc. Symp. Architectural Support for Programming Languages and Operating Systems, pp. 48-56, March, 1982.

Memory Hierarchy Reconfiguration for Energy and Performance in General-Purpose Processor Architectures*

Rajeev Balasubramonian[†], David Albonesi[‡], Alper Buyuktosunoglu[‡], and Sandhya Dwarkadas[†]

[†] Department of Computer Science
[‡] Department of Electrical and Computer Engineering
University of Rochester

Abstract

Conventional microarchitectures choose a single memory hierarchy design point targeted at the average application. In this paper, we propose a cache and TLB layout and design that leverages repeater insertion to provide dynamic low-cost configurability trading off size and speed on a per application phase basis. A novel configuration management algorithm dynamically detects phase changes and reacts to an application's hit and miss intolerance in order to improve memory hierarchy performance while taking energy consumption into consideration. When applied to a two-level cache and TLB hierarchy at $0.1\mu m$ technology, the result is an average 15% reduction in cycles per instruction (CPI), corresponding to an average 27% reduction in memory-CPI, across a broad class of applications compared to the best conventional two-level hierarchy of comparable size. Projecting to sub-.1 μm technology design considerations that call for a three-level conventional cache hierarchy for performance reasons, we demonstrate that a configurable L2/L3 cache hierarchy coupled with a conventional L1 results in an average 43% reduction in memory hierarchy energy in addition to improved performance.

1 Introduction

The performance of general purpose microprocessors continues to increase at a rapid pace. In the last 15 years, performance has improved at a rate of roughly 1.6 times per year with about half of this gain attributed to techniques for exploiting instruction-level parallelism and memory locality [13]. Despite these advances, several impending bottlenecks threaten to slow the pace at which future performance

---

*This work was supported in part by NSF grants CDA-9401142, EIA-9972881, CCR-9702466, CCR-9701915, CCR-9811929, CCR-9988361, and CCR-9705594; by DARPA/ITO under AFRL contract F29601-00-K-0182; and by an external research grant from DEC/Compaq.

improvements can be realized. Arguably the single biggest potential bottleneck for many applications in the future will be high memory latency and the lack of sufficient memory bandwidth. Although advances such as non-blocking caches [10] and hardware and software-based prefetching [14, 21] can reduce latency in some cases, the underlying structure of the memory hierarchy upon which these approaches are implemented may ultimately limit their effectiveness. In addition, power dissipation levels have increased to the point where future designs may be fundamentally limited by this constraint in terms of the functionality that can be included in future microprocessors. Although several well-known organizational techniques can be used to reduce the power dissipation in on-chip memory structures, the sheer number of transistors dedicated to the on-chip memory hierarchy in future processors (for example, roughly 92% of the transistors on the Alpha 21364 are dedicated to caches [6]) requires that these structures be effectively used so as not to needlessly waste chip power. Thus, new approaches that improve performance in a more energy-efficient manner than conventional memory hierarchies are needed to prevent the memory system from fundamentally limiting future performance gains or exceeding power constraints.

The most commonly implemented memory system organization is likely the familiar multi-level memory hierarchy. The rationale behind this approach, which is used primarily in caches but also in some TLBs (*e.g.*, in the MIPS R10000 [24]), is that a combination of a small, low-latency L1 memory backed by a higher capacity, yet slower, L2 memory and finally by main memory provides the best tradeoff between optimizing hit time and miss time. Although this approach works well for many common desktop applications and benchmarks, programs whose working sets exceed the L1 capacity may expend considerable time and energy transferring data between the various levels of the hierarchy. If the miss tolerance of the application is lower than the effective L1 miss penalty, then performance may degrade significantly due to instructions waiting for operands to arrive. For such applications, a large, single-level cache (as used in the HP PA-8X00 series of microprocessors [12, 17, 18]) may perform better and be more energy-efficient than a two-level hierarchy for the same total amount of memory. For similar reasons, the PA-8X00 series also implements a large, single-level TLB. Because the TLB and cache are accessed in parallel, a larger TLB can be implemented without impacting hit time in this case due to the large L1 caches that are implemented.

The fundamental issue in current approaches is that no one memory hierarchy organization is best suited for each application. Across a diverse application mix, there will inevitably be significant periods of execution during which performance degrades and energy is needlessly expended due to a mismatch between the memory system requirements of the application and the memory hierarchy implementation. In this paper, we present a configurable cache and TLB orchestrated by a configuration algorithm that can be used to improve the performance and energy-efficiency of the memory hierarchy. Key to our approach is the exploitation of the properties of conventional caches and future technology trends in order to provide cache and TLB configurability in a low-intrusive manner. Our approach monitors cache and TLB usage by detecting phase changes using miss rates and branch frequencies, and improves performance by properly balancing hit latency intolerance with miss latency intolerance dynamically during application execution (using CPI as the ultimate performance metric). Furthermore, instead of changing the clock rate as proposed in [2], we implement a cache and TLB with a variable latency so that changes in the organization of these structures only impact memory instruction latency and throughput. Finally, energy-aware modifications to the configuration algorithm are implemented that trade off a modest amount of performance for significant energy savings.

Our previous approaches to this problem [2, 3] have exploited the partitioning of hardware resources to enable/disable parts of the cache under software control, but in a limited manner. The issues of how to practically implement such a design were not addressed in detail, the analysis only looked at changing configurations on an application-by-application basis (and not dynamically during the execution of a single application), and the simplifying assumption was made that the best configuration was known for each application. Furthermore, the organization and performance of the TLB was not addressed, and the reduction of the processor clock frequency with increases in cache size limited the performance improvement that could be realized.

Recently, Ranganathan, Adve, and Jouppi [22] proposed a reconfigurable cache in which a portion of the cache could be used for another function, such as an instruction reuse buffer. Although the authors show that such an approach only modestly increases cache access time, fundamental changes to the cache may be required so that it may be used for other functionality as well, and long wire delays may be incurred in sourcing and sinking data from potentially several pipeline stages.

This paper significantly expands upon our results in [5] that addressed only performance in a limited manner for one technology point (0.1μm) using a different (more hardware intensive) configuration algorithm. In this paper, we explore the application of the configurable hierarchy as a L1/L2 replacement in 0.1μm technology, and as an L2/L3 replacement for a 0.035μm feature size. For the former, we demonstrate an average 27% improvement in memory performance, which results in an average 15% improvement in overall performance as compared to a conventional memory hierarchy. Furthermore, the energy-aware enhancements that we introduce bring memory energy dissipation in line with a conventional organization, while still improving memory performance by 13% relative to the conventional approach. For 0.035μm geometries, where the prohibitively high latencies of large on-chip caches [1] call for a three-level conventional hierarchy for performance reasons, we demonstrate that a configurable L2/L3 cache hierarchy coupled with a conventional L1 reduces overall memory energy by 43% while even slightly increasing performance. This latter result demonstrates that because our configurable approach significantly improves memory hierarchy efficiency, it can serve as a partial solution to the significant power dissipation challenges facing future processor architects.

The rest of this paper is organized as follows. The cache and TLB architectures are described in Section 2 including the modifications necessary to enable dynamic reconfiguration. In Section 3, we discuss the dynamic selection mechanisms, including the counter hardware required and the configuration management algorithms. In Sections 4 and 5, we describe our simulation methodology and present a performance and energy dissipation comparison with conventional multi-level cache and TLB hierarchies for the two technology design points. Finally, we conclude in Section 6.

2 Cache and TLB Circuit Structures

In this section, we describe the circuit structures of the conventional and configurable caches and TLBs that we consider. We also describe two different approaches for using configurable caches as replacements for conventional on-chip cache hierarchies.

2.1 Configurable Cache Organization

The cache and TLB structures (both conventional and configurable) that we model follow that described by Mc-

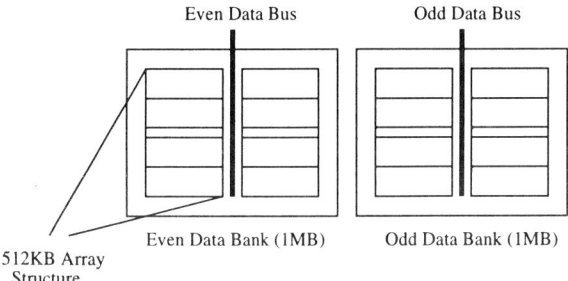

Figure 1. The overall organization of the cache data arrays

Farland in his thesis [19]. McFarland developed a detailed timing model for both the cache and TLB that balances both performance and energy considerations in subarray partitioning, and which includes the effects of technology scaling.

We start with a conventional 2MB data cache that is organized both for fast access time and energy efficiency. As is shown in Figure 1, the cache is structured as two 1MB interleaved banks[1] in order to provide sufficient memory bandwidth for the four-way issue dynamic superscalar processor that we simulate. In order to reduce access time and energy consumption, each 1MB bank is further divided into two 512KB SRAM structures one of which is selected on each bank access. We make a number of modifications to this basic structure to provide configurability with little impact on access time, energy dissipation, and functional density.

The data array section of the configurable structure is shown in Figure 2 in which only the details of one subarray are shown for simplicity. (The other subarrays are identically organized). There are four subarrays, each of which contains four ways. In both the conventional and configurable cache, two address bits (*Subarray Select*) are used to select only one of the four subarrays on each access in order to reduce energy dissipation. The other three subarrays have their local wordlines disabled and their precharge, sense amp, and output driver circuits are not activated. The TLB virtual to real page number translation and tag check proceed in parallel and only the output drivers for the way in which the hit occurred are turned on. Parallel TLB and tag access can be accomplished if the operating system can ensure that *index_bits-page_offset_bits* bits of the virtual and physical addresses are identical, as is the case for the four-way set associative 1MB dual-banked L1 data cache in the HP PA-8500 [11].

In order to provide configurability while retaining fast access times, we implement several modifications to McFarland's baseline design as shown in Figure 2:

- McFarland drives the global wordlines to the center of each subarray and then the local wordlines across half of the subarray in each direction in order to minimize the worst-case delay. In the configurable cache, because we are more concerned with achieving comparable delay with a conventional design for our smallest cache configurations, we distribute the global wordlines to the nearest end of each subarray and drive the local wordlines across the entire subarray.

- McFarland organizes the data bits in each subarray by bit number. That is, data bit 0 from each way are grouped together, then data bit 1, *etc*. In the configurable cache, we organize the bits according to ways as shown in Figure 2 in order to increase the number of configuration options.

- Repeater switches are used in the global wordlines to electrically isolate each subarray. That is, subarrays 0 and 1 do not suffer additional global wordline delay due to the presence of subarrays 2 and 3. Providing switches as opposed to simple repeaters also prevents wordline switching in disabled subarrays thereby saving dynamic power.

- Repeater switches are also used in the local wordlines to electrically isolate each way in a subarray. The result is that the presence of additional ways does not impact the delay of the fastest ways. Dynamic power dissipation is also reduced by disabling the wordline drivers of disabled ways.

- *Configuration Control* signals from the *Configuration Register* provide the ability to disable entire subarrays or ways within an enabled subarray. Local wordline and data output drivers and precharge and sense amp circuits are not activated for a disabled subarray or way.

Using McFarland's area model, we estimate the additional area from adding repeater switches to electrically isolate wordlines to be 7%. In addition, due to the large capacity (and resulting long wordlines) of each cache structure, a faster propagation delay is achieved with these buffered wordlines compared with unbuffered lines. Moreover, because local wordline drivers are required in a conventional cache, the extra drivers required to isolate ways within a subarray do not impact the spacing of the wordlines, and thus bitline length is unaffected. In terms of energy, the addition of repeater switches increases the total memory hierarchy energy dissipation by 2-3% in comparison with a cache with no repeaters for the simulated benchmarks.

---

[1] The banks are word-interleaved when used as an L1/L2 replacement and block interleaved when used as an L2/L3 replacement.

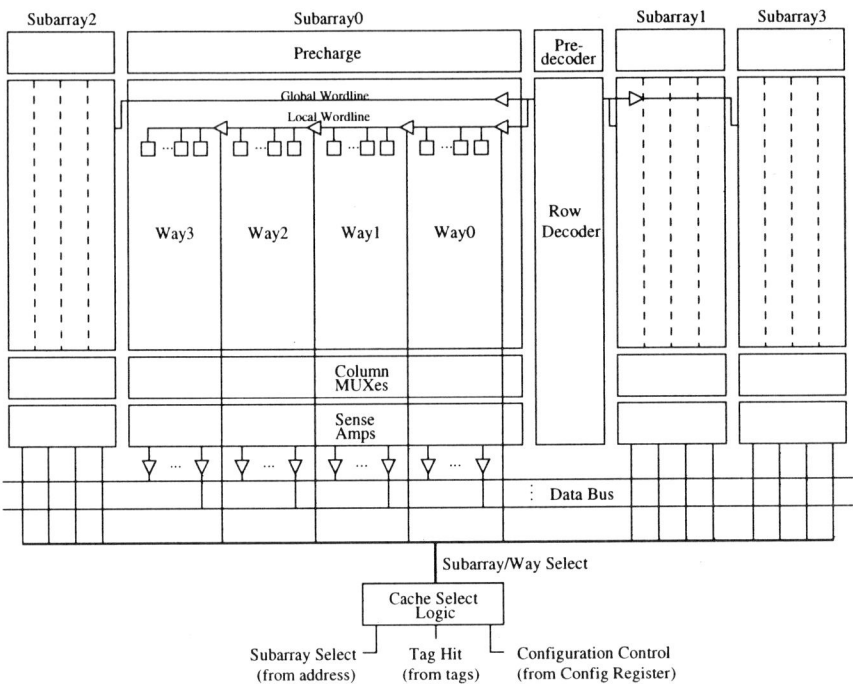

Figure 2. The organization of the data array section of one of the 512KB cache structures

2.2 Configurable Cache Operation

With these modifications, the cache behaves as a *virtual two-level, physical one-level* non-inclusive cache hierarchy, with the sizes, associativities, and latencies of the two levels dynamically chosen. In other words, we have designed a single large cache organization to serve as a configurable two-level non-inclusive cache hierarchy, where the ways within each subarray that are initially enabled for an L1 access are varied to match application characteristics. The latency of the two sections is changed on half-cycle increments according to the timing of each configuration (and assuming a 1 GHz processor). Half cycle increments are required to provide the granularity to distinguish the different configurations in terms of their organization and speed. Such an approach can be implemented by capturing cache data using both phases of the clock, similar to the double-pumped Alpha 21264 data cache [16], and enabling the appropriate latch according to the configuration. The advantages of this approach is that the timing of the cache can change with its configuration while the main processor clock remains unaffected, and that no clock synchronization is necessary between the pipeline and cache/TLB.

However, because a constant two-stage cache pipeline is maintained regardless of the cache configuration, cache bandwidth degrades for the larger, slower configurations. Furthermore, the implementation of a cache whose latency can vary on half-cycle increments requires two pipeline modifications. First, the dynamic scheduling hardware must be able to speculatively issue (assuming a data cache hit) load-dependent instructions at different times depending on the currently enabled cache configuration. Second, for some configurations, running the cache on half-cycle increments requires an extra half-cycle for accesses to be caught by the processor clock phase.

When used as a replacement for a conventional L1/L2 on-chip cache hierarchy, the possible configurations are shown in Figure 3. Although multiple subarrays may be enabled as L1 in an organization, as in a conventional cache, only one is selected each access according to the *Subarray Select* field of the address. When a miss in the L1 section is detected, all tag subarrays and ways are read. This permits hit detection to data in the remaining portion of the cache (designated as L2 in Figure 3). When such a hit occurs, the data in the L1 section (which has already been read out and placed into a buffer) is swapped with the data in the L2 section. In the case of a miss to both sections, the displaced block from the L1 section is placed into the L2 section. This prevents thrashing in the case of low-associative L1 organizations.

The direct-mapped 512KB and two-way set associative 1MB cache organizations are lower energy, and lower performance, alternatives to the 512KB two-way and 1MB four-way organizations, respectively. These options activate half the number of ways on each access for the same capacity as their counterparts. For execution periods in which there are few cache conflicts and hit latency tolerance is high, the low energy alternatives may result in compara-

				Subarray 2				Subarray 0				Subarray 1				Subarray 3			
Cache Configuration		L1 Size	L1 Assoc	L1 Acc Time	W3	W2	W1	W0	W3	W2	W1	W0	W0	W1	W2	W3	W0	W1	W2	W3
	256-1	256KB	1 way	2.0	L2	L2	L2	L2	L2	L2	L2	*L1*	*L1*	L2	L2	L2	L2	L2	L2	L2
	512-2	512KB	2 way	2.5	L2	L2	L2	L2	L2	L2	*L1*	*L1*	*L1*	*L1*	L2	L2	L2	L2	L2	L2
	768-3	768KB	3 way	2.5	L2	L2	L2	L2	L2	*L1*	*L1*	*L1*	*L1*	*L1*	*L1*	L2	L2	L2	L2	L2
	1024-4	1024KB	4 way	3.0	L2	L2	L2	L2	*L1*	*L1*	*L1*	*L1*	*L1*	*L1*	*L1*	*L1*	L2	L2	L2	L2
	512-1	512KB	1 way	3.0	L2	L2	L2	*L1*	L2	L2	L2	*L1*	*L1*	L2	L2	L2	*L1*	L2	L2	L2
	1024-2	1024KB	2 way	3.5	L2	L2	*L1*	*L1*	L2	L2	*L1*	*L1*	*L1*	*L1*	L2	L2	*L1*	*L1*	L2	L2
	1536-3	1536KB	3 way	4.0	L2	*L1*	*L1*	*L1*	L2	*L1*	*L1*	*L1*	*L1*	*L1*	*L1*	L2	*L1*	*L1*	*L1*	L2
	2048-4	2048KB	4 way	4.5	*L1*	*L1*	*L1*	*L1*	*L1*	*L1*	*L1*	*L1*	*L1*	*L1*	*L1*	*L1*	*L1*	*L1*	*L1*	*L1*

Subarray/Way Allocation (L1 or L2)

Figure 3. Possible L1/L2 cache organizations that can be configured shown by the ways that are allocated to L1 and L2. Only one of the four 512KB SRAM structures is shown. Abbreviations for each organization are listed to the left of the size and associativity of the L1 section, while L1 access times in cycles are given on the right. Note that the TLB access may dominate the overall delay of some configurations. The numbers listed here simply indicate the relative order of the access times for all configurations and thus the size/access time tradeoffs allowable.

ble performance yet potentially save considerable energy. These configurations are used in an energy-aware mode of operation as described in Section 3.

Note that because some of the configurations span only two subarrays, while others span four, the number of sets is not always the same. Hence, it is possible that a given address might map into a certain cache line at one time and into another at another time (called a *mis-map*). In cases where subarrays two and three are disabled, the high-order *Subarray Select* signal is used as a tag bit. This extra tag bit is stored on all accesses in order to detect mis-maps. Mis-mapped data is handled the same way as a L1 miss and L2 hit, *i.e.*, it results in a swap. Our simulations indicate that such events are infrequent.

In sub-0.1μm technologies, the long access latencies of a large on-chip L2 cache [1] may be prohibitive for those applications which make use of only a small fraction of the L2 cache. Thus, for performance reasons, a three-level hierarchy with a moderate size (*e.g.*, 512KB) L2 cache will become an attractive alternative to two-level hierarchies at these feature sizes. However, the cost may be a significant increase in energy dissipation due to transfers involving the additional cache level. We demonstrate in Section 5 that the use of the aforementioned configurable cache structure as a replacement for conventional L2 and L3 caches can significantly reduce energy dissipation without any compromise in performance as feature sizes scale below 0.1μm.

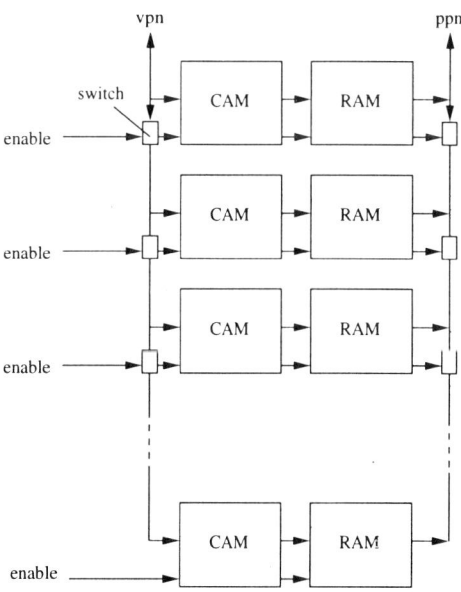

Figure 4. The organization of the configurable TLB

2.3 Configurable TLB Organization

Our 512-entry, fully-associative TLB can be similarly configured as shown in Figure 4. There are eight TLB increments, each of which contains a CAM of 64 virtual page numbers and an associated RAM of 64 physical page numbers. Switches are inserted on the input and output buses to electrically isolate successive increments. Thus, the ability to configure a larger TLB does not degrade the access time of the minimal size (64 entry) TLB. Similar to the cache design, TLB misses result in a second access but to the backup portion of the TLB.

3 Dynamic Selection Mechanisms

In this section, we first describe selection mechanisms for the configurable cache and TLB when used as a replacement for a conventional L1/L2 on-chip hierarchy. In the last subsection, we discuss the mechanisms as applied to a configurable L2/L3 cache hierarchy coupled with a conventional fixed-organization L1 cache.

Our configurable cache and TLB approach makes it possible to pick appropriate configurations and sizes based on application requirements. The different configurations spend different amounts of time and energy accessing the L1 and the lower levels of the memory hierarchy. Our heuristics improve the efficiency of the memory hierarchy by trying to minimize idle time due to memory hierarchy access. The goal is to determine the right balance between hit latency and miss rate for each application phase based on the tolerance of the phase for the hit and miss latencies. Our approach is to design the selection mechanisms to improve performance and then to introduce modifications to the heuristics that opportunistically trade off a small amount of performance for significant energy savings. These heuristics require appropriate metrics for assessing the cache/TLB performance of a given configuration during each application phase.

3.1 Search Heuristics

Large L1 caches have a high hit rate, but also have higher access times. To arrive at the cache configuration that is the optimal trade-off point between the cache hit and miss times, we use a simple mechanism that uses past history to pick a size for the future, based on CPI as the performance metric.

Our initial scheme is tuned to improve performance and thus explores the following five cache configurations: direct-mapped 256KB L1, 768KB 3-way L1, 1MB 4-way L1, 1.5MB 3-way L1, and 2MB 4-way L1. The 512KB 2-way L1 configuration provides no performance advantage over the 768KB 3-way L1 configuration (due to their identical access times in cycles) and thus this configuration is not used. For similar reasons, the two low-energy configurations (direct-mapped 512KB L1 and two-way set associative 1MB L1) are only used with modifications to the heuristics that reduce energy (described shortly).

At the end of each *interval* of execution (100K cycles in our simulations), we examine a set of hardware counters. These hardware counters tell us the miss rate, the IPC, and the branch frequency experienced by the application in that last interval. Based on this information, the selection mechanism (which could be implemented in software or hardware) picks one of two states - stable or unstable. The former suggests that behavior in this interval is not very different from the last and we do not need to change the cache configuration, while the latter suggests that there has recently been a phase change in the program and we need to explore and pick an appropriate size.

The initial state is unstable and the initial L1 cache is chosen to be the smallest (256KB in this paper). At the end of an interval, we enter the CPI experienced for that cache size into a table. If the miss rate exceeds a certain threshold (1% in our case) during that interval, we switch to the next largest L1 cache configuration for the next interval of operation in an attempt to contain the working set. This exploration continues until the maximum L1 size is reached or until the miss rate is sufficiently small. At this point, the table is examined, the cache configuration with the lowest CPI is picked, the table is cleared, and we switch to the stable state. We continue to remain in the stable state while the number of misses and branches do not significantly differ from that in the previous interval. When there is a change, we switch to the unstable state, return to the smallest L1 cache configuration and start exploring again. The pseudo-code for the mechanism is listed below.

```
if (state == STABLE)
    if ((num_miss-last_num_miss) < m_noise
        && (num_br-last_num_br) < br_noise)
        decr m_noise, br_noise;
    else
        cache_size = SMALLEST;
        state = UNSTABLE;

if (state == UNSTABLE)
    record CPI;
    if ((miss_rate > THRESHOLD)
        && (cache_size != MAX))
        cache_size++;
    else
        cache_size = that with best CPI;
        state = STABLE;
        if (cache_size == prev_cache_size)
            incr br_noise, m_noise;
```

Different applications see different variations in the number of misses and branches as they move across application phases. Hence, instead of using a single fixed number as the threshold to detect phase changes, we change this dynamically. If an exploration phase results in picking the same cache size as before, the noise threshold is increased to discourage such needless explorations. Likewise, every interval spent in the stable state causes a slight decrement in the noise threshold in case it had been set to too high a value.

The miss rate threshold ensures that we explore larger cache sizes only if required. Note that a high miss rate need not necessarily have a large impact on performance because of the ability of dynamic superscalar processors to hide L2 latencies.

Clearly, such an interval-based mechanism is best suited to programs that can sustain uniform behavior for a number of intervals. While switching to an unstable state, we also move to the smallest L1 cache configuration as a form of "damage control" for programs that have irregular behavior. This choice ensures that for these programs, more time is spent at the smaller cache sizes and hence performance is similar to that using a conventional cache hierarchy. In addition, we keep track of how many intervals are spent in stable and unstable states. If it turns out that we are spending too much time exploring, we conclude that the program behavior is not suited to an interval-based scheme and simply remain fixed at the smallest sized cache.

Our earlier experiments [5] used a novel hardware design to estimate the hit and miss latency intolerance of an application's phase (which our selection mechanism is attempting to minimize). These estimates were then used to detect phase changes as well as to guide exploration. As our results show in comparison to those in [5], the additional complexity of the hardware is not essential to obtaining good performance. Presently, we envision that the selection mechanism would be implemented in software. Every 100K cycles, a low-overhead software handler will be invoked that examines the hardware counters and updates the state as necessary. This imposes minimal hardware overhead and allows flexibility in terms of modifying the selection mechanism. We estimated the code size of the handler to be only 120 static assembly instructions, only a fraction of which is executed during each invocation, resulting in a net overhead of less than 0.1%. In terms of hardware overhead, we need roughly 9 20-bit counters for the number of misses, loads, cycles, instructions, and branches, in addition to a state register. This amounts to less than 8,000 transistors.

In addition to cache reconfiguration, we also progressively change the TLB configuration on an interval-by-interval basis. A counter tracks TLB miss handler cycles and the L1 TLB size is increased if this counter exceeds a threshold (3% in this paper) of the total execution time counter for an interval. A single bit is added to each TLB entry that is set to indicate if it has been used in an interval (and is cleared at start of an interval). The L1 TLB size is decreased if the TLB usage is less than half.

For the cache reconfiguration, we chose an interval size of 100K cycles so as to react quickly to changes without letting the selection mechanism pose a high cycle overhead.

For the TLB reconfiguration, we used a larger one million cycle interval so that an accurate estimate of TLB usage could be obtained. A smaller interval size could result in a spuriously high TLB miss rate over some intervals, and/or low TLB usage.

3.2 Reconfiguration on a Per-Subroutine Basis

As previously mentioned, the interval-based scheme will work well only if the program can sustain its execution phase for a number of intervals. This limitation may be overcome by collecting statistics and making subsequent configuration changes on a *per-subroutine* basis. The finite state machine that was used for the interval-based scheme is now employed for each subroutine. This requires maintaining a table with CPI values at different cache sizes and the next size to be picked for a limited number of subroutines (100 in this paper). To focus on the most important routines, we only monitor those subroutines whose invocations exceed a certain threshold of instructions (1000 in this paper). When a subroutine is invoked, its table is looked up and a change in cache configuration is effected depending on the table entry for that subroutine. When a subroutine exits, it updates the table based on the statistics collected during that invocation. A stack is used to checkpoint counters on every subroutine call so that statistics can be determined for each subroutine invocation.

We investigated two subroutine-based schemes. In the *non-nested* approach, statistics are collected for a subroutine and its callees. Cache size decisions for a subroutine are based on these statistics collected for the call-graph rooted at this subroutine. Once the cache configuration is changed for a subroutine, none of its callees can change the configuration unless the outer subroutine returns. Thus, the callees inherit the size of their callers because their statistics played a role in determining the configuration of the caller. In the *nested* scheme, each subroutine collects statistics only for the period when it is the top of the subroutine call stack. Thus, every single subroutine invocation is looked upon as a possible change in phase.

Because the simpler non-nested approach generally outperformed the nested scheme, we only report results for the former in Section 5.

3.3 Energy-Aware Modifications

There are two energy-aware modifications to the selection mechanisms that we consider. The first takes advantage of the inherently low-energy configurations (those with direct-mapped 512KB and two-way set associative 1MB L1 caches). With this approach, the selection mechanism simply uses these configurations in place of the 768KB 3-way L1 and 1MB 4-way L1 configurations.

A second potential approach is to serially access the tag and data arrays of the L1 data cache. Conventional L1 caches always perform parallel tag and data lookup to reduce hit time, thereby reading data out of multiple cache ways and ultimately discarding data from all but one way. By performing tag and data lookup in series, only the data way associated with the matching tag can be accessed, thereby reducing energy consumption. Hence, our second low-energy mode operates just like the interval-based scheme as before, but accesses the set-associative cache configurations by serially reading the tag and data arrays.

3.4 L2/L3 Reconfiguration

The selection mechanism for the L2/L3 reconfiguration is very similar to the simple interval-based mechanism for the L1/L2. In addition, because we assume that the L2 and L3 caches (both conventional and configurable) already use serial tag/data access to reduce energy dissipation, the energy-aware modifications would provide no additional benefit for L2/L3 reconfiguration. (Recall that performing the tag lookup first makes it possible to turn on only the required data way within a subarray, as a result of which, all configurations consume the same amount of energy for the data array access.) Finally, we did not simultaneously examine TLB reconfiguration so as not to vary the access time of the fixed L1 data cache. Much of the motivation for these simplifications was due to our expectation that dynamic L2/L3 cache configuration would yield mostly energy saving benefits, due to the fact that we were not altering the L1 cache configuration (the organization of which has the largest memory performance impact for most applications). To further improve our energy savings at minimal performance penalty, we also modified the search mechanism to pick a larger sized cache if it performed almost as well (within 95% in our simulations) as the best performing cache during the exploration, thus reducing the number of transfers between the L2 and L3.

4 Evaluation Methodology

4.1 Simulation Methodology

We used Simplescalar-3.0 [8] for the Alpha AXP instruction set to simulate an aggressive 4-way superscalar out-of-order processor. The architectural parameters used in the simulation are summarized in Table 1.

The data memory hierarchy is modeled in great detail. For example, contention for all caches and buses in the memory hierarchy as well as for writeback buffers is modeled. The line size of 128 bytes was chosen because it yielded a much lower miss rate for our benchmark set than smaller line sizes.

For both configurable and conventional TLB hierarchies, a TLB miss at the first level results in a lookup in the second

Fetch queue entries	8
Branch predictor	comb. of bimodal & 2-level gshare; bimodal/Gshare Level1/2 entries - 2048, 1024 (hist. 10), 4096 (global), resp.; Combining pred. entries - 1024; RAS entries - 32; BTB - 2048 sets, 2-way
Branch mispred. latency	8 cycles
Fetch, decode, issue width	4
RUU and LSQ entries	64 and 32
L1 I-cache	2-way; 64KB ($0.1\mu m$), 32KB ($0.035\mu m$)
Memory latency	80 cycles ($0.1\mu m$), 114 cycles ($0.035\mu m$)
Integer ALUs/mult-div	4/2
FP ALUs/mult-div	2/1

Table 1. Architectural parameters

level. A miss in the second level results in a call to a TLB handler that is assumed to complete in 30 cycles. The page size is 8KB.

4.2 Benchmarks

We have used a variety of benchmarks from SPEC95, SPEC2000, and the Olden suite [23]. These particular programs were chosen because they have high miss rates for the L1 caches we considered. For programs with low miss rates for the smallest cache size, the dynamic scheme affords no advantage and behaves like a conventional cache. The benchmarks were compiled with the Compaq cc, f77, and f90 compilers at an optimization level of O3. Warmup times were determined for each benchmark, and the simulation was fast-forwarded through these phases. The window size was chosen to be large enough to accommodate at least one outermost iteration of the program, where applicable. A further million instructions were simulated in detail to prime all structures before starting the performance measurements. Table 2 summarizes the benchmarks and their memory reference properties (the L1 miss rate and load frequency).

4.3 Timing and Energy Estimation

We investigated two future technology feature sizes: 0.1 and $0.035\mu m$. For the $0.035\mu m$ design point, we use the cache latency values of Agarwal et al. [1] whose model parameters are based on projections from the Semiconductor Industry Association Technology Roadmap [4]. For the $0.1\mu m$ design point, we use the cache and TLB timing model developed by McFarland [19] to estimate timings for both the configurable cache and TLB, and the caches and TLBs of a conventional L1/L2 hierarchy. McFarland's model contains several optimizations, including the automatic sizing of gates according to loading characteristics, and the careful consideration of the effects of technology

Benchmark	Suite	Datasets	Simulation window (instrs)	64K-2way L1 miss rate	% of instrs that are loads
em3d	Olden	20,000 nodes, arity 20	1000M-1100M	20%	36%
health	Olden	4 levels, 1000 iters	80M-140M	16%	54%
mst	Olden	256 nodes	entire program 14M	8%	18%
compress	SPEC95 INT	ref	1900M-2100M	13%	22%
hydro2d	SPEC95 FP	ref	2000M-2135M	4%	28%
apsi	SPEC95 FP	ref	2200M-2400M	6%	23%
swim	SPEC2000 FP	ref	2500M-2782M	10%	25%
art	SPEC2000 FP	ref	300M-1300M	16%	32%

Table 2. Benchmarks

scaling down to $0.1\mu m$ technology [20]. The model integrates a fully-associative TLB with the cache to account for cases in which the TLB dominates the L1 cache access path. This occurs, for example, for all of the conventional caches that were modeled as well as for the minimum size L1 cache (direct mapped 256KB) in the configurable organization.

For the global wordline, local wordline, and output driver select wires, we recalculate cache and TLB wire delays using RC delay equations for repeater insertion [9]. Repeaters are used in the configurable cache as well as in the conventional L1 cache whenever they reduce wire propagation delay. The energy dissipation of these repeaters was accounted for as well, and they add only 2-3% to the total cache energy.

We estimate cache and TLB energy dissipation using a modified version of the analytical model of Kamble and Ghose [15]. This model calculates cache energy dissipation using similar technology and layout parameters as those used by the timing model (including voltages and all electrical parameters appropriately scaled for $0.1\mu m$ technology). The TLB energy model was derived from this model and included CAM match line precharging and discharging, CAM wordline and bitline energy dissipation, as well as the energy of the RAM portion of the TLB. For main memory, we include only the energy dissipated due to driving the off-chip capacitive busses.

For all L2 and L3 caches (both configurable and conventional), we assume serial tag and data access and selection of only one of 16 data banks at each access, similar to the energy-saving approach used in the Alpha 21164 on-chip L2 cache [7]. In addition, the conventional L1 caches were divided into two subarrays, only one of which is selected at each access. Thus, the conventional cache hierarchy against which we compared our reconfigurable hierarchy was highly optimized for both fast access time and low energy dissipation.

Detailed event counts were captured during SimpleScalar simulations of each benchmark. These event counts include all of the operations that occur for the configurable cache as well as all TLB events, and are used to obtain final energy estimations.

A	Base excl. cache with 256KB 1-way L1 & 1.75MB 14-way L2
B	Base incl. cache with 256KB 1-way L1 & 2MB 16-way L2
C	Base incl. cache with 64KB 2-way L1 & 2MB 16-way L2
D	Interval-based dynamic scheme
E	Subroutine-based with nested changes
F	Interval-based with energy-aware cache configurations
G	Interval-based with serial tag and data access

Table 3. Simulated L1/L2 configurations

4.4 Simulated Configurations

Table 3 shows the conventional and dynamic L1/L2 schemes that were simulated. We compare our dynamic schemes with three conventional configurations which are identical in all respects, except the data cache hierarchy. The first uses a two-level non-inclusive cache, with a direct mapped 256KB L1 cache backed by a 14-way 1.75MB L2 cache (configuration A). The L2 associativity results from the fact that 14 ways remain in each 512KB structure after two of the ways are allocated to the 256KB L1 (only one of which is selected on each access). Comparison of this scheme with the configurable approach demonstrates the advantage of resizing the first level. We also compare with a two-level inclusive cache which consists of a 256KB direct mapped L1 backed by a 16-way 2MB L2 (configuration B). This configuration serves to measure the impact of the non-inclusive policy of the first base case on performance (a non-inclusive cache performs worse because every miss results in a swap or writeback, which causes greater bus and memory port contention.) We also compare with a 64KB 2-way inclusive L1 and 2MB of 16-way L2 (configuration C), which represents a typical configuration in a modern processor and ensures that the performance gains for our dynamically sized cache are not obtained simply by moving from a direct mapped to a set associative cache. For both the conventional and configurable L2 caches, the access time is 15 cycles due to serial tag and data access and bus transfer time, but is pipelined with a new request beginning every four cycles. The conventional TLB is a two-level inclusive TLB with 64 entries in the first level and 448 entries in the second level with a 6 cycle lookup time.

For L2/L3 reconfiguration, we compare our interval-

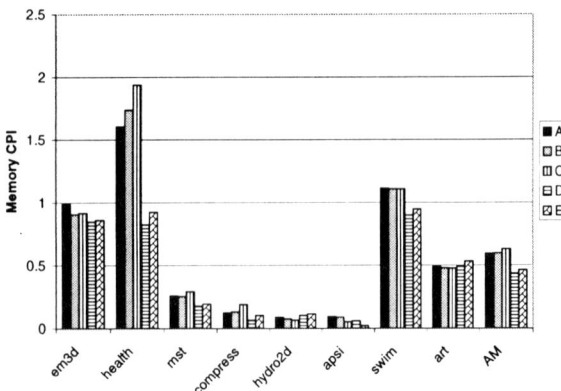

Figure 5. Memory CPI for conventional (A, B, and C), interval-based (D), and subroutine-based (E) configurable schemes

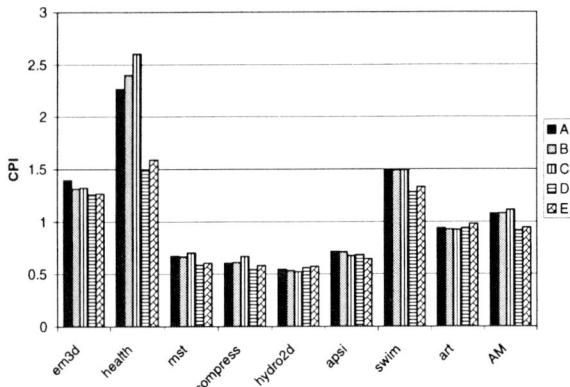

Figure 6. CPI for conventional (A, B, and C), interval-based (D), and subroutine-based (E) configurable schemes

	Cache contribution	TLB contribution	Cache explorations	TLB changes
em3d	73%	27%	10	2
health	33%	67%	27	2
mst	100%	0%	5	3
compress	64%	36%	54	2
hydro2d	100%	0%	19	0
apsi	100%	0%	63	27
swim	49%	51%	5	6
art	100%	0%	11	5

Table 4. Contribution of the cache and the TLB to speedup or slowdown in the dynamic scheme and the number of explorations

based configurable cache with a conventional three-level on-chip hierarchy. In both, the L1 cache is 32KB two-way set associative with a three cycle latency, reflecting the smaller L1 caches and increased latency likely required at $0.035\mu m$ geometries [1]. For the conventional hierarchy, the L2 cache is 512KB two-way set associative with a 21 cycle latency and the L3 cache is 2MB 16-way set associative with a 60 cycle latency. Serial tag and data access is used for both L2 and L3 caches to reduce energy dissipation.

5 Results

We first evaluate the performance and energy dissipation of the L1/L2 configurable schemes versus the three conventional approaches using delay and energy values for $0.1\mu m$ geometries. We then demonstrate how L2/L3 reconfiguration can be used at finer $0.035\mu m$ geometries to dramatically improve energy efficiency relative to a conventional three-level hierarchy but with no compromise of performance.

5.1 L1/L2 Performance Results

Figures 5 and 6 show the memory CPI and total CPI, respectively, achieved by the conventional and configurable interval and subroutine-based schemes for the various benchmarks. The memory CPI is calculated by subtracting the CPI achieved with a simulated system with a perfect cache (all hits and one cycle latency) from the CPI with the memory hierarchy. In comparing the arithmetic mean (AM) of the memory CPI performance, the interval-based configurable scheme outperforms the best-performing conventional scheme (B) (measured in terms of a percentage reduction in CPI) by 27%, with roughly equal cache and TLB contributions as is shown in Table 4. For each application, this table also presents the number of cache and TLB explorations that resulted in the selection of different sizes. In terms of overall performance, the interval-based scheme achieves a 15% reduction in CPI. The benchmarks with the biggest memory CPI reductions are health (52%), compress (50%), apsi (31%), and mst (30%).

The dramatic improvements with health and compress are due to the fact that particular phases of these applications perform best with a large L1 cache even with the resulting higher hit latencies (for which there is reasonably high tolerance within these applications). For health, the configurable scheme settles at the 1.5MB cache size for most of the simulated execution period, while the 768KB configuration is chosen for much of compress's execution period. Note that TLB reconfiguration also plays a major role in the performance improvements achieved. These two programs best illustrate the mismatch that often occurs between the memory hierarchy requirements of particular application phases and the organization of a conventional memory hierarchy, and how an intelligently-managed configurable hierarchy can better match on-chip cache and TLB resources to these execution phases. Note that while some applications stay with a single cache and TLB configuration for most of their execution window, others demonstrate the need to adapt to the requirements of different phases in each program (see Table 4). Regardless, the dynamic schemes are able to determine the best cache and TLB configurations, which span the entire range of possibilities, for each application during execution.

The results for art and hydro2d demonstrate how the dynamic reconfiguration may in some cases degrade performance. These applications are very unstable in their behavior and do not remain in any one phase for more than a few intervals. Art also does not fit in 2MB, so there is no size that causes a sufficiently large drop in CPI to merit the cost of exploration. However, the dynamic scheme identifies that the application is spending more time exploring than in stable state and turns exploration off altogether. Because this happens early enough in case of art (the simulation window is also much larger), art shows no overall performance degradation, while hydro2d has a slight 3% slowdown. This result illustrates that compiler analysis to identify such "unstable" applications and override the dynamic selection mechanism with a statically-chosen cache configuration may be beneficial.

In comparing the interval and subroutine-based schemes, we conclude that the simpler interval-based scheme usually outperforms the subroutine-based approach. The most notable exception is apsi, which has inconsistent behavior across intervals (as indicated by the large number of explorations in Table 4), causing it to thrash between a 256KB L1 and a 768KB L1. The subroutine-based scheme significantly improves performance relative to the interval-based approach as each subroutine invocation within apsi exhibits consistent behavior from invocation to invocation. Yet, due to the overall results and the additional complexity of the subroutine-based scheme, the interval-based scheme appears to be the most practical choice and is the only scheme considered in the rest of our analysis.

In terms of the effect of TLB reconfiguration, health, swim, and compress benefit the most from using a larger TLB. Health and compress perform best with 256 and 128 entries, respectively, and the dynamic scheme settles at these sizes. Swim shows phase change behavior with respect to TLB usage, resulting in five stable phases requiring either 256 or 512 TLB entries.

These results demonstrate potential performance improvement for one technology point and microarchitecture. In order to determine the sensitivity of our qualitative results to different technology points and microarchitectural trade-offs, we varied the processor pipeline speed relative to the

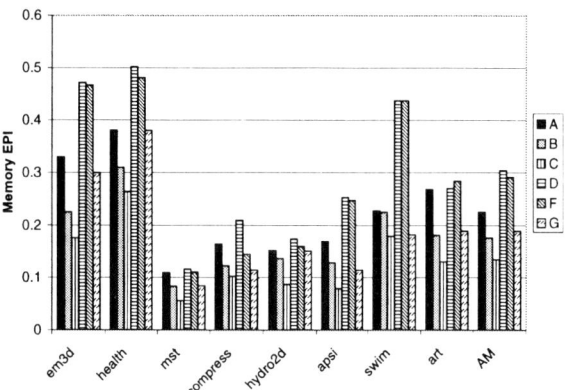

Figure 7. Memory EPI (in nanoJoules) for conventional (A, B, and C), interval-based (D), and energy-aware (F and G) configurable schemes

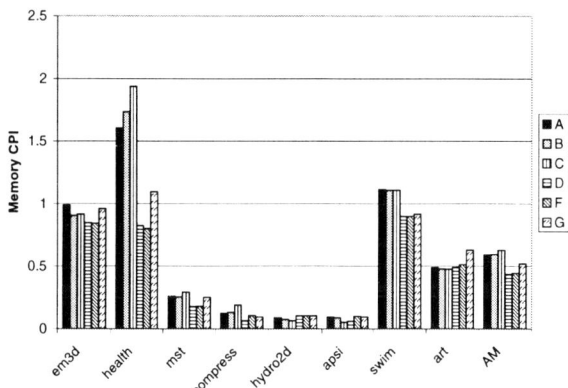

Figure 8. Memory CPI for conventional (A, B, and C), interval-based (D), and energy-aware (F and G) configurable schemes

memory latencies (keeping the memory hierarchy latency fixed). The results in terms of performance improvement were similar for 1 (our base case), 1.5, and 2 GHz processors.

5.2 Energy-Aware Configuration Results

We focus here on the energy consumption of the on-chip memory hierarchy (including that to drive the off-chip bus). The memory energy per instruction (memory EPI, with each energy unit measured in nanoJoules) results of Figure 7 illustrate how as is usually the case with performance optimizations, the cost of the performance improvement due to the configurable scheme is a significant increase in energy dissipation. This is caused by the fact that energy consumption is proportional to the associativity of the cache and our configurable L1 uses larger set-associative caches. For this reason, we explore how the energy-aware improvements may be used to provide a more modest performance improvement yet with a significant reduction in memory EPI relative to a pure performance approach.

From Figure 7 we observe that merely selecting the energy-aware cache configurations (scheme F) has only a nominal impact on energy. In contrast, operating the L1 cache in a serial tag and data access mode (G) reduces memory EPI by 38% relative to the baseline interval-based scheme (D), bringing it in line with the best overall-performing conventional approach (B). For compress and swim, this approach even achieves roughly the same energy, with significantly better performance (see Figure 8), than conventional configuration C, whose 64KB two-way L1 data cache activates half the amount of cache every cycle than the smallest L1 configuration (256KB) of the configurable schemes. In addition, because the selection scheme automatically adjusts for the higher hit latency of serial access, this energy-aware configurable approach reduces memory CPI by 13% relative to the best-performing conventional scheme (B). Thus, the energy-aware approach may be used to provide more modest performance improvements in portable applications where design constraints such as battery life are of utmost importance. Furthermore, as with the dynamic voltage and frequency scaling approaches used today, this mode may be switched on under particular environmental conditions (*e.g.*, when remaining battery life drops below a given threshold), thereby providing on-demand energy-efficient operation.

5.3 L2/L3 Performance and Energy Results

While L1 reconfiguration improves performance, it may consume more energy than conventional approaches if higher L1 associative configurations are enabled. To reduce energy, mechanisms such as serial tag and data access (as described in the previous subsection) have to be used. Since L2 and L3 caches are often already designed for serial tag and data access to save energy, reconfiguration at these lower levels of the hierarchy would not increase the energy consumed. Instead, they stand to decrease it by reducing the number of data transfers that need to be done between the various levels, *i.e.*, by improving the efficiency of the memory hierarchy.

Thus, we investigate the energy benefits of providing a configurable L2/L3 cache hierarchy with a fixed L1 cache as on-chip cache delays significantly increase with sub-0.1μm geometries. Due to the prohibitively long latencies of large caches at these geometries, a three-level cache hierarchy becomes an attractive design option from a performance perspective. We use the parameters from Agarwal et al. [1] for 0.035μm technology to illustrate how dynamic L2/L3 cache configuration can match the performance of a conventional three-level hierarchy while dramatically reducing energy dissipation.

Figures 9 and 10 compare the performance and energy,

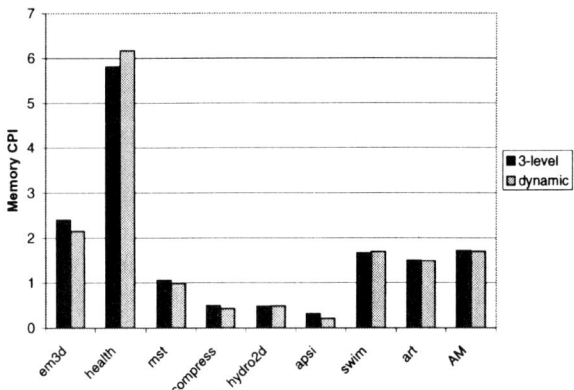

Figure 9. Memory CPI for conventional three-level and dynamic cache hierarchies

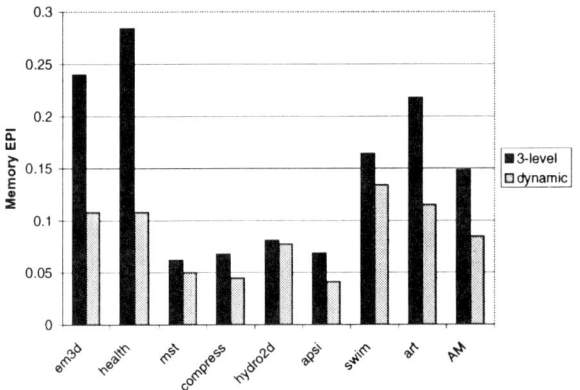

Figure 10. Memory EPI (in nanoJoules) for conventional three-level and dynamic cache hierarchies

respectively, of the conventional three-level cache hierarchy with the configurable scheme (Recall that TLB configuration was not attempted so the improvements are completely attributable to the cache.). Since the L1 cache organization has the largest impact on cache hierarchy performance, as expected, there is little performance difference between the two, as each uses an identical conventional L1 cache. However, the ability of the dynamic scheme to adapt the L2/L3 configuration to the application results in a 43% reduction in memory EPI on average. The savings are caused by the ability of the dynamic scheme to use a larger L2, and thereby reduce the number of transfers between L2 and L3. Having only a two-level cache would, of course, eliminate these transfers altogether, but would be detrimental to program performance because of the large 60-cycle L2 access. Thus, in contrast to this approach of simply opting for a lower energy, and lower performing, solution (the two-level hierarchy), dynamic L2/L3 cache configuration can improve performance while dramatically improving energy efficiency.

6 Conclusions

We have described a novel configurable cache and TLB as an alternative to conventional cache hierarchies. Repeater insertion is leveraged to enable dynamic cache and TLB configuration, with an organization that allows for dynamic speed/size tradeoffs while limiting the impact of speed changes to within the memory hierarchy. Our configuration management algorithm is able to dynamically examine the tradeoff between an application's hit and miss intolerance using CPI as the ultimate metric to determine appropriate cache size and speed. At $0.1\mu m$ technologies, our results show an average 15% reduction in CPI in comparison with the best conventional L1-L2 design of comparable total size, with the benefit almost equally attributable on average to the configurable cache and TLB. Furthermore, energy-aware enhancements to the algorithm trade off a more modest performance improvement for a significant reduction in energy. Projecting to $0.035\mu m$ technologies and a 3-level cache hierarchy, we show improved performance with an average 43% reduction in memory hierarchy energy when compared to a conventional design. This latter result demonstrates that because our configurable approach significantly improves memory hierarchy efficiency, it can serve as a partial solution to the significant power dissipation challenges facing future processor architects.

Future work includes investigating the use of compiler support for applications where an interval-based scheme is unable to capture the phase changes (differing working sets) in an application. Compiler support would be beneficial both to select appropriate adaptation points as well as to predict an application's working set sizes. Finally, improvements at the circuit and microarchitectural levels will be pursued that better balance configuration flexibility with access time and energy consumption.

References

[1] V. Agarwal, M. Hrishikesh, S. Keckler, and D. Burger. Clock rate versus IPC: The end of the road for conventional microarchitectures. *Proceedings of the 27th International Symposium on Computer Architecture*, pages 248–259, June 2000.

[2] D. Albonesi. Dynamic IPC/clock rate optimization. *Proceedings of the 25th International Symposium on Computer Architecture*, pages 282–292, June 1998.

[3] D. Albonesi. Selective cache ways: On-demand cache resource allocation. *Proceedings of the 32nd International Symposium on Microarchitecture*, pages 248–259, November 1999.

[4] S. I. Association. The National Technology Roadmap for Engineers. Technical report, 1999.

[5] R. Balasubramonian, D. Albonesi, A. Buyuktosunoglu, and S. Dwarkadas. Dynamic memory hierarchy performance optimization. *Workshop on Solving the Memory Wall Problem*, June 2000.

[6] P. Bannon. Alpha 21364: A scalable single-chip SMP. *Microprocessor Forum*, October 1998.

[7] W. Bowhill et al. Circuit implementation of a 300-MHz 64-bit second-generation CMOS Alpha CPU. *Digital Technical Journal*, 7(1):100–118, Special Issue 1995.

[8] D. Burger and T. Austin. The Simplescalar toolset, version 2.0. Technical Report TR-97-1342, University of Wisconsin-Madison, June 1997.

[9] W. Dally and J. Poulton. *Digital System Engineering*. Cambridge University Press, Cambridge, UK, 1998.

[10] K. Farkas and N. Jouppi. Complexity/performance tradeoffs with non-blocking loads. *Proceedings of the 21st International Symposium on Computer Architecture*, pages 211–222, April 1994.

[11] J. Fleischman. Private communication. October 1999.

[12] L. Gwennap. PA-8500's 1.5M cache aids performance. *Microprocessor Report*, 11(15), November 17, 1997.

[13] J. Hennessy. Back to the future: Time to return to some long standing problems in computer systems? *Federated Computer Conference*, May 1999.

[14] N. Jouppi. Improving direct-mapped cache performance by the addition of a small fully-associative cache and prefetch buffers. *Proceedings of the 17th International Symposium on Computer Architecture*, pages 364–373, May 1990.

[15] M. Kamble and K. Ghose. Analytical energy dissipation models for low power caches. *Proceedings of the International Symposium on Low Power Electronics and Design*, pages 143–148, August 1997.

[16] R. Kessler. The Alpha 21264 microprocessor. *IEEE Micro*, 19(2):24–36, March/April 1999.

[17] A. Kumar. The HP PA-8000 RISC CPU. *IEEE Computer*, 17(2):27–32, March 1997.

[18] G. Lesartre and D. Hunt. PA-8500: The continuing evolution of the PA-8000 family. *Proceedings of Compcon*, 1997.

[19] G. McFarland. *CMOS Technology Scaling and Its Impact on Cache Delay*. PhD thesis, Stanford University, June 1997.

[20] G. McFarland and M. Flynn. Limits of scaling MOSFETS. Technical Report CSL-TR-95-62, Stanford University, November 1995.

[21] T. Mowry, M. Lam, and A. Gupta. Design and evaluation of a compiler algorithm for prefetching. *Proceedings of ASPLOS-V*, pages 62–73, October 1992.

[22] P. Ranganathan, S. Adve, and N. Jouppi. Reconfigurable caches and their application to media processing. *Proceedings of the 27th International Symposium on Computer Architecture*, pages 214–224, June 2000.

[23] A. Rogers, M. Carlisle, J. Reppy, and L. Hendren. Supporting dynamic data structures on distributed memory machines. *ACM Transactions on Programming Languages and Systems*, Mar. 1995.

[24] K. Yeager. The Mips R10000 superscalar microprocessor. *IEEE Micro*, 16(2):28–41, April 1996.

Frequent Value Compression in Data Caches *

Jun Yang   Youtao Zhang   Rajiv Gupta
Department of Computer Science
The University of Arizona, Tucson, AZ 85721

Abstract

Since the area occupied by cache memories on processor chips continues to grow, an increasing percentage of power is consumed by memory. We present the design and evaluation of the **compression cache** *(CC) which is a first level cache that has been designed so that each cache line can either hold one uncompressed line or two cache lines which have been compressed to at least half their lengths. We use a novel data compression scheme based upon encoding of a small number of values that appear frequently during memory accesses. This compression scheme preserves the ability to randomly access individual data items. We observed that the contents of 40%, 52% and 51% of the memory blocks of size 4, 8, and 16 words respectively in SPECint95 benchmarks can be compressed to at least half their sizes by encoding the top 2, 4, and 8 frequent values respectively. Compression allows greater amounts of data to be stored leading to substantial reductions in miss rates (0-36.4%), off-chip traffic (3.9-48.1%), and energy consumed (1-27%). Traffic and energy reductions are in part derived by transferring data over external buses in compressed form.*

1 Introduction

The portable computing devices being designed today are typically battery powered. Thus in addition to meeting the performance goals, the designs for such devices must also be power efficient. One significant source of power consumption is the cache memory on processor chips which continue to occupy increasing amounts of chip area. Reducing the sizes of on-chip caches is not the answer because higher miss rates result in performance loss and an increase in power consumed by external buses.

By storing code and data in compressed form, smaller caches can provide lower miss rates and reduce power consumption. The power consumed by external buses can be further reduced by transferring code or data that is fetched across the buses in compressed form. Code compression is being widely studied today by researchers for the purpose of reducing power consumption [9, 11]. Recently techniques for packing of narrow width data operands in multimedia applications have been explored [4, 15, 16]. However, little work has been done on compression of data in caches for general purpose applications.

The memory compression techniques proposed in [2, 3] are applicable to data in main memory – the data is uncompressed when it is brought into any of cache levels in the memory hierarchy. In [8] authors proposed the use of the X-RL [7] data compression algorithm to achieve compression of data. The X-RL algorithm does not preserve random access of individual data elements. Therefore in [8] compressed data cannot be stored at the top level L1 cache; only at the lower levels of the memory system (L2 cache) can it be kept in compressed form. We present a compression scheme applicable to L1 caches in this paper. The only other technique which meets this requirement has been developed independently by Larin and Conte [12].

In order to achieve higher performance and lower power consumption, data compression should be applied at the first level cache. The higher performance results because by storing data in compressed form we can store greater amounts of it and therefore maximize the hits to this *fast* cache. Optimizing the performance of L1 cache has the most reduction in power consumption because the power consumed by L1 cache is over three times of that consumed by the L2 cache [5]. This is because L1 cache services far more memory references than the L2 cache.

In this paper we present the design and evaluation of the *compression cache* (CC) which not only stores data in compressed form, but it can also be used as the top level cache. This is because CC employs a

---

*Supported by DARPA award no. F29601-00-1-0183 and NSF grants CCR-0096122 and EIA-9806525 to the Univ. of Arizona.

novel compression scheme which allows random access of data elements in the cache. The CC has been designed to improve the performance of on-chip Direct-Mapped write-back data Caches (DMCs). We only consider write-back caches because write-through caches generate much greater degrees of off-chip traffic and are therefore not power efficient. In a direct-mapped CC each line of $2l$ words is also capable of storing two compressed lines as long as each of the lines can be compressed to size l. Since two compressed lines can potentially reside in a cache line simultaneously, more data can be held by the cache and reduced miss rates are observed in comparison to a conventional DMC. The compression scheme we have developed exploits *frequent value locality* [18] observed in programs. It preserves random access of data, it is applicable to all data (not just narrow width data), and is therefore useful in context of general purpose applications (not just multimedia applications).

The CC provides substantial reductions in off-chip traffic. The reduction in off-chip traffic is only in part due to reduced miss rates. There is an additional source of traffic reduction. Since cache lines can be stored into the CC in compressed form, they are compressed off-chip before they are brought into the on-chip cache. Also evicted cache lines are transmitted off-chip in compressed form where they are decompressed before being stored into memory or another off-chip cache. CC provides substantial reductions in miss rates (0-36.4%), off-chip traffic (3.9-48.1%), and energy consumed (1-27%) over a DMC.

Section 2 evaluates the potential for compressing cache lines to half their sizes by encoding frequently accessed values for SPECint95 suite. In section 3 we describe the design of CC. Section 4 presents an evaluation of CC. Related work is discussed in section 5.

2 Frequent Value Compression

In our prior work we studied the behavior of programs in the SPECint95 suite and found that six out of eight benchmarks exhibit *frequent value locality* [18]. In these six programs ten distinct values occupy over 50% of all memory locations and on an average account for nearly 50% of all memory accesses during program execution. The two benchmarks that do not exhibit high degree of frequently value locality are 129.compress and 132.ijpeg. In this paper we develop a data compression scheme for use in a first level cache which exploits frequently accessed values. Profiling techniques for identifying frequent values are described in [18].

Compression of the data in a cache line can be achieved by storing selected values in encoded form, as opposed to their original form which takes up a full word. The values that should be selected for encoding should be the frequently accessed values to maximize the compression that can be achieved. In particular, our goal is to exploit the instances in which $2l$ words of data can be compressed into l words. This would allow a cache line that holds $2l$ words of uncompressed data, to be able to hold two cache lines of compressed data.

In order to evaluate the potential of the above compression strategy, we studied the distribution of the top n frequently accessed values in individual cache lines. We pick n as power of 2 for efficient encoding. We ran the six benchmarks with frequent value locality and examined the memory contents midway through their executions. We divided the memory into blocks of 4, 8 and 16 words each to mimic cache line sizes of 4, 8 and 16 words. The number of frequent values chosen are 2, 4 and 8. In order to estimate the likelihood that a cache line could be compressed to half of its size we plotted the percentage of lines in which at least half of the values are frequently accessed values (see Figure 1). On an average nearly 40%, 52% and 51% of cache lines of sizes 4, 8 and 16 respectively can be compressed to at least half their size by exploiting top 2, 4, and 8 frequent values respectively.

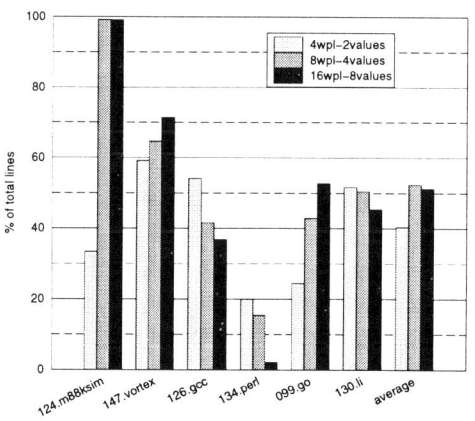

Figure 1. Lines that can be compressed to at least half of their sizes.

3 The Compression Cache

The basic idea behind the *compression cache* (CC) is to store cache lines in a compressed form so a greater number of cache lines can reside in the data cache at any given time and thus lower miss rates would result. Since we are also interested in reducing off-chip traffic, to reduce the power consumed by external buses, we compress the data in a cache line before it is brought into the on-chip cache. Also when a compressed cache line is evicted from the data cache, it is transmitted off-chip in compressed form and then uncompressed before being stored in off-chip memory (see Figure 2).

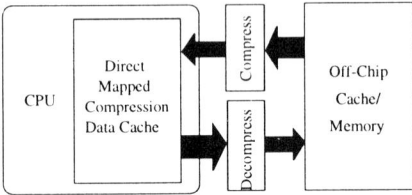

Figure 2. Compression cache.

We assume that each given cache line of $2l$ words can accommodate either one uncompressed cache line or two compressed cache lines. If the line cannot be compressed to l words we keep it in uncompressed form. However, if two lines, each of which has been compressed to l words, map to the same cache line, they can reside in that line simultaneously. It should be noted that by incorporating compression, we will always improve the hit rates of a direct-mapped cache. This is because if no compression opportunities exist, the behavior of the CC will simply be identical to that of DMC. However, if compression opportunities exist, some amount of cached data will be able to reside in the cache for a longer duration and thus potentially contribute to increased hit rate. It is possible to design more general strategies which can compact a cache line to any size less than $2l$ and thus we could allow varying number of cache lines to fit in $2l$ words. However, such complex compression strategies would make it more difficult to determine whether a hit or a miss has occurred and will therefore slow down all cache accesses.

Compression/decompression of already cached data. Compression techniques have been used effectively for instructions because typically code is not modified by a running program. However, data compression techniques have been hard to design because data values change as the program executes. As described above the data is transferred on-chip and off-chip in compressed form. However, when already cached data is modified, opportunities to compress currently uncompressed line may arise. Also if an infrequent value is written to a location in the compressed line where previously a frequent value was stored, the need to uncompress the line may arise.

We conducted experiments in which compression and decompression of already cached data was allowed to occur to see how often compression opportunities for cached data arose. We measured the percentage of total cache hits during which a compression opportunity arose. We found that such opportunities are quite infrequent for most benchmarks. As shown in Table 1, the only case in which compression opportunities are substantial is for 124.m88ksim benchmark when a line size of 8 words is used. Therefore we decided not to exploit these opportunities. Carrying out compression of cached data is an expensive operation with associated hardware and execution time costs. By sacrificing a small number of compression opportunities we greatly simplify the cache design.

Assuming that no compression of already cached data will be carried out, we next determined how often a compressed cache line must be decompressed as a result of writing an infrequent value to a location in the compressed line. In Table 2 the percentage of total cache hits during which a need for decompression arose is given. Although decompression operations cannot be avoided, they are so infrequent (a maximum of 0.367% of the hits was observed) that they will not seriously effect cache performance. During decompression a compressed line can be read out of the cache in a buffer, decompressed, and then written back to the cache line. Alternatively we can also send it to memory thereby evicting the decompressed line from the cache. We opted for the former solution since it is faster to update a cache line on-chip than transferring its contents off-chip.

From the above experiments we can conclude that if data is brought on-chip in compressed form, it generally continues to stay in compressed form. The reverse is also true, that is, in most benchmarks if data is brought on-chip in uncompressed form it cannot often be compressed later on.

CC design details. As shown in Figure 3, the cache entries must be modified to indicate whether or not they contain compressed lines. The C bit is used for this purpose. We must also modify the entries so that they can hold the relevant information for the two compressed cache lines. Each of the lines has its own tag (Tag1, Tag2) as well as valid (V1, V2) and dirty (D1, D2) bits. In addition, the mask fields (mask1, mask2) provide useful information for compressed lines. The determination of a cache hit is straightforward. If there is a match with any of the valid tags we have a hit. The retrieval of the value requires examining the mask. If the mask indicates that the value is one of the frequent value, then the mask can provide the value as it stores the value in encoded form. On the other hand if the mask indicates that the value is not one of the frequent values, then it identifies the word in the cache line where it is stored. When compressed cache lines

benchmark	line size = 4 words = 16 bytes				line size = 8 words = 32 bytes				line size = 16 words = 64 bytes			
	4Kb	8Kb	16Kb	32Kb	4Kb	8Kb	16Kb	32Kb	4Kb	8Kb	16Kb	32Kb
124.m88ksim	0.897	0.901	0.965	0.983	8.249	8.194	16.060	16.077	0.341	0.379	8.243	8.297
147.vortex	5.746	5.974	6.358	6.591	2.566	2.650	2.833	2.923	1.147	1.241	1.336	1.410
126.gcc	2.630	2.859	3.095	3.340	1.656	1.787	1.944	2.072	0.890	0.970	1.051	1.091
134.perl	7.152	8.423	7.039	7.048	4.303	2.283	4.963	4.964	2.112	1.219	2.907	2.907
099.go	2.042	2.323	2.718	2.778	0.941	1.093	1.261	1.319	0.816	0.890	1.147	1.798
130.li	4.031	4.083	4.472	5.123	2.523	2.514	2.591	2.868	0.384	0.381	0.393	0.536

Table 1. % of cache hits creating compression opportunities.

benchmark	line size = 4 words = 16 bytes				line size = 8 words = 32 bytes				line size = 16 words = 64 bytes			
	4Kb	8Kb	16Kb	32Kb	4Kb	8Kb	16Kb	32Kb	4Kb	8Kb	16Kb	32Kb
124.m88ksim	0.284	0.282	0.277	0.277	0.207	0.208	0.204	0.205	0.015	0.006	0.003	0.003
147.vortex	0.304	0.232	0.123	0.087	0.143	0.110	0.063	0.044	0.075	0.058	0.037	0.023
126.gcc	0.242	0.197	0.167	0.153	0.151	0.132	0.109	0.102	0.071	0.058	0.051	0.048
134.perl	0.183	0.009	0.179	0.178	0.093	0.005	0.005	0.004	0.266	0.003	0.003	0.003
099.go	0.203	0.136	0.081	0.058	0.136	0.093	0.056	0.039	0.154	0.110	0.062	0.038
130.li	0.404	0.367	0.284	0.118	0.136	0.128	0.112	0.045	0.064	0.063	0.059	0.022

Table 2. % of cache hits requiring decompression.

are transmitted across the chip boundary, the contents of the masks must also be transmitted along with the frequent values. Figure 3 depicts the logic for retrieving a value from a cache line size of four words.

Next let us consider the encoding scheme in greater detail. When a cache line has been compressed to at least half its size, access to data requires consulting the mask corresponding to the compressed line. The mask contains as many fields as the original line size. Each field provides us with the necessary information regarding the data value at the corresponding location in the cache line. Each field is $log_2 l$ bits long where l is the line size. The first bit in a field is 0 if the corresponding location contains a frequent value; otherwise it is 1. The remainder of the bits serve a dual purpose. If the value at the corresponding location is a frequent value, the remaining bits of the field provide an encoding of this frequent value. Since $log_2(l/2)$ bits are available for encoding frequent values, at most $l/2$ frequent values can be exploited by the above design. On the other hand if the corresponding value is an infrequent value, then the remaining bits in the field indicate the position in the compressed data line at which that value is stored. Notice that the increase in cache line lengths due to additional information we store is quite modest. For cache line size of 32 bytes or 8 words, the increase is 6 bytes.

The example in Figure 4 illustrates the above encoding scheme. We assume that the line size is eight words and therefore four frequent values can be exploited. The frequent values and their encodings are given in the figure. Note that the leading bit is zero for all four frequent value codes. The size of an uncompressed line is 256 bits (= 8 × 32) while the size of a compressed line is 152 bits(= 8 × 3 + 4 × 32). We show the contents of corresponding uncompressed and compressed cache lines and describe how the contents to the latter change with changes to the former.

In its initial state the uncompressed line contains four frequent and four infrequent values and therefore it can be compressed as shown in the figure. The leading bit is zero for the fields at positions 1, 3, 5, and 8 because they correspond to frequent values, 0 and -1, which are appropriately encoded by the remaining two bits. The fields at positions 2, 4, 6, and 7 have their leading bits as one to indicate the presence of four infrequent values which are stored in uncompressed form in the first half of the cache line. The last two bits of the mask encodes the positions in the first half of the cache line where the infrequent values are stored.

Next we illustrate how the changes in the contents of an uncompressed line are reflected by changes in the corresponding compressed line. The example illustrates the following cases: (a) the overwriting of a frequent value (0) by a different frequent value (1) results only in a change in the appropriate field of the mask; (b) the overwriting of an infrequent value (1000) by a different infrequent value (2000) results only in a change in the location in the cache line indicated by the appropriate field of the mask; (c) increase in the number of frequent values, due to overwriting of 99999 by -1, changes the mask; (d) decrease in the number of frequent values, due to overwriting of -1 by 6a8d, changes the mask and the cache line; and (e) finally the over-

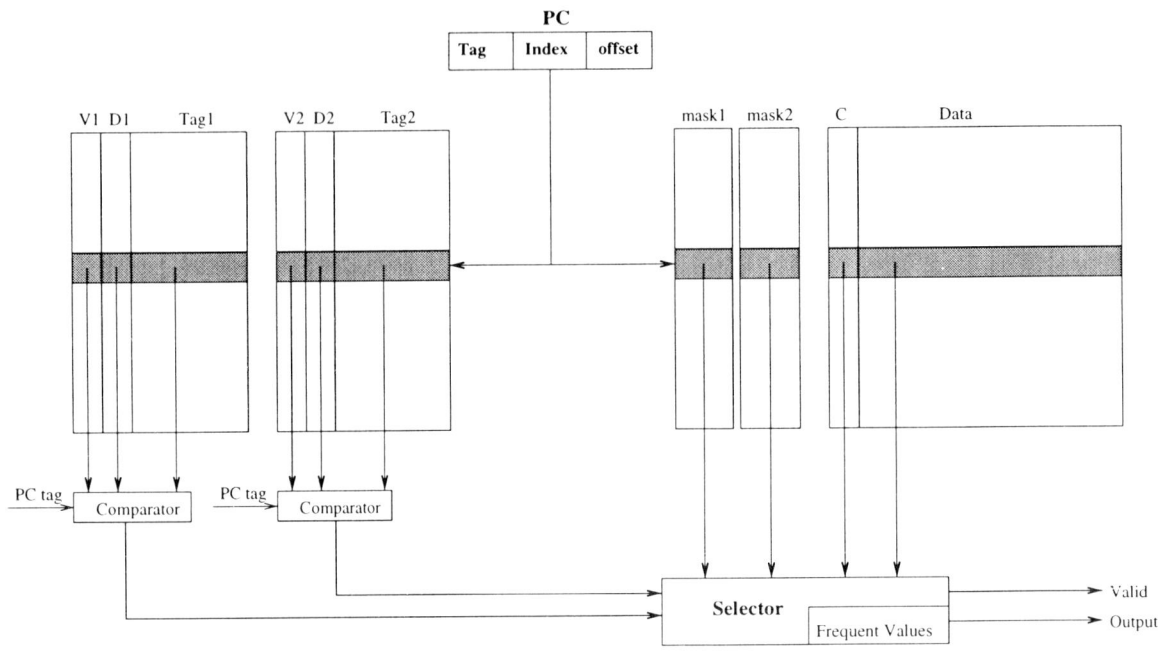

Figure 3. Compression cache design details.

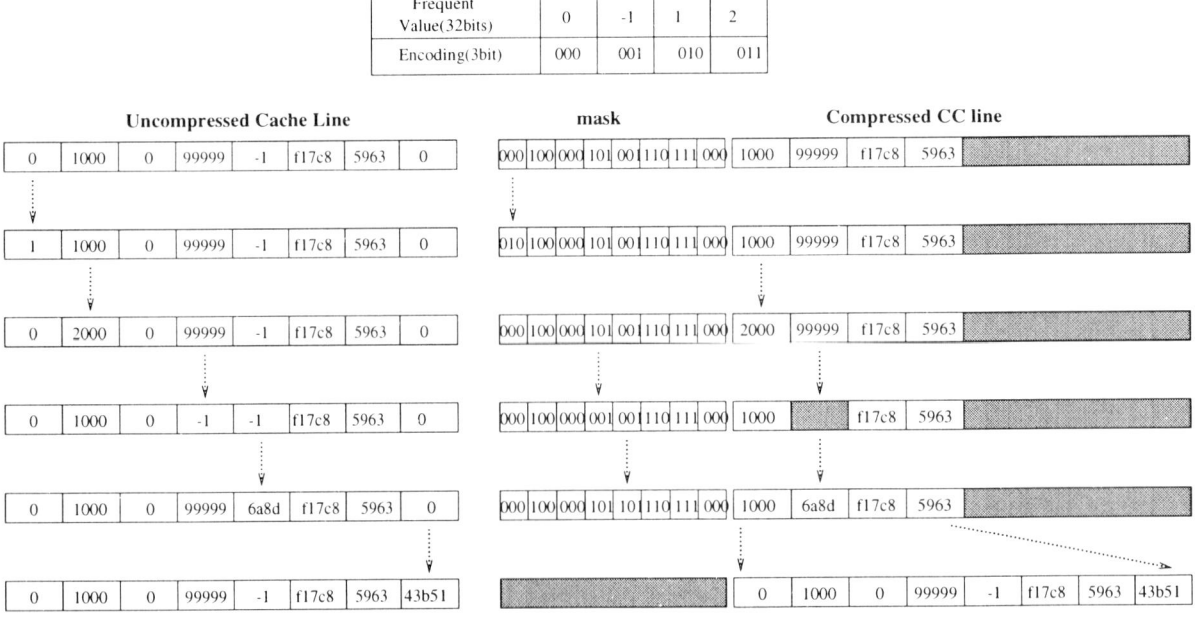

Figure 4. Compressed encoded data in CC.

writing of the frequent value (0) by an infrequent value (43b51) causes the line to be decompressed.

4 Experimental Evaluation

The goal of the experimentation was to determine by how much can the CC enhance the performance of DMCs of varying configurations. We considered DMCs of sizes 4, 8, 16, and 32 Kbytes for line sizes of 4, 8, and 16 words in our experiments. The corresponding CC therefore could potentially hold two lines each compressed down to a size of 2, 4, and 8 words respectively. Moreover these caches could exploit 2, 4, and 8 frequent values respectively. All programs were compiled using the gcc 2.7.2 compiler with the -O3 level of optimization, the instruction set used was MIPS-I, and the programs were executed using simulators generated using the FAST system [13].

Miss rate reductions. The cache miss rates of the DMC and CC data caches for the six integer benchmarks are shown in Table 3. In every single case the miss rate of CC is lower than that of DMC which shows that CC only improves performance. The percentage reduction in miss rate given by the column IMP varies from 0% to 36.4%.

In the above comparisons due to the additional information in the CC's cache lines, actually the sizes of the CC's are somewhat larger than that of corresponding DMC's. In fact the CC cache lines are longer by 1 to 2 words depending upon the configuration. However, this does not mean that the same improvements could have been obtained by simply constructing a larger DMC. For example, if we look at the miss rates shown in Table 3, we notice that for the 124.m88ksim benchmark the performance of the 8Kb CC is very close to the performance of a 16Kb DMC. In contrast the increase in size of the CC due to additional information stored in each cache line is quite modest (15% - 36%).

Traffic reduction. The reductions in traffic are substantial for most benchmarks and cache sizes as shown in Figure 5. They vary from 3.9% to 48.1%. The percentage reductions in the traffic are higher than the miss rate reductions because only part of the traffic reductions are derived from miss rate reductions. The remaining traffic reduction is due to transmission of data across the processor chip boundary in compressed form.

The relative improvements provided by CC do not necessarily correspond to the relative degree of compressibility observed in the data presented in Figure 1. For example, in Figure 1 we observed that 134.perl demonstrated much lower levels of compressibility than 099.go. However, CC provides greater performance improvements for 134.perl than those achieved for 099.go. This is due to a number of reasons. First, in the study the compressibility was measured at one program point during program's execution while the performance of CC depends upon the compressibility of cache lines over the entire execution of the program. Second, in the study all memory lines are treated equally while CC will benefit most from the compressibility of the most frequently referenced cache lines. Finally, compressibility of a cache line is only beneficial to CC if other conflicting cache lines are also compressible.

Energy savings. The energy savings were computed using an energy model for 0.8 micron technology used in the *Simplepower* tool [17]. This model computes the energy consumed by cache memory cells, address and data buses, address and data pads, and main memory. The savings in energy consumed by using CC instead of DMC are shown in Figure 6. The energy savings are also significant and vary from 1% to 27%.

Access times. The additional logic in CC should result in greater access time than the same sized DMC. However, since the CC provides a more cost effective solution for improving miss rates, than simply increasing the size of the DMC, we expect that the access time of a CC would be close to the access time of a DMC which provides comparable miss rates. This is because the access time of a cache typically depends upon the size of the cache and larger caches have longer word line lengths and bit line lengths which leads to greater word line and bit line capacitances. Therefore a CC should provide energy savings over a DMC with similar access times and miss rates.

5 Related Work

Data Compression. Recently Larin and Conte [12] have also proposed data compression schemes which share an important characteristic with our compression scheme. Both preserve random access to data since they encode individual values to achieve compression. They explore three different encoding schemes (Rigid Huffman, Flexible Huffman, and Flexible Huffman with Long Memory) in their work. There are two key differences between our approaches. First, while we encode a very small number of frequently accessed values, they encode a larger number of values. Therefore while a simple encoding scheme suffices in our

benchmark	4Kb			8Kb			16Kb			32Kb		
	DMC	CC	IMP	DMC	CC	IMP	DMC	CC	IMP	DMC	CC	IMP
	line size = 4 words = 16 bytes											
124.m88ksim	2.1	1.4	33.3	1.4	0.9	35.7	1.1	0.7	36.4	1.0	0.7	30.0
147.vortex	5.2	4.6	11.5	3.7	3.1	16.2	1.7	1.6	5.9	1.1	1.0	9.1
126.gcc	6.0	5.5	8.3	4.1	3.8	7.3	2.9	2.7	6.9	2.2	2.0	9.1
134.perl	5.8	4.4	24.1	4.2	3.4	19.0	3.5	2.7	22.9	3.5	2.7	22.9
099.go	14.4	14.1	2.1	9.4	9.3	1.1	5.7	5.6	1.8	3.3	3.2	3.0
130.li	4.8	4.5	6.2	3.2	3.1	3.1	2.2	2.2	0.0	1.3	1.3	0.0
	line size = 8 words = 32 bytes											
124.m88ksim	1.9	1.6	15.8	1.3	1.0	23.1	0.9	0.7	22.2	0.9	0.6	33.3
147.vortex	5.5	4.6	16.4	3.9	3.2	17.9	1.8	1.5	16.7	1.2	0.9	25.0
126.gcc	5.9	5.5	6.8	3.9	3.7	5.1	2.6	2.4	7.7	1.9	1.7	10.5
134.perl	6.5	5.8	10.8	4.5	4.0	11.1	3.9	3.3	15.4	3.8	3.3	13.2
099.go	17.3	16.6	4.0	11.2	10.7	4.5	6.4	6.1	4.7	3.5	3.2	8.6
130.li	3.7	3.5	5.4	2.4	2.3	4.2	1.4	1.4	0.0	0.8	0.8	0.0
	line size = 16 words = 64 bytes											
124.m88ksim	2.4	1.7	29.2	1.2	0.9	25.0	0.8	0.6	25.0	0.8	0.5	37.5
147.vortex	6.0	5.0	16.7	4.3	3.7	14.0	2.0	1.5	25.0	1.4	0.9	35.7
126.gcc	6.2	5.8	6.5	4.0	3.7	7.5	2.6	2.3	11.5	1.8	1.6	11.1
134.perl	6.3	5.3	15.9	3.7	3.0	18.9	2.9	2.5	13.8	2.8	2.5	10.7
099.go	21.9	20.4	6.8	14.4	13.5	6.3	8.2	7.5	8.5	4.4	3.9	11.4
130.li	3.4	3.2	5.9	2.0	2.0	0.0	1.0	1.0	0.0	0.5	0.5	0.0

Table 3. DMC vs CC : % miss rates (DMC,CC) and % miss rate reduction (IMP).

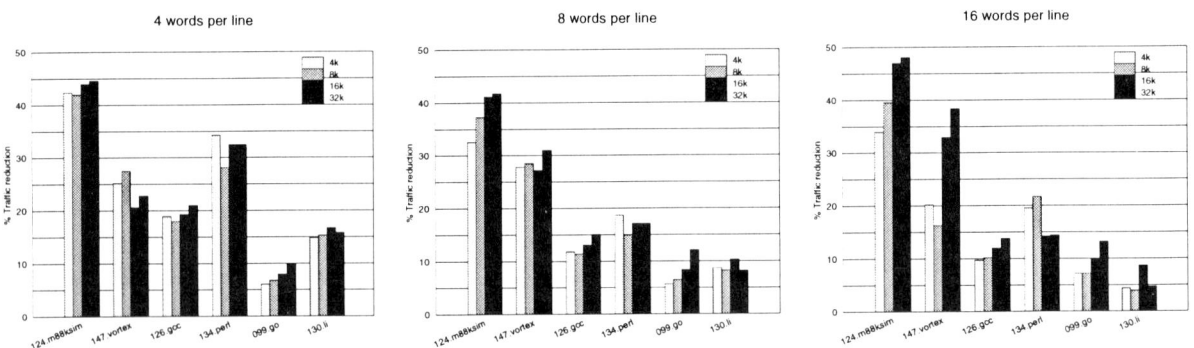

Figure 5. % Traffic reduction.

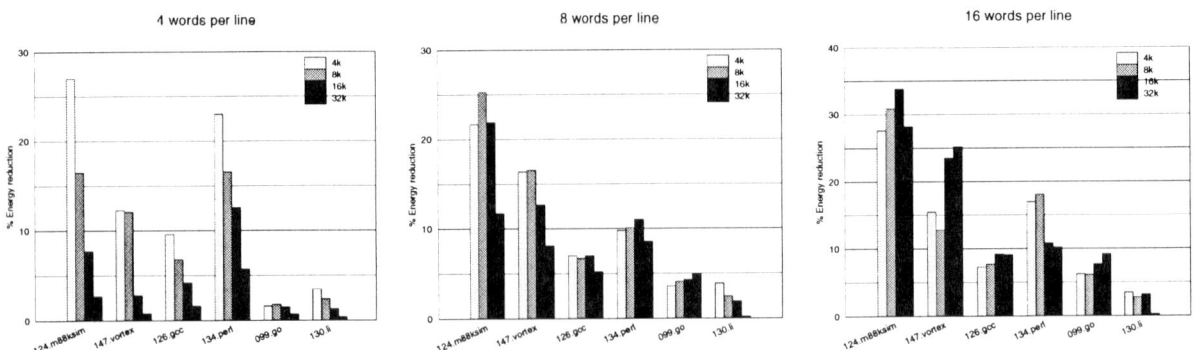

Figure 6. % Energy savings.

case they require more sophisticated compression encodings. Second, while the list of frequent values is kept fixed for the entire execution of the program in our approach, they dynamically adapt the encodings according to changing frequency distribution of data values. Therefore the two designs of data compression schemes represent two points in a spectrum of techniques that are possible by trading off generality with hardware and runtime costs.

Data cache. In [18] we proposed the *frequent value cache* (FVC) which is a type of a victim cache designed to exploit frequent value locality. FVC is a small direct-mapped cache which is dedicated to holding only frequent values. We conducted an experiment in which we measured the improvements in traffic and miss rates that can be obtained by a combination of CC and FVC. We considered line size of 8 words with CC and FVC configurations that exploit top four frequent values. The results show that the combination of CC and FVC can result in traffic reductions of 2-72% over a DMC and miss reductions of 3-69.5%. Therefore a combination of CC and FVC is highly effective. We are currently exploring the impact of compression on other power efficient cache organizations [1, 15, 14, 10, 5].

References

[1] D.H. Albonesi, "Selective Cache Ways: On Demand Cache Resource Allocation," *32nd Annual International Conference on Microarchitecture*, pages 248-259, 1999.

[2] B. Abali and H. Franke, "Operating System Support for Fast Hardware Compression of Main Memory Contents," *Workshop on Solving the Memory Wall Problem*, June 2000.

[3] C.D. Benveniste, P.A. Franaszek, and J.T. Robinson, "Cache-Memory Interfaces in Compressed Memory Systems," *Workshop on Solving the Memory Wall Problem*, June 2000.

[4] D. Brooks and M. Martonosi, "Dynamically Exploiting Narrow Width Operands to Improve Processor Power and Performance," *Fifth International Symposium on High-Performance Computer Architecture*, Orlando, Florida, January 1999.

[5] K. Ghose, "Reducing Power in Superscalar Processor Caches using Subbanking, Multiple Line Buffers, and Bit Line Segmentation," *International Symposium on Low Power Electronics and Design*, pages 70-75, 1999.

[6] N.P. Jouppi, "Improving Direct-Mapped Cache Performance by the Addition of a Small Fully-Associative Cache and Prefetch Buffers," *17th Annual International Symposium on Computer Architecture*, Seattle, pages 364-373, 1990.

[7] M. Kjelso, M. Gooch, and S. Jones, "Empirical Study of Memory-data: Characteristics and Compressibility," *IEE Computers and Digital Techniques*, Vol. 145, No. 1, pages 63-67, January 1998.

[8] J-S. Lee, W-K. Hong, and S-D. Kim, "Design and Evaluation of a Selective Compressed Memory System," *IEEE International Conference on Computer Design*, Austin, TX, pages 184-191, October 1999.

[9] C. Lefurgy, P. Bird, I.-C. Chen, and T. Mudge, "Improving Code Density Using Compression Techniques," *30th Annual ACM/IEEE International Symposium on Microarchitecture*, pages 194-203, 1997.

[10] J. Kin, M. Gupta, and W.H. Mangione-Smith, "The Filter Cache: An Energy Efficient Memory Structure," *30th Annual ACM/IEEE International Symposium on Microarchitecture*, pages 184-193, 1997.

[11] D. Kirovski, J. Kin, and W. H. Mangione-Smith, "Procedure Based Program Compression," *30th Annual ACM/IEEE International Symposium on Microarchitecture*, pages 204-217, 1997.

[12] S. Y. Larin, "Exploiting Program Redundancy to Improve Performance, Cost and Power Consumption in Embedded Systems," Ph.D. thesis, ECE Dept., North Carolina State Univ., Raleigh, North Carolina, August 2000.

[13] S. Onder and R. Gupta, "Automatic Generation of Microarchitecture Simulators," *IEEE International Conference on Computer Languages*, pages 80-89, Chicago, Illinois, May 1998.

[14] M.D. Powell, S-H. Yang, B. Falsafi, K. Roy, T.N. Vijaykumar, "Gated Vdd: A Circuit Technique to Reduce Leakage in Deep-submicron Cache Memories," *ACM/IEEE International Symposium on Low Power Electronics and Design*, 2000.

[15] P. Ranganathan, S. Adve, and N. Jouppi, "Reconfigurable Caches and their Application to Media Processing," *27th Annual International Symposium on Computer Architecture*, Vancouver, British Columbia, Canada, June 2000.

[16] M. Stephenson, J. Babb, and S. Amarasinghe, "Bitwidth Analysis with Application to Silicon Compilation," *ACM SIGPLAN Conference on Programming Language Design and Implementation*, Vancouver, British Columbia, Canada, June 2000.

[17] W. Ye, N. Vijaykrishnan, M. Kandemir, and M.J. Irwin, "The Design and Use of Simplepower: A Cycle-accurate Energy Estimation Tool," *37th Design Automation Conference*, Los Angeles, CA, June 2000.

[18] Y. Zhang, J. Yang, and R. Gupta, "Frequent Value Locality and Value-centric Data Cache Design," *The Ninth International Conference on Architectural Support for Programming Languages and Operating Systems*, Cambridge, MA, November 2000.

Dynamic Translation and Multithreading

A Study of Slipstream Processors

Zach Purser Karthik Sundaramoorthy Eric Rotenberg

North Carolina State University
Department of Electrical and Computer Engineering
Engineering Graduate Research Center, Campus Box 7914, Raleigh, NC 27695
{zrpurser, ksundar, ericro}@ece.ncsu.edu, www.tinker.ncsu.edu/ericro/slipstream

Abstract

A slipstream processor reduces the length of a running program by dynamically skipping computation non-essential for correct forward progress. The shortened program runs faster as a result, but it is speculative. So a second, unreduced copy of the program is run concurrently with and slightly behind the reduced copy — leveraging a chip multiprocessor (CMP) or simultaneous multithreading (SMT). The short program passes its control and data flow outcomes to the full program for checking. And as it checks the short program, the full program fetches and executes more efficiently due to having an accurate picture of the future. Both programs are sped up: combined, they outperform conventional non-redundant execution.

We study slipstreaming with the following key results.

1. *A 12% average performance improvement is achieved by harnessing an otherwise unused, additional processor in a CMP. Slipstreaming using two small superscalar cores often achieves similar instructions-per-cycle as one large superscalar core, but with a potentially faster clock and a more flexible architecture.*

2. *A majority of the benchmarks show significant reduction in the short program (about 50%). Slipstreaming using an 8-way SMT processor improves their performance from 10% to 20%.*

3. *For some benchmarks, including gcc, performance improvement is due to the short program resolving branch mispredictions in advance. Others benefit largely due to value predictions from the short program, and the effect is not always reproducible by conventional value prediction tables.*

4. *As execution bandwidth is increased, slipstreaming provides less of a performance advantage — unless instructions are removed in the short program before they are fetched. A simple program sequencing mechanism is developed to bypass instruction fetching.*

1. Introduction

The slipstream paradigm [21,27] proposes only a fraction of the dynamic instruction stream is needed for a program to make full, correct, forward progress. For example, some instruction sequences have no observable effect. They produce results that are not subsequently referenced, or results that do not change the state of the machine. And then there are instruction sequences whose effects are observable, but the effects are invariably predictable. Computation influencing control flow is the most notable example.

Ineffectual and branch-predictable computation can be exploited to reduce the length of a running program, speeding it up. Unfortunately, we cannot know for certain what instructions can be validly skipped. Constructing a shorter program is speculative and, ultimately, it must be checked against the full program to verify it produces the same overall effect.

Therefore, a slipstream processor concurrently runs two copies of the program, leveraging either a single-chip multiprocessor (CMP) [17] or a simultaneous multithreading processor (SMT) [28,31] (the user program is instantiated twice by the operating system and each copy has its own context). One program always runs slightly ahead of the other: the leading program is called the *advanced stream*, or A-stream, and the trailing program is called the *redundant stream*, or R-stream. Hardware monitors the R-stream and detects 1) instructions that repeatedly and predictably have no observable effect (e.g., unreferenced writes, non-modifying writes) and 2) branches whose outcomes are consistently predicted correctly. Future instances of the ineffectual instructions, branch instructions, and the computation chains leading up to them are speculatively removed in the A-stream — but only if there is high confidence correct forward progress can still be made, in spite of removing the instructions.

The reduced A-stream fetches, executes, and retires fewer instructions than it would otherwise, resulting in a faster program. To verify that the A-stream makes correct forward progress, all control and data flow outcomes of the A-stream are passed to the R-stream. The R-stream checks the outcomes against its own and, if a deviation is detected, the R-stream's architectural state is used to selectively repair the A-stream's corrupted architectural state (an infrequent event).

A key point is the R-stream uses the outcomes it is checking as predictions [20]. This has two advantages.

- First, the R-stream fetches and executes more efficiently due to having near-ideal predictions from the A-stream. Thus, although the unreduced R-stream retires more instructions, it keeps pace with the A-stream and the two programs combined finish sooner than a single copy of the program would. The slipstream processor's approach of speeding up a single program via redundancy is analogous to "slipstreaming" in car racing, where two cars race nose-to-tail to increase the speed of *both* cars [19].

- Second, by using A-stream outcomes as predictions, *the R-stream leverages existing speculation mechanisms for checking the A-stream*. Conventional processors typically have mechanisms in place to check control flow speculation, and future processors may incorporate value prediction and mechanisms to check data flow speculation.

Another benefit of slipstreaming is improved reliability. Transient faults that affect redundantly-executed instructions are transparently detectable and recoverable [20,27]. Fault detection/recovery is transparent because transient faults are indistinguishable from prediction-induced deviations.

1.1. Contributions

This paper is a follow-up study of our recent slipstream proposal [27] and makes four new contributions.

1. *Understanding slipstreaming.*

    Slipstreaming can be explained and understood in several ways. We describe two different interpretations of slipstreaming, qualitatively explain where its performance improvement is derived from, and expose its limitations. Insight into the limitations of slipstreaming allows us to focus efforts on areas that are likely to payoff.

    More comprehensive experimental results provide important insight and confirm the expectations of our qualitative arguments. Multiple CMP configurations are explored — examining multiple CMP configurations is relevant because conclusions change as the processor cores scale.

2. *Slipstreaming using SMT processors.*

    Slipstreaming was not previously implemented on an SMT processor. Insufficient reduction in the A-stream made SMT-based slipstreaming less viable. Artifacts of our previous instruction-removal mechanism have been addressed (see next item below), so SMT-based slipstreaming is now viable and this paper provides results.

3. *More effective instruction-removal.*

    Previously, removal-confidence was measured for a group of instructions as a whole, i.e., for a trace [27]. A trace-based approach ensures producer instructions are not removed from the A-stream unless corresponding consumer instructions are also removed. Not enforcing this constraint leads to spurious instruction-removal mispredictions.

    Trace-based removal has severe limitations, however [27]. Frequently-varying removal patterns within a trace cause the overall confidence to be low, despite stable patterns among certain dependence chains. As a result, no instructions in the trace are removed even if many are removable. And although traces ensure dependence chains are removed together, chains are confined to the same trace.

    Our new approach measures confidence for instructions individually, so unrelated instructions do not dilute confidence. Yet dependence chains still tend to be removed together and chains are not confined within a small region.

4. *Bypassing instruction fetching.*

    The A-stream is most effective when both the number of instructions fetched and executed are reduced. Reducing the number of fetched instructions requires a different sequencing model than conventional branch predictors currently provide. A conventional branch predictor is modified in a novel and simple way to bypass fetching of large, dynamic instruction sequences.

1.2. Paper outline

The paper is organized as follows. Section 2 develops models for understanding slipstreaming and examines its fundamental limits. Section 3 reviews the slipstream microarchitecture and introduces the new instruction-removal mechanisms. In sections 4 and 5, the simulation environment and results are presented, respectively. Related work is discussed in Section 6 and conclusions in Section 7.

2. Understanding slipstreaming

We present two different interpretations of slipstreaming to better understand the paradigm. In subsection 2.1, the A-stream is interpreted as the "main" thread and the R-stream "assists" the A-stream. In subsection 2.2, roles are reversed: the R-stream is the "main" thread and the A-stream "assists" the R-stream. Actually, the two programs in a slipstream processor are functionally equivalent and mutually beneficial, so either interpretation is valid.

We next examine limits of the paradigm to motivate removing instructions from the A-stream before they are fetched. Finally, we consider other ways of reducing the A-stream to highlight the conceptual simplicity of our chosen approach.

2.1. R-stream: a fast checker

The A-stream does not explicitly derive any performance benefit from the R-stream. Rather, the R-stream checks (and occasionally redirects) the A-stream without slowing it down. This is possible because *checking is inherently parallel* [13,20]. As depicted in Figure 1, *the R-stream is a fast checking assist to the A-stream* [20,21,2].

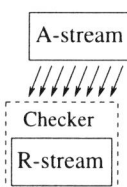

FIGURE 1. A fast checking assist to the A-stream.

2.2. A-stream: a program-based predictor

Alternatively, *the A-stream is a program-based predictor for the R-stream* [7,23,33,5]. For example, the A-stream assists the performance of the R-stream by improving its branch prediction accuracy. Dynamic branch predictions are classified into two groups, *confident* and *unconfident* [10], as shown in Figure 2. Confident branch predictions are more likely to be correct and the corresponding branches and computation feeding the branches are removed from the A-stream. Confident predictions represent the most accurate predictions, therefore, removing the computation needed to verify them is sound, and it allows the A-stream to focus instead on verifying unconfident branch predictions. As a result, *many branch mispredictions are resolved by the A-stream in advance of when the R-stream reaches the same point.*

The A-stream also serves as an accurate value predictor [13] for the R-stream. Although only the results of A-stream-executed instructions are available, the predictions are potentially more accurate than those provided by conventional value predictors: A-stream "predictions" are produced by program computation as opposed to being history-based. Perhaps there is some overlap in what the A-stream provides and what a conventional value predictor could provide. Initial investigations in Section 5.3 indicate some benchmarks (e.g., *gcc*) benefit primarily from the short program resolving branch mispredictions in advance; others benefit largely due to value predictions from the A-stream, and the effect is not always reproducible by conventional value prediction tables. However, comprehensive comparisons are left for future work.

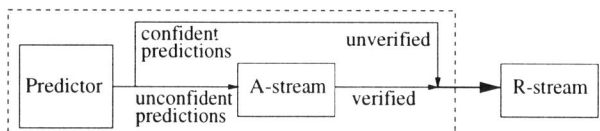

FIGURE 2. A combined predictor/program for improving R-stream branch prediction accuracy.

2.3. Importance of bypassing instruction fetch

Prior research has shown that in the absence of any resource constraints, performance is generally dictated by mispredicted branches [30,11]. That is, in an ideal processor with unconstrained fetch and execution bandwidth, mispredicted branches and their dependence chains tend to dominate the critical path of the program. *The A-stream cannot reduce this critical path* because the dependence chains of mispredicted branches are not safely removable from the A-stream — only correctly predicted branches are safely removable. The A-stream, like a full version of the program, encounters the same mispredictions and resolves them in program order. Therefore, slipstreaming is not likely to provide performance advantages if fetch and execution bandwidth are unconstrained.

Understanding slipstreaming's limitations enables us to focus research efforts on areas that are likely to pay off. For example, we can reason about the relative importance of bypassing instruction fetch and execution in the A-stream. Consider a slipstream processor that reduces the number of instructions *executed* in the A-stream, but not the number of instructions *fetched*. The A-stream runs on one core of a CMP and the R-stream on a second core (for example). As raw execution bandwidth of both cores is increased, the A-stream starts to lose its edge with respect to the R-stream. Instruction fetching becomes the bottleneck and, from a practical standpoint, the A-stream is not truly reduced if the number of fetched instructions is not reduced.

Fortunately, it is possible to bypass even instruction fetching in the A-stream. The A-stream has a distinct advantage in this regard because raw instruction fetch bandwidth cannot be as easily extended as raw execution bandwidth, e.g., due to taken branches and branch predictor bandwidth.

2.4. Other ways of reducing the A-stream

One method for reducing the A-stream is removing branch-predictable computation. Another possibility is removing value-predictable computation. As was described in Figure 2 in the context of branch prediction, an overall better value predictor may be possible by combining a conventional value predictor with the A-stream: the value predictor identifies and removes highly value-predictable computation, and the A-stream focuses instead on hard-to-predict values. The R-stream observes a stream of accurate values comprised of both unverified confident values and computed values.

This approach complicates the mechanism for reducing the A-stream, however. For the A-stream to make correct forward progress, the effects of removed, value-predictable computation must be emulated by updating the state of the A-stream with values directly, similar to block/trace/computation reuse [9,8,6] but without the reuse test. This is why we focused initially on the special cases of ineffectual and branch-predictable computation: this computation can be literally removed (i.e., replaced with nothing), and only the program counter needs to be updated to skip instructions.

3. Microarchitecture description

A slipstream processor requires two architectural contexts, one for each of the A-stream and R-stream, and new hardware for directing instruction-removal in the A-stream and communicating state between the threads. A high-level block diagram of a slipstream processor implemented on top of a two-way chip multiprocessor is shown in Figure 3, although an SMT processor might also be used. The shaded boxes show the original processors comprising the multiprocessor. Each is a conventional superscalar/VLIW processor with a branch predictor, instruction and data caches, and an execution engine — including the register file and either an in-order pipeline or out-of-order pipeline with reorder buffer.

Slipstreaming requires four new components.

1. The *instruction-removal predictor*, or IR-predictor, is a modified branch predictor. It generates the program counter (PC) of the next block of instructions to be fetched in the A-stream. Unlike a conventional branch predictor, however, *the predicted next PC may reflect skipping past any number of dynamic instructions* that a conventional processor would otherwise fetch and execute. Also, the IR-predictor indicates which instructions *within* a fetched block can be removed after the instruction fetch stage and before the decode/dispatch stage.

2. The *instruction-removal detector*, or IR-detector, monitors the R-stream and detects instructions that could have been removed from the program, and might possibly be removed in the future. The IR-detector conveys to the IR-predictor that particular instructions should potentially be skipped by the A-stream when they are next encountered. Repeated indications by the IR-detector build up confidence in the IR-predictor, and the predictor will remove future instances from the A-stream.

3. The *delay buffer* is used to communicate control and data flow outcomes from A-stream to R-stream [20].

4. The *recovery controller* maintains the addresses of memory locations that are potentially corrupted in the A-stream context. A-stream context is corrupted when the IR-predictor removes instructions that should not have been removed. Unique addresses are added to and removed from the recovery controller as stores are processed by the A-stream, the R-stream, and the IR-detector. The current list of memory locations in the recovery controller is sufficient to recover the A-stream memory context from the R-stream's memory context. The register file is repaired by copying all values from the R-stream's register file.

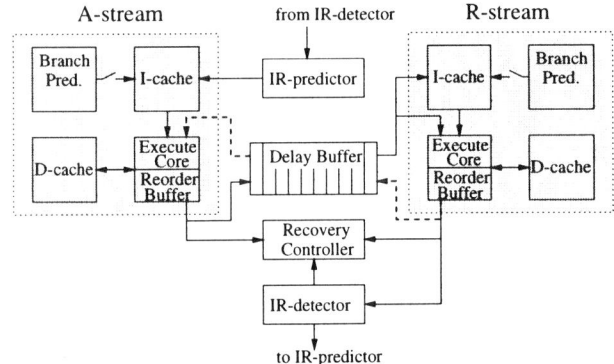

FIGURE 3. Slipstream processor using a two-way chip multiprocessor [27].

The diagram in Figure 3 shows the A-stream on the leftmost core and the R-stream on the rightmost core. This is arbitrary and does not reflect specializing the two cores. A real design would have one core that flexibly supports either the A-stream or R-stream. In any case, there is a clear symmetry that makes designing a single core natural. In both cores, there is an interface to the fetch unit that overrides the conventional branch predictor, indicated symbolically with an open switch and a second interface to the fetch unit. Likewise, both cores show symmetric interfaces to and from the execution pipeline.

3.1. Creating the shorter program

3.1.1. Base IR-predictor.
The IR-predictor resembles a conventional branch predictor. In this paper, the IR-predictor is indexed identically to a *gshare* predictor [15], i.e., an index is formed by XORing the PC and the global branch history bits. Each table entry contains information for a single dynamic basic block.

- *Tag*: This is the start PC of the basic block and is used to determine whether or not the entry contains information for the desired block.
- *2-bit counter*: If the block ends in a conditional branch, the 2-bit counter predicts its direction.
- *Confidence counters*. There is a resetting confidence counter [10] for each instruction in the block. The counters are updated by the IR-detector: a counter is incremented if the corresponding instruction is detected as removable, otherwise the counter is reset to zero. If a counter is saturated, then the corresponding instruction will be removed from the A-stream when it is next encountered.

Every fetch cycle, the IR-predictor supplies a branch prediction and an *instruction-removal bit vector* to the A-stream fetch unit. The branch prediction is used to select a PC for the next fetch cycle; potential target PCs are stored within existing structures of the processor, e.g., pre-decoded targets in the instruction cache or branch target buffer.

The instruction-removal bit vector reflects the state of the confidence counters for the basic block being fetched. A bit is set in the vector if the corresponding confidence counter is saturated, and this directs the fetch unit to remove the corresponding instruction from the A-stream. Thus, although all instructions in the basic block are fetched, potentially many instructions are removed before the decode stage of the pipeline.

In Figure 3, the IR-predictor is shown as a new component outside the processor core that overrides the conventional branch predictor. Alternatively, since the IR-predictor is built on top of a conventional branch predictor, the core's predictor and the IR-predictor may be integrated.

3.1.2. Improved IR-predictor: bypassing instruction fetch.
With the base IR-predictor described in Section 3.1.1, the A-stream is not reduced in terms of the number of instructions *fetched*. Only the number of instructions *executed* is reduced. If execution bandwidth is relatively unconstrained, then the A-stream will not be effectively reduced.

The A-stream is more effective if *fewer fetch cycles* are expended on it than on the full program. In Figure 4, we show an example of how the number of fetch cycles can potentially be reduced. Four basic blocks, labeled A through D, are to be predicted and fetched. The corresponding table entries in the IR-predictor are shown; shaded entries indicate that all of the confidence counters are saturated and the entire basic block is predicted for removal. The base IR-predictor predicts each block in sequence, requiring four cycles. During two of these cycles, the instruction cache fetches instructions and then throws them all away (basic blocks B and C). Clearly, only two fetch cycles are required, but it is not known in advance that instruction fetching of blocks B and C can be bypassed.

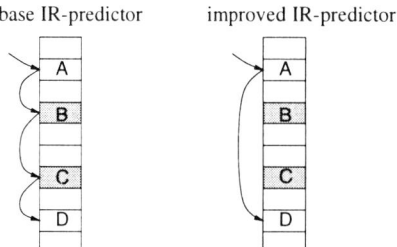

FIGURE 4. Reducing fetch cycles in the A-stream.

Interestingly, the effect we want to produce — bypassing basic blocks — is the same effect produced by taken branches. The improved IR-predictor shown on the right-hand side of Figure 4 exploits the analogy. The improved predictor "converts" the branch terminating block A into a taken branch whose target is block D. Below, we consider two possible ways to implement this conversion.

- Two additional pieces of information are stored in block A's table entry. First, the predicted directions of any bypassed branches must be stored, in this case, the predicted directions of the branches in blocks B and C. The reason is all control flow information must be pushed onto the delay buffer to be consumed by the R-stream, in spite of partially bypassing instruction fetching in the A-stream. Second, a target address must be stored, in this case, the start PC of block D. The target address overrides the next PC computation performed by the fetch unit. The additional information (bypassed predictions and corresponding target address) is accumulated for block A's entry as the IR-detector sequentially updates the entries of blocks B, C, and D.

- Effectively, the branch terminating block A is now a multi-way branch. It has more potential targets than its original taken and fall-through targets because it inherits the targets of skipped blocks. The processor's branch target buffer may be modified to store multiple targets per branch. Now, dynamically-created target addresses do not have to be stored in the IR-predictor.

The bypassed predictions still need to be stored and, conveniently, this path information is sufficient to select the appropriate target address from the branch target buffer.

3.1.3. IR-detector. The IR-detector consumes retired R-stream instructions, addresses, and values. The instructions are buffered and, based on data dependences, circuitry among the buffers is dynamically configured to establish connections from consumer to producer instructions. In other words, a reverse dataflow graph (R-DFG) is constructed. The graph is finite in size, so the oldest instructions exit the graph to make room for newer instructions. Removal information for exiting instructions are used to update the IR-predictor.

As new instructions are merged into the R-DFG, the IR-detector watches for any of three triggering conditions for instruction removal. Triggering conditions are unreferenced writes (a write followed by a write to the same location, with no intervening read), non-modifying writes [12,14,16,29] (writing the same value to a location as already exists at that location), and correctly-predicted branch instructions. When a triggering condition is observed, the corresponding instruction is selected for removal. Then, the circuits forming the R-DFG back-propagate the selection status to predecessor instructions. Predecessors may also be selected if certain criteria (described later) are met.

The IR-detector is shown in Figure 5. A single R-DFG is shown, however, the buffering could be partitioned into multiple smaller R-DFGs. The latter approach reduces the size/complexity of each individual R-DFG but still allows a large analysis scope for killing values (observing another write to the same location).

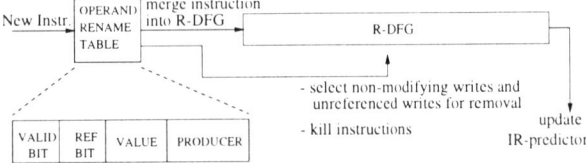

FIGURE 5. IR-detector.

The operand rename table in Figure 5 is similar to a register renamer but it can track both memory addresses and registers. A single entry of the operand rename table is shown in Figure 5. To merge an instruction into the R-DFG, each source operand is checked in the rename table to get the most recent producer of the value (check the *valid bit* and *producer* field). The instruction uses this information to establish connections with its producer instructions, i.e., set up the back-propagation logic (if the buffering is partitioned into smaller R-DFGs, connections cannot be made across partition boundaries). The *ref bit* is set for each source operand indicating the values have been used. If the instruction writes a register/memory location, the corresponding operand rename table entry is checked to detect non-modifying/unreferenced writes and to kill values, as follows.

1. If the *valid bit* is set, and the current instruction produced the same value as indicated in the *value* field, then the current instruction is a non-modifying write. The current instruction is selected for removal as it is merged into the R-DFG. No fields are updated in the rename table entry since the old producer remains "live" in this case.
2. If the *valid bit* is set and the new and old values do not match, the old producer indicated by the *producer* field is killed. Furthermore, if the *ref bit* is not set, then the old producer is an unreferenced write and is selected for removal. Finally, all fields in the rename table entry are updated to reflect the new producer.

Correctly predicted branch instructions are selected for removal when they are merged into the R-DFG.

Finally, any other instruction x may be selected for removal via the R-DFG back-propagation circuitry, if three conditions are met.

1. All of x's dependent instructions must be known, i.e., x's production(s) must be killed by other production(s).
2. All of x's dependent instructions must be selected for removal.
3. *All of x's dependent instructions must have been removed by the IR-predictor this time around.*

When a basic block becomes the oldest basic block in the analysis scope, the appropriate entry for that basic block is updated in the IR-predictor, i.e., confidence counters are incremented for selected instructions and reset for non-selected instructions.

The third (highlighted) condition above is the major innovation with respect to our previous instruction-removal mechanism. Previously, this constraint was not needed because dependence chains were confined to a trace and a single confidence counter was maintained for the entire trace; this ensured producers and consumers were removed together or not at all, but it also resulted in unrelated chains diluting overall confidence. The dilution problem is fixed by maintaining confidence for instructions individually; however, this can lead to partial-chain removal and the specifically bad situation of removing a producer but not the consumer. The third constraint above ensures a producer's counter saturates only after all consumers' counters saturate. The end result: 1) our new approach measures confidence for instructions individually, so unrelated instructions do not dilute confidence, yet 2) dependence chains still tend to be removed as a unit, and chains are not confined within a small region other than to reduce R-DFG complexity.

3.2. Delay buffer

The delay buffer is a simple FIFO queue that allows the A-stream to communicate control flow and data flow outcomes to the R-stream. The A-stream pushes both a *complete* history of branch outcomes and a *partial* history of operand values onto the delay buffer. This is shown in Figure 3 with a solid arrow from the reorder buffer of the A-stream (left-most processor) to the delay buffer. Value history is partial because only a subset of the program is executed by the A-stream. Complete control history is available, however, because the IR-predictor predicts all branches even though the A-stream may not fetch all instructions (Section 3.1.2).

The R-stream pops control and data flow information from the delay buffer. This is shown in Figure 3 with solid arrows from delay buffer to the instruction cache and execution core of the R-stream (right-most processor). Branch outcomes from the delay buffer are routed to the instruction cache to direct instruction fetching. Source operand values and load/store addresses from the delay buffer are merged with their respective instructions after the instructions have been fetched/renamed and before they enter the execution engine. To know which values/addresses go with which instructions, the delay buffer also includes information about which instructions were skipped by the A-stream (for which there is no data flow information available).

3.3. IR-misprediction recovery

An *instruction-removal misprediction*, or IR-misprediction, occurs when A-stream instructions were removed that should not have been. The A-stream has no way of detecting the IR-misprediction, therefore, it continues instruction retirement and corrupts its architectural state. Two things are required to recover from an IR-misprediction. First, the IR-misprediction must be detected and, second, the corrupted state must be pinpointed for efficient recovery actions.

IR-mispredictions are detectable by the R-stream because either the control or data flow outcomes from the delay buffer will not match its redundantly computed outcomes. In other words, IR-mispredictions usually surface as branch or value mispredictions in the R-stream.

Some IR-mispredictions take awhile to cause any visible symptoms in the A-stream. For example, a store may be removed incorrectly and the next load to the same location may not occur for a very long time. The IR-detector can detect these IR-mispredictions much sooner by comparing its computed removal information against the corresponding predicted removal information — if they differ, computation was removed that should not have been. Thus, the IR-detector serves the dual-role of updating the IR-predictor *and* checking for IR-mispredictions.

When an IR-misprediction is detected, the reorder buffer of the R-stream is flushed. The R-stream architectural state now represents a precise point in the program to which all other components in the processor are re-synchronized. The IR-predictor is backed up to the precise program counter, the delay buffer is flushed, the reorder buffer of the A-stream is flushed, and the A-stream's program counter is set to that of the R-stream.

All that remains is restoring the corrupted register and memory state of the A-stream so it is consistent with the R-stream. Because register state is finite, the entire register file of the R-stream is copied to the A-stream register file. The movement of data (both register and memory values) occurs via the delay buffer, in the reverse direction, as shown with dashed arrows in Figure 3.

The *recovery controller* receives control signals and the addresses of store instructions from the A-stream, the R-stream, and the IR-detector, as shown in Figure 3. The control signals indicate when to start or stop tracking a memory address (only unique addresses need to be tracked). After detecting an IR-misprediction, stores may either have to be "undone" or "done" in the A-stream.

- The recovery controller tracks addresses of stores retired in the A-stream but not yet retired in the R-stream. After detecting an IR-misprediction, these A-stream stores must be "undone" since the R-stream has not yet performed the companion, redundant store.

- The recovery controller tracks addresses of stores retired in the R-stream and skipped in the A-stream, only until the IR-detector verifies that the stores are truly ineffectual. When an IR-misprediction is detected, all unverified, predicted-ineffectual stores are "done" in the A-stream by copying data from the redundant locations in the R-stream.

4. Simulation environment

We developed a detailed execution-driven simulator of a slipstream processor. The simulator faithfully models the architecture depicted in Figure 3 and outlined in Section 3: the A-stream produces real, possibly incorrect values/addresses and branch outcomes, the R-stream and IR-detector check the A-stream and initiate recovery actions, A-stream state is recovered from the R-stream state, etc. The simulator itself is validated via a functional simulator run independently and in parallel with the detailed timing simulator [26]. The functional simulator checks retired R-stream control flow and data flow outcomes.

The Simplescalar [3] compiler and ISA are used. We use the SPEC95 integer benchmarks (-O3 optimization) run to completion (Table 1).

TABLE 1. Benchmarks.

benchmark	input dataset	instr. count
compress	40000 e 2231	124 million
gcc	cccp.i -o cccp.s	265 million
go	9 9	133 million
jpeg	vigo.ppm	166 million
li	test.lsp (queens 7)	202 million
m88ksim	-c < ctl.in (dcrand.big)	121 million
perl	scrabble.pl < scrabble.in	108 million
vortex	vortex.in (persons.250)	101 million

TABLE 2. Microarchitecture configuration.

single processor core	
instruction cache	size/assoc/repl = 64kB/4-way/LRU
	line size = 16 instructions
	2-way interleaved
	miss penalty = 12 cycles
data cache	size/assoc/repl = 64kB/4-way/LRU
	line size = 64 bytes
	miss penalty = 14 cycles
superscalar core	reorder buffer: 64, 128, or 256 entries
	dispatch/issue/retire bandwidth: 4-/8-/16-way
	n fully-symmetric function units (n = issue b/w)
	n loads/stores per cycle (n = issue b/w)
execution latencies	address generation = 1 cycle
	memory access = 2 cycles (hit)
	integer ALU ops = 1 cycle
	complex ops = MIPS R10000 latencies
new components for slipstreaming	
IR-predictor	2^{20} entries
	gshare-indexed (16 bits of global branch history)
	block size = 16
	16 confidence counters per entry
	confidence threshold = 32
IR-detector	R-DFG = 256 instructions, unpartitioned
delay buffer	data flow buffer: 256 instruction entries
	control flow buffer: 4K branch predictions
recovery controller	# of outstanding store addr. = unconstrained
	recovery latency (*after* IR-misp. detected):
	• 5 cycles to start up recovery pipeline
	• 4 reg. restores/cycle (64 regs performed 1st)
	• 4 mem. restores/cycle (mem performed 2nd)
	• ∴ min. latency (no memory) = 21 cycles

Microarchitecture parameters are listed in Table 2. The top half of the table lists parameters for individual processors within a CMP or, alternatively, a single SMT processor. The bottom half describes the four slipstream components. A large IR-predictor is used for accurate instruction removal. The removal confidence threshold is 32. The IR-detector has a scope of 256 instructions and the R-DFG is unpartitioned. The delay buffer stores 256 instructions (data flow buffer) and 4K branch predictions (control flow buffer). The recovery controller tracks any number of store addresses, although we observe not too many outstanding addresses in practice. The recovery latency (*after* the IR-misprediction is detected) is 5 cycles to startup the recovery pipeline, followed by 4 register restores per cycle, and lastly 4 memory restores per cycle.

5. Results

5.1. Slipstream performance results

In this section, we compare the performance of eight models. Three are superscalar configurations (SS). Four are chip-multiprocessor configurations (CMP) with slipstreaming. One is a simultaneous multithreading configuration (SMT) with slipstreaming.

- **SS(64x4)**: A single 4-way superscalar processor with 64 ROB entries.
- **SS(128x8)**: A single 8-way superscalar processor with 128 ROB entries.
- **SS(256x16)**: A single 16-way superscalar processor with 256 ROB entries.
- **CMP(2x64x4)**: Slipstreaming on a CMP composed of two SS(64x4) cores.
- **CMP(2x64x4)/byp**: Same as previous, but A-stream can bypass instruction fetching.
- **CMP(2x128x8)**: Slipstreaming on a CMP composed of two SS(128x8) cores.
- **CMP(2x128x8)/byp**: Same as previous, but A-stream can bypass instruction fetching.
- **SMT(128x8)/byp**: Slipstreaming on SMT, where the SMT is built on top of SS(128x8).

For consistent comparisons, the same (*gshare*-based) IR-predictor provides branch predictions in all of the processor models, and the base superscalar processor models ignore the instruction-removal information. Performance is measured in retired instructions-per-cycle (IPC). For slipstream models, IPC is computed as the number of retired R-stream instructions (i.e., the full program, counted only once) divided by the number of cycles required for both the A-stream and R-stream to complete (total execution time).

IPC performance of the eight models is shown in Figure 6. The first conclusion is a slipstream processor can exploit a second, otherwise unused processor to dramatically improve single-program performance. From Figure 7, CMP(2x64x4) performs on average 12% better than using only a single SS(64x4) processor. And CMP(2x128x8) performs on average 7% better than using only a single SS(128x8) processor. Slipstreaming degrades performance in *jpeg*, by 1% and 5% for CMP(2x64x4) and CMP(2x128x8), respectively. *Jpeg*'s A-stream is not reduced much and *jpeg* is already quite parallel; IR-mispredictions cause an overall degradation.

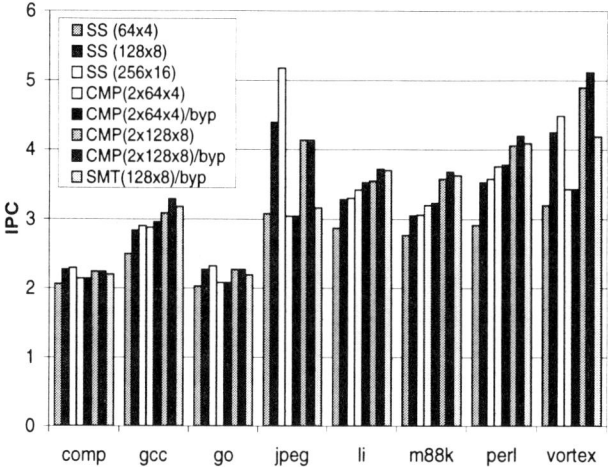

FIGURE 6. IPC results.

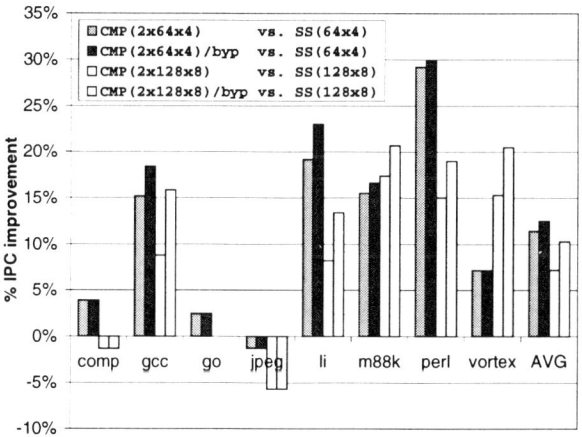

FIGURE 7. Performance improvement using a second processor for slipstreaming.

The second conclusion is the benefit of slipstreaming decreases as more execution bandwidth is made available. This is evident from the first and third bars of Figure 7. For all except *m88ksim* and *vortex*, the performance improvement of CMP(2x128x8) over SS(128x8) is less than the improvement of CMP(2x64x4) over SS(64x4). For example, *perl* drops from a 30% improvement down to a 15% improvement as the window size and issue bandwidth of the processor core is doubled. This is evidence for the arguments made in Section 2.3.

The above result motivates reducing the number of instructions *fetched* in the A-stream, using the improved IR-predictor (Section 3.1.2). From Figure 7, CMP(2x64x4)/byp on average performs 13% better than SS(64x4), a modest change from CMP(2x64x4). As expected, it is more important to bypass instruction fetching for larger processor cores. CMP(2x128x8)/byp on average performs 10% better than SS(128x8), whereas CMP(2x128x8) performs 7% better. With the improved IR-predictor, slipstream performance improvement increases from 8% to 16% for *gcc*, from 8% to 14% for *li*, from 17% to 21% for *m88ksim*, from 15% to 19% for *perl*, and from 15% to 20% for *vortex*.

In Figure 8, we compare the performance of slipstreaming on two small processors to the performance of a larger processor. The larger processor has the same total number of ROB entries and issue bandwidth as the two smaller processors combined. For half of the benchmarks (*perl*, *gcc*, *li*, *m88ksim*), CMP(2x64x4)/byp actually performs from 4% to 8% better than SS(128x8). Overall, CMP(2x64x4)/byp performs comparably to the more complex, less flexible SS(128x8) processor — within 5% on average. The results are more pronounced for CMP(2x128x8)/byp, which on average performs 7% better than SS(256x16).

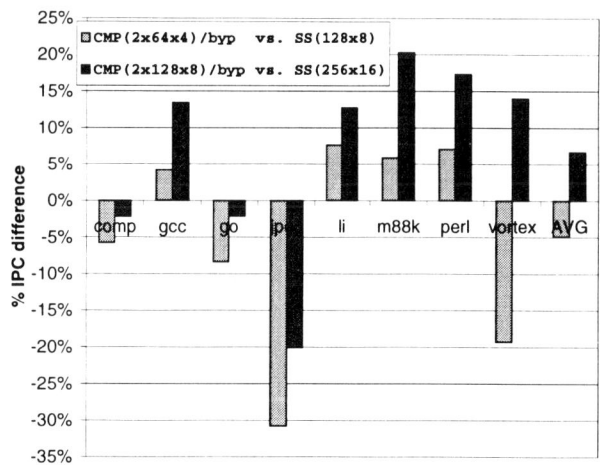

FIGURE 8. Perf. of slipstreaming on two small processors vs. perf. of a single large processor.

Finally, we examine the performance of slipstreaming on an SMT processor. The performance improvement of SMT(128x8)/byp over SS(128x8) is shown in Figure 9. For half of the benchmarks, performance improves by more than 10%. *Gcc*, *li*, *perl*, and *m88ksim* improve by 12%, 13%, 16%, and 19%, respectively. Performance is degraded between 1% and 4% for *compress*, *go*, and *vortex*, and over 25% for *jpeg*. *Compress* showed a small loss even for the CMP(2x128x8) model, so one would expect the same for SMT(128x8)/byp. The reason is the A-stream is less effective for *compress* and IR-mispredictions degrade performance. *Go* was also borderline in the

CMP(2x128x8) case. *Vortex* and *jpeg* utilize the SS(128x8) processor well — in fact, they exceed half of the peak IPC — and the A-stream steals useful processor bandwidth from the R-stream. The effect is more pronounced for *jpeg* than for *vortex* because *jpeg* exhibits little reduction in its A-stream (Figure 10).

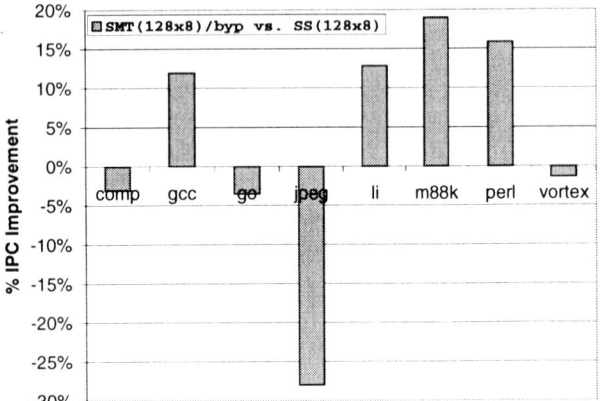

FIGURE 9. Performance improvement of SMT(128x8)/byp over SS(128x8).

5.2. Instruction removal

Figure 10 shows the fraction of original dynamic instructions removed from the A-stream. Nearly half of the program is removed for *gcc*, *li*, *perl*, and *vortex*, and about two-thirds of *m88ksim* is removed. About 20% of *compress* is removed, and only 10% for *go* and *jpeg*.

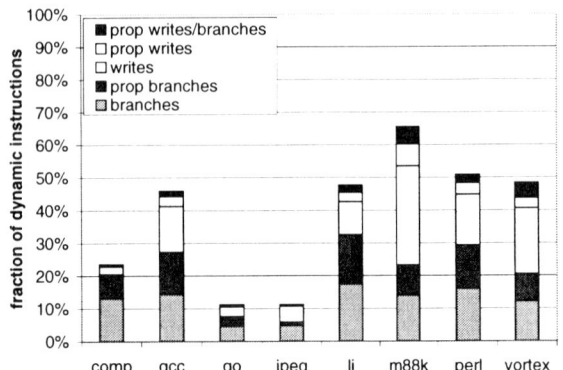

FIGURE 10. Breakdown of instruction removal.

Removing only 10% of the program simply does not buffer the R-stream from many branch mispredictions. But 20% removal in *compress* is significant, and it is surprising slipstream performance improvements are not higher. The problem with *compress* is three-fold: there are frequent branch mispredictions, their dependence chains are quite long, and the chains have long-latency arithmetic operations. Removing 20% of *compress* can perhaps buffer the R-stream against any one of these three, but not two or three combined.

Figure 10 also breaks down the reasons for instruction removal. On average, branches are the primary source, at just over a third of the removed instructions ("branches"). Ineffectual writes are about a third of removed instructions ("writes"). Among instructions removed due to back-propagation ("prop —"), most are in dependence chains of removed branches ("prop branches").

5.3. Prediction

In Figure 11, we show the performance improvement of three models with respect to SS(64x4). The first is SS(64x4) with conventional value prediction added. A large context-based value predictor (CVP) [24] is used (2^{18} and 2^{20} entries in the first and second levels, respectively). The second is CMP(2x64x4)/byp, but the R-stream does not use A-stream values speculatively ("no value prediction"). The third is CMP(2x64x4)/byp.

We only consider benchmarks that show reasonably large improvements with any of the models (eliminating *compress*, *go*, *jpeg*). For *gcc* and *li*, better branch prediction is the largest benefit due to slipstreaming, not value prediction (we can tell because the second and third bars are close). Also, CVP provides only minor improvements for these benchmarks. For *m88ksim*, value prediction is the dominant factor and CVP is superior. For *perl* and *vortex*, value prediction is the larger benefit due to slipstreaming, however, CVP does not provide the same benefit. Perhaps in *perl*, better branch prediction is needed to better exploit value predictions.

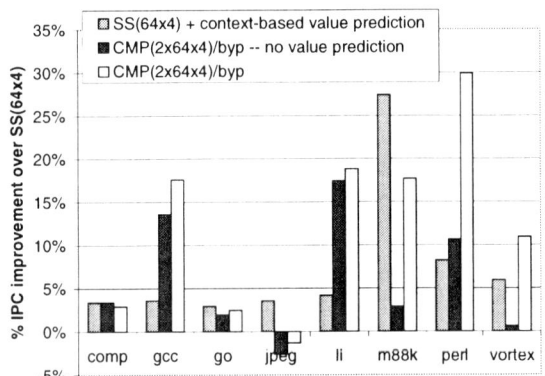

FIGURE 11. Measuring the relative importance of branch and value prediction benefits.

6. Related work

Advanced-stream/Redundant-stream Simultaneous Multithreading (AR-SMT) [20] is based on the realization that microarchitecture performance trends and fault tolerance are related. Time redundancy — running a program twice to detect transient faults — is cheaper than hardware redundancy but it doubles execution time. AR-SMT runs the two programs simultaneously [28] but delayed (via the delay buffer), reducing the performance overhead of time redundancy. Results are compared by communicating all retired A-stream results to the R-stream, and the R-stream performs the checks. Here, the R-stream leverages speculation concepts [13] — the A-stream results can be used as ideal predictions. The R-stream fetches/executes with maximum efficiency, further reducing the performance overhead of time redundancy. And the method for comparing the A-stream and the R-stream is conveniently in place, in the form of misprediction-detection hardware. In summary, AR-SMT leverages the underlying microarchitecture to achieve broad coverage of transient faults with low overhead, both in terms of performance and changes to the existing design.

DIVA [2] and SRT [18] are two other examples of fault-tolerant architectures designed for commodity high-performance microprocessors. DIVA detects a variety of faults, *including design faults*, by using a verified checker to validate computation of the complex processor core. DIVA leverages an AR-SMT technique — the simple checker is able to keep pace with the core by using the values it is checking as predictions. SRT improves on AR-SMT in a variety of ways, including a formal and systematic treatment of SMT applied to fault tolerance (e.g., *spheres of replication*).

Researchers have demonstrated a significant amount of redundancy, repetition, and predictability in general purpose programs [6,8,9,12,13,14,16,24,25,29]. This prior research forms a basis for creating the shorter program in slipstream processors. A technical report [21] showed 1) it is possible to ideally construct significantly reduced programs that produce correct final output, and 2) AR-SMT is a convenient execution model to exploit this property.

Tullsen et. al. [28] and Yamamoto and Nemirovsky [31] proposed simultaneous multithreading for flexibly exploiting thread-level and instruction-level parallelism. Olukotun et. al. [17] motivate using chip multiprocessors.

Farcy et. al. [7] proposed resolving branch mispredictions early by extracting the computation leading to branches. Zilles and Sohi [33] similarly studied the computation chains leading to mispredicted branches and loads that miss in the level-two cache. They suggest identifying a difficult subset of the program for *pre-execution* [22,23], potentially prefetching branch predictions and cache lines that would otherwise be mispredictions and cache misses. Pre-execution typically involves pruning a small kernel from a larger program region and running it as a prefetch engine [22]. Roth and Sohi [23] developed a new paradigm called *Speculative Data-Driven Multithreading* that implements pre-execution generally. Rather than spawn many specialized kernels on-the-fly, our approach uses a single, functionally complete, and persistent program (A-stream). Slipstreaming avoids the conceptual and possibly real complexity of forking private contexts, within which the specialized kernels must run.

Speculative multithreading architectures [e.g.,1,17,26] speed up a single program by dividing it into speculatively-parallel threads. The speculation model uses *one architectural context* and future threads are spawned within temporary, private contexts, each inherited from the preceding thread's context. Future thread contexts are merged into the architectural context as threads complete. Our speculation model uses redundant architectural contexts, so no forking or merging is needed. And strictly speaking, there are no dependences between the architecturally-independent threads, rather, outcomes are communicated as predictions via a simple FIFO queue. Register and memory mechanisms of the underlying processor are relatively unchanged by slipstreaming (particularly if there is an existing interface for consuming value predictions at the rename stage). In contrast, speculative multithreading often requires elaborate inter-thread register/memory dependence mechanisms.

SSMT [5] runs microthreads simultaneously with an application to optimize its performance. Microthreads are small routines designed in conjunction with applications and the processor. For example, microthreads may perform cache prefetching, improve branch prediction accuracy [5], or optimize exception handling [32].

The DataScalar paradigm [4] runs redundant programs on multiple processor-and-memory cores to eliminate memory read requests.

7. Summary and conclusions

Integrating multiple architectural contexts on a single chip is an important trend, and it is difficult to conceive of more effective uses for a billion transistors. The slipstream paradigm extracts more functionality from a CMP or SMT processor, without fundamentally reorganizing it. The operating system may flexibly choose among multiple operating modes based on system and user requirements: high job throughput and parallel-program performance (conventional SMT/CMP), improved single-program performance and reliability (slipstreaming), or fully-reliable operation with low impact on single-program performance (AR-SMT / SRT).

In this paper, we developed a new and more effective instruction-removal mechanism for creating the shorter program. It measures removal-confidence on a per-instruction basis, eliminating many flaws of the prior trace-based approach and leveraging conventional branch predictors. The new approach reduces the A-stream significantly (often by 50%), but also accurately.

We also developed a new and simple sequencing mechanism that enables the A-stream to skip over large dynamic sequences of instructions.

Finally, we reasoned about the sources of slipstream performance, and its limitations. This focused our exploration of the architecture and led us to some key results.

- A 12% average performance improvement is achieved by harnessing an otherwise unused, additional processor in a CMP. Slipstreaming using two small superscalar cores often achieves similar IPC as one large superscalar core, but with a potentially faster clock and a more flexible architecture. For programs with sufficiently reduced A-streams, slipstreaming on an 8-way SMT processor improves performance from 10%-20%.

- For some programs, performance improvement is due to the A-stream resolving branch mispredictions in advance. Others benefit largely from A-stream value predictions, and the effect is not always reproducible using conventional value prediction tables.

- As more execution bandwidth is made available, slipstreaming provides less performance improvement. But if the A-stream is able to bypass instruction fetching, slipstreaming retains its edge — because raw instruction fetch bandwidth is not as easily extended as raw execution bandwidth.

References

[1] H. Akkary and M. Driscoll. A Dynamic Multithreading Processor. *31st Int'l Symp. on Microarch.*, Dec 1998.

[2] T. Austin. DIVA: A Reliable Substrate for Deep Submicron Microarchitecture Design. *32nd Int'l Symp. on Microarch.*, Nov. 1999.

[3] D. Burger, T. Austin, and S. Bennett. Evaluating Future Microprocessors: The Simplescalar Toolset. Tech. Rep. CS-TR-96-1308, CS Dept., Univ. of Wisconsin, July 1996.

[4] D. Burger, S. Kaxiras, and J. Goodman. DataScalar Architectures. *24th Int'l Symp. on Comp. Arch.*, June 1997.

[5] R. Chappell, J. Stark, S. Kim, S. Reinhardt, and Y. Patt. Simultaneous Subordinate Microthreading (SSMT). *26th Int'l Symp. on Comp. Arch.*, May 1999.

[6] D. Connors and W.-M. Hwu. Compiler-Directed Dynamic Computation Reuse: Rationale and Initial Results. *32nd Int'l Symp. on Microarch.*, Nov. 1999.

[7] A. Farcy, O. Temam, R. Espasa, and T. Juan. Dataflow Analysis of Branch Mispredictions and its Application to Early Resolution of Branch Outcomes. *31st Int'l Symp. on Microarch.*, Dec. 1998.

[8] A. González, J. Tubella, and C. Molina. Trace-Level Reuse. *Int'l Conf. on Parallel Processing*, Sep. 1999.

[9] J. Huang and D. Lilja. Exploiting Basic Block Value Locality with Block Reuse. *5th Int'l Symp. on High-Perf. Comp. Arch.*, Jan. 1999.

[10] E. Jacobsen, E. Rotenberg, and J. Smith. Assigning Confidence to Conditional Branch Predictions. *29th Int'l Symp. on Microarch.*, Dec. 1996.

[11] M. Lam and R. Wilson. Limits of Control Flow on Parallelism. *19th Int'l Symp. on Comp. Arch.*, May 1992.

[12] K. Lepak and M. Lipasti. On the Value Locality of Store Instructions. *27th Int'l Symp. on Comp. Arch.*, June 2000.

[13] M. Lipasti. Value Locality and Speculative Execution. PhD Thesis, Carnegie Mellon University, April 1997.

[14] M. Martin, A. Roth, and C. Fischer. Exploiting Dead Value Information. *30th Int'l. Symp. on Microarch.*, Dec 1997.

[15] S. McFarling. Combining Branch Predictors. Tech. Rep. TN-36, WRL, June 1993.

[16] C. Molina, A. Gonzalez, and J. Tubella. Reducing Memory Traffic via Redundant Store Instructions. *HPCN* 1999.

[17] K. Olukotun, B. Nayfeh, L. Hammond, K. Wilson, and K.-Y. Chang. The Case for a Single-Chip Multiprocessor. *ASPLOS-VII*, Oct. 1996.

[18] S. Reinhardt and S. Mukherjee. Transient Fault Detection via Simultaneous Multithreading. *27th Int'l Symp. on Comp. Arch.*, June 2000.

[19] D. Ronfeldt. Social Science at 190 MPH on NASCAR's Biggest Superspeedways. *First Monday Journal* (on-line), Vol. 5 No. 2, Feb. 7, 2000.

[20] E. Rotenberg. AR-SMT: A Microarchitectural Approach to Fault Tolerance in Microprocessors. *29th Int'l Symp. on Fault-Tolerant Computing*, June 1999.

[21] E. Rotenberg. Exploiting Large Ineffectual Instruction Sequences. Tech. Rep., ECE Dept., NC State, Nov. 1999.

[22] A. Roth, A. Moshovos, and G. Sohi. Dependence Based Prefetching for Linked Data Structures. *ASPLOS-VIII*, Oct. 1998.

[23] A. Roth and G. Sohi. Speculative Data-Driven Multithreading. Tech. Rep. CS-TR-2000-1414, CS Dept., Univ. of Wisconsin, April 2000.

[24] Y. Sazeides and J. E. Smith. Modeling Program Predictability. *25th Int'l Symp. on Comp. Arch.*, June 1998.

[25] A. Sodani and G. S. Sohi. Dynamic Instruction Reuse. *24th Int'l Symp. on Comp. Arch.*, June 1997.

[26] G. Sohi, S. Breach, and T. N. Vijaykumar. Multiscalar Processors. *22nd Intl. Symp. on Comp. Arch.*, June 1995.

[27] K. Sundaramoorthy, Z. Purser, and E. Rotenberg. Slipstream Processors: Improving both Performance and Fault Tolerance. *ASPLOS-IX*, Nov. 2000.

[28] D. Tullsen, S. Eggers, J. Emer, H. Levy, J. Lo, and R. Stamm. Exploiting Choice: Instruction Fetch and Issue on an Implementable Simultaneous Multithreading Processor. *23rd Int'l Symp. on Comp. Arch.*, May 1996.

[29] D. Tullsen and J. Seng. Storageless Value Prediction Using Prior Register Values. *26th Int'l Symp. on Comp. Arch.*, May 1999.

[30] D. Wall. Limits of Instructional-Level Parallelism. *ASPLOS-IV*, April 1991.

[31] W. Yamamoto and M. Nemirovsky. Increasing Superscalar Performance through Multistreaming. *Parallel Architectures and Compilation Techniques*, June 1995.

[32] C. Zilles, J. Emer, and G. Sohi. The Use of Multithreading for Exception Handling. *32nd Int'l Symp. on Microarch.*, Nov. 1999.

[33] C. Zilles and G. Sohi. Understanding the Backward Slices of Performance Degrading Instructions. *27th Int'l Symp. on Comp. Arch.*, June 2000.

Relational Profiling: Enabling Thread-Level Parallelism in Virtual Machines

Timothy Heil   James E. Smith
University of Wisconsin – Madison
Madison, WI 53706
{heilt, jes}@ece.wisc.edu

Abstract

Virtual machine service threads can perform many tasks in parallel with program execution such as garbage collection, dynamic compilation, and profile collection and analysis. Hardware-assisted profiling is essential for providing service threads with needed information in a flexible and efficient way. A relational profiling architecture (RPA) is proposed for meeting this goal.

The RPA selects particular instructions for profiling, and communicates collected information to service threads through shared memory message queues. The RPA's capabilities lead to new profiling applications, such as concurrent garbage collection.

Simulations indicate that a low-cost implementation of the RPA should be able to profile four in-flight instructions simultaneously, and provide storage for eight profile records. Profiling overhead is less than 0.5% for concurrent garbage collection and edge profiling.

1 Introduction

Two important trends are shaping the processing paradigm of the future. First, technology and the demand for higher performance are leading to on-chip multithreading, both within a large single processor and across multiple on-chip processors. Second, the emergence of binary translation, dynamic optimization, and virtual machine (VM) technologies is leading to a re-definition of the traditional hardware/software interface.

Our research is targeted at this future environment and is centered on the development and application of co-designed virtual machines. Co-designed VMs combine hardware and software to implement a virtual instruction set architecture on hardware directly supporting an implementation-specific instruction set architecture [10, 11, 12, 18, 20]. Co-designed virtual machines and on-chip multithreading complement each other very well. In particular, the co-designed VM paradigm naturally leads to a form of thread-level parallelism (TLP) where *service threads* perform tasks such as dynamic profile collection and processing, dynamic re-compilation, and garbage collection in parallel with program execution (which may also be multithreaded).

Efficient hardware-assisted profiling is central to the dynamic optimization paradigm. We have taken a top-down approach to hardware-assisted profiling. The goal is to develop profiling mechanisms flexible enough to satisfy not only known applications, but also future applications that will develop as the VM paradigm evolves. At the top level, the *relational profiling architecture* (RPA) summarizes and passes profile information to service threads in a flexible and efficient way, enabling them to perform their tasks.

We propose a *relational profiling model*, which provides the framework for designing the RPA. The relational profiling model allows software to form general queries regarding program behavior. These queries may request information regarding instruction types, hardware events, specific instructions, or ranges of instructions, as well as various combinations. A hardware implementation processes the queries, collects the requested information, and passes it back to software in the form of standard format messages. Service threads read these messages to perform optimizations and other tasks to support the main computation thread(s).

The relational profiling model is discussed in Section 2. Section 3 describes the RPA using examples. Section 4 discusses an implementation of the RPA and analyzes hardware costs at the microarchitectural level. Sections 5 and 6 evaluate the utility and performance of the RPA using one traditional profiling application, edge profiling, and one new application, concurrent garbage collection. Related work is described in Section 7, and Section 8 concludes the paper.

2 The Relational Profiling Model

The relational profiling model can uniformly specify the collection of a wide range of information. Conceptually, the relational profiling model is similar to a table in a relational database. See Figure 1. Each column represents a dynamic instruction; each row represents a possible event. This model leads to two basic forms of queries.

1) Instruction-based queries. "For certain instructions, what events occurred?" These queries select columns from the table. To collect this information, the profile mechanism essentially follows the instruction as it flows

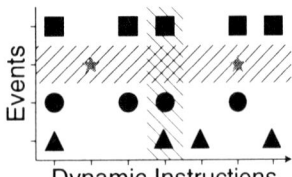

Figure 1. The relational profiling model organizes instructions and events in a table.

through the pipeline, collecting event information regarding its behavior. This is similar to ProfileMe [9].

2) Event-based queries. "For some events, what instructions were involved?" These queries select rows from the table. To collect this information, the profile mechanism essentially sits at some point(s) in the pipeline, recording information about instructions that flow past. This is similar to the counter profiling mechanisms common in processors today. In contrast to counter-based methods, however, the relational model can provide detailed information about specific dynamic instructions. Nevertheless, hardware counters may sometimes be useful as an efficient summarizing mechanism.

Hybrids queries are also possible. For instance, the definition of, "some instructions," in instruction-based queries may contain event-related conditions (i.e. "For all load instructions that miss in the cache...").

3 The Relational Profiling Architecture

Given the relational model, the goal was to produce a profile architecture that allows queries to be conveniently expressed, and that leads to an efficient implementation. This pursuit led to the development of the relational profiling architecture (RPA).

3.1 RPA Assembly Language

Profile queries are most easily expressed via an assembly language. An RPA assembly language program or *query* 1) describes records of information to be collected, 2) specifies a rate at which the information should be collected, 3) describes selection criteria for which a record should be checked, and 4) indicates actions to be taken for the selected records.

To facilitate RPA research, an assembler was developed using the ANTLR tool [16]. Unlike typical assembly languages, RPA queries invoke a number of machine level instructions that manage structures in the profile hardware. These structures are described in Section 3.4. Examples in Figure 2 describe the RPA and its usage.

An RPA program is broken into a series of queries. Each query begins with a *query header* that indicates which instructions should be profiled, what information should be collected and how often. Instructions are divided into the eight classes shown in Table 1. For example, the statement in Figure 2a specifies that conditional

a) for opBRANCH * every 256 collect pc misc ;
   send 1 stop;

b) for evL2DMISS * always collect pc res2 ;
   send 2 stop;

c) for opSTORE 1 always collect op1 op2 op3;
   if op1 <> 0 then send 3 stop else stop;

d) for opJMP * opBRANCH * opLOAD *
   opSTORE * opALU * opMULT *
   opFLOAT * opSYS *
   every 1024 collect pc rrate;
   send 4 stop;

Figure 2. Example RPA assembly language queries.

Table 1 Instruction profiling classes.

Mnemonic	Instructions
opJMP	Unconditional jumps
opBRANCH	Conditional branches
opLOAD	Load instructions
opSTORE	Store instructions
opALU	Simple arithmetic and logical instr.
opMULT	Multiply/divide instructions
opFLOAT	Floating point operations
opSYS	SYSCALL, BREAK, etc.

branch instructions should be profiled. Additional software-controllable classification is made available by a two-bit profile tag per instruction in the program binary being profiled. This yields a total of 32 instruction classes. Note that the VM paradigm allows instruction fields to be added to the implementation ISA. An alternative is to add additional hardware tables to hold software-controlled classification information. The statement in Figure 2c indicates that only stores with a profile tag of "1" should be profiled.

For the specified instruction classes the query header indicates the information to be collected and a random sampling rate. Simple random sampling reduces the rate at which profile information is collected. The header uses mnemonics from Table 2 to list the information collected. Types of collected information include both *architected* and *implementation* information. Each item in Table 2 represents one 32-bit word of information, which is collected and packed into a record by the RPA. The proposed RPA limits the information collected to seven words per record. This limits records to a manageable size, and still supports most profiling tasks. Example 2b collects the PC and Result 2 (the effective address) of L2 data misses.

Following the query header, *query clauses* select certain records and perform actions on them. Each query clause can perform up to two comparisons to check for properties within the record. Comparisons operate on 8,16 or 32 bit integer values. Both the size and location of the data within a record are encoded in the query comparison.

Table 2 Proposed information collectible by RPA.

Mnemonic	Information
pc	Instruction PC
thread	Thread ID
op1, op1up, op2, op2up, op3	Input operand values
res1, res1u, res2	Output results
misc	Exceptions and branch outcome
ftime	Cycle when instruction fetched
frate, drate, irate	Fetch, dispatch and issue rates
wlat	Execution window latency
elat	Execution latency
rtime	Cycle when instruction retired
rrate	Retire rate

Table 3 Comparison types

Mnemonic	Comparison
< = >	All unsigned integer magnitude comparisons
BCLR	True if bits under mask are clear
BSET	True if bits under mask are set
FILTER 2/4/16/256	Random filtering. Succeed once in 2/4/16/256 executions.
TRUE/FALSE	Always/never succeed.

Each comparison may use a 16-bit immediate value. Table 3 lists the comparison types available. All standard relational operations are available. Other comparisons check for set or cleared bits in the record or perform further random sampling. The example in Figure 2c checks if operand 1 has a nonzero value. If the comparison(s) match, an action may be performed, or there may be a branch to another query clause. Otherwise, execution falls through to the next sequential query clause. Query clauses can form if-then-else decision trees to compute arbitrary Boolean expressions. The *stop* keyword within the query clause indicates that query is completed.

Query clauses perform profile actions to communicate collected information to VM software. The most common action is the *message action*, indicated by the *send* keyword in the assembly code. The message action writes a copy of the record into a message queue where it can be examined by a service thread. Message queues are held in shared memory, and are accessed by service threads using normal loads and stores. Typically a single service thread is assigned to each queue to reduce synchronization between the service threads. The RPA can send different messages to different queues, so service threads can be specialized to a particular type of information. If processing power beyond a single service thread is needed, the RPA can disburse messages to multiple queues so multiple service threads can consume the messages.

A *counter action* increments a counter embedded in the query clause itself. This allows software to construct custom counters for arbitrary events using the query engine. When the counter is close to overflowing, the thread being profiled is interrupted.

An *interrupt action* interrupts a thread directly. The interrupt may be synchronous or asynchronous. For synchronous interrupts, the profiled instruction retires, but subsequent retirement stalls until the query is completed.

3.2 Examples

The four example queries shown in Figure 2 illustrate how the RPA can specify different profiling applications.

Example a) Edge Profiling -- Edge profiles, counts of how often conditional branches are taken and not-taken, are one of the most useful types of profiles, enabling or improving several important optimizations [2, 4, 26]. These profiles are also relatively easy to collect. Figure 2a shows the RPA assembly for the query. The *query header* indicates the PC and branch outcome (taken/not-taken) result as well as a branch misprediction flag (*misc*) for branch instructions should be collected. Random sampling is used to select one out of 256 branches. This query performs no comparisons. It simply sends the message to a service thread(s) that tabulates the information.

Example b) Prefetching -- It has been proposed that data prefetching can be done by *assistant threads* or *nanothreads* [19] which are essentially types of service threads. An RPA query for performing this profiling is in Figure 2b. The RPA is used to monitor L2 cache misses. For each L2 cache miss the instruction PC and effective address are collected. These records are sent to a service thread that executes prefetch instructions on behalf of the application. This is straightforward if the service thread and application thread share the L2 cache. In other situations, a dynamic optimizer running in a service thread could insert prefetch instructions into the binary, or the service thread could configure an existing hardware prefetch mechanism.

Example c) Garbage Collection (GC) -- Figure 2c shows the RPA query used in a low-overhead concurrent GC algorithm we proposed [13]. GC is the process of automatically reclaiming memory that is no longer needed by an application. Details of the algorithm are given in Section 5. Briefly, to perform GC without stopping the application, the GC thread must monitor certain application stores. This is typically done by adding *store-barrier* code around each store in the application, thereby slowing the application. RPA solves this problem by profiling all instructions that store references to the heap. By using the RPA, the time overhead of GC was reduced to 0.6% on average [13]. In Figure 2c, input operand 1, op1, contains the value being written. If this value is not null (zero), then the record is passed to GC service threads that execute the store barrier code.

Example d) Concurrency Metrics -- ProfileMe [9] uses paired sampling to estimate *concurrency metrics*, such as wasted issue slots in the vicinity of a given instruction. The RPA can compute similar concurrency metrics without using paired sampling. For instance, the query in Figure 2 can be used to compute cycles-per-instruction (CPI) for individual instructions and regions, such as loops and functions. The query collects the PC and retirement rate data for all instruction types. Retirement rate data, *rrate* in Figure 2d and Table 2, contains two basic pieces of information. The first is the number of instructions, n, that retired during the same cycle as the sampled instruction. The second is the number of preceding cycles in which no instructions retired, c. These cycles can be attributed to the sampled instruction only if it was the head instruction during these stalled cycles. Hence, c is zero if the sampled instruction was not the first instruction retired after the stalled cycles.

The execution cycles for one instruction sample is computed as $C = c + 1/n$. The total cycles spent executing the instruction can be computed by summing all the samples, and dividing by the sample rate. The CPI for one instruction can be computed as the arithmetic average over all samples collected for that instruction.

The total time spent in a region of code can be computed by summing the total cycles for each instruction in the region. The CPI over a region can be computed using an arithmetic average weighted by relative instruction execution frequency.

To locate bottlenecks, RPA collects not only the number of retirement stall cycles (c), but categorizes stall cycles by the reason for the stall. Example categories are an empty window, the head instruction not yet issued, or the head instruction not yet completed. Because stalls often have multiple causes, information gained from such categorization is usually approximate. The RPA can collect stall information at other stages in the pipeline as well.

3.3 Simplifications

In the example applications given above, the queries are very simple -- one query clause for each, and message passing is used exclusively. We expect this to be the common case. Essentially, the query engine filters unnecessary messages, and passes only the necessary records on to service threads for more involved processing. This reduces the work for the service threads. A lower-cost design could replace the query engine with a table able to do a small fixed number of comparisons per record, followed by a message action.

In addition, messaging may make counter actions redundant. Counters can be maintained by service thread software. While this is less efficient than the counter increment operation, simple random sampling can reduce counter increments to a reasonable rate and still maintain good counter accuracy. Rare events use a high frequency sampling rate, while common events require a low sampling rate.

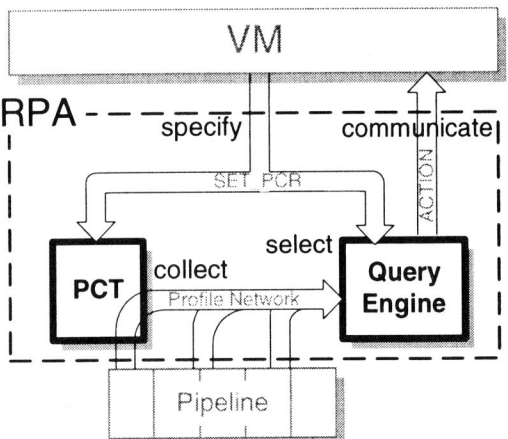

Figure 3. The RPA contains the profile control table (PCT) and the query engine.

3.4 Low-Level Architecture

Figure 3 shows an implementation of the RPA. Specific queries are formed by software -- virtual machine software, using the query language as described in the preceding section. The assembler divides query processing into two components shown in the figure. A configuration for the *profile control table* (PCT) is derived from the query headers. The PCT is a set of architected *profile control registers* (PCRs). Software loads the PCT using a special SET_PCR instruction, also used to configure other parts of the RPA.

Each query clause generates one *query instruction* to be executed by the *query engine*, a simple processor capable of performing the comparisons and actions dictated by the query. Query instructions may be stored in memory, or, to reduce implementation costs, in a special-purpose table constructed out of PCRs.

3.4.1 The Profile Control Table (PCT).
The PCT implements two PCRs for each of the 32 instruction classes. The first PCR sets the sampling rate and selects information from Table 2 to be collected. The second PCR contains the starting *query PC* (QPC), the address of the initial query instruction for the query engine to execute.

The PCT also controls event-based profiling. Theoretically, event-based profiling hardware could be dispensed with entirely by collecting instruction records and using the query engine to select only those instructions with the desired event. For rare events this yields very long profile times, however. The proposed RPA specifies event-based profiling for ITLB, DTLB and L2 cache misses. Two PCRs are provided for each of these three events. Due to implementation constraints, only a subset of the informa-

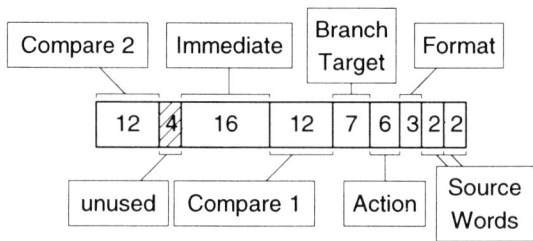

Figure 4. Query instructions contain up to two comparisons, a branch and an action.

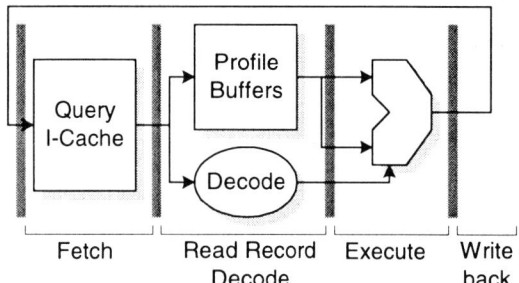

Figure 5. The query engine four stage pipeline.

tion in Table 2 may be collected for event-based profiling. The processor implementation may not detect an instruction needing to be profiled until the event occurs, which is likely to be too late to collect information from earlier pipeline stages. At least the instruction PC, a cycle count, and the effective address are expected to be available.

3.4.2 The Query Engine. Profile records collected at the behest of the PCT are passed to the query engine, which begins executing query instructions at the initial QPC location indicated in the PCT. Query instructions perform the comparisons, branches and actions specified by the equivalent query clauses.

Query instructions are encoded in a 64-bit two-comparison format shown in Figure 4. Instructions encode two comparisons, a 16 bit immediate value, branch target and an action. The query instruction reads two values from the record. To reduce implementation costs, one even word and one odd word from the profile record are selected.

The application program continues to execute in parallel with the query engine, and multiple comparisons may be executed in parallel. To simplify the implementation there is no guarantee of the order in which separate queries are executed or completed.

To implement message actions, the query engine manages message queues in memory. Each message uses eight words of memory, and the size of the queue is configurable up to 128 messages. To write a record into a queue, the query engine writes the seven words of the record. The eighth word is used to indicate that the record is available. To read a record, a service thread polls the ready word, reads the record from memory, and clears the ready word. The service thread also informs the query engine how many messages have been read by storing the total messages read into the *buffer read status* word in memory. The buffer read status word is examined periodically by the query engine. The query engine uses the number of messages read, along with the number written (which it knows), to determine if space is available for another message, reducing polling by the query engine.

4 RPA Implementation and Cost

The query engine pipeline that we simulated is shown in Figure 5. The query engine is designed to execute up to four queries simultaneously using a simple barrel-and-slot design [21]. The pipeline is four stages long, and one query instruction is executed for each active query once every four cycles in a round-robin fashion. The barrel-and-slot design eliminates all interlocks and dependences in the pipeline. As the profile records fill, the processing power of the query engine increases to one query instruction per cycle.

The first pipeline stage fetches the query instruction from the small query instruction array. At 512 bytes, this cache holds 64 instructions, which appears to be plenty. Decode is performed in stage 2. The record buffers are also accessed in this cycle. They are word-interleaved; the query engine accesses one word from the even bank, and one word from the odd bank each cycle. The query ALU performs the comparison(s) in stage 3 using a masked magnitude comparator. The fourth stage selects and drives the next query PC back to the fetch stage. Query actions are also initiated in the write-back stage.

An interconnection network carries profile information from the pipeline to the profile buffer. Though a complete design of this network is beyond the scope of this paper, the size of the network will scale linearly with the number of simultaneously profiled instructions [9]. The latency of this network is not a concern; the profile buffers can be relatively distant from the core pipeline.

A typical implementation contains a number of identical profile networks to carry information from the pipeline to the profile buffers. The number of networks determines how many in-flight instructions can be profiled simultaneously. Instructions are selected for profiling during instruction dispatch, and a profile network and profile buffer are allocated to the instruction. Instruction dispatch stalls if either is unavailable. Hence enough of each should be provided to make this a rarity. When the instruction retires the profile network is freed, but the profile buffer remains allocated until the query completes.

The fixed costs of the RPA are the 280-byte PCT and

the query engine with its 512B I-cache. Two remaining important cost variables are the number of profile networks and the number of 32-byte profile buffers. These are evaluated in the following sections.

5 Simulated Applications of the RPA

To determine how many profile networks and buffers are needed for low-overhead profiling, we simulated two example applications. These are the edge profiling and the concurrent GC applications shown in Figure 2.

The concurrent GC algorithm is described in detail in [13]. A short overview is provided here. Object-oriented languages such as Java organize memory into objects that contain *references* to other objects. This forms a graph with objects as nodes and references as directed arcs between the nodes. Tracing GC finds all objects reachable, directly or indirectly, from a set of *root references* -- object references in global or local variables. This reachability analysis involves *marking* objects directly reachable from the roots, and then iteratively marking all objects reachable (via references) from previously marked objects. This iterative processes terminates when no more unmarked objects can be reached from marked objects. At this point all unmarked objects are unreachable by the application and can be collected, freeing the storage space for future objects.

Concurrent GC algorithms must handle modifications to the object graph performed concurrently by the application to avoid erroneously collecting reachable objects. The RPA supports this function by profiling store instruction addresses and values. This information is sent to *store barrier* service threads that perform simple book keeping operations for the garbage collector, running on another service thread. Storing a reference to an object causes a store barrier thread to mark the object live so it will not be collected. This is called an *incremental update* mechanism in Wilson's survey of GC algorithms [24].

Only instructions that store object references need to be profiled. The VM distinguishes these stores from others using the profile tag described in Section 3.1. In addition, if a null reference store is performed, no profiling is needed. Hence, the query discards profile records in which the stored value is null (zero). Because the GC algorithm relies on observing every non-null reference store, random sampling is not appropriate.

The result is an extremely efficient garbage collector. Using the RPA, GC overhead is reduced to 0.6% of the total runtime [13].

5.1 Simulation Methodology

Simulation experiments are based on the Strata VM research infrastructure and the SimpleMP simulator [17]. SimpleMP is a version of the SimpleScalar [3] execution-driven timing simulator that was extended to simulate

Table 4 Benchmark characteristics.

	Inputs	Duration	
		Instr. (M)	Cycles (M)
strata	Database	517	222
db	input/db2 input/src3	206	79
jack	10	648	234
javac	-verbose JavaLex.java	432	190
jess	zebra.clp wordgame.clp	596	220
raytrace	50 500 time-test.model	246	84

multiple processors. We extended it further to simulate multithreaded processors and the RPA. The Strata VM contains a static compiler from Java bytecodes to SimpleScalar PISA assembly code. The Strata compiler is itself written in Java and forms one of our benchmarks.

5.2 The Strata Compiler

The Strata compiler performs typical optimizations such as global register allocation, constant propagation, local common sub-expression elimination and global copy propagation. It also performs Java specific optimizations aimed at eliminating null-pointer checks, type checks and array bounds checks.

The runtime system, which contains the GC algorithm, is written in C. Running a Java application involves compiling the bytecodes using the Strata compiler, and then linking the resulting assembly with the runtime system.

5.3 Benchmarks

Six benchmarks shown in Table 4 are simulated. The first is the Strata compiler. The other five are taken from the SPECjvm98 suite. They are *jess*, an expert system, *raytrace*, a 3-D rendering tool, *db*, a simple relational database, *javac*, the Java compiler, and *jack*, a parser generator. Simulations began at about 10 million instructions before the first GC, until completion, except for *javac*, which was terminated at 200M cycles.

5.4 Processor models

Ways to exploit thread-level parallelism include chip multiprocessing (CMP) [15] and multithreading. The particular design explored in this paper, Figure 6, uses fine-grain multithreading (FGMT) [1] and CMP. On one chip, there is a large high-ILP processor supplemented by three service processors. The computation of greatest concern, the application, runs on the high-ILP processor. Lower priority VM tasks run on three service processors concurrently with application execution. One service processor consumes the edge profile information. A second processor consumes the store-barrier records for the garbage collector. A third service processor executes the garbage collector.

Parameters for the processor models are shown in Ta-

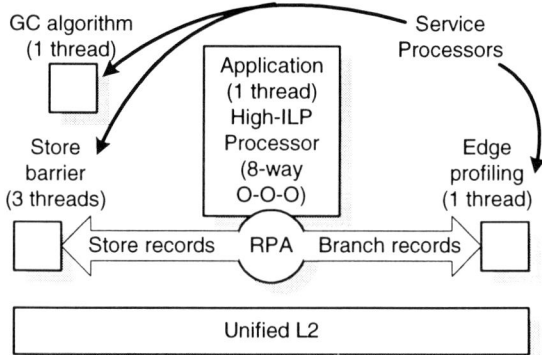

Figure 6. The system on a chip

Table 5 Processor model parameters

Parameter	High-ILP Proc.	Service Proc.	Units
Number	1	3	Proc.
Threads	1	3	Threads
Width	8	1	Instr.
Instr. Win.	128	(in-order)	Instr.
Br. Pred.	4KB gshare	Not-taken	
Min. penalty	8	4	Cycles
I-Cache	32KB 2-way	1KB 4-way	
D-Cache	64KB 4-way	2KB 4-way	
Unified L2	Perfect		

ble 5. The ILP processor is an 8-way super-scalar, out-of-order processor, running only one thread. The service processors are designed to maximize throughput per unit area, rather than single-thread performance. Each service processor is a six stage scalar pipeline capable of running three threads using FGMT. To keep these processors small and simple, they have small L1 caches and predict-not-taken branch prediction. All three processors connect to a perfect L2 with a 12 cycle round-trip access time.

6 Results

This section uses simulations to determine the number of profile buffers and networks needed by the profiling hardware. Further simulations examine the performance overhead of profiling and the sampling rates that the RPA implementation can support.

6.1 Resource Usage

Figure 7 shows results from simulating the edge profiling and GC queries from Figure 2. One out of 256 branches are sampled. Profile resources were essentially unrestricted with 32 profile buffers and 32 profile networks. The histograms on the left show the percentage of cycles (y-axis) in which at least x profile buffers were in use (x-axis).

The benchmarks *raytrace*, *db* and *jess* stress the RPA very little, rarely using more than a single profile buffer. Hence we omitted these plots. The three benchmarks *strata*, *javac* and *jack* load the RPA more heavily. We observe that eight profile buffers, 256 bytes of storage, appear to be sufficient. Only *jack* can utilize more than eight buffers, although eight are nearly enough.

The right histograms show the number of profiled instructions simultaneously in flight. The histograms show the percentage of cycles (y-axis) in which at least x profiled instructions were in flight (x-axis). This includes profiled instructions between the dispatch and retire stages. Under the interconnect model described in Section 4, one profile network is need for each in-flight instruction. The histograms are very similar to the left histograms, though they are slightly lower because profile buffers remain allocated longer than the flight time of an instruction. The benchmarks *strata* and *javac* should run well with four profile networks. The *jack* benchmark appears to need as many as eight. Direct measurement of profiling overhead in the next section shows far fewer networks are actually needed.

6.2 Profiling Performance Overhead

Based on the previous results, the number of profile buffers was reduced to eight, and the number of profile networks was varied from one to four. Figure 8a plots the percentage of cycles for which dispatch was stalled due to limited RPA resources. Only *jack* and *strata* are plotted in Figure 8; *javac* generally shows about half the stalls of *strata*, and the other benchmarks show very few or no stalls. Other simulation results not presented here indicate that limited profile networks cause these stalls. *Strata* stalls vary from 3.8% with one profile network, to 0.5% with four networks. *Jack* stalled dispatch 12.4% of the time with a single profile network. Despite the results in Figure 7, however, stalling was reduced to only 1.7% with four networks.

Figure 8b plots the percent slow-down resulting from these stalls, as compared to the unrestricted results in Section 6.1. Note that the y-axis scale changes between Figures 7 and 8; generally about half of the dispatch stalls are covered by the out-of-order execution window. Three profile networks reduce profiling overhead below 0.5% for all benchmarks. Four networks make it effectively zero. In fact, *jack* shows a slight speedup (negative slow-down), likely resulting from system-level interactions with the garbage collector.

To understand how profiling overhead varies with the sample rate, four sampling rates for edge profiling were simulated; rates simulated were one in 32, 64, 128 and 256 branches. Note that the GC query is still included. Figure 8c plots the slow-downs for these rates. *Strata* and *jack* show a mild increase in profiling overhead as the profiling rate is increased. This suggests that the RPA

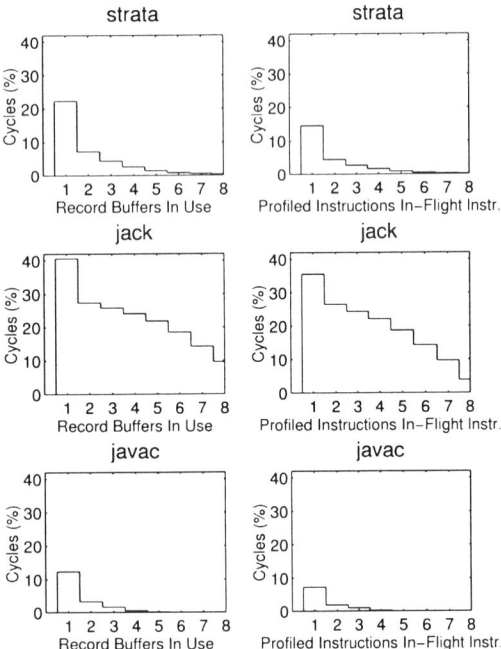

Figure 7. Resources used by the RPA for *strata*, *jack* and *javac*.

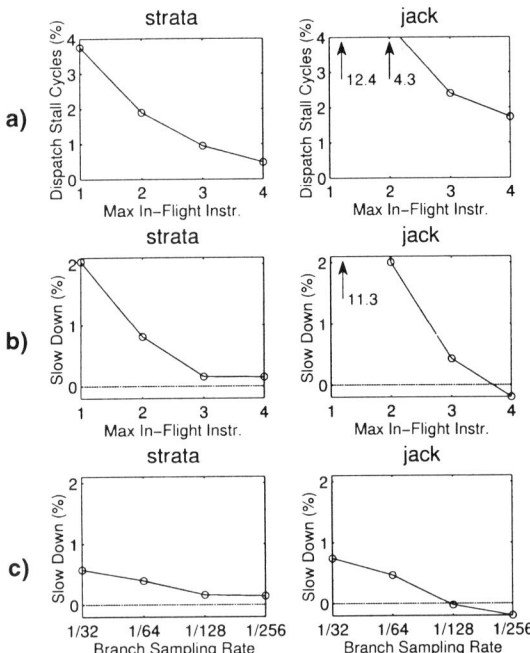

Figure 8. Profiling overhead for the *strata* and *jack* benchmarks. a) Percentage of cycles that the RPA stalled dispatch. b) Slow-down resulting from profiling. c) Variation in the slow-down with the sampling rate.

should monitor its own behavior. Sample rates can be throttled back if dispatch stalls increase.

Table 6 shows the load that these rates place on the profile mechanism. Table 6 contains the instructions executed per profiled instruction, and the cycles per profiled instruction. The instructions executed per cycle (IPCs) are generally a little above two for these benchmarks and this CPU model, so instructions-per-sample is about twice the cycles-per-sample.

Comparing Table 6 to Figure 8 shows *jack* can profile about one in 41 instructions, or one sample every 15 cycles. At higher rates, profiling begins to stall the processor. *Strata* also has measurable stalls for higher sampling rates, though Table 6 shows many fewer instructions are profiled than *jack* due to variation within the benchmark. Stalls in *strata* occur during bursts of profiling for the GC application.

6.3 Reducing Profile Stalls

The above results are based on a network model that collects information throughout the pipeline. However, information available at instruction retirement may often be sufficient. Such information could include the instruction PCs, branch targets and directions, and effective ad-

Table 6 Profiling rates for different branch sampling rates.

	Instr. per sample				Cycles per sample			
	1/32	1/64	1/128	1/256	1/32	1/64	1/128	1/256
strata	110	149	182	205	47	64	78	88
db	113	173	237	290	44	67	91	112
jack	35	38	41	42	13	14	15	15
javac	128	212	317	420	57	94	139	184
jess	166	299	499	750	62	111	185	277
ray	289	468	676	869	99	160	230	296

dresses. If a profile record only contains retire-time information, it is wasteful to allocate a profile network for the entire lifetime of the instruction.

This leads to a model that supports both cheap and expensive profiles. A cheap profile only contains information available during retirement. Instructions profiled this way must allocate profile buffers, but need not allocate a profile network. An expensive profile includes information not available during retirement and must allocate a profile network, as assumed in the above results. Mechanisms that collect all information for all instructions, like ProfileMe, cannot take advantage of this optimization.

288

7 Related work

Special-purpose mechanisms have been proposed for many of the profiling operations discussed above. These require special hardware, software, or both.

Conte et al. propose two hardware methods [6, 7] for edge profiling. The first samples the values of the branch-target-buffer and branch prediction array to derive estimates of the edge profile. The second method improves the accuracy using a small special-purpose array, the *Profile Buffer*, to count taken and not-taken branches indexed by PC. In both methods the tables are periodically read by software using interrupts.

Merten et al. [14] develop a scheme for identifying *hot spots* in programs. Their scheme works by collecting branch taken/not-taken counts in the Branch Behavior Buffer (BBB), a structure similar to the Profile Buffer, though much larger. The BBB also identifies frequently seen branches and uses this information to identify hot spots. A separate structure, the Monitor Table prevents hot spot re-detection.

As noted earlier, Song and Dubois [19] investigate data prefetching with *assisted execution*, a service thread-like paradigm. Both sequential and stride prefetching are implemented with assisted execution. Simultaneous Subordinate Microthreads (SSMT) [5] is another paradigm similar to service threads. SSMT executes multiple *microthreads* in parallel with the application using simultaneous multithreading [8, 21, 25].

Several elements of the ProfileMe mechanism [9] also appear in the RPA. ProfileMe provides a simplified form of instruction-based profiling. The hardware picks one instruction from the stream, using a software settable decrementing counter. Simple random sampling is performed by resetting the counter to randomized values. ProfileMe allows information to be collected for both retiring and squashed instructions.

To keep costs low, ProfileMe keeps sampling rates low, e.g. one sample every 10^3 to 10^5 instructions, much lower than the one in forty instructions sampled by the RPA. Although more research is needed to determine whether higher sampling rates will benefit dynamic optimization, some non-traditional applications, such as concurrent GC, will require a much higher sampling rate.

ProfileMe also supports *paired sampling*, a simple and powerful form of clustered sampling. Paired sampling collects two instruction samples close to each other using a *major* and *minor* sampling interval. Paired sampling is useful for measuring interactions between instructions.

RPA is not incompatible with paired sampling, and future research will consider adding paired sampling to the RPA. Paired sampling does have some drawbacks. First, it will likely increase the number of in-flight instructions that must be tracked. Second, paired sampling can further increase the profiling latency if representative samples must be gathered for all nearby pairs of instructions. Furthermore, the RPA can gather some of the same information as paired sampling by collecting the proper per-instruction data, as illustrated by the concurrency metric example in Section 3.1.

A method described in a patent by Westcott and White [23] is also very similar to both RPA and ProfileMe. The processor uses a counter to randomly select instructions for profiling. Like ProfileMe, a standard profile record is collected. Like RPA's query engine, *triggers* can be used to scan for records of interest. Also like RPA, the records are stored to a buffer in memory. However, the buffer is read following an interrupt when the buffer fills.

Contemporaneous with this work, Zilles and Sohi developed a profiling mechanism with many similarities to the RPA [27]. It selects instructions for profiling based on their opcode class and the low-order bits of the instruction PC using a *hardware filter* similar to the PCT. Collected information is held in a *sample buffer* (like RPA's profile buffers), until examined by a programmable *profile co-processor*. This co-processor summarizes information before it is relayed to software via an interrupt. The co-processor is a more complete processor than the query engine, having registers, a private data memory and an associative array for hash tables. The RPA off-loads much of this computation to service threads.

The RPA has some additional capabilities. Working in the context of service threads leads RPA to focus on communicating profiled information through shared memory. All previous profile mechanisms use interrupts to record or sample profiled information. More importantly, the RPA can guarantee some instructions are always profiled. This allows the profiler to be used for new applications that require correctness.

8 Conclusions

The relational profiling architecture (RPA) provides a powerful and flexible profiling mechanism. It can enable the same optimizations as several previous mechanisms, and has additional capabilities. Since the RPA can guarantee that certain instructions are always profiled it is useful when the information is required for correctness. Working in the context of service threads leads to messages communicating profile information, which increases the sampling rate and lowers profiling overhead, compared to previous interrupt-driven approaches. This leads to new applications for hardware-assisted profilers such as concurrent garbage collection.

Simulation results shed light on the implementation requirements and profiling overhead of the RPA. Profiling four simultaneous in-flight instructions and storing eight profile records is sufficient to make losses negligible. Eight profile records require only 256 bytes of storage. The profile interconnection network, which scales linearly with the number of simultaneously profiled instructions, appears to be the greatest cost of profiling. The PCT reduces this cost by selectively profiling only the particular data that is needed. This reduces the size of the profile records, and could also be used to intelligently allocate profile resources.

The PCT allows the sampling rate to be tuned to match the frequency with which the profiled event occurs. For common events, low sampling rates reduce the bandwidth required. For rare events, high sampling rates reduce the time required to obtain a representative sample. In addition, different benchmarks stress the profiling mechanism to different degrees. This suggests that the RPA should monitor its own behavior to adapt the sampling rate to the application.

The query engine is a powerful and relatively low-cost mechanism for selecting and communicating collected profile information. Queries are generally simple and result in sending the profile record to a service thread. In fact, a simple table-driven engine which can do a small fixed number of comparisons, conditionally followed by sending the record to a service thread may be sufficient. The RPA effectively enables a virtual machine to exploit the abundant thread-level parallelism expected to be available on-chip in the future. This configuration will reduce the overheads of VM technology by running VM tasks such as dynamic compilation and garbage collection concurrently.

Acknowledgements

This work was supported by NSF Grant CCR-9900610, by Sun Microsystems, by an IBM Partnership Award, and by Intel Corporation.

References

[1] R. Alverson et al., "The Tera Computer System," 1990 Intl. Conf. on Supercomputing, pp. 1-6, 1990.

[2] R. Bodik, R. Gupta, M. L. Soffa, "Complete Removal of Redundant Expressions," 1998 Conf. on Programming Language Design and Implementation, pp.1-14, June 1998.

[3] D. C. Burger, T. M. Austin, "The SimpleScalar Tool Set, Version 2.0," Univ. of Wisconsin - Madison Comp. Sci. Tech. Rep. #1342, June 1997.

[4] P. P. Chang, S. A. Mahlke, W. W. Hwu, "Using Profile Information to Assist Classic Code Optimizations," Software-Practice and Experience, vol. 21, pp. 1301-1321, Dec. 1991.

[5] R. S. Chappel et al., "Simultaneous Subordinate Microthreading (SSMT)," 26th Intl. Symp. on Computer Architecture, pp. 186-195, May 1999.

[6] T. M. Conte, B. A. Patel, J. S. Cox, "Using Branch Handling Hardware to Support Profile-Driven Optimization," 27th Intl. Symp. on Microarchitecture, pp. 12-21, Nov. 1994.

[7] T. M. Conte, K. N. Menezes, M. A. Hirsch, "Accurate and Practical Profile-Driven Compilation Using the Profile Buffer," 29th Intl. Symp. on Microarchitecture, pp. 36-45, Dec. 1996.

[8] G. E. Daddis, Jr., H. C. Torng, "The Concurrent Execution of Multiple Instruction Streams on Superscalar Processors," Intl. Conf. on Parallel Processing, pp. I:76-83, Aug. 1991.

[9] J. Dean et al., "ProfileMe: Hardware Support for Instruction-Level Profiling on Out-of-Order Processors," 30th Intl. Symp. on Microarchitecture, pp. 292-302, Dec. 1997.

[10] K. Ebcioglu, E. R. Altman, "DAISY: Dynamic Compilation for 100% Architectural Compatibility," IBM Research Rep. RC 20538, Aug. 1996.

[11] M. Gschwind et al., "Dynamic and Transparent Binary Translation," Computer, 33(3):54-59, Mar. 2000.

[12] A. Klaiber, "The Technology Behind Crusoe Processors," a Transmeta technical brief, 2000.

[13] T. Heil, J. E. Smith, "Concurrent Garbage Collection Using Hardware Assisted Profiling," to appear Intl. Symp. on Memory Management, Oct. 2000.

[14] M. C. Merten et al., "A Hardware-Driven Profiling Scheme for Identifying Program Hot Spots to Support Runtime Optimization," 26th Intl. Symp. on Computer Architecture, pp. 136-147, May 1999.

[15] K. Olukotun et al., "The Case for a Single-Chip Multiprocessor," 7th Intl. Symp. on Architectural Support for Programming Languages and Operating Systems, pp. 2-11, Oct. 1996.

[16] T. Parr, ANother Tool for Language Recognition (ANTLR), available at http://www.ANTLR.org.

[17] R. Rajwar, A. Kagi, J. Goodman, private correspondence. The SimpleMP simulator was produced by the Galileo group at the University of Wisconsin - Madison.

[18] J. E. Smith, T. Heil, S. Sastry, T. M. Bezenek, "Achieving High Performance via Co-Designed Virtual Machines," Intl. Workshop on Innovative Architecture, pp. 77-84, Oct. 1999.

[19] Y. H. Song, M. Dubois, "Assisted Execution," Tech. Rep. CENG 98-25, EE-Systems, University of Southern California, Oct. 1998.

[20] "MAJC Architecture Tutorial", Sun Microsystems White Paper, May 1999.

[21] J. E. Thornton, "Design of a Computer – The Control Data 6600," Scott, Foresman and Co., 1970.

[22] D. M. Tullsen et al., "Exploiting Choice: Instruction Fetch and Issue on an Implementable Simultaneous Multithreading Processor," 23rd Intl. Symp. on Computer Architecture, pp. 191-202, May 1996.

[23] D. W. Westcott, V. White, "Instruction Sampling Instrumentation," U.S. Patent #5151981, assigned to IBM, Sept. 1992.

[24] P. R. Wilson, "Uniprocessor Garbage Collection Techniques," 1992 Intl. Workshop on Memory Management, pp. 1-42, Sept. 1992.

[25] W. Yamamoto et al., "Performance Estimation of Multistreamed, Superscalar Processors," 27th Hawaii Intl. Conf. on System Sciences, pp. I:105-204, Jan. 1994.

[26] C. Young, D. S. Johnson, D. R. Karger, M. D. Smith, "Near-Optimal Intraprocedural Branch Alignment," 1997 Conf. on Programming Language Design and Implementation, pp. 183-193, June 1997.

[27] C. Zilles, G. Sohi, "A Programmable Co-processor for Profiling," to appear 7th Intl. Symp. on High Performance Computer Architecture, Jan. 2001.

Calpa: A Tool for Automating Selective Dynamic Compilation

Markus Mock, Craig Chambers, and Susan J. Eggers
Department of Computer Science and Engineering
University of Washington
Box 352350, Seattle WA 98195-2350
{mock, chambers, eggers}@cs.washington.edu

Abstract

Selective dynamic compilation systems, typically driven by annotations that identify run-time constants, can achieve significant program speedups. However, manually inserting annotations is a tedious and time-consuming process that requires careful inspection of a program's static characteristics and run-time behavior and much trial and error in order to select the most beneficial annotations. Calpa is a system that generates annotations automatically for the DyC dynamic compiler. Calpa combines execution frequency and value profile information with a model of dynamic compilation cost and dynamically generated code benefit to choose run-time constants and other dynamic compilation strategies. For the programs tested so far, Calpa generates annotations of the same or better quality as those found by a human, but in a fraction of the time. The result was equal or better program speedups from dynamic compilation, but without the need for programmer intervention.

1. Introduction

Dynamic compilation optimizes programs at run time, based on information available only at run time, thus offering the potential for greater performance than purely statically compiled code. Some dynamic compilation systems, including Smalltalk-80 [27], Self [28, 29], and just-in-time compilers for Java (for example, [30]), perform virtually all compilation during program execution. Others are selective about which parts of programs they dynamically compile. *Selective* dynamic compilation systems can focus the additional run-time effort of dynamic compilation on those portions of the program that most benefit from dynamic compilation, leaving the remainder of the program to be compiled statically.

Selective dynamic compilers usually base their optimizations on run-time-computed values of particular variables and data structures (called *run-time constants*). A region of a procedure that references these run-time constants (called a *dynamic region*) is *specialized* at dynamic compile time for the particular run-time values of these variables, with the dynamic compiler performing various constant-propagation- and loop-unrolling-like optimizations on the dynamic region. The specialized code can be reused for any future executions of the dynamic region where the run-time constants have the same values as was assumed when the code was specialized. If a dynamic region is invoked with different values for the run-time constants, multiple specialized versions of the dynamic region can be generated and maintained. On entry to the dynamic region at run time, a *dispatcher* selects the appropriate specialized version, based on the values of the run-time constants, or invokes the dynamic compiler to produce a new version.

Dynamic compilation involves additional overheads during program execution that statically compiled programs don't incur, namely, specialization and dispatching. In order for dynamic compilation to be profitable, the run-time benefits dynamic compilation obtains must outweigh these run-time costs. This requires that the code that is specialized to the values of the run-time constants be sufficiently better optimized and reused sufficiently often to more than recoup the costs of producing it and dispatching to it; typically, this precludes performing any expensive analysis at run time. Hence, the effectiveness of a selective dynamic compilation system depends critically on choosing good run-time constants and dynamic regions. On the positive side, since the actual values of the constants don't have to be known until run time, dynamic compilation systems can optimize code in situations where a compile-time specializer can either not be used at all, or may suffer from code explosion because code may have to be specialized for *all possible* values instead of only the values that *actually occur* at run time.

Previous dynamic compilation systems require the programmer to choose run-time constants and dynamic regions manually. The selections are communicated to the dynamic compilation system through declarative annotations. Fabius [17] and Tempo [5,20] allow the user to annotate formal parameters of procedures as run-time constants, causing the annotated procedures to be specialized for the particular values of the annotated parameters. DyC [10,12,11] provides finer-grained dynamic optimization, by allowing users to annotate individual variables at arbitrary points within a procedure; the variables are treated as run-time constants up to the end of their scope, or until another annotation returns them to run-time-variable status. DyC also has a set of annotations with which programmers can regulate the aggressiveness of specialization and certain other dynamic compilation costs.

For the most part, annotations do not affect the behavior of the program, only how it is implemented. However, because they do not include a whole-program side-effect analysis, Tempo and DyC include some annotations that the statically compiled portions of the program may render unsafe; if the programmer uses an unsafe annotation incorrectly, the program's behavior can be changed through dynamic compilation. (Fabius avoids the need for unsafe annotations by handling only purely functional programs.)

To manually select annotations that will produce program speedups. programmers must gain a good knowledge of the application's run-time behavior, perhaps aided by an execution frequency profile of the various regions of the program and a log of the values of variables and selected data structures. They must understand the effects of candidate annotations on the relative quality of the dynamically compiled code versus the statically compiled code, and on the run-time cost to produce it and dispatch to it. They must anticipate how often the specialized version(s) will be reused on a typical application execution. Finally, when using an unsafe annotation, they must be confident that the annotation's assumptions about program behavior are satisfied.

Consequently, manually annotating programs so that they achieve good speedups is difficult and time consuming, and often becomes the bottleneck for many applications that could benefit from dynamic optimization. Our experience with DyC serves as a case in point. To annotate the applications for our initial evaluation of DyC's run-time optimizations [12], we first profiled them with `gprof`. We then examined the functions that comprised the most execution time, searching for invariant or *quasi-invariant* function parameters, i.e. function parameters with only one or a few values, respectively. In cases when invariance was too difficult to infer by inspection, we logged the values of the functions' parameters by manually inserting code into the applications, and then searched the logs. Optimization opportunities were determined by trial and error. For example, to determine whether complete loop unrolling was beneficial, we generally first performed the unrolling, but then disabled it (by removing an annotation) if it did not improve performance. Since some of DyC's annotations control the aggressiveness of specialization and the cost of run-time compilation, choosing the best combination here turned out to be laborious and time-consuming as well. All in all, although DyC's annotations are few and conceptually simple, finding good candidates for run-time constants and picking appropriate specialization strategies turned out to be a very tedious process, taking us several weeks to annotate the applications for that study.

Calpa[1] [19] is the first system to automate this process. Calpa combines program analysis and profile information to automatically derive the annotations that drive dynamic compilation (in our case, of C programs using DyC). Calpa consists of two modules: an *instrumentation tool* and an *annotation selection tool*. The programmer first runs the instrumentation tool on the program to produce an instrumented version of the program that will generate and summarize value and frequency data. (Figure 1 presents an overview of the process for using Calpa and DyC.) The instrumented version is then executed on some representative input, yielding an execution profile of this run-time information. The programmer then invokes the annotation selection tool on the program and the profile. The annotation selector searches the space of possible dynamic compilation annotations, using an internal model of the costs and benefits of dynamic compilation and the execution profile to estimate the overall impact of each candidate annotation. The selection tool reports its choices by producing an annotated program. This annotated program is then compiled by DyC to yield a final executable program that contains specialized dynamic compilers. In essence, Calpa uses DyC as a back-end to carry out its chosen dynamic compilation strategy; Calpa encapsulates the *policy* decisions about where, on what and how aggressively to dynamically compile, while DyC encapsulates the *mechanism* of performing dynamic compilation. Unlike programmer-inserted annotations, Calpa's selected dynamic compilation strategy is guaranteed to be safe, i.e., it will not change the observable behavior of the program.

To test Calpa's effectiveness in automatic annotation against the "gold standard" of manual annotation, we used Calpa to derive annotations for some kernels and applications we had previously hand-annotated. The entire profiling and annotation process was completed for the kernels within seconds and for the applications either in minutes or hours, depending on the program. Calpa produced all the annotations that we had identified with our manual process, and, in addition, for some programs,

---

[1] Calpa was an important Inca oracle ritual, which was performed before making important decisions.

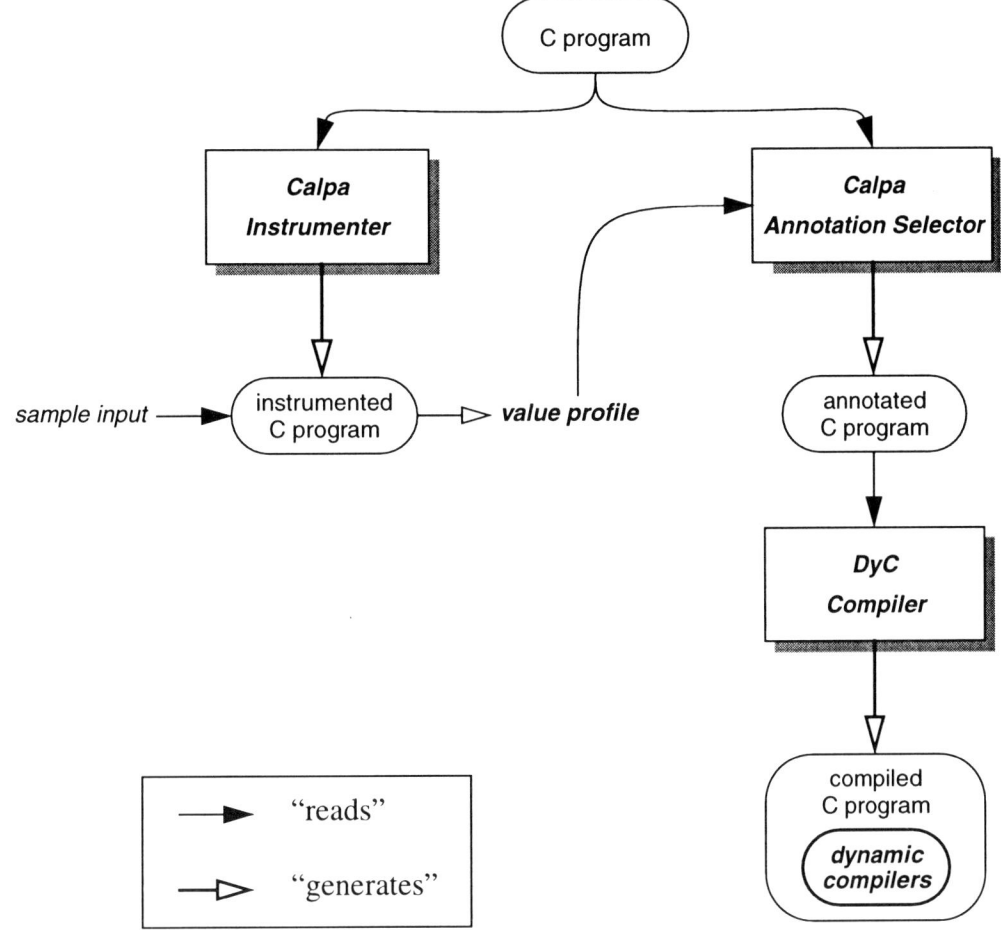

Figure 1. Overview of Calpa

inserted others that improved their performance.

This paper presents Calpa's approach to automating selective dynamic compilation. We describe Calpa's instrumentation and annotation selection tools and the interface between them. We also report our initial performance results using a prototype implementation of Calpa, including the time and space it takes to instrument and profile the applications and to derive the annotations, and the speedups of Calpa-annotated, dynamically optimized programs relative to those that were manually annotated. The paper makes the following contributions:

- We present a program analysis that combines various static analyses with value profile information to identify good candidate variables and dynamic regions for dynamic compilation.

- We develop a multi-faceted cost/benefit model based on run-time specialization that enables the automatic evaluation of the costs and benefits of dynamically compiling different annotation choices.

- We demonstrate experimentally that these techniques produce annotations for a dynamic compiler that results in comparable or better program speedups than manual annotations, at a small fraction of the time a human annotator would need to understand and profile the programs. While each of the techniques by itself is not new, Calpa's merit lies in its special combination of techniques that provides useful value.

In the next section we summarize Calpa's targeted dynamic compilation system, DyC. Section 3 describes Calpa. Section 4 describes the experiments we carried out to assess the effectiveness and the resource use of Calpa. Section 5 discusses related work and section 6 concludes.

2. Overview of DyC

DyC is an annotation-driven, selective dynamic compilation system that attains speedups of up to 4.6× on a group of medium-sized (< 15K lines of code) C programs [12]. To achieve this level of performance, DyC contains

(1) a sophisticated form of partial-evaluation-style binding time analysis (BTA) that supports program-point-specific polyvariant division and specialization,[1] (2) low-cost, dynamic versions of traditional global optimizations that include zero and copy propagation and dead-assignment elimination, and (3) dynamic peephole optimizations, such as strength reduction.

To trigger dynamic compilation, programmers annotate their source code to identify *static variables* (run-time constants) on which many calculations depend. Loads from memory can be annotated as static if their contents are static, and called procedures can be annotated as static if their results are static whenever given static arguments. DyC's BTA analyzes code downstream of the annotations, intraprocedurally, to separate those computations that depend solely on the annotated static variables, plus additional static variables that are derived from them, (called the *static computations*) from the computations that depend at least in part on run-time variables (called the *dynamic computations*). Static computations are executed just once, at dynamic compilation time. By delaying final compilation of the dynamic computations until run time, the results of the static computations can be treated as embedded constants in the dynamic computations. A part of a procedure that contains static computations and the directly dependent dynamic computations constitutes a dynamic region. Since the BTA is program-point-specific and flow-sensitive, a dynamic region can start and stop at any program point, and a variable may be static at some program points and not at others.

For each dynamic region, DyC builds a custom dynamic compiler (also called a *generating exten*sion [16]) that generates code at run time, using the values of the static variables once they become known. To minimize dynamic compilation overhead, DyC performs much of the analysis and planning for dynamic optimization during static compile time, freeing the custom dynamic compiler from needing an intermediate representation and iterative analyses at run time.

When a dynamic region is entered at run time, the region's dispatcher checks an internal cache of previously dynamically generated code for a version that was compiled for the current values of the annotated variables. If one is found, it is executed. If not, the dispatcher invokes the region's custom dynamic compiler to generate code specialized to the current values of the annotated variables. The custom compiler evaluates the static computations and emits machine code for the dynamic computations. When done, the newly generated code is saved in the dynamic-code cache and then executed. Invoking the dynamic compiler and dispatching to dynamically generated code are the principal sources of run-time overhead.

If a load is annotated as static, the dynamic compiler assumes that the contents of the referenced memory location remains the same for all invocations of the dynamic region. If the memory location is later updated, then the affected dynamically compiled code should be thrown away and redynamically compiled for the new value. In the current DyC system, whenever a store changes the contents of a memory location upon which code might be specialized, the program must invoke DyC's `invalidate()` operation, which flushes the compiled code caches of all affected functions, and resets the dynamic region's code pointer to point to the dynamic compiler. The dynamic compiler will then produce new code for the invalidated dynamic region, based on the new contents of the memory location.

DyC is driven primarily by annotations that identify initial run-time constant variables and data structures. Optional policy annotations allow the programmer to specify whether specialization and division should be mono- or polyvariant, whether code downstream of conditional branches or switches should be dynamically compiled eagerly or lazily, and whether the dynamic code cache for each region should keep many, one, or zero code versions. A final annotation identifies program points where `invalidate()` should be inserted. DyC's annotations are described in detail elsewhere [11].

3. The Calpa System

Calpa combines program analysis and profile information to automatically derive annotations that drive selective dynamic compilation systems like DyC. These systems specialize parts of programs for particular values of run-time constants, dynamically generate the specialized code, and cache it for later reuse. They implement a variety of dynamic optimizations and techniques for caching and dispatching to the compiled code. Calpa models all these

---

[1] Polyvariant division allows the same piece of code to be analyzed with different combinations of variables being treated as run-time constants; each combination is called a *division*. Polyvariant specialization allows multiple compiled versions of a division to be produced, each specialized for different values of the run-time-constant variables. Program-point-specific polyvariance commences at arbitrary points in programs, not just at function entries. Polyvariant specialization can result in complete loop unrolling by creating a specialized copy of a loop body for each set of values of the run-time-constant loop induction variables. Complete loop unrolling is unlike unrolling done by traditional static compilers in that the loop is eliminated rather than enlarged. For simple loops, such as those that merely increment a counter until an exit condition is reached, a linear chain of unrolled loop bodies results (which we call *single-way loop unrolling*). For more complex loops, however, one iteration may lead to several alternative loop iterations (e.g., if it contains branch paths that update the loop induction variables differently), or even return to a previously executed loop iteration, producing in general a directed graph of unrolled loop bodies (which we call *multi-way loop unrolling*).

capabilities and automatically selects and places annotations to govern them.

Calpa consists of two components, an instrumentation tool and an annotation selection tool, both of which analyze C source code. The job of the instrumenter is to provide the selection tool with profile information from an application execution that will aid it in making reasonable annotation choices. It does this by automatically instrumenting its input application to track the execution frequencies of basic blocks and log the values of variables at all definitions and uses. The Instrumenter performs a pointer analysis to compute a conservative approximation to the set of variables referenced by each load and store instruction. Finally, to enable cache invalidation costs to be assessed, the instrumenter tracks the execution frequencies of store instructions and the targets they are updating.

Calpa's annotation selection tool first identifies, for each instruction in potential dynamic regions, the minimal set of static variables that cause the instruction that uses them to be static. In order to increase the number of simultaneously static computations, the selection tool combines the sets, and uses its cost/benefit model, with key parameters derived from the profile log information, to estimate the run time for each combination. If a new combination is predicted to produce faster dynamically generated code, it is retained as the current best choice. After all combinations have been considered, Calpa automatically generates the selected DyC annotations and outputs annotated C source code, which DyC compiles.

At Calpa's core is the cost/benefit model that predicts the effect of annotations on the run time of a dynamically compiled application. The model's cost function estimates the run-time overhead of dynamically generating and dispatching to specialized code. It is comprised of several subfunctions, all of whose parameters are derived from actual costs in DyC. It includes the following:

- The basic cost function accounts for specializing a region of code for a particular combination of run-time constant values. The function takes into account the frequency of static variable value changes, i.e., the number of re-dynamic compilations.
- Optimization-specific cost functions reflect the additional dynamically generated code needed to implement code-expanding optimizations, such as complete loop unrolling.
- Other cost functions account for dispatching to the correct dynamically generated code version. Calpa handles two basic dispatch models: *cache-lookup* and *invalidation-based caching*. In cache-lookup, the values of the static variables and data structures are used as a lookup key into the dynamic-code cache. If the key matches, the cached code is executed; otherwise a new version is dynamically compiled.

Invalidation-based caching dispatches according to the value of the pointer that is set by the `invalidate()` operation. If the pointer contains a code address, the previously generated code version is reused, avoiding a code-cache lookup; otherwise, it will contain a pointer to the customized dynamic compiler that will generate a new version. Both models have several implementations (including one that combines them) that trade off dispatch speed, lookup key size, and frequency and cost of invalidations [8].

The benefit function predicts the execution-time savings when running the dynamically generated code. It takes into account the savings obtained by executing static instructions only once for each dynamic code version and executing the optimized, dynamically generated code instead of the original instructions. Since instructions not on the critical path of a specialized procedure are unlikely to contribute to saved cycles on a wide-issue processor, Calpa computes the critical path of the procedure to determine which instructions qualify; because it ignores instructions off the critical path, Calpa conservatively underestimates the potential benefit of executing them only once during specialization. All qualifying instructions are weighted by their latency and the frequency of their execution.

The following subsections provide more detail on Calpa's features that comprise our current prototype and on which our experimental results are based.

3.0.1. Calpa's Instrumenter

To provide the necessary data for the cost/benefit analysis, the instrumenter instruments an application to collect information about program variables and program point execution frequencies during its execution. The instrumenter inserts code into the application to monitor and summarize three kinds of information: basic block frequencies (currently the number of executions, not execution time), variable definitions, and variable uses. When a variable or data structure is accessed via a pointer, the instrumenter uses the results of its pointer analysis[1] to insert code that associates the pointer's value with a corresponding variable or data structure from its points-to set.[2] This serves two purposes: first, it attributes the use or definition of a particular value to the variable or data

---

[1] Calpa's current default pointer analysis uses Das' improvement [32] over Steensgaard's almost linear-time context- and flow-insensitive algorithm [23] for pointers to static and stack-allocated variables and data structures; heap-allocated data is handled by creating one distinct variable for each allocation site. In lieu of Das' algorithm the standard Steensgaard algorithm, or an extension proposed by Shapiro & Horwitz [31] can also be chosen for stack-allocated variables. In addition, Ghiya & Hendren's algorithm [7] can be run for pointers to heap-based data structures, after one of the previously mentioned points-to algorithms has been run.

```
           i = 0                    {}
    L1:    if i >= size goto L2     {i,size}
           uelem = u[i]             {i,u[]}
           velem = v[i]             {i,v[]}
           t = uelem * velem        {i,u[],v[]}
           sum = sum + t            {i,sum,u[],v[]}
           i = i + 1                {i}
           goto L1                  {}
    L2:
```

Figure 2. Example of Candidate Static Variable Sets

structure that is defined or used; second, it identifies potential invalidation points of variables and data structures, so that the instrumenter can insert code to monitor the points' execution frequencies. To account for definitions that take place in library functions for which no source code is available, Calpa conservatively assumes that any variable or data structure that escapes to a library function is possibly modified by it.

An instrumented application logs values of definitions and uses as they occur, storing them as a per-invocation histogram of values and their number of occurrences. Each value-occurrence pair is tagged by the invocation number of the procedure in which it was produced (to obtain more accurate cost information for loop indices that are dependent on procedure parameters (see section 3.1.2)). Data is kept in a hash table in memory up to a user-specifiable maximum memory usage. When necessary, the values for the least recently used variables or data structures are written out to disk to make room for new values. To limit overall log size, monitoring is dynamically disabled for variables and data structures for which more than a user-specified number of distinct values have been recorded. (Because of dynamic compilation overhead, it is unlikely that these data will be run-time constants.) Before the application terminates, the profile data is written to a log file.

3.1. Calpa's Annotation Selection Tool

3.1.1 Candidate Static Variable and Candidate Division Sets

The first task in Calpa's annotation selection tool is the computation of the basic sets of variables which, if annotated as static, cause the operations that use them to become static. We call these sets *candidate static variable (CSV) sets*. The dot-product code fragment shown in Figure 2 illustrates CSV sets; next to each statement is the CSV set that makes the statement static. In general, the CSV set for an instruction is the set of variables used as source operands to the instruction, or the empty set if there are no source variable operands. For example, the comparison between i and size is static if and only if both variables are static; hence the statement's CSV set is {i,size}. For memory loads, the contents of the memory must also be static for the load to be static. For example, the load of u[i] is static if and only if both i and the array u is static, so the statement's CSV set is {i,u[]}, where u[] represents both the address u and its contents. Since DyC's binding time analysis will determine that instructions are static if their arguments are computed by unique static instructions, Calpa treats operands with a single reaching definition specially. In this case, the static variables for the operand are those that correspond to the CSV set of the reaching definition (instruction). For example, in the statement t=uelem*velem, since uelem and velem each have exactly one definition, the CSV set for this statement is {i,u[]} ∪ {i,v[]} = {i,u[],v[]}.

Calpa can build bigger dynamic regions with greater degrees of run-time optimization by merging CSV sets into larger sets of variables, called *candidate divisions* (*CDs*). The set of static instructions for a CD is the union of the instructions whose CSV sets are subsets of the CD. In general, if there are n CSV sets, there are 2^n ways to combine them. However, since CSV sets tend to overlap, not all combinations will produce different sets. For instance, if we combine {u[],i} and {u[],v[],i}, we obtain the same set as when we combine {v[],i} and {u[],v[],i}. In the dot-product example above, we get the following set of possible CDs (called the *CD set*): {}, {i}, {i,size}, {i,u[]}, {i,v[]}, {i,u[],v[]}, {i,size,u[]}, {i,size,v[]}, {i,size,u[],v[]}, {i,sum,u[],v[]}, and {i,size,sum,u[],v[]}.

The CD set captures all possible combinations of annotated variables that result in distinct collections of static instructions, i.e., distinct dynamic regions. Other combinations of static variables never have to be considered, since they will produce the same results as some CD already in the CD set. For instance, {sum,i} leads to the same instructions being static as {i}, which is

---

[2] Where these analyses determine that only one monitored variable or data structure can be accessed (a points-to set of size 1), no run-time matching is performed.

already included in the CD set. Therefore, it suffices to evaluate only the CDs in the CD set to estimate the potential benefits that specialization can achieve, rather than evaluating all 2^k possible combinations of k variables; for instance, in the dot-product example, the CD set size is only 11, whereas there are 32 sets in the power set of the five variables.

For each procedure, Calpa first computes the CSV sets of all instructions. The CD set is then enumerated, using a gradient search strategy. Variables are first sorted by their number of distinct values, obtained from the profile. Then, beginning with the CSV sets that contain the more invariant variables, new candidate divisions are generated and their run-time benefit and cost estimated. The search process remembers the best candidate division choice and its estimated speedup. The search terminates if all choices have been enumerated (feasible for small applications, such as dotproduct), a set time quota has expired, or the gradient of improvement over the best choice so far drops below a preset threshold.

3.1.2 The Cost Model

The DyC system incurs three different costs when dynamically compiling a program: a one-time specialization cost for producing a dynamically compiled region for particular static values, periodic dispatching costs which are paid each time a section of dynamically generated code is executed, and an invalidation check cost for variables and data structures for which invalidation-based caching is used.

Specialization Cost

The specialization cost is roughly proportional to the number of dynamic instructions generated for all code versions. Therefore, when computing its specialization cost estimate, Calpa uses the profile data to estimate the number of different code versions that will be produced. Its estimate of the total number of instructions generated at run time is proportional to the product of the number of specializations and the number of dynamic instructions generated for each.

In more detail, for each procedure and each of the procedure's choice of static variables, the following steps are performed. First, for each basic block the number of dynamic instructions d is computed. Then, for each static variable, d is multiplied by the number of the variable's profiled values v. If a loop induction variable is static, different versions of the loop iteration, one for each value of the induction variable, will be produced. To account for this additional generated code, a second multiplier is used for each static loop induction variable, based on the number of profiled induction variable values. For multi-way loops, in which the choice of the next loop path is determined at run time, Calpa scales d * v, based on the number of different paths and how often each is executed. Finally, to obtain the estimated specialization time, the estimate for the total number of instructions generated is multiplied by a constant factor. (We currently use 40 cycles per instruction generated[1]).

When loops are completely unrolled, Calpa constrains code blowup by guarding the loop-unrolling annotation with a condition that is generated by the specialization cost model. It generates the expression d * range(i) < limit, where range(i) is the actual number of different values observed for the loop induction variable i and limit is a predetermined constant (modifiable by a Calpa command-line argument) to guard the unrolling. Hence, the loop unrolling will only be performed if the number of values of i remains below the threshold of limit generated instructions. If the preset limit is too large (causing performance degradation due to cache effects) or too conservative, limit can be changed. Currently Calpa makes the programmer do this; however, future work will automate this process by observing the resulting cache behavior of the generated application and dynamically adjusting the limit.

Code Caching Cost

Using a simple binding-time analysis, Calpa identifies program points at which dynamically-generated-code cache lookups are necessary. However, a cost need not be incurred at all cache lookup points. For example, DyC includes a caching policy (*cache_one_unchecked*) to specify that it is safe to omit a cache lookup for invariant static variables – in this case, specialized code is generated for the variable's first encountered value, cached and used thereafter without a cache lookup. Alternatively, *cache_all_unchecked* is used for variables that step through a small sequence of values. When the cache lookup point is encountered, a new version of code is generated without a lookup. This policy is useful for complete (single-way) loop unrolling, where the induction variable is monotonically incremented.

Calpa uses profile information as a hint to decide whether an unchecked policy should be used; if a variable has only one value, it becomes a candidate for *cache_one_unchecked*; if it has only a few values and the variable is a loop index, then it may be suitable for *cache_all_unchecked*. To guarantee the safety of the *cache_one_unchecked* policy, the invalidation point analysis will ensure that the variable, once defined, will not be redefined. The *cache_all_unchecked* policy is always safe when specialization is performed on demand. Calpa can choose eager specialization if it can determine that the loop termination condition is static; if it cannot (e.g., for

---

[1] DyC typically takes between tens to a few hundred cycles per instruction generated, depending on the dynamic optimizations being applied [9].

Table 1. Workload

Program	Size (lines)	Description	Input
`binary`	111	binary search over an array	array of 4K entries
`dotproduct`	136	dot-product of two integer vectors	vectors of size 100 that were 90% zero-filled
`query`	226	database query for an exact match	a query with 21 comparisons
`romberg`	134	function integration by iteration	an iteration bound of 8
`dinero` (version III)	2,397	cache simulator [13]	L1 cache (8KB, 32B blocks, direct-mapped)
`pnmconvol`	333	image convolution routine that is part of the netpbm toolkit for image transformations	3×3 convolution matrix on a 2.2 MB image file
`m88ksim`	11,549	Motorola 88000 simulator, taken from the SPEC95 benchmark suite [21].	SPEC-provided null breakpoint set

multi-way loop unrolling), it chooses the safe, lazy option.

When Calpa uses the more costly *cache_all* policy (which does a cache lookup), it assesses a per-lookup fee to allocate memory for a cache key and do a hash table lookup (85 cycles in the model), plus a small additional cost to construct the cache key from the set of variables whose values must be checked in order to dispatch to the correct version of code (5 cycles per variable). Since the caching cost is paid each time the cache point is executed, it is multiplied by the execution frequency of the point, obtained from the profile.

Invalidation Cost

When Calpa uses invalidation-based caching for a variable or data structure, it first computes its invalidation points. The cost of each invalidation point is the product of its execution frequency and some fixed cost (100 cycles in the model). The sum over all invalidation points is the variable or data structure's total invalidation cost.

3.1.3 The Benefit Model

Calpa's benefit estimation identifies all instructions that are made static by the particular CD being evaluated. For each procedure and choice of static variables, it runs a simple and fast binding time analysis (a simplified version of DyC's BTA [11]) to compute the derived static variables and the division of variables and instructions into static or dynamic. (The BTA also computes the program points that require dynamically-generated-code cache lookups, important for the estimation of caching costs, described above.) In the current implementation, the BTA assumes that the variables are specialized throughout the procedure. In some cases, specializing a smaller region of the procedure may result in the same number of static instructions, but with a smaller specialization or caching cost. In such a case, the current implementation will tend to overestimate these costs.

The benefit of specializing a procedure for a particular choice of static variables is computed by estimating the number of saved cycles that will result from their instructions becoming static.[1] Since static instructions off the critical path of the specialized procedure are unlikely to contribute to saved cycle time, Calpa first computes the critical path of the procedure. The total number of cycles saved is obtained by multiplying the latency of each static instruction on the critical path by its profile-derived execution frequency.

4. Experiments and Results

Calpa's instrumentation and annotation selection tools are implemented using the SUIF compiler infrastructure [26], together with the Machine SUIF libraries for CFG-construction and data flow analysis [14]. All analysis, instrumentation, and insertion of annotations are carried out on the SUIF intermediate representation (IR). Processed IR is converted back to C code and then compiled with the GNU gcc compiler (for the instrumented application) or DyC (for the annotated application).

Our experiments profile and automatically annotate a number of commonly used kernels and applications, described in Table 1. In this initial study, the same inputs were used for profiling and the final performance runs that determine application speedup. Studying the variance of value profiles across different inputs and the effects of varying levels of precision of different alias analysis algorithms is beyond the scope of this paper; we will analyze Calpa's sensitivity to these factors once we finish calibrating our cost/benefit model. All experiments were done on a lightly loaded DEC Alpha 21164 workstation with 1.5GB of physical memory. Timings were obtained by using the UNIX `time` command; reported times are wall clock time.

---

[1] We use instruction latencies, and currently assume L1 cache hits, again a conservative estimate.

Table 2. Profiling Results. This table shows the effects of instrumentation on application code size and execution time, and the resulting profile log size.

Program	Instrumentation Time	Original Binary Size	Instrumented Binary Size [a]	Binary Expansion Factor	Original Run Time (seconds)	Instrumented Run Time	Profile Log File Size
`binary`	0.2 seconds	25 KB	224 KB	9.0	< 0.1	1.9 seconds	275 KB
`dotproduct`	0.1 seconds	25 KB	224 KB	9.0	< 0.1	0.3 seconds	92 KB
`query`	0.4 seconds	27 KB	224 KB	8.3	< 0.1	7.8 seconds	939 KB
`romberg`	0.3 seconds	26 KB	224 KB	8.6	< 0.1	0.4 seconds	102 KB
`dinero`	4.6 seconds	57 KB	448 KB	7.9	1.3	13.8 minutes	6.8 MB
`pnmconvol`	1.2 seconds	66 KB	288 KB	4.4	3.0	17.1 minutes	266 KB
`m88ksim`	10.7 minutes	213 KB	2.6 MB	12.6	180.1	3.5 hours[b]	7.5 MB

a. Instrumented binary sizes include required portions of a 409KB instrumentation library.
b. Using a limited amount of binary patching improved m88ksim's instrumented run time from 18 to 3.5 hours.

4.1. Instrumentation and Profiling Results

To assess the viability of our profiling tool, we measured (1) the time to instrument the applications, (2) the impact of instrumentation on the size and execution time of the applications, and (3) the size of the resulting log files. The results are summarized in Table 2.

Instrumenting the source code was fast, ranging from fractions of a second for the kernels to 10 minutes for `m88ksim`.

Instrumenting programs increased their size by roughly an order of magnitude. For most of the applications, this increase is predominantly due to including portions of Calpa's instrumentation library. Making this a dynamically linked library and removing its debugging support would greatly reduce the code space cost of instrumentation.

The run time of the instrumented executables was 1 to 3 orders of magnitude slower than that of the original code. In contrast, Calder et al. [4] report average slowdowns in the range of 10× to 33× for their profiling schemes. Calpa's much slower profiling performance is caused by its straightforward tracking of *all* variables, at all definition and use points. While Calpa currently disables tracking for variables with more than a thousand values, a much lower cut-off point seems more appropriate, i.e., the costs of *re*dynamic compiling for each of a thousand values will surely swamp the gains of executing the specialized code. In addition, simple static analysis could be applied to reduce the number of redundant points of instrumentation, e.g., attributing dominated use counts to the instrumented, dominating use in the same control region (assuming no intervening definition), and binary patching schemes could be used to eliminate, for example, cut-off-point checking. Both techniques would reduce the costs associated with over-profiling variables [33]; for instance, binary patching of disabled tracking calls alone improved the run time from 18 to 3.5 hours for m88ksim. However, despite its straightforward instrumentation approach, Calpa's instrumented run times were a matter of seconds or minutes for the kernels and medium-sized applications, and hours for m88ksim.

Monitoring and storing data for all variables produced profile log files that ranged from 92KB to 275KB for the kernels and 266KB to 7.5 MB for the applications. Summarizing profile data in memory, rather than simply saving values to a file as they stream out of the instrumented program, turned out to be a good time-space trade-off; in particular, high repeat counts for value uses indicate that a non-summarizing profile log would be much larger.

4.2. Annotation Generation Results

Based on the profile data, Calpa generated annotations for all programs. We measured the execution time of the annotation selection tool and compared the set of Calpa's annotated variables to those chosen by a programmer. The results are shown in Table 2.

For all programs Calpa generated the same set of annotations that had been produced by the manual methodology. In addition, despite the current simple functionality of the profiling tool and the coarse-grain estimates of the analysis cost/benefit model, Calpa occasionally annotated other variables. The additional annotations increased the speedups of the dynamically compiled programs over their statically compiled versions. Although preliminary, the results demonstrate the promise for automatic dynamic compilation based on the approach taken by Calpa. A discussion of the individual programs follows.

- In `binary`, the procedure search is called repeatedly for the same array of values. We had manually

Table 3. Application & Annotation Characteristics. This table shows, for each program, the variables that were automatically annotated, and the selection tool annotation time. The variables in **bold** are those that Calpa annotated, but the human missed.

Program	Annotated Static Variables	Annotation Time
binary	size & contents of the input array induction variable for the search loop **the search key**	6 seconds
dotproduct	the contents of vector u the loop index and duration bound **the contents of vector v**	2 seconds
query	a query	15 seconds
romberg	the iteration bound	26 seconds
dinero	cache configuration parameters	27 minutes
pnmconvol	4 loop indices in two doubly-nested loops 3 color arrays image format flag maximum size of the image array	75 seconds
m88ksim	an array of breakpoints loop index flag that indicates whether breakpoint-checking is enabled	8.0 hours

annotated as static this array, its size and the loop induction variables used to search it. This resulted in a complete unrolling of the search loop. Calpa identified the same variables for annotation, and, in addition, decided to make the search key static. The driver routine that calls search uses only 3 different key values to do the search, making the search key appear quasi-invariant, an artifact of this particular use of the search routine by the driver. Therefore, Calpa chose to specialize for the search key values thereby increasing binary's speedup from 2.3 to 3.1.

- For dotproduct Calpa also generated the same annotations as had been done manually (vector u). In addition, it annotated the second vector v, which was also constant, an artifact of the use of the dotproduct procedure by the driver routine. Annotating both vectors instead of one, improved the speedup from 6.6 to 22.6.
- For the remaining programs, the set of variables automatically annotated by Calpa exactly matched the manual annotations. Speedups for those programs were 1.4 (query), 1.2 (romberg), 1.5 (dinero), 1.1 (m88ksim), and 3.0 (pnmconvol).

The column named "annotation time" shows the time to generate annotations from the profile data logs. It took only a few seconds to generate the annotations for the kernels, and minutes for most applications (the exception, m88ksim, took eight hours).

5. Related Work

Calder *et al.* [3] were the first to expose quasi-invariant behavior by profiling. They then went on to show [4] that the values found during profiling could be used to potentially guide automated optimization by demonstrating via hand optimization that two codes could get substantial benefit from using the value profiles. Their value profiler identifies (quasi-) invariant variables and their top n values; two metrics are defined to measure the invariance of variables, and a cache is used during profiling to store the values. They do not collect information about particular sequences of variable values, which we need to compute precise caching and specialization costs. An advantage of their tool is that no recompilation of a program is necessary in order to profile it, since they instrument the executable using ATOM [22]. However, to exploit the invariance information, a mapping of the instruction-level information back to the source code is necessary.

Value prediction [18] is a hardware technique that is complementary to our compiler- and profiler-based approach of value-specific optimizations. It uses processor hardware to predict instruction results and speculatively executes subsequent data-dependent instructions, based on the predicted values.

Dynamo [2] is a run-time optimizer that tries to improve performance by identifying frequently taken paths (traces) through a program. Speedup results from accumulating the traces in a code cache and executing the streamlined code instead of the original code with branches. To obtain control over an application's execution and monitor its performance, execution starts in Dynamo, which interprets native code until it finds a hot path. Hot paths execute from the code cache and return control to Dynamo when finished. When a path is no longer hot, the code cache is flushed and monitoring and interpretation of the code is resumed. If too much time is spent in interpretation mode, Dynamo bails out to native execution. Because of bail-out, Dynamo can limit the maximum slowdown an application may suffer. Since Dynamo tries to speed up an application in executable format, its approach is complimentary to Calpa's. Applications annotated by Calpa and compiled by DyC could be run under Dynamo, which might further improve their performance.

While there is a large body of research on dynamic compilation, only a small fraction relates to automation. Autrey and Wolfe [1] proposed a loop-level analysis to identify variables that are modified much less frequently than they are referenced, which they call *glacial variables*. Variables that are defined at loop nesting level n, and not modified at any higher nesting levels are identified as candidates for dynamic compilation at loop nesting level n. They do not report results of applying their analysis in a real dynamic compilation system. TypeGuard and MemGuard are two tools used in the Synthetix project [24] to identify where invariant values are modified. In TypeGuard the programmer tags fields in C struct types with a *guard specification*. TypeGuard then analyzes the C program and identifies all places where the tagged fields are potentially modified. This information is used by the Synthetix system to trigger respecialization for the field's new value. However, due to pointer type casts, TypeGuard can not safely identify all potential definition points. In addition, since struct types rather than particular variables are guarded, scalar variables cannot be handled, because too many (mostly spurious) messages would be generated. MemGuard puts a static data structure into a protected memory page. On a write to the page, the page fault handler triggers respecialization for the new values in the data structure. The MemGuard approach requires a modification to the operating system, something we did not want to do.

IPERF [15] is a framework for the automatic construction of performance prediction models. It uses a database of performance models of computation, the memory hierarchy, and virtual address translation and tries to fit a linear combination of these as closely as possible to observed performance. In its model of computation it distinguishes only between different compiler optimization levels (e.g., -O2); in contrast, Calpa takes both the estimated benefit from dynamically compiling code and the compilation cost into account when deciding whether to use dynamic compilation. Wang [25] proposed a framework for the performance prediction of superscalar-based computers to guide the optimization in the PTRAN2 compiler for High Performance Fortran. He reported results for straight-line code only (no loops or other control structures). Dean *et al.* [6] estimated the benefit of function inlining in an object-oriented language by performing the inlining and subsequent optimization in a trial; their approach was able to amortize the trial cost by reusing the benefit estimate for call sites whose receiver arguments belonged to the same type groups. Calpa's approach of specializing conditionally, using conditions that are based on variable values and architecture-specific parameters, such as I-cache size, is similar to Debray's concept of resource-bounded partial evaluation [34], where a cost-benefit model is used to prevent a partial evaluator from specializing too aggressively, e.g., producing too much code for the I-cache.

6. Conclusions

In selective dynamic compilation systems like DyC, finding the right annotations is a major challenge to profitable run-time optimization. Sometimes several person-weeks are spent in a tedious, trial-and-error process until successful annotations are found. We have shown that Calpa can quickly produce annotations for small- and medium-sized programs, using its unique combination of techniques, and its particular choice of parameters (for example, cutoff limits for value profiling). While the current combination provides useful value, it represents only one particular point the design space. Our next step is to explore this design space by varying Calpa's parameters and examining the trade-offs of different choices, in particular, studying the sensitivity of Calpa results with respect to different value profiles, alias algorithms, and cut-off limits. With that study, we hope to come closer to the long-term goal of making dynamic compilation just another in a series of optimizations performed automatically by compilers.

Acknowledgments

We'd like to thank Brian Grant, Matthai Philipose and our anonymous reviewers for valuable comments on an earlier draft, and Mike Smith and Glenn Holloway for Machine SUIF source and technical help in using it. This work was supported by ONR contract N00014-96-1-0402, NSF grant CCR-9503741, and NSF Young Investigator Award CCR-9457767.

References

[1] T. Autrey and M. Wolfe. Initial results for glacial variable analysis. In *Proceedings of the 8th International Workshop on Languages and Compilers for Parallel Computing*, pages 120–134, August 1996.

[2] V. Bala, E. Duesterwald, and S. Banerjia. Dynamo: A transparent dynamic optimization system. In *SIGPLAN '00 Conference on Programming Language Design and Implementation*, pages 1–12, June 2000.

[3] B. Calder, P. Feller, and A. Eustace. Value profiling. In *Proceedings of the 30th Annual International Symposium on Microarchitecture*, pages 259–269, December 1997.

[4] B. Calder, P. Feller, and A. Eustace. Value profiling and optimization. *Journal of Instruction Level Parallelism*, 1:1–37, March 1999.

[5] C. Consel and F. Noël. A general approach for run-time specialization and its application to C. In *Symposium on Principles of Programming Languages*, pages 145–156, January 1996.

[6] J. Dean and C. Chambers. Towards better inlining decisions using inlining trials. In *Proceedings of the ACM Conference on LISP and Functional Programming '94*, pages 273–282, June 1994.

[7] R. Ghiya and L.J. Hendren. Connection analysis: A practical interprocedural heap analysis for C. *International Journal of Parallel Programming*, 24(6):547–578, December 1996.

[8] B. Grant, C. Chambers, and S.J. Eggers. Efficiently dispatching to run-time specialized code. Submitted for publication.

[9] B. Grant, M. Mock, M. Philipose, C. Chambers, and S.J. Eggers. The benefits and costs of DyC's run-time optimizations. Submitted for publication.

[10] B. Grant, M. Mock, M. Philipose, C. Chambers, and S.J. Eggers. Annotation-directed run-time specialization in C. In *Symposium on Partial Evaluation and Semantics-Based Program Manipulation*, pages 163–178, June 1997.

[11] B. Grant, M. Mock, M. Philipose, C. Chambers, and S.J. Eggers. DyC: An expressive annotation-directed dynamic compiler for C. *Theoretical Computer Science*, 248(1-2):147–199, October 2000.

[12] B. Grant, M. Philipose, M. Mock, C. Chambers, and S.J. Eggers. An evaluation of staged, run-time optimizations in DyC. In *Conference on Programming Language Design and Implementation*, pages 293–304, May 1999.

[13] M.D. Hill and A.J. Smith. Experimental evaluation of on-chip microprocessor cache memories. In *Proceedings of the International Symposium of Computer Architecture*, pages 158–166, June 1984.

[14] G. Holloway and C. Young. The flow and analysis libraries of machine SUIF. In *Proceedings of the 2nd SUIF Compiler Workshop*, August 1997.

[15] C-H. Hsu and U. Kremer. A framework for automatic construction of performance predication models. In *Proceedings of the 1st Workshop on Feedback-Directed Optimization*, October 1998.

[16] N.D. Jones, C.K. Gomarde, and P. Sestoft. *Partial Evaluation and Automatic Program Generation*. Prentice Hall, 1993.

[17] M. Leone and P. Lee. Optimizing ML with run-time code generation. In *Conference on Programming Language Design and Implementation*, pages 137–148, May 1996.

[18] M.H. Lipasti, C.V. Wilkerson, and J.P. Shen. Value locality and load value prediction. In *Proceedings of the Seventh International Conference on Architectural Support for Programming Languages and Operating Systems*, pages 138–147, October 1996.

[19] M. Mock, M. Berryman, C. Chambers, and S.J. Eggers. Calpa: A tool for automating dynamic compilation. In *2nd Workshop on Feedback-Directed Optimization*, November 1999.

[20] F. Noël, L. Hornof, C. Consel, and J. L. Lawall. Automatic, template-based run-time specialization: Implementation and experimental study. In *International Conference on Computer Languages*, pages 132–142, May 1998.

[21] SPEC CPU, August 1995. http://www.specbench.org/.

[22] A. Srivastava and A. Eustace. ATOM: A system for building customized program analysis tools. *SIGPLAN Notices*, 29(6):196–205, June 1994. Conference on Programming Language Design and Implementation.

[23] B. Steensgaard. Points-to analysis in almost linear time. In *Symposium on Principles of Programming Languages*, pages 32–41, January 1996.

[24] SYNTHETIX TOOLKIT. http://www.cse.ogi.edu/projects/synthetix/toolkit/.

[25] Ko-Yang Wang. Precise compile-time performance prediction for superscalar-based computers. In *Conference on Programming Language Design and Implementation*, pages 73–84, June 1994.

[26] R. Wilson, R. French, C. Wilson, S. Amarasinghe, J. Anderson, S. Tjiang, S.-W. Liao, C.-W. Tseng, M. Hall, M.S. Lam, and J. Hennessy. SUIF: An infrastructure for research on parallelizing and optimizing compilers. *ACM SIGPLAN Notices*, 29(12), December 1994.

[27] L.P. Deutsch and A.M. Schiffman. Efficient Implementation of the Smalltalk-80 System. In *Conference Record of POPL '84: Symposium on Principles of Programming Languages*, pages 297-302, January 1984.

[28] C. Chambers and D. Ungar. Making Pure Object-Oriented Languages Practical. In *Proceedings OOPSLA '91*, pages 1-15, November 1991.

[29] U. Holzle and D. Ungar. Optimizing Dynamically-Dispatched Calls with Run-Time Type Feedback. In *Proceedings of the ACM SIGPLAN '94 Conference on Programming Language Design and Implementation*, pages 326-336, June 1994.

[30] V.C. Sreedhar and M. Burke and J.-D. Choi. A Framework for Interprocedural Optimization in the Presence of Dynamic Class Loading. In *Proceedings of the ACM SIGPLAN '00 Conference on Programming Language Design and Implementation*, pages 208-218, June 2000.

[31] M. Shapiro and S. Horwitz. Fast and Accurate Flow-Insensitive Points-To Analysis. In *Conference Record of POPL '97: Symposium on Principles of Programming Languages*, January 1997.

[32] M. Das. Unification-Based Pointer Analysis with Directional Assignments. In *Proceedings of the ACM SIGPLAN '00 Conference on Programming Language Design and Implementation*, pages 35-46, June 2000.

[33] O. Traub and S. Schechter and M.D. Smith. Ephemeral Instrumentation for Lightweight Program Profiling. Technical report, Harvard University, 2000.

[34] S.K. Debray. Unfold/Fold Transformations and Loop Optimization of Logic Programs. In *Proceedings of the ACM SIGPLAN '88 Conference on Programming Language Design and Implementation*, pages 297-307, June 1988.

Increasing the Size of Atomic Instruction Blocks using Control Flow Assertions

Sanjay J. Patel   Tony Tung   Satarupa Bose   Matthew M. Crum

Center for Reliable and High-Performance Computing
Department of Electrical and Computer Engineering
University of Illinois at Urbana-Champaign
{sjp, tonytung, sbose, mcrum}@crhc.uiuc.edu

Abstract

For a variety of reasons, branch-less regions of instructions are desirable for high-performance execution. In this paper, we propose a means for increasing the dynamic length of branch-less regions of instructions for the purposes of dynamic program optimization. We call these atomic regions frames and we construct them by replacing original branch instructions with assertions. Assertion instructions check if the original branching conditions still hold. If they hold, no action is taken. If they do not, then the entire region is undone. In this manner, an assertion has no explicit control flow. We demonstrate that using branch correlation to decide when a branch should be converted into an assertion results in atomic regions that average over 100 instructions in length, with a probability of completion of 97%, and that constitute over 80% of the dynamic instruction stream. We demonstrate both static and dynamic means for constructing frames. When frames are built dynamically using finite sized hardware, they average 80 instructions in length and have good caching properties.

1 Introduction

An atomic region of code has the following properties: execution of the region begins at a single instruction, ends at a single instruction, and the region contains a single path of execution. The region is considered atomic because if one instruction in the region is committed to architectural state, then all instructions are committed. A basic block, for example, is an atomic region.

Atomic regions consisting of many instructions are desirable for a variety of reasons. They allow a compiler maximum flexibility for optimizations. Code scheduling in atomic regions, for example, need not account for side entrances, side exits, or divergent paths of execution. Atomic regions provide hardware with a sequential stream of instructions with no control flow. Instruction fetch mechanisms can stream out an atomic region with a single PC and a single branch prediction. Optimistic state recovery mechanisms need only save state at boundaries of atomic regions.

The nature of programs, however, is such that atomic regions typically consist of very few instructions. Basic blocks are the most familiar notion of atomic regions. The data in Table 1 shows that dynamic basic block size for a majority of the SPEC2000 integer benchmarks is below 9 instructions. The benchmarks were compiled using the Compaq Alpha compiler with a high level (-O4) of optimization including function in-lining and loop unrolling.

Benchmark	Average block size
bzip	9.17
crafty	9.23
eon	7.45
gap	8.52
gcc	6.43
gzip	11.07
mcf	5.33
parser	5.30
twolf	7.36
vortex	7.20
vpr	8.56

Table 1. Dynamic basic block size.

In this paper, we present an effective technique for generating longer atomic regions with the use of control flow *assertions*. An assertion is an instruction that verifies that the original branching conditions still hold. If the conditions are still true, then no action is taken. If they are not, then the entire region is undone and control is diverted to an original copy of the code.

The atomic regions formed using our technique are called *frames*. A frame is a region of code where all internal branches have been promoted into assertions. Frame creation can be done statically by a profiling compiler, or dynamically with a hardware fill unit. We demonstrate that with a dynamic technique using branch correlation, frames can be very long—an order of magnitude longer than a basic block—with several properties that make them very compelling for further investigation.

In addition to the reasons mentioned earlier in the introduction, long atomic regions are useful for low-level dynamic translation and optimization, as exemplified by several recent proposals such as the rePLay Framework [10], the Transmeta Code Morphing System [5], and HP Dynamo [1]. An atomic region can serve as the basic unit of optimization. It can be as small as an instruction, but longer regions are preferred in order to give a dynamic optimizer greater opportunity for optimization. Further benefits are had if recently optimized regions occur frequently—the overhead costs of translation and optimization are amortized over each occurrence. While the frame construction techniques presented here are specifically tailored for rePLay, they can be extended for use by a variety of dynamic optimization schemes.

In this paper, we contribute the following. We present a technique for constructing logically atomic regions called frames by using control flow assertions. We measure the effectiveness of our construction technique when applied to static code versus applying it dynamically using branch correlation. We provide metrics for evaluating the effectiveness of frame construction. We propose and evaluate a hardware mechanism for constructing frames.

2 Basic concepts : assertions and frames

There are two basic concepts proposed in this paper: assertions and frames. An assertions is a type of branch instruction that has no explicit control flow associated with it [6]. An assertion verifies that certain conditions are true during execution, and initiates a recovery action if they are not. Frames are logically atomic blocks of instructions where all internal control flow has been replaced by assertions. In this section, we elaborate further on these concepts.

2.1 Assertions

A conditional branch instruction and an assertion instruction are similar in that they both test a condition. They are different, however, in the actions taken after the condition is tested. A conditional branch instruction will either divert the instruction stream to the taken target of the branch instruction if the condition is true, or allow the program to progress sequentially if the condition is false. An assertion does nothing if the condition is true. If the condition is false, however, the assertion triggers a recovery action and diverts control back to a recovery point. The recovery action involves reverting the architectural state to that of the beginning of the block that contains it. Essentially, an assertion that fires causes its entire block to be undone. We discuss the specifics of the recovery action later in this section.

This undoing of state creates an important distinction between a conditional branch and an assertion: subsequent instructions in the same block are not control dependent upon the assertion. An assertion therefore requires no prediction when fetched. An implicit prediction is made that the assertion will follow the direction the original branch instruction was biased towards.

We demonstrate the concept with an example. Figure 1 shows the difference between original code and code with assertions. The original code contains three basic blocks: BlockA, BlockFallThroughA, and BlockZ. BlockA contains a conditional branch that is taken to BlockZ. BlockA and BlockZ can be coalesced using an assertion. In Frame1, the instructions in BlockZ are not control dependent on the assertion, and can be safely moved ahead of the assertion. If the condition checked by the assertion is true, nothing happens. If it is not true, the entire block is flushed (i.e., architectural state is recovered back to the beginning of Frame1), and control is transfered to BlockA. We say that in this case, the assertion has fired.

```
BlockA:
        :
        BRz  r3, BlockZ ; BR 1
BlockFallThroughA:
        :
BlockZ:
        :
        BRz  r4, BlockK ; BR 2
        :
Frame1:
        :
        <insts from Block A and Z>
        :
        ASSERTz r3, BlockA
        :
        BRz     r4, BlockK ; BR 2
```

Figure 1. Example of a frame. BlockA, BlockFallThroughA, and BlockZ constitute the original control flow. Frame1 contains copies of Blocks A and Z joined by an assertion. If the assertion fires, control is diverted to BlockA.

We will demonstrate that using assertions in place of highly biased branches allows for the creation of large atomic regions (like Frame1). The objective is to promote conditional branches into assertions in situations where they are unlikely to fire.

The three general forms of a conditional assertion are shown below.

```
ASSERT    Rx, Ry, <cond>, assert_tgt
ASSERTi   Rn, <imm>, <cond>, assert_tgt
ASSERTil  Rn, <long_imm>, <cond>, assert_tgt
```

All three versions compare a register with either a register, a short immediate value, or a long immediate value. A PC-relative assertion target (assert_tgt) specifies where control is to be redirected in the case the condition is not true. The conditional field can be any standard relational comparison (i.e., less than, less than or equal to, etc). Most ISAs only support conditional branches that compare a register with the value zero (i.e., the relational comparison is less than zero, less than or equal to zero, etc.). This is to allow high-speed implementation of branch execution logic; performing a register-to-register comparison and initiating a possible misprediction recovery in a single cycle at high frequencies can be problematic. Since the case of an assertion firing is by design the uncommon case, we allow two register values to be compared within assertions. As a result, the recovery due to a fired assertion might start a cycle after the comparison is done. There is no direct performance advantage in doing this, and this can be done with branches also. It does, however, allow the removal of an extra instruction in certain situations when converting from basic blocks into frames.

As we will show, our technique for converting branches into assertions also allows indirect branches to be converted. The third form shown above, ASSERTil, compares a register with a 32-bit (or 64-bit) immediate value, and therefore an ASSERTil takes the space of 2 (or 3) regular 32-bit instructions. Highly biased indirect branches or returns can be converted into assertions and their target blocks encapsulated with a frame. The address of the expected target is the immediate value field of the ASSERTil instruction.

2.2 Frames

A section of code in which all internal branches have been promoted into assertions is called a frame. A frame is an atomic region. If any instruction within the frame commits, then they all commit. Figure 2 shows how a likely path through a section of a program can be converted from original basic blocks into a frame.

The frame in Figure 2 has four assertions. These assertions test that the original branching conditions that would have taken program control from block A to block B to

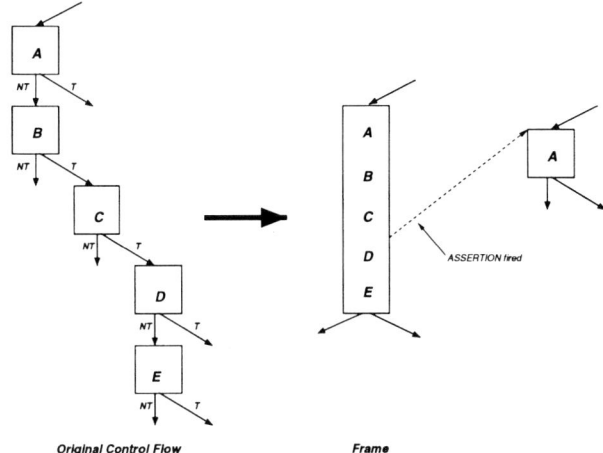

Figure 2. A frame is a region where all internal branches are promoted to assertions.

block C to block D to block E still hold. If they hold, then the frame completes. If any one of them do not hold, then an assertion will fire, the frame will be undone, and program control will transfer to the original block A and proceed from there.

An optimization can be done in the mapping between branches and assertions. Assertions need only check for the most restrictive condition that must be true in order for a frame to execute. For example, if the branch at the end of block A tested for (x < 10) and the branch at the end of block B tested for (x < 4) then only an assertion to verify the condition (x < 4) is required (provided the value of x does not change in the interim).

Because a firing assertion can have a higher execution penalty than a mispredicted branch, frames should not be constructed unless the paths that they encapsulate are determined to have high likelihood of execution. The penalty of a firing assertion depends on two factors: (1) the dataflow depth of that assertion and (2) the efficiency of the processor in meeting that depth during execution.

Frames have a similarity to other types of regions identified by optimizing compilers, but are nonetheless different. Hyperblocks, superblocks, and traces from a trace scheduling compiler are not strictly atomic regions—all can have side exits or divergent paths. The use of the control flow assertion in frame construction alleviates an obvious limitation to region size imposed by atomicity. We will also demonstrate that frame construction can be carried out dynamically.

Recovery involves two things: (1) reverting architectural state back to what it was before the frame started execution, and (2) directing control back to the original (non-frame) version of the code. Reverting state is done using a state recovery mechanism similar to what is required for a deeply-pipelined dynamically-scheduled processor, such as checkpointing or a reorder buffer. A large store buffer is required to hold values stored to memory by instructions within a frame. Once the frame is determined to execute completely, the stores are committed to memory and the register values produced by the frame are committed to the architectural register set.

2.3 The rePLay Framework

The techniques presented in this paper can be applied directly to a hardware/software framework for dynamic optimization called rePLay [10]. In rePLay, frames are constructed by hardware using some of the techniques described in this paper. A software-driven optimization engine optimizes each frame before storing it within the frame cache. The atomic property of frames enables the optimization engine to perform aggressive optimization with lower overhead than if frames were non-atomic. A sequencer speculates through the control flow, initiating fetches of both frames and regular basic blocks. Figure 3 shows a high-level diagram of the rePLay framework.

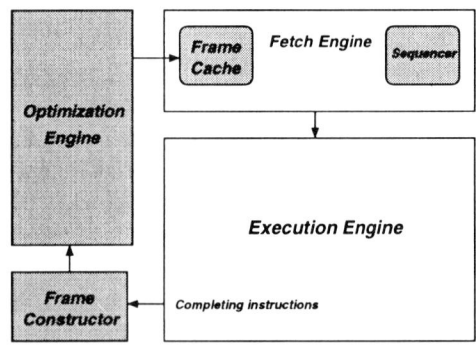

Figure 3. The rePLay Framework.

Since we are investigating frame construction for use with dynamic optimization, we are faced with two competing objectives: we want frames to be long in order to boost the potential of optimization, and we want frames to completely execute. In this paper, we examine frame construction techniques that achieve both.

3 Related Work

The fundamental elements of this work are derived from work done by Melvin and Patt on the Block-Structured ISA [6]. They proposed the concept of developing an ISA centered around atomic regions. In a similar vein to frame construction, trace scheduling [3] exploits infrequent branch paths by removing them from a trace and branching to compensation code if an infrequent path should have been executed. Assertions (and dynamic branch correlation) improve upon trace scheduling.

Much of this work builds upon previous trace cache research [11, 12, 9], in particular that of Branch Promotion [8]. Recently, Merten et al [7] have investigated identifying hot traces to focus the benefits of a trace cache-like mechanism. The one key difference between most previous trace cache work and this work is that here frames are considered atomic entities; traces in previous trace cache work could have side exits. Furthermore, we consider frames for dynamic optimization, and thus frames are required to be long. Trace caches were primarily investigated to boost instruction fetch bandwidth.

The concept of dynamic compilation and optimization is an emerging area. The desire to boost performance and efficiency by exploiting run-time behavior has spawned several alternative proposals [1, 5, 4, 10]. All of these systems rely on identifying good candidate regions for optimization. In this paper, we provide a region-identification mechanism that can be used by most of these run-time systems.

4 Experimental Model

4.1 Benchmarks

For this study, we used all but one of the SPEC2000 integer benchmarks. We omitted the benchmark *perlbmk* because of problems in running it within our simulation environment. All benchmarks were simulated to completion except the benchmark *vpr*, which was simulated for 1B instructions[*]. Table 2 shows the number of simulated instructions for each benchmark. For most benchmarks, we used modified versions of the input sets provided by SPEC in order to get benchmark instances that simulated completely in a reasonable amount of time.

All benchmarks were compiled using the Compaq Alpha C compiler DEC C V5.9 with optimization level 4. At this level of optimization, the compiler performs in-lining, loop unrolling, and code replication to eliminate branches.

4.2 Simulation Environment

Our simulation framework is built upon the Alpha instruction-level simulator provided as the core of the SimpleScalar 3.0 tool set. For the studies done in this paper, we use an instruction trace analyzer that emulates a frame constructor and models a frame cache and branch bias table.

---
[*]The benchmark vpr undergoes to two phases of execution (placement and routing). We cover all of the placement phase and part of the routing phase in our simulations.

Benchmark	Instructions	Input Set
bzip2	289M	modified SPEC test input
crafty	620M	modified SPEC test input
eon	609M	SPEC test input (cook)
gap	490M	modified SPEC test input
gcc	283M	jump.i -o jump.o
gzip	870M	modified SPEC test input
mcf	413M	modified SPEC train input
parser	508M	modified SPEC test input
twolf	574M	modified SPEC train input
vortex	265M	modified SPEC train input
vpr	1000M	SPEC test input

Table 2. Benchmarks used in simulations.

5 Evaluation

In this section we evaluate two techniques for frame construction. The first technique is based on a simple static analysis of branch behavior. Branches that are highly biased above a particular threshold are promoted into assertions. The second technique uses branch correlation to identify instances of branches for promotion.

Since we are proposing a frame construction technique for use with dynamic optimization, we have only considered frames above a minimum size. Small frames are unlikely to provide substantial benefit over basic blocks in terms of optimization opportunity, and instead can incur performance overhead that cannot be recovered. We therefore discard frames consisting of fewer than 3 basic blocks or fewer than 16 instructions from consideration. We also set an upper limit on frame size to accommodate restrictions imposed by real hardware (for instance, line size in the frame cache or number of outstanding stores in a store queue). Frames are truncated at the 256th instruction.

We use three primary metrics to evaluate our frame construction techniques: average dynamic frame size, frame completion rate, and coverage of the instruction stream. Average frame size is the average size in number of instructions of a frame measured over all committed frames. The frame completion ratio measures how likely a frame is to commit once issued. A frame does not commit if any of its assertions fires. The completion rate therefore is a measure of how often all assertions within a frame are correct. Frame coverage measures the fraction of the dynamic instructions that is derived from committed frames. For example, 80% coverage indicates that 80% of the i-stream came from instructions encapsulated within a frame.

5.1 Static frame construction

Static frame construction is performed by using a profiling compiler to first identify branches to promote into assertions. The compiler then promotes candidate branches and arranges their blocks into sequential frames, keeping the original copies to handle a firing assertion. An example of static frame construction is demonstrated in the example in Figure 1.

We evaluated a scheme for static frame construction by emulating an idealized compiler technique within our experimental framework. We first profiled each benchmark on a training input set to identify branches that are 97%[†] likely to go to a particular target. These candidate branches are treated as assertions in subsequent simulations of each benchmark on the measurement input sets listed in Table 2. In effect, we are modeling a compiler that is ideally able to promote every highly biased branch (conditional, indirect, and return) into an assertion and construct frames out of all paths containing sequences of 2 or more assertions.

Table 3 shows the average frame size, completion rate and coverage for each of the benchmarks. Also included is the number of unique frames generated by this static technique. With static frame construction, frames average 66 instructions in length, have a 97% probability of complete execution, and cover 50% of the instruction stream.

	Ave Frame Size	Completion Rate	Coverage	Assertions per Frame	Unique Frames
bzip2	137	91%	61%	15.9	1412
crafty	64	98%	42%	3.2	3954
eon	78	99%	57%	3.1	7210
gap	48	95%	53%	3.6	3844
gcc	37	99%	40%	3.6	21720
gzip	98	95%	59%	5.9	1423
mcf	93	96%	33%	6.1	1092
parser	33	99%	50%	4.1	3835
twolf	39	99%	54%	3.4	4497
vortex	58	99%	82%	5.2	8178
vpr	42	99%	18%	2.7	3428
Ave	66	97%	50%	5.2	5508

Table 3. Effectiveness of Static Frame Construction.

Figure 4 shows the distribution of frame sizes observed during execution, averaged over all benchmarks. Each bar represents a span of four sizes. For example the bar labeled 16 represents the dynamic frequency of frames of size 16, 17, 18, and 19 instructions. It indicates that frames of this

---
[†]We chose the 97% after investigating several thresholds. We selected one that maximizes size while not compromising completion rates.

size account for slightly over 9% of all frames. The distribution is wide, however the bulk of frames are between 16 and 48 instructions long.

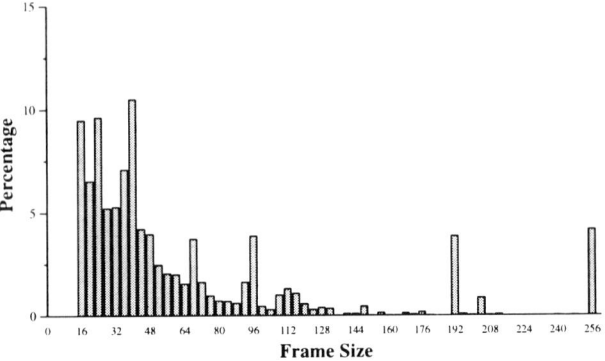

Figure 4. Distribution of statically-generated frame sizes at run-time.

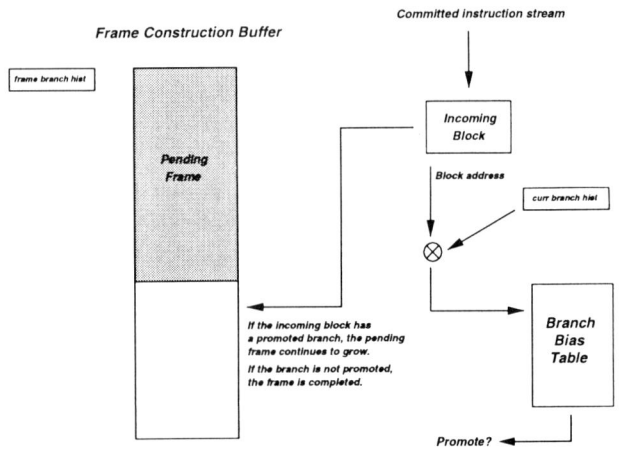

Figure 5. A hardware-based constructor that utilizes branch correlation.

5.2 Dynamic frame construction

A variety of basic research in branch prediction [14, 2] has provided substantial insights into the relationships among dynamic branch instructions. These studies have identified two types of basic correlation: *local correlation*, where a branch's current direction is highly correlated to its previous directions, and *global correlation*, where a branch's current direction is highly correlated to the direction of any previous branch or branches.

The dynamic techniques we explore in this section rely upon global correlation between branches to guide promotion from branches to assertions. Figure 5 provides a high-level view of the construction technique.

The frame constructor hashes (using XOR) the fetch address of each incoming block of committed instructions with the committed branch history to index into the branch bias table [8]. The bias table keeps track of whether the branch ending the block has gone in the same direction for a particular number of successive occurrences. If it has, the bias table indicates that the branch should be promoted. In our experiments, the bias table is configured to promote if the branch repeats its direction 32 consecutive times. Figure 6 shows the structure of the bias table. Once the 5-bit counter has saturated, the branch is promoted and the entire block is added to the frame construction buffer and the pending frame continues to grow. Once a branch is encountered that is not promoted, the block is added and the pending frame is considered complete. A separate bias table is maintained for indirect branches and returns. For such branches, a single bit for last direction does not suffice. A target address must be kept in each entry.

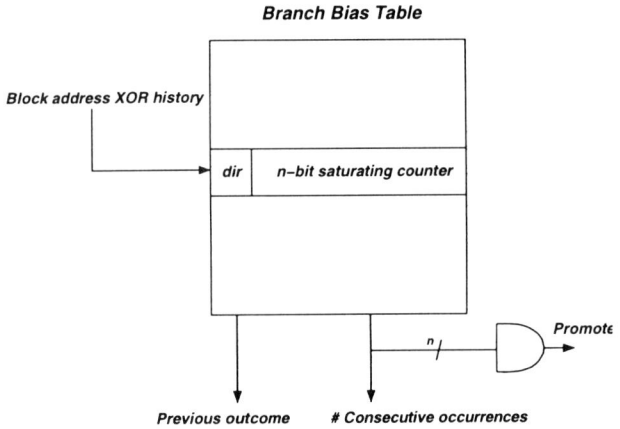

Figure 6. Branch bias table for conditional branches.

We also *demote* assertions back into branches when we detect that their behavior has changed. Using the branch bias table, we also track firing assertions to determine if they should be demoted back into branches. An assertion is allowed to fire once before it is demoted. A demoted assertion causes the frame containing it to be discarded.

The starting branch history of each frame (i.e., the committed history at the first branch in the frame) is kept with each frame. This history is essentially a prefix that identifies the instance of each promoted branch within a frame. For example, if the history of frame ABCDE is XYZ, then XYZ was used to decide whether or not to promote branch A, YZA was used to decide the promotion of B, and so forth. The starting history XYZ forms a *signature* for the frame and specifies when it should be invoked. Whenever the current history contains XYZ and the current fetch address is

A, the frame sequencing mechanism attempts to fetch the frame ABCDE.

The crux of this frame construction technique hinges on the observation that a branch can be separated into instances based on the path leading up to the branch. Once separated this way, a greater number of branches tend to exhibit biased behavior. This is the same phenomenon exploited by two-level branch predictors. Said another way, the outcome of a branch tends to be correlated to the outcomes of branches, or path, before it. The history used in the promotion decision helps separate branches into these biased instances.

We gathered branch information in two ways: global history and path history. Global history is a recording of the n most recent conditional branch outcomes. Path history is a recording of the n most recent branch target addresses. Global history can more compactly represent branch history because only a single bit is required to encode a branch direction. Path history is less compact. It requires more bits per target in order to uniquely identify the target from all others. In this way, the information stored in the path history can completely identify paths in cases where global history would be ambiguous. Also, path history can capture targets of indirect branches whereas global history cannot.

First we measure the fraction of all dynamic branches that are promoted into assertions as a function of path history length. Figure 7 demonstrates that as path history is increased beyond 6 targets, fewer than 20% of all dynamic branches actually remain as branches. The rest are promoted into assertions. Of these assertions, less than 0.5% ever fire. This data was collected using a bias table that promoted after 32[‡] consecutive similar occurrences.

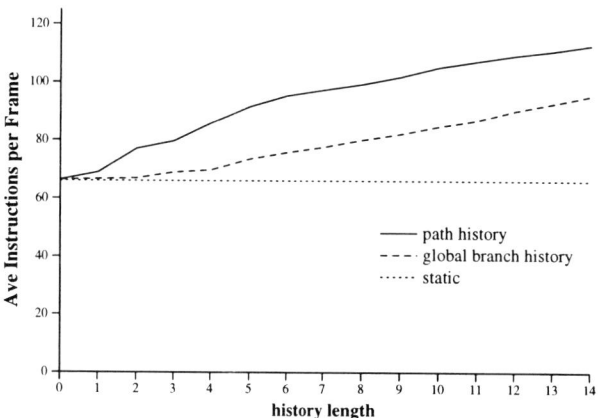

Figure 8. Average dynamic frame size as a function of history used in frame construction. Bias threshold = 32.

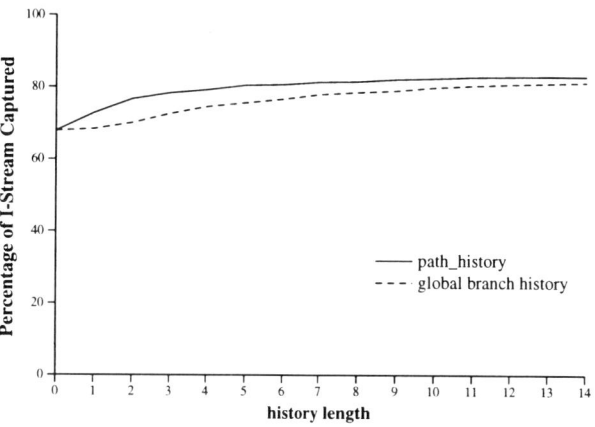

Figure 9. Frame coverage of the i-stream as a function of history. Bias threshold = 32.

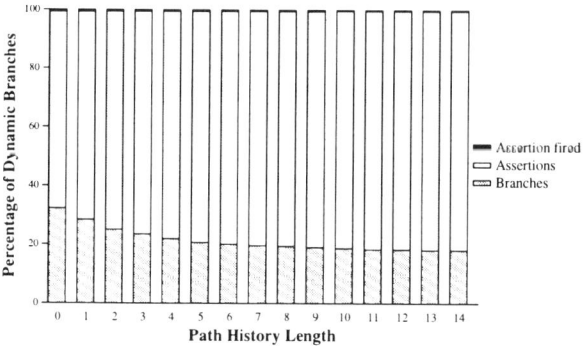

Figure 7. Fraction of dynamic branches converted into assertions. Bias threshold = 32.

Using an ideal version of this frame construction technique (i.e., a bias table that suffers no interference and an ideal hardware frame cache), we measured the effects of branch correlation on frame construction.

Figure 8 demonstrates the average size of frames as measured on the benchmark set using both global branch history and path history. Figure 9 shows the coverage of the instruction stream. In these experiments, the bias table was configured to promote branches into assertions after 32 consecutive similar outcomes. The important trend is that even adding a small amount of branch correlation to the promotion decisions causes the size and coverage of the instruction stream increase. The completion rate of the frames remains nearly constant at 97% (this indicates that the per-assertion fire rate actually decreases because the average number of assertions per frame increases).

The data in Figures 7 and 8 indicate that decreasing the total dynamic branch count by even a small percent-

---

[‡] We use a threshold of 32 throughout this paper. After extensive studies on promotion thresholds, we determined that a threshold of 32 produces large frames with low assertion rates.

age causes a significant increase in frame size. This is because, after a certain critical number of branches have been promoted into assertions, promoting more branches causes adjoining frames to be coalesced into larger frames.

Average frame size serves as a gross summary of behavior. Firstly, this is because frame size has a wide distribution as demonstrated in Figure 10. There are small frames and very large frames (almost 12% of all frames are the maximum 256 instructions long). Also, each benchmark has its own characteristic distribution. Due to space constraints we have omitted the per benchmark distribution data here.

	Ave Frame Size	Completion Rate	Coverage	Assertions per Frame	Unique Frames
bzip2	180	89%	79%	18.9	1108
crafty	88	96%	85%	6.7	15432
eon	179	98%	89%	8.6	1515
gap	155	98%	96%	15.4	5662
gcc	70	96%	77%	8.2	24687
gzip	89	95%	79%	5.6	1505
mcf	52	96%	71%	6.7	2097
parser	46	98%	78%	6.2	7629
twolf	66	99%	82%	6.8	2533
vortex	135	99%	94%	13.4	3273
vpr	61	99%	74%	4.8	2656
path	102	97%	82%	9.2	6191
global	82	97%	79%	7.4	13324
static	66	97%	50%	5.2	5508

Table 4. Per benchmark statistics for a constructor using a 9 element path history.

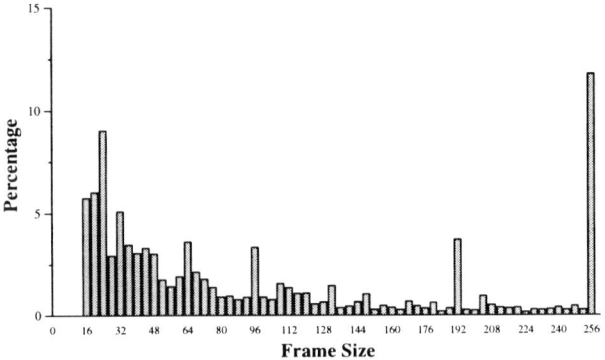

Figure 10. Distribution of dynamic frame sizes constructed using a 9 element path history.

We do however include a per benchmark average of the 9 element path history scheme on the three important metrics, plus the average number of assertions per frame, and the overall number of dynamically generated frames. Included for reference is the overall average of the static scheme and the dynamic scheme utilizing a 9-bit global history.

The frame properties resulting from path-history based frame construction are superior. One particular item of note is the relatively high number of unique frames generated via global history. We suspect this has to do with the ambiguity surrounding global history.

Overall, the results are promising. With a dynamic frame construction utilizing a 9 element path history, we are able to construct frames that span an average of 102 instructions, encapsulate over 9 branches, and have a 97% chance of complete execution. These frame characteristics make atomic frame construction useful for optimization. The reduction in dynamic branches opens opportunity for less complex fetch hardware. In the next section, we demonstrate that even with the simulated effects of finite hardware, our frame constructor is able to sustain good results.

While we have been calling this frame construction technique a dynamic frame construction technique because of its use of run-time branch information, Young et al [15] proposed a mechanism that can be adapted to exploit such dynamic information statically by creating duplicate versions of branches specific to an execution path.

5.3 Hardware for frame construction

In this section, we examine the effects of using a finite sized branch bias table and a finite sized frame cache on the frame constructor.

In the first experiment, we examine the effects of bias table size. The data plotted in Figure 11 demonstrate the effects on frame size of using 16KB, 32KB, and 64KB bias tables. Also, each configuration uses a 4KB indirect branch bias table. The threshold for promotion was set to 32.

The bias table uses a 9 element path history maintained as suggested by Stark et al [13]. They proposed maintaining path history by XORing new targets into the path history and XORing old targets out. Along the way, each target is rotated to encode each target's position within the history. The number of bits selected from each target address depends on the size of the bias table. For example, a 32KB bias table uses 15 bits from each target address in forming the path history.

The frames generated by using finite sized bias tables peak at slightly over 80 instructions. The drop in frame length between a 64KB bias table and a 16KB bias table is significant but not severe.

Two things of note: First, the hardware frame constructor mechanism uses committed branch information and therefore requires no recovery mechanism for misspeculations as would a branch predictor in the frontend of a processor. Second, our bias table suffers from negative interference (as

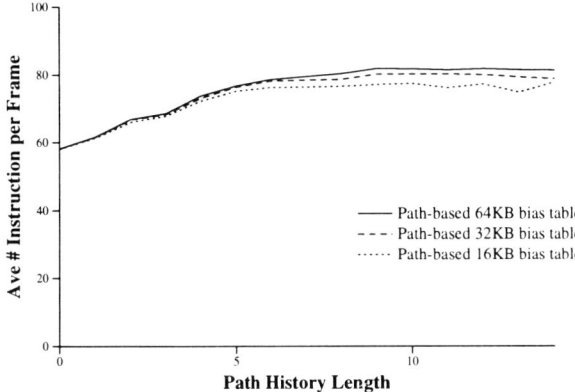

Figure 11. Dynamic frame size for various sized hardware bias tables.

demonstrated by the degradation from ideal to finite-sized). Many of the proposed interference reduction techniques explored for branch predictors such as filtering and agree prediction can be applied here to improve performance of the bias tables.

Next, we evaluate the effects of a finite sized frame cache. The data presented in Table 5 lists the results of using a 256 element frame cache with a 32KB branch bias table and a 4KB indirect branch bias table. Frame construction uses a 9 element path history. Promotion threshold is again set to 32 consecutive occurrences.

The data indicate that the constructor is able to coalesce almost 8 basic blocks together to form atomic regions of over 80 instructions, 7 of which are assertions. Almost 70% of the dynamic instruction stream is covered by these frames. These characteristics of frames not only present useful opportunity for dynamic optimization, but the increase in the span of branchless regions makes the job of a processor's fetch engine much simpler. A single fetch can produce 80 instructions with only a single branch prediction.

To give further context to the frame characteristics presented in Table 5, we also include the branch prediction accuracy of a small 4KB gshare using 14-bits of global branch history. Frame completion rates are high even though branch prediction accuracy is not. However, most benchmarks that suffer from low branch prediction accuracies also have smaller average frame sizes.

We measure frame cache size by the number of elements cached rather than number of bytes of storage because frame size is dependent on optimizations performed by an optimizer. Hand optimizations of high frequency frames in the SPECint95 benchmarks suite resulted in considerably smaller frames than we started with. When smaller frame cache sizes are evaluated, the primary change in metrics is a reduction in coverage. A 64 element frame cache gets a coverage of 58%, a 128 element frame cache gets 64%, and a 256 element frame cache gets 67%. Frame size remains nearly constant.

Degradation from ideal hardware is significant, but there is opportunity for increasing the effectiveness of a frame cache using the hot spot identification techniques of Merten et al [7]. They have determined that the behavior of frame-like regions of the control flow exhibit hot-cold behavior. At certain regions of execution, some frames are likely to be more frequently utilized than others. Using their technique it is possible to only cache frames that are detected to be hot, and to drop cold frames, and thereby use the limited capacity of the frame cache more effectively.

6 Analysis

In this section, we provide some insight into the frame construction techniques. We provide some ancillary data to shed light on the types of program behavior that are being exploited by the frame constructor.

6.1 Rationale behind what is happening

Frame construction, both dynamic and static, exploit biased branches. Based on our experimentation, we found that via profiling approximately 55% of all branches are categorized as promotable biased branches using the criterion we mention in Section 5.1. This number increases to 67% when the classification is done dynamically using a bias table. The number increases to over 80% when branch correlation is added to the classification.

The phenomenon being captured by the dynamic frame constructor is very similar to the phenomenon captured by a 2-level branch predictor. Take for example a string of correct predictions made by a 2-level predictor such as gshare. The initial correct prediction is made by indexing the predictor with the starting global branch history and a fetch address. At the end of the cycle the fetch engine provides a fetch block of instructions, a new global history, and a new fetch address. In the next cycle, the new history and fetch address index the fetch mechanism to produce another fetch block, history, and fetch address. This cycle continues until an event such as a branch misprediction, or BTB miss, or cache miss causes a disruption. The process begins with an initial history and an initial fetch address. The frame constructor *unfurls* this process by prepackaging the fetch blocks with the predictions; both can be known *a priori* by traversing history information stored in the bias table. Since the cost of an assertion can be higher than that of a branch misprediction, we use larger counters in the bias table than in the standard pattern history table (5-bit as opposed to 2-bit) to gain more confidence about branch behavior. The

	Average Frame Size	Completion Rate	Coverage	Assertions per Frame	Unique Frames	4KB gshare
bzip2	179	89%	78%	18.9	1151	97.4
crafty	75	96%	61%	5.3	13643	92.4
eon	87	98%	46%	4.1	1613	97.1
gap	114	96%	88%	11.1	7569	98.0
gcc	51	97%	36%	5.7	21033	89.4
gzip	89	95%	77%	5.6	1579	90.7
mcf	53	96%	68%	6.6	2051	90.1
parser	43	99%	69%	5.9	6946	93.1
twolf	56	99%	67%	5.6	3569	90.4
vortex	89	98%	76%	8.4	5769	97.6
vpr	52	99%	75%	4.1	3085	85.0
Average	81	97%	67%	6.9	6182	
Ave - Ideal Dynamic	102	97%	82%	9.2	6191	
Ave - Ideal Static	66	97%	50%	5.2	5508	

Table 5. Frame stats with 256 entry frame cache, 32KB+4KB bias tables, and 9 element path history.

starting address and starting branch history serve as a fetch signature for a frame created with this technique.

6.2 Is it simply loop unrolling?

One phenomenon that both static and dynamic frame construction may be capturing is loop unrolling. For all data presented thus far, the loop unrolling option was enabled when the benchmarks were compiled using the Compaq Alpha compiler, so frame construction was able to boost atomic region size beyond the loop unrolling performed by a production C compiler.

We explored the effects of compiler loop unrolling on the frame constructor by running an experiment with binaries generated with loop unrolling disabled. Table 6 presents the results. The table contains the average across all benchmarks for a frame constructor utilizing a 9 element path history. The first two data rows of the table present the results with compiler unrolling enabled and with it disabled. The data in the third row was measured using a frame constructor that was inhibited from adding duplicate blocks to a pending frame (i.e., if a frame already contained block X, then the frame would be considered complete if another copy of X were attempted to be added). This is a very severe way of restricting the effects of loop unrolling because it factors out loops that would be otherwise difficult for a compiler to unroll, such as loops with complex control paths or function calls. This test was run on binaries generated with compiler unrolling enabled.

Based on the data collected with loop unrolling disabled, the effect of compiler unrolling on frame construction is minimal. The frame constructor exploits loops, as demonstrated by the sharp drop in frame size and coverage when

	Ave Frame Size	Completion Rate	Coverage	Unique Frames
W/ unrolling	102	97%	82%	6191
W/o unrolling	105	96%	90%	6774
No duplicates	74	98%	71%	4581

Table 6. The effects of loop unrolling on frame construction using a 9-element path history.

duplicate blocks are inhibited. Nonetheless, frame size and coverage is still substantial.

6.3 Phased behavior

Static construction relies on profiling and is therefore brittle to the difference in behavior between the execution profiles and actual execution. Dynamic construction, with extra hardware costs, can adapt to actual execution behavior.

Another benefit of dynamic frame construction over static construction is the ability for frames to be generated and destroyed depending on the dynamic behavior. A branch may be biased during a section of a program, and not biased during another. Such phased behavior is more easily exploited by a dynamic mechanism than a static one.

We measured the dynamic variation in branch promotions throughout the execution of each benchmark. For every branch instance (branch preceded by specific path) that executed at least 3200 times (this number was chosen because our promotion threshold is 32, thus the warmup cost is a smaller factor), we counted how often the branch instance was observed as an assertion and how often it was not. We found that a majority of such branches were encountered as promoted only between 90% and 95% of the time, indicating that there are periods of execution where these branches have irregular behavior.

7 Conclusion

Frame construction using assertions creates large atomic regions of instructions that have a very high probability of complete execution. We demonstrate that incorporating branch correlation into the branch promotion decision results in larger frames with a larger degree of coverage of the instruction stream, even when finite sized hardware is used for frame construction and frame caching.

We submit that the dynamic frame constructor is pre-packaging the instructions associated with easy-to-predict branches into a frame, leaving the harder-to-predict branches as the connective branches between one frame and the next. From a hardware standpoint, this is good because with a single fetch, several cycles worth of instructions can be streamed out of the frame cache allowing multiple cycles for the prediction of these connective branches.

Our analysis demonstrates that the frame constructor is able to unroll loops and in-line function calls in situations difficult for a compiler to exploit. In addition to unrolling, the frame constructor is able to exploit run-time control stability in paths that contain no loops as well.

We view these results as preliminary; they are the first step for rePLay, which is a hardware/software framework for dynamic optimization. Frames serve as the regions of optimization within rePLay in the same way that a trace is the basic unit within a trace scheduling compiler. Frames are different from superblocks and hyperblocks in that they contain only a single path of execution and no side entrances or side exits. This gives a dynamic optimizer with greater leeway in performing low-overhead optimizations.

8 Acknowledgments

We thank both the other members of the Advanced Computing Systems group and Prof. Steve Lumetta for their valuable insights in the development of these ideas. We also thank Intel and Hewlett-Packard for their generosity in providing equipment.

References

[1] V. Bala, E. Duesterwald, and S. Banerjia. Transparent dynamic optimization: The design and implementation of Dynamo. Technical Report HPL-1999-78, Hewlett-Packard Laboratories, June 1999.

[2] M. Evers, S. J. Patel, R. S. Chappell, and Y. N. Patt. An analysis of correlation and predictability: What makes two-level branch predictors work. In *Proceedings of the 25th Annual International Symposium on Computer Architecture*, pages 52 – 61, 1998.

[3] J. A. Fisher. Trace scheduling: A technique for global microcode compaction. *IEEE Transactions on Computers*, C-30(7):478–490, July 1981.

[4] B. Grant, M. Mock, M. Phillipose, C. Chambers, and S. J. Eggers. DyC: An expressive annotation-directed dynamic compiler for C. Technical Report UW-CSE-97-03-03, University of Washington, May 1999.

[5] A. Klaiber. The technology behind Crusoe processors. Technical report, Transmeta Corporation, Jan. 2000.

[6] S. Melvin and Y. Patt. Enhancing instruction scheduling with a block-structured ISA. *International Journal of Parallel Programming*, 23(3):221–243, June 1995.

[7] M. C. Merten, A. R. Trick, E. M. Nystrom, R. D. Barnes, and W. W. Hwu. A hardware mechanism for dynamic extraction and relayout of program hot spots. In *Proceedings of the 27th Annual International Symposium on Computer Architecture*, 2000.

[8] S. J. Patel, M. Evers, and Y. N. Patt. Improving trace cache effectiveness with branch promotion and trace packing. In *Proceedings of the 25th Annual International Symposium on Computer Architecture*, 1998.

[9] S. J. Patel, D. H. Friendly, and Y. N. Patt. Evaluation of design options for the trace cache fetch mechanism. *IEEE Transactions on Computers*, 48(2):435–446, Feb. 1999.

[10] S. J. Patel and S. S. Lumetta. rePLay : a hardware framework for dynamic program optimization. Technical Report CRHC-99-16, University of Illinois Technical Report, Dec. 1999.

[11] A. Peleg and U. Weiser. Dynamic flow instruction cache memory organized around trace segments independent of virtual address line. U.S. Patent Number 5,381,533, 1994.

[12] E. Rotenberg, S. Bennett, and J. E. Smith. Trace cache: a low latency approach to high bandwidth instruction fetching. In *Proceedings of the 29th Annual ACM/IEEE International Symposium on Microarchitecture*, 1996.

[13] J. Stark, M. Evers, and Y. N. Patt. Variable length path branch prediction. In *Proceedings of the 8th International Conference on Architectural Support for Programming Languages and Operating Systems*, pages 170 – 179, 1998.

[14] T.-Y. Yeh and Y. N. Patt. Two-level adaptive branch prediction. In *Proceedings of the 24th Annual ACM/IEEE International Symposium on Microarchitecture*, pages 51–61, 1991.

[15] C. Young and M. D. Smith. Improving the accuracy of static branch prediction using branch correlation. In *Proceedings of the 6th International Conference on Architectural Support for Programming Languages and Operating Systems*, pages 232–241, 1994.

Superscalar Architecture II

Reducing Wire Delay Penalty through Value Prediction

Joan-Manuel Parcerisa and Antonio González
Dept. d'Arquitectura de Computadors, Universitat Politècnica de Catalunya
c/. Jordi Girona, 1-3 Mòdul C6
08034 Barcelona, Spain
{jmanel,antonio}@ac.upc.es

Abstract

In this work we show that value prediction can be used to avoid the penalty of long wire delays by predicting the data that is communicated through these long wires and validating the prediction locally where the value is produced. Only in the case of misprediction, the long wire delay is experienced.

We apply this concept to a clustered microarchitecture in order to reduce inter-cluster communication. The predictability of values provides the dynamic instruction partitioning hardware with less constraints to optimize the trade-off between communication requirements and workload balance, which is the most critical issue of the partitioning scheme. We show that value prediction reduces the penalties caused by inter-cluster communication by 18% on average for a realistic implementation of a 4-cluster microarchitecture.

1. Introduction

Recent studies point out that two major problems for scaling-up current superscalar microarchitectures will be the growing impact of wire delays [1, 2, 13], and the increasing complexity of some critical components, such as the issue logic, the bypass, the register file and the rename logic [16], since they may have a direct influence on the clock cycle time.

One of the proposed solutions to this problem is based on clustering. In a clustered microarchitecture some of the critical components are partitioned into simpler structures, and the impact of wire delays is reduced as far as signals are kept local within the clusters. In a clustered architecture, deciding which instructions are executed in each cluster becomes a key issue. We will refer to this task as code partitioning. A code partitioning scheme determines how the dynamic instruction stream is split among the different clusters. Data dependences among instructions in different partitions correspond to inter-cluster communications, which use long wires and have a high associated latency. In this work we will focus on dynamic mechanisms for partitioning the instruction stream, implemented through a small hardware that steers instructions to clusters, the steering logic.

Minimizing the impact of inter-cluster communication delays is one of the main objectives of any code partitioning scheme. The solution that we propose in this work is to eliminate data dependences that cross the partition boundaries by predicting the values that flow among them. Value prediction has been largely investigated in the context of superscalar processors, and it is not our purpose to design another predictor but to investigate its potential to reduce slow inter-cluster communications on a clustered architecture, and to provide a new source of performance improvements. In this paper we show that value prediction can significantly improve the performance of the steering logic by providing a less dense data dependence graph which results in less communication requirements and better opportunities to balance the workload.

It is known that the IPC of a clustered architecture is lower than that of an equivalent centralized organization without the inter-cluster communication delays. It is also expected that value prediction may increase the IPC in both cases. However, we show that the clustered architecture benefits from value prediction more than a centralized one, since value prediction removes some inter-cluster communications. In particular, we show that the IPC degradation caused by inter-cluster communications can be reduced by 18% through a simple value prediction scheme when the steering logic is designed to take advantage of the value predictor.

The rest of this paper is organized as follows. Section 2 presents the assumed clustered architecture. Section 3 presents the partitioning heuristic implemented by the steering logic, and its specific adaptations to take advantage of value prediction, and provides a performance evaluation. In Section 4, a sensitivity analysis regarding communication latency, communication bandwidth and predictor table size is performed. Section 5 reviews other related work. And finally, the main conclusions are summarized in Section 6.

2. Microarchitecture

The target processor microarchitecture is a clustered implementation of an 8-way out-of-order issue superscalar processor with a 6 stage pipeline (fetch, decode, issue, execute, writeback and commit). The processor front-end (fetch and decode stages) is a centralized structure, and we assume that it has an aggressive instruction fetch mechanism to stress the instruction issue and execution subsystems. The processor core is divided into N homogeneous clusters: each cluster has its own instruction queue, a physical register file, a set of functional units, and the corresponding data bypasses among these functional units. We experiment with several configurations (targeting different technologies and clock rates) having 1, 2 and 4 clusters. While the register file access time and issue time are assumed to be constant in all cases, structure sizes are scaled down with the degree of clustering. Therefore, register files have respectively 128, 80 and 56 physical registers per cluster, and instruction queue lengths are 64, 32 and 16 entries. The reorder buffer length (128 entries), the total number of functional units (8), and the total issue width (8) is kept constant through all the configurations. The main architectural parameters are described in Section 2.4.

Local bypasses within a cluster are responsible for forwarding result values produced in the cluster to the inputs of the functional units in the same cluster. A local bypass takes 0 cycles, i.e. a value produced in cycle i can be an input of a local functional unit in cycle $i+1$. Inter-cluster bypasses are responsible for forwarding values among functional units of different clusters. Since inter-cluster bypasses require long wires, they will likely take several cycles in future technologies [1]. Therefore, we have assumed a one-cycle latency for inter-cluster bypasses in the basic configurations, although we also evaluate the effects of longer latencies. Latency is not the only penalty of inter-cluster communications. Also bandwidth is relevant, since it directly affects the number of register file write ports, and the complexity of the bypass logic. We first assume an unbounded number of interconnection paths in order to isolate our experiments from the effect of possible bandwidth bottlenecks, and then we evaluate the effects of having a limited inter-cluster communication bandwidth.

2.1. Handling register copies

In a processor with N clusters, instructions are renamed at the decode stage, by means of a register map table with N fields per logical register, that allows up to N different mappings of the same register. An additional bit per

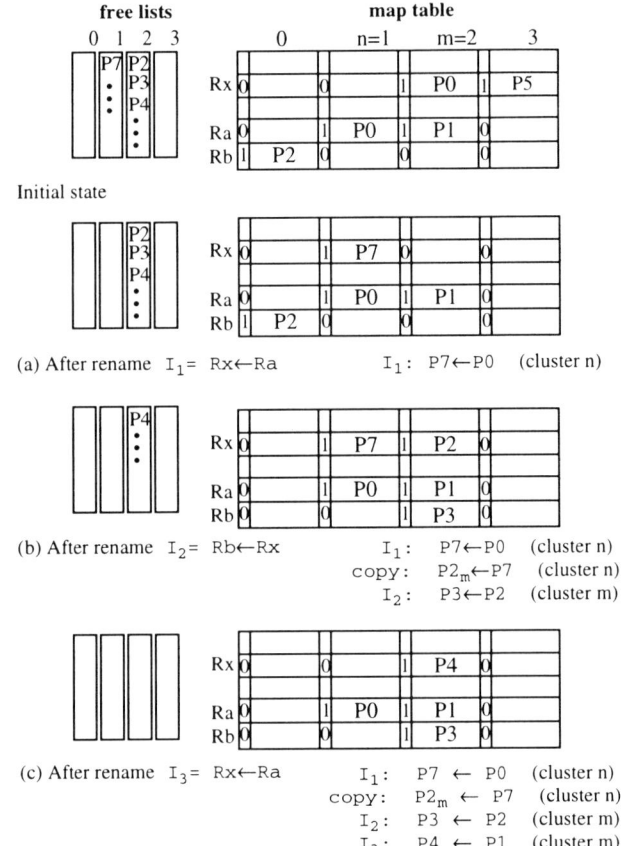

Figure 1. Example of renaming 3 instructions. I_2 requires to copy Rx from cluster n to m

field indicates whether the mapping is valid and if so, it points to a physical register in the corresponding cluster. All logical registers must have at least one valid mapping. Each cluster has a free pool of physical registers from where they are allocated when needed.

When an instruction I_1 is decoded (see Figure 1(a)), and it is assigned to cluster n by the steering logic, its source operands are renamed by looking at the field n of the map table. If the instruction has a destination register Rx, a new free physical register is allocated from the free-list of cluster n, the new mapping is written in the field n of the map table, and the other fields are set invalid, to denote that Rx is not currently mapped to any physical register in these clusters.

Let us assume that a subsequent dependent instruction I_2, that reads register Rx, is decoded and steered to cluster m, different from n (see Figure 1(b)). When I_2 is renamed, the field m of the map table entry for register Rx is found invalid. Normal instructions are not allowed to access the register files of remote clusters. Instead, they require remote operands to be copied from one register file to another by means of special *copy* instructions generated on demand during the renaming stage. Therefore, in this example a new physical register is allocated in cluster m, to store the copy of register Rx for future reuse, and its mapping is written in the field m of the map table entry for Rx. This field becomes valid, and its mapping is used to rename the source operand of I_2. Then, a *copy* instruction is dispatched to cluster n. This instruction will forward the value of the physical register in cluster n to the physical register in cluster m. This *copy* instruction will be handled by the issue logic as any other instruction, i.e., it will be executed once its source operand and the needed resources are available.

Note that during the renaming of an instruction, just one physical register for its destination register is allocated. Additional physical registers to store copies of it in other clusters are only allocated on demand if they are required by subsequent instructions that do not execute in the same cluster. All these physical registers will be freed by the first subsequent instruction that writes to the same logical register, when it is committed (see instruction I_3, in Figure 1(c)). This scheme requires some degree of register replication which dynamically adapts to the program requirements and is much lower than replicating the whole register file. Compared with a full replication scheme, it has also less communication requirements and thus, less inter-cluster bypass paths and less register file write ports.

If the processor has a limited number of inter-cluster bypass paths, they must be reserved by the issue mechanism like any other resource. Copy instructions provide a simple mechanism to allocate the required bypasses and schedule inter-cluster communications. They also provide a simple method for precise state recovery, since copy instructions are inserted in the reorder buffer like normal instructions. However, since a copy instruction makes the dependence chain one node longer, it increases by one cycle the total effective latency between the producer and the remote dependent instruction (in addition to the bus latency). A particular implementation could optimize this, either by shortening the tags propagation delay between clusters or by implementing specific hardware that avoids generating copy instructions. However, we have not assumed any of these optimizations in this work.

2.2. Value prediction

The microarchitecture implements a stride value predictor [8, 9, 19] that predicts the source operands of the instructions. There is a value prediction table indexed by the PC and the operand order (left/right). We first assume a very large table (128K entries) to isolate the results from the effects of a limited table size, and we later evaluate the impact of a table with sizes ranging from 1K to 16K entries. Each entry contains the last value, the last observed stride and a 2-bit counter that assigns confidence to the prediction. Since each prediction involves a table access and an addition, we assume that value predictions are available 1 cycle after the fetch, i.e. at the decode stage. Table updates are done at decode time.

When a source operand is not yet available at decode time, and its predicted value is confident (the counter value is greater than 1), the instruction is dispatched speculatively and may use the predicted value. The instruction that will produce this value is identified, and it is assigned the task of verifying that its output matches the prediction. The verification occurs during the writeback stage of the producer instruction, and it takes one cycle. If it fails, the dependent misspeculated instruction is invalidated and reissued.

We have assumed a selective invalidation and reissue mechanism [17], i.e. after the mispredicted instruction is reissued and executed, a new value is produced and propagated to dependent instructions, which in turn reissue, and so on. Only the instructions that depend on the mispredicted instruction are invalidated. The mechanism is in fact the existing issue mechanism, and therefore we have assumed no additional penalty for each instruction restart.

For a clustered architecture, this speculation procedure is further extended, in order to reduce inter-cluster communications. The extension apply to the case when a source operand is not currently mapped on the cluster where the instruction is being dispatched. In this case, the operand is predicted regardless of whether it is available, the instruction is dispatched speculatively, and a special *verification-copy* instruction is dispatched to the cluster where the operand is produced. When issued, the verification-copy compares locally the operand with the predicted value, and just in case of mismatch, it forwards the correct value through an inter-cluster bypass, and the remote misspeculated instruction is reissued.

2.3. Steering logic

Code partitioning can be done at compile time (static) or at run time (dynamic). The first method relies on the compiler, which allocates each static instruction to a cluster, while the second method is based on a specialized hardware that decides where to distribute each dynamic instruction. The main advantage of a static partitioning is that it requires minimal hardware support, but its downside is that it requires to recompile the applications because it extends the ISA for encoding the steering information. Furthermore, it will require to recompile for each new microarchitecture generation that changes the number of clusters.

In contrast, a dynamic partitioning method does not require to recompile, because it makes clustering transparent to the compiler. In addition, the information used by the dynamic steering logic (workload balance, data dependences) is obtained directly from the actual pipeline state, rather than estimations of the compiler. Therefore, a dynamic steering scheme is more effective than a static approach because it is more adaptable to the actual processor state. This work focuses on this type of steering.

In order to maximize performance, the dynamic steering logic must address two main goals: to minimize inter-cluster communications (or their associated penalties) and to maximize the workload balance.

On one hand, inter-cluster communications introduce delays between dependent instructions, which may result in a performance loss if they stay in the critical path of execution. Determining whether a communication is critical is a hard problem, therefore a more simple goal for the steering heuristic is to minimize the number of communications.

On the other hand, when there are more ready instructions in a cluster than functional units to execute them, the excess of instructions are forced to wait, incurring an additional delay. If at the same time, another cluster has idle functional units, this additional delay would have been avoided if the steering logic had sent some instructions to a different cluster. We refer to this situation as a workload imbalance among clusters, and since it may potentially degrade the performance, a major goal of the steering logic is to prevent it from happening.

Intuitively, both goals (reducing communications and balancing workload) are sometimes conflicting, and therefore a good steering algorithm must find the optimal trade-off between them. We outline below how these two issues are addressed by the steering logic from a conceptual standpoint. Particular steering techniques are defined in Section 3

2.3.1. Communication. The valid bit associated to each field of the map table indicates whether the logical register may be directly read in the corresponding cluster without requiring a communication. Therefore, the steering logic uses this information to minimize communications by choosing a cluster where all or most of the source operands of an instruction are currently mapped. In some cases, when an operand is mapped in more than one cluster due to previously dispatched copy instructions, but the value is not yet available, the choice of clusters should be narrowed to the cluster where the value will be available sooner, to avoid the instruction being needlessly delayed by a communication.

2.3.2. Workload balance. To improve the workload balance, the steering logic must detect when there is a workload imbalance and how much unbalanced it is, and must also determine which is the least loaded cluster. There are many alternatives to determine at run-time the individual workloads of the clusters and their relative workload imbalance. In other words, there are several figures that can be used to measure these features. From the description given above, we intuitively define the workload imbalance at a given instant of time as the total number of ready instructions that cannot issue, due to having exceeded the issue width in their respective clusters, but could have issued in other clusters since they have idle functional units. This figure (we will refer to it as metric NREADY), is what we report in our experiments as "workload imbalance", because it corresponds to our definition. However, we also experimented several other imbalance figures to guide the steering decisions, and found the following scheme (we will refer to it as metric DCOUNT) to give the best performance:

- The processor has a signed counter in each of the N clusters that measures its workload. Its value is initially zero, and it is updated in the following way: for every instruction dispatched to a cluster, the corresponding counter in that cluster is increased by N-1, while the other N-1 counters are decreased by 1 (i.e. the sum of the counters is kept always zero). Therefore, the value stored in the counter of a given cluster is N times the difference between the total number of instructions dispatched to that cluster and the average number of instructions dispatched per cluster. The workload imbalance is calculated as the maximum absolute value of the workload counters. Note also that in the case of two clusters, a single counter will suffice.

The NREADY figure matches more exactly our definition of workload balance. However, when it is used by the steering logic, the actions taken to compensate a workload imbalance (sending instructions to the least loaded cluster) may not update immediately the NREADY figure, if some of the steered instructions are not ready. When this occurs, the corrective action may result disproportionate, and cause an imbalance in another direction or some unnecessary inter-cluster communications. This does not happen with the DCOUNT figure, since it varies instantly and in proportion to the steering decisions, which allows the steering logic to gauge more accurately the actions to compensate a workload imbalance. Thus, the steering logic uses the DCOUNT figure to determine balancing actions and we use the NREADY figure to measure and report workload balance.

2.4. Experimental framework

We perform our microarchitectural timing simulations with a modified version of the SimpleScalar tool set [3], version 3.0. It was extended to include register renaming through a physical register file, instruction queues (separate integer and FP), stride value prediction, steering logic, and a clustered processor core.

Three different configurations were simulated, having 1, 2 and 4 clusters respectively. Each was simulated with and without value prediction. The total issue width, number

Table 1. Main architecture parameters, for configurations with 1, 2 and 4 clusters

Parameter	1 Cluster config.	2 Clusters config.	4 Clusters config.
Fetch, decode & retire width	8 instructions		
Branch Predictor	Combined predictor of 1K entries with a Gshare with 64K 2-bit counters, 16 bit global history, and a bimodal predictor of 2K entries with 2-bit counters.		
ROB size	128		
Instruction queue size	64	32	16
Functional units	8 int (4 include mul/div) 4 fp (2 include fp mul/div)	4 int (2 include mul/div) 2 fp (include fp mul/div)	2 int (1 include mul/div) 1 fp (includes fp mul/div)
Issue width	8 int/ 4 fp	4 int/ 2 fp	2 int/ 1 fp
	Out-of-order issue. Loads may execute when prior store addresses are known		
Communications	1-cycle latency. Communications consume issue width and instruction queue entries		
Register file sizes	128	80	56
I-cache L1	64KB, 2-way set-associative. 32 byte lines, 1 cycle hit time, 6 cycle miss penalty		
D-cache L1	64KB, 2-way set-associative. 32 byte lines, 1 cycle hit time, 6 cycle miss penalty, 3 R/W ports		
I/D-cache L2	256 KB, 4-way set associative, 64 byte lines, 6 cycle hit time.		
Memory	8 bytes bus bandwidth to main memory, 18 cycles first chunk, 2 cycles interchunk.		

Table 2. The Mediabench benchmark suite[1]

program	input	instr. count (millions)	description
cjpeg	testimg.ppm	18.8	image
djpeg	testimg.jpg	6.0	image
epicdec	test_image.pgm.E	11.1	image
epicenc	test_image.pgm	70.6	image
g721dec	clinton.g721	421.1	audio
g721enc	clinton.pcm	440.6	audio
ghostscript	tiger.ps	899.5	PS interpreter
gsmdec	clinton.pcm.gsm	115.1	audio
gsmenc	clinton.pcm	307.1	audio
mesamipmap	m.ppm	75.2	3D graphics
mesaosdemo	o.ppm	29.7	3D graphics
mesatextgen	t.ppm	129.4	3D graphics
mpeg2dec	test.m2v	12.6	video
mpeg2enc	test.par	222.0	video
pgpdec	pgptext.pgp	108.6	encryption
pgpenc	pgptest.plain	130.6	encryption
rasta	ex5_c1.wav	26.4	audio
rawcaudio	clinton.pcm	8.7	audio
rawdaudio	clinton.adpcm	7.1	audio

(1) Many program names are renamed for convenience

of functional units, and reorder buffer length was kept constant along the configurations while the sizes of register files and instruction queues were scaled down with the number of clusters. The most relevant architecture parameters are detailed in Table 1.

We simulate all Mediabench benchmark programs [14, 12], (except for Pegwit, which could not be compiled). We chose this benchmark suite because they are representative of modern multimedia applications, which is a growing segment of the commercial workloads. In addition, they exhibit a quite high ILP, which makes them suitable for testing a wide issue superscalar architecture like the one we present here. Table 2 lists briefly program input data and run lengths. All the benchmarks were compiled for the Alpha AXP using Compaq's C compiler with the -O4 optimization level, and they were run till completion.

We define a new metric to evaluate the performance of a clustered configuration relative to that of a centralized one, with similar characteristics: the normalized N-clusters IPC Ratio ($IPCR_N$ for short) is the quotient $IPC_{N\text{-clusters}}/IPC_{1\text{-cluster}}$. It indicates the IPC degradation caused by inter-cluster communication delays on a clustered architecture, and its maximum value is 1. This metric is useful to evaluate the impact of a particular technique (e.g. value prediction) on a clustered architecture, by comparing the IPCR obtained with and without implementing the technique. An IPCR increase would indicate that the technique produces higher IPC improvements in the clustered architecture than in the centralized one, thus measuring the benefits that are exclusive to the clustered architecture, isolated from other more general improvements that affect both configurations.

3. A steering scheme for value prediction

In this section, we first introduce a steering scheme that is very effective but does not include any technique to leverage value prediction. Then we present a steering mechanism that exploits value prediction as a way to reduce communication requirements.

3.1. The baseline steering algorithm

We have evaluated several steering strategies described in previous works [4, 5], and variations of them. Finally, the best performance was obtained with an enhanced version of the "Advanced RMBS" heuristic [4], generalized for an arbitrary number of clusters, which will be the Baseline scheme considered in this paper. This algorithm

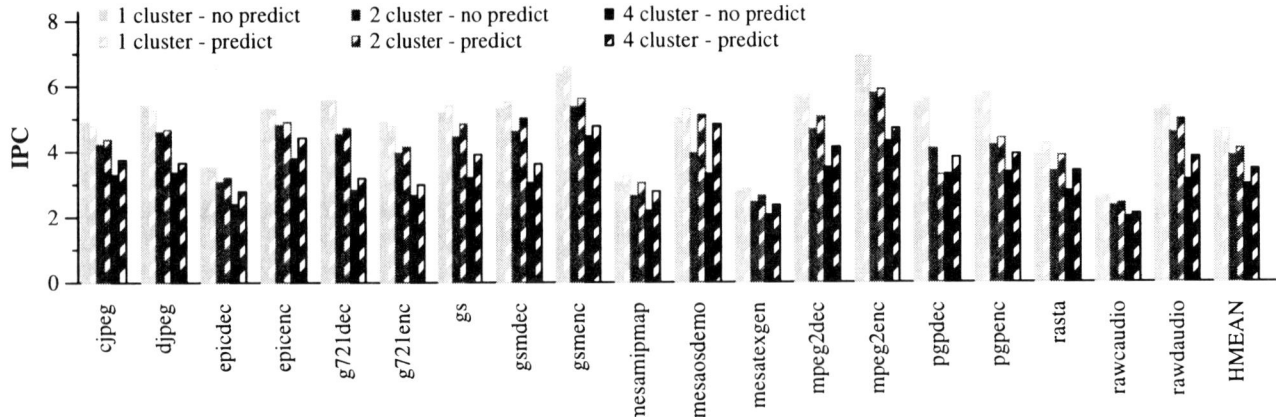

Figure 2. IPC of a 1, 2 and 4-cluster configurations (baseline steering), with value prediction, and without it

applies the criteria discussed above in the following way: in most cases, as a primary rule, it gives the highest priority to the reduction of communication penalties, and as a second rule, it tries to improve the workload balance. However, in some cases, when the workload imbalance is considered too high, the balance criterion takes precedence. The algorithm is described next, in more detail.

1. If the workload imbalance is higher than a given threshold, the current instruction is sent to the least loaded cluster.
2. Else, the clusters that will cause minimum communication penalties are identified:
   2.1. If any source operand is not available at dispatch time, select the cluster(s) where the pending operand(s) are to be produced.
   2.2. If all source operands are available, select the clusters that have the greatest number of operands currently mapped.
   2.3. If it has no source operands, select all clusters.
3. Finally, choose the least loaded cluster among those selected in step 2.

The threshold mentioned in rule 1 was set experimentally to DCOUNT=32 and DCOUNT=16 on a 4-cluster and a 2-cluster configurations, respectively.

Figure 2 shows the IPC obtained with the baseline steering algorithm for 1, 2 and 4 clusters, with value prediction and without it. The IPCs are higher when value prediction is implemented, although the improvement is rather low for the centralized configuration (2% on average, and negative for several benchmarks). The benefits are higher for the clustered organization (5% and 16% for the 2 and 4-cluster configurations respectively).

The two leftmost bars in each group in Figure 3 depict other interesting figures from the same previous experiments. Graph c shows the IPCR ratio increase provided by value prediction, which is a performance improvement specific to each clustered architecture, as discussed in Section 2.4. This graph shows a notable increase of the IPCR ratios when value prediction is implemented (in spite of a slight increase in the average workload imbalance, see graph a) which is due to a drastic communication reduction (graph b), especially for the 4-cluster configuration, where communications are also higher: $IPCR_4$ increases by 14%, from 0.65 to 0.74, and the communications rate is reduced by 44%, from 0.22 to 0.12.

3.2. Enhancing the partitioning scheme through value prediction

In this paper we focus on how value prediction may improve the performance of the steering logic in a clustered processor. We propose some modifications of the Baseline steering heuristic, based on the assumption that the predicted source operands will never cause communications or delays, and thus the steering may concentrate on improving the workload balance. The assumption is true if the prediction does not fail, but it may not hold otherwise. However, as far as the misprediction rate is kept low, these modifications may improve significantly the workload balance. The first two modifications to the steering strategy are described below, in more detail:

First, when the source operand of an instruction is predicted and it is not yet available, the steering algorithm considers it as available. By doing so, the algorithm does not force to steer the instruction to the cluster where the operand is going to be produced (if it is the only operand, rule 2.1 is not applied).

The second modification consists on considering any predicted source operand to be mapped in all clusters because, regardless of the cluster it is sent to, it will not cause any additional inter-cluster communication (unless the prediction fails and the operand is remote). In consequence, communication issues do not impose any restriction on the

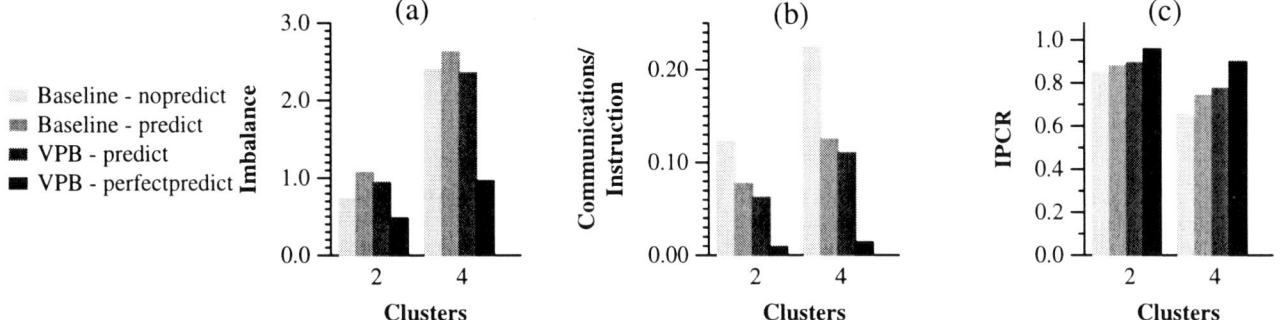

Figure 3. Comparison of 4 configurations: Baseline without and with prediction, VPB with prediction and VPB with perfect prediction. (a) Workload Imbalance (b) Communications/Instruction (c) Normalized IPCR

choice of clusters (i.e. this operand does not constrain the set of candidate clusters, if rule 2.2 is applied).

In summary, these two modifications to the baseline steering algorithm eliminate in some cases the constraints imposed by communications/delays issues (in rule 2), so that the algorithm has better opportunities for balancing the workload (since rule 3 selects one cluster from a wider choice of clusters).

We evaluated the impact of these two modifications on a 4-cluster configuration, and found that they produce a negligible average performance improvement over the baseline scheme. The average workload balance is reduced by 31% and, since imbalance correction actions (which ignore communication issues) are less frequent, one would expect also to have less communications. However, the communications ratio (which mostly determines the IPC) remains constant because there is also a communications increase due to an indiscriminate use of the optimistic initial assumptions. More specifically, if an instruction that uses a predicted source operand is sent to a cluster where it is not mapped, and the prediction fails, then this instruction will be re-issued non-speculatively, and a communication will be required to read the correct operand from a remote cluster.

3.3. The VPB steering scheme

In consequence, to minimize the above mentioned communications increase, the second modification to the Baseline steering scheme should only apply to those cases in which there is a potential for improving the workload balance. In particular, we propose that the steering logic considers predicted source operands to be mapped in all clusters only when the workload imbalance is higher than a given threshold (that we set empirically to DCOUNT=16 and DCOUNT=8, for a 4-cluster and a 2-cluster configurations, respectively). In other words, if the workload is very well balanced, the steering does not rely on value prediction to improve workload balance, since it may increase the communication requirements. We refer to this technique as the Value Prediction Based scheme (VPB).

Figure 3 compares workload imbalance, communication rate and IPCR for 4 different configurations: the Baseline without and with value prediction, the VPB scheme, and VPB with perfect prediction. Comparing the results for a 4-cluster configuration with value prediction, the VPB scheme has 12% less communications than the Baseline and a 10% lower workload imbalance, which results in a significant performance improvement ($IPCR_4$ increases from 0.74 to 0.77).

The rightmost bar in each group in Figure 3 show an upper bound for the VPB scheme, assuming a perfect predictor. Communications are not zero because of fp values, that are not considered by our predictor. IPCR ratios are 0.90 and 0.96 for a 4- and a 2-cluster configurations respectively, which suggests that the performance of the VPB scheme may significantly be improved by a more effective predictor.

So far, all the reported experiments assumed that the rename/steering logic takes a single cycle. However, due to the additional complexity introduced by the steering logic, it might require 2 cycles, for some particular technology. We simulated a 2-cycle rename/steer stage and obtained that, for a 4-cluster configuration with VPB, the IPC is degraded by less than 2%.

In summary, we observe that value prediction produces significant performance improvements for a cluster organization, which are higher than those observed for a centralized one, especially when adequate steering techniques are implemented. In particular, we have found that for a 4-cluster configuration the $IPCR_4$ ratio increases on average by 18%, from 0.65 to 0.77, and for a 2-cluster configuration $IPCR_2$ increases by 5%, from 0.85 to 0.89. This is due to the drastic 50% reduction of the communication rate (from 0.22 to 0.11 for 4 clusters, and from 0.12 to 0.06 for 2 clusters). We can thus conclude that value prediction is a very effective technique to reduce the communication requirements of clustered processors.

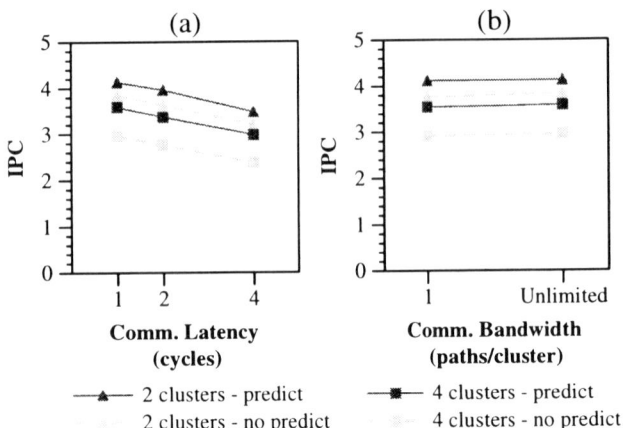

Figure 4. Impact of (a) communication latency and (b) communication bandwidth, on the IPC

The overall benefits of value prediction translate into an increase in IPC of 21% on average (from 2.96 to 3.59) for a 4-cluster architecture, and a smaller increase for a 2-cluster configuration (8%, from 3.84 to 4.14), whereas for a centralized processor the benefits are almost negligible (2%, from 4.54 to 4.63). Note that we assumed a simple value predictor and the results will likely be better with more complex and effective predictors

4. Sensitivity analysis

In future technologies the widening gap between the relative speeds of gates and wires will decrease dramatically the percentage of on-chip transistors that a signal can travel in a single clock cycle [1]. Using high clock rates will require not only to reduce the capacity of many components like register files and issue windows, but also to pipeline more deeply the access to other structures.

In this work we focus on the inter-cluster communication bypasses. In the previous sections we have assumed that these communications take 1 cycle (there is a 1 cycle "bubble" between the copy instruction and the dependent instruction, in another cluster). In this section, we study the sensitivity of clustered architectures to the communication latency, measured by the IPC degradation caused by a communication latency of 1, 2, and 4 cycles. In all cases we assume that communications are fully pipelined, that is, for a given bypass path, one communication may begin per cycle regardless of its total latency. We also analyze the impact of the communication bandwidth and value predictor table size on the performance of the processor.

4.1. Communication latency

Figure 4(a) shows that there is a significant performance degradation when the communication latency increases from 1 to 4 cycles. For instance, on a 4-cluster configuration, the IPC decreases by 17% (and by 20% without prediction, because of its higher communication requirements). Similar trends are observed on a 2-cluster configuration, although the performance degradation is slightly smaller (16% with prediction and 17% without prediction).

4.2. Communication bandwidth

The inter-cluster communication bandwidth has a direct impact on the complexity and delay of the register files [7, 16] and the bypass network, since it determines the number of register file write ports devoted to remote accesses, the number of bypass multiplexer's inputs coming from remote clusters, and the number of outputs from the bypass network to the interconnection network. Furthermore, the inter-cluster communication bandwidth also determines the number of tags that are broadcast to the instruction queues of remote clusters. Therefore, it has a direct impact on the complexity and delay of the wake-up logic, which depends quadratically on the total number of tags crossing its CAM cells [15, 16].

So far, we have assumed an unbounded bandwidth for the interconnection network to isolate our results from possible communication bandwidth bottlenecks. Here we study the impact of having a limited bandwidth. For an N-cluster configuration, we assume a simplified model with NxB independent paths. Each path is implemented through a pipelined bus where any cluster can send a value and each bus is connected to the write port of a single cluster register file. Therefore, we assume that each register file has B write ports for inter-cluster communications. Any cluster may allocate one of these paths to write a value to a remote register file, and holds it during a single cycle, since the communication is fully pipelined. Obviously, this model is somewhat idealized, since it omits the complexities due to the pipelining, arbitration, or variable latencies dependent on the topology, but it may provide a first order approach to evaluate the problem.

Figure 4 (b) shows that when the communication bandwidth is limited to a single path per cluster there is very little performance degradation compared to the unbounded model. For instance, on a 4-cluster configuration, the IPC decreases only by 1% (1.4% without value prediction), and a small IPC decrement is also observed for a 2-cluster configuration (0.2% and 1.8% respectively). In consequence, for inter-cluster communications in a cost-effective architecture, it may suffice just a single write port in each register file, a single incoming tag per issue window, and a single remote bypass attached to the input multiplexers of the functional units.

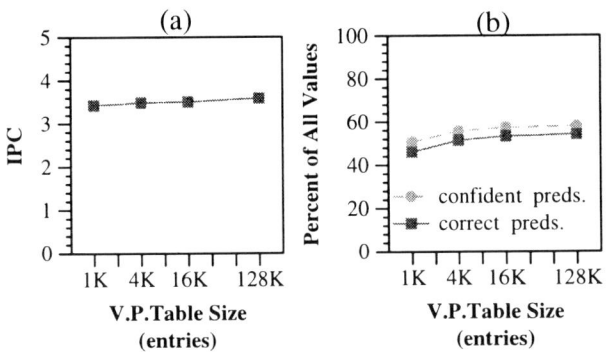

Figure 5. Impact of value predictor table size for 4 clusters on (a) IPC (b) predictor accuracy.

4.3. Value predictor table size

The predictor table size determines the prediction accuracy, which has a significant influence on the performance. We have evaluated the impact of the predictor table size on a clustered architecture. Figure 5(a) shows that on average, for a 4-cluster configuration, there is less than 4.5% IPC degradation when the predictor table size is reduced from 128K to just 1K entries.

Figure 5(b) shows the predictor accuracy for the same range of predictor sizes. We can observe that for 42% of the values, the predicted value was not used because it was not confident. The percentage of non-confident predictions is a bit high because we chose a rather simple value predictor. In addition, the hit ratio (correctly predicted values over predicted values) decreases from 93.4% to 90.9% when the predictor size is reduced from 128K to 1K.

5. Related work

The main contribution of this work is realizing that value prediction can eliminate many of the long wire communication penalties in the context of a clustered architecture. We have also presented a new steering algorithm, the VPB scheme, that takes advantage of value prediction to further reduce inter-cluster communications. Moreover, this paper extends the techniques used in previous works [4, 5] (for register renaming, dynamic steering of instructions and forwarding values among different clusters) from a configuration with 2 heterogeneous clusters to a more general design with an arbitrary number of homogeneous clusters.

Other relevant works on dynamically scheduled clustered processors are the Dependence-based, the Multicluster and the Pews architectures. In the Dependence-based paradigm [15, 16], instructions are steered to several FIFO queues instead of a conventional issue window, according to a heuristic that ensures that two dependent instructions are only queued in the same FIFO if there is no other instruction in between. This heuristic lacks of any explicit mechanism to balance the workload, which is instead adjusted implicitly by the allocation algorithm of new free FIFO queues. This allocation algorithm generates many communications when it assigns a FIFO to a non-ready instruction, since it does not consider in which cluster the operands are to be produced [5].

The Multicluster architecture [6] also used run-time generated copy instructions for inter-cluster communication. In that architecture the register name space is partitioned into two subsets, and program partitioning is done at compile time without any ISA modification, by the appropriate logical register assignment for the result of each instruction. Both the workload balance and inter-cluster communication are estimated at compile time. The same authors proposed a dynamic scheme [7] that adjusts run-time excess workload by re-mapping logical registers. However, they found most heuristics to be little effective since the re-mapping introduces communication overheads that offset almost any balance benefit.

Kemp and Franklin proposed the Pews clustered architecture [11] where instructions are assigned to clusters based on register dependences. However, since they assume a centralized register file, the steering scheme only needs to group two dependent instructions in the same cluster when the value from the producer is not still available at the time the consumer is decoded. This simple scheme is not suitable for our "distributed" register file, and in addition, it does not address the load balancing problem.

The Alpha 21264 [10] is also a 2-cluster organization that duplicates the integer register file, one copy in each cluster. The two register file copies are kept consistent by writing any result in both clusters. Instructions are dynamically steered at issue time by a central instruction queue, that sends an instruction to the cluster where its operands will be available earlier. This organization does not reduce the number of register write ports nor the number of registers per cluster. Besides, it does not reduce the complexity of the issue logic, although it requires a simpler partitioning scheme.

The Trace Processors [17, 20] dynamically partition the code sequence into chunks of consecutive instructions, called traces. Instruction steering to clusters is then performed at run-time in a per-trace basis. This partitioning may result in an acceptable workload balance since traces have similar sizes but it is likely to result in many inter-cluster communications since they are not taken into account by the partitioning scheme.

Sastry, Palacharla and Smith proposed a static code partitioning technique [18]. The partitioning scheme is constrained to dispatching loads, stores and complex integer instructions to the same cluster. In addition, it requires some extensions to the ISA in order to specify to the hardware the target cluster of each instruction. Moreover, their scheme is less flexible and less effective than a dynamic approach as shown elsewhere [4], since all dynamic instances of the same static instruction are executed in the same cluster regardless of run-time conditions, such as the workload balance, that are difficult to estimate at compile time.

6. Conclusions

Future microprocessors are likely to be communication bound due to the increasing penalty of wire delays. In this paper we show that value prediction can be an effective instrument to improve communication locality. In particular, we have presented an approach to reduce inter-cluster communication by means of a dynamic steering logic that leverages value prediction. Values produced in a cluster and consumed in another one may not require long wire delays to propagate from the producer to the consumer if the consumer can correctly predict the value. The validation required by the prediction is locally performed in the producer cluster.

We have shown that value prediction removes communications even for previously proposed steering schemes not specially designed to exploit value prediction. However, performance is higher if the steering logic exploits the predictability of values. We have presented a novel steering scheme (VPB), and we have shown that it outperforms previous proposals. This benefit mainly comes from a 50% reduction in the amount of communications. We observed that value prediction reduces the penalties caused by inter-cluster communications by 18% on average. Moreover, whereas value prediction increases the IPC of a centralized architecture by just 2%, the same predictor increases the performance of a 4-cluster microarchitecture with VPB steering by 21%.

Acknowledgements

We thank the anonymous referees for their valuable comments. This work was developed using the resources of the CEPBA, and is supported by the Ministry of Education of Spain under contract CYCIT TIC98-0511.

References

[1] V.Agarwal, M.S.Hrishikesh, S.W.Keckler and D.Burger. "Clock Rate versus IPC: The End of the Road for Conventional Microarchitectures", in *Proc. of the 27th Annual Int. Symp on Comp. Architecture*, June 2000.

[2] Bohr, Mark T. "Interconnect Scaling - The Real Limiter to High Performance ULSI". in *Proc. of the 1995 IEEE Int. Electron Devices Meeting*, pp. 241-244, 1995.

[3] D. Burger, T.M. Austin, S. Bennett. "Evaluating Future Microprocessors: The SimpleScalar Tool Set", *Tech. Report CS-TR-96-1308*, Univ.Wisconsin-Madison, 1996.

[4] R.Canal, J-M.Parcerisa, A. González. "A Cost-Effective Clustered Architecture". In *Proc. of the Int. Conf. on Parallel Architectures and Compilation Techniques (PACT 99)*, Newport Beach, CA, pp. 160-168, Oct. 1999.

[5] R.Canal, J-M.Parcerisa, A. González. "Dynamic Cluster Assignment Mechanisms". In *Proc. of the 6th. Int. Symp. on High-Performance Computer Architecture*, pp.132-142, Jan. 2000.

[6] K.I.Farkas, P.Chow, N.P.Jouppi, Z.Vranesic. "The Multicluster Architecture: Reducing Cycle Time Through Partitioning", in *Proc of the 30th. Ann. Symp. on Microarchitecture*, pp. 149-159, December 1997.

[7] K.I.Farkas. "Memory-system Design Considerations for Dynamically-scheduled Microprocessors", *Ph.D. thesis*, Department of Electrical and Computer Engineering, Univ. of Toronto, Canada, January 1997.

[8] F.Gabbay and A.Mendelson. "Speculative Execution Based on Value Prediction", TR. #1080, Technion, 1996.

[9] J.González and A.González. "Memory Address Prediction for Data Speculation". Tech. Report UPC-DAC-1996-50, Univ. Politècnica de Catalunya, Spain. 1996.

[10] L. Gwennap. "Digital 21264 Sets New Standard", *Microprocessor Report*, 10 (14), Oct. 1996.

[11] G.A.Kemp, M.Franklin, "PEWs: A Decentralized Dynamic Scheduler for ILP Processing", in *Proc. of Int. Conf. on Parallel Processing*, pp. 239-246, August 1996.

[12] C. Lee, M. Potkonjak and W. H. Mangione-Smith, "Mediabench: A Tool for Evaluating and Synthesizing Multimedia and Communications Systems", *Proc. of the Int. Symp. on Microarchitecture* (Micro 30), pp. 330-335, Dec. 1997.

[13] D.Matzke, "Will Physical Scalability Sabotage Performance Gains", *IEEE Computer 30(9)*: 37-39, Sept. 1997.

[14] Mediabench Home Page. URL: http://www.cs.ucla.edu/~leec/mediabench/

[15] S. Palacharla, N.P. Jouppi, and J.E. Smith, "Complexity-Effective Superscalar Processors" in *Proc of the 24th. Int. Symp. on Comp. Architecture*, pp. 1-13, June 1997.

[16] S.Palacharla. "Complexity-Effective Superscalar Processors". Ph.D. thesis, Univ. of Winsconsin-Madison, 1998.

[17] E.Rotenberg, Q.Jacobson, Y.Sazeides and J.E.Smith, "Trace Processors", in *Proc. of the 30th. Ann. Symp. on Microarchitecture*, pp. 138-148, December 1997.

[18] S.S.Sastry, S.Palacharla and J.E.Smith, "Exploiting Idle Floating-Point Resources For Integer Execution", in *Proc. of the Int. Conf. on Programming Lang. Design and Implementation*, pp. 118-129, June 1998.

[19] Y.Sazeides, S.Vassiliadis, J.E.Smith."The Performance Potential of Data Dependence Speculation & Collapsing", *Proc.of Int. Symp. on Microarchitecture*, pp.238-247, 1996.

[20] S. Vajapeyam and T. Mitra, "Improving Superscalar Instruction Dispatch and Issue by Exploiting Dynamic Code Sequences", in *Proc.of the Int. Symp. on Computer Architecture*, pp. 1-12, June 1997.

Compiler Controlled Value Prediction using Branch Predictor Based Confidence

Eric Larson and Todd Austin
Electrical Engineering and Computer Science
University of Michigan
{larsone,austin}@eecs.umich.edu

Abstract

Value prediction breaks data dependencies in a program thereby creating instruction level parallelism that can increase program performance. Hardware based value prediction techniques have been shown to increase speed, but at great cost as designs include prediction tables, selection logic, and a confidence mechanism. This paper proposes compiler-controlled value prediction optimizations that obtain good speedups while keeping hardware costs low. The branch predictor is used to estimate the confidence of the value predictor for speculated instructions. This technique obtains 4.6% speedup when completely implemented in software and 15.2% speedup when minimal hardware support (a 1 KB predictor table) is added. We also explore the use of critical path information to aid in the selection of value prediction candidates. The key result of our study is that programs with long dynamic dependence chains benefit with this technique while programs with shorter chains benefit more so from simple selection methods that favor optimization frequency. A new branch instruction that ignores innocuous value mispredictions is shown to eliminate unnecessary mispredictions when program semantics aren't violated by confidence branch mispredictions.

1. Introduction

High performance computing requires high throughput instruction execution. Control and data hazards impede this goal, preventing programs from using all of the available resources. Research has shown that the outcomes of many instructions are highly predictable leading to a growing body of work in value prediction. Values are predicted for selected instructions, breaking output dependencies that allow dependent instructions to execute concurrently. This technique breaks data hazards, extracting additional instruction level parallelism (ILP) and increasing the number of instructions executed per cycle (IPC). There are several different types of value predictors: last value predicted [10], stride [3], context-based [19], or hybrid [3].

To date, most value prediction research has focused on hardware-based schemes. In these predictors, the prediction table is indexed very early in the pipeline using the PC. Typically, the prediction is known in the fetch and/or dispatch stages, such that predicted values can be forwarded immediately to dependent instructions stalled waiting for inputs. Speculative instructions must delay retirement until the value prediction is verified. If the prediction is correct, any dependent instructions that have executed can retire immediately. If the prediction is wrong, the errant instruction and all dependent instructions must be re-executed. The high cost of value mispredictions (tens of cycles in proposed microarchitectures) limits the application of value prediction to only the most highly predictable instructions.

To increase the scope of value prediction, it is possible to employ confidence mechanisms to reduce the probability that a value is mispredicted [7]. A confidence mechanism is a meta-predictor, it predicts if the prediction of the value predictor is correct. If the confidence mechanism is not very confident that a prediction will be correct, it will not predict the value, thereby avoiding an expensive misprediction. Many instructions with low overall prediction accuracies do have highly predictable confidence, making it possible to leverage more predictions without incurring more mispredictions.

One technique to measure the confidence of value prediction is to use a saturating counter [3] where the counter is incremented on every correct prediction and subtracted or reset to zero when an incorrect prediction occurs. If the value of the counter is greater than some threshold, it will be considered a high-confidence prediction and will be subject to value prediction. Another scheme to measure confidence is to base predictions on the past n predictions [3]. This implementation allows for highly confident predictions on instructions that exhibit a specific pattern of correct and incorrect predictions. This scheme is very similar to pattern-based branch predictors.

Hardware-based value predictions, while efficient, have significant hardware costs. Value predictors are often on the order of cache sizes before they attain respectable accuracies and coverage. In addition, misprediction recovery mechanisms, especially partial re-execution techniques [20], are quite complex. Efforts have been made to address these costs through software-based value prediction optimizations. For these techniques, the compiler is responsible for locating prediction candidates, implementing the prediction optimization, verifying the prediction, and providing fixup code in case of a misprediction [5]. Typically, the compiler chooses value prediction candidates based on profiling data.

To date, software-based value prediction techniques have only rendered small speedups compared to hardware-based techniques. The primary reason for this disparity is because software-based techniques have not employed confidence mechanisms that can increase the coverage and accuracy of value prediction. Without a confidence mechanism, software-based techniques must choose between either low accuracy or few candidates - neither choice provides much opportunity for performance gains. Moreover, candidates are selected using profiles from a particular input set; choices made for a particular input set may hinder performance for another.

Another factor that limits software-based speedups is the cost of applying the technique. Instructions must be added to implement predictions, update predictor tables, and fix up mispredictions. To limit these costs, most previous work has employed simple predictors such as last-value predicted or static stride. More powerful methods require too many instructions and consumes too much code and data space to be efficiently handled by software. Moreover, the additional instructions required to maintain software-based predictors increase register pressure and consume valuable memory bandwidth. One technique for solving both problems is to add explicit predict and update instructions to the instruction set architecture (ISA) [6]. The prediction state is completely stored in hardware and allows for more sophisticated context-based predictors. Candidate selection and misprediction recovery is still implemented by the compiler.

In this paper, we present an optimized approach to compiler-controlled value prediction. Our approach improves the performance of compiler-controlled value prediction while keeping hardware costs significantly lower than hardware-only based techniques. It also addresses many of the drawbacks endemic to compiler-controlled value prediction.

Low coverage and accuracy can be addressed by adding confidence. We implemented a confidence prediction mechanism using the underlying branch predictor. The branch predictor has a choice of executing a section of code using the predicted value or the actual value. Based on previous history, the branch predictor will make an informed decision on which section of code should be executed. If a selected candidate turns out to be unpredictable, the branch predictor will predict that the non-speculative value should be used, resulting in performance comparable to the original code. Assuming a fixed accuracy, a scheme with confidence will have higher coverage and a higher potential for speedup.

To address overhead concerns, we propose improvements to the optimized instruction selection process. By selecting more gainful sites for selection, we can select fewer of them, thus limiting the overheads associated with software-based value prediction. Typically, the basis for choosing candidates is based upon the prediction accuracy and the number of times it is executed. While these are good characteristics, it does not tell the complete story. Research has shown [3, 12] that selecting candidates on the critical path is important to realize the maximum potential of value prediction.

Ideally, a long chain of dependent instructions should be split in half resulting in two chains that can be executed in parallel. Past work [4] has employed static analysis to identify instructions in the middle of these output dependence chains. This approach does not provide complete information regarding true critical paths, since it is difficult to tell where the performance degrading (e.g., long latency) instructions lie and how much of a particular chain actually resides in the instruction window. As a result, we analyze the dependence chains at runtime in the instruction window of a detailed processor simulator. Instructions are given scores based on how far they are to either end of a dependence chain. The final candidates are selected as a function of this critical path metric, optimization frequency, and optimization accuracy.

In all software-based value prediction techniques, a branch is used to validate the prediction. If a prediction is incorrect, the branch will re-direct the program to the fixup code where the computation proceeds with the non-speculative value. We use a similar approach when mapping confidence to the branch predictor. This approach introduces unnecessary branch misprediction when the branch predictor directs instruction fetch down the fixup path and the value prediction is correct. When the branch direction is verified to be incorrect (i.e., the value prediction was correct), the pipeline is flushed and instruction fetch is redirected to the value speculative code. Since the fixup path is always correct, regardless of the value prediction, this branch misprediction is superfluous. We create a misprediction tolerant branch that eliminates the misprediction recovery when this situation occurs.

The rest of this paper is organized as follows: Section 2 describes our three value prediction optimizations in more detail: compiler-controlled value prediction with confidence, critical path based selection, and a special branch that tolerates certain mispredictions. Section 3 describes our results. Section 4 describes related work in value prediction and Section 5 gives a conclusion and some ideas for future work.

2. Value prediction optimizations

This section details techniques used to improve compiler-controlled value prediction while keeping implementation costs low. The first technique described employs the existing branch predictor as a confidence mechanism. This allows for additional optimization candidates to be selected while keeping the accuracy high. The second technique is a critical path based selection technique which selects instructions based on their position in the critical path. The approach reveals to the compiler the best candidates to select for optimization. The final optimization is a misprediction tolerant branch that will remove unnecessary mispredictions when program correctness remains intact.

2.1 Branch based confidence

In order to reap the full benefits of value prediction, it is necessary to have a confidence scheme. This is difficult to implement directly in software since the data used to keep track of the previous history must be stored in data memory and additional instructions will be needed to extract and update this confidence data. To avoid adding this complexity, we propose using the branch predictor to measure the confidence of a value prediction. The primary benefit is that the information needed to make the confidence estimate and the misprediction recovery scheme is already built into the processor. In addition, a good branch predictor will provide a better measure of confidence than any reasonable software implementation could attain because the predictor implements powerful algorithms directly in hardware. For value predictions, it is necessary to record if a value was correctly predicted or not. To use the branch predictor for value prediction confidence, we map "value prediction was correct" to "not taken" and "value prediction was incorrect" to "taken" by bracketing value prediction sites with a controlling confidence branch.

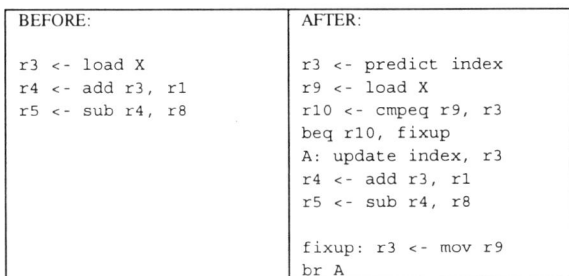

Figure 1: Software Value Prediction with Confidence Example. Value prediction is applied to the initial load instruction. The branch predictor will try to predict if the predicted value (r3) matches the actual value (r9).

Our technique is illustrated by the example in Figure 1. The code before the optimization shows a chain of two instructions that are dependent on a load instruction. In this example, the optimization is applied to the load instruction. The destination register of the load is replaced by a register that is free during this segment (r9 in this case). The prediction is written into the original destination register of the load (details on the predict and update instructions are given later; assume for now that the destination register automatically contains a prediction for the load instruction). After the load, compare and branch instructions are added to validate the prediction. If the prediction is incorrect, the branch is taken where fixup code will place the proper value into the destination register. If correct, no fixup code is executed, and the program proceeds with the speculated value. The dependent instructions that follow the prediction remain unchanged.

The branch instruction gauges the confidence of the prediction. If the branch predictor predicts the branch not taken, it is predicting with high confidence that the value will be predicted correctly. In this case, execution of the dependent instructions can begin as soon as the predicting instruction has completed (and, if necessary, data from other sources is also ready). If the branch predictor predicts the branch taken, it predicts low confidence and speculates down the unoptimized path. The instruction on the unoptimized path is dependent on the actual value of the load instruction (or whatever instruction was being predicted) so progress will not be made until this instruction has completed. If the branch predictor was wrong, the penalty is the cost of a branch misprediction.

Our approach assumes the underlying machine contains a dynamic scheduling mechanism. Using this mechanism, we can dynamically select speculative or non-speculative code sequences knowing that the scheduler will extract all available instruction level parallelism. In a statically scheduled machine, extracting instruction level parallelism from the value speculative code sequence requires that the compiler commit to applying the optimization at compile time, otherwise, no benefits are found. For instance, the compare instruction in Figure 1 will stall on a statically scheduled machine, eliminating the benefit of predicting the load.

The example in Figure 1 uses the predict and update instructions that were proposed in [6]. These instructions are additions to the ISA that contain an index which refers to a specific entry in a hardware value prediction table. Predict instructions employ different indices to distinguish between different prediction sites. Each predict instruction also has a corresponding update instruction which informs the predictor of the last correct value. The predictor used by these instructions is transparent to the programmer, permitting the hardware predictor mechanism to be changed without impacting correctness of programs.

A static stride predictor [5] is used for all experiments. The static stride is determined by profiling. This predictor works well and is fairly straightforward to implement in software. Implementing more powerful predictors in software incur significantly more overhead in terms of instructions and memory operations.

The software-only version is applied in a similar manner. The major difference is where the predictions are stored. Without hardware support to store the predictions in a table, predictions must be stored in memory and/or registers. We chose to keep the predictions in memory until we enter the function where the instruction resides. At that time, the prediction is transferred into a register. Throughout the function, all updates are done by updating the register. At the end of the function, the value is stored back into memory for future use. This approach cannot always be applied as it requires that the prediction consume a register throughout the entire function. The optimization was applied at link-time when sufficient free registers were available (no spills). As a result, fewer sites were optimized in the software-only implementation. For some benchmarks, we were unable to apply the optimization to any site. We also explored loading and storing the prediction to and from memory instead of using a register but this resulted in consistent slows down due to the high number of additional memory operations.

Any instruction can be selected as a value prediction candidate. This includes floating-point instructions as well as integer instructions. Floating-point predictions are restricted to last-value only since there is no floating point immediate instruction to add a static stride. This is not a significant concern since there are very few floating point instructions that are predictable with nonzero static strides.

2.2 Value prediction candidate selection

Profiling data is used to select candidates for value prediction. We examine two techniques to determine which instructions are the best candidates for applying the optimizations. It it best to apply the optimization when the following equation holds true:

$$OPT_{accuracy} \times OPT_{benefit} \gg OPT_{inaccuracy} \times OPT_{penalty}$$

Optimization accuracy and inaccuracy is only gauged at sites where the branch predictor indicates a high-confidence prediction. The optimization accuracy ($OPT_{accuracy}$) is computed (using profiling) as the number of times a value was correctly predicted divided by the number of high-confidence predictions. Similarly, the optimization inaccuracy ($OPT_{inaccuracy}$) is the percentage of incorrect high-confidence predictions (or $1 - OPT_{accuracy}$). When a misprediction tolerant branch is implemented (described in the next section), the low-confidence case is equivalent to no optimization being applied at all. Therefore, we do not consider low-confidence predictions when computing the optimization inaccuracy. There is a small penalty due to the instructions added as a result of the optimization and increased pressure of the branch predictor. We ignore this effect in order to simplify the selection process.

The optimization penalty ($OPT_{penalty}$) is equivalent to a branch misprediction plus the overhead of executing the fixup code. In addition, there are issues such as increasing code size and branch predictor pressure that could adversely affect performance. Since the number of optimized candidates is small, the effect is a second order consideration and is not considered further.

The optimization benefit ($OPT_{benefit}$) is much more difficult to measure in an out-of-order microarchitecture. Instead of trying to derive an equation, we estimate the benefit using two techniques: a naive approach that assumes a fixed benefit each time the optimization is executed and a critical-path based approach which looks at how often the instruction is on critical paths in the processor instruction window.

In the naive approach, we assume the benefit is fixed with a value of one, making the overall benefit equal to the number of times the optimization was successfully applied. This fixed benefit model does not hold true in modern out-of-order machines as reducing the latency of different instructions will have varying levels of benefit. For example, a load instruction that misses the cache and heads a long chain of dependent instructions will have a higher benefit than a load instruction that hits in the cache and has no dependencies.

Previous research [3] has shown that applying value prediction to instructions on the critical path will have a higher benefit than applying it to instructions that are not on the critical path. In order to maximize the benefit of value prediction, it is desirable to split long chains of dependent instructions in half so the two halves can execute in parallel, improving performance. Our critical-path based selection technique estimates the benefit by looking at how often it is in the middle of a dependence chain.

An example of a dependence chain is given in Figure 2. From each instruction in the dependence chain, a "middle metric" is computed by taking the minimum distance from the endpoints of the chain. The profiled latencies of the instructions are used in calculating the distance to properly weight long latency instructions. This middle metric is an estimate of the parallelism gained by splitting the chain at that particular instruction. In the example, the subtract instruction has the best middle metric, and thus is the best candidate to apply value prediction to in this dependence chain. When the chain is split, each chain requires only four cycles to execute. Since both chains can be executed in parallel, the savings is three cycles over the original execution.

Obtaining the required data for profiling in this step requires the use of a detailed microarchitectural simulator that captures the state of the instruction window for each cycle of execution. Examples of tools that could perform this analysis include the SimpleScalar tool set [1] or Intel's VTune [24]. Addressing the performance of these analyses is beyond the scope of this paper, however, we believe techniques such as microarchitectural memoization [21] or sampling could be used to limit the cost of dependence chain profiling.

2.3 Misprediction tolerant branches

An important optimization scenario occurs when the value is predicted correctly but the branch predictor indicated it would be predicted incorrectly. With a normal branch instruction, the processor will speculate down the path using the actual value of the instruction assuming the prediction is incorrect. When the branch

Initial chain of dependent instructions	Lat.	Dist. Top	Dist. Bottom	Middle Metric
lda r0 <- 40(r29)	1	1	7	1
load r3 <- 0(r0)	2	3	6	3
sub r9 <- r5, r3	1	4	4	4
sll r13 <- r9, 8	1	5	3	3
add r8 <- r6, r13	1	6	2	2
cmpeq r11 <- r8, 3	1	7	1	1

Resulting chain 1	Resulting chain 2
lda r0 <- 40(r29)	predict r9
load r3 <- 0(r0)	sll r13 <- r9, 8
sub r9 <- r5, r3	add r8 <- r6, r13
	cmpeq r11 <- r8, 3
Latency: 4 cycles	Latency: 4 cycles

Figure 2: Example of computing the middle metric and the resulting chains. The left diagram shows the computation of the middle metric and indicates that the subtract instruction is the best choice. The right diagram shows the resulting chains when the initial chain is split at the sub instruction. This results in a potential savings of three cycles over the initial chain.

executes, a misprediction takes place and control is transferred down the path which uses the predicted value. However, using the actual value of the predicted instruction does not violate the semantics of the program. Useful instructions are thrown away when recovering from the misprediction. To solve this particular problem, we add a special branch instruction that will not recover from such a misprediction. We call this branch BEQIT, which stands for "Branch if EQual to zero Ignoring mispredictions down the Taken path". If the branch predictor speculates down the taken path, no misprediction will take place if the branch was mispredicted. The branch predictor is still updated with the correct choice so it can potentially make a better choice in the future. If the predictor speculates the branch is not taken but should be, a branch misprediction will be declared as normal (to fix the incorrect value). While it is still preferable to go down the optimized code path, there is no overall benefit to reaching it by taking a misprediction.

One advantage to the misprediction tolerant branch is that it is inexpensive to implement. It only requires some additional decoding logic and a few gates to prevent the processor from entering a speculative state when the branch is mispredicted in the taken direction.

3. Results

In this section, the results of our experimental evaluation are detailed. The initial experiment looks at the coverage and accuracies of a value predictor with and without confidence. This is followed up with simulation-based performance analysis. Next, we look at the effectiveness of software-only value prediction. The final experiments evaluate the utility of various selection mechanisms, and analyzes the performance impact of the misprediction tolerant branch.

3.1 Experimental framework

We obtained our results using a mix of SPEC95 and SPEC2000 benchmarks including integer and FP benchmarks. The benchmarks were compiled using the Compaq C (version 5.9) and Fortran (version 5.3) compilers under using full compiler optimization (-O4). The benchmarks used are listed in Table 1. The train input set was used during all profiling runs.

Table 1: Benchmarks used in simulation

Name	Fastfwd Cycles	Sim. Cycles	Base IPC (train)	Base IPC (ref)
art (2000 FP)	100 M	250 M	0.8988	0.9106
compress (95 INT)	none	51M	2.1864	1.4796
crafty (2000 INT)	100 M	250 M	1.7819	1.7524
equake (2000 FP)	100 M	250 M	2.6225	2.5963
go (95 INT)	100 M	250 M	1.5356	1.5478
m88ksim (95 INT)	none	150 M	2.3362	2.2220
mcf (2000 INT)	100 M	250 M	2.5588	2.5630
tomcatv (95 FP)[1]	none	85 M	2.3905	2.1885

1. For tomcatv, the reference set was used for profiling and will be referred to train throughout the paper and vice versa.

The simulators used in this study are derived from the SimpleScalar/Alpha 3.0 tool set [1], a suite of functional and timing simulation tools for the Alpha AXP ISA. The timing simulator executes only user-level instructions, performing a detailed timing simulation of an aggressive 4-way dynamically scheduled microprocessor with two levels of instruction and data cache memory. Simulation is execution-driven, including execution down any speculative path until the detection of a fault, TLB miss, or branch misprediction.

Initially, the benchmarks were run with SimpleScalar twice to obtain profiling information. In the first pass, the best static stride and average latencies were determined for each instruction that wrote to an output register. In this phase, all instruction latencies are assumed to be one cycle except loads and branches. The latency for each load is the average latency given an L1 cache hit is one cycle and an L1 miss is eight cycles. The average latency for branches is computed given that a correct prediction executes in one cycle and an incorrect prediction recovers in six cycles. In the second profiling pass, the predictability, optimization accuracy, and the middle metric was computed for each instruction. The predictability was determined by using an infinite sized static stride predictor to eliminate conflicts. Optimization accuracies were determined using a 16k gshare branch predictor to estimate confidence.

Statistics gathered from profiling were then used to select the candidates to apply the value prediction optimization. The optimization was applied using ALTO [16] - a link time optimizer that provides a set of classic compiler optimizations that can be applied to Alpha COFF object files. To normalize results, we disabled all ALTO optimizations, only utilizing its intermediate representation construction and analysis features.

Finally, the optimized program was simulated using SimpleScalar. Our baseline simulation configuration models a modern out-of-order processor microarchitecture. The processor has a large window of execution; it can fetch and issue up to 4 instructions per cycle. It has a 32 entry re-order buffer with a 16 entry load/store buffer. Loads can only execute when all prior store addresses are known. In addition, all stores are issued in program order with respect to prior stores. A 4k entry gshare branch predictor was used and there is an six cycle minimum branch misprediction penalty. The processor has 4 integer ALU units, 2-load/store units, 2-FP adders, 1-integer MULT/DIV, and 1-FP MULT/DIV. The latencies are: ALU 1 cycle, MULT 3 cycles, Integer DIV 12 cycles, FP Adder 2 cycles, FP Mult 4 cycles, and FP DIV 12 cycles. All functional units, except the divide units, are fully pipeline allowing a new instruction to initiate execution each cycle.

The processor we simulated has 32k 2-way set-associative instruction and data caches. Both caches have block sizes of 32 bytes. The data cache is write-back, write-allocate, and is non-blocking with 2 ports. The data cache access latency is one cycle (for a total load latency of two cycles). There is a unified second-level 512k 4-way set-associative cache with 32 byte blocks, with a six cycle cache hit latency. If there is a second-level cache miss it takes a total of 60 cycles to make the round trip access to main memory. We model the bus latency to main memory with a six cycle bus occupancy per request. There is a 16 entry 4-way associative instruction TLB and a 32 entry 4-way associative data TLB, each with a 30 cycle miss penalty.

The value prediction table used by the PREDICT and UPDATE instructions contains enough entries so that each optimization site gets a unique entry. The number of entries in the table ranges from 22 (*m88ksim*) to 136 (*mcf*) when using the best set of candidates. The best set of value prediction candidates is determined in Section 3.5. This set is used for all other experiments (except for the software-only section - see Section 3.4).

3.2 Coverage and accuracy

Value predictors can be measured by their coverage and accuracy, giving a clear indication how well the predictor will perform. In profile based candidate selection, a threshold is used to filter out bad candidates. An instruction is only a candidate if its accuracy exceeds this threshold. Using this approach, there is a trade-off between coverage and accuracy. When the threshold is increased, the accuracy increases by only allowing the most accurate candidates; and coverage decreases since the higher threshold will eliminate many candidates. Conversely, decreasing the threshold increases the coverages but lowers the accuracy.

Figure 3 looks at the confidence and accuracy for all value prediction candidates within each of the benchmarks. The baseline statistics are updated each time the instruction is executed while statistics in the branch based confidence scheme are only updated when the branch predictor indicates a high confidence prediction. A static stride predictor is used in both instances. The accuracy for the static predictor is equivalent to the value prediction accuracy, and the coverage is the percentage of instructions (using a dynamic instruction count) that meet or exceed the threshold. For the predictor with confidence, the accuracy is equal to the number of times a prediction is correct when the branch predictor indicates a high confidence prediction and the coverage is the percentage of instructions that were predicted to have high confidence.

The results in Figure 3 show that the value predictor with confidence has better coverage - accuracy pairs than with no confidence. Even with a threshold of zero, accuracy is high for almost all of the benchmarks. Six of the eight benchmarks have accuracies greater than 94% with *crafty* (87.6%) and *go* (79.8%) being the two exceptions. As threshold increases the predictor with no confidence obtain high accuracies, but coverage decreases. This result is expected since using confidence will add candidates that have a pattern of predictability but do not necessarily have overall high predictability.

3.3 Value prediction with confidence

Now, we measure the actual performance benefit of the value prediction technique using confidence. We compare each program to a baseline with no value prediction and to a model of the value prediction scheme

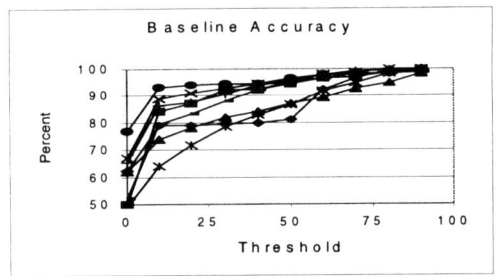

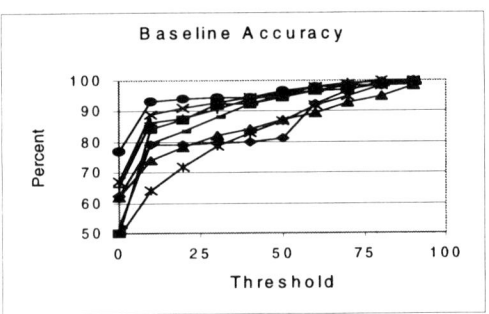

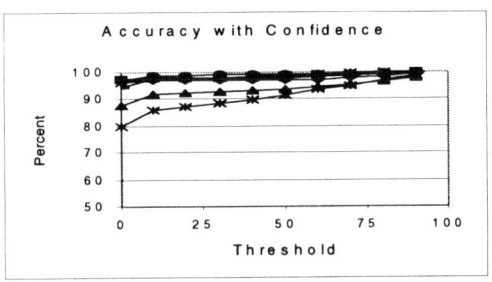

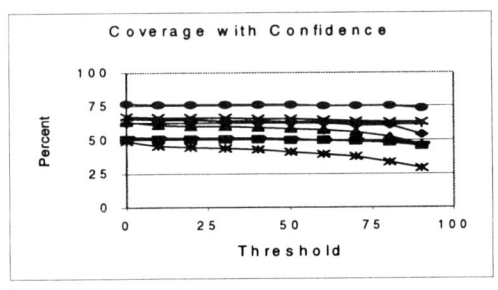

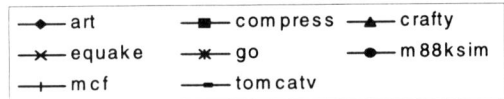

Figure 3: Coverage and accuracy results. The top plots show baseline value prediction coverage and accuracy with no confidence and the bottom plots show coverage and accuracy when the branch predictor is used to estimate confidence. Given a fixed accuracy, the coverage is higher when confidence is used resulting in more candidates for value prediction.

implemented in [6]. This scheme is also compiler-controlled and uses the PREDICT and UPDATE instructions. It is applied using a statically scheduled compiler where speculative code is executed before a branch that will verify if the prediction was correct. The fixup code re-executes all of the instructions using the correct value. This is modeled in our implementation by forcing execution down the "not taken" or "use value prediction" path. If the value shouldn't be used, control will be transferred to the fixup code. However, a misprediction penalty is only assessed if the branch predictor predicted not taken.

The results of this experiment are shown in Figure 4. An average speedup of 15% is obtained over the baseline with no value prediction and up to 38.1% for *m88ksim* with reference input. The value predictor with confidence was, on average, 3.3% faster than the model, but only three benchmarks (*compress*, *equake*, and *mcf*) exhibited any significant speedup. The static predictor even did slightly better for the *crafty* benchmark.

We also ran experiments using an identically-sized bimodal and a hybrid branch predictor (profiling was still done using a gshare predictor). Not surprisingly, the gshare predictor outperformed the bimodal predictor (average gain of 5.4%) but was not as good as the hybrid predictor (average gain of 2.9%).

3.4 Software value prediction

The results of software-only value prediction are shown in Figure 5. Speedups were a mixed bag, ranging from 1% for *art* and *mcf* to 13% for *m88ksim*. The average speedup for the five benchmarks is 4.6%. Compiler-controlled value prediction with ISA support did much better. The slower performance can be attributed to the fact that the predictor state is stored in memory, resulting in larger overheads compared to hardware. Another problem can be attributed to the fact we do not allow register spills in our implementation. Candidates were rejected if there wasn't a free register to hold the prediction. This means far fewer candidates were optimized (a subset of the best set as determined in section 3.5) compared to the experiments with ISA support. In fact, no instructions were optimized for this reason in three of the benchmarks (*compress*, *crafty*, and *tomcatv*). A possible improvement is to include more sophisticated register allocation techniques but this require balancing register files spills in to memory and the benefit of applying the value prediction optimization.

3.5 Selecting value prediction candidates

Selecting proper candidates is an important aspect to obtaining the maximum speed up for value prediction. In this experiment, we look at three different selection criteria. In the first case, we assume that each time the optimization is executed, it has a constant or *fixed* benefit. As a result, this selection criteria is tied to the number of times the instruction will successfully execute the optimization. In the second case, the benefit is tied to its estimated position and frequency in the *critical path*. This middle metric is computed for each instruction by determining the distance from the closest end-

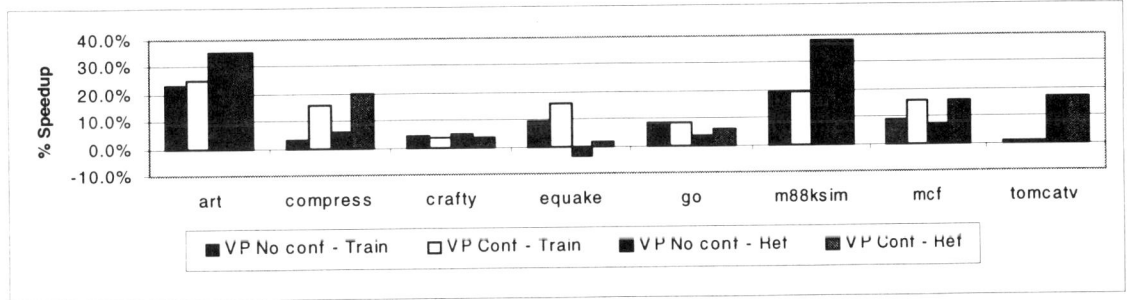

Figure 4: Measuring value prediction with confidence. Using the branch predictor with confidence obtains an average speedup of 15.2% compared to a program with no value prediction and an average speedup of 3.3% speedup over programs with value prediction but no confidence.

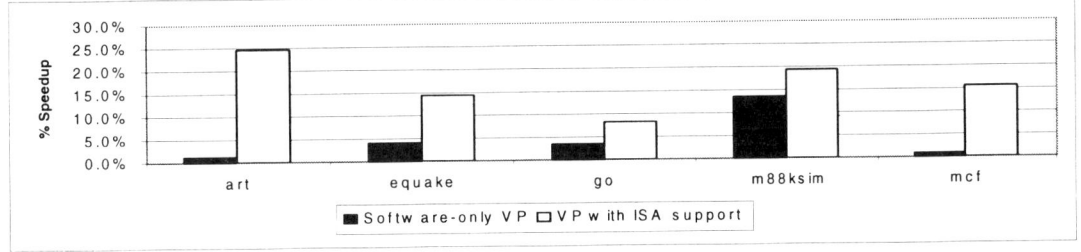

Figure 5: Comparing software-only value prediction to value prediction with ISA support. Software-only value prediction leads to a average speedup of 4.6% Speedups of at least 1% for each of the five benchmarks including a 13% speedup for *m88ksim* but value prediction with ISA support does significantly better. Insufficient free registers were available to apply the optimization to the three other benchmarks (*compress*, *crafty*, and *tomcatv*).

point in the dynamic instruction window dependence chain. This result is averaged over the duration of the simulation and then multiplied by the number of times the optimization is executed. The third selection criterion is a *union* of the two previous techniques in an attempt to gather the best candidates from both selection criteria. The final selection is based on multiplying the benefit by the optimization accuracy.

When selecting candidates, only the best instruction was selected for each basic block since adjacent instructions tended to have similar benefit scores and applying optimizations too close together results in overheads that reduce the effectiveness of value prediction. This heuristic is simple but may be wrong in situations where the basic blocks are small. We plan to address this problem in future work.

For each benchmark, four to five sets of candidates were analyzed for each selection method. The sets were obtained by taking the best *n* candidates where *n* was a different number for each set. The numbers used to determine the sets were the same for each criterion within a benchmark except for the union which contained the union of the two other selection methods. The numbers used varied from benchmark to benchmark due to different static instruction counts.

The results of this experiment are shown in Figure 6. The graph compares the best performing set of each selection technique. For most benchmarks, there isn't significant differentiation between the three selection methods. There are three benchmarks (*crafty, go,* and *tomcatv*) where the critical path based techniques did poorly. This can be explained using the data in Table 2. This table shows the average number of unique dependence chains present in the instruction window during execution, the average size of each chain, and the average length of the longest size chain present in the instruction window each cycle. Benchmarks *crafty, go,* and *tomcatv* all had an average long chain of 4.2 or less while the other five benchmarks had an average longest chain greater than 5.0. Since the longest chain is short, the benefit of splitting up the chains is reduced since less instructions are executed in parallel. For benchmarks that did well, such as *m88ksim* and *equake*, there are a large number of long chains. The other benchmarks saw little difference between the two techniques despite long chain sizes. This is due to the selection methods picking similar lists of candidates.

Table 2: Chain statistics for benchmarks

Benchmark	Avg. Num. of Chains	Avg. Size of Chain	Avg. Longest Sized Chain
art	1.7572	5.2454	5.5716
compress	6.6651	3.3440	5.3126
crafty	4.7575	2.6762	3.0922
equake	6.4199	2.9883	5.2122
go	3.8074	3.1829	3.7823
m88ksim	7.4921	4.3198	5.0041
mcf	7.1499	3.1283	5.7780
tomcatv	4.8718	2.8814	4.1790

Table 3: Number of optimized instructions. This table indicates the number of instructions that were optimized by the compiler.

Benchmark	Optimized Instructions	Benchmark	Optimized Instructions
art	26	go	78
compress	59	m88ksim	22
crafty	87	mcf	136
equake	134	tomcatv	61

Table 3 shows the number of instructions that are optimized in the best case and gives a rough estimate of the size of the value predictor table needed. In the worst case, *mcf* optimized 136 instructions, assuming 8 bytes (standard Alpha data size) for each entry, the predictor will have an overall size of just over 1 KB. This is significantly smaller than hardware-only solutions that require tables in the 16 - 32 KB range [19]. In addition, hardware cannot do selection so it must indiscriminately apply value prediction to highly predictable instructions while the compiler can selectively apply the optimization to only the most gainful sites requiring significantly fewer resources.

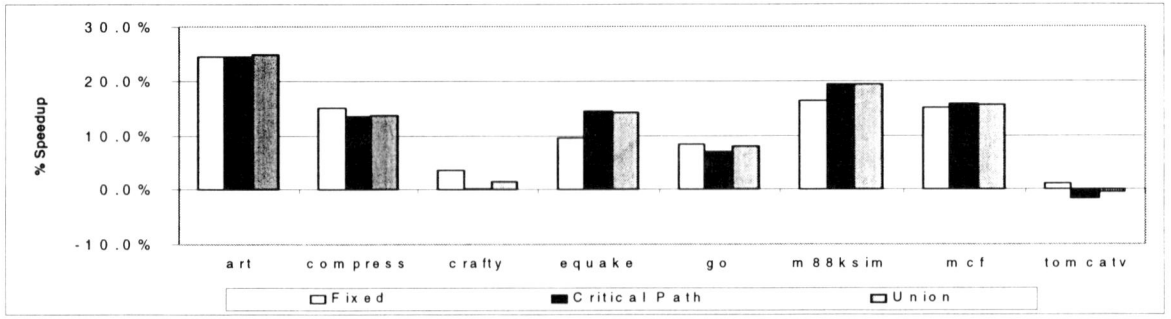

Figure 6: Analyzing different techniques for selecting value prediction candidates. The critical path based technique works best for benchmarks that have long chains such as *equake* and *m88ksim*. Using a fixed benefit model worked best for benchmarks with short chains such as *crafty* and *go*. In other cases, the two techniques were about equal.

3.6 Mispredication tolerant branches

The special branch BEQIT is used to ignore branch mispredictions when the branch predictor mistakenly uses the actual value when the predicted value is indeed correct. Using the actual value does not cause incorrect program behavior so a misprediction is unnecessary in this case. The results of applying the BEQIT branch are shown in Figure 7. The misprediction tolerant branch improved the performance of many of the benchmarks, especially for *compress* where a speedup of 13% was realized for the reference input set. A few programs, such as *m88ksim* and *tomcatv*, saw little benefit as these programs have few mispredicted value speculation branches.

4. Related work

Several studies have looked at the predictability of the instructions and the overall performance potential of value prediction [2, 9, 10, 11, 13, 19]. Lepak and Lipasti [9] show that the data used in store instructions is predictable. Marcuello and Gonzalez [13] look at how various microarchitectural parameters affect value prediction performance. They show that small instruction windows only render moderate speedups, making the criticality of instructions important. Calder *et. al.* [2] found that loads in general are predictable and have invariant values. They also use this knowledge to specialize code sequences.

Fu *et. al.* [4, 5, 6] first examined compiler controlled value prediction. They applied value prediction optimizations to selected candidates based on profiling data. In [5], the value prediction is completely software based. Speedups were obtained for a few benchmarks. In [6], PREDICT and UPDATE instructions are added to the instruction set, resulting in better speedups since predictions could be stored more efficiently in hardware. In [4], the design is modified to incorporate a CHECKPRED instruction which will rewind the architectural state in the event of a value misprediction. The main advantage of this approach is that it eliminates the need of explicit fixup code since the original code is re-executed with the proper value. They also look at the predictability of instructions based on their location in the static dependence graph and found that instructions in the middle of dependence chains do not necessarily lead to the best speedup.

Many researchers have developed techniques for more accurate value prediction [3, 8, 17, 19, 23]. Calder *et. al.* [3] adds the notion of confidence to value predictors so the hardware can identify when it should predict values. Unlike our scheme, the confidence is completely implemented in hardware.

Recent research has provided a better understanding of the behavior of long latency instructions. Zilles and Sohi [25] looked at the backward slices of performance degrading instructions. The slice is formed by looking at the instructions that lead up to the performance degrading event. The slices can be pre-executed to hide the latency of the event improving performance. Srinivasan and Lebeck [22] found that many load instructions can tolerate long latencies without hindering performance. Value prediction tries to remove these long latencies and this research implies that effort should be concentrated on predicting load instructions where the long latency cannot be tolerated without hindering performance.

Other value prediction research has focused on separating the value prediction hardware from the rest of the machine or applying it to different microarchitectures [12, 14, 15, 18]. Lee *et. al.* [12] describes an implementation where the value prediction hardware is decoupled from the instruction fetch stage. Nakra *et. al.* [18] applies value prediction to VLIW machine that uses two execution engines. One engine is for VLIW code that uses value prediction to remove data dependencies and the other executes compensation code when there is a misprediction. Marcuello *et. al.* [14, 15] added value prediction to multithreaded architectures and found it is important to eliminate serialization caused by inter-thread dependencies.

5. Conclusions

In this paper, we have shown that using a branch predictor as a confidence mechanism for value prediction was effective in improving performance while minimizing hardware costs. The speedup on average is 15.2% over a program with no value prediction and 3.3% over a program with a static value predictor without confidence. Hardware can be further reduced by implementing value prediction completely in software. Moderate speedups were obtained for some benchmarks (average of 4.6%); others were excluded due to a lack of free registers to implement the optimization.

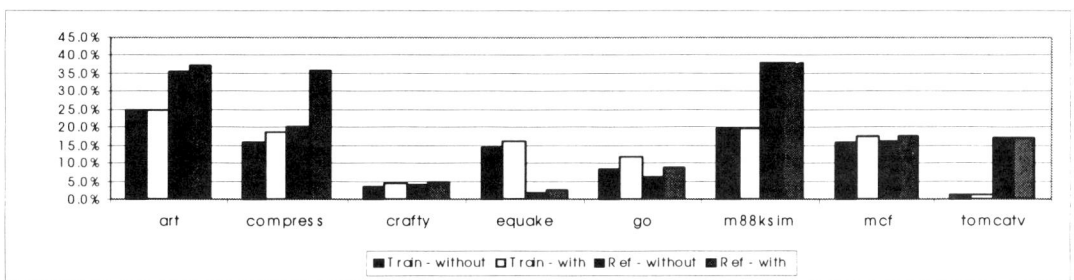

Figure 7: Speedup with and without a misprediction tolerant branch. There were speedups of greater than 1% in four of the eight benchmarks. The branch performed well in *compress* with the reference data set with a speedup of 13%.

The best method for selecting candidates differs upon the size and number of dependence chains in a program. Using a constant fixed benefit was better for programs with fewer and shorter chains while the critical path technique was better for programs with more and longer chains. The largest number of optimized instructions in any one benchmark was 136 for *mcf*, requiring a value prediction table of only slightly larger than 1 KB, much smaller than required by similar performing hardware techniques. A low-cost misprediction tolerant branch was used to avoid misprediction, resulting in speedups for most benchmarks, including a 13% speedup in *compress*.

There are several opportunities for future work. One possibility is to further understand the best set of value prediction candidates. A factor not looked at in this paper is the spacing of the optimized instructions. If optimized instructions are too close together, there will be too much splitting of dependence chains and the overhead of the optimization will dominate. On the other hand, if the optimized instructions are too far apart, the maximum benefit of value prediction is not obtained. There may be other uses for the optimizations outlined in this paper. The branch predictor could be used to estimate confidence for other forms of speculation, or the misprediction tolerant branch can be used in optimizations that contain a programmatically correct path regardless of the actual outcome of the branch.

Acknowledgements

We would like to thank the anonymous reviewers for their valuable comments. This material is based upon work supported under a National Science Foundation Graduate Fellowship. Equipment support was provided by Intel Corporation.

References

[1] D.C. Burger and T. M. Austin, "The SimpleScalar Tool Set, Version 2.0", *University of Wisconsin Computer Sciences Technical Report #1342*, June 1997.

[2] B. Calder, P. Feller, and A. Eustace, "Value Profiling and Optimization", in *Journal of Instruction-Level Parallelism*, March 1999.

[3] B. Calder, G. Reinman, and D. M. Tullsen, "Selective Value Prediction", in *26th International Symposium of Computer Architecture*, May 1999.

[4] C. Fu. and T. M. Conte, "Value Speculation Mechanisms for EPIC Architectures", *Technical Report. Dept. of Electrical and Computer Engineering, North Carolina State University, Raleigh, NC 27695-7911*, October 1998.

[5] C. Fu, M. D. Jennings, S. Y. Larin, and T. M. Conte, "Software-Only Value Speculation Scheduling", *Technical Report. Dept. of Electrical and Computer Engineering, North Carolina State University, Raleigh, NC 27695-7911*, June 1998

[6] C. Fu, M. D. Jennings, S. Y. Larin, and T. M. Conte, "Value Speculation Scheduling for High Performance Processors", in *8th International Conference on Architectural Support for Programming Languages and Operating Systems*, October 1998.

[7] D. Grunwald, A. Klauser, S. Manne, and A. Pleskun, "Confidence Estimation for Speculation Control", in *25th International Symposium of Computer Architecture*, June 1998.

[8] J. Huang, Y. Choi, D. J. Lilja, "Improving Value Prediction by Exploiting Both Operand and Output Value Locality", *Laboratory for Advanced Research in Computing Technology and Compilers Technical Report No. ARCTiC 99-06*, July 1999.

[9] K. M. Lepak and M. H. Lipasti, "On the Value Locality of Store Instructions", in *27th International Symposium of Computer Architecture*, June 2000.

[10] M. H. Lipasti and J. P. Shen, "Exploiting Value Locality to Exceed the Dataflow Limit", in *29th International Symposium on Microarchitecture*, December 1996.

[11] M. H. Lipasti and J. P. Shen, "The Performance Potential of Value and Dependence Prediction", in *EUROPAR-97*, August 1997.

[12] S. Lee, Y. Wang, P.Yew, "Decoupled Value Prediction on Trace Processors", in *6th International Symposium on High Performance Computer Architecture*, January 2000.

[13] P. Marcuello and A. Gonzalez, "The Potential of Data Value Speculation to Boost ILP", in *12th International Conference on Supercomputing*, July 1998.

[14] P. Marcuello and A. Gonzalez, "A Quantitative Assessment of Thread-Level Speculation Techniques", in *1st International Parallel and Distributed Processing Symposium*, May 2000.

[15] P. Marcuello, J. Tubella, and A. Gonzalez, "Value Prediction for Speculative Multithreaded Architectures" in *32th International Symposium on Microarchitecture*, November 1999.

[16] R. Muth, S. Debray, S. Watterson, and K. De Bosschere, "alto: A Link-Time Optimizer for the Compaq Alpha", *University of Arizona Computer Sciences Technical Report 98-14*, December 1998.

[17] T. Nakra, R. Gupta, and M. L. Soffa, "Global Context-Based Value Prediction", in *5th International Symposium on High Performance Computer Architecture*, January 1999.

[18] T. Nakra, R. Gupta, and M. L. Soffa, "Value Prediction in VLIW Machines", in *26th International Symposium on Computer Architecture*, May 1999.

[19] Y. Sazeides and J. E. Smith, "The Predictability of Data Values", in *30th International Symposium on Microarchitecture*, December 1997.

[20] A. Sodani and G. Sohi, "Dynamic Instruction Reuse", in *24th International Symposium on Computer Architecture*, June 1997.

[21] E. Schnarr and J. Larus, "Fast Out-Of-Order Processor Simulation Using Memoization", in *8th International Conference on Architectural Support for Programming Languages and Operating Systems*, October 1998.

[22] S. T. Srinivasan and A. R. Lebeck, "Load Latency Tolerance in Dynamically Scheduled Processors", in *31st International Symposium on Microarchitecture*, December 1998.

[23] D. M. Tullsen, J. S. Seng, "Storageless Value Prediction Using Prior Register Values", in *26th International Symposium on Computer Architecture*, May 1999.

[24] VTune[TM] Performance Analyzer Home Page, http://developer.intel.com/vtune/analyzer/index.htm

[25] C. B. Zilles and G. Sohi, "Understanding the Backwards Slices of Performance Degrading Instructions", in *27th International Symposium of Computer Architecture*, June 2000.

Instruction Distribution Heuristics for Quad-Cluster, Dynamically-Scheduled, Superscalar Processors

Amirali Baniasadi
Electrical and Computer Engineering
Northwestern University
amirali@ece.northwestern.edu

Andreas Moshovos
Electrical And Computer Engineering
University of Toronto
moshovos@eecg.toronto.edu

Abstract

We investigate instruction distribution methods for quad-cluster, dynamically-scheduled superscalar processors. We study a variety of methods with different cost, performance and complexity characteristics. We investigate both non-adaptive and adaptive methods and their sensitivity both to inter-cluster communication latencies and pipeline depth. Furthermore, we develop a set of models that allow us to identify how well each method attacks issue-bandwidth and inter-cluster communication restrictions. We find that a relatively simple method that changes clusters every other three instructions offers only a 17% performance slowdown compared to a non-clustered configuration operating at the same frequency. Moreover, we show that by utilizing adaptive methods it is possible to further reduce this gap down to about 14%. Furthermore, performance appears to be more sensitive to inter-cluster communication latencies rather than to pipeline depth. The best performing method offers a slowdown of about 24% when inter-cluster communication latency is two cycle. This gap is only 20% when two additional stages are introduced in the front-end pipeline.

1 Introduction

Exploiting instruction-level parallelism via out-of-order execution facilitated rapid performance improvements during the past decade. An evolutionary path to continuing this performance growth calls for larger and wider instruction windows. The hope is that such instruction windows will expose more parallelism leading to higher concurrency and hence higher performance. Unfortunately, it is now widely believed that simply scaling the existing centralized window designs may not be possible without adversely affecting clock cycle and consequently performance. There are several reasons why including fundamental scaling limitations of centralized designs [12] and changing semiconductor technology trade-offs, e.g., [2,10] (e.g., it may not be possible to route results within a single cycle in a wide superscalar processor).

Accordingly, *clustering* has been proposed as an alternative to wide and deep organizations. In clustering, a collection of smaller windows with associated functional units is used to approximate a much wider and deeper window. Compared to a centralized organization, clustered designs trade-off scheduling flexibility for higher clock rates. Consequently, to achieve high performance we need to distribute instructions among the clusters so that clustering-induced stalls are minimized. Such stalls are primary the result of restricted intra-cluster issue bandwidth and of increased inter-cluster communication latency.

Previous work investigated various instruction distribution (or, cluster assignment) methods for dual-cluster designs [4,6,12] (see Section 6 for additional information). Moreover, the ALPHA 21264 processor already uses a dual-cluster core [9]. Building even wider and deeper windows may require additional clusters. However, whether such designs are appropriate requires close investigation of the underlying trade-offs. Accordingly, in this work we investigate instruction distribution methods for a quad-cluster, dynamically-scheduled superscalar organization. We investigate a variety of methods with various cost, complexity and performance characteristics including *adaptive* and *non-adaptive* methods. Non-adaptive methods use fixed policies that do not change during run-time, while adaptive methods may change their decisions based on past behavior. We study methods that utilize various types of information, including dependences, dataflow graph depth, instruction types and past behavior. To gain additional insight we also vary intra-cluster issue and inter-cluster communication restrictions. Finally, we investigate the sensitivity of these methods to relevant architectural parameters, i.e., inter-cluster communication latency and pipeline depth.

Some (i.e., the non-adaptive), but not all of the methods have been proposed and evaluated before in the context of dual-cluster processors. To the best of our knowledge, no other study of instruction distribution heuristics for quad-clustered, dynamically-scheduled superscalar processors has been published. Of course, there is a multitude of architectural parameters that are relevant for clustered designs and for the methods we studied. Moreover, cluster-aware compiler scheduling techniques warrant further attention. However, such an extensive investigation is not possible given the limited space available. Nevertheless, we study a variety of representative configurations varying a set of key architectural parameters.

The rest of this paper is organized as follows. In Section 2, we briefly discuss a number of trade-offs relevant to the design of instruction distribution methods. Here, we also discuss our methodology. In Section 3 we present a number of non-adaptive heuristics and evaluate their performance. In Section 4, we discuss a number of adaptive heuristics. In Section 5, we investigate the sensitivity of the better performing heuristics to increased inter-cluster communication latency and front-end pipeline stages. In Section 6 we review related work. Finally, in Section 7 we summarize our findings and offer concluding remarks. For clarity we use the term *distribution method* in place of *instruction distribution method*. We also use *communication* instead of *inter-cluster communication*. Finally, we use the terms *centralized* and *non-clustered* architecture interchangeably.

2 Distribution Trade-offs and Methodology

In this Section, we discuss the trade-offs involved in developing instruction distribution methods. Throughout this study we assume a uniform, quad-cluster organization (the details are given later in this Section). The front-end delivers instructions which are then distributed to the four clusters via a distribution mechanism. Our focus is on this distribution mechanism. As we later show, this assignment process can dramatically impact performance. We assume that each cluster contains each own scheduler and set of functional-units. Furthermore, we assume that once an instruction is assigned to a cluster the decision is final. An alternative would be to decouple execution resources and schedulers, however, such a study is beyond the scope of this paper. Each cluster has its own set of functional units including data cache ports. Dependent instructions can issue back-to-back provided that they both reside in the same cluster. However, propagating results across clusters requires additional cycles.

Throughout this study, our goal is to maximize performance through appropriate distribution methods. To achieve maximal performance an ideal schedule is needed. However, this is a hard problem even for a centralized architecture. Accordingly, it is convenient to approach distribution as a problem of minimizing clustering-induced stalls compared to an equivalent (i.e., same overall instruction window and resources) centralized architecture. Clustering-induced stalls are either the result of limited per cluster issue bandwidth (and in general, resource distribution including functional units) or of inter-cluster communication latencies.

In contrast to a centralized configuration, each cluster is limited to only a fraction of the total issue slots per cycle (for example, each of the four clusters can issue only 2 instructions of the total of 8 per cycle). Accordingly, it is possible for an otherwise ready-to-issue instruction to get stalled in one cluster while free issue slots exist in other clusters. Moreover, since we assume that it takes additional cycles to propagate results across clusters, it is possible for an instruction to get stalled waiting for data that is currently available at another cluster. However, it is not strictly true that our mechanism should minimize such stalls. To be precise, it is only those stalls that impact the critical path through the computation that are really important. It may be possible to tolerate some stalls. Accordingly, we can categorize stalls into *benign* (those that do not affect performance compared to a centralized organization) and *harmful*. An example illustrating some of the trade-offs is given in Figure 1.

While maximum performance is desirable, the potential performance benefits of a distribution method should be weighted against its cost and complexity. Of particular concern is the size of any auxiliary structures used. For example, in Section 4, we will study a number of methods that significantly improve performance while utilizing sizeable cache-like structures.

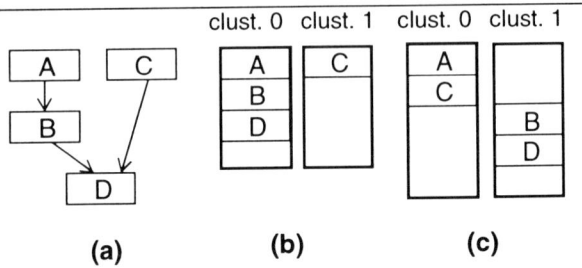

Figure 1: *Example illustrating some of the performance trade-offs in instruction distribution. We assume a dual-cluster configuration and unit latencies for all operations. Furthermore, we assume single-issue clusters. (a) Code fragment with arrows representing data dependences and boxes instructions. (b) A cluster assignment that maximizes performance. Notice that while it takes an additional cycle to propagate C's result, this does not negatively impact performance. (c) A non-optimal cluster assignment. Execution is delayed while A's result is propagated between the two clusters.*

Depending on the real-estate available on-chip, this space may be better used for other purposes (e.g., branch prediction).

Moreover, care must be taken to consider not only IPC improvements but also the potential impact on clock cycle and pipeline depth. Besides the number of steps required by the method, particular attention should also be given to the type of information used. It is desirable to use information that is readily available at the decode stage or earlier and preferably early in the clock cycle. For example, in Section 3, we will examine methods that utilize dependence information. While such information can be easily determined (e.g., via the register renaming mechanism), we may not have enough time to utilize it during the decode phase without introducing an additional stage or prolonging the clock cycle.

Before we start to describe and evaluate various methods we first discuss our methodology. We have used the SPECint'95 programs which we compiled for the MIPS-4-like architecture used by the Simplescalar simulation toolset [3]. We used GNU's *gcc* compiler (flags: -O2 -funroll-loops -finline-functions). To attain reasonable simulation times we modified the standard *train* or *test* inputs. Table 1 reports the dynamic instruction count. In the interest of space, we use the abbreviations shown under the "Ab." column.

We have modified Simplescalar's out-of-order simulator to model a variety of clustering configurations and instruction distribution methods. The base configuration is detailed in Table 2. Our base processor is capable of executing up to 8 instructions per cycle and is equipped with a 256-entry instruction window. Moreover, an 128-entry load/store scheduler (load/store queue) capable of scheduling up to four loads and stores per cycle is used to schedule load/store execution. This scheduler implements ideal memory dependence speculation [11]. Previous work has shown that memory dependence speculation is particularly important for clustered architectures. Moreover, it has been shown that it is possible to approach ideal memory dependence speculation via prediction [5,11].

Program	Ab.	IC	Program	Ab.	IC
126.gcc	gcc	1,317 M	130.li	li	207 M
129.compress	com	154 M	124.m88ksim	m88	196 M
099.go	go	134 M	134.perl	per	177 M
132.ijpeg	ijp	130 M	147.vortex	vor	377 M

Table 1: *Benchmark Execution Characteristics. Instruction counts ("IC" columns) are in millions.*

Default Non-Clustered Configuration			
Branch Predictor	64K GShare+64K bimodal w/ 64K selector	Fetch Unit	Up to 16 instr. per cycle.
Instruction Window Size	256 entries	Load/Store Queue	128 entries, 4 loads or stores per cycle
Issue/Decode/Commit Bandwidth	8 instructions / cycle	Functional Unit Latencies	same as MIPS R10000
L1 - Instruction cache	64K, 2-way SA, 32-byte blocks, 2 cycles	L1 - Data cache	64K, 4-way SA, 32-byte blocks, 2 cycles
Unified L2	256K, 4-way SA, 64-byte blocks, 12 cycles	Main Memory	Infinite, 100 cycles
Default Clustered Configuration			
Clusters	4, each 2-way issue w/ uniform distribution of functional units 64-entry windows and 32-entry load/store queues per cluster	Inter-cluster delay	1 cycle both for registers and store-load forwarding

Table 2: *Base configuration details. We model an 8-way aggressive, dynamically scheduled superscalar processor having a 256-entry scheduler and an 128-entry load/store queue. Also shown is the default quad-cluster configuration.*

3 Non-Adaptive Methods

We have investigated both *adaptive* and *non-adaptive* methods. Non-adaptive methods use fixed policies that do not change during run-time. For example, always selecting the cluster with fewest instructions. Adaptive methods, on the other hand, base their decisions on dynamically collected information. For example, whether the cluster assignment for a particular instruction resulted in a stall last time it was executed. In this Section, we are concerned with non-adaptive methods. Further information on adaptive methods is given in Section 4.

We have investigated a variety of non-adaptive heuristics with varying complexity and performance characteristics. Here we restrict our attention to the following representative subset: First-Fit (FF), Modulo (MOD_1 and MOD_3), Dependence-based (DEP), Slice (SLC), Branch-Cut (BC), Load-Cut (LC) and Dependence-Depth-based (DDB). The first two methods do not utilize program-related information, while the rest do. We have considered dependences, instruction types and dataflow depth as alternative sources of program-related information.

First-Fit (FF): In this method we assign instructions to the same cluster until it fills up completely. Then we move to the next cluster and do the same. The primary advantage of this method is its simplicity. A possible implementation comprises a per cluster global-AND of the occupied flags of the cluster's reservation stations (assuming an RUU-like implementation [15]) and a global current-cluster pointer. An incoming instruction is assigned to the current cluster so long there is space available (the cluster's global-AND signal is 0, i.e., there is at least one free slot available). Otherwise, the current-cluster pointer advances to the next in order cluster[1]. The impact of this method on decode/dispatch latency should be minimal as the information required is independent of the instructions themselves and can be made available early in the pipeline. While simple, this method makes no explicit attempt to minimize neither communication- nor issue-induced stalls. Nevertheless, dependent instructions tend to be close in the instruction stream. This often helps control communication-induced stalls.

Modulo Methods (MOD_n): As we will see in Section 3.1, the first-fit method fails to use issue-bandwidth efficiently. To improve issue-bandwidth utilization while keeping complexity at a minimum, we have investigated a variety of *modulo n* (MOD_n) methods. In these methods, instructions are assigned to clusters in a modulo n fashion where n is a small integer. For example, in the modulo 3 (MOD_3) method the first three instructions are assigned to cluster 0, the next three to cluster 1 and so on. Compared to FF, these methods distribute instructions more fairly among clusters resulting in a better utilization of issue-bandwidth. We have experimented with a variety of values for n and found that the optimal value differs per program. Here, we restrict our attention to MOD_1 and MOD_3. As with first-fit, the information required by modulo methods can be made available early in the pipeline. While fairly simple, MOD_3 performs surprisingly well.

Dependence-based (DEP): Neither of the methods described so far leverages program-related information. The dependence-based method uses data-dependence information in an attempt to reduce communication-induced stalls. In this method we aim to assign dependent instructions to the same cluster. This is done as follows: When decoding an instruction, we attempt to

---

1. Using a global "is there a free slot available?" signal per cluster makes distribution a serial process; we have to wait until the first instruction is assigned before probing for slot availability for the second instruction. To do in-parallel cluster assignment of multiple instructions we may use a population count circuit per cluster. This does not have to be complete population count circuit as the number of instructions that can be assigned per cycle is limited (i.e., decode width). Accordingly, we only care whether up to that number of slots are available per cluster.

assign it to the same cluster as its parents. If an instruction has multiple parents that are assigned to different clusters we pick the cluster holding the youngest in program order parent (i.e., closest to this instruction). (We have experimented with other alternatives and found no significant performance variations.) If the parents have long committed, we just pick the cluster with the fewest instructions. The data-dependence information required by this method can be made available via the register renaming mechanism. Depending on the particular implementation, deferring cluster assignment till after register renaming may negatively impact the clock cycle or force us to introduce additional pipeline stages.

Slice (SLC): Using the DEP method, we often find that the parents of an instruction are assigned to different clusters. This is the result of the limited, forward-dependence-based scope of the DEP method. To further reduce communication-induced stalls it would be better to assign all parents and their consuming child to the same cluster. This is the goal of the slice method. To do so, we employ the method proposed by Canal, Parcerisa and González [4]. An auxiliary, PC-indexed table (the slice table) is used to re-construct the data-flow graph on the fly. Eventually, a common tag is assigned to all instructions belonging to the same *slice*. This tag is used to assign all dependent instructions to the same cluster the next time they are encountered. If no space is available in that cluster we pick the cluster with the fewest instructions. This method reduces communication stalls since instructions within a slice will reside mostly in the same cluster. Moreover, our results show that issue bandwidth is used efficiently. However, these improvements come at the expense of an auxiliary table. Compared to DEP, the slice-table-provided tag can be made available much earlier than the register-dependence information (since the slice table is PC-indexed). We classify this technique as non-adaptive as it does not utilize explicit information about the success of past cluster assignment decisions. We assume infinite slice tables in our experiments.

Branch- and Load-Cut (BC and LC): While DEP and SLC offer superior performance they may be too complex or costly to implement depending on implementation specifics. Accordingly, we investigated methods that leverage other program-related information that can be easily extracted at run-time. In particular, we investigated methods that utilize instruction-type information. In the branch-cut method we assign consecutive instructions to the same cluster till we reach a branch instruction. The intuition behind this heuristic is that instructions within a basic-block are mostly dependent. We also investigated variations of the branch-cut method where we changed clusters only on backward branches. In doing so, we were motivated by work in thread-level speculation where loop iterations may be assigned to separate clusters for parallel execution (see Section 6). However, we didn't observe significant performance improvements. Accordingly, we restrict our attention to the general, all branch-cut method.

We also experimented with a load-cut method where instructions are assigned to the same cluster until a load is encountered. The load and the instructions that follow (till the next load) are then assigned to the next available cluster. The intuition behind this method is that loads often lead a chain of dependent instructions. Accordingly, the hope is that changing clusters upon encountering a load should force mostly dependent instructions to the same cluster, while distributing independent instructions across clusters. Whenever a sequence of adjacent loads is encountered we do not change clusters.

Dependence-Depth-based (DDB): Finally, in this method we categorize instructions based on its position (depth) in the DFG (Data Flow Graph). Only instructions currently active in the instruction window are considered in this process. If an instruction has no parents alive in the window, it belongs to depth 0. If it has only its direct parents alive it belongs to depth 1, and so on. We assign an instruction to the cluster having the least number of instructions of the same level while taking dependence information also into account (when a choice exists, we will assign to the same cluster as its closest parent). The intuition behind this method is that in a centralized configuration, instructions at the same level would probably issue around the same time (ignoring cache misses and other multi-cycle operations). Therefore by distributing them among clusters we could use the available issue bandwidth more efficiently. While this method may be fairly complex to implement, we include it as it approximates a resource-based scheduling algorithm.

3.1 Non-Adaptive Method Performance

In this Section, we present our analysis of the non-adaptive methods. We approach each method from two different perspectives. First we approach each method as an improvement over the most simple non-adaptive method (FF). Ultimately however, clustering is viable only if it results in a sufficiently higher operating frequency compared to a non-clustered implementation. For this reason, we also compare each method with a non-clustered architecture with the same overall resources.

While performance is our ultimate metric, it is desirable to get additional insight on how each method attacks issue-bandwidth restrictions and inter-cluster communication delays. To do so, we use a two tiered approach. First we report the fraction of instructions that are delayed as a result of communication or of issue bandwidth limitations. However, the two performance degrading factors interact with each other making it difficult to isolate their impact. Accordingly, we also study each performance degrading factor independently (more on this later on).

Figure 2(a) reports relative performance for DEP, BC, LC, MOD_1, SLC, DDB and MOD_3 from left to right. The base configuration is a clustered architecture utilizing the FF method. We can see that on the average, DEP performs the worst among all heuristics (excluding FF of course). With this method instructions find that their two parents are assigned to different clusters. Also, this method tends to assign too many dependent instructions to the same cluster. The first phenomenon results in inter-cluster communication induced delays, while the second phenomenon results in under-utilized issue bandwidth. As expected, (with the exception of *go*) the SLC method improves performance over DEP by placing all dependent instructions in the same cluster while distributing unrelated slices across clusters. The instruction-type-based heuristics LC and BC offer competitive and some times better performance even though they do not require an auxiliary table. The DDB method also performs similarly for most benchmarks. Further improve-

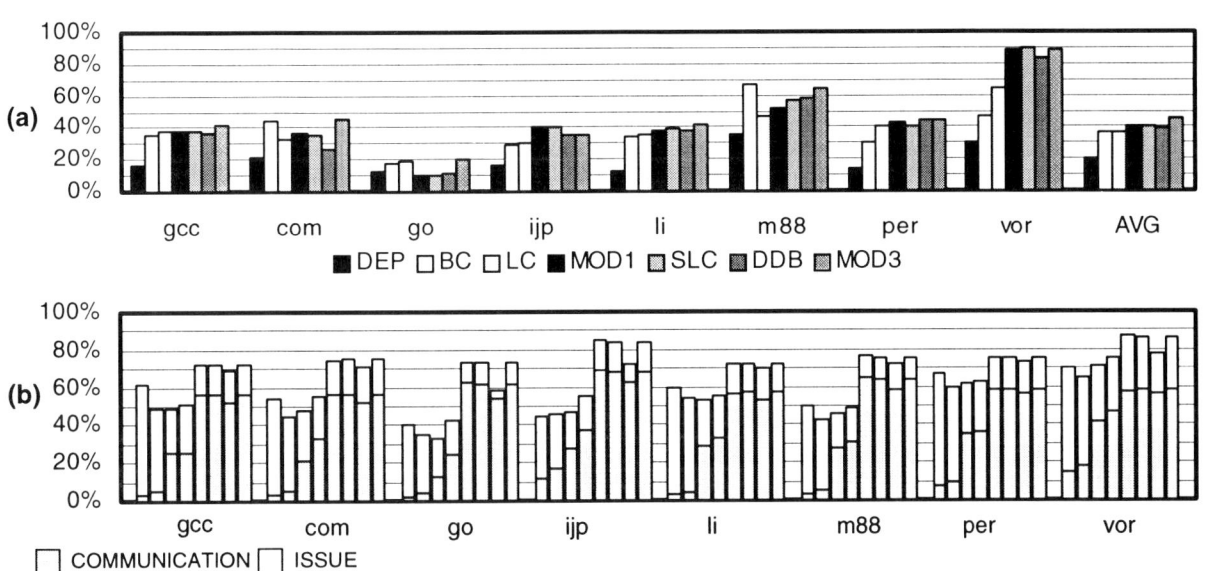

Figure 2: *(a) Performance of non-adaptive heuristics over a base configuration utilizing the first-fit (FF) method. Here we approach each method as an improvement over the simplest method we studied. Higher is better. (b) Fractions of committed instructions that are stalled as the result of inter-cluster communication (lower part) or issue-bandwidth restrictions (upper part). The following methods are reported: FF, DEP, BC, LC, MOD_1, SLC, DDB and MOD_3 from left to right per benchmark (same order as in part (a) with the addition of FF).*

ments may be possible by utilizing better instruction latency estimates (currently DDB assumes unit latencies for all instructions). Finally, MOD_3 performs the best. It offers a 45.6% improvement over FF. Apparently, this method strikes a good balance in assigning some dependent and some independent instructions to the same cluster. *Go* seems to benefit less from the various methods compared to the other benchmarks. This is mostly due to the relatively low branch prediction accuracy for this benchmark which results to relative small number of simultaneously active instructions. Consequently there isn't much parallelism and little room for improving performance over the simple FF method. Branch prediction accuracy is also mostly responsible for the higher performance benefits observed for vortex and to a lesser extend for m88ksim. In these programs, the vast majority of reservation stations are occupied. Moreover, these programs exhibit relatively high parallelism. Consequently, there is much to be gained by carefully distributing instructions across clusters. Moreover, these programs tend to be more tolerant to inter-cluster communication overhead (parallelism helps to tolerate these delays).

Figure 2(b) reports the fraction of committed instructions that are delayed waiting for a result from a different cluster (lower bar) or because issue-bandwidth was unavailable (upper bar). Whenever an instruction is delayed both due to inter-cluster communication and issue-bandwidth limitations we assign it to the inter-cluster communication delayed category. In general, performance and the fraction of instructions that are delayed are not correlated. However, in most cases, the best a method is, the higher the fraction of instructions that are delayed. This is the result of higher concurrency. (When distribution is not good, very few instructions are executing at any given point, resulting in very few instructions that are ready, or that would be ready if they had immediate access to the results in other clusters.) An observation can also be made about the relative fractions of instructions delayed due to communication or issued-bandwidth and performance. For the worse performing methods (FF and DEP), most instructions are delayed due to insufficient issue-bandwidth (upper bar). As we distribute instructions to better utilize issue-bandwidth, communication delays start to become more common (lower bar).

In a realistic clustered configuration, issue-bandwidth restrictions and communication delays interact making it difficult to draw conclusions. Accordingly, we introduce four machine models: NI-NC, I-NC, NI-C and I-C. In this notation, I indicates that the model includes per cluster issue bandwidth restrictions, while C indicates that communication delays are incurred. The inverse notation, NI and NC, indicates that the model does not include per cluster issue-bandwidth restrictions or inter-cluster communication delays respectively. The NI-NC model corresponds to a non-clustered architecture while the I-C model corresponds to a realistic, clustered architecture. The two other models do not correspond to realistic architectures. However, they provide additional insight on the effectiveness of each method. The NI-C model shows how well we could have done if no issue-bandwidth restrictions were applicable (total issue bandwidth is still limited to 8 instructions per cycle, however, these instructions can come from any cluster, possibly all from the same one). Similarly, the I-NC model shows how well the heuristic performs in attacking issue bandwidth restrictions (no communication stalls possible).

Figure 3 reports performance improvements over the base clustered configuration that uses the FF method. Due to space limitations we restrict our attention to FF, MOD_3, the instruction-type-based BC and the dependence-based SLC. As

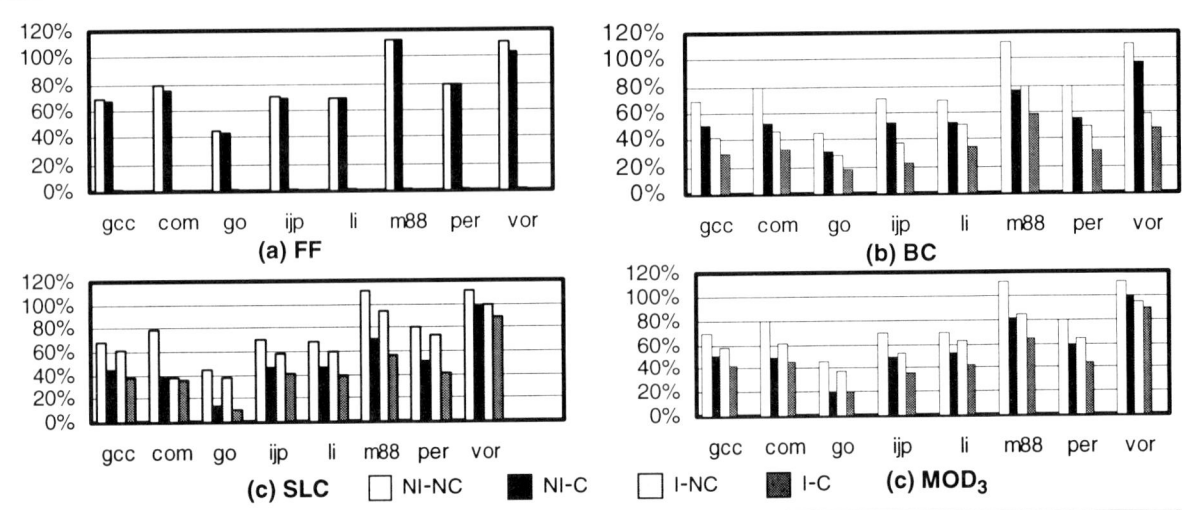

Figure 3: *How well some of the non-adaptive methods attack issue-bandwidth and communication restrictions. Four models are simulated per method. The four models are derived by selectively modeling issue-bandwidth and communication restrictions. The models are labeled with an X-Y notation, where X is either I or NI and Y is either C or NC. I indicates that issue bandwidth restrictions are imposed, while NI that they are not. Similarly, C and NC indicate that inter-cluster communication delays are modeled or that they are not respectively. NI-NC corresponds to a non-clustered architecture, while I-C corresponds to a realistic clustered one. Relative performance is reported over the base clustered configuration that utilizes the FF (first-fit) method. Higher is better.*

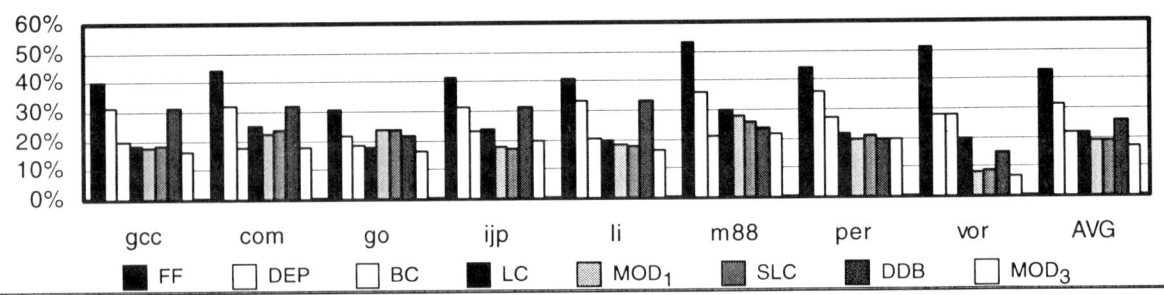

Figure 4: *Relative performance of non-adaptive method over a non-clustered organization assuming the same clock rate. Reported are slowdowns (lower is better). These slowdowns can serve as bounds on how much faster a clustered implementation's clock rate has to be over an non-clustered implementation.*

expected, the FF method (part (a)) does not perform well compared to the non-clustered architecture (NI-NC) (there are no I-C bars here since I-C with FF is the base case). In the best case of *go*, the difference is about 45%, while, it grows as large as approximately 110% for *m88ksim*. The two models NI-C and I-NC reveal that much of this performance loss is the result of issue-bandwidth distribution. When issue bandwidth is not restricted (NI-C), performance is very close to that of the non-clustered architecture (NI-NC). However, when issue is restricted and even without any communication delays (I-NC), performance drops rapidly and is very close to the realistic clustered architecture (I-C). While, the FF method is somewhat sensitive to communication delays, it is primarily crippled by inefficient use of issue-bandwidth. Issue-bandwidth restrictions seem to be more important than communication delays for BC also (part (b)). With the exception of *m88ksim*, BC performs better under NI-C than under I-NC. This trend is reversed for most benchmarks for both SLC and MOD_3 (parts (c) and (d)). As we have seen in Figure 2, these methods perform much better than either FF or BC. This result suggests that once we begin using issue bandwidth more effectively, then inter-cluster communication latencies become more important. Interestingly, the differences between I-NC and NC-I are smaller for MOD_3 for most benchmarks. This result supports our previous observation that MOD_3 strikes a better balance in attacking issue-bandwidth and communication restrictions. Notably, I-C and NI-C perform almost identical in *go*, suggesting that in this benchmark it is communication that is most important. This can be explained by the relatively low branch prediction accuracy and the resulting low instruction level parallelism.

Ultimately, a clustered architecture may be viable only if it offers better performance compared to a centralized one. For the methods we studied this can only be the result of higher operating frequency. It is desirable to know how much faster the clock rate of the clustered architecture has to be (vs. the centralized architecture's clock rate) to result in higher performance. Accordingly, we report performance slowdowns compared to a non-clustered architecture assuming the same clock frequency. These slowdowns can serve as bounds on how much faster the clock cycle of the clustered implementation must be. The results are shown in Figure 4. MOD_3, the best non-adaptive method, is 17% slower than the centralized configuration. Notice that some minor differences in the trends exhibited compared to Figure 2, are the result of using a different base configuration (in Figure 2, we used the FF-based clustered configuration as our base).

In this Section, we have discussed and evaluated the performance of various non-adaptive heuristics. We have found that it is possible to significantly improve performance over the simplistic first-fit method. However, we have also found that there is still a sizeable gap in performance (17% on the average for the best performing method) compared to a centralized architecture operating at the same frequency. In the next section we propose methods that aim at reducing this performance gap.

4 Adaptive Methods

In this section, we present and evaluate a number of adaptive methods. The intuition behind these methods is that programs tend to exhibit non-random behavior. Accordingly, it may be possible to learn and avoid inefficient cluster assignments. We have investigated two classes of adaptive techniques. The first class is based on voting, while the second attempts to improve over the fixed modulo techniques we described in the previous section.

Voting-based Methods (CNT-X): The idea behind these methods is to identify problematic instruction assignments and try to avoid them the next time the same instructions are encountered. For example, these methods can improve instruction distribution whenever a program follows the same path repeatedly. In these methods we start with an underlying non-adaptive technique. Upon executing an instruction we record information about the success or failure of the current cluster assignment in a *Cluster Prediction Table* (CPT). We experimented with PC-indexed CPTs so that they can indexed early the pipeline. A CPT entry contains four 2-bit up/down saturating counters one per cluster. The counters indicate how appropriate a cluster might be for the matching instruction, with 11 being the best and 00 the least. Initially, all counters are set to 01, indicating that all clusters are equally appropriate. As soon an instruction becomes ready we update the corresponding counter in the CPT. If the instruction can issue immediately, we increment the counter, otherwise we decrement it[2]. The next time the same instruction is encountered, the CPT is accessed in parallel with the non-adaptive method. The instruction is then assigned to the cluster with the highest counter value (most appropriate based on past experience). If there are more than one qualifying clusters, we use either the non-adaptive

---

2. Actually, updates are done at commit time. To do so, a bit is kept in the reservation station. This bit is set when the reservation station's ready signal is set, but the ready-select logic does not allow the instruction to execute. Upon commit, the corresponding CPT entry is updated accordingly.

method's recommendation (so long as it is one the clusters with the highest counter values) or choose the cluster with less instructions.

As described, the *voting-based* method reacts only to issue-bandwidth-induced stalls. We used these stalls as they can easily identified locally at each reservation station (ready signal vs. allowed to issue). In our simulation environment it is straightforward to also detect scenarios where inter-cluster communication is at fault. However, the specifics of a realistic implementation are beyond the scope of this paper. Accordingly, we restrict our attention to using only issue-bandwidth related stalls for our adaptive methods.

Adaptive-Modulo (MOD_a): As we have seen in Section 3, MOD_3 performed best among the non-adaptive techniques. We have also noted that the best modulo value varied per benchmark, with 3 being a good enough comprise across all benchmarks we studied. Motivated by these observations we have developed the adaptive-modulo method. In this method, we start with an initial modulo value of 3. However, as execution progresses we keep statistics on how often instructions are stalled as the result of insufficient issue-bandwidth. After a prespecified number of instructions have executed (1 million in our experiments) we try a different modulo value (e.g., increase to 4). If the new modulo value results in fewer instructions being stalled, we continue changing the modulo value (e.g., move to 5). Otherwise, we alter our direction of change (e.g., decrement as opposed to increment). Using this policy, the modulo value is dynamically adjusted to one that offers better performance. As described, this policy can get stuck to a local maximum since it relies on comparisons between adjacent values. Accordingly, we have also tried a different policy where we sweep over a pre-specified range of modulo values (i.e., 1 to 16) before deciding on the best one (this scan is repeated at regular intervals, i.e., 100M instructions). However, we did not find significant performance improvements.

The primary advantage of this method is that it offers some adaptability without requiring many additional resources. A similar method was proposed for selecting an appropriate history-depth for branch prediction [8].

4.1 Adaptive Method Performance

We report results assuming infinite cluster prediction tables. We have also experimented with finite prediction structures and found that 16K-entry non-tagged, counter-based prediction tables perform very close and sometimes better than the infinite table (better accuracy is possible via constructive interference). As with the non-adaptive techniques, we first compare their performance using the most simple method (FF) as our base. Moreover, we report a breakdown of stalled instructions and use our four models (presented in Section 3.1) to isolate issue-bandwidth and communication related stalls. Finally, we compared with a non-clustered architecture assuming the same clock rate.

We have experimented with various voting-based methods. Here we restrict our attention to voting-based extensions to MOD_1[3], Branch-Cut (BC) and Slice (SLC). We also study the adaptive-modulo technique. Figure 5(a) shows relative performance improvements over the FF-based clustered architecture.

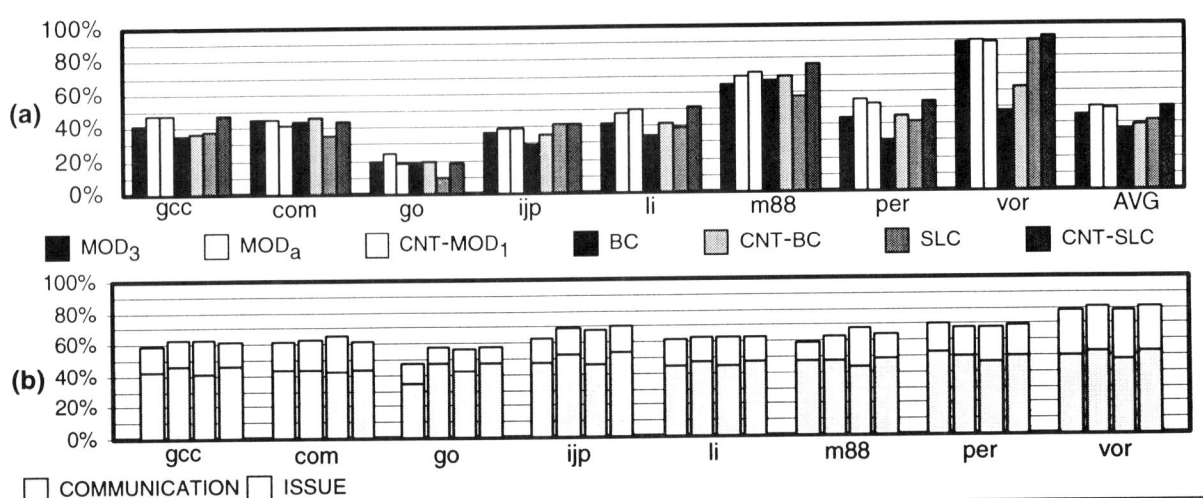

Figure 5: *(a) Adaptive Method Performance. Performance improvements are over the clustered architecture using the FF method. For ease of comparison we also include the corresponding non-adaptive methods. A CNT-X notation indicates a counter-based extension of the X non-adaptive method. Higher is better. (b) Fractions of committed instructions that are stalled as the result of inter-cluster communication (lower part) or issue-bandwidth restrictions (upper part). The following methods are reported: MOD_a, $CNT\text{-}MOD_1$, $CNT\text{-}BC$ and $CNT\text{-}SLC$ from left to right per benchmark (same order as in part (a) excluding the non-adaptive methods).*

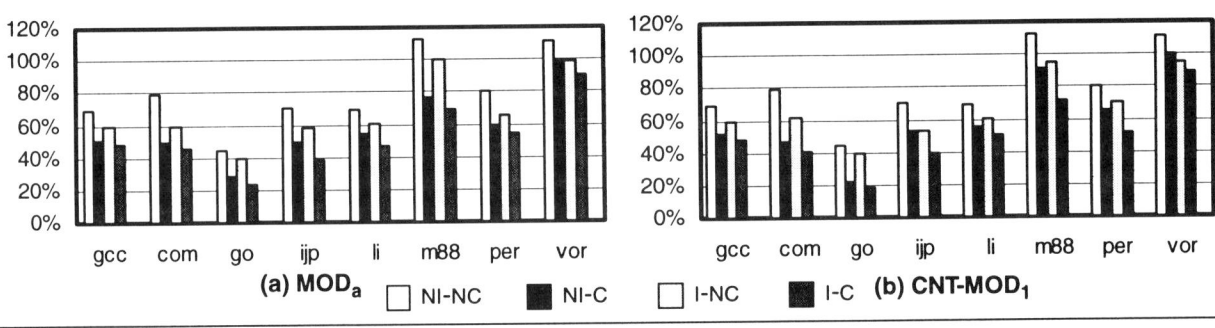

Figure 6: *How well some of the adaptive methods attack issue-bandwidth and communication restrictions. Four models are simulated per method. See Figure 3 for an explanation of the four models. Higher is better.*

For ease of comparison, the relevant non-adaptive methods are also included (repeated from Figure 2). As expected, for most cases the adaptive-techniques improve performance over the underlying non-adaptive method. On the average, the performance improvements over FF are approximately 50%, 49%, 39% and 50% for MOD_a, $CNT\text{-}MOD_1$, $CNT\text{-}BC$, and $CNT\text{-}SLC$ respectively. The performance improvements over FF for MOD_3, BC and SLC were 46%, 37% and 41% respectively. The best performing method is $CNT\text{-}SLC$. However, $CNT\text{-}MOD_1$ and MOD_a offer very similar performance improvements. Recall, that $CNT\text{-}SLC$ requires both a slice table and cluster prediction table. In contrast, $CNT\text{-}MOD_1$ requires only a cluster prediction table. Finally, MOD_a has minimal space requirements.

Figure 5(b) shows a breakdown of delayed instructions for the adaptive methods. The lower part of each bar reports the fraction of committed instructions that were delayed due to inter-cluster communication. The upper part shows the fraction of committed instructions delayed due to issue-bandwidth unavailability. Again, it appears that a better a method performs the more instructions are stalled. However, the differences among the various methods are small. This further justifies using the four models of issue-bandwidth and communication (see Section 3.1) to determine how sensitive each method is to each of these restrictions. The results are shown in Figure 6 where the base case is the clustered FF-based configuration. We restrict our attention to MOD_a and $CNT\text{-}MOD_1$. The general trends with respect to issue-bandwidth and communication restrictions have not changed by much. However, the gap between NI-NC and the other models has been reduced and so have, for the most part, the differences between NI-C and I-NC.

Finally, in Figure 7 we report the relative performance of our adaptive methods over a non-clustered architecture with the same clock rate. The voting-based methods perform very simi-

---

3. We did not observe a significant difference compared to counter-based extensions to MOD_3.

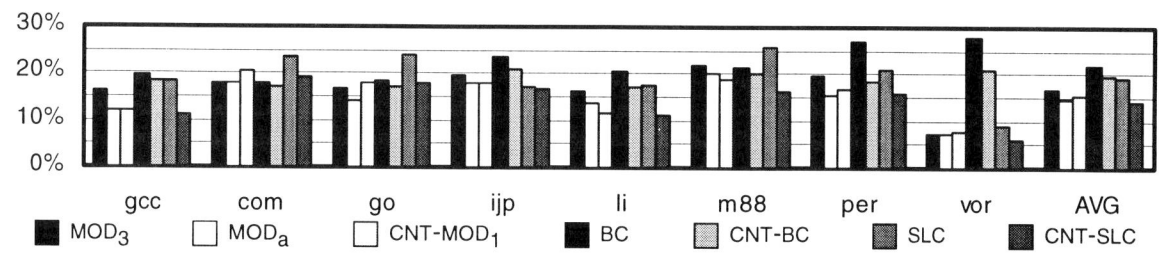

Figure 7: *Performance of the adaptive methods over a non-clustered architecture with the same clock rate. Shown are slowdowns, accordingly, lower is better.*

larly, with MOD_a offering competitive performance. CNT-MOD_1 has narrowed the gap down to 15.2%, CNT-SLC to 14.1% while MOD_a to 14.6%. In absolute terms, the improvements appear relatively minor. However, they are sizeable when compared to the original gap between the best non-adaptive method and the centralized architecture (about 3% off the maximum possible of 17%).

In this section, we have shown that it is possible to further improve performance using adaptive techniques. The best performing methods where the adaptive-modulo and the counter-based extension to MOD_1.

5 Sensitivity Analysis

In this section, we investigate the sensitivity of some methods to key architectural parameters. In Section 5.1, we vary inter-cluster communication latency, while in Section 5.2, we investigate how tolerant our mechanisms are to increases in the front-end pipeline depth. Finally, in Section 5.3, we we study configurations with 4-way, 2-way and single-issue clusters.

5.1 Inter-Cluster Communication Latency

Figure 8 reports performance when the inter-cluster communication delay is increased to two cycles. We report slowdowns over the default centralized configuration operating at the same frequency. No additional communication delays are imposed for the base configuration. As expected, the performance gap increases. CNT-SLC is the best performing method being about 24% slower than the base. MOD_3 remains the best non-adaptive method. While MOD_a still improves over the non-adaptive methods, the other, voting-based adaptive methods now perform significantly better.

5.2 Front-End Latency

We also take a look at how increasing the number of front-end pipeline stages impacts some of the best performing methods. As we discussed in Section 2, depending on the specifics of the pipeline, the information utilized and the steps required by a distribution method, we might be forced to introduce additional pipeline stages. Figure 9 reports how performance varies for one (part (a)) or two (part (b)) additional decode stages. We restrict our attention to BC, CNT-BC, SLC, and CNT-SLC. We choose these methods since they utilize program-information and/or auxiliary tables. Consequently, they are more likely to impact the depth of the front-end pipeline. We report slowdowns with respect to the default centralized configuration that does not include any additional decode stages. Inter-cluster communication latency is one cycle. Overall, the performance gap has increased. However, the relative trends do not change by much. The adaptive methods still perform better than the non-adaptive ones, with CNT-SLC being the best one.

5.3 Issue-Bandwidth

Finally, we experiment with three quad-cluster configurations: One made up of 4-way clusters, one with 2-way clusters and another with single-issue clusters. The total issue bandwidth is 16, 8 and 4 respectively. In all cases, we assume 2 cycles for inter-cluster communication. The results are shown in Figure 10, parts (a) through (c). For ease of comparison we use the 4-way centralized configuration as our base case. Numbers greater than 1 represent speedup while numbers lower than 1 represent slowdown.

As expected, the higher the issue bandwidth of each cluster the higher the performance. For the single-issue cluster configuration of part (c) all distribution methods perform similarly with the exception of BC and CNT-BC. Notably, CNT-BC performs worse that its non-adaptive counterpart BC. This is because rarely free issue-slots exist in other clusters or because selecting an alternate cluster introduces additional communication delays.

As we move to dual-issue and quad-issue clusters (parts (b) and (a)) the BC- and SLC-based methods perform better than MOD_a and MOD_3. CNT-MOD_1, however, remains competitive. SLC performs poorly for the 4-way cluster configuration. Recall that SLC will spread "unrelated" slices accross clusters. However, since it does not consider memory dependences, it often assigns dependent load-stores to different clusters. This results in increased store-load forwarding delays. Given that clusters are 4-way issue, we are better off assigning multiple slices to the same cluster rather than distributing them in a round-robin fashion. CNT-SLC detects innefficient cluster assignments and improves upon them. Notably, BC perfoms very close to both CNT-SLC and CNT-BC. This makes BC an attractive choice for this configuration. Recall, that the cost of BC is low compared to both CNT-BC and CNT-SLC.

6 Related Work

A plethora of studies have investigated partitioning as a way of scaling over existing, centralized dynamically-scheduled superscalar architectures. A class of methods aims at extracting parallelism by making non-continuous or large prediction-based steps in the dynamic instruction stream, e.g., [1,7,13,14,16]. Here we restrict our attention to works that

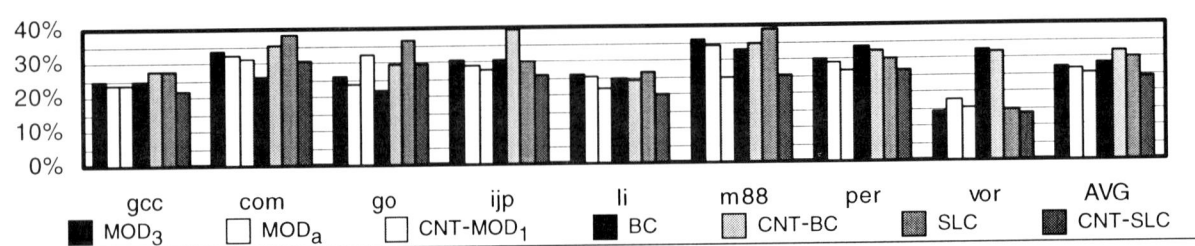

Figure 8: *Performance of some methods when inter-cluster communication latency is increased to 2 cycles. The default centralized configuration without (no communication delays) is the base. Lower is better.*

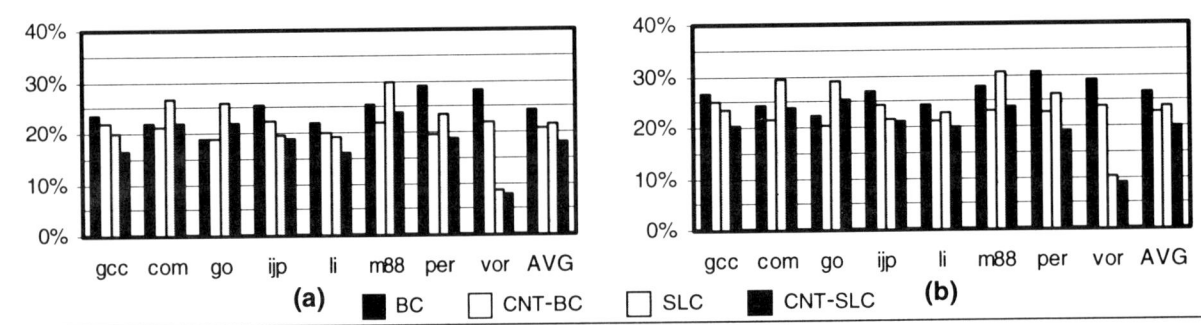

Figure 9: *Performance of some methods with deeper front-end pipelines. We include methods that utilize instruction-type and dependence information. Slowdowns are reported over the default non-clustered architecture without any additional front-end stages. Part (a) introduces one more decode stage while part (b) two.*

investigated partitioning a traditional architecture.

Palacharla, Jouppi and Smith studied the delay characteristics of key processor structures [12]. They demonstrated that it will not be possible to naively scale existing designs without adverse effects on clock cycle. They proposed using clustering as a solution and studied various non-traditional scheduling mechanisms for dual-clustered architectures (e.g., FIFO-based schedulers) and also used dependences to optimize cluster assignment. Due to the limited space available, an investigation of these alternative scheduler organizations is beyond the scope of this paper.

Farkas, Chow, Jouppi and Vransevic proposed and studied a dual-clustered architecture along with a cluster-aware static scheduling technique [6]. Canal, Parcerisa and González studied a variety of non-adaptive instruction distribution methods also for a non-uniform dual-clustered architecture [4]. They also proposed the slice-based method and explained how slice information can be extracted dynamically. Finally, the ALPHA 21264 already employs a dual-cluster micro-architecture [9].

7 Conclusion

Clustering provides a potentially viable path for wider and deeper instruction windows and higher operating frequencies. In this work, we have studied a variety of instruction distribution methods for quad-cluster processors. We studied non-adaptive methods and adaptive techniques with varying complexity and cost requirements. These methods utilized various types of information, including instruction-type, dependences and past history to better distribute instructions across clusters.

We have found that a relatively simple method, MOD_3 offers competitive performance. It was within 17% of a non-clustered organization operating at the same frequency. Moreover, we have seen that it is possible to reduce this gap down to about 14% via a counter-based prediction scheme. While in absolute terms this is a minor improvement, it does represent a sizeable reduction in relative terms (as compared to the 17% gap with MOD_3). We have also investigated the sensitivity of our methods to inter-cluster communication latency and front-end pipeline depth. We found that performance is much more sensitive to inter-cluster communication for the better performing methods. The performance gap for the best performing method increased to 24% when inter-cluster communication latency was increased two cycles. In contract, even when two additional front-end pipeline stages were introduced, this gap was only 20%.

While we studied a reasonable set of configurations and methods, there is still a plethora of design points and possible other methods that warrant further study. There are multiple directions for further experimentation, including non-uniform cluster organizations, restrictions on inter-cluster communication bandwidth, the effect of previously proposed compiler optimizations [6] and alternative scheduler designs such as those appearing in [12]. Of particular interest are organizations where execution clusters (i.e., functional units, register files and cache ports) and schedulers are decoupled. In such a design, an instruction is first assigned to a scheduler, and then, based on input operand availability is sent to the appropriate execution cluster.

Acknowledgements

We thank the anonymous reviewers and Eric Sprangle for their insightful suggestions. We also thank Scott

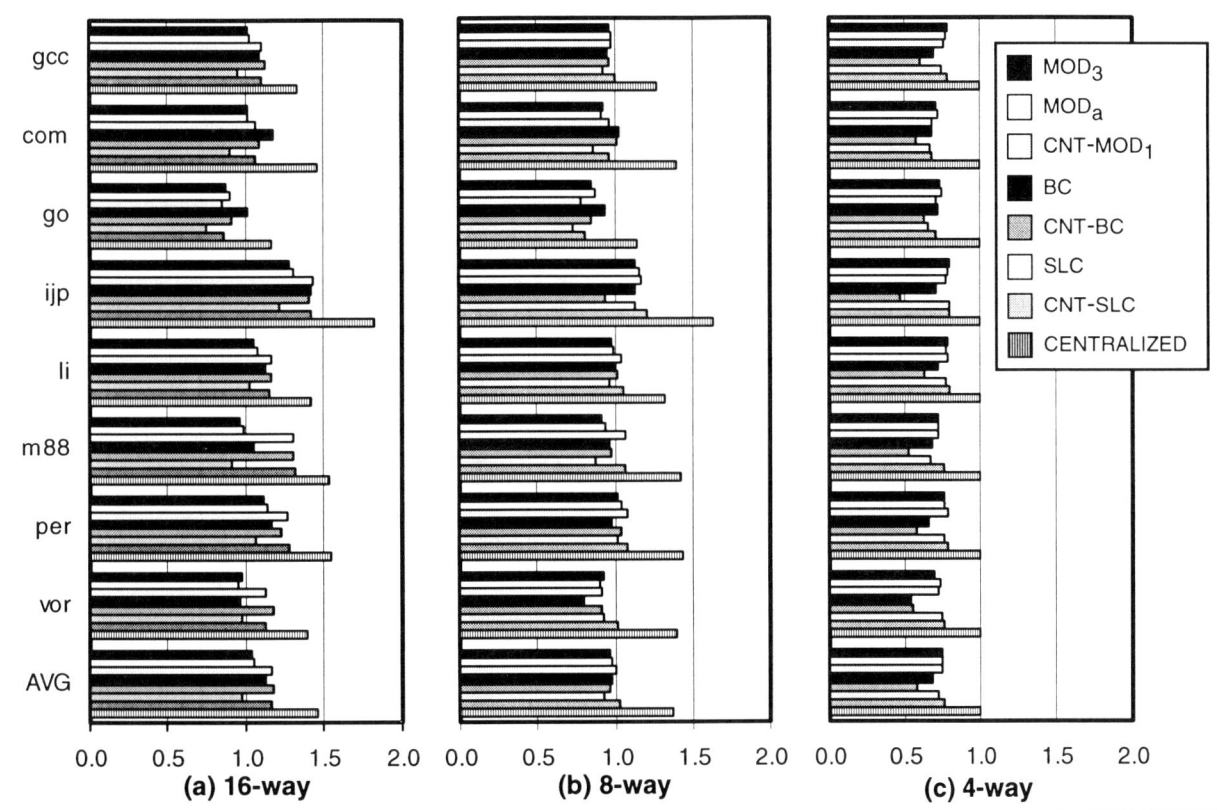

Figure 10: *Performance as a function of total issue bandwidth. All configurations use four clusters. (a) 4-way clusters (16-way total), (b) 2-way clusters (8-way total), and (c) single-issue clusters (4-way total). Performance is normalized to a 4-way centralized configuration. All clustered configurations incur 2 cycles for inter-cluster communication. The base, centralized configuration does not incur any communication delays. Higher is better.*

Breach for early discussions that lead to this study. This research was supported by an NSF Career Award.

References

[1] H. Akkary and M. A. Driscoll. A dynamic multithreading processor. In *Annual International Symposium on Microarchitecture-31*, Nov. 1998.

[2] M. T. Bohr. Interconnect scaling - the real limiter to high performance ULSI. *International Electron Devices Meeting Technical Digest*, 1995.

[3] D. Burger and T. M. Austin. The SimpleScalar tool set, version 2.0. Technical Report Computer Sciences Tech. Report #1342, University of Wisconsin-Madison, June 1997.

[4] R. Canal, J. M. Parcerisa, and A. Gonzalez. Dynamic Cluster Assignment Mechanisms. In *Proc. High Performance Architecture 6*, Jan. 2000.

[5] G. Z. Chrysos and J. S. Emer. Memory dependence prediction using store sets. In *Proc. International Symposium on Computer Architecture-25*, June 1998.

[6] K. I. Farkas, P. Chow, N. P. Jouppi, and Z. Vranesic. The Multicluster Architecture: Reducing Cycle Time Through Partitioning. In *Proc. Annual International Symposium on Microarchitecture-30*, Dec. 1997.

[7] L. Hammond, M. Willey, and K. Olukotun. Data speculation support for a chip multiprocessor. In *Proc. Symposium on Architectural Support for Languages and Operating Systems VIII*, Oct. 1998.

[8] T. Juan, S. Sanjeevan, and J. J. Navarro. Dynamic history-length fitting: A third level of adaptivity for branch prediction. In *Proc. 25th Annual International Symposium on Computer Architecture*, pages 155–166, June-July 1998.

[9] R. E. Kessler, E. J. McLellan, and D. A. Webb. The Alpha 21264 architecture. In *Proc. of International Conference on Computer Design*, Dec. 1998.

[10] D. Matzke. Will Physical Scalability Sabotage Performance Gains?. In *IEEE Computer, 30(9)*, Sept. 1997.

[11] A. Moshovos, S. Breach, T. Vijaykumar, and G. Sohi. Dynamic speculation and synchronization of data dependences. In *Proc. International Symposium on Computer Architecture-24*, June 1997.

[12] S. Palacharla, N. P. Jouppi, and J. E. Smith. Complexity-effective superscalar processors. In *Proc. International Symposium on Computer Architecture-24*, June 1997.

[13] E. Rotenberg, Q. Jacobson, Y. Sazeides, and J. Smith. Trace processors. In *Proc. on Annual International Symposium on Microarchitecture-30*, Dec. 1997.

[14] G. S. Sohi, S. E. Breach, and T. N. Vijaykumar. Multiscalar processors. In *Proc. International Symposium on Computer Architecture-22*, June 1995.

[15] G. S. Sohi and S. Vajapeyam. Instruction issue logic for high-performance, interruptible pipelined processors. In *Proc. 14th Annual International Symposium on Computer Architecture*, pages 27–34, Pittsburgh, PA, June 1987.

[16] J. G. Steffan and T. Mowry. The potential for using thread-level data speculation to facilitate automatic parallelization. In *Proc. High Performance Computer Architecture-4*, Jan. 1998.

Performance Improvement with Circuit-Level Speculation

Tong Liu and Shih-Lien Lu
Intel Corporation
tl999@yahoo.com; shih-lien.l.lu@intel.com

Abstract

Current superscalar microprocessors' performance depends on its frequency and the number of useful instructions that can be processed per cycle (IPC). In this paper we propose a method called approximation to reduce the logic delay of a pipe-stage. The basic idea of approximation is to implement the logic function partially instead of fully. Most of the time the partial implementation gives the correct result as if the function is implemented fully but with fewer gates delay allowing a higher pipeline frequency. We apply this method on three logic blocks. Simulation results show that this method provides some performance improvement for a wide-issue superscalar if these stages are finely pipelined.

1. Introduction

The performance of microprocessor has been accelerating rapidly in recent years. This gain has been achieved through two fronts. On one front, microarchitecture innovations have been able to take advantage of the increase number of devices to process more useful instructions per cycle (IPC). Superscalar is the predominant scheme used. A superscalar processor issues multiple instructions and execution them with multiple identical function unit. It employs dynamic scheduling techniques and executes instructions out of the original program order. The main goal is to exploit as much instruction level parallelism as possible in the program. On the other front, the miniaturization of devices improves layout density and makes the circuits run faster since electrons and holes need only to travel shorter distance. Clever circuit techniques have also been invented to further speed up the logic. Together with finer pipestages, modern microprocessor has accelerated its frequency greatly in recent years.

However, it is believed more complexity is necessary to continue the exploitation of parallelism. This complexity increase tends to cause more circuit delay in the critical path of the pipeline, thus limiting the frequency to go up further. The current approach is to allow logic structures with long delays to spread over multiple pipe-stages resulting in structures that complete the computation in single pipe-stage previously to take more than one cycle. However, finer pipelined machine leads to longer pipeline latency and imposes higher penalty due to branch missprediction and miss-speculation. Moreover, other instructions that depend on the results of these multi-staged functional blocks will have to wait until they finish in order to move forward in the pipeline. Figure 1 illustrates the effect of executing consecutive dependent instructions. Therefore, these long delay structures may become the performance bottleneck of microprocessor as clock frequency continues to rise in the future. Thus, one of the essential challenges in achieving performance in future microprocessors is the ability to increase IPC without compromising the ever-increasing clock frequency.

Much work had been devoted to finding methods to increase IPC. One possible approach is to increase the width of the superscalar processor [1-6]. Another approach considered by many researchers is multi-threading [7-12]. Both methods tend to increase the size of the structures used internally such as instruction window and re-order-buffer. Larger size means longer delay and may affect the growth in clock frequency. Work done by Cotofana and Vassiliadis [13] identified the delay complexity of issue logic in a superscalar processor to be a function of issue

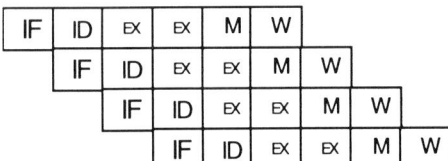

(a) Pipeline with Independent Instructions

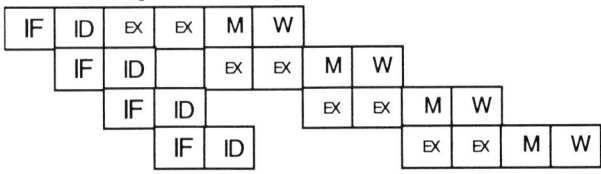

(b) Pipeline with Dependent Instructions

Figure 1. Example of Dependent and Independent Instructions Pipeline Execution

width. Work by Palacharla et. al. [14, 15] concluded that possible clock limiting structures in a superscalar processor include, register rename logic and issue logic. Also as the machine data and address width increases (currently moving from 32 to 64 bits), we believe adder may also become a bottleneck limiting the increase in frequency because many groups reporting the design of high performance microprocessors include their add circuits in their papers [16-18]. This suggests that adder may limit the frequency of microprocessor if we want to have finer pipeline stages in the future.

In this paper, we propose to use circuit level "prediction" to "speculate" the output of critical logic blocks. The approach calls for a simpler and faster circuit implementation to approximate the original complex function. We termed this technique *approximation*. Approximation circuit should be designed so that it produces the correct result most of the time. Since it is not 100% correct it does require a way to verify the correctness of the approximation. A duplicated logic block, which implements the true function and samples the output at the original worst case delay is used for verification. Results from the approximation and verification blocks are compared to determine if the approximated result used to advance the pipeline is correct or not. When the comparison result is negative we kill the instruction and use the correct result to continue. The recovery mechanism is similar to what is reported in [19]. A modified SimpleScalar [20] tool set in section is used to compare performance.

2. Background and Baseline Design

The logic structures we have considered are adder, issue logic and register rename logic. Adder circuit delay is not related to issue width. However address calculation done by integer adder is the key operation for instruction fetch, branch prediction and data supply from memory [21]. Moreover, we are observing a trend in the growth of datapath width. Currently we are in transition from 32 bits to 64 bits. Designing very fast large adder has been a constant research topic [22, 23]. The latter two are key structures used to exploit ILP in a wide-issue superscalar microprocessor and generally considered as single cycle function logic that are proved to be difficult to pipeline inside. We called these structures cycle limiter. In order to compare performance improvement, a baseline microarchitecture is needed. There are different ways to implement an out-of-order superscalar. Our baseline uses a centralized issue window, which combines the reorder buffer and instruction window together, and can provide precise interrupt [1, 14, 24].

2.1. Adder

Many instructions contain add. Load, store and branch use adder for address calculation. Arithmetic instructions use adder for add, subtract, multiply and divide. There are many different kinds of adders. Due to performance requirement, most of the current high performance processors employ one of the known parallel adders [25]. These parallel adders, such as Carry Look Ahead (CLA), Brent-Kung Adder (BKA), Kogge-Stone Adder (KSA) and Carry Select Adder (CSA), all have comparable asymptotic performance [26] proportional to log (N), where N is the number of bits of the adder. The cost complexity of parallel adders approaches N^2 when fan-in and fan-out of gates used are fixed.

2.2. Register Rename Logic

Register renaming eliminates storage conflicts (anti- and output dependencies). When an instruction is decoded, its destination register is assigned to a physical register (renamed). Usually the number of physical registers is greater than the number of architectural or logical registers. When a later instruction refers to a previously renamed destination register (with its logical binding), it must be able to traverse the renaming and obtains the value stored inside the corresponding physical register or just the tag of the physical register if the value has not yet been produced. Thus, the register rename logic is used to translate logical register designators into physical register designators and is accomplished by accessing a mapping table with the logical register designator as the index. From [14, 15], there are two different implementations: RAM and CAM. In the RAM scheme, the number of entries (i.e., rows) in the mapping table is equal to the number of logical registers and is independent of the number of physical registers. However the mapping table's entry length (i.e., columns) of the RAM scheme depends on the number of checkpoints needs to be stored. As we issue more instructions per cycle we need to predict over nested branches that will increase the width of the mapping table. The CAM scheme, on the other hand, has fixed table width but requires a larger number of entries. We use the CAM structure in our baseline machine. A block diagram of the renaming logic is shown in Figure 2 (in this figure the horizon entries are rows). It consists of a set of physical registers, a mapping table and a priority encoding logic block. The number of entries in the mapping table is equal to the number of physical registers. When a decoded instruction enters into the rename logic, its destination register is assigned a new entry in the physical register and the corresponding physical register is stored with the logical register binding. The same decoded instruction's source registers binding will be used to lookup the mapping table associatively. Since it is possible that a logical register can match multiple physical registers due to earlier instructions specify the same destination registers, the result from this associative lookup is channeled into the priority encoding logic. The priority encoder converts the multiple ones into a single active line to be used to access the physical register. The critical path

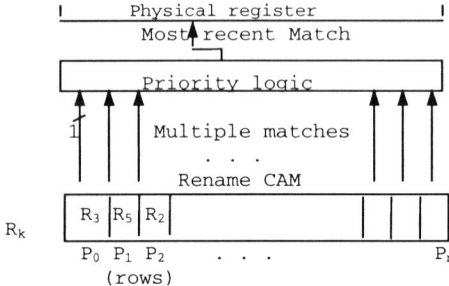

Figure 2. Rename CAM and priority logic, R is logical register, and P is physical register

of register rename using this scheme is the time for mapping table lookup and the priority encoding logic when multiple matches are found. In the worst case, when the matched entry is at the head of the mapping table, N-bit adder-like ripple structure will be formed through the entire priority encoder. A carry look ahead structure (parallel-prefix) can be used and the delay will be in the order of log (N), where N is number of physical registers.

2.3. Instruction Issue Logic

The issue logic contains three different parts, and all of them are speed critical [13, 14, 15]. When an instruction is finished from the functional unit, it writes result back to its destination register. Status of its dependent instructions will be updated by broadcasting the tag associated with the result register to all the instructions in the issue window. If there is a match that particular operand is marked ready. If all operands of an instruction are marked ready, it is ready to be issued. If multiple dependent instructions are ready to issue, there may be contentions on issue bandwidth and functional unit. A selection logic is needed to arbitrate which ready instruction to be issued first. There are different kinds of selection policy, and oldest-first policy, which grant instruction occurs earliest in program order first, is one of most popular policies. In a superscalar machine, since out-of-order issued instructions usually retire in-order, this policy is necessary because issuing old instruction first can resolve dependency quicker and committing earlier instruction first can leave space in the instruction window for newly decoded instructions. When a ready instruction is granted to issue, writeback data of the instruction it depends on will be bypassed from output of the corresponding functional unit to the source register. The delay of wakeup-selection-bypass logic increases with increasing issue window size. The selection logic will start to check the request of instructions from earliest to latest in program order, which is the order of RUU [28] from head to tail. In the worst case, when the only request is from tail of RUU, an adder like ripple carry will be formed through all entries of RUU. A carry look ahead structure can be used to make this process parallel and the delay is the order of log (N), where N is the window size. For wakeup and bypass logic, the RC delay dominates the circuit speed. Circuit simulation shows that RC delay is more sensitive to window size than logic gate level [14]. For the multiple issue case, the delay analysis will be similar.

3. Circuit Level Speculation

Previous study [29] shows that for random input data, the average carry length of a CLA is only 1/3 of its data length. Moreover, other works have shown that there is redundancy exits in programs [30-32], i.e., many instructions perform the same computation with similar input data pattern repeatedly. This could be used for adder output speculation. For example, in address calculation, one of the input to the adder is static. Moreover the other operand is usually incrementing with a regular stride. Therefore the actual adder delay is much shorter than the worst case maximum delay. We use the approximation technique described in the introduction section by generating a part of the whole carry chain. As for the register renaming logic, we believe that the renaming will mostly happen among instructions close to each other, so we employ the approximation method described previously and use a simpler priority encoding logic. For issue logic, we only select among a small group of instructions close to the head of instruction queue to issue. Due to this selection strategy, the wakeup and bypass logic can be prioritized to work on the corresponding instructions closer to head of instruction queue first, and work on the rest of instructions later. Because of the approximation techniques, the total pipestages of machine are shorter, the dependency chain will be resolved faster, and results in higher IPC. As other prediction methods, circuit level value prediction is not 100% accurate. If the prediction is wrong, the false speculated instruction has to be re-issued and re-executed. This will cause more resource contention, and dependency chain will be resolved even slower than the baseline structure. If the prediction accuracy goes down to a certain point, the speculatively architecture will perform worse than the baseline architecture. So we can only work on the logic structure whose behavior is highly predictable. If the prediction accuracy is high enough to overcome the replay penalty of false speculation, the performance improvement is expected. Also the wrongly speculated instruction output will trigger its dependent instructions to start execution and produce more false result. These false results will trigger their own dependent instructions to execute, and cause a chain reaction resulting in large overhead and overall performance loss. Therefore it is important to stop the write-back of the speculative instructions as soon as the false prediction is detected. We describe the details of our design and analysis used in the following sections.

3.1. Adder

The critical path of an adder is its full carry chain. For an N-bit adder, we denote the individual bits of the two input operands as a_i, b_i and intermediate carries as c_i ($i=0, ..., N-1$). Each intermediate carry signal - c_i depends on all its previous input bits. i.e.,

$$c_i = f(a_{i-1}, b_{i-1}, a_{i-2}, b_{i-2}, ..., a_0, b_0)$$

Thus, in order to generate the correct final result, we must consider all input bits (look ahead all inputs) to obtain the final carry out. However in real programs, inputs to the adder are not completely random and the effective carry chain is much shorter for most cases. Our approximated design considers only the previous k inputs (lookahead k-bits) instead of all previous input bits for the current carry bit. i.e.,

$$c_i = f(a_{i-1}, b_{i-1}, a_{i-2}, b_{i-2}, ..., a_{i-k}, b_{i-k}) \text{ where } 0 < k < i+1 \text{ and}$$
$$a_j, b_j = 0 \text{ if } j<0$$

If we choose $k = \sqrt{N}$, our new approximation adder only need half of the original delay ($\log \sqrt{N} = \frac{1}{2} \log N$). The prediction rate of an N-bit adder with k bits carry chain is:

$$P(N, k) = (1 - \frac{1}{2^{k+2}})^{N-k-1}$$

For example, a 64-bit approximation adder with 8-bit ($8 = \sqrt{64}$) look-ahead gives correct result 95% of the time assuming random input data.

3.2. Rename Logic

As mentioned previously, the critical path of the register rename logic is the delay of the associative lookup and the priority logic when multiple matches are found. By experimenting with benchmarks, we found that dependent instructions may have spatial locality. In other words, they are most likely to be close to each other. Thus, we propose to use a smaller CAM to implement the mapping table. The CAM table basically contains a portion of the whole map. When a new instruction enters the rename logic, its destination binding is assigned a new physical binding. The mapping table is updated if the table is not full. Otherwise the oldest one is dropped to leave room for the newly renamed destination binding. At the same time the source bindings are used to lookup the partial CAM. If there is no physical mapping found in the small CAM but the mapping does exist in the full CAM, A mis-speculation occurs. Since the number of inputs to the priority encoder is equal to the number of entry in the smaller CAM, the delay for the rename logic is also smaller. In order to double the speed, we propose to use a much smaller CAM table containing only the latest $\sqrt{N}$ number of instruction's register mapping table in it, where N is the window size. Because of the locality property of register dependency, we hope to get most of the reading operation from the rename logic correctly. Beside the faster (approximation) renaming logic, we still keep a regular full CAM and the associated full length priority encoder. It will be used to recover the mis-speculation and provide the correct renaming result in the next cycle.

3.3. Issue Logic

We use the same idea as rename logic by targeting the issue logic on the earliest $\sqrt{N}$ entries (N = window size), so that the issue logic only needs to consider waking up, selecting and bypassing data to instructions within $\sqrt{N}$ entries to the head of RUU. Since the wakeup and bypass delay are RC dominated, and RC delay is more sensitive to the window size, we will have more than twice speed up in these two logics. So the total speculative issue logic delay will be less than half of the issue logic in baseline microarchitecture if only $\sqrt{N}$ entries are considered. There is no replayed needed for the approximated issue logic since there is no false result generated.

4. Implementation and Recovery

4.1. Implementation Cost

Our new microarchitecture uses the speculative adder, rename and issue logic as described previously. A pair of duplicated normal adders and rename logic is also included in the machine being sampled at a slower frequency. Since the slower verification logic is running half speed as the speculative logic in the main data path, two identical ones are needed to interleave the input data so as to catch up with the fast frequency. The size of the above mentioned circuit-level speculation logic for rename and issue is smaller than the original logic used in the baseline machine, since the speculative window size is scaled down (in our case the size is the square root of the original size). For an N-bit adder with k-bit carry look-ahead, a total of N k-bit adders are needed. When k is large, the new design may have a significantly larger area. Fortunately, from our benchmark experiment, 4 bits of carry look-ahead can achieve an average of 85% prediction rate for 64 bits adder (random inputs give only 40% accuracy), this is due to the redundancy in program data. Each pieces of small carry chain only has local wire routings, so the device size can be smaller and layout can be rather compact. Thus, in general, our duplicated hardware used to speculate is smaller in size than the original hardware. This is different from DIVA processor proposed by Austin [33], which requires an almost identical hardware as checker. Both approaches speculate on circuit timing and both can avoid metastability.

4.2. Recovery

After the verification logic finished, the result is compared with corresponding "speculative result". If they match, no other action is required. Otherwise instructions, which generate a false result, will be issued again and write back with the correct result from verification logic. We assume that it takes an extra cycle for the slow (original) logic to finish and verify the speculative result. Also, as soon as the false speculation is known, the writeback of the speculative instruction is stopped so that it won't trigger the next dependent instructions. For issue speculation, there won't be any false result generated, so no replay is needed.

The issue mechanism in the superscalar microarchiteture is event triggered. This means an instruction will check the readiness of all of the source registers and decide to send a request to issue only when new data is written to any of the source registers. This can happen in two cases:

I. In rename stage, if all source register data are available, either in physical register it matched with, or direct from architectural register file, then the instruction is ready to issue immediately.

II. In writeback stage, when an instruction finishes execute and writeback data, its dependent instructions will be waked up, instructions with all source data available are ready to issue.

We now discuss the detail on how the newly proposed microarchitecture handles speculation and replay. In our design, RUU has the same content as baseline microarchitecture except every entry has flags showing the bogus speculation, one per each source register. We call it value prediction flag (VPF). Initially all VPFs are reset. The VPF of a register will be set when the verification logic finds out that the speculation done on the corresponding instruction before is wrong, or that register is written back by an earlier instruction whose VPF has been set. The VPF will be cleared when the corresponding register is written back by an earlier instruction whose VPF is cleared. VPF will gate the writeback of the instructions so that they won't contaminate its dependents. Because it takes one extra pipestage for the verification logic to figure out the result of the speculation, VPF will be updated one cycle later than the speculation stage. If an instruction's writeback stage is immediately following it speculation stage, it will trigger its dependent instruction to issue because VPF hasn't been set yet. However, after the dependent instruction issues, its VPF will be assigned and its writeback will be stopped if false speculation happens. Since updating VPF for the dependent instructions can be done in parallel with their executions,

it won't degrade the performance. We didn't use speculative adder for branch instruction. The reason is that branch will be resolved in the next cycle immediately after the adder calculates the address, and before VPF of the branch instruction is assigned. The false speculation of adder will cause spurious branch mispredictions. In other words, a correctly predicted branch will be considered mispredicted because the adder that is used to calculate target address and to verify the branch prediction is wrong. The penalty of recovering from spurious branch mispredictions will be higher than the benefits we get from the value prediction of add. For rename speculation, because it happens at front end of the machine pipeline, the VPF of the false speculated instruction would be set before the branch resolved. So no spurious branch miss-predictions will happen.

5. Simulation Result

Table 1. Common parameters of base simulator

Fetch width	4 inst. per cycle
Instruction cache	16K byte, Direct mapped, 32 byte line, 6 cycle miss latency
Branch Predictor	Bimodel, 2048 BTB entries with 2 bit saturating counter
Issue mech.	Out-of-order issue, commit at 4 operations per cycles, load may execute when all prior store addresses are known
FU	2 load/store, 4 fp adders, 1 fp MUL/DIV
FU latency (total/issue)	load/store 1/1, int ALU 1/1, int MUL 3/1, int DIV 29/19, fp adder 2/1, fp MUL 4/1, fp DIV 12/12, fp SQRT 24/24
Data cache	16K byte, 4 way set associate, 32 byte line, 6 cycle miss latency

Table 2. Parameters of four cases of base simulator

	Issue width	RUU, LSQ	ALU	MUL	Speculation window	carry chain
I4R64	4	64, 64	4	1	8	4
I8R64	8	64, 64	8	2	8	4
I4R32	4	32, 32	4	1	4	4
I4R16	4	16, 16	4	1	4	4

We use SimpleScalar tool set to compare the performance of our speculative microarchitecture with the baseline machine. Assume both models run with the same frequency. In the baseline machine, in order to keep up the frequency the cycle limiter logic blocks all take 2 cycles. While in the new speculative machine with approximation circuits, these same logic blocks take only 1 cycle. However the speculative machine will need to replay when the result is incorrectly generated and incur miss speculation (replay) penalty. Independent simulation experiment is performed for each of the above mentioned cycle limit logic - rename logic, issue logic and adder, with the assumption that only one of them is the main performance limiter. We run eight integer benchmarks from the spec95 suite, using the reference input database. First, we set the RUU window size = 64, issue width = 4, integer adder number = 4, integer multiplier number = 1, and run 2 billion instructions for each benchmark. Then by shuffling the parameters: window size of 16, 32, issue width of 8, integer adder number of 8 and integer multiplier number of 2, we run each benchmark for 500 million instructions. These parameters are listed in Table 1 and 2. The speedup results are summarized in Figure 3-5. The speedup is basically the ratio of IPC with baseline machine normalized to one. Bars labeled HM in all figures are the harmonic mean over all the benchmarks simulated.

From these diagrams, we can see that circuit-level speculation method described does improve the overall performance of the new microarchitecture. Also from simulation result, the average prediction rates for speculative adder, rename logic and issue logic are 88%, 80% and 36% respectively. For adder speculation, the performance improvement is less than the other two speculations. This is because addition completes close to the back end of the machine, it is more likely to pollute the dependent instructions by false writeback and cause more penalties. By reducing window size, the adder speculation performance relative to the baseline machine increased. This reason is smaller number of independent instructions is available in a smaller issue window. So the speculation is more important and efficient to resolve dependencies. On the other hand, increasing issue width and number of function units degrades the relative performance, since wider issue width, larger window size and more functional units potentially cause larger instruction level parallelism, and the mis-speculation penalty will overcome the performance gain by resolving dependency chain. However, for rename and issue speculation, the speculative window size will change to match the baseline window size so that to achieve the circuit speedup of twice fast. This will compromise the relationship between relative performance and window size, issue width and functional unit. For case I8R64, which means wide issue, large window and more functional unit, the relative performance of ijpeg degrades a lot in issue and add speculation. The predication accuracy of issue speculation means the percentage of ready instructions in speculation window over the total ready instructions. It is as low as 24% for ijpeg, causing huge waste of execution bandwidth. Since ijpeg is a computational intensive program, it is full of independent data processing instructions, which means there are fewer dependencies than other benchmarks. This explains the low performance

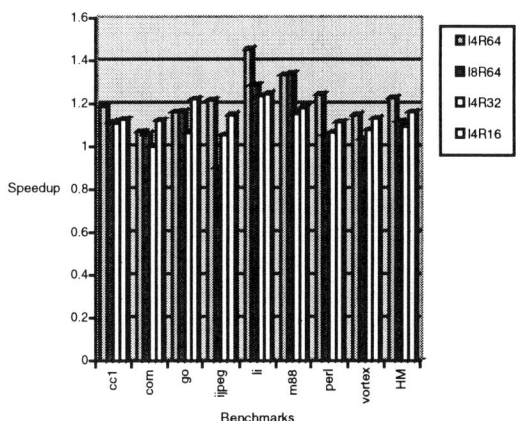

Figure 3. Speedup by speculative issue logic

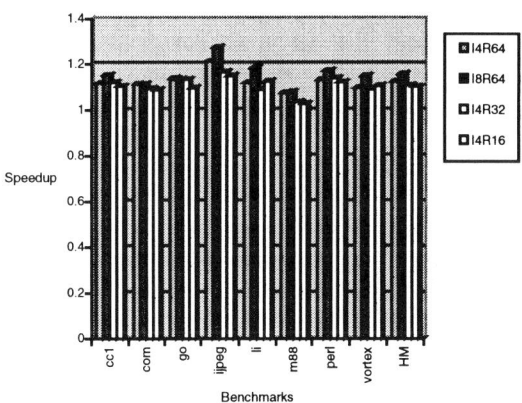

Figure 4. Speedup by speculative rename logic

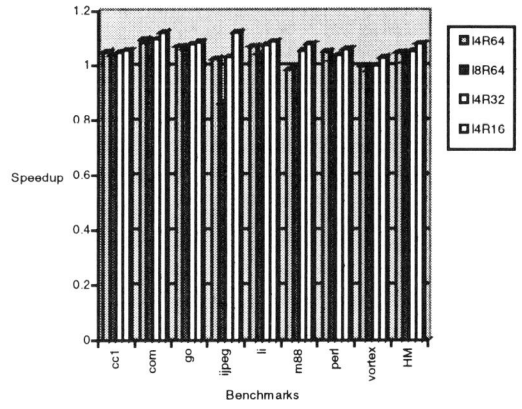

Figure 5. Speedup by approximation adder

gain with issue and adder circuit-level speculation.

6. Conclusion

In this paper, we first try to identify some possible cycle limiters in a superscalar microprocessor, namely adder, rename logic and issue logic and analyze their speed path. Then we propose a circuit level speculation method – approximation to speedup these critical logic blocks. For adder, carry chain is generated by a subset of the input data. For rename and issue logic, we only target on a subset of instructions in the issue window. For adder and rename logic, the corresponding verification logic must be duplicated to detect the correctness of value prediction. In case of false speculation, the instruction will be replayed. Our simulation of SPEC95 benchmarks with different window size, issue width and number of function units shows performance improvement for this newly proposed microarchitecture over the baseline machine. Our conclusion is that circuit level speculation method is a potential way to speedup some cycle limiting logic structures and achieve better performance in wide issue superscalar microprocessor. Approximation method works better on program with more dependencies than that with high ILP originally. The extra hardware cost both for duplicated logic blocks and verification logic is somewhat limited.

References

[1] James E. Smith, and Gurindar S. Sohi, "The Microarchitecture of Superscalar Processors," in Proc. of the IEEE, Vol.: 83 12, Dec. 1995, pp. 1609–1624.

[2] P. Michaud, A. Seznec, and S. Jourdan, "Exploring instruction-fetch bandwidth requirement in wide-issue superscalar processors," in Proc. of the Int. Conf. on Parallel Architectures and Compilation Techniques, 1999, pp. 2–10.

[3] S. Dutta, and M. Franklin, "Control flow prediction schemes for wide-issue superscalar processors," IEEE Transactions on Parallel and Distributed Systems, Vol.: 10 4, April 1999, pp. 346–359.

[4] Sangyeun Cho; Pen-Chung Yew; Gyungho Lee, "Decoupling local variable accesses in a wide-issue superscalar processor," in Proc. of the 26th Int. Symp. on Comp. Arch., 1999, pp. 100–110.

[5] J. Farrell and T. C. Fischer, "Issue Logic for a 600-MHz Out-of-Order Execution Microprocessor," IEEE JSSC, Vol. 33, No. 5, May 1998, pp. 707-712.

[6] S. J Patel, D. H. Friendly and Y. N. Patt, "Evaluation of design options for the trace cache fetch mechanism," IEEE Transactions on Computers, Vol.: 48 2, Feb. 1999, pp.193 - 204

[7] D. M. Tullsen, S. J. Eggers, and H. M. Levy, "Simultaneous multithreading: Maximizing on-chip parallelism," in Proc. of 22nd Ann. Int. Symp. Comp. Arch., 1995, pp. 392–403.

[8] C. B. Zilles, J. S. Emer and G. S. Sohi, "The use of multithreading for exception handling," in Proc. of 32nd Ann. Int. Symp. on Microarchitecture, 1999, pp. 219–229.

[9] P. Marcuello, J. Tubella, and A. Gonzalez, "Value prediction for speculative multithreaded architectures," in Proc. of 32nd Ann. Int. Symp. on Microarchitecture, 1999, pp. 230–236.

[10] S. Wallace, D. M. Tullsen and B. Calder, "Instruction recycling on a multiple-path processor," in Proc. of Fifth Int. Symp. On High-Performance Comp. Arch., 1999, pp. 44–53.

[11] J. -M. Parcerisa, and A. Gonzalez, "The synergy of multithreading and access/execute decoupling," in Proc. of Fifth Int. Symp. On High-Performance Comp. Arch., 1999, pp. 59–63.

[12] H. Akkary, and M. A. Driscoll, "A dynamic multithreading processor," in Proc. of 31st Ann. Int. Symp. on Microarchitecture, 1998, pp. 226–236.

[13] S. Cotofana, and S. Vassiliadis, "On the Design Complexity of the Issue Logic of Superscalar Machines," in Proc. of the 24th Euromicro Conf., 1998, pp. 277–284.

[14] Subbarao Palacharla, Norman P. Jouppi, J. E. Smith, "Complexity-Effective Superscalar Processors," in Proc. of the 24th Int. Symp. on Comp. Arch., June 1997.

[15] Subbarao Palacharla, Norman P. Jouppi, J. E. Smith, "Quantifying the Complexity of Superscalar Processors," Technical Report CS-TR-96-1328, University of Wisconsin-Madison, November 1996.

[16] R. Bechade et. al., "A 32b 66 MHz 1.8 W microprocessor," in Digest of Technical Papers of the 41st IEEE Int. Solid-State Circuits Conf., 1994, pp. 208–209.

[17] D. Dobberpuhl et. al., "A 200 MHz 64 b dual-issue CMOS microprocessor," in Digest of Technical Papers of the 39th IEEE Int. Solid-State Circuits Conf., 1992, pp. 106 -107, 256.

[18] H. Sanchez et. al., "A 200 MHz 2.5 V 4 W superscalar RISC microprocessor," in Digest of Technical Papers of the 43rd IEEE Int. Solid-State Circuits Conf., 1996, pp. 218 -219, 448.

[20] M. H. Lipasti, and J. P.Shen, "Exceeding the dataflow limit via value prediction," in Proc. of the 29th Ann. IEEE/ACM Int. Symp. on Microarchitecture, 1996, pp. 226–237.

[21] D.C. Burger and T.M. Austin, "The SimpleScalar Tool Set, Version 2.0," University of Wisconsin Computer Science Technical Report #1342, June 1997.

[22] Y. Shintani et. al., "A Performance and Cost Analysis of Aplying Superscalar method to Mainframe Computers," IEEE Trans. On Computers, Vol. 44, No. 7, July 1995, pp. 891-902

[23] Wei Hwang; Gristede, G.; Sanda, P.; Wang, S.Y.; Heidel, D.F, "Implementation of a Self-resetting CMOS 64-bit Parallel Adder with Enhanced Testability," IEEE JSSC, Vol.: 34 8, Aug. 1999,.pp. 1108 –1117.

[24] L.A. Lev et. al., "A 64-b microprocessor with multimedia support ," IEEE JSSC, Vol.: 30 11 , Nov. 1995 , pp. 1227 -1238.

[25] Mike Johnson, Superscalar Microprocessor Design. Prentice Hall Series in Innovative Technology. 1991.

[26] C. Nagendra, M.J. Irwin, and R.M. Owens, "Area-time-power tradeoffs in parallel adders," Circuits and Systems II: Analog and Digital Signal Processing, IEEE Transactions on Vol.: 43 10 , Oct. 1996 , pp. 689–702.

[27] T. Lynch, and E. Swartzlander, "The redundant cell adder," in Proc..of the 10th IEEE Symp. on Computer Arithmetic, 1991, pp. 165–170.

[28] G. Sohi, "Instruction Issue Logic for High Performance, Interruptible, Multiple Functional Unit, Pipelined Computers," IEEE T. on Computers, Vol. 39, No. 3, March 1990, pp.349-359.

[29] R. Ramachandran and S. L. Lu, "Carry Logic," Wiley Encyclopedia of Electrical and Electronics Engineering, Edited by John G. Webster, 1999.

[30] Avinash Sodani and Gurindar S. Sohi, "Dynamic Instruction Reuse," Proc. of the 24th Int. Symp. on Comp. Arch., June, 1997.

[31] Avinash Sodani and Gurindar S. Sohi, "An Empirical Analysis of Instruction Repetition," in Proc. of 8th Int. Conf. on Architectural Support for Programming Languages and Operating Systems (ASPLOS-VIII), Oct 1998.

[32] Avinash Sodani and Gurindar S. Sohi, "Understanding the Differences between Value Prediction and Instruction Reuse," in Proc. of 31st Int. Symp. on Microarchitecture, Nov-Dec 1998.

[33] T. M. Austin, "DIVA: a reliable substrate for deep submicron microarchitecture design," in Proc. of the 32nd Ann. Int. Symp. on Microarchitecture, 1999, pp. 196-207.

Author Index

Albonesi, D. 245
Asanović, K. 214
August, D. I. 112
Austin, T. 327
Austin, T. 87
Ayguadé, E. 137
Baker, D. 3
Balasubramonian, R. 245
Baniasadi, A. 337
Boggs, D. 5
Bose, S. 303
Brown, M. D. 57
Butts, J. A. 191
Buyuktosunoglu, A. 245
Calder, B. 42
Canal, R. 181
Catthoor, F. 171
Chambers, C. 291
Chatterjee, S. 87
Chou, Y. 147
Crum, M. M. 303
Dally, W. J. 159
Davidson, E. S. 77
De Man, H. 171
Dwarkadas, S. 245
Eggers, S. J. 291
Eichenberger, A. 101
Farrens, M. K. 11
González, A. 124, 181, 317
Greene, D. 235
Gupta, R. 258
Heil, T. 281
Huang, M. 202
Hwu, W. W. 112
Jiménez, D. A. 67
Kapasi, U. J. 159
Keckler, S. W. 67
Keukes, P. 7
Khailany, B. 159
Larson, E. 327
Lee, H.-H. S. 11
Lepak, K. M. 22
Lin, C. 67
Lipasti, M. H. 22
Liu, T. 348
Llosa, J. 137
Lu, S.-L. 348
Maradani, S. 101
Mattson, P. R. 159
Meleis, W. 101
Mock, M. 291
Moshovos, A. 337
Mudge, T. 235
Nachtergaele, L. 171
Owens, J. D. 159
Parcerisa, J.-M. 317
Patel, S. J. 303
Patt, Y. N. 57
Pillai, P. 147
Postiff, M. 235
Purser, Z. 269
Renau, J. 202
Rixner, S. 159
Rotenberg, E. 269
Roth, A. 223
Sair, S. 42
Sánchez, J. 124
Schmit, H. 147
Shen, J. P. 147
Sherwood, T. 42
Sias, J. W. 112
Smith, J. E. 181, 281
Sohi, G. S. 191, 223
Stark, J. 57
Sundaramoorthy, K. 269
Torrellas, J. 202
Tung, T. 303
Tyson, G. S. 11, 77
Valero, M. 137
Verkest, D. 171
Vermeulen, F. 171
Villa, L. 214
Vlaovic, S. 77
Weaver, C. 87
Yang, J. 258
Yoo, S.-M. 202
Zalamea, J. 137
Zhang, M. 214
Zhang, X. 32
Zhang, Y. 258
Zhang, Z. 32
Zhu, Z. 32

Notes

Notes

Press Activities Board

Vice President and Chair:
Carl K. Chang
Dept. of EECS (M/C 154)
The University of Illinois at Chicago
851 South Morgan Street
Chicago, IL 60607
ckchang@eecs.uic.edu

Editor-in-Chief
Advances and Practices in Computer Science and Engineering Board
Pradip Srimani
Colorado State University, Dept. of Computer Science
601 South Hows Lane
Fort Collins, CO 80525
Phone: 970-491-7097 FAX: 970-491-2466
srimani@cs.colostate.edu

Board Members:
Mark J. Christensen
Deborah M. Cooper – Deborah M. Cooper Company
William W. Everett – SPRE Software Process and Reliability Engineering
Haruhisa Ichikawa – NTT Software Laboratories
Annie Kuntzmann-Combelles – Objectif Technologie
Chengwen Liu – DePaul University
Joseph E. Urban – Arizona State University

IEEE Computer Society Executive Staff
T. Michael Elliott, Executive Director and Chief Executive Officer
Angela Burgess, Publisher

IEEE Computer Society Publications

The world-renowned IEEE Computer Society publishes, promotes, and distributes a wide variety of authoritative computer science and engineering texts. These books are available from most retail outlets. Visit the Online Catalog, *http://computer.org*, for a list of products.

IEEE Computer Society Proceedings

The IEEE Computer Society also produces and actively promotes the proceedings of more than 141 acclaimed international conferences each year in multimedia formats that include hard and softcover books, CD-ROMs, videos, and on-line publications.

For information on the IEEE Computer Society proceedings, send e-mail to *cs.books@computer.org* or write to Proceedings, IEEE Computer Society, P.O. Box 3014, 10662 Los Vaqueros Circle, Los Alamitos, CA 90720-1314. Telephone +1 714-821-8380. FAX +1 714-761-1784.

Additional information regarding the Computer Society, conferences and proceedings, CD-ROMs, videos, and books can also be accessed from our web site at *http://computer.org/cspress*

Revised 9 November 1999